WATER FROM THE ROCK

WATER FROM THE ROCK

BLACK RESISTANCE IN A REVOLUTIONARY AGE

Sylvia R. Frey

PRINCETON UNIVERSITY PRESS

PRINCETON, NEW JERSEY

LIBRARY OF CONGRESS CATALOGING-IN-PUBLICATION DATA

FREY, SYLVIA R., 1935–

WATER FROM THE ROCK : BLACK RESISTANCE IN A REVOLUTIONARY AGE /
SYLVIA R. FREY.

P. CM.

INCLUDES BIBLIOGRAPHICAL REFERENCES AND INDEX.

ISBN 0-691-04784-7

1. UNITED STATES—HISTORY—REVOLUTION, 1775–1783—PARTICIPATION,
AFRO-AMERICAN. 2. UNITED STATES—HISTORY—REVOLUTION, 1775–1783—
SOCIAL ASPECTS. 3. SOUTHERN STATES—HISTORY—REVOLUTION,
1775–1783—PARTICIPATION, AFRO-AMERICAN. 4. SOUTHERN STATES—
HISTORY—REVOLUTION, 1775–1783—SOCIAL ASPECTS. 5. AFRO-AMERICANS—
SOUTHERN STATES—HISTORY—18TH CENTURY. 6. SOUTHERN STATES—
HISTORY—1775–1865. 7. SLAVES—SOUTHERN STATES—HISTORY—
18TH CENTURY. I. TITLE.

E269.N3F74 1991   973.3'15'0396073—DC20   90-46655

THIS BOOK HAS BEEN COMPOSED IN LINOTRON GALLIARD

PRINCETON UNIVERSITY PRESS BOOKS ARE PRINTED
ON ACID-FREE PAPER, AND MEET THE GUIDELINES FOR
PERMANENCE AND DURABILITY OF THE COMMITTEE ON
PRODUCTION GUIDELINES FOR BOOK LONGEVITY
OF THE COUNCIL ON LIBRARY RESOURCES

PRINTED IN THE UNITED STATES OF AMERICA BY
PRINCETON UNIVERSITY PRESS, PRINCETON, NEW JERSEY

1 3 5 7 9 10 8 6 4 2

TO THE MEMORY OF

Helen D., John H., and John David Frey

WHOSE LOVE WAS FOR ME

WATER FROM THE ROCK

Speak ye unto the rock before their eyes, that it give forth to
them water out of the rock

Numbers 20:8

CONTENTS

ACKNOWLEDGMENTS

ALTHOUGH *Water from the Rock* bears my name as author, the book owes its existence to a number of colleagues, friends, and institutions, who contributed to it in various ways. To the extent that this work represents an achievement, it is theirs as much as mine. There are, of course, substantial areas of disagreement between me and even my kindest critics. I would, therefore, like to absolve them from all responsibility for the book's shortcomings.

John B. Boles, who was the first person to read any part of the manuscript, helped me to believe in the project. Ira Berlin suggested a biracial approach. Peter H. Wood and Jeffrey Crow drew my attention to important sources and gave me encouragement and useful criticism. The anonymous readers of Princeton University Press read the manuscript with painstaking care that went far beyond the usual requirements. Their meticulous attention to detail saved me from embarrassing errors and helped me to clarify my own ideas and to focus the material more sharply. Betty Wood read the manuscript in its entirety, made very helpful comments, and shared several useful sources with me. Raymond Diamond and Liva Baker read parts of the manuscript and made significant suggestions. Nan Woodruff spent endless hours talking with me about it and gave judicious advice. My greatest debt is to Eugene D. Genovese for his thorough reading of the manuscript, for his urging me on at a discouraging stage of my work, for the example of his own exceptional scholarship, which has shaped significantly the scholarly debate of an entire generation. Gail Ullman, Social Science Editor of Princeton University Press, has been involved with this project from its inception. She has waited patiently for it to end and through all the years has been my trusted counselor and friend. I owe special thanks to my copy editor, Virginia Barker, who treated my manuscript as though it were her own.

I am also indebted to a number of institutions for financial support. The American Philosophical Society, Tulane University's Council on Research, the Murphy Institute of Political Economy, and the National Endowment for the Humanities awarded me summer stipends and travel grants to undertake research in British and American archives and libraries. A year in residence as a senior postdoctoral fellow at the Smithsonian's National Museum of American History made it possible for me to engage in interdisciplinary research with the generous help and advice of museum curators, among them Theresa Singleton and Christine Mullen Kreamer of the Museum of Natural History, Roslyn Walker of the Museum of African Art, and Spencer Crew of the Museum of American History. The Research

Facilities Office of the Library of Congress, particularly Bruce Martin, gave me office space where I could write and use the vast resources of the library. The Virginia Baptist Historical Society not only gave me access to their fine collection of Baptist church records, but provided me with convenient and comfortable housing on the University of Richmond campus.

The librarians and archivists at various institutions in Britain and the United States were, without exception, helpful and accommodating. The Archives and Manuscripts Division of the Virginia State Library, especially Brent Tarter, Phoebe Jacobsen of the Maryland State Archives, Wylma Wates of the South Carolina Department of Archives and History, and Mattie Russell of the Perkins Library of Duke University were especially cooperative in helping me to locate important records and in making manuscript collections available quickly and efficiently. I also wish to express my appreciation to the libraries and archives listed separately for giving me permission to quote from manuscripts in their collections. Parts of chapters one, six, and ten have previously appeared in a different form in *The Historian*, the *Journal of Southern History*, and the United States Capitol Historical Society Symposia Series and are published here with their permission.

Last but not least, I would like to thank my family—immediate and extended—for their tolerance and especially for their love. I want to express special thanks to Jean Veta—for her patience in seeing the book through, for her unfailing support and encouragement, for her intelligent insights on many difficult questions, for her friendship, for all she gave and all she shared. Thanks, too, to Ann and Steve Brick for the serene weekend in Monterey when these acknowledgments were composed.

WATER FROM THE ROCK

INTRODUCTION

THE DECADES preceding and following the American Revolution constituted a revolutionary period for the black and white communities of the American South. The era involved two separate but related processes. The first, the actual conflict of the 1760s–1780s, was a period of prolonged crisis marked by social and economic upheaval and loosening of the fabric of community life. The lingering state of crisis and anxiety that followed the end of hostilities produced a second, or quiet, revolution that continued through the first quarter of the nineteenth century. Together, the two revolutions produced a great torrent of historical change: the destruction of the old colonial empire and the emergence of a new political order; the shift of the population center, and hence, of political gravity; the collapse of the old economic system and the gradual rise of a new staple crop economy and new patterns of labor use; the end of slavery in the North and of the transatlantic slave trade, and the formulation of a new ideological basis for the domination of slaves in the South and the developing Southwest; the decline of the old Anglican church establishment and the emergence of a new religious configuration. When the rushing waters of change subsided at last, community life in the South flowed in two streams: a white slaveholders' stream and a black slaves' stream, each with its own values, its separate way of life.

When analyzing the causes of the revolutionary war and assessing its consequences, most historical studies emphasize the seminal role of slavery. Few recognize the vital role played by slaves in the entire series of events that made up the great drama. Research in British military records made it clear to me that slave resistance during the revolutionary conflict was far more extensive than had hitherto been recognized and that significant aspects of that resistance remained essentially unexplored. Building and expanding upon the earlier works of Herbert Aptheker and Benjamin Quarles, I began to focus my attention on slave resistance and to ask of the sources, both British and American, public and private, a number of questions. What forms did slave resistance take? Was it individual more than collective? Was it gender specific? What were the conditions affecting slave resistance? What were the sources of resistance? Was there a connection between the ideology of equality and freedom and slave resistance? Were there continuities or adaptations of African patterns of resistance? Did the British army create slave resistance or was resistance already there? Was there, perhaps, a dialectical relationship between slave resistance and Britain's Southern strategy and between slave resistance and the white independence movement in the South? Did wartime slave resistance alter the environment of slavery? Did it endanger slavery?

Although the black liberation movement did not achieve its revolutionary goals, it did exert deep pressure on the slave system, which required energetic response or adjustment in the postwar period. The postwar period seemed to me to be a time of transition from an older prewar world of values and structures to a new, objectively different situation, which provided the framework for the subsequent development of a mature plantation society. In attempting to understand the direction and dynamics of change, I singled out three spheres of life in which the transformations seemed especially significant—the economy, the law, and religion. To them I addressed a second set of questions. Were the social and economic structures of postwar slave society significantly different from the prewar period? What was the precipitating force behind the emergence of a durable ethos of racial superiority? Did the revolutionary war experience alter the nature and scale of black resistance? Did ideology influence slave resistance in a manner that was different from that in earlier periods? Did the spread of evangelical religion in the postwar period produce changes in the character of slavery, or major qualitative changes in the lives of slaves, or in the patterns of race relations? What did Christianity mean to slaves? What did it do to them and for them? What was the social function of religion in the black community?

As I began to map overall patterns, two major themes emerged: a black liberation movement was central to the revolutionary struggle in the South, and the failure of that movement did not dissipate the black revolutionary potential, which reemerged in the postwar period as a struggle for cultural power. It is to these subjects that *Water from the Rock* seeks to contribute.

ONE

THE PREREVOLUTIONARY SOUTH:

FOUNDATIONS OF CULTURE AND COMMUNITY

B Y THE EVE of the American Revolution a triad of plantation economies based on the production of plantation staples with bound
labor had emerged throughout the South. The development of staple crop agriculture was not, however, uniform, but was a complex matrix
of systems, each exhibiting characteristics peculiar to the staples it exported.

One hundred and fifty years after English settlement began, the Chesapeake Bay region of British North America seemed to a foreign traveler
"an immense forest, extended on a flat plain, almost without bounds."[1]
Bounded by the Patapsco River on the north, the Blue Ridge Mountains
on the west, and the Dismal Swamp on the south, the region was divided
into two shores by the great Chesapeake Bay. From north to south the
country was broken into a series of necks by six deep rivers: the Susque-
hanna, Patuxent, Potomac, Rappahannock, York, and the James. Some
one hundred and fifty miles inland, waterfalls separated the country into
two distinct areas, tidewater and piedmont. The face of the tidewater was
generally low, flat, and densely wooded, much spread with marshes and
swamps. Along the river banks the soil was rich and deep, although by the
eve of the American Revolution there were extensive tracts of wasteland,
worn out by the cultivation of tobacco.[2] As the land receded from the
coast, it gradually rose, swelling into the hills of the piedmont. Beyond
were the mountains, severed by rivers that raged in torrents through rugged chasms or glided silently along deep valleys and into rich meadows.

Although not visible from the coast, small towns, farmsteads, and plantations were interspersed throughout the Chesapeake interior, linked by a
system of public roads.[3] In 1773 the total population of the region was at
least 646,300, most of whom were in one capacity or another involved

---

[1] J.F.D. Smyth, *A Tour of the United States of America*, 2 vols. (Dublin: G. Perrin, 1784),
1:10.

[2] Isaac Weld, Jr., *Travels Through the States of North America, and the Provinces of Upper and
Lower Canada. During the Years 1795, 1796, and 1797*, 2 vols. (London: John Stockdale,
1799), 1:151.

[3] Allan Kulikoff, *Tobacco and Slaves. The Development of Southern Culture in the Chesapeake,
1680–1800* (Chapel Hill: University of North Carolina Press, 1986), 94, 207, 209–14.

with tobacco production.[4] Despite the expansion of tobacco culture up to the Revolution, tobacco was a volatile economy. Recurring depressions during the first half of the eighteenth century led farmers on Maryland's Eastern Shore to begin shifting to wheat as early as the 1740s and 1750s.[5] Severe food shortages caused by rapid population growth and a series of bad harvests created an enormous European demand for wheat, which encouraged debt-burdened planters in the lower James Valley of Virginia and in the sandy low-lying Northern Neck to begin experimenting with the cultivation of wheat in the middle 1760s. By the 1770s, the Chesapeake colonies were exporting approximately 2.3 million bushels of grain or grain-equivalent.[6] On the eve of the Revolution, wheat was Virginia's second staple. Much of it either was consumed locally or was traded in the developing coastal and overland trade.

A very different plantation economy developed in the coastal region of the lower South. On the narrow band of land extending from the Cape Fear River in North Carolina to the Saint Johns River in Florida, the economy centered largely around the production of rice. The Lower Coastal Plain, where early colonial settlement concentrated, was ideally suited to the peculiar requirements of rice. A wet culture, rice demands systematic irrigation and a large labor force. From the northernmost point to the southernmost tip, South Carolina stretched some two hundred miles, with approximately one hundred and twenty miles of coastline. Protected from the sea by sandbanks alternately cast up only to be swallowed again by the sea, most of the coast consisted of low-lying islands and marshes cut by rivers and by innumerable creeks and narrow, muddy channels. Some fifteen or twenty miles inland, the sandy coastal soil began to give way to clay and to rich loams, covered in many places by dense forests of oak, cedar, and cypress, often interspersed with tracts of pine. The pine yielded most of the tar, turpentine, pitch, and rosin for Carolina's commercially significant naval stores industry. Rice was, however, the main crop.

Because of its adaptiveness to the coastal environment and because of the availability of West African slaves already familiar with the cultivation of the crop, rice agriculture developed quickly in the low-lying, swampy areas enriched by regular washings from the uplands.[7] Carolina's first rice

[4] Paul G. E. Clemens, *The Atlantic Economy and Colonial Maryland's Eastern Shore. From Tobacco to Grain* (Ithaca, N.Y.: Cornell University Press, 1980), 119n.

[5] Ibid., 170–205.

[6] Carville V. Earle and Ronald Hoffman, "Urban Development in the Eighteenth-Century South," *Perspectives in American History* 10 (1976): 30.

[7] The highly profitable rice plantation system that made South Carolina one of the wealthiest colonies in British North America, relied heavily on the technical knowledge of slaves imported directly from the Windward Coast, a major rice region of West Africa. Until the introduction of rice mills after 1830, West African traditions of seeding and hoeing and methods of threshing and winnowing continued in almost unchanged form in the low country of

crops were harvested late in the seventeenth century. By the eve of the Revolution, rice production reached 140,000 barrels in some years. The production of rice concentrated in the vicinity of Charleston, the capital and leading seaport, and around Georgetown, seventy miles to the north of Charleston, and Beaufort on Port Royal Island in the Broad River. Both towns served mainly as collection points for agricultural commodities shipped to Charleston. Lowland planters also cultivated indigo, first produced successfully in the 1740s by enslaved workers on Eliza Lucas's Wapoo Creek plantation; by 1770 indigo production had reached 500,000 pounds a year.[8] During slack periods in the rice-growing season, planters produced naval stores and, in the estuarine regions, planted cotton to supplement the rice.

To the south of Carolina lay the province of Georgia, its low, flat coastal lands gradually rising to hilly country some one hundred and fifty miles inland. Like the Carolina lowlands, Georgia's fertile black soil was interspersed with pine barrens. But the similarity was more than physical. In many ways Georgia was an extension of South Carolina's low-country plantation society. From the beginning of its settlement in 1733, the rich lands south of the Savannah River had attracted migrants from South Carolina. Although other groups, including Germans and Scots-Irish, settled in Georgia after 1750, the lure of comparatively cheap rice land continued to draw Carolina migrants, some of them with a few slaves. After slavery was legalized in 1751, they poured into the colony, bringing with them an estimated one thousand slaves in the year 1752 alone. During the 1750s and 1760s, the now-dominant Carolina migrants forged a plantation economy that closely resembled that of South Carolina: a biracial planting society based upon autonomous, self-contained plantation units whose pros-

---

South Carolina and Georgia. The wooden mortars and pestles used in processing the rice and the large round winnowing baskets used to separate the grain and chaff were of West African design. So too was the cooperative work pattern adapted by the slaves to the individualistic task system. As they moved through the fields during the warm growing season, slave workers slashed their hoes to the rhythm of work songs, a deep-rooted tradition that calls to mind the group labor songs of West Africa. See Peter H. Wood, *Black Majority. Negroes in Colonial South Carolina. From 1670 through the Stono Rebellion* (New York: Alfred A. Knopf, 1974), 35; Daniel C. Littlefield, *Rice and Slaves. Ethnicity and the Slave Trade in Colonial South Carolina* (Baton Rouge: Louisiana State University Press, 1981), 74–114, agrees that West Africans probably "had something to do" with the development of rice cultivation in South Carolina. Littlefield notes that although knowledge of rice cultivation was widespread, different varieties and methods of cultivation were in use in West Africa. According to Littlefield, the Baga system most closely approximated the Carolina system. See also Charles W. Joyner, *Down by the Riverside* (Urbana: University of Illinois Press, 1984), 58–59, 89; and Dale Rosengarten, *Row Upon Row: Sea Grass Baskets of the South Carolina Lowcountry* (Columbia, S.C.: McKissick Museum, University of South Carolina, 1986).

[8] Julian P. Boyd, ed. *The Papers of Thomas Jefferson*, 24 vols to date (Princeton, N.J.: Princeton University Press, 1950–), 8:197.

perity was derived from staples produced by slave labor and marketed by factorage houses in Charleston.[9] A lively trade in timber and timber products and in barreled beef and pork produced in lower Georgia was also carried on from Savannah and its commercial rival Sunbury.[10]

North Carolina was both similar to and different from the adjacent colonies of Virginia and South Carolina. The eastern section of its coastal plain was formed by sandbanks and shallow sounds, into which a series of necks of land protruded. Flat and poorly drained, it contained large areas of swamps and tidal marshes. To the west the land rose gradually, merging in the north with the rolling upland of the piedmont, in the south joining the region of sand ridges known as the Sandhills. Much of the piedmont and a small part of the coastal plain were covered with oak-pine forest. The Cape Fear River and its tributaries flowed through the heart of the longleaf pine country and served as conduits for the forest products that were shipped out of the colony through Wilmington and Brunswick.[11]

Between 1750 and 1770 the population of North Carolina increased very dramatically, primarily as a result of immigration. A heterogeneous group, including Scots-Irish, Scottish Highlanders, and Germans, the newcomers entered North Carolina from the north through Virginia and from the south via Charleston. Most of them headed for the westernmost parts of the colony. The highest densities were concentrated, however, in the northeast, north of Albemarle Sound, which received a heavy influx of migrants from Virginia, and in the lower Cape Fear region, which was settled by men of wealth and substance, many from South Carolina. Although most immigrants did not bring slaves with them, migrants from Virginia and South Carolina probably did, with the result that slaveholding was much more widespread in areas such as Albemarle and Cape Fear. By contrast, comparatively few slaves were in the western portions of the colony, where the antislavery Moravians had settled in large, compact blocks.

Like her northern neighbor, Virginia, North Carolina grew tobacco, mainly in the northern part of the colony, but in quantities substantially smaller than in Virginia and Maryland. For environmental reasons, rice cultivation was confined to a small area within the Cape Fear Valley. North Carolina's most distinctive contribution to colonial commerce was, however, forest products. A wide range of wood products, principally shingles,

[9] Betty Wood, *Slavery in Colonial Georgia, 1730–1775* (Athens: University of Georgia Press, 1984), 92–93; Julia Floyd Smith, *Slavery and Rice Culture in Low Country Georgia, 1750–1860* (Knoxville: University of Tennessee Press, 1985), 78.

[10] Smith, *Slavery and Rice Culture*, 23–24.

[11] Harry Roy Merrens, *Colonial North Carolina in the Eighteenth Century. A Study in Historical Geography* (Chapel Hill: University of North Carolina Press, 1964), 37, 39, 46, 90–91.

staves, and sawn lumber, were produced commercially in the region around Albemarle Sound. The mainstay of the colonial economy was naval stores, most of which were produced in the southern part of the colony where longleaf pine was native to the Sandhills and the coastal plain. Access to the longleaf pine forests, rivers and streams that provided routeways to Wilmington and Brunswick for thousands of barrels of pitch, tar, and turpentine, and most importantly, the availability of slave labor, contributed to the growth and eventual localization of the large-scale production of naval stores in the Cape Fear region.[12]

Large slaveholding provided the bedrock upon which each plantation system was built. Over 270,000 slaves lived in the area bounded by the tossing waters of Chesapeake Bay and the rocky falls that divide the tidewater from the piedmont regions of Virginia and Maryland. Although the geographical balance of the black population had begun to shift around midcentury, in 1775 more than half of Virginia's slaves still lived in the counties between the Rappahannock and the James rivers. In parts of the tidewater, blacks constituted a majority of the population. In the Northern Neck and in counties adjacent to the piedmont, they made up between 40 and 50 percent of the population. Although some households owned no slaves, slave distribution was becoming more widespread in the tidewater due to outmigration of poor people and because slaveholders customarily divided their slaves among all of their children. By the Revolution an estimated two-thirds of the planters in nine tidewater counties and approximately 40 percent of piedmont families held slaves.[13]

The slave population of the South Carolina and Georgia low country shared some characteristics with that of the Chesapeake. Although the low country's slave population was beginning to grow by natural increase, it continued to be dominated by young and predominantly male, African-born slaves, many of whom still carried ritual scars and spoke the distinctive dialects of West Africa.[14] Heavily concentrated in the low-country parishes, blacks increasingly outnumbered whites, particularly in the plantation parishes surrounding Charleston, the center of the lowland slave trade.[15] In 1775 South Carolina's white population was an estimated 70,000, the slave population approximately 100,000. Of these, 14,302

[12] Ibid., 55, 61, 73, 88–90, 93–107, 120, 122, 175.

[13] Kulikoff, *Tobacco and Slaves*, 136, 153, 340; Richard S. Dunn, "Black Society in the Chesapeake, 1776–1810," in Ira Berlin and Ronald Hoffman, eds., *Slavery and Freedom in the Age of the American Revolution* (Charlottesville: University Press of Virginia, 1983), 56, 58. See also Philip D. Morgan, "Slave Life in Piedmont Virginia," in Lois Green Carr, Philip D. Morgan, and Jean B. Russo, eds., *Colonial Chesapeake Society* (Chapel Hill: University of North Carolina Press, 1988).

[14] Wood, *Black Majority*, 69–70, 140, 154; Wood, *Slavery in Colonial Georgia*, 99.

[15] Philip D. Morgan, "Black Society in the Lowcountry, 1760–1810," in Berlin and Hoffman, eds., *Slavery and Freedom*, 93.

whites and 72,743 blacks clustered in the three low-country districts of
Beaufort, Charleston, and Georgetown; 55,689 whites and 27,253 blacks
lived in the backcountry districts of Camden, Cheraw, Ninety Six, and
Orangeburg[16] Because the interior regions were unsuitable for the cultivation of either rice or indigo, Georgia's population of 33,000, roughly
15,000 of whom were black, was heavily concentrated in the low country.
Ten years after slavery was legalized in Georgia perhaps one-quarter of all
households had at least one slave and the average size of slaveholdings was
over twenty-three slaves.[17]

A large labor force was essential to staple crop agriculture, whether tobacco or rice was the product grown for export, but the time and labor
requirements were different. Tobacco growing was a specialized occupation that required close supervision of all phases of production.[18] The kinds
of activities involved in tobacco cultivation—hoeing, raking, plowing,
planting, transplanting, weeding, worming, and cutting—were best carried out by small work gangs supervised by an owner or overseer. Perhaps
half of all tidewater slaves lived on farms of more than twenty slaves, while
another 25 percent labored on units of eleven to twenty slaves. On smaller
farms, masters worked side by side with their slaves on every step of the
production cycle. On larger units, gangs were often divided according to
skills, e.g., plowman or mower. After 1750 larger quarters began to employ slave drivers and foremen; by the 1770s between one-third and one-
half of all slaves in the tidewater lived on plantations with overseers, but
the overseers had little real authority. In the mature plantation societies of
the upper South, where a distinctive form of patriarchy had developed,
patriarchal norms required that planters retain control over land and slaves,
the basis of patriarchal power, and planters delegated authority very reluctantly. Their preference for centralized control is apparent in the frequent
conflicts between masters and overseers, which resulted in a high turnover
of overseers, and in the spatial arrangement of the tidewater plantation
itself, which was designed to provide maximum surveillance and control.[19]

Whereas in the older plantation societies of the Chesapeake, plantation
management tended to be patriarchal, in the low country it was delegated.
Unlike tobacco, where strict regimentation required gang labor, all work
on the rice coast was done by tasks. The reclamation of swamp land was a

[16] Stella H. Sutherland, *Population Distribution in Colonial America* (New York: AMS Press,
1966), ix, 139, 239, 240.
[17] Ibid., 259–60; Wood, *Slavery in Colonial Georgia*, 107–8.
[18] Philip D. Morgan, "Work and Culture: The Task System and the World of Lowcountry
Blacks, 1700 to 1880," *William and Mary Quarterly*, 3d ser., 39 (1982): 568.
[19] Allan Kulikoff, "The Origins of Afro-American Society in Tidewater Maryland and Virginia, 1700–1790," *William and Mary Quarterly*, 3d ser., 35 (1978): 246; idem, *Tobacco and
Slaves*, 173, 187, 408, 410–11.

laborious process that could take several years to complete. Rice cultivation required an enormous amount of hand labor, and the work was grueling and unwholesome. Although a high incidence of the sickle-cell trait provided blacks with some protection against malaria, environmental conditions in the rice fields made slaves particularly vulnerable to pleurisy and pneumonia.[20] The laborious and even hazardous nature of field work made the task system a more practical organization of labor than the gang system.[21] Under tasking, slaves were assigned a specified task or a certain amount of land to tend. The basic unit of measurement for all tasks was a quarter-acre, although the standard varied according to heavy, moderate, or light work.[22] Once the task was complete, slaves were free to engage in stock raising, fishing, or hunting, or to work their own garden lots.

The labor of slaves and the commercialization of agriculture created a distinctive social structure in the southern staple colonies. A pyramid, its broad base was composed of slaves; its ascending face comprised freeholders, the majority of whom lived on small inland farms averaging around two hundred acres; and its apex was crowned by a small planter elite. Rhetorically, at least, white southerners constituted a unified community, although as the region became more densely populated, class distinctions and differences based on wealth, landholding, and slaves became increasingly apparent. Although racial interaction was constant, largely through the labor process, and their various destinies were intertwined, black and white southerners participated in two separate cultural worlds.[23] Each had its own traditions of life and thought, which in most cases antedated the development of the plantation economy; each was still in the process of evolving. Although the degree of separation varied considerably through time and space and according to the relative economic status of the owner, the dichotomy was inherent in the historical experiences of each group and in the system of slavery itself.

Over a century and a half, those whites who had survived the harsh en-

[20] Wood, *Black Majority*, 85–91; Wood, *Slavery in Colonial Georgia*, 150.

[21] Scholars do not agree about the origins of the task system. Ira Berlin, "Time, Space, and the Evolution of Afro-American Society in British Mainland North America," *American Historical Review* 85 (1980): 44–78, contends that similarity to conditions in West Africa and the slaves' familiarity with field-crop production, contributed to the development of tasking. Philip Morgan, "Work and Culture," 563–99, emphasizes that rice production required less direct supervision and that productivity could be easily measured on a task basis.

[22] Smith, *Slavery and Rice Culture*, 45–46.

[23] Recent studies of the plantation system have emphasized the cultural interrelationships between master and slave in the Chesapeake, if not in the low country. See, for example, Mechal Sobel, *The World They Made Together. Black and White Values in Eighteenth-Century Virginia* (Princeton, N.J.: Princeton University Press, 1987), 11 and throughout. Kulikoff, *Tobacco and Slaves*, 381–420, also discusses cultural interrelationships, but argues for the existence of two southern cultures in the Chesapeake.

vironment of the southern coastal plains were able to patent large amounts of land. Using slave labor, they placed more land under cultivation. With the profits earned, they bought out small landowners. Over time they accumulated extensive holdings, which they passed on to future generations. Through marriage within kinship groups, their descendants consolidated family fortunes and cemented familial bonds. During the eighteenth century this small elite increasingly monopolized wealth and power.[24] Because their wealth and social status were based on foundations built by a system of forced, lifetime labor, relationships between masters and slaves, although they were continually being negotiated, were fundamentally antagonistic. For the slaveholding elite, the central dilemma was how to defend slavery against slaves. Those who claimed the mandate to order society developed a protective shield of symbols and institutions, which created the apparent unity of the white community and thereby helped to secure its well-being: the great house, the courthouse, and the church. Together these institutions generated social and cultural life within the white community and simultaneously operated as a single social and cultural system of domination within plantation society.

The plantation house, which first appeared early in the eighteenth century, was the most powerful metaphor for the culture of the plantation aristocracy. The seat of the gentry's economic power, the estates of great planters generally conformed to a common pattern that reflected the requirements of a slave-based system of plantation agriculture. The plantation of the average wealthy tidewater planter consisted of some three thousand acres of land that generally were broken up into small tracts called "quarters." Separated from the home plantation, sometimes by a considerable distance, the quarters were physically isolated by the woods, swamps, and uncleared land that surrounded them. Although variation was considerable, after 1740 both the size of quarters and the number of large estates increased. By 1770 the home plantation of the wealthiest tidewater planters contained over one hundred slaves, the quarters from thirty to fifty slaves. Piedmont plantations were usually smaller, but they too increased in size during the 1760s and 1770s.[25]

The home plantation generally was located on the lower reaches of one of the Chesapeake's rivers, which offered the easiest means of transportation and trade, and was usually placed on a branch road that led into a main road. The rivers connected the planters' world with the British mer-

---

[24] Kulikoff, *Tobacco and Slaves*, 134, 165–313, offers an excellent discussion of the rise of the gentry class in the Chesapeake; for South Carolina, see Jerome J. Nadelhaft, *The Disorders of War. The Revolution in South Carolina* (Orono: University of Maine at Orono Press, 1981), 3–5.

[25] Gerald W. Mullin, *Flight and Rebellion. Slave Resistance in Eighteenth-Century Virginia* (New York: Oxford University Press, 1972), 47, 61; Kulikoff, *Tobacco and Slaves*, 337.

cantile community; the roads provided a link to local commerce. The typical plantation consisted of various dependencies, service buildings, and slave quarters grouped compactly around the main dwelling. This configuration was apparently a function both of the economic role of the plantation—the large-scale production of staples for a nondomestic market—and of the need for effective, centralized estate management. George Washington's home plantation in Fairfax County, Virginia, is representative of the pattern developed in the eighteenth century.[26] Seen from the land side, Mount Vernon resembled a small village.[27]

Low-country estates had similar spatial layouts. Archaeological data from two eighteenth-century plantations in the South Carolina low country, Middleton Place, the principal family residence of a wealthy planter, Henry Middleton, and Hampton Plantation, established by Daniel Horry in midcentury, suggest the same systematic arrangement of the main house complex.[28] But the need for continuous irrigation combined with the low country's distinctive ethnic configuration gave Georgia and South Carolina plantations a somewhat different character.

The first rice crops in South Carolina were planted in open fields without irrigation, but the discovery that yields were higher if rice was grown in moist places led to the transition to swamp rice culture sometime in the early eighteenth century. Because South Carolina's coastal swamps were often brackish, the best environment for rice growing was inland floodplain swamps that were normally beyond the push of the tides and were fresh, fed by streams. The problems associated with controlling the freshwater streams led to experiments in the 1750s with tidewater rice culture, which used the tidal flow of fresh water and, therefore, required that rice fields be located adjacent to estuaries to facilitate irrigation. By the American Revolution both methods of cultivation were in use, sometimes simultaneously, and rice cultivation was slowly beginning to shift toward the tidal portions of the major coastal rivers.[29] Middleton Place, for example, was situated on the west bank of the Ashley River northwest of Charleston and apparently employed the tidal method; Hampton Plantation, on the southern bank of the South Santee River, was on the edge of the Santee Delta, an area of extensive rice cultivation southwest of Georgetown. An

[26] Kenneth E. Lewis, "Plantation Layout and Function in the South Carolina Lowcountry," in Theresa A. Singleton, ed., *The Archaeology of Slavery and Plantation Life* (Orlando, Fla.,: Academic Press, 1985), 37, 38.

[27] The general description is from Jedidiah Morse, *American Geography*, 3d ed. (Dublin, FreLand: John Jones, 1792), 381, and Weld, *Travels*, 1:92.

[28] Lewis, "Plantation Layout," 35–65.

[29] Smith, *Slavery and Rice Culture*, 21, claims that tidal culture was established by 1750. Converse D. Clowse, *Economic Beginnings in Colonial South Carolina, 1670–1730*, 1st ed. (Columbia: University of South Carolina Press, 1971), 167, which draws heavily on contemporary sources, dates the wide practice of tidal culture to the American Revolution.

early plan of the plantation shows both impounded and tidal rice fields.[30] The high proportion of Africans, particularly in rural parishes, and the need to locate rice plantations in malaria-ridden swamps, caused many low-country planters to set up summer residences in Charleston, whose brackish saltwater environment kept it relatively free of malaria.[31]

The progressive separation of masters and slaves on larger estates, which is reflected in changes in the plantation layout, mirrors what Fraser D. Neiman has described as a "dramatic restructuring of the basis of social relations." The appearance of the great house, the detachment of work structures and outbuildings, and the separation of all service-related tasks from the main dwelling are the manifest embodiments of slaveowners' growing intolerance of racial intermixing and their increasing concern with dominance and subordination, with peace and with order.[32]

The facade of order the great house presented was, however, often at odds with reality. To reinforce social boundaries and to bolster their claim to civil authority, the planter elite relied upon the legal and judicial system. The development of a large body of criminal laws and the creation of a separate judicial system for slaves reinforce the impression of a new adversarial relationship, or perhaps the aggravation of the existing one, between master and slave. Barely twenty years after the arrival of the first Africans in Virginia, the colony began to write legislation affecting black labor.

Through the passage of piecemeal legislation, slavery was by 1682 firmly established on a racial basis in Virginia. In 1705 the assembly approved the Virginia code, the major provisions of which were retained in subsequent revisions. The first comprehensive effort to regulate slaves in South Carolina followed shortly after the passage of the act of 1712, which is generally exemplary of later revised codes including the 1740 statute passed in the wake of the Stono Rebellion. That same statute served as the model for Georgia's slave act of 1755, written after the metropolitan law banning the importation of slaves into Georgia was repealed under intense local pres-

---

[30] Lewis, "Plantation Layout," 44; see also Sam B. Hilliard, "Antebellum Tidewater Rice Culture in South Carolina and Georgia," in James R. Gibson, ed., *European Settlement and Development in North America: Essays on Geographical Change in Honour and Memory of Andrew Hill Clark* (Toronto: University of Toronto Press, 1978), 91–115, especially p. 99.

[31] Black population by density was highest in the Santee region; see Philip D. Morgan, "The Development of Slave Culture in Eighteenth Century Plantation America" (Ph.D. diss., University College, London, 1977), 1, 7.

[32] Fraser D. Neiman, "Domestic Architecture at the Clifts Plantation: The Social Context of Early Virginia Building," *Northern Neck Historical Magazine* 28 (1978): 3121. See also William M. Kelso, *Kingsmill Plantations 1619–1800. Archaeology of Country Life in Colonial Virginia* (Orlando, Fla.: Academic Press, 1984); Lynne G. Lewis, "The Planter Class: The Archaeological Record at Drayton Hall," and Kenneth E. Lewis, "Plantation Layout," in Singleton, ed., *Archaeology of Slavery*, 121–40, 35–65.

sure.[33] Although the slave codes of the several colonies differed in minor details, they all sharply curtailed slave mobility, limited their personal liberties, and prescribed severe punishments for a large number of "criminal" offenses.

The expansion of the criminal codes during the seventeenth and eighteenth centuries was, to a large extent, a reaction to long-term changes in slave behavior, which emanated from developments within the various slave communities. The numerical increase in the number of slaves, their rising percentage of the total population, and the gradual coalescence of networks of various kinds, produced changes in slaves' criminalized behavior and corresponding changes in the development of slave laws.[34] The growing racial tension, particularly in the low country, where a black majority had emerged by the 1720s,[35] is reflected in the increasing severity of the penalties for such "offenses" as running away or resisting a white person. Because the successful flight of slaves effectively ended their bondage and created the possibility for concerted aggressiveness, colonial assemblies developed elaborate deterrents, including branding, maiming, and arbitrary killing of runaways.[36] Because the death of a slave represented a capital loss to the owner, it became economically unfeasible to enforce such brutal punishments and later codes abandoned branding, maiming, and killing runaways in favor of severe corporal punishment.[37] Penalties for actual insurrection, however, grew increasingly harsh during the eighteenth century.

Until the development of a cohesive slave community, collective rebellion did not pose a serious threat to white society. The gradual reformation of families, fictive and real, and the simultaneous development of kinship networks in the upper South contributed to a series of plots and risings in

[33] A. Leon Higginbotham, Jr., *In the Matter of Color. Race and the American Legal Process. The Colonial Period* (New York: Oxford University Press, 1978), 32, 37, 55, 169, 216–17; for details of the Georgia code, see Wood, *Slavery in Colonial Georgia*, 111–30.

[34] I am following the argument made by Philip J. Schwarz, *Twice Condemned. Slaves and the Criminal Laws of Virginia, 1705–1865* (Baton Rouge: Louisiana State University Press, 1988), 14, 16, 68, 73–74, and throughout.

[35] Wood, *Black Majority*, 130–32.

[36] William W. Hening, ed., *The Statutes at Large. Being a Collection of All the Laws of Virginia from the First Session of the Legislature in the Year 1619*, 13 vols. (Richmond, 1809–23), 7:352–65; Thomas Cooper and David J. McCord, eds., *The Statutes at Large of South Carolina*, 10 vols. (Columbia, S.C.: A. S. Johnston, 1836–41), 7:352–65; Allen D. Candler, comp., *The Colonial Records of the State of Georgia* (1732–1782), 27 vols. (Atlanta: C. P. Byrd, 1904–16), 18:105–6, 137–38 (hereafter cited as *CRG*).

[37] The South Carolina act of 1735 reduced the penalty to corporal punishment; see Cooper and McCord, *Statutes of South Carolina* 7:390. The Virginia law allowing dismemberment of runaways was repealed in 1769; the same law, however, conferred new authority on county courts to castrate slaves convicted of attempted rape of a white woman; see Schwarz, *Twice Condemned*, 22.

Virginia between 1709 and 1723. These in turn led the assembly to pass the first insurrection legislation in the colonies' history.[38] In the wake of the Stono Rebellion of 1739, which confirmed white fears of the potential for a massive slave revolt, most colonies passed laws designed to crush even the possibility of slave rebellion.[39] As part of the deterrent process, the southern colonies also created elaborate surveillance systems. By midcentury responsibility for colonial defense not only against external enemies but also against the "internal" enemy was concentrated in the hands of local militia units composed of white adult males between the ages of sixteen and sixty. The provisions of South Carolina's patrol law of 1743, passed in response to the "many late horrible massacres" committed by blacks during the Stono Rebellion, were typical of other colonial statutes. The act ordered militia officers, most of whom were of the slaveholding class, to set up patrol districts, not to exceed fifteen miles in extent, within each of the militia districts. Plantation owners within each district, women as well as men, were required to perform patrol service or procure a substitute. Patrol duty consisted of visiting each plantation within the district at two-week intervals to search slave quarters for concealed weapons or stolen goods and to check "disorderly tipling houses" or other places suspected of harboring fugitive slaves.[40] In Georgia the patrols were empowered to arbitrarily "correct every such slave or slaves by whipping with a switch or cowskin, not exceeding twenty lashes."[41]

The ultimate power of legal punishment was in the hands of the county courts. The center of institutional power in the Chesapeake and in tidewater North Carolina, the county courts exercised full judicial and administrative powers, including licensing ordinaries, laying out roads, building bridges and ferries and regulating the credit system. Located at major crossroads, these neat brick buildings also served as the principal centers for social and business activities, where cockfights, fairs, horse sales, slave sales and auctions took place, and where the reciprocal exchanges between gentry and yeomen, which formed the basis for gentry rule, were worked

[38] Schwarz, *Twice Condemned*, 85, 88.

[39] Georgia prohibited slaves from owning canoes, breeding livestock, or trading goods or provisions; see Candler, *CRG* 18:128, 136; South Carolina passed a law against teaching slaves to read or write and fined whites who violated the law, Cooper and McCord, *Statutes of South Carolina* 7:397–417; North Carolina's code of 1741 declared any gathering of three or more slaves to "consult, advise or conspire to rebell" a capital crime, Walter Clark, ed., *The State Records of North Carolina*, 26 vols. (Raleigh: P. M. Hale, 1886–1907), 22:202–3. In times of crisis, such as a fire, most southern states required the militia to turn out under arms as a precaution against a slave rising; see Henry Melchoir Muhlenberg, *The Journals of Henry Melchoir Muhlenberg*, Theodore G. Tappert and John W. Doberstein, eds., 3 vols. (Philadelphia: Evangelical Lutheran Ministerium of Pennsylvania and Adjacent States, 1942–58), 2:593, 658.

[40] Cooper and McCord, *Statutes of South Carolina* 7:417–19.

[41] Candler, *CRG* 18:232–33.

out.[42] In South Carolina the rural courthouse had less legal, political and social importance, perhaps because the great low-country planters and even small up-country planters spent so much time in Charleston, the seaport capital.[43]

Beginning with the passage in 1692 of Virginia's "Act for the speedy prosecution of slaves committing Capitall Crimes," the county courts also functioned as separate slave tribunals. Composed of the most prominent and powerful citizens, Virginia's courts of oyer and terminer operated without juries and, after 1765, under blanket gubernatorial commissions issued expressly for the trial of slaves. Special courts of oyer and terminer were also created in all other southern colonies except South Carolina, whose slave courts functioned at the parish level of government.[44] The creation of a separate judicial process for slaves was in large measure a reaction to the growing assertiveness of the South's swelling slave population, which manifested itself in a marked increase in criminalized activity. A cycle of insurrectionary activity beginning in the 1750s and the general growth of violent racial confrontation produced an increase in the prosecutions of slaves for various felonies and misdemeanors and, in the late colonial period, a steady increase in convictions and in the rate of sentences of execution. The great majority of those convicted of capital crimes were either hanged or burned alive, their bodies often dismembered or hung in chains for public display.[45] Executions, floggings, and mutilations did not put an end to slave resistance, although they did, perhaps, make it more difficult.

If the county court was frequently the locus of political and legal power,

[42] For the functions of the Chesapeake courts, see Kulikoff, *Tobacco and Slaves*, 95–96, 129–30, 285–87, 289, 292–95; for the development of the courts in a frontier area, see Richard R. Beeman, *The Evolution of the Southern Backcountry. A Case Study of Lunenburg County, Virginia, 1746–1832* (Philadelphia: University of Pennsylvania Press, 1984), 83, 86.

[43] Richard Beale Davis, *Intellectual Life in the Colonial South, 1758–1763*, 3 vols. (Knoxville: University of Tennessee Press, 1978), 3:1187; Nadelhaft, *Disorders of War*, 4.

[44] See, for example, Betty Wood, " 'Untill He Shall Be Dead, Dead, Dead': The Judicial Treatment of Slaves in Eighteenth-Century Georgia," *Georgia Historical Quarterly* 71 (1987): 380; Mark J. Stegmaier, "Maryland's Fear of Insurrection at the Time of Braddock's Defeat," *Maryland Historical Magazine* 71 (1976): 473. For South Carolina, see John E. Douglass, "Judiciary Without Jurisdiction: South Carolina's Experiment With a County and Precinct Court System, 1720–1730," *South Carolina Historical Magazine* 90 (1989): 237–56.

[45] Schwarz, *Twice Condemned*, 96, 109, 110, 116, 122, 143, 151, 174–76 notes a sharp increase in convictions for poisonings in the late 1740s and 1750s and in insurrectionary activity during the 1750s; Wood, "Untill He Shall Be Dead," 378, 381–82, 383, 384, 387; reports at least seventeen slave executions in Georgia between 1766 and 1773 and three in 1774–75, two of whom were sentenced to be burned alive for their involvement in the St. Andrew parish "revolt" of 1774, the third for burning his master's house; Stegmaier, "Maryland's Fear of Insurrection," 474, 482, found a rise from a frequency of one reported crime per year between 1745 and 1748 to fifteen reported acts between 1753 and 1755. Significantly over half of the reported crimes involved two or more slaves or servants acting together.

in the white southern community the parish church was its spiritual and moral counterpart. The small brick, stone, or wooden structures with their box pews, galleries, and cupola-topped pulpits were generally designed to meet the needs of rural congregations composed of royal officials, great and small planters, merchants, artisans, and indentured servants. Legally established in all of the southern colonies except Maryland, the Anglican church was charged with responsibility for sustaining and supporting the social and moral order. In the southern backcountry before the formation of counties and courts, churches also carried out a wide range of social and civic activities. Not everyone accepted the institutional church, particularly in the backcountry where, beginning in the 1740s, evangelical missionaries launched the first of the sporadic revivals in the Virginia backcountry. Dissenters constituted a small minority, however, and the majority of the white churched population subscribed to the Anglican faith.[46]

Although Anglicanism commanded a clear majority of the white religious population of the South, the region as a whole lagged behind the rest of the country in the growth and expansion of religion. Southern parishes were large and often extended up to one hundred miles. Even in the tidewater parishes of Virginia and the low-country parishes of South Carolina, which were generally well-churched and where the establishment was strongest, Anglican preachers were often obliged to itinerate between churches. Many rural parishes were without churches, glebes, or even chapels of ease. Georgia did not achieve a religious establishment until 1758, and even then it consisted of only six ministers to serve a population of approximately ten thousand.[47] In his tour of North Carolina in 1772, Joseph Pilmore found only six ministers to serve an area two hundred miles wide. The Great Awakening of 1739–1745 did produce a surge in church admissions everywhere, particularly among men, young people, and blacks, but on the eve of the Revolution only about half of the white population and a very small percentage of the black population of the southern colonies was churched.[48]

[46] Patricia U. Bonomi and Peter R. Eisenstadt, "Church Adherence in the Eighteenth-Century British American Colonies," *William and Mary Quarterly*, 3d ser., 39 (1982): 262–63, 67n; for the Great Awakening in the backcountry, see Beeman, *Evolution of Southern Backcountry*, 53, 97–119.

[47] In 1761 Governor James Wright estimated the population to be no more than 6,100 whites and about 3,600 blacks; quoted in Wood, *Slavery in Colonial Georgia*, 89.

[48] Bonomi, "Church Adherence," estimates the churched population in all colonies as 56 to 80 percent, with the South at the bottom end of the range. Bonomi, *Under the Cope of Heaven: Religion, Society and Politics in Colonial America* (New York: Oxford University Press, 1986), 6, 50, 55, 123, 126, refutes the traditional interpretation of religious declension and argues that the prerevolutionary years were a time of "rising vitality in religious life," even in the South. Compare Bonomi to the more negative view offered by Donald G. Mathews, *Religion in the Old South* (Chicago: University of Chicago Press, 1977), 4–10. For the state

Most of the gentry class were members of the Anglican church and membership in the ruling vestry usually overlapped with membership in the county court. The educated gentry shared various degrees of humble faith, deism, and skepticism. Under the influence of Enlightenment thinkers such as Newton, Bacon, and Locke, many subscribed to rational religious ideas. Even so, most of the great planters had an appreciation of devotional religion. Many of them studied the Scriptures and theology, conducted family prayers, attended church services regularly, and participated in the practical affairs of the church. By and large they believed in the importance of religion to the psychological well-being and to the moral order of society.[49] Although they recognized the church's important role as one of the basic institutions for stabilizing white society, the gentry who dominated parish vestries expended great energy in trying to prevent slaves from becoming Christians, in their minds the best means of defending slavery.

The first systematic if tentative efforts to Christianize slaves in the South were made early in the eighteenth century by missionaries of the Society for the Propagation of the Gospel (SPG), the missionary arm of the Anglican church. In South Carolina, the Reverend Thomas of Goose Creek parish taught native Americans and blacks and by 1705 had twenty black communicants. Two white women took "extraordinary pains" to instruct slaves in St. Andrew parish in 1713.[50] Despite owner opposition and the inability of many Africans to understand or to speak English, by 1724 Anglican clergymen had established small groups of African converts in a number of parishes in Virginia and Maryland. They enjoyed their greatest success in Bruton parish in Williamsburg, where approximately 200 Africans were baptized by the Reverend William Black.[51]

Orthodox on slavery, the Anglican church nonetheless took seriously its sacred duty to save souls, regardless of race, and sought to encourage the missionary efforts of its ministers. In 1727 the bishop of London addressed two pastoral letters to British colonials and to SPG missionaries,

of religion in North Carolina, see Frank Baker, "The British Background of North Carolina Methodism," in O. Kelly Ingram, ed., *Methodism Alive in North Carolina* (Durham, N.C.: Duke University Press, 1976), 515.

[49] See, for example, Ralph L. Ketcham, "James Madison and Religion—A New Hypothesis," *Journal of the Presbyterian Historical Society* 38 (1960): 65–90; David Duncan Wallace, *The Life of Henry Laurens* (New York: Russell and Russell, 1967), 438; Charles B. Sanford, *The Religious Life of Thomas Jefferson* (Charlottesville: University Press of Virginia, 1984), 3, 4, 5.

[50] C. E. Pierre, "The Work of the Society for the Propagation of the Gospel in Foreign parts among the Negroes in the Colonies," *Journal of Negro History* 1 (1916): 350.

[51] William Stevens Perry, ed., *Historical Collections Relating to the American Colonial Church*, 5 vols. in 4 (1870–78; reprint, New York: AMS Press, 1969), 1:261, 264, 267, 269, 277, 278, 280, 281, 287, 291, 293, 297, 299, 301, 310, 327, 360.

urging them to provide religious instruction for slaves. To counter planter fears that slave conversions might interfere with their legal right to their slaves' labor, the bishop insisted that Christianity "does not make the least Alteration in Civil Property." Rather than "discharging Men from the Duties of the Station and Condition in which it found them," Christianity "lays them under stronger Obligations to perform those Duties with the greatest Diligence and Fidelity, not only from the Fear of Men, but from a sense of Duty to God, and the Belief and Expectation of a future Account." Ten thousand copies of the pastoral letter were published by the SPG for distribution in the colonies. During the next twenty-five years it was followed by a series of sermons and tracts all aimed at persuading British Americans that as Christians, they had a moral responsibility to develop a more "Humane and Christian system of slavery."[52]

Thus encouraged by the church, a number of ministers began to instruct blacks in the principles of the Christian faith. During his first tour of the Virginia backcountry in 1738, the Reverend Anthony Gavin baptized 229 white and 172 black persons in the frontier parish of St. James in Goochland County.[53] In 1742 the Reverend Alexander Garden established the first school for slaves in Charleston. Under two black instructors, Harry and Andrew, the school flourished, and taught an average of fifty or sixty children. After twenty-two years it closed when Andrew died and Harry "turned out profligate."[54] Shortly after slavery became legal in Georgia, the SPG founded a similar school in Savannah and appointed Joseph Ottolenghe, a convert from Judaism, its first schoolmaster. For eight years Ottolenghe held classes three nights a week, but because the still small black population in Georgia was dispersed, the school was forced to close.[55]

A few planters were receptive to these early missionary efforts. Prominent planters like James Habersham, secretary of the colony of Georgia, president of the Governor's Council and, for a time, acting governor, read the bishop's annual sermons and took seriously the argument that owners had a fundamental responsibility to provide a Christian education for their slaves. The "inoffensive and pious behavior" of Anglican clerics in their educational work among slaves also helped to alleviate the planters' fears. Bartholomew Zouberbuhler, rector of Christ Episcopal Church in Savan-

---

[52] Frederick Dalcho, *An Historical Account of the Protestant Episcopal Church in South Carolina. From the First Settlement of the Province, to the War of the Revolution* (Charleston, S.C.: E. Thayer, 1820), 149, 156–58, 174, 178, 193, 336–37.

[53] Perry, *Historical Collections* 1:360.

[54] Dalcho, *Historical Account*, 149, 156–58, 174, 178, 193, 336–37.

[55] James B. Lawrence, "Religious Education of the Negro in the Colony of Georgia," *Georgia Historical Quarterly* 14 (1930): 41, 47, 49, 51. For the attitude of Georgia whites see Wood, *Slavery in Colonial Georgia*, 85, 114–15, 161–62. The Georgia Trustees first required attention to the spiritual welfare of slaves, but the 1755 code omitted any reference to their spiritual life.

nah and one of the principal organizers of the Savannah school for slave children, was himself a slave owner. In his will Zouberbuhler left in trust a sizeable portion of his estate for the support of an Anglican minister "properly qualified to instruct" his own slaves and any others whose masters would permit it.[56]

Cornelius Winter, a Methodist preacher, was appointed by the executors of Zouberbuhler's will and began preaching to blacks in 1769. A "Condescending and patient" man, Winter quickly found several white patrons, among them James Habersham. Habersham, a friend of George Whitefield and of Zouberbuhler, became on the latter's death in 1769, a warm advocate of moral and religious instruction for slaves. Motivated by the newfound conviction that slaves had souls, Habersham invited Winter to preach to nearly two hundred of his slaves. Unlike most "narrow minded, formal, and high flying" Anglican ministers, Winter proved willing to "stoop to the unimproved Capacities of these poor Creatures." Although slaves responded well to his simple style of preaching, Habersham was convinced that to win acceptance from whites, Winter must be ordained. He therefore carried on a letter-writing campaign with a number of prominent people in England, and Winter himself traveled to London in 1770 in a vain effort to obtain ordination.[57]

The insistence of the church on maintaining an educated clergy destroyed the appeal of the Anglican faith to blacks and forced owners like Habersham and his good friend William Knox, who not only pressed for the religious instruction of slaves but forced his own to attend divine services, to turn to more radical sects.[58] In 1775 Knox, who had been removed as provincial agent of Georgia because of his opposition to the Stamp Act, sent over two Moravian preachers to teach his slaves. Although one was college educated, the other was a tailor who, because he barely spoke English, seemed to Habersham "an improbable instrument of doing good." Nevertheless, they founded a school for black children, which had on the eve of the Revolution about thirty children.[59]

Anglican efforts to Christianize slaves met with competition from dissenters. The first to come were the New Light Presbyterian missionaries. Young, fervent, eager, in the 1740s they launched the first of the sporadic revivals in the backcountry of Virginia. Staid sermons by university graduates were no match for the powerful rhetoric of the sectarians, whose themes of tyranny, slavery, and spiritual equality, often delivered in coarse

[56] "Letters of the Honorable James Habersham, 1756–1775," Georgia Historical Society, *Collections* 6 (1904): 95, 96, 99, 135 (hereafter cited as GHS *Coll.*).

[57] Ibid., 95, 96, 100, 130.

[58] Wood, *Slavery in Colonial Georgia*, 161. In 1768 Knox published *Three Tracts* to encourage planters to permit religious instruction of their slaves.

[59] GHS *Coll.*, "Letters of James Habersham," 241.

language embellished by colorful metaphors, had an electrifying effect on blacks and poor whites alike. Nevertheless, the efforts of the Anglican church and of the SPG had paved the way for the itinerants. Hardy pioneers, they traveled on horseback thousands of miles on a stretch on the frontiers of civilized life.

The moving spirit behind the early frontier revival was the Reverend Samuel Davies, a frail but eloquent young graduate of William Tennent, Sr.'s little seminary, derisively dubbed "the Log College" by its detractors. Settlement in Hanover County, where Davies formed his first church, was sparse, but pious people came from miles away to hear the ebullient preacher. Among the devout who crowded into his rough meeting house were a number of slaves, who represented about 50 percent of the population of the county. Davies was captivated by their "artless simplicity, their passionate Aspirations after Christ, their incessant Endeavors to know and do the will of God," and so he began to devote more time to their religious instruction. Profoundly moved by their piety, he began to teach a few of them to read. Free from work on Saturday evenings, they crowded into Davies' home, "begging for books," sent for their instruction by sympathetic friends in England. When his supply was exhausted, Davies wrote for more, especially Bibles and Watt's psalms and hymns, because "the Negroes, above all the Human Species that I ever know, have an Ear for Musick, and a kind of extatic Delight in Psalmody; and there are no books they learn so soon, or take so much pleasure in, as those used in that heavenly Part of divine worship."[60] By 1750 Davies had baptized forty African-Americans in Hanover County, seven or eight of whom were in full communion.[61]

Davies' work among slaves met neither serious opposition nor much sympathy from white owners. Reluctant perhaps to alienate the white support his moderate evangelism had attracted, in 1757 he preached a sermon which neither inveighed against slavery nor gave religious sanction to it. Instead it echoed many of the themes laid out by Anglican bishops and SPG missionaries: that Christianity was "the universal Religion of Mankind," its message intended by God to be propagated among Jews and Gentiles, masters and slaves; that "the meanest slave" was "as much a Candidate for Heaven or Hell," as was his master and, therefore, slave conversion was a duty "of utmost importance and Necessity"; that the "Order of the World" required civil distinctions, and Christianity did not destroy them but instead "establishes and regulates them, and enjoins every Man to conduct himself according to them"; finally, that the Christianization of

[60] Excerpts of Davies' letters were reprinted in the appendix of Benjamin Fawcett, *A Compassionate Address to the Christian Negroes in Virginia, and Other British Colonies in North-America*, 2d ed. (London: J. Eddowes and J. Colton, 1756), 35–37.

[61] Perry, *Historical Collections* 1:369.

slaves was a matter of self-interest because "there never was a good Christian yet, who was a bad servant."[62]

Revivalist sects, particularly the Baptists and Methodists, also shared a passion for evangelizing the "heathens." During the Baptist revival in Virginia beginning about 1760 and in the Methodist phase beginning around 1770, itinerants as eagerly sought black as white converts. The Baptists, who were readier than most other groups to extend membership in the moral community to blacks, established several predominantly black churches, most of them in Southside and the central piedmont. The Baptist church constituted in 1758 at Bluestone in Mecklenburg County, for example, was composed of "several white members, besides a large number of Blacks" from William Byrd's estate. The church lasted until the Revolution, when the breakup of Byrd's quarters scattered the slave membership. Even then evangelism spread, carried afield by "the bright and shining Christian" slaves from the Byrd plantation, who "through their labors in the different neighbourhoods into which they fell," made numerous converts, including several "persons of distinction."[63]

Perhaps because their social policies placed them in fundamental tension with organized society and with the conventional churches, Methodist leaders also identified more closely with slaves and labored to convert them. Following the example of John Wesley, who in 1758 baptized the first black Methodist in Antigua, the English minister Francis Asbury began preaching to "the poor negroes" soon after his arrival at Head of Elk, Maryland, in 1771. Alarmed by the equalitarianism of Methodism, some "unhappy masters" forbade their slaves to attend Asbury's open air services, and Methodism won few black converts. But a major wave of revivalism was launched at White Oak in 1770 and from there the evangelical itinerancy spread into Sussex and Brunswick counties and into Amelia, which "for many years [had] been notorious for carelessness, profaneness, and immoralities of all kinds"; by 1775 lines of itinerant activity reached into Dinwiddie, Lunenburg and Mecklenburg counties. Although Asbury praised it as a "great, a deep, a swift, and an extensively glorious work," the revival affected only seven or eight of Virginia's fifty-two counties, almost

[62] Samuel Davies, *The Duty of Christians to Propagate Their Religion Among Heathens, Earnestly Recommended to the Masters of Negro Slaves in Virginia. A Sermon Preached in Hanover, January 8, 1757* (London: J. Oliver, 1758), 31.

[63] Robert A. Semple, *A History of the Rise and Progress of the Baptists in Virginia* (Richmond: John O'Lynch, 1810), 222–23. For a general history of black Baptists, see Mechal Sobel, *Trabelin' On: The Slave Journey to an Afro-Baptist Faith* (Westport, Conn.: Greenwood Press, c. 1979); and James Melvin Washington, *Frustrated Fellowship. The Black Baptist Quest for Social Power* (Macon, Ga.: Macon University Press, 1986). See also Luther P. Jackson, "Religious Development of the Negro in Virginia from 1760 to 1860," *Journal of Negro History* 16 (1931): 168–239.

all of them in Southside, an area with the Chesapeake's highest concentration of "new Negroes."[64]

Methodist efforts at evangelizing slaves also met with limited success in the low country. Although John and Charles Wesley had visited Georgia in the 1730s and founded a society in Savannah, it disintegrated soon afterwards and no other was formed for seventy years. The Wesleys had also preached in South Carolina, and in 1740 George Whitefield visited there. Among Whitefield's converts was Hugh Bryan, a well-to-do planter from St. Helena Parish. Persuaded by Whitefield's warning that slaveholders must Christianize their slaves or face God's wrath, Bryan determined to fulfill his Christian obligation. At Whitefield's urging, he opened a school for slaves and became one of the first of Carolina's dissenter gentry to hold religious meetings for slaves from his own and neighboring plantations. Alarmed by reports of "great Bodies of Negroes" meeting together, in 1742 the South Carolina Common House of Assembly appointed a committee to investigate the matter. A month later, Bryan appeared before the assembly and volunteered the information that he had prophesied that Charleston would be destroyed and that slaves would be delivered from servitude by "fire and sword." Two weeks later, the Assembly ordered the arrest of Hugh, his brother Jonathan, and several other evangelicals for preaching to slaves. It is not known what punishment was meted out to the evangelicals, but Hugh recanted and confessed that his apocalyptic vision was "a Delusion of Satan."

The chastened Bryan continued to teach his own slaves, however, and in 1745 the first black converts were recorded at Stoney Creek Independent Congregational Church, formed by the Bryans and some of their neighbors. Over the next ten years, nearly thirty other blacks joined the congregation, the majority of them slaves of the Bryans or of the Reverend William Hutson, pastor at Stoney Creek. Beginning in 1746, Jonathan Bryan took over as family leader, and his plantation became the focus for dissenter gentry efforts to convert slaves. Neither of the Bryans freed their slaves, but Hugh Bryan's Biblical theme of liberation was appropriated by Christian slaves and became a central motif of African-American Christianity, if not of Anglo-American Christianity. Later, Jonathan Bryan became one of the first southern planters to promote the evangelization of slaves by black preachers at his Brampton plantation near Savannah. His coachman and body servant, Andrew Bryan, was one of the founding fathers of the Afro-Baptist church in Georgia.[65]

<hr/>

[64] Francis Asbury, *The Journal and Letters of Francis Asbury*, Elmer T. Clark, J. Manning Potts, and Jacob S. Payton, eds., 3 vols. (London: Epworth Press, 1958), 1:55, 219, 235, 249, 251, 262, 265–66; Thomas Coke and Henry Moore, *The Life of the Reverend John Wesley, A.M. Including an Account of the Great Revival of Religion in Europe and America* (Philadelphia: Larry Hall, 1793), 347.

[65] See Leigh Eric Schmidt, "'The Grand Prophet,' Hugh Bryan: Early Evangelicalism's

Despite Methodism's later dominance in North and South Carolina, Baptists took an early lead in establishing themselves in the lower South.[66] A group of Baptists from Maine formed the first Baptist church in South Carolina, and apparently in the South, in Charleston perhaps as early as 1682.[67] In 1737 a small group of Welshmen from Welch Tract, Pennsylvania, later Delaware, moved to the Pee Dee River and established the Welsh Neck Church, the second center of Baptist influence in the province.[68] All white when formed, the Welsh Neck church became predominantly black following a long period of general decline in white membership. By the eve of the Revolution there were forty Baptist churches in South Carolina, most of them scattered through the Pee Dee and the Congaree regions. Despite official hostility to white efforts to stir up slaves "in the name of religion," nearly all of the early Baptist churches in South Carolina had black members.[69]

After nearly three-quarters of a century of itinerancy, Christian missionaries had little to show for their efforts. Some slaves had been baptized and some had become communicants, but the mass of slaves were still "as great strangers to Christianity, and as much under the influence of Pagan darkness, idolatry and superstition, as they were at their first arrival from Africa."[70] In part this was due to the resistance of slaves to missionary efforts to convert them; in part, to the strong resistance of the great majority of slaveholders, who feared the radicalizing effects of Christianity on their slaves.

Historically Christianity had been ambiguous on the question of slavery. Christian theology advanced the notion of one community of men under God, with heavenly justice for all. For slaveowners, however, the problem was complicated by the suspicion that black people were a special creation

Challenge to the Establishment and Slavery in the Colonial South," *South Carolina Historical Magazine* 87 (1986): 238–30; Harvey H. Jackson, "Hugh Bryan and the Evangelical Movement in Colonial South Carolina," *William and Mary Quarterly*, 3d ser., 43 (1986): 594–614; Allan Gallay, "The Origins of Slaveholder's Paternalism: George Whitefield, the Bryan Family, and the Great Awakening in the South," *Journal of Southern History* 53 (1987): 369–94. See also Allan Gallay, *The Formation of a Planter Elite: Jonathan Bryan and the Southern Colonial Frontier* (Athens: University of Georgia Press, 1989), 23, 44–46, 52, 164.

[66] Jesse Lee, *A Short History of the Methodists in the United States of America; Beginning in 1766, and Continued till 1809* (Baltimore, Md.: Magill and Clime, 1810), 12, 121, 344.

[67] Leah Townsend, *South Carolina Baptists 1670–1805* (Florence, S.C.: Florence Printing, 1935), 5, 8.

[68] Welsh Neck Baptist Church, Society Hill Minutes, 1737–1841, South Carolina Baptist Historical Society, Furman University Library, Greenville, South Carolina.

[69] Townsend, *South Carolina Baptists*, 255; Margaret Washington Creel, *"A Peculiar People": Slave Religion and Community-Culture Among the Gullahs* (New York: New York University Press, 1988), 212, says that slaves were "only nominally represented in a few white congregations."

[70] Alexander Hewatt, *An Historical Account of the Rise and Progress of the Colonies of South Carolina and Georgia*, 2 vols. (London: Alexander Donaldson, 1779), 2:100.

and, therefore, not meant to share in the benefits of Christianity and by the fear that once a slave was baptized, he became "enfranchised."[71] Although most colonies passed laws explicitly declaring that baptism did not confer freedom or alter the state of bondage, the Calvinist notion of an elite continued to militate against the Christianization of slaves. This attitude weakened in the Middle Colonies and in New England during the Great Awakening in the 1740s. In the South, where religious revivalism was localized and sporadic before 1800, the radical religious doctrines of the unity of single creation and the implied equality among the saved, served merely to intensify and intellectualize differences and prejudices. Although the clergy, which was dependent upon the goodwill of planters, did not attack the slave system, their work among slaves heightened the anxiety of slaveowners, particularly as the proportion of blacks in the population increased, and opposition to the conversion of slaves hardened.[72]

The church, the courthouse and the plantation house gathered white society together in several overlapping networks of relationships that continued to function despite differences and discord within the white community. The central institutions of patriarchal control, they reinforced and transformed one another, evolving in the postwar era into new structures and forms of dominance. The growing physical separation of the races that these structures both reflected and enforced, contributed significantly to the creation of asymmetrical cultural situations. On the one hand, they reinforced patterns of white domination and control. On the other hand, racial separation made it possible for slaves to begin to develop their own separate culture in the quarters.

While the white culture world was embodied in three central institutions, which supplied the framework of plantation society, a black culture world was developing within the contours of the institution of slavery. By contrast to the kin-oriented world of the white gentry, black society was made up of loose networks of kinship and friendships that often extended beyond individual plantations. However strong the ties between individuals and small groups of family members and friends, the black population of the South did not as yet constitute a unified community, but functioned as an aggregation of relatively separate, embryonic communities. Three elements were crucial in developing and sustaining these emerging communities: the particular complex of values that were common to all or most of the West African societies from which African-Americans were drawn; the relative isolation of the various communities from competing values and

---

[71] The fear was apparently based upon an English ruling of 1677, Butts v. Penny, 3 Keble 185. Slaveholders maintained that as "beings of an inferior rank," slaves had no souls and, therefore, "no concern need be taken about their salvation"; see Hewatt, *Historical Account* 2:101.

[72] Bonomi, *Under the Cope of Heaven*, 119.

social systems; and the gradual emergence of a common religious culture that ultimately formed around the church, the quintessential instrument for the transmission of essential values.

Historical and archaeological research has made it possible to identify various stages in the development of the black community. The earliest is a complex mix, the roots of which are found in the social environment of Africa, where clan life under the chief and the influence of the priest were the dominating characteristics. Only scraps of historical evidence survive about African traditions in the New World. Almost certainly the earliest Africans continued to follow the basic cultural patterns and structures in which they lived prior to slavery. Under the constraint of constant surveillance by the plantation system, much of the African cultural heritage was, of course, lost. Clearly some continued covertly on the plantation and was transmitted through the generations as the basis for the development of a new cultural entity whose source was first and foremost African.

A crucial step in the cultural process can be isolated in the historical and archaeological record of plantation slavery in the revolutionary era. On the eve of the Revolution only the contours were visible, principally in the form of language, values, and customs of African derivation and in the appearance of localized kinship groups. During the postrevolutionary era, by an incremental process, the primary character of kin relationships was extended into important social institutions outside the family, principally the church and religious groups and associations with African affinities. Because slaves entered British North America with no single group identity, the group and culture-building process began in slavery. To a large extent the parameters of the emerging culture were dictated by the conditions of servitude and by the sociocultural environment of the various slave communities. The social survival of the group involved more than adaptation to the dominant cultural patterns. It involved the novel creation of an ethnic culture based on resolute adherence to a system of values and beliefs and to various customs of African derivation.

The African populations of the southern colonies were, on the eve of the Revolution, of different historic ages and ethnic origins. Although after 1700 the vast majority of slaves came from West and Central Africa, they represented a wide variety of cultural provinces. Studies of ethnic distribution in the South suggest that the majority of slaves in the upper South were from the Niger Delta, with an estimated 37.7 percent from the Bight of Biafra and another 15.7 percent from Angola.[73] South Carolina planters, who demonstrated an acute awareness of enthnicity, preferred slaves

[73] Darold D. Wax, "Preferences for Slaves in Colonial America," *Journal of Negro History* 58 (1973): 371–401. The estimates are from Philip D. Curtin, *The Atlantic Slave Trade. A Census* (Madison: University of Wisconsin Press, 1969).

from the Guinea coast, Gambia, Sierra Leone, and Angola.[74] During the eighteenth century, 40 percent of all African imports were from the Kongo-Angola region, 43 percent from everywhere else. Because Georgia and North Carolina absorbed a substantial portion of the slaves entering British North America through Charleston, the principal entrepôt for the North American slave trade, the ethnic composition of their slave populations was probably similar.[75] As a result of a higher rate of natural increase, most slaves in the upper South by the late eighteenth century were American-born, although in certain piedmont counties the adult population remained heavily African.[76] In the lower South, where the rate of natural increase was lower and where slave imports continued to 1808, a high percentage of slaves were African-born or of recent African origin. The histories of the black populations of the upper and the lower South were thus different.

Nonetheless, as a result principally, though by no means exclusively, of strong Euro-American opposition to biological assimilation, African-American slaves were, as one scholar has put it, "functionally members of the same caste."[77] Moreover, as Africans they shared certain common theological and philosophical similarities and certain broad cultural and religious affinities, which ultimately formed the basis for the development of an ethnic culture. Although there are approximately eight hundred ethnic groups and one hundred or more languages, some linguistic anthropologists believe that all linguistic groupings in West Africa ultimately derive from the same language stock, the Western Sudanic family. As a consequence, perhaps, of a common language stock, certain common concepts and fundamental ideas and practices obtained among all West African peoples.[78] As slaves, Africans were prevented from bringing material objects

[74] Littlefield, *Rice and Slaves*, 8–9, 21, 113, 150, observes that the "overwhelming predominance" of Angola slaves, which characterized the first decades of the eighteenth century, was counteracted in the second half by rising importations of Senegambian peoples. Creel, who traces Gullah peoples in detail, agrees with Littlefield on the early cultural dominance of BaKonga peoples of Kongo-Angolan origins, followed by the growing importance of Upper Guinea Africans of the Senegambia and Windward coasts; see Creel, *A Peculiar People*, 29–44.

[75] W. Robert Higgins, "Charleston: Terminus and Entrepôt of the Colonial Slave Trade," in Martin L. Kilson and Robert I. Rotberg, eds., *The African Diaspora. Interpretative Essays* (Cambridge, Mass.: Harvard University Press, 1976), 114–31.

[76] Morgan, "Slave Life in Piedmont Virginia," 435. Morgan maintains that the piedmont received the majority of the approximately fifteen thousand Africans imported between 1755 and 1774. He estimates the number of Africans still alive in Virginia's slave population in 1782 at fourteen thousand.

[77] Richard A. Long, *Africa and America: Essays in Afro-American Culture* (Atlanta, Ga.: Atlanta University, 1981), 23.

[78] Cyril Daryll Forde, "The Cultural Map of West Africa: Successive Adaptations to Trop-

and institutions to the New World, but, as the French sociologist Roger Bastide has observed, they did carry with them concepts and values and ideas and practices, which they transmitted to their children and which were reinforced by continual infusions of Africans. Many of them took root and survived, albeit in more highly visible form in some areas than in others, due principally to radically different sociocultural conditions and different political regimes.

The patterns of racial demography, which produced different forms of plantation management, gave low-country slaves comparatively little contact with whites prior to the Revolution. Free from the watchful paternalism of owners, the black majority of the rice coast counties were able to develop and maintain a culture strongly influenced by African cultural patterns. The numerical dominance of peoples from the Kongo-Angola region and their cultural concentration in particular areas, made it possible for aspects of their particular group culture to enjoy prominence in the emerging culture. In keeping with a tradition found in parts of Africa to develop a special language distinct from that spoken by the master class,[79] low-country slaves created their own form of communication. Known as Gullah in South Carolina and Geechee, the roughly synonymous slave dialect spoken in the Georgia Sea Islands, it resulted from a fusion of African and English words.[80] Although increasing contact with whites in the post-Revolutionary War period led to gradual slave acculturation, low-country slaves successfully conveyed this linguistic tradition from one generation to the next. Moreover, as Charles Joyner has observed, marginal contact with Gullah playmates and nurses produced a corresponding African influence on the speech of many planters of the Sea Island Region. Tidewater

---

ical Forests and Grasslands," in Simon Ottenberg and Phoebe Ottenberg, eds., *Cultures and Societies of Africa* (New York: Random House, 1960), 116–38.

[79] Michael Craton, *Testing the Chains: Resistance to Slavery in the British West Indies* (Ithaca, N.Y.: Cornell University Press, 1982), 47.

[80] Linguists do not agree completely about the origins of Gullah. Early works emphasized the importance of BaKongo influence. Other scholars pointed out that a large proportion of Africanisms came from Liberia and Sierra Leone. Peter Wood, and more recently Margaret Creel, have argued for the possibility of two or more original derivations, including Upper Guinea and Kongo-Angolo, but influenced mainly by the Tshi (Gold Coast), KiKongo (Kongo-Angolo) and Mande (Upper Guinea) linguistic patterns. Compare Lorenzo Dow Turner, *Africanisms in the Gullah Dialect* (Chicago: University of Chicago Press, 1949), to more recent works such as Wood, *Black Majority*, 166–91 and Creel, *A Peculiar People*, 15–19, 208. Recent studies of present-day Gullah emphasize that although the lexicon is English, certain distinctive features, including verb reduplication, the pronominal system, and certain grammatical rules, distinguish Gullah speech; see Joyner, *Down by the Riverside*, 196–224; Patricia Jones-Jackson, *When Roots Die. Endangered Traditions on the Sea Islands* (Athens: University of Georgia Press, 1987), 132–46. Joyner and Jones-Jackson studied Gullah in different areas of the Sea Islands and adjacent coasts and found that there were different varieties.

slaves apparently also developed an African pidgin language, but closer contact with whites and the growth of the slave population by natural increase probably forced them to learn English sooner to communicate with masters and native slaves.[81]

Evidence of African cultural survivals is also found in low-country slave housing patterns. Building materials similar to those used by their African ancestors were used by slave laborers in a variety of construction types. The slave houses of the rice coast were generally made of tabby, a lime and seashell aggregate used throughout the Guinea coast of West Africa. Tabby was also used in other construction, including walls, fences, and roadways, and in owners' houses as well, which suggests the reciprocal nature of cultural development in the plantation south. Local building materials similar to those found in Africa, such as the leaves of the palmetto tree, were also used in the construction of slave huts throughout the low country. African design forms, such as the steeply pitched roofs that distinguished many low-country slave houses, and the circular form, useful for dispersing the sun's rays evenly to keep the interiors of buildings like icehouses cool, had their antecedents in coastal areas of West Africa.[82]

Archaeological data collected from the slave quarters at the Yaughan and Curriboo plantations in St. Stephen's Parish, Berkeley County, South Carolina, both of which were established in the 1740s following twenty years of enormous importations of Africans, reveal that the earliest slave and domestic structures on the plantations were mud-walled huts. Wall trenches with cob-wall construction was a familiar architectural mode in West Africa. Demographic recontact with Africa until the turn of the century was conducive to the perpetuation of these architectural traditions; at the same time the high ratio of blacks to whites made it less likely that slaves would adopt European cultural forms, although the presence of iron nails and small amounts of window glass in the slave quarters at the Curriboo and Yaughan plantations suggests at least limited contact with and influence of white cultural forms in the period prior to the Revolution. Artifact patterns from the same slave quarters show that colonoware ceramics distinctive of West Africa were being made at the plantations by slaves for their own use.[83]

Architecture and pottery are important visible manifestations of group culture. A more important factor in the creation of community was the gradual development of a number of institutions to guide and to support the separate slave communities and to tie the scattered members to the

[81] Smyth, *Tour* 1:24; Kulikoff, *Tobacco and Slaves*, 335.

[82] Steven L. Jones, "The African-American Tradition in Vernacular Architecture," in Singleton, ed., *Archaeology of Slavery*, 119, 199, 200.

[83] Thomas R. Wheaton and Patrick H. Garrow, "Acculturation and the Archaeological Record of the Carolina Lowcountry," in Singleton, ed., *Archaelogy of Slavery*, 242, 244, 248.

common values of the group. Kinship and inherited values and beliefs were critically important to the formation of African-American culture. In their struggle to retain their sense of identity, slaves had to determine which aspects or traits of their African heritage to retain and which to discard. The choices they made were based on an awareness of where their strength derived. Kinship and family solidarity, the most important elements of African culture, also became the primary sources of the distinctive value system of African-Americans.

Throughout West and Central Africa, kinship was the basis of social life. The household, including both the elementary or nuclear family, and the compound or polygynous family,[84] was the basic unit of the kinship system. Both in concept and in structure, the African family was vastly different from the Euro-American family of the eighteenth century, although in some respects it resembled Anglo-Saxon English marriages.[85] In traditional society the family consisted of the unborn, all living members, including parents, children, grandparents, uncles, aunts, cousins and other immediate relatives, and the departed or living dead as long as they existed in the personal memory of living relatives. Numerous households consisted of only parents and children and, in some cases, grandparents. In many areas, however, extended families were common. In patrilocal societies two or more brothers might establish joint households consisting of ten or even a hundred persons, including several wives. In many systems the structural unit consisted of a woman and her children. In polygynous families of patrilineal societies, two or more mother-child groups, each with a separate hut and food supply but united by relationships with the man who was the husband and father, formed compound families.[86]

The structure of the mainland British-North American plantation economy, characterized by relatively small landholdings dispersed over a large area and the policy of deliberate separation of members of the same tribe or kin group, permanently destroyed African kinship organizations such as the clan, although some elements survived and were reconstituted as kin-

---

[84] Most Africans were monogamous by choice, but only in exceptional cases was monogamy compulsory. Permanent unions were the ideal everywhere, but numerous groups permitted easy dissolution of the marriage, ordinarily by interfamily agreement rather than at the whim of the parties. The great emphasis on fertility and procreation, by which means individuals ensured the continuation of the family and the future of the group, in part explains the African institution of polygyny. See Edward Geoffrey Parrinder, *Sex in the World's Religions* (New York: Oxford University Press, 1980), 137–38; John S. Mbiti, *Love and Marriage in Africa* (London: Longman, 1973), 81–82, 189–201; George Thomas Basden, *Among the Ibos of Nigeria* (London: Seeley, Service and Co., 1921), 97.

[85] A. R. Radcliffe-Browne and Cyril Daryll Forde, eds., *African Systems of Kinship and Marriage* (London: Oxford University Press, 1987), 45, 46.

[86] John S. Mbiti, *African Religions and Philosophy* (New York: Frederick A. Praeger, 1969), 106–7; Radcliffe-Browne and Forde, *African Systems of Kinship*, 81, 84.

ship networks, and temporarily shattered the household structure. Early studies of the slave family have suggested that the black family never recovered from the devastating experience.[87] More recent works concede that the traditional African domestic organization was severely disrupted by conditions under slavery. But, they maintain, as a result of the growth of the size of quarters after 1740, the increase in the proportion of slaves in the population, and the decrease in the adult sex ratio, slaves were in a position to begin re-forming families by the mideighteenth century.[88] Owing to sexual exploitation, miscegenation, and various legal impediments, by the 1830s the traditional African family had been largely transformed.[89] By 1863 the typical family in the last slave generation lived in a two-parent household characterized by enduring marital unions and strong family ties.[90]

Evidence from birth lists, ration rolls, estate censuses, plantation business records, and advertisements for runaway slaves provides compelling proof that slaves valued marriage and family highly and maintained long

[87] The debate whether African-Americans lost their African heritage originated in the 1930s with the publication of E. Franklin Frazier, *The Negro Family in the United States* (Chicago, 1939); in part 2, "The House of the Mother," Frazier argued that slavery "stripped [African-Americans] of [their] social heritage," destroyed households, and "dissolved the bonds of sympathy and affection between members of the same blood and household," a view promoted in the 1950s by Kenneth Stampp, *The Peculiar Institution* (New York: Vintage Books, 1956), 362–63, and Stanley Elkins, *Slavery: A Problem in American Institutional and Intellectual Life* (Chicago: University of Chicago Press, 1959), 53–54, 101. See also E. Franklin Frazier, *The Negro in the United States*, rev. (New York: Macmillan, 1957), 10–14. That interpretation was challenged by Melville J. Herskovits, *The Myth of the Negro Past* (Boston: Beacon Press, 1958), which insisted upon the persistence of African cultural influence, particularly in social organization, religious philosophy, and in certain aesthetic aspects. The French sociologist, Roger Bastide, who has studied African influences in the Caribbean and in Central America, found greater influence in the Caribbean and in Central America, but identified two strong centers of African influence in the United States: the Sea Islands off the coasts of Georgia and South Carolina and the New Orleans area; see Roger Bastide, *African Civilizations in the New World* (London: C. Hurst, 1971). Recent work by Sobel, *World They Made Together*, Creel, *A Peculiar People*, and Sterling Stuckey, *Slave Culture. Nationalist Theory and the Foundations of Black America* (New York: Oxford University Press, 1987) have discovered compelling evidence of pervasive African influence in the white as well as in the black community.

[88] Kulikoff, "Origins of Afro-American Society," 226–58, and Russell R. Menard, "The Maryland Slave Population, 1658–1730: A Demographic Profile of Blacks in Four Counties," *William and Mary Quarterly*, 3d ser., 32 (1975): 29–54. Jean Butenhoff Lee, "The Problem of Slave Community in the Eighteenth-Century Chesapeake," *William and Mary Quarterly*, 3d ser., 43 (1986): 333–61 finds evidence that stable family life probably developed much more slowly. My findings agree with Lee's.

[89] John W. Blassingame, *The Slave Community. Plantation Life in the Antebellum South*, rev. and enl. (New York: Oxford University Press, 1979), 149–91.

[90] Herbert G. Gutman, *The Black Family in Slavery and Freedom, 1750–1925* (New York: Pantheon Books, 1976), 11.

and enduring unions in the face of incredible odds. The frequent naming of children for parents, siblings, and blood relatives, suggests the strength of family and kinship ties, which in many cases was further cemented by the slave practice of passing on economic skills, often the slaves' most valuable possession, to sons and daughters. The essential character of the slave family, family solidarity, had thus everywhere emerged. Its function, the survival of a people, remained everywhere the same.[91]

The monogamous slave family as a single model did not, however, exist on the eve of the Revolution. Slave marriages must, of necessity, be discussed in relationship to the institution of slavery. In the plantation colonies slave marriage had no status at law. Marriage rites lacked the permanence implied by the Christian marriage ceremony. Whether for humane or practical reasons, some white owners recognized the importance of stable slave unions and encouraged their slaves to take a marriage partner, preferably on the same estate; but many slaves still lived on small or middling units and, therefore, often had to find partners on neighboring plantations. Many plantations still had communal housing of groups ranging in size from eight to twenty-four slaves. Moreover, the needs of the plantation usually took precedence over black familial bonds. The practice of hiring out slaves often separated families because slaves usually lived on the farm where they were assigned to work. Systems of inheritance also strained familial ties. Although many planters tried to preserve the nuclear unit when dividing their estates, older children, particularly males, were frequently separated from their parents and adults were separated from their elderly parents and extended kin. Because the practice was to divide slave property equally among heirs, slave families often remained within the extended white family in a restricted geographic area.[92] The existence of cross-quarter networks and the practice, common in the colonial period, of permitting visiting in the evening and on Sundays and holidays, allowed slaves to maintain some contact with family members and preserve family ties. Nevertheless, a majority of slave couples remained separated for much of their married lives.

By the eve of the Revolution, a variety of different kinds of households had emerged. Slave marriages were extremely complex, with significant

---

[91] See Cheryll Ann Cody, "Naming, Kinship and Estate Dispersal. Notes on Slave Family Life on a South Carolina Plantation, 1786 to 1833," *William and Mary Quarterly*, 3d ser., 39 (1982): 192–211; Michael P. Johnson, "Runaway Slaves and the Slave Communities in South Carolina, 1799–1830," ibid., 3d series, 38 (1981): 418–41; Mary Beth Norton, Herbert G. Gutman, Ira Berlin, "The Afro-American Family in the Age of Revolution," in Berlin and Hoffman, eds., *Slavery and Freedom*, 175–91.

[92] Amy Friedlander, "Establishing Historical Probabilities for Archaeological Interpretations: Slave Demography on Two Plantations in the South Carolina Lowcountry, 1740–1820," in Singleton, ed., *Archaeology of Slavery*, 230–31; Cody, "Naming, Kinship and Estate Dispersal," 192–211.

differences in marital stability and in types of conjugal relations, none of which were legal, none of which corresponded to white marriages. On large tidewater plantations, where some two-fifths of slave women lived in two-parent nuclear families, a family structure similar to the white nuclear family had emerged. On small farms, however, less than one-fifth of blacks lived in two-parent households, and a majority of men and a substantial number of women lived with neither spouse nor children. The records of at least one planter suggest that in the low country mean family size was probably two.[93] Although the African-American household clearly developed within the limitations of the institution of slavery, African-Americans did not immediately renounce traditional marriage forms any more readily than had the first European settlers in the New World. Even though the forms that some slave marriages assumed undoubtedly differed from their African prototypes, they shared more similarity with them than with the Euro-American family type. Mother-headed households and polygyny, characteristic of many West African societies, were functionally useful under conditions of slavery and both forms survived until the end of slavery. Demographic factors, particularly the sex ratio and the sexual division of labor common in urban areas, led to the predominance of the female-headed household, even among free blacks, in cities such as Charleston.[94]

Polygyny, a respected and formally sanctioned arrangement throughout West Africa, was also prevalent throughout the South. Some polygynous alliances, such as that of Carpenter Bill who lived at Mount Airy in Virginia while his two wives, Ester and Winney, lived at Landsdown with parallel sets of young children, were strongly reminiscent of West African polygynous families of patrilineal societies. To be sure, the institution of slavery, particularly its residential instability, produced unique polygynous arrangements, which might be more accurately described as consecutive polygyny or serial monogamy, and which in certain essential features anticipated the later emergence of the new cultural system of marriage among whites.[95]

Despite the various institutional impediments slaves did not mate promiscuously, nor did they abandon traditional customs. Because slaves had

[93] Kulikoff, *Tobacco and Slaves*, 371, 374; Friedlander, "Slave Demography," 233.

[94] In Savannah women outnumbered men by approximately 115 to 100; see Betty Wood, "Some Aspects of Female Resistance to Chattel Slavery in Low Country Georgia, 1763–1815," *Historical Journal* 30 (1987): 606 n. 16; by midcentury black women also outnumbered black men in Charleston; see Philip D. Morgan, "Black Life in Eighteenth-Century Charleston," *Perspectives in American History*, n. s., 1 (1984): 189.

[95] See, for example, Richard S. Dunn, "A Tale of Two Plantations: Slave Life at Mesopotamia in Jamaica and Mount Airy in Virginia, 1799 to 1828," *William and Mary Quarterly*, 3d ser., 34 (1977): 32–65; Johnson, "Runaway Slaves," 418–34; George Blackburn and Sherman L. Ricards, "The Mother-Headed Family Among Free Negroes in Charleston, South Carolina, 1850–1860," *Phylon* 42 (1981): 11–25.

no legal right to marry, Euro-American observors like Philip Georg Frie- . drich Von Reck, who conducted the first transport of Salzburgers to Georgia in 1733, made the unverified assumption that "marriage is not in use amongst them; but they are suffer'd promiscuously to mix, as if they were a part of the Brute Creation."[96] Such documentary evidence as survives indicates that slaves created their own marriage ceremonies, some of which apparently had African antecedents. During his second tour of the South, the Quaker leader John Woolman noted that "Negroes marry after their own way."[97] Woolman provided no details, but John Brickell, a physician who lived and practiced medicine in Edenton, North Carolina, around 1731, decribed a common ceremony: "Their *Marriages* are generally performed amongst themselves, there being very little ceremony used upon that Head; for the Man makes the Woman a Present, such as a *Brass Ring* or some other Toy, which if she accepts of becomes his Wife; but if ever they part from each other, which frequently happens, upon any little Disgust, she returns his Present: These kind of Contracts no longer binding them, than the woman keeps the pledge given her."[98]

A similar custom among Georgia slaves was reported early in the nineteenth century: "The man would go to the cabin of the woman he desired, would roast peanuts in the ashes, place them on a stool between her and himself, and while eating propose marriage." If she agreed, they were immediately regarded as husband and wife.[99] Euro-American descriptions tend to trivialize or negate the significance of these ceremonies, which in fact appear to be variations of a practice common among the Igbira and other West African groups. After all family arrangements were complete, the prospective bridegroom visited his intended, offering her money or cowries. If she accepted the gift, the engagement was considered settled and elaborate wedding ceremonies followed at a later date.[100] Under slavery many crucial elements of African marriage customs, such as the involved family negotiations, marriage payments, and elaborate ceremonies necessarily disappeared, but simple rituals probably continued on a private basis until superceded by Christian ceremonials.[101]

[96] "An Extract of the Journals of Mr. Commissary Von Reck," in Peter Force, comp., *Tracts and Other Papers, Relating Principally to the Origin, Settlement and Progress of the Colonies in North America from the Discovery of the Country to the Year 1776*, 4 vols. (Washington, D.C.: P. Force, 1836–46), 4:9.

[97] Amelia Mott Gummere, ed., *The Journal and Essays of John Woolman* (New York: Macmillan, 1922), 194.

[98] John Brickell, *The Natural History of North Carolina* (New York: Johnson Reprint, 1969), 274.

[99] Quoted in Gutman, *Black Family*, 348.

[100] Paula Brown, "The Igbira," in *Peoples of the Niger-Benue Confluence* (c. 1955; reprint, London: International African Institute, 1970), 67.

[101] Blassingame, *Slave Community*, 166–67, notes that the celebrated "jumping the broom-

Of equal and, perhaps, even of greater importance than the family in reconstructing cultural integrity was the preservation of traditional spiritual values and religious practices. West Africans were often described by Europeans as "pagans" when, in fact, they were a deeply religious people. Even as slaves African-Americans retained their strong religious commitments, which continued to shape their values, the principal differentiating factor between the dominant white culture and the emerging black culture. During the early history of slavery many specific African beliefs and practices survived. Evidence is found in the complaints of Maryland colonial authorities about the use of "Negro Drums" that called slaves together for gatherings and religious rituals.[102] Slaves on Virginia's Northern Neck continued to hold mass funerals until 1687, when public funerals were banned by Westmoreland County authorities after a large-scale conspiracy was apparently planned at such a gathering. Maryland and other colonies also passed laws "to suppress tumultous meetings of slaves" in an obvious effort to check independent religious gatherings. On an individual level, slave masters universally disdained the "heathen" survivals of African heritage and forbade all religious activities.[103]

The systematic repression of the African heritage is strikingly apparent in the absence of African-related or African-derived ritual objects in archaeological deposits where they would be expected to appear. Slavery dictated a very limited number of personal possessions, which affected first and foremost the material expressions of African religion. Objects for use in worship, shrines, cult insignia, altarpieces, divination paraphenalia, masks, funerary art, clothing, all largely disappeared, although a handful of deliberately shaped polygonal artifacts discovered in the excavation of the slave quarters at the Garrison Plantation near Baltimore, Maryland, are possibly amulets or ritual objects, testaments perhaps to the secret religious rituals conducted in slave cabins or dense forests away from the watchful eyes of masters and overseers.[104] Although the material expressions of African religion were largely destroyed by the slave regime, slaves were able to maintain generalized West African religious forms through the eighteenth century. Even after Christianization, African concepts and practices continued to flourish within African-American Protestantism.

The spiritual odyssey of African-Americans from traditional religion to

---

stick" was not part of the wedding ceremony but part of the postnuptial revelries. A humorous creation, it was meant to demonstrate who would exercise the most authority in the union.

[102] Quoted in Menard, "Maryland Slave Population," 37.

[103] Herbert Aptheker, *American Negro Slave Revolts* (London: P. S. King and Staples, 1943; New York: Columbia University Press, 1977), 166.

[104] Eric Klingelhofer, "Aspects of Early Afro-American Material Culture: Artifacts from the Slave Quarters at Garrison Plantation, Maryland," *Historical Archaeology* 21 (1987): 115–17.

Protestant Christianity forms a critical chapter in the history of the emerging black community and indeed in the history of slavery. Three elements were crucial in the creation of a common religious culture: the particular complex of values that were common to traditional religion; the relative isolation of black communities from competing values; and the committed efforts of the handful of white planters and missionaries who brought the faith to blacks, together with the work of a larger number of black converts who were the principal carriers of the faith. What emerged in the end was a religious system that stood alongside the white system rather than within it. As the various institutions within the two systems evolved, the differences between them became greater rather than less.

The beginnings of a settled religious life for African-Americans are found in the late colonial period, when numbers of slaves were first exposed to Christianity by aggressive missionaries of the SPG and, in the Chesapeake, by white evangelical preachers during the bursts of revivalism associated with the first Great Awakening. The growth of an organized religious life, however, was a product of the revolutionary era and was largely the work of African-Americans themselves.[105] The chief carriers of the church, they constituted its early leadership. Indeed it was indigenous leadership and initiative in the propagation of the early black church that gave African-American Christianity its distinctive African traits. Although the piedmont was the center of early white evangelical efforts among slaves, the first black congregations were formed in tidewater Virginia by self-appointed urban black leaders. In 1776 a black Baptist named Moses organized a congregation among the slaves at Williamsburg. Gowan Pamphlet, a free black from Middlesex, moved to Williamsburg and formed his own Baptist church after he and a number of his followers were expelled by the Dover Association for defying an order against preaching.[106]

The most illuminating example of aggressive black evangelism is found in the history of the black Baptist church in Georgia. The first black Baptist church in Georgia, and perhaps in the United States, developed from the efforts of a Virginia slave, George Liele.[107] Brought to Georgia by his

[105] Although his work was limited to Virginia, Luther P. Jackson, "Religious Development of the Negro," was one of the first scholars to distinguish various periods in the process of Christianizing slaves. My periodization is somewhat different; however, I have benefited a great deal from Jackson's work.

[106] Semple, *History of the Baptists in Virginia*, 97, 115. There were, however, a number of biracial churches in piedmont counties during the revolutionary era; see Morgan, "Slave Life in Piedmont Virginia," 474.

[107] Some dispute whether the Silver Bluff church or Bryan's First African is oldest. On June 3, 1888, the African Missionary Baptist State Convention reviewed the evidence and decided unanimously that the distinction belonged to the First African church. The convention's report is cited in Edgar Garfield Thomas, *The First African Church of North America* (Savannah, Ga.: n.p., 1925), 104–5.

owner, Henry Sharpe, Liele was converted and baptized by Matthew Moore, an ordained Baptist minister. The first black Baptist in Georgia, Liele carried his religious zeal to other slaves on the rice and indigo plantations. Finding nothing objectionable in Liele's preaching, a white Baptist congregation invited him to preach. Impressed by his "ministerial gifts," the congregation voted unanimously to license him as a probationer. Before he was killed in the revolutionary war, Sharpe, a loyalist, freed Liele, who was subsequently jailed by Sharpe's heirs. A British officer secured his release, but at the British evacuation of Savannah Liele was embarked for Jamaica as an indentured servant for money he owed the officer.

Before leaving, Liele baptized several slaves, including his own wife; one of his "black hearers," Andrew Bryan, servant of Jonathan Bryan; David George, a Virginia runaway who eventually ended up as a slave on the Thomas Galphin plantation about twelve miles below Augusta in the Edgefield District in South Carolina, where Liele had obtained permission to preach; and Jesse Peter, or Jesse Galphin, another slave on the Galphin plantation. Following in Liele's footsteps, Bryan began to preach to slaves on his master's plantation at Brampton, three miles west of Savannah. Soon he was conducting regular services in a small, rough church in Yamacraw Village. But wartime tensions generated by black desertions to the British led to harrassment by whites. Slaves were prevented from attending church, services were interrupted, and members of the congregation were hauled before magistrates for violation of the laws against assembly. Some fifty of them, including Andrew Bryan, were severely whipped. At the intercession of James Habersham and several other sympathetic planters, the black Baptists were released by Chief Justice Henry Osborne, who also gave Bryan permission to continue conducting religious services in a barn on Jonathan Bryan's plantation between sunrise and sunset.[108]

In the meantime, David George had been baptized in a millstream on the Galphin plantation by an itinerating preacher named Brother Joshua [?] Palmer. After hearing Liele preach in a cornfield, George was seized with a desire to preach and, on Liele's advice, began to "pray with slaves between services." After Brother Palmer "formed us into a church at Silver Bluff," George began to exhort and to take instruction from Palmer on "how to conduct myself" as a preacher. During the Revolution, itinerating preachers were not allowed to continue their evangelical work among slaves "lest they should furnish us with too much knowledge." In Palmer's absence, George began to preach and, with the assistance of white children, to learn to read. Soon he had "the whole management" of the Silver Bluff church. At the time of the British invasion in 1779, membership in

[108] "Letters Showing the Rise and Progress of the Early Negro Churches of Georgia and the West Indies," *Journal of Negro History* 1 (1916): 70–71, 77–78.

the Silver Bluff church had increased from eight to thirty. When Thomas Galphin fled during the British occupation, George went to the British in Savannah, where his wife washed for the army and George "kept a butcher's stall." With money borrowed from other blacks he bought passage to Charleston and at the evacuation went to Nova Scotia where he established a Baptist church, the second in Nova Scotia.[109] In the meantime, Jesse Galphin, or Jesse Peter as he was also known, had organized three or four Baptist churches in rural South Carolina and Georgia and preached at each of them alternately.[110]

Although the developing religious community of necessity paid obeisance to white Christian beliefs and practices, black Christians proceeded both consciously and unconsciously to reinstate certain traditional values and beliefs, as a consequence of which emerging African-American Christianity retained an immutable individual essence. The basic elements of African influence are apparent principally in the customs associated with death. Although funerary rites differed among various groups, in traditional West African practice complex rites dramatized the African belief in a life cycle composed of three levels of being—the unborn, the living and the dead—all three levels of which were united by mystical links. Although death separated the individual from the community of the living, it returned the deceased to the land of the ancestors and thereby completed the life cycle. Among West African peoples, death was viewed as a transition, a journey from the physical world of the living to the world of spirits.[111] Elaborate funeral rites were performed by most peoples to allow the deceased to enter the spirit world. Although ceremonies varied according to age, sex, and status of the deceased, burial rites generally consisted of two phases. The first involved preparation of the corpse and the actual interment. Because the presence of the corpse was disturbing, the burial ceremony usually took place soon after death. To make the journey to the world beyond easier, the body was carefully prepared for burial and various

[109] "An Account of the Life of Mr. David George, from Sierra Leone in Africa; given by himself in a Conversation with Brother Rippon of London, and Brother Pearce of Birmingham," in John Rippon, ed., *The Baptist Annual Register (1790/93–1801/02)*, 4 vols. (London: n.p., 1791), 473–77.

[110] George Liele to the editor, December 18, 1791, ibid., 336. Walter Brooks, "Priority of the Silver Bluff Church and Its Promoters," *Journal of Negro History* 7 (1922): 172–96, claims that the Silver Bluff church was the first black Baptist church. According to George Liele, Jesse Galphin and David George were both members of the Savannah church; see "An Account of Several Baptist Churches, consisting chiefly of Negro Slaves," in Rippon, ed., *Baptist Annual Register* (1791), 336.

[111] For traditional beliefs, see Edward Geoffrey Parrinder, *West African Religion. A Study of the Beliefs and Practices of Akan, Ewe, Yoruba, Ibo and Kindred Peoples* (New York: Barnes and Noble, 1970), 106–7; Dominique Zahan, *Religion, Spirituality and Thought of Traditional Africa* (Chicago: University of Chicago Press, 1979), 44.

personal possessions were placed in the coffin for use on the journey. Among most groups a second ceremony took place at a later date. It was widely believed that the dead do not enter the world of ancestral spirits until this ceremony is performed. It was characterized by feasting, singing, dancing, and general rejoicing, all of which assure the deceased a triumphant entry into the spirit world.

Burials were the principal festivals of New World slavery, occasions of exuberance and celebration when ancestral spirits mingled with the living. Slave funerals were more than social events, however. Death provided slaves with an occasion for very broad statements or restatements of their religious beliefs as well as their social values and ideology. Burial customs in slave societies varied widely from urban to rural areas, even from plantation to plantation. Although African death rites were clearly brought to the New World, systematic repression of African influence destroyed the most distinctive burial practices associated with the African heritage.

Archaeological evidence collected from burial grounds in Maryland and Virginia from the late seventeenth to the early nineteenth centuries reveal minimal African influence and suggest the forced extinction of African practices. At the excavated slave sites at the Cliffs Plantation, a prosperous tobacco farm occupied from around 1670 to 1730, at Catoctin Furnace in Maryland, one of some sixty-five ironworks in the Chesapeake, and at College Landing, which served Williamsburg as a commercial center and supply point, burial customs seemed to follow traditional Christian standards with respect to coffin burial, the extended position of the corpse, and the use of shrouds. Gravemarkers and decorations typical of African practice are largely absent from these early sites, perhaps because they did not exist, perhaps because they were perishable and did not survive, perhaps because they were mistaken as junk and were destroyed. Because, however, osteological analysis indicates that the skeletal remains at Catoctin Furnace and probably at the Cliffs Plantation were of first- or second-generation slaves, who probably would have retained African customs, the Christian rites probably were dictated by the master.

There is, moreover, suggestive if not conclusive evidence that slaves surreptitiously continued practices that were not conspicuously African. Copper and bronze stains on the skeletal remains of some of the adults, left perhaps by bracelets, and a string of beads interred with an infant at the College Landing site suggest survival of the African custom of including personal possessions of the deceased for use on the journey to the world of spirits.[112] At the Catoctin site three graves, one an infant and two adults,

[112] Carter L. Hudgins, "Historical Archaeology and Salvage Archaeological Excavations at College Landing. An Interim Report," Virginia Research Center for Archaeology (1977), 63–81. The author is grateful to Professor Hudgins for permitting the use of the full unpub-

had botanical offerings—a formal wreath for the child and concentrations of seeds on the coffin surfaces of the adults. Reminiscent of African grave goods, these modest burial offerings survive as reminders of slave austerity, and perhaps as eloquent, if necessarily understated, cultural assertions. At the College Landing site, females and children were buried unshrouded in imitation, perhaps, of the custom in parts of West Africa symbolic of birth in the hereafter.[113] A chronological and geographic comparison of historical and archaeological evidence reveals the persistence of these same spiritual motifs in slave cemeteries throughout the South until well into the twentieth century.

The African practice of a second funeral characterized by music and dancing also survived everywhere in the South in attenuated form.[114] Although much of what slaves did or believed was not considered worthy of record, dancing, singing, and rejoicing that accompanied final rites was documented because it was unusual and was considered abberrant behavior. References to the practice are found throughout the low country. In 1755, for example, James Murray, writing from the slave-rich Cape Fear, noted that "the Negroes . . . are at a great loss this Christmas for want of a death to play for."[115] In 1766 a grand jury in Savannah, Georgia, demanded the enforcement of the Negro Act to prevent slaves from "attending funerals in large bodies in the night, rioting . . . and in a most notorious manner breaking the Lord's day."[116] In 1774 Janet Schaw, a Scottish traveler, attended the funeral of Jean Corbin, the wife of both James Innes and Francis Corbin, of Point Pleasant Plantation, North Carolina. After the white ritual was over and the guests had departed, Schaw reported that

lished report and for other details provided during a telephone conversation September 26, 1988.

[113] Sharon Ann Burnston, "The Cemetery at Catoctin Furnace, Maryland: The Invisible People," *Maryland Archaeology* 17 (1981): 19–31; Carter L. Hudgins, Report on College Landing Site, Williamsbury, Virginia, cited in Jennifer Olsen Kelley and J. Lawrence Angel, "The Workers of Catoctin Furnace," *Maryland Archaeology* 19 (1983): 9; Arthur C. Aufderheide, Fraser D. Neiman, Lorentz E. Wittmers, Jr., and George Rapp, "Lead in Bones II: Skeletal-Lead Content as an Indicator of Lifetime Lead Ingestion and the Social Correlates in an Archaeological Population," *American Journal of Physical Anthropology* 55 (1981): 285–93.

[114] Albert J. Raboteau, *Slave Religion. The "Invisible Institution" in the Antebellum South* (New York: Oxford University Press, 1978), 231, notes the practice of a second funeral, but concludes that "it is difficult to say whether this practice reflected an African system of multiple funerals or was simply a necessity dictated by the uncertainty of permission and the lack of time available to slaves to attend such services."

[115] James Murray, Cape Fear, to "Sister Clark," December 26, 1755, Robbins Papers, Massachusetts Historical Society (Mf. CRP), typescript copy in Historical Publications Section, Division of Archives and History, Raleigh, North Carolina. I am indebted to Jeffrey Crow for this reference.

[116] December 24, 1766, *Georgia Gazette*.

"the Negroes assembled to perform their part of the funeral rites, which they did by running, jumping, crying and various exercises."[117] The singing, dancing, and general rejoicing dismissed by whites as "festive accompaniments" of "an elaborate social function," was in fact an unmistakable ritual celebration of the traditional African belief in the successful culmination of the journey of the soul of the deceased and its triumphant entry into the world of the spirits.[118]

The rituals of death provide evidence of the persistence of traditional religious concepts and practices. Through them black Christians expressed their pervading faith in a source of power outside humanity and in a certain continuity of physical existence. The rituals also served important social functions. The long period of mourning and the public manifestations of grief provided solace to the families of the deceased in a situation where impersonal relationships offered no sustaining support. As an expression of traditional belief in the continuing existence of ancestral spirits, funeral rituals served as a link between the living, their ancestors, and the unborn, thus symbolically uniting the past, present, and future. The sense of continuity it engendered strengthened social bonds. Singing and dancing, the artistic expressions of religious faith, enhanced and protected that sense of community by affirming a common African heritage.

The continuation of relevant traditional concepts and practices thus satisfied individual psychological needs and helped to create and to sustain a sense of community. The drastically altered conditions of life under slavery, however, required new patterns of social organization and norms and values appropriate to the situation. It required as well institutions capable of embodying and transmitting those new patterns. The African-American Protestant church was the institution that would fulfill this function. Although wartime conditions, particularly in occupied areas, favored black evangelicalism and the modest expansion of Afro-Christianity, official hostility and popular preoccupation with political concerns caused the white evangelical movement to falter in the 1770s. British occupation completely disrupted the white Baptist movement in South Carolina. For two years there were no meetings of the Charleston Association. In Charleston itself religious activities came to a halt as both Baptist churches were taken over by the army, one for storing beef, the other for forage.[119] By contrast, the black churches in certain occupied areas, such as Georgia, expanded. Al-

[117] Janet Schaw, *Journal of a Lady of Quality. Being the Narrative of a Journey from Scotland to the West Indies, North Carolina, in the Years 1774 to 1776*, Evangeline Walker Andrews, ed. (New Haven, Conn.: Yale University Press, 1939), 171.

[118] William E. Hatcher, *John Jasper. The Unmatched Negro Philosopher and Preacher* (New York: Negro Universities Press, 1969), 37.

[119] Loulie Owens, *Saints of Clay: The Shaping of South Carolina Baptists* (Columbia, S.C.: R. L. Bryan, 1971), 50; Townsend, *South Carolina Baptists*, 26.

though the Chesapeake was spared the bitterness of the internecine warfare that tore congregations asunder and shattered churches in the low country, the revolutionary war scattered Baptist ministers and destroyed most of the once flourishing and prosperous churches in the piedmont and South-side.[120] During the war years, many Methodists "through fear, necessity, or choice," moved into the backcountry, although once peace was restored they began to petition for preachers "to come among us." Most of Wesley's English preachers "were obliged to fly for their lives," except for Asbury, who stayed "to bear the heat and burden of that day." For three years the intrepid Asbury continued to preach in Maryland and parts of Virginia, where the effects of the White Oak revival still lingered. Despite Asbury's complaint that Virginia was "in a very dark and deplorable condition," large numbers of people, black and white, turned out to hear him speak. Asbury avoided direct discussions of slavery and generally held separate meetings for blacks and whites, but sporadic Tory outbursts and raids by British forces after 1778 whipped up wartime passions and the English-born Asbury, who declared himself a non-juror on conscientious principles, was finally prohibited from preaching in the Chesapeake. He withdrew to Delaware, where the clergy were not required to take a state oath.[121]

Although the vast majority of slaveholders obstinately resisted efforts to Christianize their slaves, during the prerevolutionary years race was not a major issue in the consciousness of white southerners nor was it a special concern of the evangelical churches.[122] For all their solicitude for the spiritual well-being of slaves, except for the Quakers, the evangelicals had not made slaveholding a vital religious matter nor had they attempted to use the state as a positive instrument to achieve their religious objectives. The intense religious excitement of the Great Awakening, which swept New England in the second quarter of the century, had, however, begun to transform traditional Christianity by emphasizing not merely freedom from the bondage of sin but emancipation from chattel slavery. As a result, radical evangelicals came to view slavery as an anomaly in the moral order, and, rather than accommodate to the mores of the larger society on the question of slavery, they began to try to shape the larger society according to their own moral ideology.

During the 1760s, this interpretation of evangelical Christianity was

[120] David Benedict, *A General History of the Baptist Denomination in America* (New York: Lewis Colby, 1848), 708–9.

[121] Lee, *Short History*, 84–85; Coke and Moore, *Life of Wesley*, 350; Francis Asbury, *An Extract from the Journal of Francis Asbury, Bishop of the Methodist Episcopal Church in America from August 7, 1771, to December 29, 1778* (Philadelphia: Joseph Crukshank, 1792), 219, 235, 265, 272, 274, 325.

[122] Sobel, *Trabelin' On*, 387.

powerfully reinforced by the secular philosophy of Republican ideology with its overlapping emphasis on liberty and equality. The fusion of evangelical faith and republican ideals produced a searing indictment of slavery, which formed the intellectual foundation for the incipient antislavery movements in England and in the northern colonies. The religious frenzy of revivalism had also penetrated the South, but it was sporadic and localized before 1800. The Quakers, who left an unmistakable mark on the antislavery movement in the North, had no readily apparent influence on the southern consciousness. The Baptists and Methodists were not yet a major force in the Chesapeake, and in the low country they were widely scattered. The antislavery assault led by evangelical sects was still to come. Before it did, the Revolution intervened.

TWO

TOWARD INDEPENDENCE: THE CONFLICT

OVER SLAVERY IN A

REVOLUTIONARY CONTEXT

THE ERA of the American Revolution was a time of violent and unpredictable social, economic, and political change. The dislocations of that period were most severely felt in the South. Although historians have tended to view the war in the South in military terms as a bipolarity, in fact it was a complex triangular process involving two sets of white belligerents and approximately four hundred thousand slaves.[1] The environment in which the revolutionary conflict developed in the South was shaped not only by British policies or white southern initiatives but also by African-American resistance.

Actual or potential resistance was a main factor in the development of Britain's southern strategy. Influenced in part by slaves' combative and aggressive behavior, British military leaders and Crown officials seized upon the idea of intimidating independence-minded white southerners with the threat of a slave rising without, however, actually inciting one. In the end the British strategy of manipulating conflict between the races became a rallying cry for white southern unity and impelled the South toward independence. The need to weaken slaves' zeal for service with the British, which threatened to expose the moral absurdity of a society of slaveholders proclaiming the concepts of natural rights, equality, and liberty, formed part of the complex interaction of events that constituted the revolutionary war in the South. To that extent, the American Revolution in the South was a war about slavery, if not a war over slavery.

Before the outbreak of the American Revolution, there were relatively

[1] An important exception is Peter Wood. In Peter Wood, " 'The Dream Deferred': Black Freedom Struggles on the Eve of White Independence," in Gary Y. Okihiro, ed., *In Resistance. Studies in African, Caribbean, and Afro-American History* (Amherst, Mass.: University of Massachusetts Press, 1986), 166–87, Wood calls attention to the triangular nature of the war in the South. The failure to recognize the degree of black resistance is the result, he maintains, of the tendency of historians to do colony-by-colony studies rather than the general survey, that Wood undertakes in "The Dream Deferred." Another recent work that emphasizes the connection between slave resistance and American independence is Robert A. Olwell, " 'Domestick Enemies': Slavery and Political Independence in South Carolina, May 1775–March 1776," *Journal of Southern History* 55 (1989): 21–48.

few overt slave conspiracies or uprisings in the thirteen British mainland colonies. Historians have, therefore, concluded that American slaves were not prone to revolt.[2] It is, however, clear from records of the revolutionary period that slaves posed a real, not imaginary, threat to the very existence of the plantation colonies of the South. The list of conspiracies and other overt acts of resistance is impressive, especially when one takes into account the tendency of slaveowners to suppress all news of revolts or plots. As historians of slavery have suggested, patterns of resistance were, by and large, influenced by internal or motivational factors and by external factors, which limited the parameters of choice and forced slaves to act within circumscribed boundaries. Slave reactions were also influenced by behavior inherited from the African past, specifically from African systems of slavery from which thousands of New World slaves were drawn, and from traditional patterns of warfare. To be sure, African-American slaves had a different set of disabilities than African slaves, but they operated in the same way to produce similar patterns of resistance.

Although research on the subject is just beginning, it appears that slave revolts were relatively rare in Africa. For such revolts to occur, anthropologists maintain, a large number of slaves must have formed "a self-conscious stratum," that is, a group that was conscious of itself. The formation of a self-conscious stratum is a necessary preliminary to group solidarity, which alone makes collective action possible.[3] The complex nature of African slavery militated against such formation.

Different in almost all respects from European forms of slavery and New World systems, African slavery existed in both voluntary and involuntary forms; as a consequence, there were various categories of slaves. Among

[2] Ulrich B. Phillips explained the absence of major revolts as evidence of the benign nature of North American slavery and the racial submissiveness of the African in Ulrich B. Phillips, *American Negro Slavery. A Survey of the Supply, Employment and Control of Negro Labor as Determined by the Plantation Regime* (Baton Rouge: Louisiana State University Press, 1966), 463–88. Stanley Elkins emphasized internal factors, specifically the socialization into the role of slave; see, Elkins, *Slavery*, 136–38. In *American Negro Slave Revolts*, Herbert Aptheker once and for all dispelled the image of the happy, submissive slave and substituted for it the idea of a latent rebel, whose hatred for a vile and brutal system frequently erupted in rebellion, individual and collective, and ultimately forged "a great tradition of militancy." More recently, Eugene Genovese has suggested that elements of Sambo and his opposite extreme were present in every slave, the preponderance of one or the other being dependent "on the totality of social conditions." Genovese's comparison of American slave insurrections with those in the West Indies and Brazil led him to the conclusion that instead of a revolutionary tradition, African-Americans created a tradition of "nonrevolutionary self-assertion." The absence of a major outbreak during the revolutionary war, when conditions seemed to invite it, apparently bears out Genovese. See Eugene D. Genovese, *Roll, Jordan, Roll. The World the Slaves Made* (New York: Vintage Books, 1976), 587–97.

[3] Igor Kopytoff and Suzanne Miers, "African 'Slavery' as an Institution of Marginality," in Suzanne Miers and Igor Kopytoff, eds., *Slavery in Africa: Historical and Anthropological Perspectives* (Madison: University of Wisconsin Press, 1977), 43–49.

the Ashanti of Ghana, for example, at least five separate terms described the various conditions and degrees of servitude.[4] Although some social disabilities were attached to enslavement, in most societies slaves enjoyed certain rights, including the right to marry, to earn an independent income, to hold property, attain wealth, and even succeed to the master's property.[5] Deeply embedded in the social and political systems, in some societies slavery was used to prevent the depletion of a family line by incorporating the "slave" into the master's lineage.[6] Although servitude was generally considered more benign than New World slavery, certain categories of slaves were subject to sacrificial death to provide companionship and service to a deceased master on the journey to the world of the ancestors.[7]

Variations in the legal and social positions of slaves, their geographical and residential scattering among dispersed households, and the absorption and assimilation of certain categories into the kinship system, created situations that were not conducive to the development of a self-conscious stratum, or consequently, to the development of a revolutionary tradition. Because of the complexity of African slavery, it is very difficult to find a single pattern of resistance. A few groups, such as the Vai slaves, did on occasion revolt.[8] Others, such as the Fulani Machube, willingly accepted the role of slave.[9] The Yoruba belief in the importance of *ori*, or destiny, led to an acceptance of the inequalities of birth and property and to the hope that by propitiating destiny slaves could improve their status within the traditional system.[10] Nor, for that matter, did traditional religion provide ideological grounds for revolt. Rather, its existence was accepted as a natural institution, practiced by the ancestors, sanctioned by the gods.[11] For these reasons, perhaps, most slaves resorted to self-reliance and survival strategies and to flight, the most usual form of resistance.[12] Flight was, as

[4] Robert S. Rattray, *Ashanti Law and Constitution* (New York: Negro Universities Press, 1969), 39–40.

[5] Victor C. Uchendu, "Slaves and Slavery in Igboland, Nigeria," in Miers and Kopytoff, eds., *Slavery in Africa*, 128.

[6] Boniface I. Obichere, "The Social Character of Slavery in Ashanti and Dahomey," *Ufahamu* 12 (1983): 201.

[7] Uchendu, "Slaves and Slavery," 129.

[8] Svend Holsoe, "Slavery and Economic Response among the Vai (Liberia and Sierra Leone)," 287–303, and Kopytoff and Miers, "African 'Slavery,' " in Miers and Kopytoff, eds., *Slavery in Africa*, 48.

[9] Bernd Baldus, "Response to Dependence in a Servile Group: The Machube of Northern Benin," in Miers and Kopytoff, eds., *Slavery in Africa*, 435–58.

[10] Babatunde Agiri, "Slavery in Yoruba Society in the Nineteenth Century," in Paul E. Lovejoy, ed., *The Ideology of Slavery in Africa* (Beverly Hills, Calif: Sage Publications, 1981), 128.

[11] Obichere, "Social Character of Slavery," 143.

[12] Kopytoff and Miers, "African 'Slavery,' " 53, and Martin A. Klein, "Servitude Among the Wolof and Sereer of Senegambia," in Miers and Kopytoff, eds., *Slavery in Africa*, 347.

Paul Lovejoy has demonstrated, a major form of resistance inasmuch as it destroyed property and thereby undermined the wealth and power of the master.[13]

If they did not have a revolutionary tradition, African slaves did have a military tradition. Everywhere in Africa and in many Middle Eastern societies, slaves had a military role: as sailors for ship captains and merchants, as palace guards, as slavers in slave raiding, as soldiers for local rulers, as members of the regular army. In Ashanti and Dahomey, in times of war slaves rendered a variety of services—as guides and scouts, as interpreters, as carriers of supplies, and in Dahomey, as foot soldiers. One reason for the popularity of the slave soldier in Africa was that slaves were believed to be more reliable than free persons, whose loyalty was generally to the kinship group rather than to any central authority. In some societies slaves occupied positions of great political and military importance, some rising to the highest ranks in the army.[14]

The traditions of nonrevolutionary resistance and slave participation in military activities, which had a long history in Africa, were carried to the New World, where they found reinforcement under the conditions of slavery in the thirteen British mainland colonies. Conditions for the development of a self-conscious stratum clearly existed in the British North American colonies. By contrast to African slavery, the status of North American slaves was formally institutionalized and, in some colonies, was unalterable. Laws establishing slavery on a racial basis raised unbridgeable boundaries between slave and master, black and white, thus institutionalizing a generalized social identity as "black slaves." More important than any common bonds based on slavery were the internal bonds created by slaves themselves: their reconstitution of the family along traditional lines; their development of a language based on two or more African linguistic derivations; their retention, in the face of incredible odds, of core traditional spiritual and social values.

Other factors, however, militated against the development of a discreet stratum: the ethnic diversity of the slave population; its broad geographic dispersal through various kinds of slave systems; the existence of effective physical controls, which destroyed tribal organization and prevented the development of alternate mechanisms for the creation of broad, inclusive bonds and the incorporation of new members into the group; the absence

[13] Paul E. Lovejoy, "Fugitive Slaves: Resistance to Slavery in the Sokoto Caliphate," in Okihiro, ed., *In Resistance*, 72–73.

[14] Frederick Cooper, *Plantation Slavery on the East Coast of Africa* (New Haven, Conn.: Yale University Press, 1977), 14, 18, 35; Allan G. B. Fisher and Humphrey J. Fisher, *Slavery and Muslim Society in Africa*, 1st U.S. ed. (Garden City, N.Y.: Doubleday, 1971), 154–70; Nehemia Levtzion, *Ancient Ghana and Mali* (New York: Africana Publishing, 1980), 111–12; Obichere, "Social Character of Slavery," 200.

of an effective ideology for revolt. Having lost their old social identity, slaves were in the midst of acquiring a new social identity. At the beginning of the American Revolution their condition was analogous to what anthropologists have called incipient stratum. It thus appears that slaves' responses to the revolutionary crisis comprised part of an evolving African-American culture. Although their reactions were complex and varied according to locality and the parameters of choice available to them, generally speaking they appear to have been largely determined by capabilities already developed in response to the institution of slavery in Africa and to familiar military tactics. During the war, types of organization and inspiration emerged that looked in important ways to the future and, in some cases, anticipated the church-connected revolts and conspiracies of the postwar period.[15]

During the two decades beginning in 1765, slave unrest was more intensive and widespread than in any previous period. In the gathering intensity of the decade beginning in 1765, white Americans in the thirteen English colonies were passing resolutions denouncing Parliament's attempt to "enslave" them by regulating and taxing their property without their consent. In discussing the scope and powers of Parliament, colonists inevitably relied upon the ideology of natural rights, which rested upon the fundamental assumption that all humans are born with the inalienable right to be free. Apart from James Otis and Benjamin Rush, who publicly acknowledged the anomaly in colonial cries for freedom and the existence of chattel slavery, and Benjamin Franklin, who for a quarter-century had denounced slavery as unconstitutional, most political leaders preferred to ignore the relationship between political slavery and chattel slavery.[16] The connection was not, however, entirely lost on black slaves who, like their white owners, responded to the political ferment of the revolutionary years.

Blacks, slave and free, urban and rural, artisan and field hand, literate and illiterate, were swept up by the force of ideological energy. Northern blacks, who were disproportionately urban, mostly native-born and English speaking, were generally more conversant with the ideology of the Revolution. When asserting their claims to freedom, they frequently invoked the philosophical arguments that white revolutionaries were making in their own fierce struggle against oppression.[17] In the South, where rev-

[15] Vincent Harding's evocative metaphor of a "river" of resistance, building in power and intensity over time, is applicable to the development of resistance I am suggesting; see Vincent Harding, *There is a River. The Black Struggle for Freedom in America*, 1st ed. (New York: Harcourt Brace Jovanovich, c. 1981).

[16] Donald L. Robinson, *Slavery in the Structure of American Politics, 1765–1820* (New York: Harcourt Brace Jovanovich, 1971), 80–83.

[17] Charles W. Akers, " 'Our Modern Egyptians': Phillis Wheatley and the Whig Campaign against Slavery in Revolutionary Boston," *Journal of Negro History* 60 (1975): 406–7; Ruth

olutionary ideology was as sincerely affirmed as in the North though the commitment to slavery was much more thorough, the large slave population perceived a change in the coherence and ideology of the master class and tried to take advantage of it.

Although the mass of southern slaves were illiterate, there is every reason to suppose that they had access to revolutionary ideology, particularly in a period of history when written communication was still hindered by undependable mail service and a paucity of printers and publishers. As late as 1775 more people probably heard the news of Lexington and Concord from riders on horseback relaying the news than read about it in newspapers. Newspaper advertisements for runaways indicate that most fugitives spoke English, some fluently.

The slave community had, moreover, the means to maintain a vital oral tradition.[18] The close physical proximity and the communality, which had disappeared among the white upper classes by the late eighteenth century, continued in a modified form among poor whites and slaves, most of whom lived in communal quarters of ten or more people.[19] With the development of larger slave quarters and the creation of a common language, a complex communication system emerged. Table talk listened to by domestic slaves, conversations overheard by slave attendants or musicians, was quickly carried back to the slave quarters and was rapidly disseminated through the cross-quarter underground to other plantations, even to other colonies. Indeed, as Archibald Bullock and John Houston, two of Georgia's delegates to the Continental Congress, confided to John Adams, the slave network could carry news "several hundreds of miles in a week or fortnight."[20]

Whether or not slaves were impelled by the subsuming power of the

---

Bogin, " 'Liberty Further Extended': A 1776 Antislavery Manuscript by Lemuel Haynes," *William and Mary Quarterly*, 3d ser., 40 (1983): 85–105; Massachusetts Historical Society, *Collections*, 5th ser., 3 (Boston, 1877): 432–37 (hereafter cited as MHS *Coll.*); George Livermore, *An Historical Research Respecting the Opinions of the Founders of the Republic On Negroes as Slaves, as Citizens, and as Soldiers*, 4th ed. (Boston: A. Williams, 1863), 116–17; Samuel Tucker to John Hancock, July 5, 1776, item 68, New Jersey State Papers 1775–1788, Papers of the Continental Congress, 1774–1789 (M247), Microfilm reproduction of the Records of the Continental and Confederation Congresses and the Constitutional Convention, RG 360, National Archives, Washington, D.C. Tucker of Trenton was president of the Provincial Congress. See also John Dennis (New Brunswick) to Samuel Tucker, July 4, 1776, Papers of the Continental Congress, RG 360, 173.

[18] Lawrence W. Levine, *Black Culture and Black Consciousness. Afro-American Folk Thought from Slavery to Freedom* (Oxford: Oxford University Press, 1977), is the most detailed work on the subject.

[19] Rhys Isaac, *The Transformation of Virginia, 1740–1790* (Chapel Hill: University of North Carolina Press, 1982), 74.

[20] L. H. Butterfield, ed., *Diary and Autobiography of John Adams*, 4 vols. (Cambridge, Mass: Harvard University Press, Belknap Press, 1962), 2:183.

ideas of liberty and equality, their actions show that they did follow the progress of the war, and they fully appreciated its implications for their own lives. Slaves tried, for example, to take advantage of the confusion generated by the Stamp Act crisis in 1765 to make good their own understanding of revolutionary ideology. In Charleston, South Carolina, they watched with interest as white crowds protested the Stamp Act by parading around the homes of suspected stamp officers shouting "Liberty! Liberty and stamp'd paper." Shortly after, in a move clearly calculated to call attention to their own clanking chains, a group of blacks threw white citizens into panic as they chanted the same cry, "Liberty."[21] In recounting the incident Henry Laurens dismissed the slaves' behavior as a "thoughtless imitation" of whites. But time and events leave no doubt that this show of consciousness and activism was no abberation.

In large measure prerevolutionary slave resistance found its ideology, strategy, and meaning in African patterns of resistance and warfare. As in African slavery, where self-reliance and survival strategies prevailed, the shape and degree of slave resistance was roughly proportional to the possibilities inherent in their situations. Extensive settlement and cultivation had greatly limited the possibilities for maroon types of resistance in the American colonies, particularly in the Chesapeake, where with the exception of the Great Dismal Swamp, which straddled the boundary with North Carolina, the absence of a large wilderness area prevented effective maroon occupation. The expanse of unsettled frontier and a comparatively large amount of swampland still offered sanctuary for maroonage in the lower South, however.[22] Acutely aware of the strategic possibilities created by the Stamp Act disorders, slaves in Georgia and South Carolina took advantage of the situation to form maroon communities, from which, for a while, they were able to defend themselves against recapture.

At the height of the Stamp Act crisis in Georgia, a group of slave men, women, and children fled to a swamp on the north side of the Savannah River. Like guerrilla fighters they supported themselves by living off the forest and the fruits of their raids on plantations on the south side of the river. Although the Georgia assembly offered a reward of £2s. "For the head of every such Slave making Resistance,"[23] the group was apparently sufficiently strong to survive because four years later the assembly was

[21] Quoted in Peter H. Wood, " 'Taking Care of Business' in South Carolina: Republicanism and the Slave Society," in Jeffrey J. Crow and Larry E. Tise, eds., *The Southern Experience in the American Revolution* (Chapel Hill: University of North Carolina Press, 1978), 277.

[22] The pioneering study on the subject of maroonage in British North America is Herbert Aptheker, *To Be Free. Studies in American Negro History* (New York: International Publishers, 1948), especially 11–30.

[23] Candler, *CRG* 14:292–93. Journal of the Commons House of Assembly, June 17, 1763, to December 24, 1768.

forced to send a detachment of militia into the swamp to destroy a settle-ment of black runaways. Either the fugitives were able to elude their cap-tors or a similar band formed in the same general area, because again in 1772 the assembly ordered a company of militia to hunt down in their hiding places on "the Creeks and Secret Places" of the Savannah River, a band of runaways who had set fire to a house near Black Creek, burning to death in it a white child.[24]

At about the same time a group of South Carolina slaves, taking advan-tage of the Christmas holidays, fled into the swamps. Fearing a general black insurrection, provincial authorities called on the Catawba Indians to "come down and hunt the Negroes." Although Indian tribes sometimes sheltered black runaways, cultural differences and the practice common throughout the South and in the Caribbean of using Indians to crush slave revolts and destroy maroon communities sometimes fomented hostility be-tween Indians and African-Americans.[25] Neither numerous enough nor sufficiently strong to resist successfully, the black fugitives were quickly dispersed or captured by the Indians, "Partly by the Terror of their name their Diligence and singular sagacity in pursuing Enemies through such Thickets." Many of the runaways surrendered to their white owners "rather than expose themselves to the attack of an Enemy so dreaded."[26]

In structural features, maroon settlements, of which there are numerous examples in Jamaica, Brazil, and elsewhere in the Caribbean, bear striking resemblance to African slave towns built by runaway or rebel slaves for self-defense and survival.[27] Rather than an innovation in resistance techniques,

[24] Statutes, Colonial and Revolutionary, 1768–1773, Candler, *CRG*, pt. 1, 14:185, Pro-ceedings and Minutes of the Governor and Council, Candler, *CRG* 12:325–26.

[25] The seminal article on this subject is William S. Willis, "Divide and Rule: Red, White, and Black in the Southeast," *Journal of Negro History* 48 (1963): 157–76.

[26] Report of a Committee of the Council of South Carolina relative to the proposed bound-ary between North and South Carolina, in Walter Clark, ed., *The State Records of North Car-olina*, 26 vols. (Raleigh, N.C., 1886–1907), 11:226–27.

[27] Richard Price, *Maroon Societies: Rebel Slave Communities in the Americas*, 2d ed. (Balti-more, Md.: Johns Hopkins University Press, 1979), 28–30, 199, noted the African character of maroon societies in the Spanish Americas, but he called attention to "their syncretistic composition," and the differences in geographical, demographic, and political conditions in New World slavery that produced important differences in maroon societies. The same qual-ifications would obviously apply to maroon communities in the British mainland colonies. For descriptions of eighteenth-century African slave towns, see Thomas Masterman Winter-bottom, *An Account of the Native Africans in the Neighbourhood of Sierra Leone*, 2d ed., 2 vols. (London: Frank Cass, 1969), 1:154–59; and Alexander G. Laing, *Travels in the Timannee, Kooranko, and Soolima Countries* (London: J. Murray, 1825), 405. The retreat to fortified towns was apparently not a tactic unique to slaves. The thick bush that covered much of coastal Sierra Leone made open fighting, even in warfare, a rare occurrence. Among the Mende, military tactics usually consisted of each side concentrating its resources and main defense inside strongly fortified towns, whose "war-fences" must be breached by the enemy; see Kenneth L. Little, *The Mende of Sierra Leone. A West African People in Transition*, rev.

maroonage in the New World appears to have been a common African heritage. Although it did not constitute a direct attack on the slave system, it was regarded by whites as a menace, primarily because it expressed the slaves' hatred of the system, but also because it emphasized the importance they attached to joining or building a community, a more insidious but no less potentially dangerous development. Because escape was intended to be permanent, maroonage had to be undertaken with a high degree of consciousness and deliberateness. Survival in the woods or the swamps required the community to be creative, enterprising, and rational, which was implicitly subversive of white supremacy. A more direct challenge to the plantation order came from the waging of guerrilla warfare, which not only theatened white security, but fomented black unrest on the plantations and thus created the danger that maroonage could, and in the Caribbean frequently did, lead to open revolt.[28] Without adequate allies or access to an isolated interior that sheltered maroon groups in the Caribbean,[29] most of the maroon settlements in the revolutionary South were eventually destroyed.

The changing political situation after 1773 exposed the slave population to new motives and greater opportunities for overt resistance. Early in 1773 a group of Boston slaves presented three petitions for freedom to the general court and to General Thomas Gage, British commander in chief in America and governor of Massachusetts Bay. A year later, Gage was presented with two more petitions from "a grate Number of Blacks," as they styled themselves, offering to fight for him if he would arm them and set them free once victory was achieved.[30] In November a group of Virginia slaves met together secretly to select a leader, "who was to conduct them when the English troops should arrive—, which they foolishly thought would be very soon and that by revolting to them they should be rewarded with their freedom." Their plans were, however, discovered and "proper precautions taken to prevent the Infection." In reporting the incident to William Bradford, James Madison cautioned that "it is prudent such things should be concealed as well as suppressed."[31]

(London: Routledge and Kegan Paul; New York: Humanities Press, 1969), 32–36. Although they waged intermittent battles, siege operations were also characteristic of Yoruba warfare through most of the nineteenth century; see J. F. Ade Ajayi, *Yoruba Warfare in the Nineteenth Century* (Cambridge, England: Cambridge University Press, 1964), 23–32, 43.

[28] For general studies of maroonage in the Caribbean, see Craton, *Testing the Chains*, and Price, *Maroon Societies*.

[29] Craton, *Testing the Chains*, 61–66.

[30] Sidney Kaplan, "The Domestic Insurrections of the Declaration of Independence," *Journal of Negro History* 61 (1976): 249–50.

[31] To William Bradford, November 26, 1774, William T. Hutchinson and William M. E. Rachal, eds., *The Papers of James Madison*, 11 vols. to date (Chicago: University of Chicago Press, 1962–), 1:129–30.

Madison's account of the abortive rising and his revealing warning to Bradford expose the dilemma of a slaveholding society about to embark on a war against tyranny: how to prevent their slaves from imbibing the heady notions of liberty and equality, which had become their own rallying cry in the contest with Britain; how to exploit white fears of a slave rebellion to unite the white population behind the patriot cause and at the same time conceal from a watching world that behind the bewitching rhetoric of liberty was the hideous face of slavery. The resolution to the dilemma began to unfold a month later in Georgia, when the prospect of black rebellion threatened to become actual. On December 7, 1774, six "new Negro fellows and four wenches," who belonged to a Captain Morris of St. Andrew parish, killed their overseer, went to his house and murdered his wife, and "dangerously wounded a carpenter named Wright" and a boy who died the next day. They then marched to a neighboring plantation and seriously wounded the owner, Angus McIntosh. From there they proceeded to the house of Roderick M'Leod, "wounded him very much," and killed his son before they were taken. Their leader and McIntosh's slave, "a sensible fellow" who had joined the rebels, were burned alive.[32]

Although the St. Andrew Parish Revolt was purely spontaneous and was apparently confined to one estate, it greatly stirred white anxiety and two months later possibly led the residents of St. Andrew parish to adopt a set of antislavery resolutions. Authored by Lachlan McIntosh, a slaveowner, the resolutions asserted that "to show the world that we are not influenced by any contracted or interested motives, but a general philanthropy for all mankind . . . , we hereby declare our disapprobation and abhorrence of the unnatural practice of Slavery in America." They then pledged "to use our utmost endeavours for the manumission of our Slaves in this Colony, for the most safe and equitable footing for the masters and themselves."[33]

In the meantime, British military leaders and Crown officials viewed with intense interest the aggressive behavior of slaves and the apprehension it excited in their owners. Although the motives of the London government were complex, from the beginning of the conflict the North ministry was tempted by the idea of using the slave population in some capacity to crush southern resistance. Early in January 1775, news reached the south-

[32] *Georgia Gazette*, (Savannah), Dec. 7, 1774.
[33] Quoted in Wood, *Slavery in Colonial Georgia*, 201. Wood, 201–3, suggests that the Darien resolution was consciously manipulative. With a cold eye critically cast on the transparent hypocrisy of white Americans demanding liberty for themselves while denying it to their slaves, they publicly condemned slavery; by thus obscuring the discrepancy between the representation and the reality, they hoped to silence critics and win skeptical white supporters to the patriot cause. Acutely aware of the danger posed by the threat of black rebellion during periods of crisis, they conjured up the dream of manumission in the hope of luring black support for the American cause or at the very least, of discouraging blacks from casting their lot with the British.

ern colonies that an extraordinary proposal had been recently introduced into the House of Commons.[34] Aimed at "humbling the high aristocratic spirit of Virginia and the southern colonies," it called for the general emancipation of slaves. The measure failed to win the necessary support in the Commons, but the idea of recruiting slaves as a disruptive tactic gained support as war with the colonies became imminent.[35] Soon afterwards, Gage, whose own experience with Boston slaves clearly heightened his appreciation of the intense psychological repercussions a war of nerves might produce, expressed interest in the idea. In what was apparently a private letter written in February or March to John Stuart, British Indian superintendent in the Southern District from 1762 to 1779, Gage warned that unless South Carolina moderated its opposition to British policies "it may happen that your Rice and Indigo will be brought to market by negroes instead of white People."[36]

The complex triangularity of events is increasingly apparent in the events leading up to independence. In April 1775, shortly after John Murray, fourth earl of Dunmore and royal governor of Virginia, seized the colony's store of gunpowder from the magazine at Williamsburg, "some Negroes (by one of his servants) had offered to join him and take up arms," thus anticipating by several months Dunmore's famous proclamation. Dunmore ordered them "to go about their business," and "threatened them with his severest resentment, should they presume to renew their application." Slaveholders were, however, suspicious.[37] Convinced that Dunmore "designed, by disarming the people to weaken the means of opposing an insurrection of the slaves," a group of citizens armed themselves and demanded that the powder be returned to the magazine.[38] "Exceedingly exasperated," Dunmore threatened to "declare freedom to the slaves and reduce the City of Williamsburg to ashes" and boasted that in the event of war "he should have . . . people and all the Slaves on the side of Government."[39]

The situation grew steadily more explosive following the actual com-

[34] From William Bradford, January 4, 1775, in Hutchinson and Rachal, eds., *Madison Papers* 1:132.

[35] Edmund Burke, *The Speeches of the Right Honourable Edmund Burke, in the House of Commons, and in Westminister-Hall*, 4 vols. (London: Longman, Hurst, Rees, Orme and Brown, 1816), 1:299. Burke's speech, which referred to the emancipation proposal, was made on March 22, 1775.

[36] Quoted in John Richard Alden, "John Stuart Accuses John Bull," *William and Mary Quarterly*, 3d ser., 2 (1945): 318.

[37] *Virginia Gazette*, (Pinckney), May 4, 1775.

[38] Edmund Randolph, *History of Virginia*, Arthur H. Shaffer, ed. (Charlottesville: University Press of Virginia, 1970), 219.

[39] "Deposition of Dr. William Pasteur, 1775," *Virginia Magazine of History and Biography* 13 (1905): 49.

mencement of hostilities at Lexington and Concord on April 19, 1775. On
May l, Dunmore wrote to William Legge, second Earl of Dartmouth and
secretary of state for the colonies, informing him of his plan "to arm all my
own Negroes and receive all others that will come to me whom I shall
declare free." Properly armed, he boasted, his force would soon "reduce
the refractory people of this colony to obedience."[40] Dunmore's threat to
recruit slaves and the arrival on May 3 of a letter from Arthur Lee, the
American correspondent in London, to Henry Laurens, confirming "that
a plan was laid before Administration, for instigating the slaves to insurrection," brought the racial issue to the forefront of public consciousness
and gave an entirely new character to the conflict in the South. "This was
the more alarming," William Drayton, a member of the South Carolina
Committee of Intelligence, remembered, "because it was already known,
[the slaves] entertained ideas that the present contest was for obliging us
to give them their liberty."[41]

The growing indentification of slave militancy and British plots to incite
slaves as part of its American policy—always a factor in the relations of
Britain and her southern colonies—became increasingly important in the
spring of 1775. The "dread of instigated Insurrections," a popular euphe-
mism for a British-inspired slave revolt, was particularly acute in South
Carolina because of its unique racial demography. In May, a report that
slaves would be set free on the arrival of the new governor, Lord William
Campbell, and that the sloop of war carrying Campbell was also bearing
fourteen thousand stand of weapons became "common talk" among slaves
throughout the province and "occasioned impertinent behaviour in many
of them."[42] The discovery of an insurrection plot, planned to coincide with
the British arrival, threw the white citizenry of Charleston into panic. "The
newspapers were full of Publications calculated to excite the fears of the
People—Massacres and Instigated Insurrections, were words in the mouth
of every Child—," recalled John Stuart, who was forced to flee the city after
he was implicated in the plan to employ Indians.[43]

When the second session of the First Provincial Congress, the patriots'
legislative body, convened June 1, the new president, Henry Laurens, jus-

[40] Dunmore to Dartmouth, May 1, 1775, CO5/1373, PRO.

[41] John Drayton, *Memoirs of the American Revolution, From Its Commencement to the Year
1776, Inclusive; As Relating to the State of South-Carolina*, 2 vols. (Charleston, S.C.: A. E.
Miller, 1821), 1:231; see also Henry Laurens, *The Papers of Henry Laurens*, Philip H. Hamer
and George C. Rogers, eds., 10 vols. to date (Columbia: University of South Carolina Press,
1968–), 10:113 n. 5, 114 n. 2.

[42] Josiah Smith, Jr. to James Poyas, May 18, 1775, in Josiah Smith, Jr. (1730–1826) Let-
tercopy Book, 1771–1784, Southern Historical Collection, University of North Carolina
Library, Chapel Hill (hereafter cited as SHC). The rumor of arms for slaves is cited in Wood,
"The Dream Deferred," 176.

[43] Alden, "John Stuart Accuses John Bull," 320.

tified the session on the grounds that the outbreak of fighting in Massachusetts, the possibility of an invasion of Charleston, or a slave uprising either independently or in conjunction with a British invasion warranted defense preparations. He called on the Congress to establish a provincial military force, to form an association of patriots, and to create a council of safety to exercise day-to-day executive power.[44] The Provincial Congress responded by approving the formation of an association of defense to which all patriots would subscribe. The text of the association placed the onus squarely on Britain for "The actual Commencement of Hostilities against this Continent—the threats of arbitrary impositions from abroad—& the dread of instigated Insurrections at home."[45] The Provincial Congress also decided to establish three regiments of troops for a dual-purpose described by the Charleston merchant, Josiah Smith: "to keep those mistaken creatures in awe, as well as to oppose any Troops that may be sent among us with coercive Orders." With white fears running high in Charleston, the Congress also ordered three companies of militia to patrol the city's streets, one by day and two at night, "to guard against any hostile attempts that may be made by our domesticks," the jittery Smith wrote to a friend in London.[46] At the height of the crisis, said one resident, the city "has rather the appearance of a garrison town than a mart for trade."[47]

Determined to quash the slaves' "high notions of liberty," the Provincial Congress also appointed a special committee to investigate the reports of black insurrections and to form further plans for the "public security."[48] In June hearings were held by the committee, and on the twenty-second of the month freeholders were summoned to try the first suspects under the provisions of the Negro Act of 1740, article 17 of which dealt with homicide and insurrection. Two of the plotters were ordered to be "Severely flogged and banished." The alleged leader, a free black man named Thomas Jeremiah, was brought to trial August 11 before a court of two justices of the peace and five freeholders on charges of plotting an insurrection and threatening to assist the royal navy over the bar in Charleston harbor when it arrived, presumably to assist slaves in gaining freedom. Jeremiah, a fisherman and pilot who, according to Henry Laurens, was "puffed up by prosperity, ruined by Luxury and debauchery and grown to an amazing pitch of vanity and ambition," was convicted of intended sedition by a

[44] To John Laurens, May 30, 1775, *Papers of Henry Laurens* 10:160, n. 14.
[45] Ibid., May 15, 1775, 118–19.
[46] Smith to Poyas, May 18, 1775, Smith Lettercopy Book.
[47] Extract of a Letter from Charleston, June 29, 1775, Peter Force, ed. *American Archives . . . A Documentary History of . . . the North American Colonies*, 4th ser., 6 vols. (March 7, 1774–August 21, 1776), 2:1129.
[48] Drayton, *Memoirs* 1:231.

unanimous decision of the judges. On August 18 he was hanged and burned to death in Charleston.[49]

During the trial, which dispensed with most of the legal niceties, a slave named Sambo testified that two or three months earlier Jeremiah had told him that "there was a great War coming soon." When Sambo, a waterman, asked Jeremiah "what shall we poor Negroes do in a schooner," Jeremiah replied that they should "set the schooner on fire, jump on shore and join the soldiers," because "the War was come to help the poor Negroes."[50] Despite the concerted effort of slaveowners to suppress any information that was likely to cause unrest, Jeremiah's message, that slaves had a powerful ally in the British, enjoyed wide credence among slaves—from the swampy rice plantations of South Carolina, to the small tobacco farms hacked out of the thick pine forests of North Carolina, to the great tobacco plantations that lined Virginia's majestic tidal rivers. During the summer of 1775, the conflict in the South increasingly took on a racial polarity. Rumors of British plans to free slaves excited slave resistance while slave militancy provided the dynamic for British "tampering." The simultaneous operation of the two fostered the feeling among slaveholders that they were beset by foes from within and without. The conviction that their society was in a great crisis contributed to the growing alienation from Britain.

Although by southern standards North Carolina had relatively few slaves, they were heavily concentrated in counties east of the fall line. The rumors of insurrections that spread across the Carolinas in the summer of 1775 caused a frenzy of action throughout the East. Upon receiving a report "that the Negroes mean to take advantage of the times," the frightened citizens of Edenton, in the heart of the tobacco-growing Northeast, "raised up a guard of Eight men in the Town every night, in the Country, the same precaution is taking."[51] In New Bern, located at the confluence of the Neuse and Trent rivers halfway between two other important ports of Edenton and Wilmington, the local committee of safety warned the citizens of Craven County that "there is much reason to fear, in these Times of general Tumult and Confusion, that the Slaves may be instigated, encouraged by our inveterate Enemies to an Insurrection" and called on them to form themselves into companies to "patrol and search the Negroes Houses" for arms and ammunition.[52]

---

[49] To John Laurens, June 18, 1775, June 23, 1775, August 20, 1775, *Papers of Henry Laurens* 10:184–5, 191, 320 n. 4, 323; William Campbell to [?], August 19, 1775, British PRO Transcripts, Colonial Williamsburg, Williamsburg, Virginia.

[50] Testimony Given in the Trial of Jeremiah, Campbell to [?], August 19, 1775, BPROT.

[51] Robert Smith to Joseph Hewes, May 23, 1775, Hayes Collection, M324, SHC.

[52] In the Committee of Newbern, May 31, 1775, in Adelaide L. Fries, ed., *Records of the*

Despite all their precautions, the political excitement stirred by rumors of emancipation produced an actual insurrection attempt. In Wilmington, in the lower Cape Fear country where slavery was most prominent, the discovery of a slave conspiracy hours before the scheduled rising was to take place produced widespread panic among whites across three counties. Apparently conceived by a slave named Merrick, the conspiracy involved slaves from Beaufort, Pitt, and Craven counties. The plot projected July 8 as the day for all slaves "to fall on and destroy the family where they lived, then to proceed from House to House (burning as they went) until they arrived in the Back Country where they were to be received with open arms by a number of Persons there appointed and armed by Government for their Protection, and as a further reward they were to be settled in a free government of their own."[53] By nightfall the revolt, which rumor had it was encouraged by John Collet, military commander of Fort Johnston and by Governor Josiah Martin, had been crushed. Patrollers from the three counties involved, who had been given discretionary power to "shoot any Number of Negroes above four, who are off their Masters Plantations, and will not submit,"[54] had killed one slave and arrested nearly forty others. Before dark five of them had been severely whipped and had "both Ears crap'd" [sic] before a crowd of spectators. For several days the interrogations and the "scourgings" continued.[55] During the crucial period political differences were temporarily set aside and the white community closed ranks against the slaves. "All parties are now united against the common enemies," as Janet Schaw, a Scottish gentlewoman, wrote at the height of the crisis. "Every man is in arms and the patroles going thro' all the town, and searching every Negro's house, to see they are all at home by nine at night." After spending a late evening with friends, Schaw was escorted to her home by the midnight patrol, commanded by a local tory.[56]

Although several issues peculiar to North Carolina were influencing provincial leaders toward revolution,[57] the insurrection scare of 1775, and the belief, particularly in the Cape Fear country, that Governor Martin and other Crown officials were "spiriting up the back counties, and perhaps the Slaves," were contributing factors to the growing alienation

---

Moravians in North Carolina, 11 vols. (Raleigh, N.C.: Edwards and Broughton, 1922), 2:929.

[53] Colonel John Simpson, Chairman of Safety Committee, Pitt Co., to Colonel Richard Cogdell, Chairman of Safety Committee, Craven Co., July 15, 1775, William L. Saunders, ed., *The Colonial Records of North Carolina*, 10 vols. (Raleigh: Printers to the State, 1886–90), 10:94–95 (hereafter cited as *CRNC*).

[54] Proceedings of the Safety Committee in Pitt County, July 8, 1775, *CRNC* 10:87.

[55] Ibid., 43, 94–95, 112.

[56] Schaw, *Journal*, 199–201.

[57] A. Roger Ekirch, *"Poor Carolina." Politics and Society in Colonial North Carolina, 1729–1776* (Chapel Hill: University of North Carolina Press, 1981), esp. 208–11.

from Britain.[58] As part of the British effort to return the southern colonies to allegiance to the Crown, the London government decided to send a small expedition to the Cape Fear region. The plan was to restore royal government to the control of loyalists and then to withdraw British troops to the north. Governor Martin was charged with responsibility for raising provincial troops, which he would lead as a provincial colonel. During the month of June, rumors began to circulate that the British plan also called for inciting the slaves to revolt, which indeed had some basis in fact.

Shortly before he was succeeded as commander in chief of British forces in the colonies by General Sir William Howe, Gage wrote to Secretary at War Barrington, warning him that "things are now come to that Crisis, that we must avail ourselves of every resource, even to raise the Negros, [sic] in our cause."[59] Rather than deny the persistent rumors, Governor Martin ambiguously replied "that nothing could ever justify the design, falsely imputed to me, of giving encouragement to the negroes, but the actual and declared rebellion of the King's subjects, and the failure of other means to maintain the King's Government."[60] As a shaken John Stuart, whose flight to East Florida before an incensed mob was interpreted as "a proof of Conscious Guilt,"[61] testified from personal experience, "nothing can be more alarming to the Carolinas than the Idea of an attack from Indians and Negroes."[62]

Thoroughly antagonized, provincial leaders were spurred to action. Local militia companies were hurriedly raised and trained, slaves were disarmed, and patrols were organized to keep them under control. Fearing for his life, Martin sent his pregnant wife to New York, spiked the palace cannon and buried the ammunition in the cellar before fleeing to Fort Johnston on Cape Fear.[63] His efforts to strengthen the garrison prompted the Wilmington Committee of Safety to raise a force of militia and minutemen to attack the fort. The "savage and audacious mob," led by Colonel Robert Howe, announced their intention to remove the guns from the fort in a letter to Martin from "The People." Listed among the reasons for the attack was Martin's "base encouragement of Slaves eloped from their Mas-

[58] The Safety Committee in Wilmington to Samuel Johnston, July 13, 1775, in Saunders, *CRNC* 10:91.

[59] To Barrington, June 12, 1775, in Clarence E. Carter, ed., *The Correspondence of General Thomas Gage with the Secretaries of State, and with the War Office and the Treasury*, 2 vols. (Hamden, Conn.: Archon Books, 1969), 2:684.

[60] Martin to Hon. Lewis Henry DeRosset, June 24, 1775, Saunders, *CRNC* 10:138. Martin's letter responding to the charge that he was encouraging slaves to revolt was published by the New Bern Committee of Safety.

[61] To James Laurens, June 24, 1775, *Papers of Henry Laurens* 10:197.

[62] John Stuart to the earl of Dartmouth, Saunders, *CRNC* 10:118.

[63] Hugh F. Rankin, "The Moore's Creek Bridge Campaign, 1776," *North Carolina Historical Review* 30 (1953): 23–60.

ters, feeding and employing them, and his atrocious and horrid declaration that he would incite them to an Insurrection."[64]

Martin's subsequent efforts to subjugate the colony with a force of loyalists supported by slaves, acting in conjunction with British troops, culminated in defeat in the Moore's Creek Bridge campaign. The decline of British authority in the colony quelled unrest among slaves. Bereft of the hope of support from a powerful ally, "The Negroes at Cape Fear," as a North Carolina planter put it shortly after the patriot victory, "were never known to behave so well as they have lately."[65]

Latent fears of a slave rising surfaced again in the spring of 1776, however, when British forces commanded by General Charles Cornwallis appeared in the Cape Fear area. Although the primary objective was Charleston, the British conducted a few raids, mostly military excercises to relieve the boredom of the troops. But the Fourth Provincial Congress sitting at Halifax took no chances. Slave owners on the south side of the Cape Fear River were instructed to move all male slaves capable of bearing arms or of otherwise assisting the British to areas remote from the sea. On April 12 the same Congress adopted the Halifax Resolves, which included among other things the penultimate charge that "Governors in different Colonies have declared protection to slaves, who should imbrue their hands in the blood of their masters." Apparently without debate the Congress unanimously agreed to authorize North Carolina delegates to the Continental Congress to recommend independence.[66]

Events in South Carolina were also pushing that province toward revolution. After a brief period of comparative calm following the trial and sentencing of Thomas Jeremiah, another insurrection scare occurred. The threatened insurrection had certain elements in common with the revolt planned in North Carolina; the most conspicuous was coincidental timing. The scene of the South Carolina conspiracy was St. Bartholomew parish. The plotters confessed to the court of freeholders convened to try them during the first week of July that they had planned a general insurrection "to take the Country by killing the whites." The St. Bartholomew scare was, however, different in one remarkable respect: its leaders included several black preachers, two of whom were women whose owners were prominent Cheraw planters, Francis Smith, William Smith, John Wells, Thomas Hutchinson, and George Austin. With the exception of Austin, who was an absentee owner, during the war all of the planters either served in the Cheraw District militia or were active supporters of the patriot cause.[67]

[64] "The People" to Gov. Martin, July 16, 1775, Saunders, *CRNC* 10:102–3.
[65] Quoted in Rankin, "Moore's Creek Bridge," 56.
[66] April 12, May 8, 1776, Journal of the Fourth Provincial Congress, Saunders, *CRNC* 10:512, 567, 569. For details of the British expedition, see Hugh F. Rankin, *The North Carolina Continentals* (Chapel Hill: University of North Carolina Press, 1971), 56, 58, 59, 60.
[67] *Papers of Henry Laurens* 10:207 nn. 3, 4, 5.

Trial testimony revealed that the insurrection had been planned at secret religious meetings held in the woods or some other secluded place, usually on one of the Austin plantations, whose day-to-day operations were left in the hands of an overseer and black driver, which probably gave the slaves greater freedom from close supervision. The meetings, which violated the law prohibiting slaves meeting for religious worship before sunrise or after sunset, were begun some two years previously by a Scottish preacher named John Burnet, who insisted that his only motive was "the salvation of those poor ignorant Creatures." After Burnet was warned that "his conduct was extremely Obnoxious to the People," he withdrew, but self-appointed black preachers began conducting services on their own. Burnet's professed efforts "to reconcile them to that Lot in Life in which God had placed them," and to teach them "the Duty of Obedience to their Masters," clearly miscarried because, according to one trial witness, the black preachers offered their own distinct rendition of Christian theology. George, the slave of Francis Smith and one of the leaders of the insurrection, told "the Great crouds of Negroes in the Neighborhood of Chyhaw" who attended the meetings in defiance of the law, that "the old King had reced a Book from our Lord by which he was to Alter the World (meaning to set the Negroes free) but for his not doing so, was now gone to Hell, and punishment—That the Young King, meaning our Present One, came up with the Book, & was about to alter the World, & set the Negroes Free." After some deliberation the court decided on "the disagreable necessity to cause Exemplary punishments" and sent George to the gallows. Although no complicity could be established, Burnet was ordered out of the province.[68]

The exodus motif also made its appearance in Savannah and created deep anxieties among white Georgians, particularly because it came from a black preacher named David. Invited to preach to a gathering of whites and blacks, David "dropped some unguarded expressions, such as, that he did not doubt, but 'God would send Deliverance to the Negroes, from the power of their Masters, as he freed the Children of Israel from Egyptian Bondage.'" Convinced that he "meant to raise rebellion among the negroes," frightened slaveowners determined to capture David, "and hang him, if they can lay hold of him." To spare his life, James Habersham helped to "send him off privately" on the ship *Georgia Planter*. Habersham's objection that, "His business was to preach a Spiritual Deliverance to these People, not a temporal one," underscores the sharp difference between Afro-Christian and Anglo-Christian theology. Used by Christian slaveholders to rationalize the brutality of slavery, the exodus motif was appropriated by Christian slaves to justify their own struggles for freedom.

[68] Thomas Hutchinson to Council of Safety, July 5, 1775, Council of Safety to St. Bartholomew Committee, July 18, 1775, *Papers of Henry Laurens* 10:206–8, 231–32.

The theme continued to resonate through the church-associated revolts of the postrevolutionary era.[69]

By the end of the critical summer of 1775 British authority had been significantly undermined by the series of crises in the low country. In South Carolina escalating violence and the patriot decision to capture Fort Johnson led to open confrontation between Governor Campbell and the Council of Safety. On September 15, Campbell dissolved the assembly, closed his offices and fled to the *Tamar* in Charleston harbor, thus suspending royal government in South Carolina until the British capture of Charleston in 1780 restored royal control.[70]

The waves of unrest that swept the South during the tumultuous summer of 1775 crested in Virginia with the so-called Dunmore rising. Dunmore's military activities in Virginia in the following months have been so frequently described and at such length, that a detailed account here is unnecessary.[71] For nearly a year he ordered spoiling operations among Virginia's waterways, causing considerably more fear than damage. After several minor clashes with militiamen, Dunmore declared martial law and on November 7, 1775, issued his proclamation from on board the *William*, which he had seized from local merchants and fitted out for war.

Although it was viewed on both sides of the Atlantic as a threat to the very foundations of slavery, Dunmore's intention was neither to overthrow the system nor to make war on it. Directed principally at "all indented servants, Negroes, or others, (appertaining to Rebels), that are able and willing to bear Arms," the proclamation was designed to encourage the defection of useful blacks without provoking a general rebellion and to disrupt the psychological security of whites without unleashing the full military potential of blacks. Practical rather than moral, it was rooted in expediency rather than humanitarian zeal. That is not, however, how it was perceived in the South.

The Continental Congress meeting in Philadelphia represented Dunmore's offer of freedom to slaves as "tearing up the foundations of civil authority and government" in Virginia, and called on the colony to estab-

---

[69] To Mr. Robert Keen, May 11, 1775, in "Letters of Hon. James Habersham," 243–44.

[70] Council of Safety to William Drayton, September 15, 1775, *Papers of Henry Laurens* 10:386–88.

[71] See, for example, Benjamin Quarles, *The Negro in the American Revolution* (Chapel Hill: University of North Carolina Press, 1961), 19–32. Quarles' is the pioneering work on the subject of black participation in the revolutionary war. It remains the standard study. See also Sylvia R. Frey, "Between Slavery and Freedom: Virginia Blacks in the American Revolution," *Journal of Southern History* 49 (1983): 375–98; and Ivor Noel Hume, *1775. Another Part of the Field* (New York: Alfred A. Knopf, 1966), which chronicles events in Virginia during the year 1775 including Dunmore's proclamation and his activities in the months of November and December.

lish a government that would produce happiness and secure peace.[72] In a vain effort to prevent word of it from reaching Maryland's slave population, the provisional government there prohibited all correspondence with Virginia, either by land or water. But in Dorchester County on Maryland's Eastern Shore, an area already troubled by persistent rumors of insurrectionist activities among slaves and lower class whites,[73] the committee of safety reported new signs of slave militancy: "The insolence of the Negroes in this county is come to such a height, that we are under a necessity of disarming them which we affected [sic] on Saturday last. We took about eighty guns, some bayonets, swords, etc."[74] In neighboring North Carolina, Howe's Continentals and the Edenton Minute Men were ordered to Pasquotank and Currituck to prevent a rumored attempt by Dunmore to march into North Carolina and to apprehend agents of Dunmore who were allegedly working to incite slaves in the Albemarle region.[75]

Nervous whites on the unsettled coast of South Carolina saw an ominous connection between Dunmore's activities and the massing of runaways on Sullivan's Island. Acting with British complicity, the runaways made nightly sorties to rob and harrass the seacoast of Christ-Church. The first reports reached the Council of Safety in Charleston on December 6, 1775. The following day the Council ordered Colonel William Moultrie to move "this ensuing night" against the runaways' encampment on Sullivan's Island. Perhaps because the seriousness of the situation was not yet fully appreciated, the assault did not take place on the seventh. On December 10, the Council received an alarming report from Fenwick Bull, a local citizen, of his conversation with Captain John Tollemache of the *Scorpion*. According to Tollemache, the runaways were not "inticed" to desert by the British but "came as freemen, and demanding protection; that he could have had near 500 who had offered; that we were all in actual rebellion," and that he had orders "to distress Americans by every means in his power."

Now fully alarmed, the Council of Safety cut off all supplies and provisions to the king's ships and ordered an immediate attack on the Sullivan's Island refuge. On the morning of December 19 a company of fifty-four rangers commanded by Lieutenant William R. Withers descended on the island. Although most of the fugitives had already escaped with the aid of boats from the British warship *Cherokee*, four blacks were killed and eleven

[72] December 4, 1775, Worthington C. Ford, ed., *Journals of the Continental Congress, 1774–1789*, 34 vols. (Washington, D.C.: USGPO, 1904–37), 3:403–4.

[73] Ronald Hoffman, *A Spirit of Dissension. Economics, Politics, and the Revolution in Maryland* (Baltimore, Md.: Johns Hopkins University Press, 1973), 147–49.

[74] Report of Dorchester County Committee, Fall, 1775, quoted in Hoffman, *Spirit of Dissension*, 148.

[75] Rankin, *North Carolina Continentals*, 24.

people were captured, including three crew members from the *Cherokee*. Destruction of the runaway haven and the summary justice meted out to them "will serve to humble our Negroes in general," the relieved Charleston Council predicted.[76]

Two of Georgia's delegates to the Continental Congress, Archibald Bullock and John Houston, were far less sanguine. Eager to seize upon any outside encouragement, Georgia slaves were, they confided to John Adams, waiting for the chance to rise. If, the two predicted, "one thousand regular troops should land in Georgia, and their commander be provided with arms and clothes enough, and proclaim freedom to all the negroes who would join his campaign, twenty thousand would join it from [Georgia and South Carolina] in a fortnight."[77] The presence of British war vessels at the mouth of the Savannah River early in January 1776, spurred a rash of slave desertions from Georgia plantations. Although the vessels were there to purchase provisions and not to liberate slaves, the Georgia Council of Safety initiated defensive preparations. The militia was ordered out to protect Savannah against any hostile attempt by the British and coastal areas were advised to increase their vigilance. Slave patrols were sent to search Negro houses throughout the province, including those on the South Carolina side of the Savannah River as far north as Purrysburg, for arms and ammunition. As an added precaution Georgia's last royal governor, Sir James Wright, and the members of his council were arrested and required to give their paroles not to leave the city or to communicate with the British vessels.[78] In February when more British ships arrived, Governor Wright and several of his councillors broke their paroles and fled Savannah "to avoid the rage and violence of the rebels."[79] While the HMS

[76] My account of the Sullivan Island incident differs somewhat from Peter Wood's account. According to Wood, the attack occurred December 7 and was led by Colonel Moultrie. It resulted in the killing of fifty runaways. See Wood, "The Dream Deferred," 178–79. That the attack ordered for December 7 did not take place as planned is suggested by the December 14 entry of the Journal of the Council of Safety, which indicates that "a few days ago, when a report prevailed, that they were to be attacked upon Sullivan's Island, [the runaways] were taken off the shore in boats sent from the ships." All accounts of the actual attack indicate that only four or five fugitives were killed. For details see "Journal of the Second Council of Safety," South Carolina Historical Society, *Collections*, 5 vols. (Charleston, 1857–1897), 3:63, 64–65, 75, 84, 88, 89, 91, 102–3, 104–5, 106, 130, 141, 142, 143, 151 (hereafter cited as SCHS, *Coll.*); Council of Safety to Richard Richardson, December 19, 1775, *Papers of Henry Laurens* 10:576 n. 5; *The South-Carolina and American General Gazette*, December 15–22, 1775; William Bell Clark, ed. *Naval Documents of the American Revolution*, 5 vols. (Washington D.C.: USGPO, 1968), 3:105, 164, 191, 202, 725.

[77] Butterfield, *Diary and Autobiography of John Adams* 2:428.

[78] Allen D. Candler, comp., *The Revolutionary Records of the State of Georgia*, 3 vols. (Atlanta: Franklin-Turner, 1908), 1:87, 92 (hereafter cited as *RRSG*); "Journal of the Second Council of Safety," SCHS, *Coll.* 3:198.

[79] Memorial of Sir James Wright, Candler, *CRG*. Copies made from original records in

Scarborough rode at anchor off Cockspur Island at the entrance to the Savannah River, between two and three hundred slaves presented themselves
to Governor Wright, declaring "they were come for the King."[80] For another month while British warships remained in the area, slaves continued
to flee from the farms and plantations along the high bluffs of the Savannah
River.

The defection of hundreds of slaves produced a powerful defensive response from white leaders. When Colonel Stephen Bull arrived with reinforcements from South Carolina early in March, he learned that some two
hundred black fugitives were massed on Tybee Island. Reasoning that if
they were successful in joining the British it would "only enable an enemy
to fight against us with our own money or property," Bull recommended
to Henry Laurens, president of the Council of Safety of Charleston, a campaign of eradication: "It is far better for the public and the owners, if the
deserted negroes on Tybee Island . . . be shot, if they cannot be taken." To
"deter other negroes from deserting," and to "establish a hatred or aversion
between the Indians and negroes," Bull asked permission to employ a party
of Creek Indians to carry out the distasteful mission.

Laurens expressed personal horror at the "awful business contained in
your letter," but he conceded that it was necessary, perhaps because South
Carolina was also losing "many hundreds" of slaves by desertion to British
coastal cruisers.[81] "We think," he wrote for the Charleston Council, that
"the Council of Safety in Georgia ought to give that encouragement which
is necessary to induce proper persons to seize and if nothing else will do to
destroy all those Rebellious Negroes upon Tybee Island or wherever else
they may be found." He approved as well the classic slaveholder policy of
pitting hostile ethnic groups against one another: "If Indians are the most
proper hands let them be employed on this Service but we would advise
that Some discreet white Men be encorporated with or joined to lead
them."[82] Because Bull and Laurens agreed that the information be selec-
tively circulated, it is not known whether the general massacre that was
planned actually occurred. Nevertheless, the event stands as a stark dram-
atization of the extreme brutality necessary to maintain the slave system.

Even without access to interministerial discussions it seems clear that the

---

England (microfilm), Howard-Tilton Library, Tulane University, New Orleans, Louisiana,
39 (1733–1783), 26–27.

[80] Memorial of Sir James Wright and several other gentlemen, Candler, *CRG*, pt. 2 (1772–
1775) 38:139.

[81] I am grateful to Peter H. Wood for this citation. Henry Laurens to Col. Stephen Bull,
"Papers of the Second Council of Safety of the Revolutionary Party in South Carolina, November 1775–March 1776," *South Carolina Historical and Genealogical Magazine* 4 (1903):
205. See Wood, "Dream Deferred," 256–57, for a further discussion of the Tybee affair.

[82] Wood, "Dream Deferred."

slaveholders' fear of a servile rising and the groundswell of slave resistance that both preceded and accompanied the development of Dunmore's experiment with armed blacks were precipitating factors in the shaping of Britain's Southern strategy. On October 15, 1775, one month before Dunmore's Proclamation, Lord North had recommended to the King an "immediate expedition against the Southern Provinces in North America." The claims of crown officials there that loyalist forces could be raised to restore royal government and pacify the South were "the more to be credited," North told the King, "as we all know the perilous situation of three of them from the great number of their negro slaves, and the small proportion of white inhabitants."[83] Although the strategy was several years away from implementation, the North ministry continued to advance the idea of employing slaves as an ingredient of military policy.

On October 26, 1775, William Henry Lyttleton, former royal governor of South Carolina (1755–1760) and of Jamaica (1760–1766) and a consistent supporter of Lord North, introduced into the House of Commons "something like a proposal for encouraging the negroes in that part of America to rise against their masters, and for sending some regiments to support and encourage them, in carrying the design into execution." Lyttleton's comparison of America to a chain, the upper part, or northern colonies, of which was strong, populous, and capable of resistance, the lower part, or southern colonies, of which was weak "on account of the number of negroes in them," reveals a keen awareness of southern vulnerability. If a few regiments were sent to the South, Lyttleton predicted, "the negroes would rise, and embrue their hands in the blood of their masters." In an acrimonious debate that continued until 4:30 A.M., Lyttleton was "most severely reprehended from the other side, and the scheme totally reprobated, as being too black, horrid and wicked, to be heard of, much less adopted by any civilized people." Lyttleton's motion was defeated by a vote of 278 to 108.[84] One month later Dunmore issued his proclamation.

Impressed by reports coming from southern refugees and exiled governors of the material advantages to be gained by the employment of slaves, British officials were reluctant to cast aside the weapon of a black force. Several of the proposals urged the home government to ride the wave of fear created in the Chesapeake by the active hostility of slaves during Dunmore's operations and by the seething discontent of the lower classes, par-

[83] Lord North to the king, October 15, 1775, in Sir John Fortescue, ed., *The Correspondence of King George the Third from 1760 to December, 1783*, 6 vols. (London: Macmillan, 1927–28), 3:266.

[84] William Cobbett and T. C. Hansard, eds., *The Parliamentary History of England from the Earliest Period to the Year 1803*, 36 vols. (London: T. C. Hansard, 1806–20), 18:733; David H. Murdoch, ed., *Rebellion in America. A Contemporary British Viewpoint 1765–1783* (Santa Barbara, Calif.: Clio Books, 1979), 334.

ticularly on Maryland's Eastern Shore.[85] In a daring proposal designed to capitalize on local fears of united action by Maryland's slaves and poor whites, Sir John Dalrymple recommended that levies of indentured servants be raised on the Pennsylvania side of the Delaware Bay and in major cities, such as Alexandria, Fredericksburg, Baltimore, and Annapolis, along with "the bravest and most ingenious of the black Slaves whom He may find all over the Bay of Chesapeake." The effect, Dalrymple confidently predicted, would be "to throw the Estates on the Delaware Bay in waste, because the Masters will carry off the Servants from their Estates upon hearing what is happening in Chesapeake Bay."[86]

Rather more remarkable because it came from a prominent Anglican cleric noted for his sermons on civil obedience and passive resistance, was a similar proposal from the Reverend Jonathan Boucher of Maryland. Government should, Boucher maintained, "keep their Fears perpetually awake, either by apprehensions of having their Slaves armed against them, or their savage Neighbours let loose on their Frontiers." Besides their slaves, Maryland and Virginia had in their indentured servants other "enemies in their bowells." As white servants they were generally better treated than were slaves and stood above slaves in social status. Nonetheless, they harbored latent hostility over social and political inequities, which sometimes erupted into open revolt, making them, Boucher insinuated, a force "not a little to be dreaded."[87]

Like Boucher himself, most of those who wrote to urge government to make use of slaves in some capacity or other had no serious intention of promoting a revolution in the South's social system. A number of them, including Moses Kirkland, a backcountry loyalist militia leader,[88] William Knox, wartime under secretary of state for the American colonies, and Sir James Wright, the last royal governor of Georgia, were themselves planters and slaveholders, who wished merely to use white fears of a servile revolt as a devastating weapon with which to beat the rebels into submission. Some, like Wright, who had lost eleven plantations and 523 slaves under the Georgia confiscation act, had a more prudential reason as well, the indemnification of loyalists. Wright, among others, argued strongly that government owed something to its "much oppressed and injured dutiful

[85] Hoffman, *Spirit of Dissension*, 57, 149, 171, 184, 188–91, 145, 152, 153, 166, 184–87, 197–203, 224–33.

[86] Sir John Dalyrymple, "Project for Strengthening Howe's Operations in the North by a Diversion in the South," n.d., George Germain, first Viscount Sackville, 1776–1785, Papers, 1683–1785, William L. Clements Library, Ann Arbor, Michigan. This was intended as a diversionary tactic to strengthen Howe's operations in the North.

[87] Boucher to [Germain], November 27, 1775, Germain Papers.

[88] Randall M. Miller, "A Backcountry Loyalist Plan to Retake Georgia and the Carolinas, 1778," *South Carolina Historical Magazine* 75 (1974): 207–14.

and loyal subjects." What he had in mind was full compensation for all losses sustained during the war by Crown officials or friends of government, restitution to be made from a loyalist fund to be derived from the confiscation of rebel property. Although Wright's earlier reports were apparently ignored, his indemnification scheme became after 1778 an essential ingredient of Britain's Southern strategy.[89]

So too did the proposal made by Lieutenant Colonel Archibald Campbell of the Seventy-first Regiment. Campbell, a veteran of the French and Indian War, proposed to bolster Britain's sagging military strength by forming a "Regiment of Stout Active Negro's." Like the provincial troops in the French and Indian War, the black regiment could be used "to ease the Soldier from many dutys, both discouraging and prejudicial to the health of them which ought to be Nurs'd and Reserved for More Active and Spirited Services, Battle or Attack."[90] For a start Campbell proposed raising a corps of some 1,400 slaves in the British West Indies. The landing of a black corps in any of the mainland colonies would, he predicted, encourage 90 percent of the slaves to desert their masters, thus depriving the South of its labor force and ruining the southern economy for "it is on the labor of their slaves that they owe their existence." Finally, Campbell concluded, slave labor could be applied to the production of supplies for the army, thereby relieving the military of reliance on the costly and inefficient system of trans-Atlantic supply.[91]

Proposals to arm slaves and the actual attempt to do so in the Chesapeake provoked an outburst of indignation in and out of Parliament. Merchants and traders in London and Bristol, where the British slave trade was centered, resolutely condemned the idea. In a petition to the Crown a group of London merchants expressed "indignation and horror" at the prospect of slaves in arms against "our *American* brethern."[92] "Very long representations" from the cities of London and Bristol were also presented to Parliament in protest of the "improper manner of carrying on the war and burning towns, savage invasions, and insurrections of negroes."[93] In a letter to a friend in Philadelphia one Londoner denounced the North ministry as "worse than barbarians" for its "thoughts of declaring all your negroes free, and to arm them."[94]

[89] "Sir James Wright Looks at the American Revolution," *Georgia Historical Quarterly* 53 (1969): 516.

[90] Campbell to Germain, January 16, 1776, Germain Papers.

[91] Ibid.

[92] "The Humble Address, Memorial and Petition of the Gentlemen, Merchants and Traders of London," October, 1775, in Force, ed., *American Archives*, 4th ser., 3:1011.

[93] Murdoch, *Rebellion in America*, 325.

[94] "Extract of a Letter Received in Philadelphia," August 24, 1775, in Force, ed., *American Archives*, 4th ser., 3:256–57.

The emotional response to the various proposals for the arming of slaves sprang from several concerns. First, the measure was viewed as a radical departure from civilized practice. Historical precedents for using slaves in a military capacity reach back to ancient societies. Normally, however, slaves played a secondary and subordinate role in the military, serving as galley slaves in ancient fleets or as fatigue men to relieve the land forces of onerous duties. Even in ancient societies the arming of slaves was a highly exceptional measure resulting usually from a desperate emergency. In part this was due to the fear that armed slaves would turn their weapons against their masters. It was also due to ideological factors. Beginning in classical antiquity, the rule obtained that military duties were proportional to social status, with the highest classes being assigned the greatest obligations; the slaves generally were excluded from military servce. Although the equivalence of political and military functions changed over the centuries, the ancient practice of exempting slaves persisted.[95]

The use of slave labor in a military capacity was also common among European powers since the seventeenth century, particularly in the Caribbean and Brazil, where shortages of manpower forced colonial nations to recruit slaves for various military functions.[96] The dangerous expedient of arming slaves was, however, generally eschewed[97] until 1795, when the problem of West Indian defense forced the British government to organize black companies.[98] The fact that the government's efforts to arm slaves ran counter to the weight of tradition caused concern in many quarters that the national honor would be impugned. It was their anxiety to "vindicate the national honour" that moved a group of London merchants to plead with the Crown to repudiate the reports circulating of "slaves incited to insurrection."[99] Britain's violation of the time-honored rule against inciting foreign slaves against their masters had, Edmund Burke lamented in Commons, "deeply wounded" the national honor and debased "our character as a people" in the estimation of foreigners. Burke's claim that the arming of slaves had served only "to embitter the minds of all men"[100]

---

[95] Jan Libourel, "Galley Slaves in the Second Punic War," *Classical Philology* 68 (1973): 116–19; Moses L. Finley, *Ancient Slavery and Modern Ideology* (New York: Viking Press, 1980), 99, 109–10; Yvon Garlan, *War in the Ancient World. A Social History* (London: Chatto and Windus, 1975), 78–95.

[96] Roger Norman Buckley, *Slaves in Red Coats. The British West India Regiments, 1795–1815* (New Haven, Conn.: Yale University Press, 1979), 2–5.

[97] David Brion Davis, *The Problem of Slavery in the Age of Revolution. 1770–1823* (Ithaca, N.Y.: Cornell University Press, 1975), 74–75, 75–79.

[98] Lowell Joseph Ragatz, *The Fall of the Planter Class in the British Caribbean, 1763–1833* (New York: Century, 1928), 32–33, 220–21.

[99] "The Humble Address, Memorial and Petition of the Gentlemen, Merchants, and Traders of London," October, 1775, in Force, *American Archives*, 4th ser., 3:1011.

[100] Cobbett and Hansard, *Parliamentary History* 19:699.

resonated through the *Annual Register's* account of Dunmore's activities in the Chesapeake: "This measure of emancipating the negroes," the *Register* regretfully reported on July 8, 1776, has been "received with the greatest horror in all the colonies, and has been severely condemned elsewhere."[101]

Critical to British concern over world reaction was the fear of retaliation. Should "the Ministry act in that way," one Londoner predicted, "the *Americans* would march (the slaves) back, and perhaps arm them all that they could trust."[102] Driven by the same fear, Burke warned the Commons that "when we talk of enfranchisment, do we not perceive that the American master may enfranchise too; and arm servile hands in defense of freedom?"[103] Although American slaveowners proved to be more reluctant than the British to put weapons into the hands of slaves, a few, including the diplomat Silas Deane, recognized that considerable psychological advantages were to be gained by threatening to do so: "*Omnia tendanda* is my motto," Deane wrote to his friend John Jay in Paris, "therefore I hint the playing of their own game on them, by spiriting up the *Caribs* in *St. Vincents*, and the negroes in *Jamaica*, to revolt."[104]

Deane's calculated suggestion is a reminder that events were being played on an international stage, which forced England to take an international view of the matter of arming slaves. Burke's recollection that "other people have had recourse more than once, and not without success," to that expedient, called to mind the Caribbean region, where recurring warfare among European powers frequently provoked slave risings. The series of revolts in Jamaica and the Guianas, comprising the territories of Essequibo, Berbice, and Demerara, in the 1760s and 1770s, breaking out as they did during a time in the history of the empire when slavery itself was under assault, was enough to arouse serious misgivings about the wisdom of arming slaves.[105] The Jamaican slave insurrection scare of 1776, which had apparent ideological connections with the American Revolution, was perhaps a more immediate cause for concern. The conspiracy took place in the sugar-growing Hanover parish in the northwest corner of Jamaica, which had a black-white ratio of twenty-six to one. The removal on July 3, 1776, of the Fiftieth Regiment from Jamaica to

[101] Murdoch, *Rebellion in America*, 313.

[102] "Extract of a Letter Received in Philadelphia," August 24, 1775, in Force, *American Archives*, 4th ser., 3:256–57.

[103] Edmund Burke, *The Speeches of the Right Honourable Edmund Burke, in the House of Commons, and in Westminister-Hall*, 4 vols. (London: Longman, Hurst, Rees, Orme and Brown, 1816), 1:299. The quote is from Burke's March 22, 1775, speech in the House of Commons.

[104] Deane to Jay, Paris, December 3, 1776, Force, *American Archives*, 5th ser., 3:1051.

[105] Eugene D. Genovese, *From Rebellion to Revolution. Afro-American Slave Revolts in the Making of the Modern World* (Baton Rouge: Louisiana State University Press, 1979), 21–22, 33–37.

strengthen General William Howe's army in North America, was to be the signal for the insurrection to begin. The plot was discovered before it could be carried out, but some prominent Jamaicans, including Stephen Fuller, the agent for Jamaica in England, believed that the conspirators had been influenced by revolutionary ideology and by inflammatory statements made by their masters in support of the rebels.[106]

The knowledge that British Caribbean colonies were susceptible to the spreading influence of slave revolts focused public discussion on two additional questions: Could an alliance with slaves succeed? and Might it succeed too well? Like many of his contemporaries Burke believed that slaves were by nature too servile to make good soldiers: "Slaves are often much attached to their masters" he reasoned, so that "a general wild offer of liberty would not always be accepted." Indeed "History furnishes few instances of it." Repeating the commonly held notion that slaves actually preferred bondage to freedom, Burke concluded that "It is sometimes as hard to persuade slaves to be free, as it is to compel freemen to be slaves; and in this auspicious scheme, we should have both these pleasing tasks on our hands at once."

Even if slavery had not dulled their desire for freedom, Burke wondered, might not blacks be skeptical of "an offer of freedom from that very nation which has sold them to their present masters? From that nation, one of whose causes of quarrel with those masters, is their refusal to deal any more in that inhuman traffic?" With a fine touch of irony Burke, a consistent supporter of abolition of the slave trade, pondered aloud whether "an offer of freedom from England, would come rather oddly, shipped to them in an African vessel, which is refused an entry into the ports of Virginia or Carolina, with a cargo of three hundred Angola negroes. It would be curious to see the Guinea captain attempting at the same instant to publish his proclamation of liberty, and to advertise his sale of slaves."[107]

The most important argument against the arming of slaves as a war measure was that it involved a social revolution that went far beyond the aim of disciplining the rebellious colonies. "This measure of emancipating the negroes," the *Annual Register* grimly warned its readers, had momentous implications. It threatened the existing social order. Whereas the conventional practice of relegating slaves to menial tasks had confirmed the validity of the social order, the plan to encourage "African negroes" to appear in arms against white men and to encounter them upon an equal footing in the field, weakened the traditional system of social relations, which turned on social discrimination and a sense of race. Furthermore, the *Reg-*

[106] Richard B. Sheridan, "The Jamaican Slave Insurrection Scare of 1776 and the American Revolution," *Journal of Negro History* 61 (1976): 290–309.
[107] Burke, *Speeches* 1:299. The quotes are from Burke's March 22, 1775, speech in the House of Commons.

ister broadly hinted, the full participation of slaves in the revolutionary crisis, with promises of freedom, endangered existing arrangements of property and wealth and the cluster of privileges and rights associated with it. Throughout the South the slave was regarded by whites as property. A capital asset, the slave was subject to taxation and was attachable for debt. From ancient times the protection of property was regarded as a fundamental obligation of the state. Now, the *Register* objected, by advancing the offer of freedom to slaves, "those who were the best friends of government" were exposed "to the same loss of property, danger, and destruction, with the most incorrigible rebels."[108]

But the gravest risk was to the slave system itself. Prior to the American Revolution the military employment of slaves was usually aimed at preserving the institution of slavery. The various proposals for arming slaves during the revolutionary war generally implied its destruction, an issue few English leaders were prepared to debate in 1776. Since the seventeenth century, Englishmen, like other Europeans, had considered black peoples different.[109] That perception of difference formed the basis for the traditional justification for slavery: a belief in the Negroes' cultural and racial inferiority, often interwoven with arguments for the utility of slave labor. Reinforced by Christian theology, which continued to distinguish between the spiritual equality of God's children and worldly enslavement, slavery enjoyed general acceptance.

Indeed, despite the confusion over the status of slaves under the common law, black servitude existed in England. Beginning with the arrival in 1555 of a group of African slaves brought from the Guinea coast by John Lok, an English trader, the importation of blacks into England continued on a small scale until 1713, when the British won from Spain the Asiento, the coveted contract for the Spanish colonial slave trade, for a period of thirty years. Chiefly as a result of the Asiento, England became the leading slave trader of the world. Gradually, black slaves were introduced into Britain itself, first by captains of slaving vessels, who were allowed to transport several slaves in each cargo for their personal profit, and then by West Indian planters, who imported slaves as body servants. By the eighteenth century a thriving trade had developed in body servants, generally regarded as an "Index of Rank" among wealthy families, and in black boys, viewed by European aristocrats as exotic curiosities since the seventeeth century.[110] By 1772, the year of the Somerset decision, informed estimates

---

[108] Murdoch, *Rebellion in America*, 313.

[109] Winthrop D. Jordan, *White Over Black: American Attitudes Toward the Negro, 1550–1812* (Chapel Hill: University of North Carolina Press, 1968).

[110] Even Lord Mansfield, the celebrated emancipator of British slaves, had a black child named Oido; see F. O. Shyllon, *Black Slaves in Britain* (London: Oxford University Press, 1974), 3–4, 11, 14.

put the number of blacks in England at twenty thousand. Overwhelmingly male, most of them were concentrated in London or other urban areas where they were employed principally as domestics.[111]

White attitudes toward blacks ranged widely from the virulent negrophobia of Edward Long, a Jamaican planter who represented West Indian interests in London, to the vociferous abolitionism of Granville Sharp, who led the fight for the emancipation of black slaves in Britain. General domestic British feeling seems to have been that blacks were, if not sub-human, at least a peculiar and inferior type of human being.[112] The attitude of the British reading public toward blacks was forged first from a literary mythology about blacks that reached back into antiquity. Focusing on the physical features of Africans, their sexual habits, heathenism, and social customs, it ultimately justified their enslavement by reason of their physical and moral inferiority. From the 1760s on, a growing concern among whites about the size of Britain's black population, which was viewed in some quarters both as a threat to racial purity and as the root cause of unemployment among London's white poor, aroused popular resentment against blacks. Fueled by racist propaganda, it reinforced the sense of blacks as inferior beings.[113]

A strong crosscurrent was developing, of course, as economic changes intersected with radical intellectual and cultural developments to begin to transform European attitudes toward slavery. The germ of the intellectual attack was contained in book 15, chapter 1 of Montesquieu's *Spirit of the Laws*, published in 1748. Montesquieu's argument that slavery was forbidden by natural law constituted the most influential intellectual attack on slavery in the eighteenth century. Its most extraordinary impact was on the Scottish philosophers, including James Beattie, Francis Hutcheson, and to a lesser extent, David Hume. Although their specific concern was not with slavery, they uniformly deplored the brutality of slavery. Their notions of morality and justice in turn directly influenced Adam Smith's utilitarian arguments.

The publication in 1776 of Adam Smith's *Wealth of Nations* reinvigorated the debate. Although Smith conceded that slavery was still profitable in tobacco and sugar cultivation, as a general system he condemned it as "the dearest of any" form of labor. His general depiction of slavery as an archaic mode of production, coinciding with the decay of the tobacco tidewater and the decline of sugar profits, helped to demolish the traditional arguments for the utility of slavery. At the same time, the emergence of British Protestantism, especially Quakerism and the Methodist movement

[111] Paul Edwards and James Walvin, *Black Personalities In the Era of the Slave Trade* (Baton Rouge: Louisiana State University Press, 1983), 19, 22.

[112] Ibid., 42–43.

[113] Shyllon, *Black Slaves in Britain*, 152.

within the Church of England, exposed the obvious contradictions between the Christian teaching of human equality and slavery.[114] The development of agitational techniques, such as the public lecture, the circulation of cheap printed abolitionist material, which coincided with the rise of literacy among artisanal classes, and the mobilization of women as fund-raisers and petitioners, finally aroused the national conscience and led to irresistible public pressure to abolish the slave trade (1787–1807) and later to emancipate slaves (1823–1838).[115]

Despite the dawn of the new moral consciousness, the sun had not set on the old slave morality. Although some moralists, like John Wesley, the gifted open-air preacher, vigorously opposed slavery, other religious leaders, like George Whitefield, who owned a plantation and slaves in South Carolina, supported or at least defended it.[116] Nor did the Somerset decision immediately resolve the slavery question in Britain. Although the West Indian interests in Commons failed in their effort to reverse the decision, they successfully circumvented the judgment, the first breach occurring within a year of the decision. Sixteen years later, blacks were still being kidnapped and sold from London streets.[117] Not until 1778, when the Joseph Knight case made slavery illegal in Scotland, was it outlawed throughout the British Isles.[118] For another century it was legal everywhere else in the empire. Until the abolition of the slave trade to foreign countries or to captured or ceded colonies in 1806, Britain continued as the leading slave-trading nation in the world.[119]

That the national interest was still served by slavery was the immediate world of affairs, as the *Register* duly noted: "For however founded distinctions with respect to colour may appear, when examined by the tests of nature, reason, or philosophy, while things continue in their present state, while commerce, luxury, and avarice, render slavery a principal object in the political system of every European power that possesses dominion in America, the ideas of a preeminence must always be cherished, and considered as a necessary policy."[120] The only alternative to white dominion and

[114] Two excellent surveys of the intellectual origins of abolition are Davis, *Problem of Slavery*, chap. 1; and Charles Duncan Rice, *The Rise and Fall of Black Slavery* (London: Macmillan, 1975), chap. 5.

[115] James Walvin, ed., *Slavery and British Society, 1776–1846* (Baton Rouge: Louisiana State University Press, 1982), 51–52, 57–61, 61–63.

[116] Frank Joseph Klingberg, *The Anti-Slavery Movement in England* (New Haven: Yale University Press; London: Humphrey Milford, Oxford University Press, 1926), 43–47. For details concerning Whitefield's plantation, see Gallay, *Formation of a Planter Elite*, 41, 49–51.

[117] Shyllon, *Black Slaves in Britain*, 157, 158, 168, 174.

[118] Klingberg, *Anti-Slavery Movement*, 38–39.

[119] Dale H. Porter, *Abolition of the Slave Trade in England, 1784–1807* (Hamden, Conn.: Archon Books, 1970), 1.

[120] Murdoch, *Rebellion in America*, 313.

social order was further discord and violence. Above all else, perhaps, it was an irrational fear of the uncontrolled behavior of freed slaves that Englishmen, like their American counterparts, most dreaded.

Debates in the House of Commons in 1778 over the North ministry's conduct of the war exposed the deepest anxieties. In Parliament, the Opposition, which frequently used government's handling of American affairs to attract public support, launched a full-scale attack on the fitful efforts to develop a general slave policy. As chief spokesman on this issue, Edmund Burke introduced a motion condemning the military employment of Indians and slaves. During the debate, which was closed to the public, Burke delivered a three and one-half hour speech described by many of the members present as the most eloquent of his career. In it Burke denounced the government for its deliberate employment of Indians and for its efforts to provoke a slave insurrection. With hyperbolic generalization he warned his colleagues in Commons of "the horrible consequences that might ensue from constituting 100,000 fierce barbarian slaves, to be both the judges and executioners of their masters." With the examples in mind of the Stono Rebellion in South Carolina in 1739 and the massive risings in Berbice and Jamaica in the 1760s, he conjured up images of murders, rapes, and "horrid enormities of every kind," which he insisted "had ever been acknowledged to be the principal objects in the contemplation of all negroes who had meditated an insurrection."[121] The same apocalyptic imagery resonates through the *Register's* account of Dunmore's efforts to arm slaves in Virginia and Maryland. The idea of emancipating slaves was generally repudiated "as tending to loosen the bands of society, to destroy domestic security, and encourage the most barbarous of mankind, to the commission of the most horrible crimes, and the most inhuman cruelties."[122]

It is highly doubtful that the North ministry ever intended to effect a general emancipation of slaves. More likely the policy represented an effort to exploit slave militancy and coerce support from their owners. Had Dunmore's efforts to crush the South with an army of blacks been successful, it is difficult to assess what public reaction might have been. Burke believed that had Chesapeake slaves "reduced the province to their obedience, and made themselves masters of the houses, goods, wives, and daughters of their murdered lords," then "Another war must be made with them, and another massacre ensue; adding confusion to confusion, and destruction to destruction." At any rate, clearly on the defensive, North weakly defended Dunmore's Proclamation on the grounds that "it did not call on them to murder their masters . . . but only to take up arms in defense of their sovereign." Hoping to lay the matter to rest, he volunteered that

[121] Cobbett and Hansard, *Parliamentary History* 19:694n, 698.
[122] Murdoch, *Rebellion in America*, 313.

"Lord Dunmore's proclamation should be laid on the table, that, if reprehensible, it might be attended to."[123] Despite North's public disavowal of attempts to incite a slave insurrection, the temptation to employ slaves in some capacity remained, particularly in the South, whose huge black population made slaves a potentially powerful political, psychological, and military weapon.

Aware of the dangers inherent in such a plan, and with the memory of the public controversy still fresh in mind, the government proceeded cautiously. But the British path toward the military employment of slaves was smoothed by the decision of Americans to accept volunteered slaves for military service. Until the late seventeenth century blacks served in colonial militias, but only in a limited capacity and usually in noncombative roles.[124] Fear of mutiny and the widely held belief that mustering slaves among freeholders was inappropriate, eventually led to their exclusion during peacetime in the mature plantation colonies of the upper South.[125] In periods of war the scarcity of manpower forced most colonies to accept slaves and free blacks for military service in exchange for the promise of freedom. Blacks fought in mixed companies in all of the colonial wars. In the lower South, frontier warfare allowed blacks to play a major role, often as combat troops. Black soldiers fought in the Tuscarora War of 1711–1712 and played an active part in the Yamasee War of 1715.[126] As late as 1755 a shortage of white manpower and imperial rivalries along the vulnerable southern frontier forced the Georgia assembly to authorize the recruitment of blacks into the militia.[127]

At the outbreak of the American Revolution several colonies, all of them in the North, accepted blacks in militia units. Blacks were with the patriot forces at Lexington and Concord and at Bunker Hill. Several served with Connecticut units during the Boston campaign.[128] At the time of the Lexington engagement, however, rumors that slaves were mobilizing to massacre the citizens left defenseless when the militia marched off to fight caused such panic among white citizens that the Massachusetts Committee of Safety decided in May to prohibit the enlistment of slaves in any of the colony's armies.[129] Five days after he was appointed commander in chief of

[123] Cobbett and Hansard, *Parliamentary History* 19:698–99, 708.

[124] Philip Foner, *Blacks in the American Revolution* (Westport, Conn.: Greenwood Press, 1976), 41.

[125] Isaac, *Transformation of Virginia*, 105.

[126] Wood, *Black Majority*, 117, 124–30.

[127] Candler, *CRG* 18:38–44, especially p. 43.

[128] Foner, *Blacks in the American Revolution*, 42; David O. White, *Connecticut's Black Soldiers, 1775–1783* (Chester, Conn.: Pequot Press, 1973), 17. The earliest effort to recount the military activities of black soldiers in the revolutionary war is Livermore, *An Historical Account*, 89–156.

[129] Foner, *Blacks in the American Revolution*, 43.

the Continental Army, George Washington, the Virginia slaveholder, issued orders against enlisting blacks, although those already in the army were allowed to remain. In a move that suggests the degree to which white attitudes toward slavery had hardened as a result of British "tampering" and escalating slave resistance, Edward Rutledge, who represented South Carolina at the Continental Congress, moved that all blacks, whether slave or free, be discharged from the Continental Army; although the motion was "strongly supported" by southern delegates, it failed.[130] The actuality of black insurrection in Virginia, however, gave the delegates second thoughts and on November 12, 1775, the Continental Congress formally declared all blacks, slave or free, ineligible for military service.[131] Similar policies were subsequently approved by the other northern states.

But the weight of common sense and military necessity compelled the abandonment of the policy. Despite his own repugnance for using slaves as soldiers, Washington was among the first to recognize that slavery had become a military weakness because of the willingness of slaves to fight for the enemy. Dunmore must be crushed instantly, he earnestly urged his countrymen, "otherwise, like a snowball, in rolling, his army will get size."[132] Convinced that the outcome of the war hinged "on which side can arm the Negroes the faster,"[133] Washington publicly advocated the recruitment of blacks into the Continental Army, otherwise "they may seek employ in the ministerial army."[134] His great influence in support of the military employment of blacks persuaded the cautious Continental Congress to agree to allow the enrollment of free blacks, although the exclusion of slaves from American armies continued.

Although Dunmore had not created slave rebellion but merely exploited it, the crisis created by his reception and use of black soldiers worked by no means entirely to the disadvantage of America. By blaming Dunmore for inciting slaves to rebellion, colonists found a strong stick with which to beat their opponents. The "dread of instigated Insurrections" combined

[130] Richard Smith, "Diary of Richard Smith," *American Historical Review* 1 (1896): 292.

[131] Foner, *Blacks in the American Revolution*, 46.

[132] Washington to Reed, December 15, 1775, in William Bradford Reed, ed., *Life and Correspondence of Joseph Reed, Military Secretary of Washington, at Cambridge. . . .* 2 vols. (Philadelphia: Lindsay and Blakiston, 1847), 1:135.

[133] Quoted in Foner, *Blacks in the American Revolution*, 46.

[134] To the president of the Congress, December 31, 1775, in John C. Fitzpatrick, ed., *The Writings of George Washington from the Original Manuscript Sources, 1745–1799*, 39 vols. (Washington, D.C.: USGPO, 1931–40), 4:195. For a discussion of two all-black units in the Continental Army, see Sidney Kaplan, *The Black Presence in the Era of the American Revolution, 1700–1800* (Washington, D.C.: New York Graphic Society and Smithsonian Institution Press, 1973), 55–59. Kaplan also identifies a number of individuals and describes some of their wartime experiences through contemporary accounts.

with the hardening of attitudes after Lexington and Concord were, even to a moderate like Henry Laurens, "causes sufficient to drive an oppressed People to the use of Arms."[135] Paradoxically, white Americans found as well a rationalization for their own incorporation of slaves, rendered necessary by a rapidly developing manpower shortage. When in 1777 Congress began to impose troop quotas on the states, a number of New England towns and state governments began quietly enrolling blacks, although their enlistment was not yet legally sanctioned. Following the military disasters at Forts Washington and Lee and Washington's shameful retreat across New Jersey, the Continental Army dissolved like a morning fog, and Congress was forced to approve the raising of eighty-eight battalions, which were assigned to the several states on the basis of population.[136] Rhode Island, with a population of little better than fifty-one thousand whites and the British in possession of most of the state, including the capital city of Newport, had difficulty in filling its quota of two battalions. Prompted by the seeming hopelessness of the situation, the legislature approved slave enlistments. Promised freedom in return for service during the duration of the war, some two hundred and fifty slaves joined Rhode Island's black battalion. Similar problems in completing continental quotas led Connecticut to form an all-black company, the Second Company of the Fourth Regiment.[137] By the end of 1777 free blacks and slaves were serving in mixed regiments in a number of states, most of them in the North.

Eager to escape blame for having first resorted to the use of slaves, Lord North later claimed that it was the American decision to enlist blacks that forced Britain to follow suit.[138] In fact the precipitating factor was the decision made in 1778 to shift the seat of the war to the South. During the revolutionary war, Britain pursued a variety of strategies for ending the rebellion: by subduing New England; by securing the Middle Colonies; by pacifying the South. Although the shifting strategies were often marked by confusion, by 1778 operations in the southern colonies clearly occupied the principal place in British planning. Britain's Southern strategy finally emerged with three crucial components: to enlist the help of loyalists to defeat the rebels and to hold territory once it was liberated by British regular forces; to weaken rebel resistance by depriving the South of its labor

---

[135] To John Laurens, May 15, 1775, *Papers of Henry Laurens* 10:118. See also Kaplan, "Domestic Insurrections," 243–255, which also argues that the fear generated by British plans to use slaves was a factor in pushing the colonies to revolution and in the writing of the Declaration of Independence.

[136] Foner, *Blacks in the American Revolution*, 46, 55.

[137] White, *Connecticut's Black Soldiers*, 32.

[138] "House of Commons," November 20, 1775, in Force, *American Archives*, 4th ser., 6:187.

force and by cutting off southern resources, such as tobacco, rice and indigo, the exportation of which helped attract foreign capital and thus sustained the rebellion; to exploit pro-British Indian tribes along the southern frontiers and the tens of thousands of slaves concentrated in the tidewater and the low country.[139] The groundswell of slave resistance that both preceded and accompanied the gradual crystallization of that strategy, played an instrumental role in Britain's decision to gamble on the dangerous expedient of recruiting slaves for military service as well as in the American decision for independence.

[139] Ira D. Gruber, "Britain's Southern Strategy," in W. Robert Higgins, ed., *The Revolutionary War in the South: Power, Conflict and Leadership* (Durham, N.C.: Duke University Press, 1979), 205–38; John Shy, "British Strategy for Pacifying the Southern Colonies, 1778–1781," in Crow and Tise, eds., *Southern Experience in the American Revolution*, 155–73.

THREE

THE STRUGGLE FOR FREEDOM:

BRITISH INVASION AND OCCUPATION

OF GEORGIA

T HIS PLACE," the King's Counsel, Chief Justice Anthony Stokes wrote of Georgia, "is the key to the southern provinces, and the Gibraltar of the Gulf passage; for to the south of this province there is not a port on the continent that will receive a sloop of war."[1] The deep-draft navigation of Savannah harbor, which led to its development as Georgia's principal port or entrepôt, combined with heavy loyalist concentration in that city and throughout the state,[2] were the principal factors in the decision made in 1778 by Lord George Germain, the American secretary, to renew offensive operations in the South. Exaggerated reports of the strength of loyalist support in the South had led Germain to conclude that renewed military operations there would lead to the restoration of royal government. Rich in supplies of ship timbers, staves, Indian corn, cattle, and hogs, Georgia was selected as the loyalist base for the reconquest of the southern colonies. Despite its rapid commercial development, at the outbreak of the American Revolution no one of the thirteen colonies was, in the words of a committee of the Georgia assembly, "so weak within and so exposed without." The presence of "vast numbers of Negroes . . . perhaps themselves sufficient to subdue us," made the prospect of an internal insurrection likely, while her defenceless borders made Georgia constantly vulnerable to external conquest.[3]

Within Georgia's borders were approximately fifteen thousand slaves, most of whom were heavily concentrated in the low country and in the hands of a relatively small planter elite. To the west were the Creeks, Cherokees, Choctaws and other small Indian tribes. Regularly supplied with arms by the British through East and West Florida, they continually harrassed the Georgia frontier. To the east stretched the flat coastal lands.

[1] Quoted in Rankin, *North Carolina Continentals*, 191.

[2] Wallace Brown, *The King's Friends: The Composition and Motives of the American Loyalist Claimants* (Providence, R.I.: Brown University Press, 1965), 213–14, 220–21.

[3] Georgia House of Assembly, Report of the Deputies of Georgia Respecting the Situation of that State, Georgia State Papers, 1778, Papers of the Continental Congress, Peter Force Historical Manuscripts, 1501–1866. Force Papers, ser. 7C, item 73, Library of Congress.

Throughout the war British cruisers plied the waters around the sea islands plundering them of livestock and slaves.[4] To the south lay the British province of East Florida, since the days of Spanish possession a haven for runaway slaves who escaped through the porous coastal passages or along the overland trails. Still a labor-scarce frontier region whose precarious circumstances probably produced relative freedom of movement for slaves, East Florida remained an attractive refuge for runaways after the British took possession in 1763. Beginning in 1776 with the collapse of the royal government and the passage of Georgia's confiscation acts, it became a haven for substantial numbers of white loyalists, many of whom migrated with their slaves. The influx of immigrants severely tested the struggling colony's resources and caused it very quickly to become a launching point for tory raiding parties and bands of "the Floridian banditti."[5] The introduction of irregular warfare and raiding added a new dimension to the war in the South, the seizure of slaves as booty. Slave raids and kidnappings inevitably brought reprisals, thus giving to the war in the southern theater a more extreme and violent form than elsewhere.

Convinced that bloody, irregular warfare along the frontier would induce "our deluded neighbors . . . to return to their allegiance,"[6] the royal governor of East Florida, Patrick Tonyn, commissioned Thomas Brown, a Georgia backcountry tory partisan, to raise a corps of rangers composed of refugees from Georgia and South Carolina. Formed initially to defend the uncultivated Georgia-East Florida frontier, the Carolina Rangers also conducted cattle raids into Georgia to feed East Florida's swollen wartime population.[7] Despite the failure of an early experiment in large-scale cattle ranching, livestock raising remained important in Georgia. Although large tracts or enclosures called cowpens protected livestock from thieves or wild animals at night, vast herds of cattle, managed by cowpen keepers, still roamed the forests in search of pasturage.[8] In the opening year of conflict, a series of raids from East Florida stripped Georgia of the rich herds of cattle and horses that were a major source of wealth and provender and caused severe economic distress to white planters along the troubled Georgia-East Florida frontier.

[4] Ibid.

[5] Patrick Tonyn to George Germain, October 10, 1776, October 30, 1776, CO5/557/3, 23.

[6] Quoted in Robert M. Calhoon, "The Floridas, the Western Frontier, and Vermont: Thoughts on the Hinterland Loyalists," in Samuel Proctor, ed., *Eighteenth-Century Florida Life on the Frontier* (Gainesville Fla.: University of Florida Press, 1976), 7–8.

[7] Gary D. Olson, "Thomas Brown, Loyalist Partisan, and the Revolutionary War in Georgia, 1777–1782," *Georgia Historical Quarterly* 54 (1970): 1–19.

[8] John Gerard William De Braham, *Report of the General Survey in the Southern District of North America*, Louis De Vorsey, Jr., ed. (Columbia: University of South Carolina Press, 1971), 95.

Beginning in the summer of 1776 a series of retaliatory raids were launched from Georgia. Georgia militia, commanded by Colonel Lachlan McIntosh, despoiled the East Florida frontier, appropriating all the cattle and slaves they could find and destroying "every plantation between the rivers St. Johns and St. Mary."[9] Terrorized planters on the exposed plantations took "the few Negroes and Effects they were able to Save" and fled to the security of St. Augustine. After "breaking up all the settlements on the other side of St. Johns," the raiders returned to Georgia.[10] But rebel bands led by McIntosh or Button Gwinnet continued to penetrate the vulnerable East Florida defenses to ravage frontier farms of livestock and slaves.[11]

In the meantime, bands of "the Floridian banditti," some of them commissioned by Governor Tonyn, waged continuous predatory war against Georgia. Operating in small groups of five or six, their annoying raids were aimed at "stealing our Horses and Negroes and doing us all the Mischief they can as thieves," as the Savannah merchant, Joseph Clay, ruefully complained.[12] In a single such incursion in the fall of 1778 by British regulars augmented by Brown's Rangers, two thousand head of cattle and two hundred slaves were seized from frontier farms.[13] By the end of the year, the incursionary attacks by both sides had "hurt us prodigiously," as John Houston, who had himself led an unsuccessful foray against East Florida, put it.[14] Although some slaves gained their freedom by joining interracial gangs, for many blacks, as for many whites, the predatory war was often a brutalizing and demoralizing experience. Capture by a partisan band meant the scattering of family and friends, black and white; it meant disruption and difficult readjustment; in countless cases it meant death.

The fate of Jermyn and Charles Wright's slaves was probably typical of many. Brothers of Georgia's last royal governor, the Wrights owned three plantations on the St. Mary's River, two on the Georgia side, one on the East Florida side. Harrassed by the banditti and by partisan gangs, they built a small fort to protect the one hundred slaves who worked their land. But the fort proved inadequate and in July 1776, rebel raiders plundered them and carried off nine to ten slaves into Georgia. Warned of another impending raid, the Wrights gathered their remaining slaves together and

[9] William Drayton, 1732–1790, Force Papers, ser. 8D, item 37.

[10] James Penman to Peter Taylor [?], September 21, 1776, Maryland State Papers, Rainbow Series, Brown Book 9:11, Library of Congress, microfilm.

[11] Olson, "Thomas Brown," 1–19.

[12] Joseph Clay to [?], September 7, 1778, and Clay to Laurens, September 9, 1778, "Letters of Joseph Clay, Merchant of Savannah, 1776–1793," GHS, Coll. (Savannah, 1913), 8:106, 109.

[13] Tonyn to Col. John Stuart, December 20, 1778, CO5/559/211.

[14] John Houston to Henry Laurens, October 1, 1778, Simms Collection of the Laurens Papers, Caroliniana Library, University of South Carolina, Columbia.

fled, moving from place to place, finally taking refuge in East Florida somewhere along the St. Johns River. There they built huts for themselves and their slaves and lived "in great distress" until February 1777, when Charles and twenty-four of the slaves died "as a result of hardships." In 1782 thirty-five of the surviving slaves died of starvation, nineteen more of "distress and sufferings."[15]

Its borders ravaged by fratricidal war, Georgia was plunged into chaos by the British invasion of 1778. The expedition began in November when Lieutenant Colonel Archibald Campbell of the Seventy-first Scottish Regiment and thirty-five hundred troops were detached by military transports to Georgia, while General Augustine Prevost was ordered to march two thousand troops from St. Augustine to the St. Mary's River to cooperate with Campbell in the conquest of Georgia. After experiencing unusually bad weather, the expedition finally landed on December 23, 1778. Intelligence reports had suggested a landing at John Giradeau's plantation two miles from Savannah as the most practical place in the area between the Savannah and Tybee rivers, a continuous tract of deep marsh interspersed by creeks of the St. Augustine and Tybee rivers and by other cuts of water. Although they encountered resistance from a rebel army led by Major General Robert Howe, "a Confidential Slave" guided the British down a path through a swamp, enabling them to surprise and rout the rebel force. On January 1 the British took possession of Savannah, a city of four hundred houses built along broad streets that intersected to divide the city into six equal parts. The following day a British force occupied Ebenezer. Within ten days the Georgia frontiers were under British control, except for Sunbury, which was taken shortly afterward by Prevost,[16] making good Campbell's claim that "I have ripped one star and one stripe from the Rebel Flag of America."[17]

After taking Sunbury, Prevost crossed the river at Purrysburg and began moving against Charleston to draw back from Georgia an American army led by the newly appointed commander of the Southern Department, Benjamin Lincoln. On May 10 Prevost reached the Ashley River and appeared before the lines of Charleston the following day. After examining the lines, however, he decided that despite their unfinished state, they could not be forced without a heavy loss of manpower. Although he had demanded the surrender of the city, Prevost decided to withdraw his troops across the

[15] "The Case and Sufferings of Jermyn and Charles Wright as Stated by Their Brother, Sir James Wright, April 30, 1778," Candler, *CRG* 39:18–19, 24–25, 218.
[16] Archibald Campbell to Henry Clinton, January 16, 1778, American Revolution MSS., misc. 0215–2254, Library of Congress. For details of the invasion, see Kenneth Coleman, *The American Revolution in Georgia, 1763–1789* (Athens: University of Georgia Press, 1958), 116–21.
[17] Quoted in Rankin, *North Carolina Continentals*, 191.

Ashley River. After foraging for several days in the area, he moved toward the seacoast, returning to Savannah by way of a chain of inland water-courses leading to the Savannah River. From the mainland he advanced to James Island and then to Johns Island, departing there for Savannah on June 16, 1779.

The capture of Georgia confronted British army officers with a host of military, administrative, and political problems. Stretched thinly over large areas, the army depended heavily on the loyalty of powerful white families and on the neutrality of others. From the beginning, however, military relations with white southerners were bedeviled by a general fear and suspicion of the potentially revolutionary effects of the army's presence on southern society. Although whites were clearly uneasy about the dangers posed by the fighting, it was the internal threat of the resistance and rebellion of their slaves that was paramount. The scale of their response indicates the degree of their concern.

The extreme political instability created by the British invasion created panic among white Georgians. The first appearance of the British army precipitated a mass exodus of whites from Georgia and from South Carolina during the brief Prevost-led incursion against Charleston. Abandoning their plantations, white families, many of them with their slaves, took refuge in the swamps, or fled to the safety of St. Augustine, or to Virginia, or to more distant areas removed from danger, such as West Florida or the West Indies. Many of the refugees were women whose fathers, husbands, and sons had rushed away to join the ranks of the state militia or had simply fled in fear of their lives. As he traveled the hard, dry road to Purrysburg on the disordered Georgia-Carolina border, the whig Major General William Moultrie encountered "the poor women and children, and negroes of Georgia, many thousands of whom I saw . . . traveling to they knew not where."[18] Accompanied by their owners or overseers, many of the slaves Moultrie saw were being moved to areas remote from the fighting to prevent them from falling into British hands, either by desertion or capture.

The case of Joseph Habersham, a wealthy rice planter, whig militia officer, and legislator, is typical of the reaction of southern slaveowners generally. When the British captured Savannah, Habersham loaded one hundred and fifty of his slaves on wagons and conducted them to Virginia, stopping along the way in temporary camps.[19] The Habersham slaves were eventually settled in the Richmond area. To continue to make profits from their labor, Habersham resorted to the well-established Georgia practice of

[18] William Moultrie, *Memoirs of the American Revolution*, 2 vols. (New York: David Longworth, 1802), 1:259.

[19] N. D. Mereness, ed., *Travels in the American Colonies* (New York: Macmillan, 1916), 598, 604.

leasing them out, some on short-term contracts, others for longer periods. The decline in the size of Virginia's own slave population after 1779 combined with wartime inflation drove the cost of hiring up from twenty-six shillings per month in July 1780, to thirty-five shillings per month by November 1782.[20] Habersham and planters like him set a pattern that was to be replicated throughout the South during the revolutionary war and later in the Civil War.

The British invasion of Georgia also alarmed white leaders in neighboring South Carolina. Keenly aware of the state's vulnerability and, in particular, of the revolutionary potential of their slaves, Isaac Huger, South Carolina's emissary to the Continental Congress, made a daring proposal that called on Congress to raise and emancipate three thousand slaves in Georgia and South Carolina. At the urging of Henry Laurens on March 18, 1779, Congress appointed a committee of five, including Chairman Thomas Burke of North Carolina, Henry Laurens of South Carolina, Thomas Nelson of Virginia, John Armstrong of Pennsylvania, and Eliphalet Dyer of Connecticut, to study "ways and means" for the defense of the southern states. The committee's report, apparently drafted by Burke, recommended that South Carolina raise two battalions of black troops and reward their service with freedom at the end of the war. On March 29 Congress voted to endorse the principal recommendations, including the raising of black troops in South Carolina at Continental expense. Despite the impending danger of a British invasion, the recommendation was rejected by state officials on the grounds that military service and emancipation would, as William Whipple, delegate from New Hampshire, put it, "lay a foundation for the Abolition of Slavery in America."[21]

If the coming of the British excited fear and anxiety in white southerners, it raised hope and expectation among enslaved southerners. Between November, when the British expedition against Georgia was launched, and January, when the conquest was complete, an estimated five thousand slaves, roughly one-third of Georgia's prewar slave population, escaped their bondage.[22] No previous occurrence in the history of North American

[20] Joseph Habersham Papers, 1769–1802, Account Book, file no. 339, Georgia Historical Society, Savannah (hereafter cited as GHS).

[21] John Henry to Thomas Johnson, January 30, 1779; William Whipple to Joseph Whipple, February 2, 1779; Henry Laurens to William Read, February 9, 1779; Thomas Burke's Committee Report, March 25, 1779; Henry Lauren's Draft Committee Report, March 25, 1779; William Whipple to Josiah Bartlett, March 28, 1779; North Carolina Delegates to South Carolina Delegates, April 2, 1779; John Armstrong, Sr. to Horatio Gates, April 3, 1779; William Whipple to Josiah Bartlett, April 27, 1779; in Paul H. Smith, Gerard W. Gawalt, and Ronald M. Gephart, eds., *Letters of Delegates to Congress, 1774–1789*, 15 vols. to date (Washington D.C.: Library of Congress, 1985–), 11:538; 12:9, 39, 200, 242–44, 280–81, 398.

[22] The estimate was made by Henry Laurens, perhaps for his private use, perhaps as part of

slavery compared with the slave exodus that began in Georgia either in scale or consequences. Because of the scale and nature of the resistance, slave flight during the war in the South might be characterized as a type of slave revolt. Ironically, the high incidence of escapes and the actions of the British army, which was perceived by slave masters as the instigator of slave resistance, lessened the possibility of organized rebellion and prevented the revolt from becoming a revolution.[23]

Despite the efforts of slaveowners to contain the exodus of their slaves, in their haste to escape, many white families left their slaves on abandoned plantations. Without supervision, restrictions, or control, thousands of slaves struck out on their own. Most fled on foot, following perhaps the same crisscross paths worn over the years by slave visits from one plantation to another. Others escaped in stolen canoes, steering a course through the small creeks and streams that in ordinary times were used to take produce to market.[24] Advertisements in surviving issues of the *Royal Georgia Gazette* suggest that many of the fugitives fled to the woods and deep river swamps, which from the early days of slavery had been a sanctuary for maroon bands. Some fled to plantations or swamp farms away from the fighting and were concealed by family or friends.[25] Although no offer of freedom had been extended, many slaves left the fields and farms to follow the British army.

Because of the special brutality of the war in the South, flight demanded genuine courage and a depth of commitment to freedom that white owners were loath to admit in their slaves. Once the initial shock of invasion had passed, whig forces began to try to recover as much of the state as possible. Georgia and South Carolina militia units, some of which had been actively engaged in defense of the frontier against Indian attack since 1775, were called up to contest British efforts to secure conquered areas with regular troops augmented by loyalist militia companies organized by Lieutenant Colonel Campbell.[26] Ordered to crush political dissent and control social disruptions, the whig militia launched a campaign of terror, characterized

---

an effort to persuade the Continental Congress to prepare for the defense of South Carolina; see Smith, Gawalt, and Gephart, eds., *Letters of the Delegates to Congress* 12:494–95.

[23] Paul E. Lovejoy's excellent analysis of resistance to slavery in the Sokoto Caliphate has contributed significantly to my understanding of slave resistance in the context of the American revolutionary war in the South. Despite the African setting, Lovejoy's analysis is clearly applicable to the situation during the American Revolution. See Lovejoy, "Fugitive Slaves," 71–95.

[24] *Royal Georgia Gazette*, February 11, 1779; August 29, 1779; August 3, 1780.

[25] Ibid., August 3, 1780; September 28, 1780; January 4, 1781.

[26] Clyde R. Ferguson, "Functions of the Partisan-Militia in the South During the American Revolution: An Interpretation," in Higgins, ed., *Revolutionary War in the South*, 239–58; Clyde R. Ferguson, "Carolina and Georgia Patriot and Loyalist Militia in Action, 1778–1783," in Crow and Tise, eds., *Southern Experience*, 174–99.

by wholesale destruction of livestock, provisions, and carriages,[27] which left the settlements from Ebenezer to Augusta "in a ruinous, neglected State; two-thirds of them deserted, some of their Owners following the King's troops others with the Rebels, and both revengefully destroying the property of each other."[28]

Fugitive slaves were profoundly vulnerable to the arbitrary violence of the white belligerents. The experience of four runaways who tried to reach British lines during the invasion suggests the formidable obstacles they faced. Armed and mounted on stolen horses, the four ran into one of the whig patrols that roamed the swamps searching for runaways. With the patrol in close pursuit and firing blindly at every noise, the runaways plunged their horses into the Savannah River, swam to the opposite bank, and surrendered themselves to the startled British picquets who made up the advance guard for the army then preparing to launch an attack against Lytell's Point near Augusta.

In the bitter battle for the up-country, slaves were used by both sides as pawns, to reward friends and punish political enemies. Informed by his scouts that Continental troops commanded by General Lincoln had captured "a large body" of loyalist-owned slaves from the once prosperous farms that lined the road from Abercorn to Ebenezer and had just ferried them across the river into Purrysburg, Colonel Campbell contrived a scheme to recover them for their owners. Campbell sent several black deserters to the riverbank with instructions to "call out to the Rebels for God's Sake to send over the Boats and save his Master's Slaves from falling into the hands of the King's Troops." While the slaves cried out "in the most pitiful manner," a company of the Seventy-first Regiment lay concealed in the woods. When the whig ferry boats returned to the Georgia bank, they were seized by British regulars, who then recrossed the river and recovered eighty-three of the slaves while General Lincoln paraded one thousand Continental troops 800 yards away. When, on the other hand, ninety slaves belonging to George Galphin, the Continental Indian commissioner, deserted his plantation near Augusta and fled to British lines, Colonel Campbell ordered them held as security against Galphin's supplying the British with information about American troop movements. Sent to General Prevost "to be preserved for Mr. Golphin, [sic] in case he continued to act the same friendly part with us, during the rest of the Campaign,"[29] the slaves were put to work on a plantation on the Ogeechee River owned by General Prevost and his brother.[30]

[27] Moultrie, *Memoirs* 1:368, 371.

[28] Quoted in Ferguson, "Functions of the Partisan-Militia," 184.

[29] Colin Campbell, ed., *Journal of an Expedition against the Rebels of Georgia in North Amer-*

The slave exodus was a result of the British conquest of Georgia, but it was not something the army had sought or encouraged. Although Parliament had briefly debated the possibility of arming slaves and Dunmore had conducted an abortive experiment with an armed black corps, the issue of using slaves as a matter of tactics remained officially unresolved, leaving commanders in the field and crown officials free to use their own discretion in deciding the question. The flood tide of runaways in Georgia transformed what had been a rather casual debate over political and diplomatic strategy into a historic decision about the future of slavery: whether to embrace the idea of an alliance with southern blacks, which implied the possibility of a political and social revolution, or to seek the thorough conciliation of white southerners, which of necessity implied the rejection of the strategy of racial manipulation.

Suddenly faced with a situation they had favored in theory, but assumed would never happen, Campbell and Prevost scrambled to catch up with events, groping for an acceptable formula to protect British military and political interests. Both officers saw the institution of slavery as the immediate panacea for some of the army's most pressing military and political problems. Neither officer was ready to promote the full military incorporation of slaves, an idea far beyond them and the nation they served. Neither were they prepared to reconcile local slaveholders at the cost of abandoning the option of using blacks in some limited military capacity. Unable to manage the issue under controlled conditions, they drifted toward a policy or policies that were not exactly opposite but grating roles— Campbell awkwardly seeking to achieve peaceful political pacification, Prevost unequivocally supporting a strategy of violent pacification.

From the British army's perspective, the complete disorganization of society and the virtual collapse of the economic system was hardly desirable. If allowed to degenerate further, it would alienate neutral and loyalist support; it would disrupt the southern labor system, which the British command increasingly saw as the solution to the army's urgent manpower problem and the equally urgent problem of supplying itself with food and provender; and it would raise the risk of inspiring slave rebellions, which went far beyond anything the architects of British strategy had in mind. Realizing that slaves represented the whigs' principal resource for carrying on the rebellion, before his departure for other duty Colonel Campbell tried to manage the slave question to the political advantage of the Crown. Shortly after the conquest of Savannah he appointed an interim government headed by Lieutenant Colonel James Mark Prevost, the brother of

ica. *Under the Command of Archibald Campbell, Esquire* (Darien, Ga.: Ashantilly Press, 1981), 33–34, 53, 56, 63–64. The incidents described occurred in January and February 1779.
[30] On Mr. Prevost's Conduct, 1779, Germain Papers.

General Prevost. At the same time he established a three-man Board of Police composed of prominent local planters, Lewis Johnston, James Mossman, and William Telfair, and ordered them to take over the care and management of the plantations of all absentee owners, whether loyal to the Crown or in rebellion. The main thrust of the Board of Police and of its successor, the office of commissioner of claims, was to prevent the collapse of the labor system in the wake of massive slave desertions; to reassure loyal slaveholders that the army's reception of slaves did not constitute a general attack on property rights; to allow white citizens to participate in the fighting while blacks continued as slaves to manage the plantation system; to, in short, reestablish the rural agricultural order and a more stable social situation. In practice this meant primarily the regulation and control of the enslaved population as a necessary labor force.[31]

The commissioners immediately conducted a survey of deserted plantations in the area between the Ogeechee River to the south side of the Altamaha and to the east from the mouths of the same rivers to the west on a line with Briar Creek, some fifty miles from Savannah. They appointed overseers to a number of plantations of disaffected persons, including those belonging to revolutionary leaders such as Thomas Savage, Benjamin and Samuel Stiles, John Habersham, and Joseph Clay, who was paymaster to the American forces, and instructed them to put the slaves to work planting crops and caring for the livestock.[32] The estates of prominent absentee loyalists, including that of Under Secretary of State William Knox, were also brought under the supervision of the commissioners of claims. At the same time the commissioners began to lease some of the sequestered estates to Georgia loyalists and to refugees from other states, on condition that they use the land and slaves to produce barrel staves and naval stores.[33]

While Campbell was pledging the army to maintain the traditional patterns of social and economic organization, his superior officer, General Augustine Prevost, was indulging his troops and Indian allies in an orgy of plunder in South Carolina, and his brother, acting Lieutenant Governor James Mark Prevost, was shaping a program of violent pacification in Georgia, producing one of the most striking anomalies of Britain's war effort in the South. Until modern times all armies had a predacious char-

[31] To Governor James Wright from Lewis Johnston, James Mossman, William Telfair, in Wright, no. 20, May 20, 1780, CO5/665/527–33. The Board of Police was also responsible for settling all private property disputes, handling breaches of the peace, granting licenses for taverns, etc. Campbell was among the first to propose the use of slaves. The details of his plan are outlined in Campbell to Germain, January 16, 1776, Germain Papers.

[32] Lilla Mills Hawes, ed., "Minute Book, Savannah Board of Police, 1779," *Georgia Historical Quarterly* 45 (1961): 245–57.

[33] Extract of a letter from Lt. Col. Thomas Brown to Governor Tonyn, May 5, 1779; extract of a letter from John Hume to Tonyn, February 13, 1779, CO5/559.

acter, which derived in part from inefficient supply systems and inadequate administrative structures. As the size of armies increased, as campaigns began to last longer, as the fields of military operations became extended, armies were forced either to develop the services necessary for their survival or to impose a system of compulsory contributions on local populations. Although the British army had developed a commissary system by the time of the American Revolution, in the South the army depended on predation for its food. It also relied on plunder to reward its poorly paid personnel.

Since ancient times custom had dictated that a conquering army enjoyed absolute and unconditional rights of property over the vanquished, including the right either to destroy or to preserve it for its own profit.[34] By the eighteenth century, however, most nations recognized the political, military, and economic implications of unrestrained plunder and attempted to regulate or limit it. Nonetheless, field commanders still enjoyed wide discretionary power over the possessions of the conquered. Private looting was severely punished during the Revolution, but systematic plundering operations, either to seize or to destroy war material or to procure provisions for the army, were regularly ordered by commanders in the field. As was customary among all European armies, the collective booty was then deposited in a common pool to be shared among the officers and men who had participated in the expedition. By custom and by law, slaves were regarded as property, subject, therefore, to the practices governing spoils.

By all accounts, British and American, during the retreat from Charleston to Savannah, Prevost's army indulged in unbridled plunder. As they swept through the rich coastal settlements of South Carolina, Prevost's troops and Indian allies burned houses and destroyed crops as they foraged and plundered their way south. Guided through the maze of waterways by a slave named Sampson, who had piloted the British fleet into Georgia and led many of her coastal cruisers on raids,[35] small galleys and barges or long boats, some of them manned by interracial crews, made regular forays up the Ashepoo, the Coosawhatchie, and others of the numerous creeks and inlets that cut the Carolina coast to form the sea islands. Small plundering parties composed of Indians and "painted white men" scoured the islands and the riverside plantations for livestock, crops, clothing, even bedding and blankets.[36] Included in the booty were an estimated three thousand

[34] Garlan, *War in the Ancient World*, 68–70.

[35] Sampson was taken by the Americans on the "Experiment." In reporting his capture, John Rutledge ordered Benjamin Lincoln to "have him secured that he may receive the punishment due his crimes," John Rutledge to Benjamin Lincoln, September 26, 1779, Benjamin Lincoln Papers, October–December 1778, September–October 1779, Library of Congress, microfilm.

[36] D. Horry to Benjamin Lincoln, June 29, 1779, James Moore to Benjamin Lincoln, August 18, 1779, Benjamin Lincoln Papers.

slaves,[37] who either fled to or were impressed by raiding parties such as the one led by Major William Gardiner, British commander at Port Royal. By making "frequent landings at different places," Gardiner told his superior officer, he had collected "some stock and Provisions and about three hundred Negroes."[38]

Whether they had volunteered for military service or were forcibly abducted, most slaves ended up, at least temporarily, as military laborers, clearing the roads of trees felled to impede British progress, or carrying the army's packs and baggage and the rice barrels filled with family possessions, jewelry, even household furniture plundered from the inhabitants.[39] By July, however, Prevost's expedition, harrassed by rebel militia, burdened by plunder and slaves, and short of water transport, was forced to surrender hundreds of the runaways. Whig intelligence reported four hundred left behind on Pine Island. The day after the British fleet evacuated Port Royal whig militia captured and restored to their owners some two hundred abandoned slaves.[40] According to contemporary histories, many of the slaves, frightened by the prospect of punishment at the hands of their former owners, tied themselves to the sides of the military transports rather than be left behind. Soldiers wielding bayonets cut them away, leaving them to drown, to perish in the woods, or face retaliation by whites angered at the excesses of the expedition.[41]

Prevost's expedition crippled British efforts to restore the South to "the peace of the king." Few families along the army's route escaped severe economic loss, much of it in slaves. No accurate figures are available, but some sense of the general slave depopulation can be gained from reports of individual claimants. Benjamin Guerard, a future governor of South Carolina, reported forty-seven slaves from his plantation near Port Royal lost to "a privateering party of the enemy."[42] All of Thomas Pinckney's slaves, except pregnant women and nursing mothers, fled or were taken by British regulars from his Ashepoo plantation.[43] George Rivers of James Island reported missing sixty-one "Mostly Young and Stout Fellows and Wenches" worth, Rivers claimed £17,000.[44] All of Mary Cowper's slaves departed or

[37] William G. Simms, *The History of South Carolina from Its First European Discovery* (Charleston: S. Babcock, 1840), 154.

[38] Campbell, *Journal of an Expedition*, 67.

[39] Capt. James Hall to Benjamin Lincoln, June 25, 1779, Benjamin Lincoln Papers.

[40] William Moultrie to Benjamin Lincoln, July 7, 1779, J. Barnwell to Benjamin Lincoln, September 14, 1779, Benjamin Lincoln Papers.

[41] David Ramsay, *History of the Revolution of South Carolina*, 2 vols. (Newberry, S.C.: W. J. Duffie, 1858), 2:178.

[42] *Virginia Gazette* (Dixon and Nicholson), May 8, 1779.

[43] Thomas Pinckney to Eliza L. Pinckney, May 17, 1779, Pinckney Family Papers, 1703–1847, South Carolina Historical Society, Charleston (hereafter cited as SCHS).

[44] Grimke Papers, 1761–1866, SCHS.

were taken by the army.[45] The whig assemblyman Peter Porcher, who listed by name two hundred and thirty-seven slaves missing, reported what was perhaps the largest number of escapes or captures.[46] In calculating the damage inflicted by Prevost's army on the slave-rich seacoast settlements, Edward Rutledge estimated that "the country in the vicinity of Beaufort has been rob'd of the value of near a million; the state has therefore lost that much for the property is carried off."[47]

The political consequences were far-reaching. James Simpson, the Crown's attorney general for South Carolina, was appointed by Lord Germain to gather information about the degree of aid and support the British might expect in a campaign to recover South Carolina, which at the outset of the war ranked behind New York and Georgia in its proportionate number of loyalists.[48] After studying conditions there and in Georgia, Simpson sadly reported that loyalists, who had welcomed the British thrust into South Carolina only to be "shamefully plundered" by them, were shocked at the wanton destruction of property and by the indiscriminate plunder of friend and foe alike.[49] Prevost's conduct "is far more obnoxious to friends of this country than enemies," complained another Crown official, probably Governor Wright. Instead of persuading wavering propertied white southerners to support the Crown, the plundering condoned by Prevost and the removal of their slaves "convinced many that he felt that he was not here to stay, and therefore was determined to make the most of the time that he was here." Such conduct, the report accurately predicted, "is likely to prove fatal to our interests."[50]

In the meantime, systematic plundering operations carried out in Georgia by civilian gangs commissioned by Lieutenant Colonel Prevost to gather intelligence and to collect provisions for the use of the army were creating widespread disillusionment with army policies in Georgia as well. While still drawing up plans for the management of Georgia's plantation economy, the commissioners of claims began to receive complaints that the civilian gangs "had committed very great waste and destruction on many well settled estates and Plantations." The commissioners' investigation proved that the charges were "but too well founded" and that in addition to rice, livestock, and other provisions "there had been a number of Negroes, Plate, Household furniture and other valuable Effects all carried off

[45] B. Beekman to Benjamin Lincoln, August 24, 1779, Benjamin Lincoln Papers.

[46] List of the Negroes Taken [by the British], November 1779, Porcher Ledger, Philip E. Porcher Papers, 1730–1800, Caroliniana Library.

[47] Edward Rutledge to [Thomas Pinckney], February 17, 1779, Miscellaneous Manuscripts, ser. 1, SCHS.

[48] Brown, *Kings Friends*, 213–14, 220–21.

[49] James Simpson to Germain, August 28, 1779, Germain Papers.

[50] On Mr. Prevost's Conduct in Georgia, Germain Papers.

in like manner under the description of Rebell property."[51] Whether or not "this booty of flesh and bone," as Marc Bloch has characterized slave captives taken by conquerors, were sold along with the spoils of war is problematic. The commissions' report concluded that "a considerable number of Negroes" had been "from time to time clandestinely ship'd or carried off to East Florida" by Benjamin Springer, Daniel McGirth, and others commissioned by the army and were there "converted to their own private use and benefit."[52]

Although its authority in the matter was unclear, the commission summoned Benjamin Springer to appear before it. When the charges were read to him, Springer produced written authorization from the acting lieutenant governor. Because the commission derived its authority from the military and was, therefore, dependent upon the cooperation and support of military commanders, it was powerless to do more than to caution Springer to be more circumspect in the future and to appeal to Lieutenant Colonel Prevost, who dismissed the complaints as "malicious persecutions against a very useful man." Although Prevost promised that the army would not interfere with the property of loyalist absentees, he insisted that rebel property "could not be better taken care of than by the army who had the best right to it." He concluded with a warning that further interference by civil authorities would "obstruct and counteract the operations of the army" and could lead to the imposition of martial law.[53]

As time and events were quickly to prove, civil and military authorities looked at slave labor from widely differing points of view. Civil authorities, whose own economic survival was closely tied to the restoration of the economic health of the state, tried to advance the pragmatic needs of the plantation economy. Because Georgia's economy was almost entirely dependent upon slave labor, they sought first and above all to check the exodus of slaves. Their efforts to assert control over the slave labor force precipitated a struggle with military authorities, who were motivated in some cases by military needs and in many cases by no larger purpose than private gain. Under the circumstances the freedom won by bondmen proved, in many cases, highly elastic.

When in July Sir James Wright, himself a casualty of the disasters wrought by war, returned to resume his duties as royal governor, he found the slave labor force severely depleted by desertion or military appropriation. A survey of plantations except those located south of the Ogeechee River, made by the commissioners of claims revealed that only nine hundred and twenty-five slaves remained on abandoned plantations in Geor-

---

[51] Report of the Commissioners of Claims, April 24, 1780, CO5/665/535–40.

[52] To Governor Wright from Lewis Johnston, James Mossman, William Telfair, in Wright, no. 20, May 20, 1780, CO5/665/527–33.

[53] Report of the Commissioners of Claims, April 24, 1780, CO5/665/534–40.

gia.[54] As a result, agricultural production was drastically down and the plantation system was in ruins. Although some of the white families who had fled to St. Augustine or the West Indies at the collapse of royal government were beginning to return, there were still more deserted estates than there were "fit persons" to manage them.[55] Unable to survive in the woods, or hoping perhaps to find refuge under the protective mantle of the British army, "a vast many" slaves had returned to Savannah on their own and "a great number" were returning to the city with Prevost's army from South Carolina. They were, however, being appropriated by the army, which resorted increasingly to taking what it needed and then using or selling them as suited its purposes.[56]

Besieged by protests from angry and disillusioned loyalists and by London merchants anxious to secure some £150,000s. in debts owed them by Georgia merchants,[57] Governor Wright, with the approval of the American secretary, tried to stop the flight of the slave population and through their forced labor restore the health of the plantation economy. To reassert control over the freedom-minded slaves, civil authorities agreed to construct "a strong and convenient house or prison," to restrain slaves who were "unruly or abscond." In a series of moves designed to keep slaves on the plantations and to sustain the authority of the master class, they agreed to restore all slaves to their loyalist owners. To relieve government of the growing burden of supporting loyalist refugees, those resident in England were instructed to return to Georgia, there to be assigned to the management of deserted estates "untill the estates are otherwise disposed of," or until such time as their property could be restored to them.[58] In an effort to balance the need for military labor with the need to maintain plantation labor, the governor and his council unanimously agreed "that they should not interfere or attempt to meddle with any of the Negroes captured by the army, but leave that matter to be conducted by General Prevost in such manner as he may think it prudent and proper for him to do." At the same time, however, they reconstituted the office of commissioner of claims and authorized it to take charge of all rebel-owned estates as well as those belonging to absentee loyalists and to take control of "all fugitive slaves found in the province," together with all those "who may have been decoyed from their owners." To defray the cost of their maintenance and to build up a fund to compensate loyalists, the commissioners were authorized to hire or rent out, slaves, houses, and plantations under their care to "proper persons."[59]

[54] Ibid., May 20, 1780.
[55] Germain to Wright, July 9, 1779, Candler, *CRG*, pt. 2, 38:165–66.
[56] Wright to Germain, July 31, 1779, CO5/665/305.
[57] At a Council held . . . at Savannah, July 23, 1779, CO5/665/309.
[58] Ibid., July 26, 1779, CO5/665/311–19.
[59] Ibid.

In a letter commending Wright's actions, Lord Germain emphasized what were, from Britain's perspective, the political advantages to be gained through proper control and use of the slave population. Because a large percentage of captured blacks were the property of South Carolinians, "the hopes of recovering [their property] might be a strong inducement to many of them to give their assistance in restoring the King's government in that province." On the other hand, the slave property of "such as continue obstinate in their rebellion, might with great justice and propriety, be appropriated to the making compensation to the king's faithful subjects for the losses they have sustained by the rebels." But, Germain cautioned, care must be taken to prevent the removal of blacks and that "good useage" must be given to those already in the king's possession so as to "encourage others to seek the same asylum."[60]

Britain's calculated attempt to develop a program that reconciled the pragmatic needs of the military and of the planter economy failed, as civil authorities steadily lost control over the carefully structured system and were forced toward accommodations by the siege of Savannah. In September 1779, a French fleet of twenty-five sail of the line and nine frigates under the command of Count D' Estaing appeared off the Georgia coast. On board were some four to five thousand troops commanded by General Benjamin Lincoln, named by Washington to command the Southern Department, and Fontages Legion, an auxiliary army of free black men from Saint Domingue, whose participation in the siege of Savannah established a vital link between the American and the Haitian revolutions.[61]

The defense of Savannah eclipsed all other issues in immediacy. The army, which already employed slaves extensively as laborers and officers' servants, began impressing hundreds more to aid in defense preparations. Two hundred and fifty of the slaves brought from South Carolina were embodied as a corps of pioneers to augment the small British garrison.[62] Five hundred more slaves were called up to serve under Major James Moncrief, chief of British engineers, in building the fortifications that enabled the city to withstand what Moses Buffington, an ensign in the South Carolina Royalist Regiment, called "as hard Sege [sic] as Ever has been sense the Rebelion [sic] began."[63]

From September 11, when Lincoln began moving his troops across the

[60] Germain to Wright, October 27, 1779, CO5/665/343.

[61] Wright to Germain, November 5, 1779, in "Letters from Governor Sir James Wright to the Earl of Dartmouth and Lord George Germain, Secretaries of State for America, from August 24, 1774, to February 16, 1782," GHS, *Coll.* 3:260–61.

[62] Regimental Order Book, Siege of Savannah, September 30, 1779, Orderly Books, British, Library of Congress.

[63] Moses Buffington to Peter Buffington, December 8, 1779, [Moses] Buffington Papers, 1779, GHS.

Savannah River at Zubly's Ferry, until October 9, when French and American troops failed in a bloody attempt to storm the city, the small garrison at Savannah lay under siege. While surrender negotiations went on, women and children and the elderly were quietly evacuated to Hutchinson Island opposite the city, where they took shelter in houses and barns. At midnight on the third of October, after the French and American demand to surrender was refused by Prevost, bombardment of the city began. For nearly a week Savannah was under constant fire from French and American forces entrenched "up to the chin" barely two hundred yards from British lines, and from French frigates in the harbor. Although most of the balls and shells sailed harmlessly over the British troops entrenched below the city, they fell on the town with great violence, crashing through roofs, tearing through houses, digging large craters in Savannah's broad, sandy streets. The rain of shot and shell sent inhabitants flying for shelter under the bluffs of the Savannah River or into cellars, which they tried to bomb proof with feather beds. Some slaves ran away during the siege, others remained in their quarters or hid out with their masters in cellars or in unoccupied houses or empty buildings. When the firing stopped to allow the artillery to cool, people emerged from their damp hiding places, all the while listening for the whistling sound of the shells, watching for the flash that defined the path of a mortar. According to one account, slave children became so accustomed to the shells "that they would run and cover them with sand, and as we were rather scarce of ammunition they would often pick up the spent balls and get for them seven-pence apiece."[64]

At daybreak on October 9, the French and Americans, led by D'Estaing himself, attacked with small arms. Although most of the slaves recruited as emergency troops labored in support positions behind British lines, two companies of black volunteers formed under white officers apparently played a significant military role in the defense of Savannah.[65] Together with some Indians, about three hundred armed blacks were placed with the picket of the line in front of the parapets and were charged with the immediate defense of the double-horn work in the center.[66] Armed black soldiers also took part in several skirmishes outside British lines. On October 16, for example, a group of blacks took on a party of rebels on McGillivray's plantation outside Savannah. In fierce fighting the rebels

[64] Chief Justice Anthony Stokes to his wife, November 9, 1779, in Henry Steele Commager and Richard B. Morris, eds. *The Spirit of 'Seventy-Six. The Story of the American Revolution. As Told by Participants* (New York: Harper and Row, 1967), 1093–95.

[65] Regimental Order Book, Siege of Savannah, September 30, 1779. See also Deposition of M. King, [Mark] King Papers, 1782, GHS. King, a deserter from Savannah, testified that about 150 blacks, "armed and equipt as infantry," served under a Colonel Brown.

[66] Bevan's History of the Siege of Savannah, [Joseph Vallence] Bevan Papers, 1733–1812, file 71, no. 71, folder 4, item 10, GHS.

were several times driven from the plantation buildings they occupied and into the woods. By nightfall the black troops had run out of ammunition and were forced to retreat, leaving one of their members dead and several wounded.[67] In reporting the successful defense of Savannah to the London government, Governor Wright singled out the work of the blacks as "they contributed greatly to our defense and safety."[68] Later in assessing the successful defense of Savannah, the *Virginia Gazette* attributed it to the unanticipated strength of the garrison, including in addition to seventeen hundred regular troops, "a greater number of sailors, marines, militia and armed blacks."[69]

The Franco-American invasion was easily repulsed, with heavy casualties by the invading force. After collecting their dead and wounded, the main bodies of French and American troops abandoned their lines, the French embarking and sailing from Cockspur, the Americans crossing into South Carolina at Zubly's Ferry. Shortly afterwards Governor Wright proclaimed a day of public thanksgiving to celebrate the city's deliverance. In the brief interlude of quiet, civil authorities struggled to restore order and return Georgia to its prewar status. Within only a few days, however, a combination of events plunged the state back into political turmoil and economic disarray. The removal of the Franco-American threat shattered the fragile consensus between civil and military authorities upon which all hope for managing the chaos to the political advantage of the Crown rested. Although British casualties during the siege were light, property damage was heavy. The incessant playing of the heavy cannon and mortars had left many of Savannah's private homes uninhabitable and had completely destroyed the military barracks. With winter approaching a bitter competition over housing developed, which brought into question the whole mandate of the civil government to manipulate private property for broad political purposes. Because all rebel property in the eyes of the army constituted spoils of war, General Prevost ordered the barrack master to take possession of all habitable rebel buildings for the troops' winter quarters. The military appropriation of some of the prime real estate in the city undercut the plans of the commissioners of claims to rent it and to dedicate the income to the support of needy loyalists. Eager to settle once and for all the jurisdictional dispute with the military, Governor Wright, at the behest of the commissioners, referred the matter to the attorney general, who advised that without legislative sanction, the powers of the commissioners were negligible.[70]

[67] "Account of the Siege of Savannah, 1779, from a British Source," GHS, *Coll.* 5:135.
[68] Quoted in Sylvia R. Frey, "The British and the Black: A New Perspective," *Historian* 38 (1976): 230.
[69] *Virginia Gazette*, (Dixon and Hunter), November 13, 1779.
[70] Report of the Third Commissioners of Claims, April 29, 1780, CO5/665/541–44.

Determined that the civil government should "Soon Strengthen and Raise its Head," Governor Wright decided to issue writs of election for a general assembly, which had not met in five years. Before it could be done partisan war erupted again. The bloody defeat of the Franco-American force at Savannah, combined with steady prodding from Lord Germain, had at last persuaded the cautious British commander in chief, Sir Henry Clinton, that the time had come to stage a full-scale invasion of the South. Launched from New York in December 1779, the expedition ended with the surrender of Charleston in May 1780. As part of the effort to restore the rest of the state to royal control, British forces were drawn from Georgia to South Carolina, so that by October the British occupied only two small garrisons in Georgia: one around Savannah, which was defended by 500 troops, the other at Augusta manned by a force of only 240.[71] Stripped of troops, the area between Savannah and Augusta lay naked before roving partisan bands and gangs of banditti.

With the restoration of royal government in Georgia, the level of partisan activity had steadily increased as whig guerrilla bands began forming under leaders like John Twiggs, Elijah Clarke, and John Dooly. Striking from Wilkes County, Georgia's backcountry, they constantly harrassed loyalist settlers and the British posts at Sunbury, Ebenezer, and Augusta. Rival tory bands sprang up as a counterforce. Some of them, like Brown's Rangers or Daniel McGirth's gang, were commissioned by British military authorities to neutralize the forces of Clarke and Dooly. Several of the loyalist leaders were well-known outlaws who, for one reason or another, enlisted in loyalist militia companies and, under the guise of military service, continued to carry out pillaging operations in Georgia and South Carolina. Although slaves were their prime targets, some of the bands, such as McGirth's, were interracial, a fact which when combined with their indiscriminate plundering, alienated potential white support for the Crown.[72]

Few white families escaped the bitter fighting peculiar to fratricidal war; the intensification of partisan activity also pressed cruelly on slaves, who lived under the constant threat of being captured by one group or another and sold away from home, family, and friends. After the failure of the siege of Savannah, a series of raids were launched across the Savannah River from South Carolina. Meeting little effective resistance from British posts at Sunbury, Ebenezer, and Abercorn, which were manned by foot soldiers, whig partisans swarmed over the loyalist plantations, which in good times

[71] Wright to Germain, October 27, 1780, "Letters from Governor Wright," GHS, *Coll.* 3:321–22.

[72] Rachel Klein, "The Rise of the Planters in the South Carolina Backcountry, 1767–1808," Ph.D. diss., Yale University, 1979, 118–19.

produced plentiful yields of rice and Indian corn.[73] Able to penetrate Georgia's inlets, creeks, and rivers all the way up to Sunbury, whig galleys and armed vessels joined the mounted troops to "plunder and carry off Negroes."[74] In a series of reprisal operations beginning in January 1780, whig raiders struck loyalist farms around Ebenezer and, emboldened by their success, began attacking unprotected plantations within twenty miles of Savannah. In one daring attack a small force plundered Lieutenant Governor John Graham's plantation just fourteen miles outside Savannah, stealing all of his horses and taking one hundred and thirty of his slaves.[75]

The frequency of whig raids soon sent white families fleeing to the safety of Savannah, which was according to American intelligence reports, protected by a garrison of Hessians, some Indians and four hundred slaves.[76] In probing the city's defenses, rebel forces several times encountered black troops. In an engagement with an interracial British party outside Savannah in April, American troops led by Colonel Andrew Pickens reported killing sixty black soldiers.[77] As conditions in Georgia rapidly deteriorated, Governor Wright called upon the assembly to enact legislation broadening his powers over the militia and authorizing him to order out slaves to construct fortifications for the security of Savannah and in case of necessity "to arm and employ Negroes for our defense." The assembly agreed to Wright's extraordinary request but stipulated that the arming of slaves must be limited to "time of Alarms actually fixed."[78] It is possible that some of those emergency troops were actually organized as military units. Shortly before the evacuation of Savannah, troops led by General Anthony Wayne routed a British force composed of Hessians, Indians, and regulars from the Seventh Regiment. After advancing within view of British lines at Savannah, Wayne detached a small force of infantry and dragoons to try to draw the British out. But the British "declined the invitation, contenting themselves with advancing a few Indians and Negroes to the skirt of a swamp from whence they commenced a scattering and ineffectual fire."[79]

For the next two years the fortunes of war seesawed violently. In January the British were forced to temporarily yield the up-country after Augusta

---

[73] Maj. John Jones to Polly Jones, October 8, 1779, Seaborn Jones, Sr. Papers, 1781–1847, William R. Perkins Library, Duke University, Durham, North Carolina.

[74] "The Proceedings and Minutes of the Governor and Council of Georgia, October 4, 1774, through November 7, 1775, and September 6, 1779, through September 20, 1780," Lilla Mills Hawes, ed., GHS, *Coll.* 10:55.

[75] Ibid., 67, 82; Wright to Germain, February 3, 1780, Candler, *CRG*, pt. 2, 38:270–71.

[76] D. Horry to Benjamin Lincoln, February 16, 1780, Benjamin Lincoln Papers.

[77] John Lewis Gervais to Henry Laurens, April 28, 1780, Simms Collection of the Laurens Papers.

[78] Wright to Germain, October 27, 1780, December 1, 1780, CO5/680/13, 14.

[79] Anthony Wayne to Nathanael Greene, May 24, 1782, M247, reel 175, item 155, Papers of the Continental Congress, National Archives.

fell into the possession of Twiggs and Dooly. The whig assembly which met there declared Augusta the seat of government, elected Richard Howley governor along with a full slate of state officers and proceeded, as Governor Wright contemptuously remarked, "to exercise some kind of civil powers" in the area controlled by the whig militia.[80] Among the first measures approved by the new state assembly set up in Augusta was the sale of slaves captured during the siege of Savannah, the proceeds to be used "for the benefit of the men then on duty under the command of Colonel John Dooly."[81] Like "Sumter's Law" in South Carolina, the Georgia statute systematized the plundering of slaves as part of the pay and recruitment procedures of the whig militia.

The removal of Continental troops from Georgia to defend South Carolina during the Charleston campaign, however, gradually weakened the whig position in Georgia and allowed Governor Wright finally to issue writs of election everywhere but St. Paul's parish in Richmond County, which remained in whig possession until May, when tory troops under Colonel Thomas Brown and James Grierson took Augusta, leaving only Wilkes County and part of Richmond County still under whig control. Back in session the provincial assembly renewed expired laws and passed several new ones. With the appointment of justices of the peace, commissioners of roads and ferries, commissioners of the loan office, and militia officers for the entire state, the political reconstruction of Georgia appeared to have been accomplished at last. There were also signs of a commercial revival. Although the season was too far advanced for planting, the commissioners of claims granted licenses to a number of loyalists, allowing them to employ slaves to produce pine lumber and staves and naval stores for export to the West Indies. In a twelve-month period over one hundred vessels entered and cleared the port of Savannah, the bulk of their cargo being lumber and naval stores. After the murder of John Dooly by a tory band lifted the threat of whig reprisals, citizens from along the coast south of Savannah began to come forward to take the oath of allegiance to the Crown.[82]

But the illusion of peace was soon shattered by new bursts of violence committed by black bands, marauding bands of whigs and tories, and by gangs of banditti. Ever alert to opportunities for freedom, several hundred slaves had volunteered to serve in the defense of Savannah during the siege. At the height of the crisis British military commanders were only too happy to accept their help. Armed and led by white officers, they had fought in the front lines and engaged in several skirmishes outside British

---

[80] Ibid. For details of whig government, see Coleman, *American Revolution in Georgia*, 159.

[81] "Minutes of the Executive Council, from January 14, 1778, to January 6, 1785," Candler, *RRG* 2:215.

[82] Coleman, *American Revolution in Georgia*, 131, 132, 133, 149–50.

lines. Eager to preserve their recently acquired freedom, some of them refused to be disarmed once the crisis had passed. Instead they boldly took over shops and abandoned houses in Savannah and began "selling and otherwise dealing or trading without any limitation or check." Much to the "terror and distress" of the white inhabitants of Savannah and Christ Church parish, who saw in armed blacks a reminder of the dangerous potential of their slaves, some slaves formed small outlaw bands, a slave inheritance as old as Graeco-Roman slavery. Although civil authorities tried to hunt them down in their wooded sanctuaries, the black brigands continued to rob and commit violence in and around Savannah for over a year.[83]

The disorganization of society and the impotence of civil and military authorities also left Georgia vulnerable to attacks by the ever-present white gangs. Beginning in the summer of 1780, there were dozens of skirmishes between partisan bands, some of them involving only a handful of whigs and tories. In a calculated attempt to eliminate opposition and to demonstrate how personally dangerous it might be, whig bands resorted to retributive bloodletting and property spoilation. One by one tory leaders who had been active in defending and consolidating support for the Crown in the backcountry were assassinated.[84] The purging of tory leadership was accompanied by the destruction of plantation crops and buildings and the expropriation of all movable property. In the milieu of chaos, bandit gangs were able to operate with impunity.

By the summer of 1780, Governor Wright agonized over events, the area between Savannah and Augusta was "infested with Partys of Robbers on Horseback." "There is one McKay," he continued, "who has a Party Some say of twelve others Say twenty, with which he Robs on the Highway between this and Augusta and goes Frequently to the Banks of Savannah River and has Stop'd Robbed and Plundered Several Boats."[85] More flamboyant and at the same time more sinister was "a Set of Men called McGirth's people." The son of a whig officer and a whig himself, Daniel McGirth switched sides after he was tried, whipped, and imprisoned by a whig officer on trumped up charges. McGirth escaped to East Florida and there joined Brown's Rangers. Later he formed his own gang and carried out pillaging operations in Georgia and South Carolina, some of which were commissioned by the British army as a counterforce to the whig gangs.[86] Despite their association with the British, McGirth's gang at-

[83] Regimental Order Book, Siege of Savannah, September 30, 1779; "Proceedings and Minutes of the Governor and Council," GHS, Coll. 10:53–54, 75, 126.

[84] Wright to Germain, March 5, 1781, Address to the Upper and Commons House of Assembly, March 5, 1781, Memorial of Sir James Wright, in "Letters of Sir James Wright," June 14, 1781, GHS, Coll. 3:335, 339, 357.

[85] Wright to Germain, August 20, 1780, GHS, Coll. 3:315.

[86] Klein, "Rise of the Planters," 121.

tacked loyalists and patriots indiscriminately, "robbing, murdering, distressing, and breaking up the Settlements in this Province," as Governor Wright plaintively put it.[87] Although McGirth's gang was interracial, slaves were a prime target. Carried into East Florida, they were sold to slave-hungry refugees there.

While the harrassing raids of mounted bands plunged Georgia's interior settlements into "a Truly Grievous Situation," her riverside and coastal settlements were "left still more exposed to the Ravages of the Enemy."[88] Georgia's coastline, deeply penetrated by rivers and inlets around which the low-country population was tightly clustered, was an inviting target for amphibious guerilla raids. Throughout the war years gangs of banditti such as the group led by "one Snipes of South Carolina," piratically ravaged Georgia's coasts and plundered "every kind of Property in some instances even the Cloaths on their backs . . . their Negroes, Horses and Cattle," as Joseph Clay, the Georgia merchant who became Deputy Paymaster General of the Southern Army, wrote during the siege of Savannah.[89] After British land troops and naval support were withdrawn from Georgia to assist in the reduction of South Carolina, Governor Wright warned in vain that "a rebel privateer or two may come up the Savannah River and cut out or carry away anything or everything in it." In the months that followed, Wright's darkest predictions were fulfilled as whig galleys and boats entered the inlets, creeks, and rivers, landing from time to time to plunder and to steal slaves from the riverside farms.[90]

During the fall of 1780 the fighting entered a final, more savage phase. In mid-September Elijah Clarke led three hundred militia in a vain assault on the British post at Augusta. In retaliatory raids sent into Wilkes County by the tory post commander, Thomas Brown, one hundred plantations were despoiled, the crops destroyed, houses and outbuildings burned.[91] In a year of escalating violence, over two hundred men were murdered "in cold blood"; their deaths, according to the provincial assembly "were attended with circumstances of wanton barbarity that would disgrace a savage."[92] Terrorized by marauding gangs, partisan bands, and regular troops alike, inhabitants of the backcountry begged for protection.[93] Belatedly,

[87] "Proceedings and Minutes of the Governor and Council," June 17, 1780, GHS, *Coll.* 10:109.

[88] Wright to Germain, April 4, 1780, Address of the Council of Georgia, in "Letters of Sir James Wright," no. 33, December 1, 1780, GHS, *Coll.* 3:281, 325.

[89] Joseph Clay to John Lewis Gervais, September 28, 1779, "Letters of Joseph Clay," GHS, *Coll.* 8:146, 147.

[90] Wright to Marriot Arbuthnot, Candler, *CRG*, pt. 2, 38:284; Wright to Germain, December 20, 1780, GHS, *Coll.* 3:327.

[91] Ibid., October 27, 1780, 321.

[92] "Selected Eighteenth Century Manuscripts," GHS, *Coll.* 20:20.

[93] Petition of the Inhabitants of the Town and District of Ebenezer, to Governor Wright,

three patrols of twenty mounted militiamen each were organized early in 1781 and two months later a troop of horse was raised to protect loyalists. But it was a case of too little, too late. In April Georgia and South Carolina militia under Micajah Williamson and Elijah Clarke lay siege to Augusta, compelling it to surrender in June. One by one the British relinquished outlying posts and retreated into Savannah, leaving all of the backcountry in whig hands. Weakened and demoralized, "naked, and destitute even of the necessaries of Life," white loyalists took refuge in the swamps or fled to the safety of Savannah and the protection of the small contingent of British regulars that remained there until evacuation.[94]

Having forced the British into a defensive posture, the whigs moved quickly to expand their political influence through the restoration of constitutional government. An assembly was chosen, which met on August 17 and elected Nathan Brownson governor. Brownson's term ended four and one-half months later when elections held early in 1781 put in a new assembly and named "a Northward Man," John Martin, governor.[95] Before he could establish full political authority, the new governor had to solve several problems of pressing concern, including the maintenance of army enlistments and army supply, the settlement of state obligations incurred during the war, and support for the refugees who began returning to Georgia in 1781. During the years of British occupation the state government had passed no tax bill, relying instead on borrowing or other informal financial arrangements for its revenue. Even though the British were more or less confined to the Savannah area after the arrival of General Anthony Wayne in January 1782, a quick expansion of revenue was impossible, given the chaotic social and economic situation. To meet its immediate financial needs, therefore, the state was forced to rely on income from the sale of estates confiscated under the acts of 1778 and 1782, which named 342 individuals, and on payments by persons named in the amercement act.[96]

In the beginning the state government tried to discharge its obligations by renting or selling tory property, excepting slaves.[97] But the desperate financial situation led authorities to try to meet expenses by the sale of slaves and by payment in kind, especially of slaves from confiscated es-

---

in Charles Cornwallis (1738–1805), second earl of Cornwallis and first marquis of Cornwallis, Papers, 1614–1854, PRO30/11/2/221–22, London.

[94] "Selected Eighteenth Century Manuscripts," GHS, *Coll.* 20:20.

[95] "Journal of the House of Assembly from August 17, 1780, to February 21, 1784," Candler, *RRG* 3:8, 34. For details regarding the reestablishment of whig government, see Coleman, *American Revolution in Georgia*, 135–36, 161, 163.

[96] Ibid., 184, 201.

[97] "Journal of the House of Assembly," Candler, *RRG* 3:12, 13, 17.

tates.[98] Bounties in slaves were offered to raise the state's Continental quota and as compensation for arrears of pay.[99] As a reward for their war service, most of the high-ranking officers who had served in Georgia and even some of the troops were given special grants in land and slaves or in specie collected from the sale of slaves.[100] Slaves from confiscated estates were also given in exchange for supplies for Continental troops.[101]

The state's struggle to stave off financial disaster and, more importantly, to rebuild Georgia's wrecked economy was closely tied to the recovery of the slave population. As they had throughout the war, slaves continued to escape whenever possible, often by concealing themselves aboard outgoing ocean vessels "in hopes of getting away."[102] Although the government seemed firmly entrenched, the state was still subject to tory raids, the objects of which were usually slaves. The result was the further dislocation of Georgia's slave population. Perhaps the largest number were removed to South Carolina, because of its proximity,[103] but many more were uprooted from their homes and families and carried into distant states. At Yadkin Ford in North Carolina General Nathanael Greene recovered a number of slaves who had been plundered from the confiscated estate of a loyalist officer, Philip Dill, Jr. On Governor Martin's orders they were sold in North Carolina to produce revenue. Although Continental and state troops were used to hunt down runaways and to guard those remaining on confiscated estates, many slaves were clandestinely conveyed to other states, in several of which slavery was still legal.[104]

Even after the British evacuation of Savannah in July 1782, harrassing activities by tory bands operating out of East Florida continued to drain away Georgia's black population. Although the size and frequency of the raids declined after Governor Martin and Governor Tonyn reached an agreement to halt the plundering operations on both sides of the St. Mary River, small groups, some of them claiming to act under commissions from the British, continued to prey on slaves on the indigo plantations border-

---

[98] "Minutes of the Executive Council," Candler, *RRG* 2:209, 327–28, 337.

[99] John Martin to General Wayne, March 23, 1782, "Official Letters of John Martin, 1782–1783," *Georgia Historical Quarterly* 1 (1917): 302.

[100] Georgia House of Representatives, July 27, 29, 1782, Bevan Papers, file 71, folder 9, item 62.

[101] "Minutes of the Executive Council," January 23, 1783, Candler, *RRG* 2:424.

[102] *Royal Georgia Gazette*, January 8, 1782, March 14, 1782, March 21, 1782, April 25, 1782, May 23, 1782.

[103] John Martin to General Wayne, March 23, 1782, John Martin to Capt. John Greene, May 3, 1782, "Official Letters of John Martin," *Georgia Historical Quarterly* 1:302, 310.

[104] "Minutes of the Executive Council," January 14, 1782, January 15, 1782, January 22, 1782, February 19, 1782, Candler, *RRG* 2:302, 310, 321; John Martin to Nathanael Greene, March 6, 1782, "Official Letters of John Martin," *Georgia Historical Quarterly* 1:292.

ing Georgia's waterways.[105] According to Patrick Carr, a Georgian active in hunting down tories, tory "traders" with a "vast property" in slaves captured in Georgia and East Florida were "continually sending Negroes to West Florida" to feed the slave-hunger of the planters and farmers, whose thin, slow stream of movement west would, by the 1790s, reach flood tide. Carr urged Governor Martin to check the slave traffic by appealing directly to the Spanish governor who, Carr maintained, had "a great regard to the Americans."[106] It was not until 1785, however, that Colonel Daniel and Captain James McGirth were finally jailed in East Florida as they prepared to move "a number of negroes and horses stolen property" from an assembly point on the Great Saltilla River to West Florida.[107]

The largest exodus of slaves occurred during the British evacuation of Savannah in July 1782, when between five and six thousand slaves were evacuated despite the vigorous protests of state authorities.[108] Beginning in 1779 with the gradual withdrawal of British forces from Georgia, the circumference of British military power had slowly shrunk. The British had seen the invasion and occupation of Georgia as the springboard from which the Southern campaign would be launched, by which first the South and then all thirteen colonies would be returned to the empire. Britain's failure in Georgia was due to a combination of factors, not the least significant of which was the flawed effort to use slavery as a tactic.

Under the pressure of practical politics, the provincial government had tried unsuccessfully to fashion a strategy for pacifying white southerners through the political manipulation of the slave population. The army's violent quest for pacification undermined those efforts. The wholesale destruction of property, the pillaging of homes, and the forcible impressment of slaves hardened the determination of many of the South's leading white families to resist British tyranny to the end. Paradoxically, by impressing slaves to work as military laborers, by forcing them back into the fields as agricultural laborers for the army or for loyalists, the army kept slavery functioning in many places and substantially reduced the enormous latent

[105] John Martin to Patrick Tonyn, August 15, 1782, October 19, 1782, John Martin to Col. Cooper, September 17, 1782, "Official Letters of John Martin," *Georgia Historical Quarterly* 1:320, 328–29, 333–34.

[106] Patrick Carr to John Martin, August 22, 1782, "Letters of Patrick Carr, Terror to British Loyalists, to Governors John Martin and Lyman Hall, 1782–1783," *Georgia Historical Quarterly* 1:339. For the postrevolutionary period, see Allan Kulikoff, "Uprooted Peoples: Black Migrants in the Age of the American Revolution, 1790–1820," in Berlin and Hoffman, eds., *Slavery and Freedom*, 143–71.

[107] Milledge and Sullivan to Governor Elbert, February 18, 1785, *Correspondence of John Milledge, Governor of Georgia, 1802–1806*, Harriet Milledge Salley, ed. (Columbia, South Carolina, 1949), 19.

[108] Lilla M. Hawes, ed., "Miscellaneous Papers of James Jackson, 1781–1798," *Georgia Historical Quarterly* 37 (1953): 78.

power of Georgia's black population; but the practice of receiving slaves, if it did not mean emancipation, at least raised the prospect of emancipation and suggested the clear possibility that some general somewhere might someday end slavery by proclamation, a fear that Clinton's pronouncement merely ratified. To the extent that it deprived slaveowners of their human property, even the highly exploitative practice of treating slaves as war contraband corroded the institution. Without meaning to do so, the British army had thus made the revolutionary war in Georgia a war about slavery. The result was to undermine British credibility and contribute significantly to Britain's ignominious retreat from Savannah, which presaged the failure of British efforts in the South and the ultimate collapse of the British cause in America.

For slaves the results were equally equivocal. Although they were not offered liberty, either as a general principle or as a reward for service, slaves generally tried to capitalize on the disruption that accompanied the war. Most made only elastic gains. Many of those who escaped in the early days of the British invasion were captured by one or the other of the contending forces and were, in many cases, reinslaved under different auspices. The constant fighting, which was a serious impediment to agricultural production, caused an increasing shortage of provisions. With no hope of permanent subsistence, and in many cases not even the hope of survival, large numbers were forced to return. Cynically mistreated by the provincial government and by state assemblies alike, they experienced massive disruptions in their lives. For those who fled to the British army, military service was, at best, a complex mixture of servitude and freedom, which for all its shortcomings, extended the tradition of slave resistance in a new direction. Although the slow growth of revolutionary consciousness did not bring Georgia's slave population all the way to revolution, the unprecedented size of the slave exodus demonstrated unequivocally that slaves constituted a potentially revolutionary force.

FOUR

THE TRIAGONAL WAR:
BRITISH INVASION AND OCCUPATION
OF SOUTH CAROLINA

IN GEORGIA, it was not British policy alone that was decisive in undermining slavery, but the actions of slaves. British policy was important principally because it created opportunities for slaves to seek their own liberation. To put it another way, the mere appearance of troops on the scene was not a sufficient cause for massive resistance, but it was a necessary one. At the same time, however, slave resistance was in a critical sense the precondition for the evolution of Britain's slave strategy. During the invasion and occupation of South Carolina, the dialectical relationship of slave resistance and the British strategy of racial manipulation culminated in the Philipsburg proclamation, which offered freedom to some slaves but upheld the institution of slavery. The operation of that dynamic, converted the Revolutionary War in South Carolina into a complex triangular process involving two sets of white belligerents and at least twenty-thousand—probably more—black slaves.

"This is the most important hour Britain ever knew," Sir Henry Clinton, the British commander in chief, declared of his decision to extend the southern campaign to South Carolina. "If we lose it we shall never see another."[1] Under pressure to launch an offensive against South Carolina, during the spring of 1779 the cautious Clinton began assembling troops in New York with which to besiege Charleston and to garrison the interior. After a five-month delay caused by the Franco-American assault on Savannah, the British expedition against Charleston finally got under way in December 1779. Because of heavy seas and violent winds mixed with snow, rain, and bitter cold, the ten-day voyage took over one month.[2] Constant storms separated the fleet and damaged many of the transports carrying

---

[1] John S. Pancake, *This Destructive War: The British Campaign in the Carolinas, 1780–1782* (University: University of Alabama Press, 1985), 57.

[2] Captain Johann Hinrichs gives a detailed description of the voyage in Bernard A. Uhlendorf, trans. and ed., *The Siege of Charleston. With an Account of the Province of South Carolina: Diaries and Letters of Hessian Officers from the von Jungkenn Papers in the William L. Clements Library* (Ann Arbor: University of Michigan Press, 1938; reprint, New York: New York Times and Arno Press, 1968), 111–17.

the artillery horses, most of which had to be thrown overboard because of injuries.[3] On February 1 the crippled fleet finally reached the shelter of the Tybee River near Savannah. After the ships were refitted and fresh water was taken on board, the fleet sailed from the Tybee to North Edisto Sound.

Ten days later the troops began disembarking on the chain of sea islands strewn along the Carolina coast. On Simmons and Johns islands they found that all the white males "had run away," leaving behind their wives and children and their slaves to manage the family farms and care for the livestock.[4] Some thirty miles of nearly impassable woods and marshland cut by swampy rivers lay between the army and the city of Charleston. Having neither maps of the area to guide them nor sufficient horses or men to haul the heavy guns, munitions, entrenching tools, gabions, fascines, and provisions, the army began immediately to look for spies and guides and military laborers among the slaves.

Many slaves, even children, had an intimate knowledge of the terrain, which proved in many cases to be indispensable to the British. It was common in the prerevolutionary war years for slaves to go visiting with a pass from the master or to be about on the master's business. Many low-country slaves also raised livestock and grew provisions in their own small garden plots for sale or barter off the plantation.[5] They were familiar with the woods because they were permitted to set traps. They knew the river crossings and the roads because it was customary in South Carolina to use slave labor to build and maintain the system of roads.[6] The detachments of the elite jager units sent out to the low-country plantations to collect slaves and livestock for troop use after the long sea voyage had, therefore, no difficulty in finding sufficient volunteers to provide each party with its own guide.

The first contact between African-Americans and British troops, most of whom had never seen Africans, produced an ambivalent response. According to Captain Johann Ewald, a Hessian officer, "none of us could manage to talk with these people because of their bad dialect, even had we spoken with the tongues of angels."[7] The "bad dialect" spoken by the Sea Island slaves was Gullah. It is not clear what racial implications the British and their German allies drew from the language differences, although clearly a rebuke is implicit in Ewald's description of Gullah as "a bad dialect." Given

[3] "Ewald Diary," in Uhlendorf, ed., *Siege of Charleston*, 23.

[4] Captain Johann Ewald, *Diary of the American War. A Hessian Journal*, Joseph P. Tustin, trans. and ed. (New Haven, Conn.: Yale University Press, 1979), 23.

[5] Morgan, "Work and Culture," 564.

[6] Klaus G. Loewald, Beverly Starika, and Paul S. Taylor, eds., "Johann Martin Bolzius Answers a Questionnaire on Carolina and Georgia," *William and Mary Quarterly*, 3d ser., 14 (1957): 232, 259.

[7] Ewald, *Diary*, 199, 203.

the long history among Anglo-Saxons of equating race and language, it is highly likely that the linguistic differences Ewald remarked on served to enhance racial distinctions between free white soldiers and black slaves and provided whatever justification was needed to treat slaves differently.

For six weeks as the army strained forward from Simmons Island to James Island, entering Stono Inlet on March 1, mounted troops continued to collect slaves to carry out the arduous work associated with the siege. Equipped with axes and shovels, black crews repaired the "miserable works [at Stono Inlet] which resembled heaps of sand."[8] Virtually every piece of equipment required for the siege had to be dragged from Gibbes Ferry, designated as the depot for the siege, to the two crescent-shaped redoubts built by the British, one on the bank of the Ashley River, the other near the Cooper River. Besieged by vermin, British sailors and several hundred African-Americans struggled in unseasonable heat to pull the heavy guns and ammunition over board roads built in a futile effort to keep the equipment from becoming mired in mud.

On March 31 the siege of Charleston began. The entire rebel force was concentrated in the city behind fortifications built by the labor of some five thousand slaves, who had been impressed into service to prepare for the British attack. With all communications cut off by the British works and the harbor in British hands, the beleaguered city began to experience food shortages by early May. Informed by black and white deserters that the city's meat ration had been cut in half,[9] and that only soldiers were allowed coffee and sugar, the British began hurling shells charged with rice and sugar into the city to demoralize the hungry population.[10] By the eighth of May all of the city's meat supplies were exhausted. On the eleventh Major General Benjamin Lincoln offered to surrender the city. The following day the articles of surrender were signed and exchanged. At 2:00 P.M. the British Major General Alexander Leslie rode into town accompanied by staff officers and adjutants. Major General Lincoln, also on horseback, formally surrendered the city while British oboists played "God Save the King."[11]

Once the British were in firm possession of Charleston, Clinton began to grapple with the problem of restoring the rest of the state to royal control. He immediately circulated proclamations throughout the state aimed at persuading the people to unite behind the King's standard. To give the

[8] Ibid., 203, 214, 221.

[9] Journal of Lt. John Peebles of the 42d or Royal Highland Regiment during the War of Independence, May 3, 1780, in GD 21, Cunningham of Thortoun Papers, 1746–1782, 1876–1883, Scottish Record Office, Edinburgh, Scotland.

[10] Journal of the Siege of Charleston, May 2, 1780, John Faucheraud Grimké, Military Records, SCHS.

[11] "Hinrichs Diary," in Uhlendorf, ed., *Siege of Charleston*, 291.

appearance if not the substance of civil authority, he organized a Board of Police modeled after similar boards established during the occupation of Georgia, New York, and Philadelphia, and appointed former attorney general James Simpson, as head. Robert William Powell, a prominent merchant and commanding officer of the royal militia at Charleston, was named to represent the "trading part of the community," and Alexander Wright, the son of Georgia's royal governor, Sir James Wright, was appointed to represent the "planting interest." Colonel Alexander Innes, a regular British officer, was named as military representative to the board, whose decisions were subject to the approval of the military commander of Charleston, who was in turn responsible to Clinton and, after Clinton's departure, to Cornwallis.[12] Although primarily a judicial body whose jurisdiction was contract obligations, the board also administered justice, regulated commercial activity, and exercised extensive police powers in the city, including the maintenance of streets and fire protection and the control and regulation of slaves and free blacks.[13]

At the same time, Clinton planned several expeditions into the interior of the state: one to move up the Savannah River into Georgia; another to cross the Saluda River to Ninety Six; a third to cross the Santee River in an effort to intercept Colonel Abraham Buford's corps, which was retreating into North Carolina with artillery and wagons loaded with arms and ammunition.[14] Before Clinton left South Carolina on June 8 to return to New York, British forces occupied Augusta, Ninety Six, and Camden, and had established small posts at Rocky Mount, Cheraw, and Georgetown. Over two hundred citizens had signed an address to Clinton congratulating him on the restoration of royal control and were granted pardon. A number of prominent whigs, including Charles Pinckney, Sr., a colonel in the state militia and a former member of the revolutionary Council of Safety, Henry Middleton, former president of the Continental Congress, and Rawlin Lowndes, who succeeded John Rutledge as governor in 1778, had all petitioned for restoration of British citizenship. Several prominent militia officers, including Andrew Pickens, Isaac Huger, Isaac Hayne, Daniel Horry, and two of his brothers, brought their commands in and accepted parole.[15] Altogether 381 persons accepted British protection.[16]

[12] Lt. Gov. William Bull to the Lords of the Treasury, February 1782, Papers from Clinton to Gage, 1781–1782, PROT1/571.

[13] For a detailed description of the board's activites see George Smith McCowen, *The British Occupation of Charleston, 1780–1782* (Columbia: University of South Carolina Press, 1972), 14, 15, 28, 30, 31.

[14] Banastre Tarleton, *History of the Campaigns of 1780 and 1781, in the Southern Provinces of North America* (London: T. Cadell, 1787), 26.

[15] Pancake, *This Destructive War*, 79–80.

[16] Nadelhaft, *Disorders of War*, 53.

Confident that the conquest of the state and of the South was complete, Clinton wrote triumphantly to Germain that "there are few men in South Carolina who are not either our prisoners, or in arms with us."[17]

Within a matter of days it was clear that Clinton had won a victory without peace. From its inception the central article of faith of Britain's Southern strategy had been the belief that the recovery of the southern provinces depended upon the loyalty and support of the king's friends who, it was widely reported, existed in formidable numbers throughout the South. Success depended in large measure on the British army's ability to defeat or contain whig forces, to give the widest support possible to the counterrevolutionary activities of loyalist forces, and to protect the lives and property of loyal citizens. But the Southern strategy was foredoomed to failure by a flawed pacification policy. Less than one month after the surrender of Charleston and the submission of some of the state's most prominent citizens, Clinton endangered the British grip on power by issuing the controversial proclamation of June 3, which required all persons on parole to take the oath of allegiance or be considered in rebellion. In effect, he revoked the paroles and forced citizens to become either active supporters of the Crown or active rebels.

The proclamation spawned a mass exodus of whites from the state. Fearing reprisals if they refused to collaborate, many individuals who had accepted neutrality fled their plantations into North Carolina during the month of June.[18] When the sympathetic Virginia assembly on July 8, 1780, exempted the citizens of Georgia and South Carolina from a state law prohibiting the further importation of slaves,[19] a number of prominent planters, among them Charles Sims and George Hancock, moved with several hundred slaves to Virginia,[20] an event noted by the Reverend James Madison, who wrote to his son in August that "Some of ye Charleston Families are fled here for Refuge."[21]

Typical, perhaps, was the experience of Stephen Bull, brigadier general of the state militia who served under Nathanael Greene. A substantial planter whose wealth consisted of slaves and "plate," Bull "did not think proper, after the capture of Charleston, to expose his wealth to the rapacity of the English." He, therefore, set off with two hundred of his slaves and

[17] Quoted in Pancake, *This Destructive War*, 72.
[18] William Richardson Davie (1756–1820) Papers, no. 1 (Addition), 1793, folder 28, pt. 2, SHC.
[19] Hening, *Statutes of Virginia* 10:307–8; see also Hutchinson and Rachal, eds., *Madison Papers* 2:57n.
[20] The law decreed that slaves brought into the state must be registered with county courts. Some of the lists survive in state records; see William R. Palmer et al., *Calendar of Virginia State Papers* 1:491, 371, 613; 2:279, 281.
[21] From the Reverend James Madison, August 3, 1780, in Hutchinson and Rachal, eds., *Madison Papers* 2:55.

his personal property and provisions loaded on wagons. Bull's "little army" travelled through South Carolina, North Carolina, and part of Virginia, pitching camp every evening until they arrived at Tuckahoe on the James River, the seat of Thomas Mann Randolph, a wealthy Virginian. On land provided by his friend Randolph, Bull built a home and lived there comfortably until Arnold and Phillips invaded Virginia. Once again Bull "departed with his treasures, his flocks and his Negroes," for the upper country near Fredericksburg, where they remained until the end of the war. When a French visitor, the Marquis de Chastellux, asked Bull at the end of the war what he would have done had the English succeeded in the conquest of Virginia, Bull replied, "I should have retired to Maryland," and if necessary, "I should have proceeded to Pennsylvania, and so on, even to New England."[22]

Smaller planters, who lacked the resources and the assistance of prominent friends, were unable to keep their slave forces intact, which caused further confusion and disruption in the lives of black families. Hancock, for example, was obliged to sell six of the sixty-three slaves he brought to Henry County in order to support himself and his family.[23]

Although many citizens took the oath of allegiance, some whigs viewed the June 3 proclamation as a violation of the surrender terms, which had promised prisoners on parole security for their property. Considering themselves released from all legal or moral constraints, a number of former militia leaders began to return to the field, among them the noted partisan leader, Thomas Sumter, whose family had been driven from its home before it was burned by Tarleton's Legion, then in pursuit of Colonel Abraham Buford. The slaughter of Buford's men at the Waxhaws near the North Carolina border and the depredations committed by British regulars and loyalist militia units unleashed some of the violent forces that had been bred by years of Indian wars and one year of bitter partisan fighting.[24] But the South Carolina pacification program broke down primarily because of British attempts to use slaves as weapons against their masters.

Before mounting the Southern campaign, General Clinton issued from his headquarters in Philipsburg, New York, the carefully worded proclamation of June 30, 1779. In it he warned that all blacks taken in rebel service by British armies would be sold for the benefit of their captors. Those who deserted the rebels for British service were, however, promised "full security to follow within these Lines, any Occupation which [they]

---

[22] François Jean, Marquis de Chastellux, *Travels in North America in the Years 1780, 1781, and 1782*, Howard C. Rice, Jr., ed., 2 vols. (Chapel Hill: University of North Carolina Press, 1963), 2:425–26.

[23] Palmer et al., *Calendar of Virginia State Papers* 2:281.

[24] Pancake, *This Destructive War*, 71, 81–82.

shall think proper."[25] Like Dunmore's proclamation before it and Lincoln's after, Clinton's Philipsburg proclamation embodied no moral or philosophical convictions. It was foremost a military measure whose stated purpose was to counteract the American "practice of enrolling Negroes Among their Troops."[26] The tacit purpose was to weaken and demoralize southern rebels by depriving them of their labor force and of their resources; to accommodate Britain's perennial needs for pioneers and military laborers in North America and for recruits for service in the West Indies; and to cement their local alliances and to keep the loyalty of their troops by distributing captured slaves after military victories. Although it did not directly alter the legal status of slaves, even those belonging to rebels, the proclamation did raise the specter of emancipation. In so doing it inspirited instead of intimidated white rebels, embittered instead of demoralized them. The predatory conduct of the army condoned by the proclamation antagonized citizens and, in many cases, created prorebel sympathies. In South Carolina it prompted a successful insurgency that turned the state into a battleground and plunged it into the most savage civil war fought in America during the Revolution. The marches and countermarches of the armies and the savage underwar that soon blazed out of control left South Carolina's once-rich plantations in ruins, the fields laid in waste, the livestock gone, and the system of labor nearly destroyed.

Slaveholders, who saw the Philipsburg proclamation as an attack on property and on the labor system of the South and an invitation to anarchy, were incensed rather than lulled by its equivocation. Blacks took every conceivable political posture in response to it, which demonstrates not that they were divided in their attitudes toward slavery but that they were pragmatic in their quest for freedom. The flight of white families following the surrender of Charleston left blacks alone on the plantations, without supervision or control for perhaps the first time in their lives. That situation presented them with an opportunity to make the hard decision to accept slavery or to resist. The choice for most was not clear-cut. Lacking either the will or the means to realize their dreams, some remained apparently loyal. Some were probably dissuaded from action by the recollection of the fate of earlier protest movements. Many had family; some owned property. Like most whites, they took a wait-and-see attitude. In many, perhaps in most, cases their inactivity was a form of passive resistance.

Although the case is by no means typical, of the two hundred slaves owned by whig General William Moultrie "not one of them left me during the war," Moultrie proudly boasted, "although they had had great offers,

---

[25] Proclamation, June 30, 1779, British Headquarters (Sir Guy Carleton) Papers, Howard-Tilton Library, Tulane University, New Orleans. Louisiana, PRO30/55, Microfilm.

[26] Negroes in North America, n.d., Plantations General, 1780–1783, CO5/8.

nay, some were carried down to work on the British lines, yet they always contrived to make their escapes and return home." When after being exchanged as a prisoner of war Moultrie returned to his plantation for a brief visit, he was greeted by his slaves singing an African war song, "welcome the war home."[27] Some slaves, like those belonging to the Reverend Archibald Simpson, pastor of the Independent Presbyterian church of Stoney Creek, apparently shared their master's distrust of the British. When Simpson returned home at the end of the war, he found his slaves at work in the woods. "They saw me," Simpson recalled in his journal, "and ran with transports of joy, holding me by the knees as I sat on horseback, and directly ran off to the plantation to give notice to Mr. Lambert." Like Moultrie's slaves, they had refused a British invitation to follow the army: "They asked me if I was going to leave them when they had stayed on the plantation when the British wanted them to go away," Simpson continued, and they "abused the two who had left me and gone with Colonel Moncrieff."[28]

Left to their own devices, slaves on many plantations conceivably ceased to be slaves. When a British army commanded by General Prevost overran most of the coastal area between Savannah and Charleston in the spring of 1779, the troops and their Indian allies raided coastal plantations and some further inland, including one belonging to Thomas Pinckney. In his account of the raid, Pinckney told how the British "took" nineteen of his slaves, leaving only "the sick women, and the young children, and about five fellows who are now perfectly free and live on the best produce of the plantation." After the British departed for Georgia, Pinckney's overseer, who had been hiding in the swamps, returned to the plantation. "I hope," Pinckney fretted, "he will be able to keep the remaining property in some order, though the Negroes pay no attention to his orders."[29] Fewer than half of the slaves of Wadboo Barony, the ancestral home of Sir John Colleton, one of the original proprietors of South Carolina, remained on the plantation, and in the breakdown of authority that followed the surrender of Charleston, they acknowledged "no subjection to the Overseers."[30]

The conditions of war made it increasingly difficult for most slaves to decide to leave the plantations. According to William Richardson Davie,

[27] Moultrie, *Memoirs* 2:256.

[28] George Howe, *History of the Presbyterian Church in South Carolina*, 2 vols. (Columbia, S.C.: Duffie and Chapman, 1870), 1:465. Lambert was apparently the white overseer. "Moncrieff" was John Moncrief, the British army engineer responsible for the construction of military defenses.

[29] Thomas Pinckney to Eliza L. Pinckney, May 17, 1779, 38–3–5, Pinckney Family Papers, SCHS.

[30] James Harold Easterby, ed., *Wadboo Barony. Its Fate as Told in Colleton Family Papers, 1773–1793* (Columbia: University of South Carolina Press, 1952), 4.

the cavalry commander who served as commissary general under Nathanael Greene, as they swept through the state, "the troops of both armies took what they wanted without ceremony or accountability and used it without measure or economy."[31] Tory and British forces and later some whig militia brigades were thorough and even wanton in their destruction. Anthony Allaire, a twenty-five-year-old loyalist officer who served with the tory forces that captured Charleston, boasted that the army foraged "by destroying furniture, breaking windows, etc., taking all their [rebel] horned cattle, horses, mules, sheep, fowls, etc. and their negroes to drive them."[32]

The unorthodox operations of the marauders were also to be dreaded. A young South Carolina widow, Eliza Wilkinson, and her two sisters were visited by turns, first by an advance party of Daniel McGirth's gang, who tried to persuade the defenceless women to "take a protection" against the loss of clothing and slaves, and then by a party of British dragoons accompanied by armed blacks, who "threatened and abused the women and then plundered them of clothing, shoe buckels, hair pens, even earrings and wedding rings." Later in the afternoon of the same day a large party of McGirth's gang returned. In an ironic gesture of chivalry the outlaws declared that "we take nothing from ladies," and then offered to try to recover the stolen property. In mortal fear for their lives, Wilkinson and her sisters deserted the family plantation on Yonge's Island and fled to the comparative safety of Charleston. En route they encountered a large boatload of women and children also on their way to Charleston, "as that place promised more safety than others." Later Wilkinson recalled the traumatic times: "The whole world seemed to me as a theatre, where nothing was acted but cruelty, bloodshed, and oppression; where neither age nor sex escaped the horrors of injustice and violence; where the lives and property of the innocent and inoffensive were in continual danger, and the lawless power ranged at large."[33]

In general, the atrocities perpetrated against women and children by British forces were individual acts and not acts of policy such as these committed later in South Carolina when, on Cornwallis's orders, terror became a basic component of policy. Indeed the British military command denounced such actions as reprehensible and instituted measures designed to prevent them.[34] But the plundering of plantations continued, disrupting production and producing severe wartime scarcities. Neglected or devas-

[31] William Richardson Davie Papers, 1, 1793, folder 28, pt. 2, SHC.

[32] Anthony Allaire, *Diary of Lieutenant Anthony Allaire* (reprint New York: New York Times, 1968), 9.

[33] Eliza [Yonge] Wilkinson, *Letters of Eliza Wilkinson*, Carolina Gilman, ed. (New York: New York Times, 1969), 14, 27, 29, 31, 46.

[34] *South-Carolina and American General Gazette*, August 23, 1780.

tated by the war, stripped of tools, farm implements, and livestock, "the plantations have been some quite, some nearly ruined and all with very few exceptions great sufferers," wrote Eliza Lucas Pinckney. "Their Crops, stock, boats, Carts, etc. all gone taken or destroyed and the Crops made this year will be very small by the desertion of the Negroes in planting and hoeing time."[35]

The conditions Eliza Pinckney described were repeated on countless plantations and farms. Situated in the upper valley of the Cooper River, Wadboo Barony suffered heavily during the war years. A shortage of slave provisions caused by low crop yields in 1779 and exacerbated by the loss of oxen and horses, the destruction of the rice fields by the different armies, and the great desertion of the slaves led to privation and suffering among those who remained.[36] The shrinking of their already meager diet reduced "the poor Negroes to a starving condition in many places hereabout," a young Scottish officer noted in his diary.[37] Although even in normal times slaves were scantily clad, especially during the summer months, wartime disruptions also created critical shortages of clothing. After commenting on the scarcity of food supplies, Josiah Smith, Jr., a Charleston merchant who served as resident manager of George Austin's properties while the latter resided in England, reported that at Austin's plantations on the Pee Dee and Ashepoo rivers "the poor Negroes were obliged to do without warm clothing the past Winter, but in the Summer I made it up to them by a double suit of Ozenbrigs to each worker and one suit to the Children."[38]

The surpassing cruelty that was the hallmark of the war in South Carolina constituted a compelling reason why many slaves viewed the British offer of freedom with caution. Severe punishment, and often death, was a virtual certainty for an unsuccessful escape. A case in point was the capture by whig forces of four men, two of them white, one a mulatto, and the fourth a black, all suspected of deserting to the enemy. Governor John Rutledge, happening by at the time, was asked what should be done with the alleged fugitives. Rutledge's reply was to "Hang them up to the beam of the gate" by which they were standing. The governor's orders were promptly carried out and the four hung there all day, a gruesome reminder of the chilling brutality of war.[39] Their choices seemingly limited to the relative security of the slave or freedom in the grave, thousands of slaves

[35] Quoted in Mary Beth Norton, *Liberty's Daughters. The Revolutionary Experience of American Women, 1750–1800* (Boston: Little, Brown, 1980), 208.

[36] Easterby, *Wadboo Barony*, 3, 4, 5, 6, 10.

[37] Journal of Peebles, May 25, 1780.

[38] Josiah Smith to George Appleby, December 2, 1780, Smith Lettercopy Book.

[39] John C. Dann, ed., *The Revolution Remembered. Eyewitness Accounts of the War for Independence* (Chicago: University of Chicago Press, 1977), 183.

stayed on the farms and plantations. These were not, as they were later made out to be, necessarily loyal slaves. Rather they were, like thousands of whites, neutral; neutrality for them was a survival mechanism. Under the circumstances, the refusal of many slaves to join the British might also be seen as a form of resistance to exploitation. Inspired by the well-established colonial tradition of freedom in return for military service, a small minority of slaves decided to throw in their lot with the Revolution and served alongside their owners.

For the vast majority of slaves who actively participated in the Revolution, the arrival of the British army was a liberating moment. Although Clinton's Philipsburg proclamation was but a pale likeness of the sweeping measure it was later made out to be, thousands of South Carolina's slaves chose to interpret his offer of freedom to "enemy Negroes" as a general emancipation. Presuming themselves to be "Absolved from all respect to their American masters, and entirely released from servitude" by it, men, women and children streamed to British lines, usually fleeing alone or in pairs.[40] Despite the greater risks of detection, some runaways traveled in groups made up of family members or friends from the same plantation, which suggests both the significance of community bonds and kinship ties and the depth of commitment to the dream of freedom.

Typical of such groups were the sixteen runaways from the plantation of the Charleston slave merchant, Andrew Lord. In the group were Sam and his twenty-year-old son George; a "well made" thirty-year-old named Coffee; Peter, "a stout young fellow," and Ned, a twelve-year-old boy, all of whom had been purchased by Lord from James Brisbane of Georgia. Ben, a thirty-year-old sawyer, and Achilles, "a very good sawyer," had formerly belonged to Alexander Wylly, also of Georgia. Tolberg, Moses, and China had all belonged at one time to Samuel Douglass of Georgia, whereas Renley, age fifteen, Seno and Titus, both twelve, had been slaves of John Lord of Amelia Township. In the group also were Jemmy, a thirty-five-year-old carpenter, and his wife Juliet.[41] The dramatic example of a family group escape offers poignant evidence of the inherent strength of kinship ties. Apparently led by Old Ross, an Ibo woman fifty-six years old, the group of runaways from Mary Thomas's plantation consisted of thirty-six-year-old Celia, the daughter of Old Ross, and Celia's sixty-one-year-old husband, Cato; Country Sue, the thirty-two-year-old daughter of Old Ross; Dick, Old Ross's twenty-two-year-old son, and Elsey, her "thick and chubbed" granddaughter. The group also contained several nonfamily members, including Kate, a recent arrival from Angola; thirty-five-year-old

<hr/>

[40] Tarleton, *History*, 89.
[41] *South-Carolina and American General Gazette*, November 29, 1780.

Town Sue, probably a creole because she was said to speak good English; Will, "a smart waiting boy"; and thirty-six-year-old Scipio.[42]

Young and old, male and female, skilled and unskilled, creole and African, alone and in groups, they streamed in like a tidal flood, their sheer numbers overwhelming the army. Although Clinton had tried to limit the effects of the Philipsburg proclamation, the magnitude of the slave response to it threatened to transcend the proclamation's carefully constructed confines and to become a mass resistance movement in which African-American resentments and aspirations could become overtly expressed in more militant form. The British response to the massive self-liberation movement was shaped by conflicting pressures and ambitions: the urge to exploit slave labor for military purposes, and the virtual impossibility of subsisting the numbers of deserters, which was, in any event, far in excess of what the army could profitably use as military laborers or train and discipline as soldiers; the urge to deprive the enemy of its most vital resource without precipitating violent and radical changes in the economic and social structures; the urge, in short, to stabilize and upset the delicate balance of southern society for British political and military advantage. Operating in the dynamic context of war, those conflicting pressures and ambitions produced an anomalous situation and in the end, an ambiguous compromise.

Discomfited by the knowledge that the Philipsburg proclamation had provided the material for a violent explosion, the military command moved quickly to confine massive slave resistance to the relative safety of military service and thereby to forestall the disintegration of the plantation economy. The army's effort to register all of the black deserters by name, owner, and former place of residence revealed ironically that many among them were the property of loyalists.[43] Anxious to avoid any suggestion of a general emancipation that would frighten away loyalist support, Clinton personally ordered nearly a hundred of the runaways restored to their owners.[44] Apprehensive of the difficulties that would arise "from a further desertion of them to us," he instructed Cornwallis "to make such arrangements as will discourage their joining us." Because the swelling number of black fugitives far exceeded the number the army could profitably employ, Clinton decided to "consider of some scheme for placing those we have on abandoned plantations on which they may subsist."[45]

Clinton's problem was not, however, merely one of subsisting slaves.

[42] *Royal Georgia Gazette*, January 4, 1781.

[43] Cornwallis to Captain Russell, December 22, 1779, PRO30/11/1/33–34.

[44] Orders to Claimants for Negroes, 1780, Negroes Delivered to Their Owners on Orders of Lord Henry Clinton, March 8, 1780, Memorandum Book, 1773–1782, Reverend Mr. Jenkins Papers, 1744–1781, SCHS.

[45] Clinton to Cornwallis, May 20, 1780, PRO30/11/2/38–39.

Wartime destruction and the desertion of slaves from almost all of the plantations within eighty miles of Charleston[46] threatened the economic system and imperiled the traditional social order. Filled with the spirit of freedom, many slaves took advantage of the confusion endemic to war to run away to their own people or to flee to urban areas like Charleston, where they tried to pass as free blacks. Living "in a state of idleness," as the *Royal Gazette* characterized slaves' unaccustomed leisure, they congregated in punch houses and dram shops that sprang up to serve the soldiers and the influx of "disorderly Persons and Negroes."[47] More importantly, slaves, who in their uncertainty about where to go had remained on the plantations, were also threatening to enter larger patterns of resistance. In July an "insurrection of Mr. [Ralph] Isard's Negroes" broke out.[48]

To dispel the specter, and in some cases the fact of social chaos, Earl Cornwallis, commander of His Majesty's forces in the South after Clinton's departure for New York in June, attempted to shore up the rapidly disintegrating social order. He first named Brigadier General James Patterson as commandant of the city of Charleston and later replaced him with Colonel Nisbet Balfour to carry out British policies in the city. Upon the recommendation of its military representative, Alexander Innes, the Charleston Board of Police requested that troops be immediately dispatched to Izard's Savannah River plantation to suppress the insurrection there and "to inflict such punishment upon the principal offenders in the insurrection as may be adequate to the crimes."[49] The speed with which the army responded was doubtless soon known to almost every slave in South Carolina. The appearance of a well-armed, united white community, quite willing to crush slave risings, must have demonstrated once again the futility of rebellion and made it abundantly clear that the only practical alternative to slavery was service with the army.

Disturbed by the fear that the slaves without masters living together in Charleston might well "contract bad habits, and such as might be dangerous to the community hereafter if they were suffered to remain in a state of idleness,"[50] the board also took steps to limit their freedom of movement and, hence, their ability to enter more militant forms of behavior. With the willing cooperation of the army, some of the features of the slave codes were applied. Slaves were, for example, not permitted to leave their places of employment without "a ticket in writing" from their owners. Those found without were to be arrested and put to forced labor on the public

[46] Josiah Smith to Mrs. Mary Hodgson, August 5, 1780, Smith Lettercopy Book.
[47] *Royal Gazette*, Garrison Orders, July 17, 1781.
[48] Proceedings of the Board of Police, July 14, 1780, CO5/519.
[49] Ibid.
[50] Ibid., June 13, 1780, CO5/520.

works.[51] Punch houses and dram shops, which served as gathering places for urban blacks, were closed on orders of the Board of Police.[52]

It was, however, the disruption of the plantation system caused by the war and by the unprecedented number of slave desertions to the British that proved most vexing to the political and military plans of civil and military authorities. To prevent the collapse of the labor system and to reassure at the same time white loyal slaveholders that the Philipsburg proclamation did not constitute a general attack on property rights, the military command quickly approved a plan proposed by the Board of Police for the immediate restoration of all slaves belonging to loyalists and to slaveholders who agreed to take the oath of allegiance, on condition only that the latter compensate the army for their maintenance at the rate of one shilling sterling per day.[53] Three prominent loyalists, William Carson, Robert Ballingall, and Thomas Inglis, were appointed commissioners of claims to supervise the delivery of runaways to claimants able to certify ownership. Early in June the commissioners called upon the various departments of the army to hand into their custody all slaves fitting the above description in anticipation of returning them to those masters "who by a public avowal of their Loyalty and Attachment to His Majesty's Government have a Right to them."[54]

The efforts of the British army to maintain the plantocracy and the slave system were only partially inspired by political considerations. The army also looked upon slaves as a labor reservoir to satisfy its chronic need for military and agricultural laborers and to satiate its appetite for booty. Army slave policy as expressed in the Philipsburg proclamation had distinguished between slaves who fled to British protection and those taken captive during military operations or on rebel plantations. The former were accepted for military service. Although nominally free once they entered British lines, the majority of blacks enrolled in the army usually served in a variety of noncombatant but vital supporting roles. Because slaves ordinarily had no training in European military skills and were, moreover, neither acquired nor trained for regular service by the British army, they were often assigned duties that allowed them to use the civilian skills they already possessed.

Both men and women served in all of the civil departments of the army. Next to engineering the Royal Artillery was the largest employer of blacks. Artificers—carpenters, wheelers, smiths, sawyers, and collar makers—repaired and built wagons, mended equipment and arms, made platforms and attended to numerous other tasks associated with the artillery. Men

[51] *Royal Gazette*, Garrison Orders, July 17, 1781.
[52] Proceedings of the Board of Police, June 13, 1780, CO5/520.
[53] Ibid.
[54] *Royal South-Carolina Gazette*, July 6, 1780.

and women made musket cartridges for ordnance.[55] The quartermaster and barrackmaster departments employed hundreds of black artificers and laborers in constructing barracks and in building and repairing boats and wagons. Commissaries used black workers to butcher livestock and to pickle, barrel, and store meat for the use of the troops.[56] The hospital department also used black men and women in a variety of capacities. Men served as orderlies, women as nurses in hospitals. The hospital frames were made in England and were then fitted and assembled by black carpenters for use as temporary hospitals in America.[57]

Black pioneers, attached either to individual regiments or organized as autonomous units under white officers, performed an assortment of garrison duties, thereby freeing white troops for field service. Paid at the rate of six pence a day, they served as guides or baggage carriers. They assisted the artificers in building and repairing bridges. They cleared the roads of stones or fallen trees, and they cleaned up the encampments. They did the heavy work of loading and hauling. When not employed on other service, they made fascines and carried out countless other noncombatant duties.[58] Scores of blacks were employed as officers' servants. Army regulations allowed field officers of the infantry two blacks, subalterns and staff, one.[59] The regulations were routinely ignored, however, and even common soldiers occasionally had black servants.

In keeping with ancient military practice, the army regarded slaves who were taken captive in war as prizes of war, title to which it claimed "as to any other acquisition or article of prize."[60] Reduced to practice this meant that captured slaves could be sold, hired out, or employed for the benefit of their captors. In the months before the surrender of Charleston, the British army in South Carolina collected vast quantities of goods, princi-

[55] See, for example, Return of Negroes Employed in the Service of the Royal Artillery, April 28, 1780, Sir Henry Clinton, 1731[?]–1795, Papers, 1750–1812, William L. Clements Library, Ann Arbor, Mich.; Return of Negroes Employed as Artificers, Labourers and Servants in the Royal Artillery, August 5, 1782, George Wray, Papers, 1770–1793, William L. Clements Library. The list included the names of fifty-five "Negro Wenches."

[56] *Royal Gazette*, February 22, 1781, March 17, 1781; see also Muster Roll of the Artificers, Labourers, Horses, etc., Employed in the Barrack Master General's Department in New York, July 16, 1781, Commissary of Captures Return of Negroes, Horses, etc., March 17, 1780, Clinton Papers.

[57] John McNamara Hayes, "Memorandum for the General Hospital, February 29, 1780," Clinton Papers; *Royal Gazette*, March 17, 1781, lists twenty female nurses.

[58] Clinton to Major General Phillips, April 25, 1781, PRO30/11/95/24–25; Clinton Orderly Book, June 1, 1780, Clinton Papers.

[59] Lord Cornwallis' Regulations Respecting the Number of Negroes and Horses, June 5, 1781, Order Book of the 43d Regiment at Yorktown, Add. MSS 42449, British Library, London.

[60] Negroes, September, 1819, PRO30/8/344/109–11. This unsigned report is a general history of British slave policy in the American Revolution.

pally indigo and livestock, and several thousand slaves from deserted estates. The British navy, in the meantime, confiscated ships and their cargoes, plus large amounts of cordage and gunpowder. Following the practice common among preindustrial empires, Clinton promised that the proceeds of victory would be distributed among the men who had served on the expedition. Indifferent to the moral side of slavery, he had originally planned to treat all captured slaves as booty. Political expediency forced him instead to remand those belonging to loyalists.[61] The rest were treated as contraband of war. Whether they were sold with the other spoils of war is subject for debate. David Ramsay, the South Carolina historian of the Revolution, claimed that over two thousand "plundered Negroes" were shipped off at a single embarkation.[62] Although it does not constitute proof, Clinton's memorandum to the commandant of Charleston seems to corroborate the substance of Ramsay's charge. In his instructions concerning the disposition of slaves, Clinton ordered "That of the Negroes who shall go with the Army to the Northward (except such as described in my orders, and those who have been brought away without their own consent) those belonging to Friends and persons under protection of Government shall be hired as was done at Savannah and in case of death paid for."[63]

In a practice reminiscent of the Romans, the British army claimed thousands of captive slaves as state property and used them on public works or as agricultural laborers, with the promise of manumission as an incentive for loyal work. For the administration of the contraband the army developed a bureaucratic structure: the Commissary of Captures for the Army and the Commissioner of Sequestered Estates. Created by Clinton during siege operations, the office of Commissary of Captures was designed to free the army from dependence on the unreliable and expensive system of transatlantic supply. Specifically it was meant to accomplish two ends: to produce economies by appropriating crops and livestock for the use of the army, thus saving the Crown the cost of prepared rations; and to save the regular British troops "much toil and fatigue" by employing captured blacks at hard labor within the various departments. Dividends

---

[61] Henry Clinton, *Memorandums etc. Respecting the Unprecedented Treatment Which the Army Have Met with Respecting Plunder Taken After a Siege, and of Which Plunder the Navy Serving with the Army Divided More Than Their Ample Share, Now Fourteen Years Since* (London, 1794), 66; Baurmeister, *Revolution in America*, 350, 363.

[62] Ramsay, *History of the Revolution of South Carolina* 2:190. Ramsay relied heavily on reports in the *Annual Register* and was sometimes uncritical of his sources. By eighteenth-century standards, however, his is good provincial history.

[63] Memorandum for the commandant of Charleston, British Headquarters Papers, Howard-Tilton Memorial Library.

accruing from the use or sale of confiscated property were to be used for the benefit of the army.[64]

Over three hundred captured slaves were assigned to work in the civil departments of the army in a system of mitigated bondage analogous to what they had known under slavery.[65] Five hundred more were taken by Clinton to New York to serve as pioneers.[66] Each regiment was allowed to embark ten blacks "to be such whose owners were not at the time of their joining under His Majesty's protection."[67] Driven by the necessity of procuring food for the army during his projected invasion of North Carolina, Cornwallis reestablished the position of Commissary of Captures and appointed a Pennsylvania loyalist, Charles Stedman, as commissary. In an effort to feed the army in the field and at the military posts at Camden, Cheraw Hill, Georgetown, Ninety Six, and later Wynnesborough, Stedman employed slaves "under proper conductors" to drive in cattle, while troops of loyal militia collected wheat and Indian corn from the farmers in the area through which the army marched. The grain was then hauled by wagon to the nearest of several mills appropriated by Stedman, where one hundred and twenty slaves threshed it out and packed it ready for use by the army.[68]

At least five thousand of the slaves fitting the description of war contraband were arbitrarily mobilized to produce supplies for the army. The British army in America consumed an average of three hundred tons of food a week, the bulk of which was sent from Europe. The hazards of the transatlantic crossing and the inadequacy of the commissariat system produced long delays in delivery and chronic shortages of food and supplies, which forced the army from time to time to live off the land.[69] The problem was

[64] Franklin Wickwire and Mary Wickwire, *Cornwallis. The American Adventure* (Boston: Houghton Mifflin, 1970), 141–42.

[65] Commissary of Captures Return of Negroes, Horse, etc., March 17, 1780, Clinton Papers.

[66] Ramsay, *History of the Revolution* 2:196.

[67] Orderly Book, June 1, 1780, Wray Papers; Orderly Book, America, June 1, 1780, 6912/14, no. 42, Order Books, Letter Books, Journals, Letters, and Other Documents of Lt. Gen. Sir Eyre Coote, Relating to the American War of Independence, 1776–1782, National Army Museum, London.

[68] Charles Stedman, *The History of the Origin, Progress and Termination of the American War*, 2 vols. (Dublin: P. Wogan; London: P. Byrne, 1794), 2:192–93, 198. Despite Stedman's attempt to discriminate between patriot and loyalist farmers, payment for much of the property seized from loyalists was refused. Moreover, payment, made by the deputy commissary general in Charleston, was often withheld, depending upon "the merit or demerit of the party at the end of the war," idem, *History*, 193–94, 206n, 225n.

[69] Sylvia R. Frey, *The British Soldier in America. A Social History of Military Life in the Revolutionary Period* (Austin: University of Texas Press, 1981), 30–32. For a comprehensive treatment of logistical problems, see R. Arthur Bowler, *Logistics and the Failure of the British Army in America, 1775–1783* (Princeton, N.J.: Princeton University Press, 1975).

exacerbated in the South by poor roads and a scarcity of wagons, which made it difficult to transport goods into the interior.[70] The confiscation of rebel-owned lands and enslaved workers offered a solution to the problem by seeming to guarantee a permanent supply of food and other necessities.

On September 7, 1780, Cornwallis announced the appointment of a commissioner to take charge of estates, both real and personal, of all disaffected persons. Cornwallis named John Cruden, a wealthy South Carolina merchant, as commissioner of sequestered estates.[71] Authorized by his commission to take control of all "capital stock, consisting of land and Negroes," and "to sell and dispose of the produce of lands and all other property,"[72] Cruden was expected not only to supply the army with food and livestock but to make the sequestered estates yield a profit that could be used "for the benefit of the suffering loyalists, who have so fair and so just a claim on it for immediate support and future indemnification."[73] The systematic exploitation of slave labor would thus serve a multiple purpose: it would satisfy the need of the military for agricultural products; it would punish the Crown's active enemies and provide a way to compensate its friends; it would allow white citizens to participate in the fighting while blacks continued as slaves to maintain the plantation system.

Cruden quickly developed a bureaucratic structure for the administration of sequestered property. The state of South Carolina was divided into districts and a deputy appointed to manage the affairs of each district.[74] In lieu of a fixed salary Cruden allowed each of the deputies a commission based on the total production of his district. These and all other of the initial operating expenses were paid for by Cruden personally. His investment was to be recovered by a five percent commission—later increased to seven and one-half percent—to be derived from anticipated profits. In organizing the one hundred plantations and over five thousand slaves ultimately sequestered,[75] Cruden continued the prewar plantation organization and routine. Overseers were appointed to control the slaves and maintain plantation efficiency on the government-operated estates. Abandoned and confiscated lands were either leased to loyalists or were worked

[70] Wickwire and Wickwire, *Cornwallis*, 138–39.

[71] Ibid., 142.

[72] Cruden's Commission, September 16, 1780, Sundry Queries from which Mr. Cruden begs to have the opinion of the Right Honorable Earl Cornwallis, Cornwallis Papers, PRO30/11/7/22–24, 25–28.

[73] Memorial of John Cruden, April 8, 1782, Cornwallis Papers, PRO30/11/7/13–15.

[74] Most deputies were prominent planters like Robert Ballingall of St. Bartholomew's parish.

[75] Lists of the sequestered slaves were published in local newspapers; see, for example, *South-Carolina and American General Gazette*, November 22, 1780, December 9, 1780; *Royal South-Carolina Gazette*, December 8–12, 1781; *Royal Gazette*, March 10, 1781.

directly for the benefit of the army.[76] On some of the government-operated estates, crops like corn and vegetables, which were "highly necessary for the Army," were cultivated by the plantation hands, although without much success.[77] Blacks who could be spared from the plantations were hired out to the civil departments of the army. Black "mechanics" supervised by "skillful whitemen," were put to work making tools and farm implements to replace those that had been stripped from exposed estates by the belligerent armies or by bands of marauders.

As part of his ambitious plan to make the sequestered estates yield "a clear permanent and increasing revenue of 50 or 60,000 pounds pr. annum,"[78] Cruden set black ship carpenters to work building vessels to transport the produce from the sequestered estates to the Charleston market.[79] The majority of sequestered blacks, including slaves seized from rebels in North Carolina, were assigned to the production of lumber, firewood, and naval stores, which Cruden expected would eventually yield the greatest profits.[80]

Pine grew profusely in the sandy soil of South Carolina, blanketing the land from the coast to the Appalachians. Its tall, straight trunk and oily wood were well suited for planks, masts, and shipbuilding in general. By the Revolution an extensive trade had developed with England, which depended upon such imports for the maintenance of the Royal Navy, and with the West Indies. Colonial South Carolinians had also built a profitable trade in naval stores by making tar, turpentine, and pitch from the oil of the pine. Because many of the sequestered estates had luxuriant tree cover—Cruden estimated that a single estate could produce ten thousand feet a year—the commissioner believed that he could adequately supply the needs of the garrison at Charleston and turn a handsome profit, which could be used to offset the cost of maintaining the black workers and to establish a fund to compensate white loyalists for their war-related losses. Although a wage system was established, which varied from two to eight pence a day for male laborers to eighteen pence a day for artificers and paid two women at a rate equivalent to that of one male laborer, in reality army blacks received no pay at all. After their wages were paid by department heads to special paymasters, deductions were made to clothe them "in uniform" and to provide for their general upkeep.[81]

[76] Mr. Cruden's Narrative, Cornwallis Papers, PRO30/11/7/38–43.
[77] John Cruden, *Report on the Management of the Estates Sequestered in South Carolina*, in *Winnowings in American History. Revolutionary Narratives*, Paul Leicester Ford, ed. (Brooklyn, 1890), 18.
[78] Mr. Cruden's Narrative, PRO30/11/7/38–43.
[79] Cruden, *Report*, 20.
[80] Balfour to Cruden, August 22, 1781, Cornwallis Papers PRO30/11/7/28.
[81] Mr. Cruden's Narrative, Cornwallis Papers, PRO30/11/7/38–43; Cruden to Skelly,

The organization of slave labor by the British army helped to defuse the potential for rebellion by drawing into the army the most courageous slaves, who had the greatest potential for revolutionary leadership and employing them at noncombatant duties. The condition of their lives once in the army further militated against a slave uprising. Although British slave policy was rooted in a clear belief in the racial inferiority of blacks, army treatment of them was restrained somewhat by conventional British morality and by the personal standards of decency of some of the officers. The well-being of army blacks was, however, frankly subordinate to purely military needs. Reasoning that military expediency justified it, the army maintained strict racial distinctions between black and white soldiers. Black soldiers were quartered in separate encampments and given inferior food. When supplies ran short, their rations were the first to be cut. Whereas many white owners recognized the potential hazards of overexertion and exposure and eased their slaves' tasks at certain times of the year, the British army, driven by the dangers and necessities of war, made excessive demands of its military laborers. Overworked and undernourished, they fell easy prey to disease, for which the army provided no effective protection or cure.

Although all eighteenth-century armies suffered high disease rates, the incidence of disease among army blacks was conspicuously higher than it was among white troops. The "fevers," typhus, typhoid, and dysentery, and smallpox, wasted thousands of army blacks. Carried by lice, the febrile diseases flourished in overcrowded and unsanitary military quarters, camps, barracks, and ships. Overcrowding and unsanitary conditions in the army camps led to an outbreak of typhus among the blacks who fled to the British during Prevost's invasion of South Carolina in 1779. Threatened by an American force on the mainland, Prevost retreated precipitantly down the chain of coastal islands, leaving the stricken blacks to perish wherever they fell. Without proper medical care, their supply of rations cut off in July by Prevost's order, several hundred died on Otter Island.[82]

Although blacks are no more or less immune to smallpox than are whites, a disproportionately high percentage of black followers of the British army was struck by that disease. As a result of inoculation, the incidence of smallpox in epidemic proportions had dropped sharply by the Revolution.[83] The revolutionary period, however, witnessed fresh outbreaks of

April 12, 1782, Cornwallis Papers, PRO30/11/7/15–16; Instructions for the Office Established to Receive the Pay of Negroes Employed in the Different Departments, Gen. Alexander Leslie, Letter Book, Emmet Collection, 15703, New York Public Library, New York City.

[82] Simms, *History of South Carolina*, 154; Ramsay, *History of the Revolution* 2:178, 179.

[83] There is evidence that some West African peoples were familiar with variolation techniques even before Europeans used the procedure in the eighteenth century; see Peter H.

the disease. Statistics on the death rate are not available; impressionistic evidence suggests that mortality was much higher, both numerically and proportionately, among black soldiers than among white soldiers, due probably to the British army's practice of inoculation to counteract the exceptional mortality suffered by troops during the Seven Years War. Perhaps because the procedure was expensive, its use was generally confined to white troops during the war.[84]

In November 1779 smallpox broke out in Charleston, which had not had a major outbreak for almost twenty years.[85] During the spring it struck among the black laborers impressed into British service during siege operations against Charleston.[86] As a result perhaps of the crowding of large numbers of unvaccinated people in unsanitary conditions, the disease gained virulence among the blacks who, as one observer put it, "have loitered in and about Charleston since the surrender." Accompanied by a "malignant fever" that "sweeps them away in great numbers," the infection spread generally, assailing white families, especially infants, as well.[87] Although the army tried to check the contagion by quarantining the stricken blacks,[88] troop movements along the coast and into the interior distributed the infection throughout the state, helped perhaps by the fact that in their haste to move, the army often left the dead unburied in the woods.[89] In July smallpox was reported among the slaves at Wadboo Barony at the head of the western branch of Cooper River, where troops were often maneuvering. By December it had struck the slaves on George Austin's plantations on the Ashepoo south of Charleston as well as those on the Pee Dee near the southern border of North Carolina.[90]

Sustained by the hope of freedom at war's end, fugitives and contrabands alike accepted the frightening risks of military life. Having placed themselves at the service of the army, they voluntarily accepted its restraining influence. Their crucial role in the British war effort, and in the political processes more generally, increased as the political situation was transformed from one in which civil war was first an imminent possibility to a grim reality. As a result of his bitter experience with vacillating loyalist support, Cornwallis reluctantly decided in the summer of 1780 to adopt

Wood, "The Impact of Smallpox on the Native Population of the Eighteenth Century South," *New York State Journal of Medicine* 87 (1987): 30–36.

[84] Frey, *British Soldier*, 43.

[85] Moultrie, *Memoirs* 2:43.

[86] Orderly Book, July 7, 1780, Wray Papers, William L. Clements Library.

[87] James Simpson to Clinton, July 16, 1780, British Headquarters Papers, Howard-Tilton Memorial Library.

[88] Orderly Book, July 7, 1780, Wray Papers, William L. Clements Library.

[89] Ramsay, *History of the Revolution* 2:190.

[90] Easterby, *Wadboo Barony*, 4, 6; Josiah Smith to George Appleby, December 2, 1780, Smith Lettercopy Book, SHC *Coll.*

terror tactics in the South. In June he instructed Lieutenant Colonel George Turnbull, a provincial officer, to "give permission to the militia to do what they please with the plantations abandoned by the rebels." That he did not intend random and wholesale destruction is, however, evident in his subsequent remarks, which substantially modified and restricted the use of terror. While Cornwallis admitted no objection "if it is convenient now and then to destroy one" [rebel plantation], he expressed a preference that "if they can get in the crops and turn them to their own use, it will be the best plan," and he absolutely forbade cruelty to the wives and children even of active rebels.[91]

After his rout of Horatio Gates at Camden on August 16, 1780, however, Cornwallis decided to carry the war to North Carolina. With his move into that state the frontiers of South Carolina exploded. General Thomas Sumter's cavalry, under orders from Gates, broke into the northern and western districts and ravaged the country from Ninety Six to Santee, while the elusive Colonel Francis Marion and Georgia Colonel Elijah Clark overran the southern and eastern parts.[92] In an effort to maintain order in the countryside and to shore up loyalist support, Cornwallis again resorted to terror. Some of the early hesitation to use violence was absent from his letter to Colonel Balfour, then commanding officer at the British base at Ninety Six: "I have given orders that all the inhabitants of this province who have subscribed and have taken part in this revolt, should be punished with the greatest rigour, and also those that will not turn out, that they may be imprisoned, and their whole property taken from them and destroyed. I have likewise ordered," he continued, "that compensation should be made out of their effects to the persons who have been injured or oppressed by them."[93] From that point South Carolina became an arena for terror and violence, as bitter partisan warfare raged through the lowcountry swamps between the Pee Dee and Santee rivers and throughout the backcountry. Inevitably plantation slaves, unarmed and unorganized, were drawn into its whirling center.

In operations throughout the middle and up-country regions of the state, the British army carried out a program of systematic destruction. During the early fall of 1780, Major John Wemyss, commanding officer of the Sixty-third Regiment, roamed the area between Black River and Lynches Creek, where Americans noted in despair, "they plunder, burn

[91] Cornwallis to Turnbull, June 16, 1780, Cornwallis Papers, PRO30/11/77/11–12.
[92] Mr. Cruden's Narrative, Cornwallis Papers, PRO30/11/7/38–43.
[93] Cornwallis to Balfour, August 1, 1780, Cornwallis Papers, PRO30/11/98/10. Franklin and Mary Wickwire claim that Cornwallis' letter to Balfour was intercepted and altered by patriots to make Cornwallis' policy seem harsher than it actually was and that the intended recipient was a provincial officer, John H. Cruger, instead of a regular British officer.

and destroy everything in their way."[94] Before he fell into the hands of whigs while attempting to surprise Sumter at Broad River in November, Wemyss "burnt and laid waste about fifty houses and plantations, mostly belonging to people who have either broke their paroles or oaths of allegiance and are now in arms against us."[95] Later in the spring of 1781, Sumter reported to General Nathanael Greene that the Broad River area was "Very bear [sic] of provisions, and striped of Chief of the Negroes and horses."[96]

Lieutenant Colonel John Harris Cruger, loyalist commander of the first battalion of De Lancey's provincial corps, successfully prosecuted the same policy in the area around Ninety Six.[97] Prominent whigs were the key targets of the attacks. On Cornwallis's personal orders, the plantation of the whig militia officer, Lieutenant Colonel Andrew Pickens, was destroyed, his home and outbuildings burned, his livestock and slaves confiscated for the use of the army.[98] When the British prepared to abandon Ninety Six, Lieutenant Colonel Balfour, who then commanded in that district, ordered abandoned and rebel plantations, including that of Governor John Rutledge, stripped of their slaves.[99] The low country, where the final campaigns of the war were staged, also felt the despoiling hand of the British. In Georgetown County, British forces arrested some thirty persons suspected of disloyalty, confined them on Johns Island, and then burned their houses, devastated their plantations, and seized their slaves, who were sent to labor on the public works at Charleston.[100]

Anxious to placate loyal whites when possible, the British assigned much of the property in land and slaves seized by the army to loyalist families for their use. Although military authorities agreed in principle with the loyalists' claim that they were entitled to some form of remuneration for their support, because of the complexity of the problem the army resisted their demand for large-scale donations of land and slaves and opted instead for a system that treated loyalists as "trustees for the Crown to whose receiver [Cruden] they must be accountable for the profits of it."[101] Informed that

[94] General H. W. Harrington to Major Gen. Gates, September 17, 1780, Clark, *State Records* 14:642.

[95] Wemyss to Cornwallis, September 20, 1780, Cornwallis Papers, PRO30/11/3/80–81.

[96] "Official Correspondence Between Brigadier-General Thomas Sumter and Major-General Nathanael Greene from A.D. 1780 to 1783," *Year-Book City of Charleston, South Carolina, 1899* (Charleston, 1899), 4:135.

[97] Cornwallis to Cruger, August 18, 1780, South Carolina Collection, Peter Force Transcripts, Ser. 7E, Box 63, Library of Congress.

[98] Cornwallis to Cruger, January 16, 1780, PRO30/11/84/66–67. [Notes 98 through 110 refer to the Cornwallis Papers.]

[99] Balfour to Cornwallis, June 24, 1780, PRO30/11/2/191–96.

[100] Moncrief to Balfour, September 22, 1780, PRO30/11/64/89–90.

[101] James Simpson to Cornwallis, September 4, 1780, PRO/11/64/18.

loyalists in the Cheraw Hill area were being harrassed by Marion and others, Cornwallis instructed Lieutenant Colonel Grey to "use your discretion about the suffering inhabitants and have my full permission to put those whose plantations have been burnt, into possession of those belonging to rebels."[102] On Cornwallis's personal orders John Lancaster, who had "rendered important service to the army," and had suffered the destruction of his property as a consequence, was given temporary use of the rebel Thomas Taylor's plantation at the Congarees with two or three slaves and two cows.[103] The inhabitants of the area were warned that if Lancaster and his family were in any way molested, they would be "severely punished."[104] Most of the slaves taken in the area around Ninety Six, including Rutledge's, were also distributed among loyalists, "taking receipts for them, making them responsible when called for." The rest were sent to labor on public works.[105]

Other captured blacks were given to loyalist militia officers as a reward for extraordinary service. The most conspicuous example was that of William Henry Mills, colonel of the Cheraw loyalist militia, who fought with Wemyss in the campaigns down the Black and up the Pee Dee rivers to Cheraw. To compensate Mills for his loss to the rebels of two sawmills, a grist mill, all of his plantation buildings, and fifty-seven slaves, Wemyss gave him one hundred slaves[106] and permission "to stay at Laurens plantation at Santee with my distressed family."[107] Cornwallis later rescinded the order on the grounds that "we cannot yet afford those kind of present." It was, however, the size of the gift to which he objected and not the gift itself, because he left it to Balfour's discretion to "let him have any small proportion you may think proper." Cornwallis found other loyalists more deserving than Mills: "The distress of himself and his family," he continued, "and his sufferings may be great, but when his behaviour is compared with that of many others, his are not [due?] from us any distinguished favors."[108]

The final irony, perhaps, is that when the imperatives of war seemed to require it, the army openly abandoned its pose as liberator by selling some of its captives and using the proceeds to buy supplies for the army. When recommending the sale of some of the blacks captured at Camden, Colonel Balfour stressed to Cornwallis the practical advantages: "Will it not be

[102] Cornwallis to Grey, October 2, 1780, PRO30/11/81/6–7.

[103] Cornwallis to Mr. Spiers, December 12, 1780, PRO30/11/83/41.

[104] Haldane to Mr. Spiers, January 9, 1781, PRO30/11/84/45–46.

[105] Balfour to Cornwallis, June 24, 1780, PRO30/11/2/191–96.

[106] Certificate by Major J. Wemyss of a Gift to Col. Mills, September 26, 1780, PRO30/11/4/231.

[107] William H. Mills to Cornwallis, November 28, 1780, PRO30/11/4/229–30.

[108] Cornwallis to Balfour, December 11, 1780, PRO30/11/83/36–37.

worthwhile," he reasoned, "to convince *Blacke* that he must not fight against us—to sell them and buy shoes for your corps?"[109] It is clear from his instructions to Lieutenant Colonel Charles Grey, a provincial officer in Colonel William Henry Mills's company, to "sell a Negro to help provide for yourself," that Cornwallis felt no moral compunction about the practice.[110]

By resorting to the burning of houses and the confiscation of crops and slaves belonging to the disaffected, Cornwallis had hoped to pacify the country. Instead, he created havoc, leaving a wide swath of bitter enemies and disappointed friends, black and white alike. Far from being intimidated, many of the disaffected were reinspirited. Paul Trapier, who sustained losses totalling almost £5,000, including crops, livestock, plantations, and fifteen slaves whose value he estimated at over £1,000, became actively rebellious and served as captain of the artillery company at Georgetown.[111] When John Postell protested the loss of some of his slaves to the British at Camden, he was told that "my property was in the hands of such as were friends to government, who had the best right to them." When in mid-October Tarleton's dragoons returned to Postell's plantation and "invited all my negroes to come to Camden, promising them rewards if they would and that I would never get them again," Postell broke his parole and joined Marion's brigade.[112]

Soon small bands under local leaders like John Postell, James Postell, Peter Horry, and Hugh Horry, began to spring up everywhere. The coalescing of newly armed patriot bands was further encouraged by Cornwallis's movement into Virginia, which left British outposts in the interior vulnerable. Fanned by the bellows of partisan passions, the war in South Carolina blazed out of control. "The division among the people," wrote the appalled new American commander General Nathanael Greene from his camp on the Pee Dee River, "is much greater than I imagined and the Whigs and Tories persecute each other with little less than savage fury. There is nothing but murders and devastations in every quarter."[113] The situation seemed much the same to British General Charles O'Hara, who from his camp on the banks of the Wateree River near Camden described "the Scenes before me" as "beyond discription wretched, every Misery

[109] Balfour to Cornwallis, September 22, 1780, PRO30/11/64/96–97.

[110] Cornwallis to Grey, October 2, 1780, PRO30/11/81/6–7.

[111] Paul Trapier, Losses Sustained by the Underwritten during the British War in America, Miscellaneous Manuscripts, ser. I, SCHS.

[112] John Postell to Major Hyune, June 24, 1781, South Carolina Collection, Peter Force Transcripts, ser. 7E, Box 63.

[113] From Major General Nathanael Greene, January 10, 1781, Harold C. Syrett and Jacob E. Cooke, eds., *The Papers of Alexander Hamilton*, 7 vols. (New York: Columbia University Press, 1961–87), 2:529.

which the bloodest cruel War ever produced we have constantly before Us." O'Hara, a rugged Irishman, was also repelled by the partisan excesses: "The violence of the passion of these People," he wrote shortly after his introduction to the bloody war in the South, "are beyond every curb of Religion, and Humanity, they are unbounded, and every Hour exhibits dreadfull, wanton Mischiefs, Murders, and Violences of every kind, unheard of before—we find the Country in great Measure abandoned, and the few who venture to remain at home in hourly expectation of being murdered, or striped of all their Property."[114]

The devastation he saw during six months of hard campaigning over some 2,000 miles also shocked Major William Pierce, an aide to General Greene. From High Hills of Santee, Pierce wrote of the destruction "of this southern country" and of the primitive spirit of tribal fanaticism that inspired it: "Such scenes of desolation, bloodshed and deliberate murder I never was a witness to before! Wherever you turn the weeping widow and fatherless child pour out their melancholy tales to wound the feelings of humanity. The two opposite principles of whiggism and toryism have set the people of this country to cutting each other's throats, and scarce a day passes but some poor deluded tory is put to death at his door. For the want of civil government the bands of society are totally disunited, and the people, by copying the manners of the British, have become perfectly savage."[115]

Caught between two fires, slaves who had remained on the plantations were among the victims of the burning partisan passions. Surrounded by the opulent ruins of war, Lewis Morris, a young New Yorker serving as an aide to Greene, sadly confessed that while the army was "enjoying our ease and fattening upon the luxury of the rice plantations" around Charleston, "I envy everything I see, except the poor unhappy blacks who, to the disgrace of human nature, are subject to every species of oppression while we are contending for the rights and liberties of mankind."[116] Morris alluded to the physical, emotional, and political suffering blacks experienced as a result of the war. Although both black and white noncombatants were deeply affected by the conditions of war, scarcities of food and clothing were felt more bitterly by slaves, who could scarcely sustain reductions in either. The whig raiding parties that surged over the low-country plantations "taking off Rice and killing of Hoggs," nearly exhausted food supplies in some areas, causing shortages for whites and severe deprivations

[114] George C. Rogers, Jr., ed. "Letters of Charles O'Hara to the Duke of Grafton," *South Carolina Historical and Geneaological Magazine* 65 (1964): 171.

[115] From William Pierce, July 20, 1781, in "Letters of Major William Pierce to St. George Tucker," *Magazine of American History* 7 (1881): 434.

[116] Lewis Morris, Jr. to Jacob Morris, December 10, 1781, in "Letters to General Lewis Morris," New-York Historical Society, *Collections*, 7 (New York, 1876), 496.

for blacks.[117] Although Francis Marion generally eschewed indiscriminate plundering, the whig partisan band he led through the low-country swamps between the Pee Dee and the Santee rivers, forbade "any Rice should be thrashed or Beat out" in order to prevent it from falling into the hands of the British.[118] Wartime disruptions also made it impossible to produce even the scanty supplies of clothing normally issued to slaves during the cold season. Many slaves like "the Poor Creatures" on George Austin's plantations, which were constantly exposed to harrassing raids, were "obliged to go without their Cloathing" for two consecutive winters.[119]

Half-starved and half-naked, slaves on the devastated plantations had also to live with the constant fear of abduction by a roving partisan band or by one of the belligerents. Throughout the war, slaves were stolen back and forth by both sides. Beginning in 1781, Sumter and Pickens systematized plundering operations as part of the pay and recruitment procedures of the whig militia. Under "Sumter's Law," slaves and goods seized from backcountry farms and plantations were used to attract recruits and to pay officers and men. For ten months of service, each lieutenant colonel was promised three grown slaves and one small one; each major, three adult slaves, and so on, diminishing by rank so that each private received one adult slave.[120] To form a body of state cavalry, Sumter seized some four hundred slaves from loyalist estates along the Congaree River;[121] similar seizures were made in Sumter's name along the Black River.[122] By such methods Sumter alone raised eleven hundred men, a substantial number of whom were from as far away as Virginia and North Carolina. In lieu of payment, two-thirds of all of the goods taken from tories were divided among the officers and men raised by Sumter's system.[123] Although some

[117] Cracked rice, considered unsuitable for export, dried peas, beans and corn were the basic staples in the slave diet, see Robert M. Weir, *Colonial South Carolina. A History* (Millwood, N.Y.: KTO Press, 1983), 187. Rice was constantly being seized by both sides, see for example, Josiah Smith to George Appleby, December 2, 1780, Smith Lettercopy Book, who reported that 3,500 bushels, most of what was produced at George Austin's Pee Dee plantation, was impressed by the Continental horse. In Smith Lettercopy Book, March 15, 1781, Smith again complained of raiding parties "taking off Rice, etc."

[118] Smith Lettercopy Book, SHC *Coll.*

[119] Ibid.

[120] Richard Maxwell Brown, *Strains of Violence. Historical Studies of American Violence and Vigilantism* (New York: Oxford University Press, 1975), 78.

[121] Thomas Sumter to the South Carolina Delegates, May 24, 1781, Papers of the Continental Congress, M247, reel 42, item 36, vol. 1:199; "Colonel Robert Gray's Observations on the War in Carolina," *South Carolina Historical and Genealogical Magazine* 11(1910): 152.

[122] Petition of Sylvester Dunn, November 18, 1792, General Assembly Papers, Petitions 1776 (1782)–1830, Record Group 0010, ser. 003, Petition of James Montgomery, Comptroller General, Accounts Audited of Claims Growing Out of the Revolution, 1778–1804, RG 0015, ser. 003, South Carolina State Archives, Columbia.

[123] Brown, *Strains of Violence*, 78; chap. 25, Clark, *State Records* 24:338; Porter v. Dunn,

whig partisans, among them Francis Marion, declined to use "Sumter's Law," countless slaves on low-country plantations shared a similar fate.

Enervated by the hundreds of small victories scored by the whig partisans, the British began to evacuate the chain of posts that had given them command of the Carolina backcountry. With their retreat from Ninety Six in July, they gave up the last post, and, thereafter, British rule was practically confined to Charleston and its immediate vicinity. The whigs, in possession of most of the rest of the state, gained the heights along the rivers leading to Charleston. From that commanding position they launched frequent raids against the sequestered estates that still struggled under John Cruden's direction to survive. Continuously exposed to guerrilla attacks, the sequestered estates and the contraband workers were particularly vulnerable. Because protection was the key to successful operation of the sequestered plantations, Cruden pleaded for regular troops to defend his shrinking holdings. Reluctant to commit scarce manpower to that purpose, the military command denied the commissioner's request, leaving Cruden to his own resources.

In October 1781, with the approval of Colonel Balfour, he embodied a corps of three companies of cavalry and assigned them to the threatened districts. After the news of Cornwallis's surrender at Yorktown, however, the South Carolina countryside was overrun with partisan bands and Cruden's corps of cavalry had to be disbanded. Stubbornly refusing to abandon the sequestered property, Cruden built and equipped galleys and manned them with the dismounted troops. These he stationed along the Cooper and the Santee rivers and along the creeks contiguous to the most valuable estates to cover the shipment of produce in small craft and to convoy them to Charleston.[124] On one expedition up the Cooper River to retrieve some valuable magazines of grain and provisions, a schooner carrying one of the companies of loyalists who made up Cruden's corps turned keel up and drowned most of the men on board.[125]

Discouraged but not defeated, Cruden devised one more plan to protect the upriver estates, this time by leading an offensive against the American privateers who hovered in the shallow inlets of South Carolina and Georgia pouncing on British trading vessels and plundering sequestered estates. He proposed to Colonel Balfour to raise at his own expense a guerrilla corps of seven hundred men to be recruited from "the people that were employed by me in various parts of the province," and from the North and

---

1 Bay 53 (1787), Elihu Hall Bay, *Reports of Cases Argued in the Superior Courts of Law in the State of South-Carolina Since the Revolution, 1783–1804* (New York: I. Riley, 1809), 1:53–58.

[124] Cruden, *Report*, 12–15; see also Cruden to Col. Stewart, October 28, 1781, Cornwallis Papers, PRO30/11/7/10–11.

[125] E. Alfred Jones, ed., *The Journal of Alexander Chesney, a South Carolina Loyalist in the Revolution and After* (Columbus: Ohio State University Press, 1920), 27.

South Carolina refugees. By "joining a few companies of determined Negroes" with them, Cruden believed that his "corps of Independent Marriners" could, by operating vessels in shallow draft, use hit-and-run tactics on the rebel privateers in their own secluded havens. Although Cruden asked for neither rank nor remuneration "until your excellency thinks I am entitled to them," Balfour refused his offer on the grounds that "he did not think himself authorized to accept of the offer without [Clinton's] previous sanction."[126] Rebuffed again, Cruden at last abandoned every hope of success. By December 1781, the remnants of his corps and what remained of the sequestered blacks had taken refuge in Charleston.[127]

Although the American recovery of South Carolina was all but complete, British forces under a new commander, General Alexander Leslie, continued to hold the capital until December 1782.[128] The brief period of relative calm that followed the demise of royal authority was, however, punctuated by the reprisal operations carried out by both sides. Acts passed by the South Carolina assembly elected under writs issued by Governor John Rutledge in August 1781, led to renewed violence, much of it directed against blacks. The new assembly that convened in Jacksonborough (Jacksonboro) on January 18, 1782, elected John Mathews to replace the aging and ailing Rutledge.[129] In February John Laurens introduced a motion calling for the embodiment under white officers of twenty-five hundred slaves to be drafted from loyalist estates. Laurens's motion failed but confiscation and amercement acts were subsequently approved by the assembly and 237 loyalist estates were designated for confiscation and forty-eight others for amercement.[130] Plagued by a lack of manpower, the assembly also approved a plan to spur enlistments by promising a bounty in slaves to new recruits.[131] Accordingly, all white males between the ages of sixteen and forty-five who enlisted were promised for each year of service the bounty of "one sound Negro" between the ages of ten and forty.[132]

Predictably the seizures that followed brought loyalist demands for re-

[126] Cruden to Clinton, February 22, 1782, in Catherine S. Crary, ed., *The Price of Loyalty. Tory Writings from the Revolutionary Era* (New York: McGraw-Hill, 1973), 292.

[127] Mr. Cruden's Narrative, Cornwallis Papers, PRO30/11/7/38–43.

[128] Leslie was ordered by Cornwallis to take command in Charleston in July, 1781; see Cornwallis to Clinton, July 26, 1781, Cornwallis Papers, PRO30/11/74/51–54. Leslie sailed for Charleston July 25 and arrived November 6 with his suite and a corps of artillery, *Royal South-Carolina Gazette*, November 7, 1781.

[129] Moultrie, *Memoirs* 2:303–4.

[130] Ramsay, *History of the Revolution* 2:268.

[131] Theodora J. Thompson, ed., The State Records of South Carolina, *Journals of the House of Representatives of South Carolina, 1783–1784* (Columbia: University of South Carolina Press, 1977), 57–58, 62, 101, 117, 125–27.

[132] An Act to procure recruits and prevent desertions, February 26, 1782, Papers of the Continental Congress, M247, reel 86, item 72, p. 550.

prisals. In response to one loyalist demand that "if the rebels will give one negro for one year's service, let us give two,"[133] General Leslie ordered a detachment of cavalry under Major Thomas Fraser and of militia led by a Colonel Thomas [?] Young to proceed from Daniels Island, ostensibly to recover slaves taken earlier from their loyalist owners in St. Thomas parish. In his orders to Fraser, however, Leslie made it clear that "the principal business to prosecute is the collecting of the Slaves who belong to those in arms against the British government." He instructed Fraser to publicize "in particular to the Negroes," the fact that the mission was retaliatory, but that "it is the determination of the General never to return them to their masters, but to take care of them and their families."[134]

Although the loyalist-owned slaves in question were not recovered, Fraser's mission was deemed successful. "We have taken," the *Royal Gazette* boasted, "at least three times the number of those we lost. The Rebels will therefore find that *their* Estates, not those of the Loyalists have been confiscated by the Assembly at Jacksonborough."[135] In April, after taking "a considerable booty in Negroes" on the south side of the Cooper River,[136] Leslie dispatched troops to the Santee, both to provide protection for the loyalists there and, as he warned General Greene, "in seizing the Negroes of your friends, that restitution may be thereby made to such of ours as may suffer under these oppressive and ruinous resolutions."[137] Leslie apparently made good on his threat because in August Governor Mathews reported sightings of the British "plundering fleet" around Georgetown. "I am in hopes," Mathews fretted, "they will not be so successful there as they were at Santee."[138] The following day British raiding parties burned William Somersall's plantation on the Ashley River and carried off his slaves; "and it is said," Governor Mathews informed Arthur Middleton, "they also burnt your father's, and carried off his negroes."[139]

Despite recurring rumors that the British intended to arm their black allies,[140] few were actually enlisted, although some did fill a variety of ancillary functions. Armed and mounted black soldiers were employed by the

---

[133] *Royal Gazette*, March 27, 1782.

[134] Leslie to Major Thomas Fraser, March 27, 1782, Leslie Letter Book, Emmet Collection, 15667.

[135] *Royal Gazette*, March 30, 1782.

[136] John Mathews to R. R. Livingston, April 4, 1782, Papers of the Continental Congress, M247, reel 99, item 78, 16:291.

[137] Leslie to Greene, April 4, 1782, CO5/109/338.

[138] Gov. Mathews to Gen. Marion, August 24, 1782, Peter Horry Papers, 1779–1807, S7E, Box 22, Peter Force Transcripts, Force Coll.

[139] Gov. Mathews to Arthur Middleton, August 25, 1782, 38–43–4, Arthur Middleton Papers, 1767–1783, SCHS.

[140] Intelligence Report to Gov. Caswell from John Penn, Thomas Burke, Allen Jones, enclosure in January 21, 1780, Saunders, *CRNC* 15:324.

British to capture deserters.[141] Blacks were systematically employed as plunderers by the British, both to forage for the army and as a psychological expedient to intimidate the opposition.[142] On the rare occasions when slaves joined the regular army, they were usually formed into auxiliary corps and were detailed for duties in support of combat operations. By 1782, however, the talk of arming black troops, largely speculative and general before, was a subject for more than academic argument. The dramatic effects of disease, particularly epidemic yellow fever and malaria among British troops in the South and in the West Indies, had already seriously compromised Britain's ability to wage war in the South. Malarial outbreaks had contributed significantly to British decisions to abandon outposts such as Ebenezer and Abercorn,[143] and extraordinary mortality generally was rapidly thinning the ranks.

During the final bitter months of British occupation, General Alexander Leslie broke away from the conventions of warfare and began forming black troops. The first reports that several black companies were being raised began circulating soon after Leslie's arrival in Charleston.[144] By the spring of 1782 some seven hundred black soldiers were reportedly under arms.[145] There is no evidence that they fought in an organized fashion, but sometimes battle came to them. On April 21 a Captain Neil of the Partisan Legion reported falling in "with one of ye British negro Captains and his Troop." Charged by the patriots, the black troops broke and fled, which suggests perhaps that they were outnumbered or that they had not undergone much training.[146] In the last engagement between the partisan leader Francis Marion and a British force, known as "the affair at Wadboo," Marion's force was attacked by a hundred British horse and "some Coloured Dragoons" led by Major Thomas Fraser. When the rapidly charging horse approached within thirty yards, Marion's force opened fire and the British troop retreated.[147] Armed blacks also did battle in less important contests, such as Fort Dreadnought near Augusta. Among the prisoners taken when the fort capitulated in May 1781, were sixty-one slaves, "principally armed," according to one patriot report.[148]

[141] Wemys to Andre, February 27, 1780, February 29, 1780, Clinton Papers.

[142] Sumter to Marion, February 20, 1781, Horry Papers, Series 7E, Box 22, Peter Force Transcripts, Force Coll.

[143] Frey, *British Soldier*, 42–43.

[144] Nathanael Greene to the president of Congress, December 9, 1781, M247, reel 175, item 155, 2:373, Papers of the Continental Congress.

[145] Greene to Marion, April 15, 1782, Gibbs, ed., *Documentary History* 2:164.

[146] "Extracts from the Journal of Lt. John Bell Tilden, Second Pennsylvania Line, 1781–1782," *Pennsylvania Magazine of History and Biography* 19 (1895): 225.

[147] Francis Marion to John Mathews, August 30, 1782, 38–43–6, Middleton Papers.

[148] John Rudolph, Report of Prisoners Taken at Fort Dreadnought, May 21, 1781, M247, reel 175, item 155, 2:109, Papers of the Continental Congress.

During the last six months of British occupation, Leslie's Black Dragoons terrorized the inhabitants of the Goose Creek area north of Charleston by "daily committing the most horrible depredations and murders on the defenceless parts of our Country."[149] Although few in numbers, their nightly raids through Goose Creek and down the Cooper River haunted the imagination of whites. Despite the efforts of state authorities to track them down, the black soldiers managed to maintain an "infamous traffic" in livestock, which kept the British markets at Charleston "daily supplied with the greatest plenty of everything they want."[150] From the patriot point of view, the knowledge that hundreds of self-liberated slaves were in possession of weapons was, as General Sumter put it, "sufficient to rouse and fix the resentment and detestation of every American who possesses common feelings."[151] Belatedly, the British army came to a different conclusion.

Impressed by the conduct of his black dragoons in South Carolina, General Leslie formed them into autonomous units for service in Florida and the West Indies, where Leslie observed "their past services will engage the grateful attention of Government to which they will continue to be useful."[152] Their experience with black troops in the American Revolution also convinced other officers that the best solution to British military problems in the West Indies was to enlist slaves by offering them freedom in exchange for military service. As military governor of Jamaica, Archibald Campbell sent recruiters to Charleston shortly before the evacuation to raise a battalion from among free blacks and "people of color" to aid regular troops in the defense of Jamaica.[153] General John Vaughan also advocated the addition of black regiments to the regular British army for service in Saint Domingue during the French Revolution and Napoleonic Wars.[154] Ultimately black troops such as these became part of the standing professional slave army upon which Britain relied increasingly after 1790 for support of its military establishment in the West Indies.

As the outlook for British arms in North America became steadily more desperate, the proposition of using slaves was raised again by John Cruden, whose reliance on black troops to protect the sequestered estates had convinced him of their military capacity. In a remarkable letter to Lord Dun-

---

[149] C. C. Pinckney to Arthur Middleton, August 13, 1782, 38–43–1, Papers of the Continental Congress.

[150] Gov. Mathews to Gen. Marion, August 29, 1782, Horry Papers, Peter Force Transcripts, Force Coll.

[151] Sumter to Marion, February 20, 1781, Horry Papers.

[152] Leslie to Carleton, July 19, 1782, Leslie Letter Book, Emmet Collection 15628.

[153] Archibald Campbell to Carleton, December 6, 1782, December 21, 1782, Carleton Papers (BHP), vols. 56, 57, PRO 30/55.

[154] Craton, *Testing the Chains*, 168–69.

more dated January 5, 1782, Cruden proposed to raise and arm ten thousand South Carolina slaves to conquer and possess the South "with its own force." Aware that it would be claimed that the idea of arming slaves was "repugnant to humanity," Cruden responded with an argument based on military necessity: that it was impossible to maintain European troops in the low country during the "Sickly season" and that "no country on earth, at such a distance, could support the loss of men" that Britain had sustained since 1780. As against the arguments that the measure raised the specter of emancipation and threatened the total disintegration of society, Cruden made a most revealing response based on political expediency: " 'Tis only changing one master for another; and let it be clearly understood that they are to serve the King for ever, and that those slaves who are not taken for his Majesty's service are to remain on the plantation, and perform, as usual, the labor of the field." Addressing himself to the anticipated dangers and consequences of such a measure he continued: "So far from ruining the property, I do aver, and experience will, I doubt not, justify the assertion, that, by embodying the most hardy, intrepid, and determined blacks, they would not only keep the rest in good order, but, by being disciplined and under command, be prevented from raising cabals, tumults, and even rebellion, what I think might be expected soon after a peace."

Cruden's boast that Britain's employment of slaves had helped to prevent a slave rebellion was correct, but his prediction that "so far from making even our lukewarm friends and secret foes greater enemies by this measure, I will, by taking their slaves, engage to make them better friends," was completely mistaken. Vast in conception and of profound significance for the future of the plantation economy of the lower South, the British program of pacification defended by Cruden was, from a political standpoint, an utter failure. It was absurdly deficient in its most important aspect, that relating to the massive employment of slaves. Equally disastrous for Britain's political aspirations in the South was the failure of Cruden and of British planners generally to recognize the importance of property to a revolutionary generation solemnly committed to the natural rights arguments of English philosophers from Harrington and Locke to Price, who had proclaimed property to be a "natural" right associated with each individual's right to life. Cruden perceived that "Property, all the world over, is dear to mankind," and that slaveowners in South Carolina "are as much wedded to it as in any other" country, and he put that argument forward as the logical and fundamental justification for "Striking at the root of all property, and making the wealth and riches of the enemy the means of bringing them to obedience."[155] The "root of all property" in the South

[155] Cruden to the Right Honorable Earl Dunmore, etc., January 5, 1782, in Livermore, *Historical Research*, 142–45.

meant slaves, who accounted for almost half of the total physical wealth of the region.[156] By "striking at the root," however ineffectually, British slave policy shook the structure of society to its very foundation, not by what it actually accomplished but by what it clearly demonstrated might be.

From the beginning, the architects of Britain's Southern strategy had been aware that without the support of propertied white Americans, British military efforts would fail.[157] Nowhere in the South were the possibilities of success greater than in Georgia and South Carolina, both of which had strong enclaves of loyalist strength as well as a high proportion of persons who were not irrevocably committed to resistance.[158] Britain's failure to win their allegiance and conquer the South was due to a number of reasons, including the failure of the army to provide adequate support for the counterrevolutionary activities of loyalists as well as the failure to reconstitute regular civil authority in occupied areas.[159] But the Southern strategy was fatally weakened by the political and military policy embodied in Clinton's Philipsburg proclamation. Despite deep divisions among Carolinians on some major issues, there was near unanimity on matters involving their slaves.[160] Vastly outnumbered, the white population lived in perpetual fear of a slave rising, which threatened both their lives and their fortunes. Clinton's policy of limited emancipation and the response of slaves to it shocked the entire system and turned a potentially loyal area into a hostile countryside. Ironically, although the British army's invitation to slaves and its wholesale appropriation of them seemed to foretell the destruction of the plantation regime, in fact emancipation as practiced by the army kept alive the plantation economy to a degree not hitherto recognized and was a major factor in preventing the outbreak of a slave rebellion. In a sense, then, the British army acted as both a sword and a shield, challenging and conserving the system at the same time.

For slaves too the war was a paradox. Clinton's Philipsburg proclamation held out the luminous hope of freedom, but time and events made it clear that the British war aim was not directed at the overthrow of the slave regime. Indeed the moral hypocrisy of the military command gave slaves good reason to doubt that the British offer of freedom could be counted upon at all. Slaves were thus faced with a fatal dilemma: to remain on the plantation and enjoy the relative freedom and comfort that the war allowed

[156] Alice Hanson Jones, ed., *American Colonial Wealth: Documents and Methods,* 3 vols. (New York: Arno Press, 1978), 3:1940, 1947.

[157] Nadelhaft, *Disorders of War*, 51; Pancake, *This Destructive War*, 25–30.

[158] Brown, *King's Friends*, 213–46.

[159] Pancake, *This Destructive War*, 243.

[160] Nadelhaft, *Disorders of War*, 8. I have argued elsewhere that the failure of the British army in America was also due to its general inability to conduct a political war; see Sylvia R. Frey, "British Armed Forces and the American Victory," in John Ferling, ed., *The World Turned Upside Down* (Westport, Conn.: Greenwood Press, 1988), 165–83.

to some, or to suffer the terrible physical deprivations that it imposed on most, and in the end still be a slave; or to risk betrayal or death in a military camp or at the hands of an outraged captor, and in the end perhaps still to be a slave. Although no precise figures are available, George Abbot Hall, a Charleston merchant and collector of customs, calculated that over twenty thousand slaves, perhaps a 'quarter of South Carolina's slave population, defied the dangers and ran away, the quintessential expression of the slave's desire for freedom. The majority were either removed from South Carolina at the British evacuation or died within British lines of smallpox, camp fevers, or other diseases.[161] Although trampled at will by both white belligerents, the tender plants of hope and passion that inspired their unprecedented challenge to the slave regime survived and were successfully cultivated in a different field in the postwar period.

[161] Enclosure 2 in From Ralph Izard, June 10, 1785, in Boyd, *Papers of Jefferson* 8:199.

FIVE

THE ENDING OF THE WAR: TRAGEDY

AND TRIUMPH AT YORKTOWN

FROM SOON AFTER the Revolution began and for some time after it ended, the Chesapeake was the scene of regular raiding operations by the British. Never occupied by them for extended periods,
it was selected instead for periodic harrassment to draw attention away
from major offensive operations elsewhere. Although the primary objective was the destruction of magazines and stores, the raids were also spoiling operations, the plunder from which was usually distributed as a reward
to the impoverished soldiers and sailors who served on each expedition.
The tobacco warehouses and granaries, the magazines and foundries, the
large herds of livestock and the vast numbers of slaves that constituted the
economic resources of the area were the prey that the raiding parties fed
upon.

The fertile tidewater peninsulas that supported the vigorous economies
of eighteenth century Virginia and Maryland were formed by the waters
of Chesapeake Bay. One hundred and ninety-five miles long, its ragged
shores were cut by forty-eight principal rivers and creeks. Although large
swamps and marshes made some of the area unsuitable for cultivation and
soil erosion made other sections barren, good agricultural lands still
abounded and produced rich yields of tobacco, wheat and corn for export
and subsistence crops of fruit and vegetables.[1] Up to the Revolution exports from the Chesapeake accounted for nearly 50 percent of all colonial
trade. Tobacco alone made up over 90 percent of the value of Chesapeake
exports and over 50 percent of colonial exports to Britain, approximately
85 percent of which was reshipped to the Netherlands, Germany, and
France.[2] Although the tobacco trade continued to expand up to the outbreak of the war, a gradual transition to grain cultivation was under way as
early as the 1760s. By the eve of the Revolution, corn and wheat exports
from Maryland's Eastern Shore alone amounted to 720,000 bushels, most
of which was transported overland to Philadelphia and Annapolis for

[1] For a thorough discussion of Maryland's eighteenth-century economy, see Clemens, *Atlantic Economy*, and Hoffman, *Spirit of Dissension*; for Virginia see Isaac, *Transformation of
Virginia*.

[2] Jacob M. Price, "The Economic Growth of the Chesapeake and the European Market,
1697–1775," *Journal of Economic History* 24 (1964): 496, 500, 501.

transshipment to southern Europe and the Caribbean.[3] The nature of the Atlantic trade determined that settlement remain close to navigable waterways.

The population of Virginia, which was divided almost equally among blacks and whites, was concentrated along the system of waterways that reached well into the interior. The center of the black population was the region south of the Rappahannock extending to the James River. There the slave population accounted for 49 percent or better of the total population. In the area south of the James and in the adjacent piedmont counties, slaves made up from 36 to 48 percent of the total population.[4] In Maryland the slave population, which constituted only 25 percent of the total population, was concentrated in Calvert, Prince Georges, Charles, Anne Arundel, and St. Marys counties on the Western Shore, and in Queen Annes, Kent, and Somerset counties on the Eastern Shore.[5] During the revolutionary war these areas were plagued by British military operations and by the relentless plundering of privateers and small armed parties that sailed at will in the bay. Although much of the Chesapeake escaped the large-scale destruction that marked the ferocious internecine warfare in Georgia and South Carolina, the punishing raids of the British wreaked economic havoc along the lower James and York rivers and along the Potomac and Chesapeake shores. The massive exodus of slaves during the war years hastened the decline of the tobacco industry, which was already reeling from the loss of British market facilities.

Following Dunmore's expulsion in 1776, the Chesapeake was not invaded for better than a year, although the area was regularly raided by British barges and by privateers and roving tory bands. Private armed vessels known as privateers played a major role in most eighteenth century wars. Commissioned by the belligerent powers, their main business was plunder. A British decision made during the Anglo-French wars to allow privateersmen and the officers and crews of royal warships to divide among themselves the proceeds of any prize vessel they might capture, greatly stimulated the growth of privateering.[6] Because the network of navigable waterways that made up the Chesapeake tidewater opened up much of the inland region to waterborne traffic, privateering played an important part in the revolutionary war in the region. So too did tory operations on the

[3] Clemens, *Atlantic Economy*, 174, 177.

[4] Marc Egnal, "The Origins of the Revolution in Virginia: A Reinterpretation," *William and Mary Quarterly*, 3d ser., 37 (1980): 406, Map 1.

[5] Hoffman, *Spirit of Dissension*, 11. During the colonial period, Maryland imported less than half the number of slaves as did Virginia; see Darold D. Wax, "Black Immigrants: The Slave Trade in Colonial Maryland," *Maryland Historical Magazine* 73 (1978): 35.

[6] Arthur Pierce Middleton, *Tobacco Coast. A Maritime History of Chesapeake Bay in the Colonial Era* (Newport News, Va.: Newport Museum, 1953), 336, 344.

bay. First inaugurated by Dunmore, tory partisan bands plundered alongside the British armies that regularly invaded Virginia and kept up continuous petty warfare in the intervals between invasions. The main targets of British and tory activity were tobacco, produce and livestock, and slaves, upon whose labor the Chesapeake economy depended.

The interruption of the tobacco trade with Britain had led to a glut of tobacco in the Chesapeake and a resulting shortage of money with which to buy war materials and support a navy for bay defence. Secret negotiations with France to restore the tobacco trade promised to relieve the sagging public credit and win French aid for the American war effort.[7] Mindful of the threat of French intervention, Britain was anxious to prevent the reopening of the tobacco trade and at the same time to suppress the interstate trade in foodstuffs, which was developing in response to the growing demands upon the upper Chesapeake to supply food for the American armies in the north and south. Late in December 1776, Admiral Richard Howe therefore ordered Commodore William Hotham to establish a naval station in the bay and from it to operate a coastal patrol to stop the flow of all supplies that might sustain the revolutionary war effort.[8]

The blockade that began in January 1777, did not completely shut down bay traffic, but it did slow it considerably. It also stirred black hopes for freedom. In February British vessels took on board approximately three hundred runaways from Northumberland, Gloucester, and Lancaster counties in Virginia.[9] In April a detachment patrolling off the coast near Lewes, Delaware, took on some runaway slaves and stimulated tory disturbances in Sussex County.[10] Local concern over the success of the British blockade and the signs of restiveness among blacks and dissident whites was intensified by reports of an impending British expedition to the Chesapeake. Alerted by Richard Henry Lee, a delegate from Virginia, the Continental Congress resolved that all livestock should be removed from the vulnerable coasts of Virginia and Maryland and that general security measures should be taken.[11] Although the alarm was sounded prematurely, six months later an expedition led by British General Sir William Howe entered the bay for an amphibious assault on Philadelphia.

Howe's fleet, consisting of over two hundred and sixty sail with several

---

[7] J. A. Robinson, "British Invade the Chesapeake, 1777," in Ernest McNeill Eller, ed., *Chesapeake Bay in the American Revolution* (Centreville, Md.: Tidewater Publishers, 1981), 357.

[8] Ibid., 358.

[9] Quarles, *Negro in the American Revolution*, 117.

[10] William Adair, "The Revolutionary War Diary of William Adair," Harold B. Hancock, ed., *Delaware History* 13 (1968): 158.

[11] Continental Congress, February, 1777, Maryland State Papers, Rainbow Series, Red Book 6:32, Library of Congress, Microfilms.

merchant ships and nearly a dozen privateers following closely in its wake, reached Chesapeake Bay in mid-August. For eight days the fleet, forming a line that extended for seven or eight miles, advanced slowly up the bay. The sight of the massive fleet with hundreds of sails spread out against the blue of the summer sky, left white inhabitants "exceedingly terrified." In response to urgent requests by the Continental Congress "to remove all boats and other crafts, provisions, grain, naval and military stores, provender, cattle and all live-stock, waggons, carts and horses in the way of the enemy's march, to places of safety and to destroy what cannot be removed in due time,"[12] many of the fleeing inhabitants gathered up "the best of their belongings" and destroyed what they could not carry. Those who remained, noted an English officer aboard the fleet, "had the melancholy prospect of seeing everything taken from them," as Howe's army "like Savages lay waste ye Country at ye Head of Chesapeake."[13]

Alternately detained by continuous calms or driven off course by strong head winds, Howe's fleet had taken five weeks and two days to make the voyage from Sandy Hook at the entrance to New York harbor to Cape Henry at the mouth of Chesapeake Bay. In the hot, crowded holds of the military transports the troops succumbed to the putrid and bilious fevers that were common to the region. Before they landed on August 25 at the head of Elk River on Maryland's Western Shore, twenty-seven men had died and one hundred and seventy horses had perished and the rest were "miserably emaciated" by the long voyage.[14] As they emptied out of the stinking transports, the sick and frustrated army of eighteen thousand began the campaign to take Philadelphia "by plundering and irregularity of every kind."[15] Eager to rally support for the Crown, Howe ordered two men hanged and had five severely whipped for plundering.[16] But systematic foraging by the army greatly distressed the counties of the upper bay, particularly Kent, Cecil, and Harford.[17] Horses, the main means of travel

[12] Ibid., August 22, 1777.

[13] For German and British accounts, see Bernhard A. Uhlendorf and Edna Vosper, eds., "Letters of Major Baurmeister during the Philadelphia Campaign, 1777–1778," *Pennsylvania Magazine of History and Biography* 59 (1935): 398–99; The Hon. Mrs. C. Stuart-Wortley, ed., *A Prime Minister and His Son. From the Correspondence of the 3d Earl of Bute and of Lieutenant-General the Hon. Charles Stuart, K.B.* (London: John Murray, 1925), 114, 116. See also Adair, "Revolutionary War Diary," 83, 162.

[14] Ambrose Serle, *The American Journal of Ambrose Serle, Secretary to Lord Howe, 1776–1778*, Edward H. Tatum, ed. (San Marino, Calif.: Huntington Library, 1943), 246; Carl Leopold Baurmeister, *The Revolution in America. Confidential Letters and Journals, 1776–1784, of Adjutant General Major Baurmeister of the Hessian Forces*, Bernhard A. Uhlendorf, trans. (New Brunswick, N.J., 1957), 98.

[15] Stuart-Wortley, *Prime Minister*, 116.

[16] Serle, *American Journal*, 245; Uhlendorf and Vosper, "Letters of Major Baurmeister," 400.

[17] See, for example, Aquila Hall, Jr. to [Governor Thomas Johnson], August 23, 1777,

for Maryland planters, were seized by the invaders to replace the draught horses lost on the voyage. The large herds of cattle, swine, and sheep kept by most Eastern Shore planters to meet the food and clothing needs of their slaves,[18] were rounded up by army drovers for delivery to the commissariat, where they were slaughtered to provide fresh meat for the troops.[19] Acres of trees that had survived the wasteful efforts of Maryland farmers to cut or burn fields out of the forest, were now cut by hundreds of soldiers for use as fuel by the army.[20]

Partly perhaps because the British army had as yet no official policy about blacks, and partly because Howe's fleet was inaccessible to runaways much of the time, slave defections were few during the first British invasion of the Chesapeake. Although the fleet moved up the bay in leisurely fashion, sailing at flood tide, anchoring at ebb tide, the width of the bay at the mouth and in the entire lower region was such that the fleet was barely visible from either shore. Only when it reached the Patuxent, where the bay narrows, did the distance between either shoreline and the fleet become relatively small. Even then only a strong swimmer or someone expert in handling a canoe or skiff could hope to survive the buffeting of the waves and the strong tidal current.

As the great flotilla slid past slave-rich Anne Arundel County on the Western Shore and Queen Anne and Kent counties on the Eastern Shore, "Scarce a white Person was to be seen," although "negroes appeared in great abundance." At several points when the fleet sailed very close to shore or to one of the numerous islands that dot the bay, slaves, in a desperate gamble for freedom, fled to it, swimming through the tossing waters or fleeing in fragile craft stolen from their masters.[21] After the troops landed at Elk Ferry, the Maryland and Delaware militias turned out in force to intercept the forage parties and to prevent desertions by slaves and white servants or other disaffected persons. Companies of militia were stationed along the broad, shallow rivers above the Patapsco to "watch there and to collect all the cannows [sic] and boats."[22] Small scouting parties of militia, one of which discovered the bodies of five slaves "drove ashore that was drowned going to the fleet," also patrolled the area.[23] The interlacing rivers

---

Maryland State Papers, Red Book 18:114. John Davis' Account Book, 1751–1782, MS1475, Maryland Historical Society, Baltimore, Md. (hereafter cited as MHS).

[18] Paul G. E. Clemens, "The Operation of an Eighteenth-Century Chesapeake Tobacco Plantation," *Agricultural History* 49 (1975): 526–27.

[19] Uhlendorf and Vosper, "Letters of Major Baurmeister," 400.

[20] Aquila Hall, Jr. to [Governor Johnson], September 13, 1777, Maryland State Papers, Red Book 18:46.

[21] Serle, *American Journal*, 244, 249, 250.

[22] Aquila Hall, Jr. to [Governor Johnson], August 28, 1777, Maryland State Papers, Rainbow Series, Red Book 18:91.

[23] Ibid. See also Thomas Jones to Governor Johnson, August 30, 1777, 14:80.

and thickly wooded shores were, however, impossible to secure absolutely and the number of runaways increased substantially during the British presence.

As word of the British presence spread up and down the bay, slaves became bolder in their quest for freedom. When early in September the fleet, because of logistical problems, was forced to double back over its original route to Newcastle, Delaware,[24] Kent County authorities posted two militia companies "to stop the Negroes flocking down from the interior parts of the country."[25] Excited by the British approach, blacks in Leonardtown in St. Marys County became "very insolent." Fearing mass escapes or worse, county officials ordered all canoes within a mile of navigable waterways to be secured or destroyed. One company of militia was sent to guard the mouth of the Patuxent River, a second was stationed on the bay near Point Lookout.[26]

Those slaves who reached the British fleet safely were, to the dismay of Maryland planters, welcomed aboard with promises of "fine cloaths and other inducements."[27] These slaves were probably taken to Philadelphia where they were formed into a company of pioneers. Dressed in white shirts and trousers, with sailor jackets and great coats, they were assigned to "attend the Scavengers," and "to assist in clearing the Streets and Removing all Newsiences [sic] being thrown into the Streets."[28] Some undoubtedly fell into the hands of the merchant vessels, of which there were several in Howe's fleet, or were taken by one of the dozen or so privateers that trailed behind. These slaves probably were sold into slavery in the West Indies. Crewmen on the merchant vessels reportedly "boasted they would make their Fortunes by selling them in the West Indies that they were kicked and cuffed on every occasion."[29] According to the Virginia *Gazette* the privateers usually lay behind the fleet as it moved up the bay and "then run along shore, and into the unguarded rivers and plunder the inhabitants. Negroes are their chief object, whom they intend to sell in the West Indies."[30]

The withdrawal of Howe's army to Philadelphia put a temporary end to the invasion threat to the Chesapeake. But ships detached from the British

---

[24] Robinson, "British Invade the Chesapeake," in Eller, *Chesapeake Bay*, 369–70.

[25] William Paca to Governor Johnson, September 26, 1777, Maryland State Papers, Rainbow Series, Red Book 4562–1, Maryland Hall of Records, Annapolis, Md.

[26] Richard Barnes to Governor Johnson, September 15, 1777, Maryland State Papers, Red Book 4580B–82.

[27] Benjamin Rumsey to Governor Johnson, Maryland State Papers, Red Book 4561–69.

[28] General Sir William Howe, Orderly Books, March 22, 1778, William L. Clements Library.

[29] Benjamin Rumsey to Governor Johnson, September 6, 1777, Maryland State Papers, Red Book 4:67.

[30] *Virginia Gazette* (Purdie), September 26, 1777.

fleet continued to harrass bay and riverfront plantations throughout 1777 and 1778. Early in December 1777, the *Phoenix* and the *Emerald* accompanied by two tenders were discovered lying in the Potomac between Sandy Point and Quantico Sound. Although their immediate purpose was to purchase provisions, which sympathetic Marylanders in the lower counties willingly sold them for sterling money,[31] they also took on board a number of fugitive slaves, five of whom managed to elude the militia shore patrols only to drown in their efforts to reach the vessels.[32]

The presence of British cruisers in the bay in the spring of 1778 again provoked large numbers of runaways from Somerset County. When residents of the county requested a flag of truce to recover their property, however, the Maryland Council of Safety refused. After noting that "we have many applications like yours," the council explained its refusal on the grounds that "the Enemy would not restore them, unless their Masters make concessions which no American ought to make."[33] Sporadic outbreaks of toryism and raids by British cruisers continued to occur in the lower counties of Maryland's Eastern Shore, where loyalists were in a majority. The militia was successful in quashing the local risings but was unable to put an end to the harrassing raids of the tory guerrilla bands that regularly plundered farms along the tidal rivers and creeks to secure provisions for the British. In the upper bay, Queen Annes and Kent counties were ravaged by a tory band led by Cheney or China Clows, the Delaware loyalist.[34] But it was the area of sprawling plantations and high slave holding between the James and Rappahannock rivers that were the main targets of amphibious operations.

In accordance with a suggestion made earlier by Lord George Germain, Sir George Collier, commander of the North American Squadron, and British commander in chief, General Sir Henry Clinton, developed a plan that called for a series of coastal raids to choke off the Chesapeake's export trade, specifically in tobacco and the produce that nourished the prosperity of the region and provided the basis of American credit in Europe.[35] The

[31] December 23, 1777, Robert Honyman, 1747–1824, Diary 1776–1782, Library of Congress.

[32] Thomas Stone to Governor Johnson, December 9, 1777, William Harrison to Governor Johnson, December 14, 1777, Maryland State Papers, Red Book 4561–81, 4583–18; *Virginia Gazette*,(Dixon and Hunter), December 19, 1777; Honyman Diary, December 23, 1777, all discuss runaways.

[33] George Dashiell to Governor Johnson, April 1, 1778, Maryland State Papers, Red Book 4584–122; Council to Dashiell, April 6, 1778, William Hand Browne, Clayton C. Hall, and Bernard C. Steiner, eds., *Archives of Maryland* MHS, 71 vols. to date (Baltimore, 1883–), 21:11–12.

[34] Edwin M. Jameson, "Tory Operations on the Bay from Dunmore's Departure to the End of the War," in Eller, ed., *Chesapeake Bay*, 379, 384–87.

[35] Robert Fallaw and Marion West Stoer, "The Old Dominion Under Fire: The Chesapeake Invasions, 1779–1781," in Eller, ed., *Chesapeake Bay*, 434–35.

first of several water expeditions into the deeply indented Virginia shore got underway in May 1779. The British force, led by Collier and Brigadier General Edward Mathew, consisted of the sixty-four gun *Raisonnable*, the forty-four gun *Rainbow*, the *Otter, Diligent*, and *Harlem* sloops, the *Cornwallis* galley, and twenty-eight transports carrying about eighteen hundred troops. The fleet, joined by a squadron of privateers, left New York on May 5 and anchored in Hampton Road on the ninth. While some of the privateers, escorted by the *Otter*, proceeded up Chesapeake Bay, the main force sailed with the tide up the Elizabeth River.

The pretty town of Portsmouth, strategically situated at the entrance to Chesapeake Bay near the Gosport shipyard, was selected as the first target.[36] Meeting little resistance from the small garrison that held the American fort in the river, the raiders quickly razed the fort and advanced to Portsmouth. There they destroyed the tobacco, tar, and other commodities stored in warehouses and seized a number of laden merchantmen in the harbor or in flight along one of the branches of the Elizabeth River. At Gosport the raiders burned 137 merchant ships, including the twenty-gun frigate *Virginia*, which was still under construction, and all of the buildings and storehouses of the best shipyard in America.[37] Using Portsmouth as a center, Collier sent out other raiding parties, one of which burned Suffolk, an important supply depot for tobacco and salted pork from other Virginia counties and for naval stores from North Carolina.[38]

Collier's "Maroding party," as Edmund Pendleton angrily described it, "too well succeeded" in its assault on the trading resources of the Chesapeake. When the fleet hoisted sail and put to sea on May 24, it brought away from two thousand to three thousand hogsheads of tobacco, several thousand head of cattle and horses and perhaps fifteen hundred slaves.[39] In their devastating sweep through the area, Collier's fleet took on board hundreds of slaves, some of them apparent victims of British or tory kidnapping. According to Pendleton's account, "The slaves did not voluntarily go to them, but they adopted the old African Mode of making up their Cargoe, sending out their parties to hunt [blurred] which many were Murdered rather than to Surrender, and giving a half Joe for such as were brought, which tempted some of our Rascals to engage in the trade and

[36] Joseph A. Goldenberg, "Virginia Ports in the American Revolution," in Eller, ed., *Chesapeake Bay*, 310.

[37] Arthur Pierce Middleton, "Ships and Shipbuilding in the Chesapeake and Tributaries," in Eller, ed., *Chesapeake Bay*, 127.

[38] Goldenberg, "Virginia Ports," 311.

[39] Edmund Pendleton to William Woodford, May 31, 1779, no. 958, folder 3, Edmund Pendleton (1721–1803) Letters, 1776–1779, SHC. Pendleton's first estimate of the number of slaves lost was five hundred. In the Pendleton Letters, June 21, 1779, he revised the estimate to fifteen hundred. Robert Honyman, a Hanover County Physician and Planter, estimated slave losses to be one thousand; see Honyman Diary, June 1, 1779.

carrying the poor wretches in." Pendleton, a slaveholder blind to the paradox of the American struggle for liberty, finished with harsh denunciation of Britain for double-dealing as it were, in the slave trade: "Thus are the Subjects of that boasted Land of Freedom practicing a Second Act of Iniquity upon this race of men, and by sending them to the West Indies, will aggravagate the horror of their Condition far beyond what the first Occasioned."[40]

The destruction of thousands of barrels of pork, immense quantities of naval stores, and well over one hundred merchant vessels during Collier's raid dealt a major blow to Virginia's military preparations and to the American war effort. Even after the fleet left the bay the privateers, still accompanied by the *Otter*, continued the campaign of attrition. Apparently acting under Collier's orders, the squadron of privateers commanded by Captain Richard Creyk cruised the capes until June 22. Early in June they entered the Wicomico River, captured two outbound vessels and carried off a number of slaves and livestock.[41] The final departure of the privateers marked the end of the first British invasion of the Chesapeake. In the coming months, however, privateering came to play an increasingly important role in naval warfare in the bay. Between August 1778 and April 1779, 100 privateers were fitted out in Liverpool, 121 in New York. In 1779 the size of the British navy increased from 432 to 481 ships. During roughly the same period, the Continental Congress granted 209 commissions to private armed vessels. In addition to the regular navy and privateers, whaleboats, barges, and various kinds of small craft manned by crews numbering anywhere from twelve to thirty men, also carried out plundering operations along the waterfronts of the Potomac, Patuxent, Pocomoke, and Nanticoke rivers and along the shores of Chesapeake Bay.[42] Although the principal purpose of the predatory war in the bay was to procure provisions to subsist British land forces, the recruitment and kidnapping of slaves for service on board the vessels or for sale for profit was also a major objective, particularly of the privateers.

Beginning in July 1780, the Maryland Council of Safety noted a marked increase in predatory activity. In an effort to clear the bay of British raiders, the state armed two brigs and several barges. Despite the success of Maryland's light cruisers and barges in capturing enemy vessels, the state's little fleet was inadequate to the task of protecting the widely scattered homes on the numerous waterways of the bay.[43] By the fall the Potomac was

[40] Edmund Pendleton to William Woodford, June 21, 1779, Pendleton Letters.

[41] For a detailed account, see Fallaw and Stoer, "Old Dominion Under Fire," 451.

[42] Gardner W. Allen, *A Naval History of the American Revolution*, 2 vols. (Williamtown, Mass.: Houghton, 1913), 2:486–87, 568.

[43] Council to Delegates in Congress, July 28, 1780, Browne, Hall, and Steiner, eds., *Archives of Maryland* 43:238, 267.

swarming with British boats and small sloops, which were apparently well suited to American coastal conditions.[44] In September after "a pack of the most abandoned Fellows that ever molested us"[45] did extensive damage in St. Marys County and carried off a number of slaves, the citizens petitioned Governor Thomas Sim Lee to send more vessels to cruise the bay and to provide transportation for those wishing to remove their property from the area.[46] On September 29 British raiders struck in Worcester County, burning a brig belonging to Robert Dashiell and a number of small craft owned by rivermen. In reporting the raid Joseph Dashiell, county lieutenant, noted that "A Number of Negroes have gone on board them."[47]

In separate raids, British barges and tenders plundered the inhabitants of Worcester and Somerset counties "in the most shameful manner of every species of property worth taking." Several barges manned by "saylors, tories and Negroes" advanced up the Nanticoke River to Vienna in Dorchester County where they "burnt several valuable vessels and plundered the inhabitants on the river of their slaves and valuable effects." Because the extraordinary accessibility of the Chesapeake rendered the state militia helpless "to prevent their depredations in many parts contiguous to the water," the inhabitants allowed them to land without opposition.[48] Lamenting the sad state of affairs, Joseph Dashiell, himself a victim of the raids, warned state authorities that "if a stop is not put to those cruisers I am convinced all our most valuable Negroes will run away."[49] Events in the coming weeks seemed to confirm Dashiell's fears. Early in November three British schooners and several small barges made up the Patuxent as far as Benedict in Charles County. On their way up the river they burned houses, seized livestock and ships loaded with tobacco, and "received a number of Slaves who flock[ed] into them from every quarter." William Fitzhugh, who lost four slaves noted that "upwards of sixty Negroes" had already joined the British and speculated that "more Black volunteers will offer than can be taken."[50]

[44] Middleton, *Tobacco Coast*, 216.
[45] Richard Barnes to Governor Thomas Sim Lee, September 20, 1780, Browne, Hall, and Steiner, eds., *Archives of Maryland* 45:113.
[46] Petition of Inhabitants of St. Marys County, September 4, 1780, to Governor Lee, Revolutionary War Collection, MS 1814, MHS.
[47] Joseph Dashiell to Governor Lee, September 29, 1777, Browne, Hall, and Steiner, eds., *Archives of Maryland* 45:125.
[48] George Dashiell to Governor Lee, September 30, 1780, Maryland State Papers, Red Book, 26:52.
[49] Joseph Dashiell to Col. Uriah Forrest, September 30, 1780, Maryland State Papers, Red Book 26:52.
[50] William Fitzhugh to [?], November 7, 1780, Revolutionary War Collection, MS 1814; see also Joseph Wilkinson to Governor Lee, November 9, 1780, Browne, Hall, and Steiner, eds., *Archives of Maryland* 45:173.

Although the white inhabitants of Maryland's eastern and western shores gained no respite from the constant danger and continual apprehension of British raids, a more serious threat was developing to the south. Near the end of October 1780, a British fleet commanded by Major General Alexander Leslie entered the capes of Virginia. Sent by Clinton to penetrate the James River valley to prevent Virginia and Maryland from sending military supplies and troops reinforcements to the American Army of the South following Horatio Gates's defeat at the Battle of Camden,[51] the expedition lay quietly for three or four weeks in the Portsmouth area, venturing out only as far as Hampton to collect five hundred head of cattle. Apart from foraging for provisions and destroying public stores, the Leslie expedition did little damage, to the immense consternation of American observers. The British forces, wrote Robert Honyman, a Hanover County physician and planter, "behaved with great moderation . . . took nothing but provisions; prohibited all plundering; dismissed the Negroes who came to join them and even gave up some vessels they took in Portsmouth harbor."[52] Finding "something Mysterious in their leaving their Slaves on shore," Edmund Pendleton speculated that the fleet lacked either the room or the manpower to accommodate them, or else that they had "designs of further hostility."[53] In fact the patriot victory at Kings Mountain, which forced Cornwallis to retreat from Charlotte to Winnsboro, and the rapid buildup of Virginia militia to oppose Leslie, led to the decision to withdraw Leslie's forces, which were needed to reinforce Cornwallis, and forced Leslie to turn away the slaves who fled to him. Before he left, however, the British commander donated one hundred guineas to the clergyman at Portsmouth for distribution among the poor "who had lossed *their all*" to plundering seamen, possibly privateers, in the several creeks of Norfolk County.[54]

Leslie's fleet had hardly cleared the bay before another small but powerful British squadron entered the Virginia capes. Commanded by Benedict Arnold, the sixteen hundred man force was sent by Clinton to conduct harrassing raids. The object of the operation was to aid Cornwallis in North Carolina by burning the Virginia stores that supplied Nathanael Greene and by perhaps forcing Greene to direct some of his troops away from North Carolina toward Virginia.[55] On December 31 the troops disembarked from the transport ships and boarded small sloops and boats

[51] Hutchinson and Rachal, eds., *Madison Papers* 2:156 n.1.

[52] Honyman Diary, December 2, 1780.

[53] From Edmund Pendleton, November 27, 1780, in Hutchinson and Rachal, eds., *Madison Papers* 2:208.

[54] General Alexander Leslie to General Henry Clinton, November 19, 1780, British Headquarters Papers, Howard-Tilton Memorial Library.

[55] Wickwire and Wickwire, *Cornwallis*, 252.

for the advance up the James River. Around nine in the morning of January 4, they anchored at Westover, the great country seat of William Byrd III. Although Westover was typical of large plantation centers in the Chesapeake, to the men of the fleet who were unfamiliar with plantation life the great house and its forty dependent structures looked like "a small town."[56] After several hours of rest, during which the officers were treated to breakfast by the Byrd family and were provided with "reliable guides," Arnold set out with about eight hundred men for Richmond, an important trading center that had recently been designated the state capital.

At 1:00 P.M. the next day the troops reached the heights of Richmond, from which they quickly dislodged the Virginia militia and entered the town. From his headquarters at the City Tavern on Main Street, Arnold sent a deputation to Governor Thomas Jefferson with an offer to spare the city on condition that the public stores kept in warehouses be loaded on British vessels without any interference. Jefferson refused and the "parricide Arnold," as Jefferson called him,[57] began the systematic destruction of everything useful to the war effort. Over five hundred hogsheads of rum, two warehouses full of salt, one hundred and twenty bushels of wheat and a number of public buildings were burned on Arnold's orders. A "very fine Rope [walk] full of material" and some private property were also burned by accident.[58]

In the meantime a detachment led by John Graves Simcoe marched to Westham, site of the state cannon foundry. Although some of the military supplies had been moved earlier to Chesterfield County, the raiders blew up the powder magazine and destroyed 330 barrels of powder, twenty-six cannon, a magazine of oats, a boring mill, and two houses and set the foundry on fire before returning to Richmond, where they found Arnold and his men "cantoned in sweet repose." Before leaving Richmond on the sixth, Arnold ordered the torch put to "all of the magazines and workshops for shipbuilding," including all of the vessels still on the blocks. With half of the place in flames the raiders departed, taking with them forty-two vessels loaded with "all kinds of merchandise for the corp's booty." Although the customary taking of spoils was something that most soldiers expected as a necessary supplement to their wretched pay, even seasoned veterans were embarrassed by the excesses of the Arnold expedition. "On the whole," wrote one Hessian officer, "the expedition resembled those of freebooters, who sometimes at sea, sometimes ashore, ravaged and laid waste everything. Terrible things happened on this excursion; churches and holy places were plundered."[59]

[56] Ewald, *Diary*, 261.
[57] Boyd, *Papers of Jefferson* 4:270.
[58] Fallaw and Stoer, "Old Dominion Under Fire," 462.
[59] Ewald, *Diary*, 268–69, 422, n. 23; Boyd, *Papers of Jefferson* 4:334.

In only forty-eight hours, as Jefferson later pointed out, the Arnold expedition had penetrated thirty-three miles, "done the whole injury and retired." Governor Jefferson had received the first intelligence that twenty-seven sail of the line had entered Chesapeake Bay at 8:00 A.M. on December 31. Two days later he was told that the British squadron had entered the James River, whereupon he immediately called up the militia and ordered the removal of military stores from Richmond.[60] The militia was slow to assemble, however, and offered only scattered and ineffective opposition to the invaders. In part this was due to the geography of the tidewater. Nowhere on the broad, flat tidal plain between the Potomac and Rappahannock, the Rappahannock and the York, and the York and the James rivers, was the land reach greater than twenty miles; frequently it was no more than five miles. Unless boats had been previously provided for crossing the numerous streams, the rapid assembly of militia was impossible. There was, however, another reason why Arnold "received less interruption than he ought among a people contending for liberty," as a chagrined Edmund Randolph put it in his *History of Virginia*. It was the haunting fear of the large black population in their midst. "The helpless wives and children," Randolph explained, "were at the mercy not only of the males among the slaves but of the very women, who could handle deadly weapons; and these could not have been left in safety in the absence of all authority of the masters and of union among neighbors."[61]

Slaveowners were right to feel threatened. Blacks constituted half or more of the population in the planting counties south of the Rappahannock. Mobilized they formed a highly potent force. The presence of the British inevitably raised their expectations, intensified their hopes for freedom, and dispelled the hesitancy many of them felt about challenging the slave regime. When, however, they set about the task of turning their expectations into actuality, they were inevitably confronted with the pervasiveness of white power on the one hand and the ambivalence of their British liberators on the other. Never at ease with their black bondmen, white Virginians kept a patient and unending vigil over them, patrolling the porous coast, securing canoes and small craft, watching the few crossing places on the numerous watercourses, guarding the deadly weapons slaves needed to challenge white authority directly. Never committed to emancipation, the British army extended an unsteady hand, sometimes welcoming black fugitives with handsome uniforms and promises of freedom, sometimes turning them away or returning them to vengeful owners, sometimes perpetrating slavery's worst evils by kidnapping and selling

[60] To George Washington, January 10, 1781, "[Jefferson's] Diary of Arnold's Invasion," Boyd, *Papers of Jefferson*, 258, 334–35.

[61] Randolph, *History of Virginia*, 285.

them to new masters in strange lands. When these and other vital factors such as geographic location and food supply were taken into account, it became clear to all but the most reckless that armed revolt was both futile and self-destructive.

Perhaps because the liberator seemed surprisingly like the master, many black Virginians consciously chose neutrality. However, other options existed in the continuum of resistance, and a surprisingly large number of slaves chose one or the other of them. At one extreme were acts of open defiance, such as violence against persons, property, or self, illustrated by the case of Jack, the property of Stephen May of Botetourt County. "[A] rebellious Servant and corrupter of other Servants," Jack had a history of violent resistance to slavery that included robbery and attempted murder. In April 1781, he was tried and convicted of "Two considerable Robberies, of attempting to procure Rats-Bane to poison Major Quirk," and of "Engaging and Enlisting several negroes to Raise in Arms and Join the British, the said Jack to be their captain." Two days before Jack's scheduled execution, he "Broke the Goal," freed a number of deserters and some tories, and escaped into hiding for several weeks before being retaken. When the court expressed concern over the legality of carrying out the execution beyond the date originally appointed by the judges, twenty-five citizens protested. Calling Jack a "dangerous and incorrigible Violator of the Laws and Peace of the Country," they demanded that the court make of him "an example of Justice and not of Mercy."[62]

Ague and her children Caesar, Jupiter, and Joe chose flight to express their resistance to slavery. Taking advantage of the panic in Richmond at Arnold's approach, Ague ran off "to one Blunt in Hanover," perhaps a relative or friend or a former master. Caesar and Jupiter fled to Point of Fork at the confluence of the Fluvanna and James rivers; Joe "ran away to the mountains,"[63] presumably the western piedmont, which was still a developing region not yet fully committed to slavery, where a runaway might conceivably hope to find freedom or locate friends.[64] Most of the slaves who wished to challenge the slave regime did so by fleeing to the British.

Black Virginians were as passionate as white Virginians in their response to the war and as practical. When division and confusion among whites improved their chances for success, when British prospects looked good, they took advantage of the opportunities and escaped in great numbers. After Arnold's sweep up the James River, the Reverend James Madison wrote to his son that "The families within the sphere of his action have suffered greatly. Some have lost 40, others 30, every one a considerable

[62] Palmer, ed., *Calendar of Virginia State Papers* 1:477–78, 2:604–05.
[63] Ibid. 1:333.
[64] Dunn, "Black Society in the Chesapeake," 63.

part of their slaves."[65] It is impossible to say whether the runaways were motivated only by the desire to achieve practical liberty for themselves or whether they perhaps believed that they were embarking on a war against slavery. What can be said with certainty is that but for their labor, Arnold's small force would probably have been destroyed, if not by the enemy then by disease.

With his immediate objective realized, Arnold retired to Portsmouth to carry out a second military objective, the establishment of a post to obstruct the American tobacco trade. The British plan was to fortify Portsmouth, the little village of Great Bridge ten miles away on the southern branch of the Elizabeth River, and Kemps Landing, a trading village of about ninety houses. Because much of Virginia's commerce and most of the tobacco grown in North Carolina passed through the capes of Virginia,[66] control of the three towns and of the James and Elizabeth rivers would guarantee the British mastery of the lower coast of Virginia and access to North Carolina through the Dismal Swamp, the great swampy woodland that extended from the edge of Portsmouth all the way into North Carolina. But the steamy heat and the swarms of vermin that flourished in the flat, marshy terrain were too much for the European troops and so the black runaways were given the heavy work of throwing up entrenchments in the sandy soil of Portsmouth. In three days, three hundred black workers built the redoubt at Great Bridge and dismantled part of the long wooden bridge that provided access to North Carolina.[67]

During the winter, however, Arnold's force found itself increasingly hemmed in: by the approach of a force of Continentals under Maria Joseph, the Marquis de Lafayette, and a large French fleet commanded by Rear Admiral Chevalier Charles René Dominique Souchet Destouches, and by the harassing attacks of the Virginia militia, which prevented the British from foraging for provisions.[68] Confined by two muddy creeks that turned Portsmouth into a kind of half-island, the garrison appeared to be trapped. Arnold, who always carried a small set of pistols in his pocket to avoid being hanged if captured,[69] ordered his black troops and the entire garrison to work day and night to make the post impregnable. Already under severe strain, the troops began to grow hungry, the horses to starve for lack of forage. Soon the black followers of the army, upon whom military duties fell most heavily, were struck by "a contagious Distemper,"

[65] From the Reverend James Madison, January 18, 1781, Hutchinson and Rachal, eds., *Madison Papers* 2:293.

[66] To John Adams, May 17, 1780, James Curtis Ballagh, ed., *The Letters of Richard Henry Lee*, 2 vols. (New York: Macmillan, 1914), 2:183.

[67] Ewald, *Diary*, 278.

[68] Fallaw and Stoer, "Old Dominion Under Fire," 464–65.

[69] Ewald, *Diary*, 925.

which "swept off numbers every Day."[70] Fortunately for the imperiled garrison, a large squadron under Admiral Marriot Arbuthnot was sent from New York to rescue it, and plans were made for General William Phillips to follow soon with reinforcements.[71] On March 27, Phillips arrived with two thousand troops and orders to take command of the entire force and proceed in a series of raids up the James River to destroy stores.

For the next several weeks, the combined forces of Phillips and Arnold conducted raids of exceptional severity in the James River valley. Pursuing a policy of systematic destruction, they struck first at the large state shipyard at Chickahominy, twelve miles above the mouth of the Chickahominy River, a tributary of the James, where they destroyed the shipyard, warehouses, and several armed ships. With undiminished ferocity they advanced on Petersburg, the tobacco capital of Virginia and the center of an extensive wagon trade with North Carolina. There they destroyed four thousand hogsheads of tobacco, one ship, and a number of small vessels on the stocks and in the river. While Phillips led a small force to Chesterfield Court House to burn a range of barracks used by the new levies of Virginia, Arnold marched with another force to Osbornes Wharf, where a number of impressed merchantmen and privateers and state warships had earlier been assembled by Jefferson as part of the failed assault on Arnold at Portsmouth.[72] Undermanned, the entire flotilla was taken. According to Arnold, "Two ships, three brigantines, five sloops, and two schooners, loaded with tobacco, cordage, flour, etc. fell into our hands. Four ships, five brigantines, and a number of small vessels were sunk and burnt. On board the whole fleet (none of which escaped) were taken and destroyed about 2,000 hogsheads of tobacco."[73]

The reunited forces of Phillips and Arnold then marched unopposed to Manchester, a small town directly across the James River from Richmond, and burned all the tobacco warehouses there. Their advance on Richmond, where large amounts of military supplies had been stored, was, however, blocked by the appearance of some two thousand militia reinforced by Lafayette's Continentals. Phillips and Arnold, therefore, withdrew from the James River "sweeping all the slaves and other property and pillaging and destroying houses," as they went. "Their plunder is immence particularly

[70] From James Innes, March 6, 1781, Boyd, *Papers of Jefferson* 5:74.

[71] Fallaw and Stoer, "Old Dominion Under Fire," 466.

[72] Goldenberg, "Virginia Ports," 194–95, 311.

[73] Quoted in Isaac N. Arnold, *The Life of Benedict Arnold* (c. 1885; reprint, New York: Arno Press, 1979), 345. For other British accounts, see Tarleton, *History*, 335–40; Samuel Graham, "An English Officer's Account of His Services in America, 1779–1781: Memoirs of Lt. General Samuel Graham," *Historical Magazine* 9(1865): 241–49, 267–74, 301–8, 329–35; John Graves Simcoe, *Simcoe's Military Journal: A History of the Operations of a Partisan Corps Called the Queen's Rangers . . . , during the War of the American Revolution* (1844; reprint, New York: New York Times and Arno Press, 1968).

in slaves," Edmund Pendleton informed fellow Virginian James Madison.[74] There is every reason to believe that the majority of slaves who fled to the British first observed the seeming impotence of the Continental and state forces on the one hand and the apparent invincibility of the British on the other, and decided that their moment had come. They "flocked to the enemy from all quarters, even from very remote parts,"[75] Dr. Robert Honyman wrote from the piedmont county of Hanover, which reported a decline in slave population at the end of the war.[76]

Faced with the prospect of losing all of their slaves, a few planters began to move them "up the country,"[77] thus initiating a major geographical redistribution of the Chesapeake slave population away from tidewater counties to piedmont counties.[78] Planters who did not own land in the piedmont or for one reason or another were unable to relocate their slaves reported high desertion rates: "Some lost 30, 40, 50, 60 or 70 Negroes besides their stocks of cattle, sheep and horses," according to Dr. Honyman.[79] So consuming was the slaves' desire for freedom an astonished Edmund Pendleton admitted, "that [they] continue to go to [the British], notwithstanding many who have escaped inform others of their ill treatment, those who are not sent off to the West Indies being kept at hard labour upon very short allowance, so as to perish daily."[80]

There is no documented proof that slaves were systematically transported and sold as spoils of war, as American sources regularly claimed, although an illicit traffic in slaves by individuals was indisputably a constant feature of the war in the South.[81] There is, moreover, highly suggestive evidence that a market in slaves existed. After the military operations that devastated the Chesapeake in 1779, General Edward Mathew and Sir George Collier "divided one-eighth of the total prize money between themselves," the rest between the army and navy. Before launching the second invasion of Virginia, Major General Alexander Leslie gave orders against plundering but promised his troops "that all Publick Stores taken during ye expedition Shall be Lodged in proper hands that an equitable division May thereafter be made." Arrangements to divide the spoils of war

[74] To James Madison, May 7, 1781, David John Mays, ed., *Letters and Papers of Edmund Pendleton, 1734–1803*, 2 vols. (Charlottesville: University Press of Virginia, 1967), 1:354–55.

[75] Honyman, Diary, May 11, 1781.

[76] Dunn, "Black Society in the Chesapeake," 58 n. 13.

[77] Honyman, Diary, May 11, 1781.

[78] Dunn, "Black Society in the Chesapeake," 54–59.

[79] Honyman, Diary, May 11, 1781.

[80] From Edmund Pendleton, May 7, 1781, in Hutchinson and Rachal, eds., *Madison Papers* 3:111.

[81] Colonel Jarvis, Loyalist. A Voice from 1776, 30–31, notes by Thomas Stinson Jarvis, ed., William R. Perkins Library, Duke University, Typescript.

were made by Arnold and Captain Thomas Symonds, commanding officer of the *Charon*, before their Virginia expedition. En route to Virginia the two officers agreed to an equal division of the spoils between the services. Disagreements wrecked the accord, and the case was remanded to the New York vice-admiralty court. The court awarded half the proceeds to the two hundred and eighty sailors, but retained the other half pending the king's pleasure. Finally, in March 1782, after Clinton personally interceded with the Crown on behalf of the army, the king ruled that one-eighth of the sum remaining should be paid to Arnold, the rest to be divided among the officers and soldiers "as had been done on former occasions."[82] Testimony given by British prisoners taken during the final British campaign in Virginia indicates that Watts Island on the west central coast of Accomac County in lower Chesapeake Bay, and Devils Island, one of the upper Tangier islands, were collection points for "the Negroes that had been plundered in the Rappahannock" and along the Chesapeake shores.[83] General Leslie's statement to Clinton, written the same day that the prisoners' depositions were taken, that the smallpox epidemic at Portsmouth "will ruin our market, which was bad enough before," apparently supports the contention that the army carried on a large-scale clandestine traffic in slaves.[84]

Simultaneously with the Phillips-Arnold river raids, the Royal Navy and privateers, often acting independently, pillaged the shores of Chesapeake Bay and the streams tributary to it. Using St. George's Island, conveniently located at the mouth of the St. Marys River, as a base, the British launched a series of bruising raids all the way up the bay as far as Baltimore and up the many tidal tributaries of the bay. In January they anchored off St. Georges Island and plundered several inhabitants, one of whom reported that "Many negroes have gone from this Neighbourhood since the time the enemy Anchored of [sic] St. Mary's." Several days later privateers landed at Smith Creek and seized a schooner loaded with tobacco.[85] Barely two weeks later they returned,[86] keeping "the inhabitants on the Waters of Potomac in constant alarm."[87]

To make matters worse, tory bands became active again in the spring. Dodging in and out of the bays and rivers, they plundered the waterfront plantations relentlessly. From Worcester County Joseph Dashiell reported

[82] Frey, "Between Slavery and Freedom," 396–97.
[83] William Paca to General Washington, February 21, 1783, William Paca in Council, March 21, 1783, Browne, Hall, and Steiner, eds., *Archives of Maryland* 48:366, 388–89.
[84] Leslie to Cornwallis, July 13, 1781, Cornwallis Papers, PRO30/11/6/280–81.
[85] Robert Armstrong to Governor Lee, January 26, 1781, January 30, 1781, Browne, Hall, and Steiner, eds., *Archives of Maryland* 47:39, 41.
[86] Richard Barnes to Governor Lee, February 16, 1781, Executive Papers, Maryland State Papers, 6636–25–101, Maryland Hall of Records.
[87] Richard Barnes to Thomas Sim Lee, February 18, 1781, Browne, Hall, and Steiner, eds., *Archives of Maryland* 47:75.

that "not a week goes by that friends are not robed [sic] by sum of those Retches under Color of belonging to the British cruisers." In nearby Somerset County an interracial band of "daring and desperate Villians" led by a man named McMullin, plundered the area throughout the summer.[88] To white citizens, the British and tory raids appeared particularly dangerous because they exacerbated slave unrest. "They have," one owner confessed, "great success in procuring our slaves."[89] The British presence in the vicinity of St. Marys County prompted a call to the governor from Colonel Richard Barnes for militia to constantly patrol "from one part of the county to the other in order to prevent dissatisfaction of the negroes going to the Enemy." Judging from "the late conduct of the Negroes when those Ships were in St. Mary's," Barnes recalled of an earlier raid, "I am well satisfied the greatest number of them that are in the County would join them, as I am well informed of twenty-five offered themselves to those Ships the night they were in St. Mary's."[90]

In an effort to shut down every avenue of escape, Maryland state authorities "posted guards at the most convenient places to prevent the Negroes from going to the enemy and secur'd all boats and canoes."[91] But the poorly trained and equipped militia was powerless to prevent British landings.[92] Frustrated by the state's inability to drive the raiders from the bay, private citizens took matters into their own hands. Fears of an impending raid and "the recent desertion of several negroes from the neighbourhood of this Town" persuaded a group of citizens from Baltimore to fit out at their own expense two look-out boats to warn of a British approach.[93] Twenty-two prominent citizens of the upper bay, including the popular leader William Paca of Annapolis, Matthew Tilghman of Talbot County and his cousin Edward Lloyd, also of Talbot, privately agreed to supply and maintain a barge to cruise between Kent Point and Tilghman's Island in the eastern bay.[94]

[88] George Dashiell to Governor Lee, March 4, 1781, Council to Philip Thomas, August 5, 1781, Browne, Hall, and Steiner, eds., *Archives of Maryland* 47:104, 45:545. See also George Dashiell to Matthew Tilghman, July 21, 1781, The Defense of Thomas Doyle, March 4, 1778, Revolutionary War Collection, MS 1814, MHS.

[89] John Mercer to [?], February, 1781, Maryland State Papers, Red Book 4563–48.

[90] Richard Barnes to Governor Lee, March 25, 1781, Browne, Hall, and Steiner, eds., *Archives of Maryland* 47:148.

[91] John Weems to Governor Lee, March 21, 1781, Maryland State Papers, Executive Papers 6636–26–50. See also George Dashiell to Matthew Tilghman, April 5, 1781, Browne, Hall, and Steiner, eds., *Archives of Maryland* 47:163.

[92] Richard Barnes to Governor Lee, April 3, 1781, Browne, Hall, and Steiner, eds., *Archives of Maryland*, 47:159; George Dashiell to Matthew Tilghman, April 5, 1781, Revolutionary War Collection MS 1814.

[93] James McHenry to Governor Lee, April 7, 1781, Browne, Hall, and Steiner, eds., *Archives of Maryland* 47:167.

[94] Subscription for the Experiment, Maryland State Papers, Red Book 4601–41.

Although there were short intervals of peace, there was no real respite from the raids. Throughout the spring of 1781 local leaders continued to report the operations of British vessels. In early April two barges manned mostly by blacks sailed all the way up the Patuxent River to Lower Marlboro in Calvert County. Under cover of darkness a landing party plundered the town, seized all the vessels there, and loaded them with tobacco taken from the warehouse. When they departed the following day, they took Colonel William Fitzhugh hostage. Taking advantage of their master's predicament, "Most of Fitzhugh's Negroes went with them."[95] At about the same time a British warship landed at Robert "Councillor" Carter's Cole's Point plantation in Westmoreland County on the Virginia side of the Potomac; despite Carter's personal appeal to his slaves, thirty deserted to the British vessel.[96] On April 18, the British sloop of war *Savage*, commanded by Captain Richard Graves, visited George Washington's estate, Mount Vernon, and took "a very valuable Boat" and seventeen slaves, most of them young, skilled artisans, and house servants.[97]

The success of the Phillips-Arnold river raids and of the pillaging strikes carried on simultaneously by the Royal Navy and privateers spread alarm among planters in vulnerable counties along the Potomac River, where slaves represented from one-half to two-thirds of the total population.[98] Their apprehension is reflected in Richard Henry Lee's plea to Governor Jefferson for military assistance so that "a tract of country an hundred miles in length and abounding with Slaves, Stocks, and much Tobacco—both public and private may be saved from the hand of ravage and destruction."[99] Although rumors ran ahead of the actual invasion, the final Chesapeake Bay campaign was rapidly taking shape.

After his Pyrrhic victory over Nathanael Greene at Guilford Court House in March, Cornwallis drew down the west side of the Cape Fear River to Wilmington, North Carolina, to rest his battered troops and to secure provisions. Located at the mouth of the Cape Fear, Wilmington was the entrepôt for the state's rice and naval stores industries, both of which depended heavily upon the hand labor of slaves.[100] As a consequence, slaves constituted 60 percent of all taxables in Wilmington and surrounding New Hanover County.[101] The disquieting memory of the abortive

[95] Stephen West to Governor Lee, April 10, 1781, Maryland State Papers, Red Book 18:8.
[96] To [the Governor of Virginia?], April 13, 1781, Ballagh, *Letters of Richard Henry Lee* 2:221.
[97] To Lund Washington, April 30, 1781, Fitzpatrick, *Writings of George Washington* 22:14, n. 20.
[98] Dunn, "Black Society in the Chesapeake," 57, map 2.
[99] To the Governor of Virginia, May 10, 1781, Ballagh, *Letters of Richard Henry Lee* 2:222.
[100] Jeffrey J. Crow, *Black Experience in Revolutionary North Carolina* (Raleigh, 1983), 8–11.
[101] Jeffrey J. Crow, "Slave Rebelliousness and Social Conflict in North Carolina, 1775–1802," *William and Mary Quarterly*, 3d ser., 37(1980): 83.

slave rebellion of July 1775, and the recollection of their slaves' fevered response to the British army during earlier offensive operations in the state[102] made whites very uneasy at the approach of the British. While slaves followed Cornwallis's movements furtively and expectantly, whites watched their slaves warily and fearfully and were struck by their grim determination to join the British. Cornwallis had scarcely opened the North Carolina campaign before blacks began to circulate "strange storys [sic]. They say," Jean Blair nervously wrote to Nelly Blair, that "people are getting ready to run again and the English are to be in Edenton by Saturday."[103]

In fact a remarkable exodus of slaves had already begun during the British march from South Carolina. In an effort to deal with the unexpected influx, Cornwallis at first tried to expel those the army could not profitably use. At Camden he ordered all blacks employed by the army to be identified "with the Number of the Regiment or the Initial Letters of the Department" to which they were attached and he instructed the provost marshal to "take up, and flog out of the Encampment all those who are not Mark'd." A week later, under obvious pressure from officers, he relented and agreed to allow officers to retain slaves in a semi-servile capacity: cavalry officers with the rank of lieutenant colonel were permitted to keep four black servants, captains and subalterns two and surgeons and quartermasters four each; infantry field officers were permitted two black servants each, all other officers one each. Shortly afterwards, Cornwallis, expressing a desire to allow his army "every Convenience," relaxed the restrictions about the number of servants each officer might keep.[104] Astonished at Cornwallis's "indulgent character," Johann Ewald, a Hessian officer who served with Cornwallis in Virginia, recalled that during that campaign "every soldier had his Negro, who carried his provisions and bundles." Ewald deplored the fact that "Every officer had four to six horses and three or four Negroes, as well as one or two Negresses for cook and maid. Every soldier's woman was mounted and also had a Negro and Negress on horseback for her servants. Each squad had one or two horses and Negroes, and every noncommissioned officer had two horses and one Negro."[105]

Day after day as Cornwallis's army pursued Greene across the red hills of piedmont North Carolina, and later as it pushed wearily south along the high bluffs of the Cape Fear River to Wilmington, slaves continued to

[102] Lt. Col. Hardy Murfree to Governor Abner Nash, November 1, 1780, Clark, *State Records* 15:138.

[103] Jean Blair to Helen "Nelly" Blair, January 4, 1781, Don Higginbotham, ed., *The Papers of James Iredell*, 2 vols. (Raleigh, N.C.: Division of Archives and History, 1976), 2:203.

[104] A. R. Newsome, ed., "A British Orderly Book, 1780–1781," *North Carolina Historical Review* 9 (1932): 276, 277, 280.

[105] Ewald, *Diary*, 305, 306.

pour in. With his army for all practical purposes destitute of food, Cornwallis began to organize the fugitives into foraging parties.[106] Although they were unarmed except for the weapons they found in "the houses they plunder," the reported two thousand black foragers[107] took advantage of their newfound freedom to "plunder and [use] violence to the Inhabitants." Unable to control them, Cornwallis ordered the provost marshal to seize and punish on the spot any black caught abusing civilians.[108] The unrestrained plunder by black followers of the army in North Carolina was exceptional. Even when opportunities were present, former slaves did not ordinarily engage in wanton acts of destruction. It is possible that their behavior in North Carolina was influenced by a desire to claim for themselves some of the fruits of years of unpaid labor, or by the conduct of Cornwallis's troops, who conquered Wilmington and put it to sack, leaving ruin in their wake as they began to withdraw from the state on May 19.

While his army rested at Wilmington, Cornwallis decided to launch a full-scale offensive against Virginia to cut off permanently the flow of supplies that sustained the Revolution. His plan was to continue to advance north to join Phillips and with their combined forces to conduct a major offensive.[109] At his departure Cornwallis left Major James Craig in command at Wilmington. Until the British evacuation of Wilmington in November, Craig continued to carry out raids up the Cape Fear River and as far north as New Bern.[110] Because planters usually fled in advance of the British arrival,[111] unsupervised slaves were able to easily escape. Nathan Bryan, a whig officer, reported that sixty of his "prime slaves" fled to the British during the New Bern raid,[112] and Craig was rumored to be able to field five hundred blacks.[113]

Cornwallis in the meantime was moving rapidly to his final destination in North America. Cutting a jagged course over the Neuse and the Tar rivers to Halifax, he crossed the Roanoke into Virginia late in May. After a march of over three weeks, which left his troops wearing pieces of cow-

[106] Twenty slaves belonging to Whitmell Hill, the state's largest slave owner, escaped in two nights; see Jean Blair to Hannah Iredell, May 10, 1781, Jean Blair to James Iredell, July 21, 1781, Higginbotham, *Papers of Iredell* 2:239, 266.

[107] Ibid.

[108] Newsome, "British Orderly Book," 296.

[109] See Wickwire and Wickwire, *Cornwallis*, 318–26 for details.

[110] General Sumner to General Greene, June 25, 1781, Clark, *SRNC* 15:495.

[111] Andrew Armstrong to Thomas Burke, August 22, 1781, 104, box 1, folder 9, Thomas Burke (c. 1747–1783), Papers, 1763–1852, SHC; William Hooper to James Iredell, February 17, 1782, Higginbotham, *Papers of Iredell* 2:327–28.

[112] Nathan Bryan to Governor Burke, September 6, 1781, Burke Papers 104, box 1, folder 9.

[113] General William Caswell to Governor Burke, September 4, 1781, Clark, *SRNC* 22:593.

hide wrapped around their feet in place of shoes,[114] he reached Petersburg and joined forces with Benedict Arnold, Phillips having died of a fever five days earlier. The next several weeks were spent in cavalry raids up the York and down the James rivers. All along his route, from North Carolina into Virginia, Cornwallis confiscated horses, of which every planter owned at least one for hauling carts, for travelling about the plantation or to marriages, funerals, or family gatherings. Fondly called "everlasters" because of their endurance, horses represented the principal means of transportation in the eighteenth century. By seizing some eight hundred horses in the James River valley alone, Cornwallis was able to form "a numerous and powerful Cavalry,"[115] which gave him an enormous advantage in speed and mobility. Able to cover fifty, even a hundred miles a day, his forces ranged over vast distances with a speed that chilled Virginia's white leaders.[116]

Despite a conspiracy of silence surrounding the possibility of a slave revolt, slaveowners clearly feared their slaves. Virginia contained over half of the black population of the United States, the vast majority of whom were held in servitude against their wills. Acutely aware of the fact that given the hope of freedom slaves would rise in rebellion, and apprehensive that a just God would be on their side, white leaders trembled at the prospect of a massive British-inspired slave revolt.[117] With great urgency several Virginia delegates in Congress implored General Washington, who had decided in favor of operations in New York instead of the South, to rush to the aid of Virginia.[118] Goaded by "many members of weight" in the General Assembly, Governor Jefferson too appealed to Washington to consider whether it would not "be best for the whole that you should repair to [Virginia's] assistance."[119] Convinced that Virginia's resources were inadequate for its own defense and that only the "most vigorous administration of public affairs" could save the state from "the ruin determined for us by the enemy," Richard Henry Lee proposed that Washington be given dictatorial powers in the state until the crisis passed.[120]

[114] Ewald, *Diary*, 303.

[115] To Arthur Lee, June 4, 1781, Ballagh, *Letters of Richard Henry Lee* 2:231. See also Randolph, *History of Virginia*, 294; Barrister to Governor Burke, July 8, 1781, Clark, *SRNC* 15:519.

[116] Reverend Edward I. Devitt, S.J., ed., "Letters of Fr. Joseph Mosely, S.J. and Some Extracts from his Diary (1757–1786)," American Catholic Society of Philadelphia, *Records* 17 (1906): 190–91.

[117] See, for example, John C. Miller, *The Wolf by the Ears: Thomas Jefferson and Slavery* (New York: Free Press, 1977), 24–25, 45, 62–64.

[118] Ernest McNeill Eller, "Washington's Maritime Strategy and the Campaign That Assured Independence," in Eller, ed., *Chesapeake Bay*, 491.

[119] To George Washington, May 28, 1781, Boyd, *Papers of Jefferson* 6:32–33.

[120] To George Washington, June 12, 1781, Ballagh, *Letters of Richard Henry Lee* 2:234; To the Virginia Delegates in Congress, June 12, 1781, Boyd, *Papers of Jefferson* 5:90–92.

Despite Washington's promise to hurry to Virginia to take command of the gathering forces, panic spread, leading to a general exodus of whites from threatened areas. As Cornwallis moved steadily northward across the James River to Westover, across the Chickahominy to New Castle and on to Hanover Court House, frenzied families, many of them with their slaves, hurried to Albemarle County,[121] which showed a gain in both the number of slaves and in the slave proportion of the population at the end of the war.[122] Urged by his friends to run to avoid capture, Edmund Pendleton, the Caroline County lawyer who had headed the first revolutionary government and now served as president of Virginia's Supreme Court of Appeals, loaded his possessions onto wagons, gathered together some of his slaves and retired to the mountains, where he remained until Cornwallis turned to the east.[123]

Reports of British landings in Gloucester County on the coast and of British designs on the large tobacco warehouses on the Rappahannock and the Potomac rivers spread alarm among the great planter families whose estates bordered the banks of both rivers.[124] Assessing the situation in Virginia as "truly critical and dangerous," George Mason, a member of the Virginia Convention that drafted the instructions to Virginia delegates in Congress in support of independence, collected "as many of my effects, as I can readily remove" and fled his Gunston Hall plantation on the Virginia side of the Potomac for Maryland.[125] Mason's neighbor, Richard Henry Lee, had already been driven from Chantilly, his home on the high bluffs of the Potomac, during the Phillips-Arnold forays into Virginia.[126]

Apparently wishing to avoid needlessly frightening the populace, which was already panic-stricken over the British invasion, Virginia's leaders remained largely silent on the possibility that a slave rising might be triggered by the turmoil of war. Their unspoken fear is, however, evident in Richard Henry Lee's subtle message to his brother, Arthur: "What will become of these lower parts heaven knows," he wrote after first describing reports of imminent hostilities. "We and our property here are now within the power of the enemy." Although he made only passing reference to the catalytic effect of the British presence, Lee, a landlord whose income was

[121] William Withers to St. George Tucker, May 20, 1780, Tucker-Coleman Papers, Earl Gregg Swem Library, College of William and Mary, Williamsburg, Va.

[122] Dunn, "Black Society in the Chesapeake," 63 n. 24 and map 4.

[123] To James Madison, July 6, 1781, July 23, 1781, Mays, *Letters and Papers of Edmund Pendleton* 1:365, 267. Pendleton spent some time in Staunton; his exact location at the time this letter was written is, however, unknown, 366 n. 1.

[124] To Arthur Lee, June 4, 1781, Ballagh, *Letters of Richard Henry Lee* 2:230.

[125] To Pearson Chapman, May 31, 1781, Robert A. Rutland, ed., *The Papers of George Mason, 1725–1792*, 3 vols. (Chapel Hill: University of North Carolina Press, 1970), 2:688.

[126] To Arthur Lee, May 31, 1781, Ballagh, *Letters of Richard Henry Lee* 2:224.

derived from tenant rents and the hire of slaves,[127] implicitly expressed the popular dread of social upheaval: " 'Tis said that 2 or 3000 negroes march in their train, that every kind of Stock which they cannot remove they destroy—eating up the green wheat and by destroying of the fences, expose to destruction the other growing grains."[128]

The confused situation in Virginia did not ignite a general slave uprising, although there were scattered attempts by individual slaves to form companies of black soldiers to join the British. As soon as they were discovered, they were quickly quashed by local authorities.[129] Instead, the widespread slave rebelliousness that was latent in Virginia and elsewhere in the South manifested itself in flight to the British. Except for the planters who moved their slaves beyond the reach of the army, virtually every family along its route lost slaves by desertion. After the army passed Matoax near Petersburg, William Withers reported to St. George Tucker that Tucker's wife's plantation had lost its work force.[130] Thirty of Jefferson's slaves ran away to the British during the ten days that Cornwallis's army lay encamped on the James River from Point of Fork to Jefferson's Elk Hill plantation. Ten years later Jefferson recorded in graphic detail what was probably a typical experience: "[Cornwallis] destroyed all my growing crops of corn and tobacco, he burned all my barns containing the same articles of last year, having first taken what he wanted, he used, as was to be expected, all my stocks of cattle, sheep and hogs for the sustenance of his army, and carried off all the horses capable of service: of those too young for service he cut the throats, and he burned all the fences on the plantations, so as to leave it an absolute waste."[131]

Although the great estates along the Potomac and Rappahannock rivers escaped the destruction done to plantations in the James River valley, British military operations in the area also led to widespread slave desertions. In a well-intentioned effort to console his brother William for the loss of sixty-five slaves, including "about 45 valuable grown slaves and useful Artisans," Richard Henry Lee summarized the losses of other planters: "Your neighbors Col. Taliaferro and Col. Travis lost every slave they had in the world, and Mr. Paradise has lost all but one—This has been the general case of all those who were near the enemy." In Lee's attempt to absolve

[127] Pauline Maier, "Early Revolutionary Leaders in the South and the Problem of Southern Distinctiveness," in Crow and Tise, eds., *Southern Experience*, 10.

[128] To Arthur Lee, June 4, 1781, Ballagh, *Letters of Richard Henry Lee* 2:230.

[129] Patrick Lockhart to Governor Nelson, November 17, 1781, To the Governor and Council of Virginia, July 2, 1781, Palmer et al., *Calendar of Virginia State Papers* 2:604–5, 5:333–34.

[130] William Withers to St. George Tucker, May 20, 1780, August 10, 1781, May 20, 1781, Tucker-Coleman Papers.

[131] To Dr. William Gordon, July 16, 1778, Paul Leicester Ford, *The Writings of Thomas Jefferson*, 10 vols. (New York: Putnam's 1892–99), 5:420.

himself and William's overseer, Valentine, from all responsibility for their escape can be read the story of the slaves' grim determination to find freedom: "All that I can say is, that every precaution for security was taken that could have been which has occasioned your loss to be so much less than that of others in similar circumstances of situation etc."[132]

Some slaves probably went to the British under duress; at least that is what most planters preferred to believe. Although he conceded that Cornwallis's army "did not compel any" slaves to desert, Dr. Robert Honyman nonetheless insisted that "wherever they had an opportunity the soldiers and inferior officers likewise, enticed and flattered the Negroes and prevailed on vast numbers to go along with them."[133] A variation of the same theme can be read in Richard Henry Lee's charge that "force, fraud, intrigue, theft, have all in turn been employed to delude these unhappy people and to defraud their masters!"[134] It would be erroneous to infer from these charges, however, that most slaves were helpless victims of white villainy. To be sure, blacks were shamelessly exploited by both sides, but such exploitation usually followed a conscious choice blacks made based upon their assessment of the situation.

John, the servant of William Hooper, is a case in point. When the Hooper family was expelled from Wilmington by Major Craig, the army did not permit John to accompany them. Instead he was "offered clothes, money, freedom, every thing that could captivate a youthful mind," if he would agree to serve with the army. John pretended to accept the British offer, but when the opportunity arose, he slipped past British sentries and fled seventy miles on foot to overtake the Hooper family.[135] John was a "loyal slave" of the type that more often existed in the dreams of white planters than in reality. It is impossible, of course, to determine his personal motivation. Perhaps he sought to rejoin other family members; perhaps, as Hooper preferred to believe, he chose the security of slavery and the apparent affection of his white owners over the uncertainties of freedom and the protection of unreliable strangers.

Given a similar set of alternatives, thousands of other slaves whose names are lost to history chose to wait out the war quietly on the plantations. Despite the fact that slaveowners generally viewed them as potential enemies, history has tended to regard these as loyal slaves. Although their reasons, like their names, are forever obscure, it is possible, even probable,

[132] To the Commander in Chief of the Armies of the United States, September 17, 1781, To William Lee, July 15, 1781, Ballagh, *Letters of Richard Henry Lee* 2:242, 256.

[133] Honyman, Diary, May 27, 1781.

[134] To the Commander in Chief of the Armies of the United States, September 17, 1781, Ballagh, *Letters of Richard Henry Lee* 2:256.

[135] William Hooper to James Iredell, February 17, 1782, Higginbotham, *Papers of Iredell* 2:328–29.

that their choice had nothing to do with the slave regime. There were after all, compelling reasons to reject the British offer of freedom, prominent among which were attachment to home and family, the enjoyment of the informal freedom that wartime conditions sometimes permitted, or the physical or psychological inability to run. Whatever hopes the war might have raised in these black men and women sank under the combined weight of prudence, caution, fear, and realism.

There was, however, in thousands of slaves a heightened sense of expectations that no amount of realism could dispel. In defiance of staggering odds they militantly rejected slavery by running to the British. Between four thousand and five thousand men and women of all ages followed behind the baggage train of Cornwallis's army on its doomed journey to Yorktown. Free of the dictates of the master and of the rigorous regime of the plantation, they fell comfortably into the role of wartime auxiliaries, the women working as cooks and maids for the officers, their wives, and mistresses, the men serving as batmen or foragers for the army. Although when free, blacks seldom indulged in revenge or destructiveness for its own sake, on the march they took what the army needed to survive. "Any place the horde approached," a Hessian officer wrote with a tone of moral superiority that belied the army's responsibility, "was eaten clean, like an acre invaded by a swarm of locusts." Either to compensate for the pathetic material poverty of their lives, or in an effort perhaps at role reversal, they "plundered the wardrobes of their masters and mistresses," and then in a touching display of the sense of community that had developed in the quarters' clustered dwellings, they "divided the loot, and clothed themselves piecemeal with it." For example, the Hessian officer wrote after an encounter with the baggage train, "a completely naked Negro wore a pair of silk breeches, another a finely colored coat, a third a silk vest without sleeves, a fourth an elegant shirt, a fifth a fine churchman's hat, and a sixth a wig.—All the rest of the body was bare," he marveled. "The one Negress wore a silk skirt, another a lounging robe with a long train, the third a jacket, the fourth a silk-laced bodice, the fifth a silk corset, the seventh, eighth, and ninth—all different styles of hats and coiffures." To the scornful officer, "These variegated creatures on thousands of horses" galloping behind the baggage train made the army look like "a wandering Arabian or Tarter horde."[136] To white planters the exotic spectacle was probably a frightening reminder of the dangerous potential of their slaves.

For white planters, however, the nightmare was almost over. For black bondmen the dream was about to end. After trying unsuccessfully to engage "the boy," as he called the young French officer Lafayette, Cornwallis abandoned Richmond on June 20 and advanced by way of Bottoms Bridge

[136] Ewald, *Diary*, 305.

to Williamsburg, which he occupied for ten days before moving on to Jamestown. Under orders from Clinton to establish a base on the Chesapeake, Cornwallis and his engineers decided to occupy the little tobacco port of Yorktown, situated close to the mouth of the York River. While several thousand black followers of the army labored under the hot August sun to fortify the village of Yorktown and Gloucester Neck across the river, a fleet of twenty-eight sail of the line commanded by Count de Grasse was approaching the capes of Virginia. Soon land forces commanded by the Marquis de St. Simon began disembarking at Jamestown Island while thirty-two hundred militiamen were assembling at Williamsburg to block the British peninsula escape route.[137]

On September 28 the Franco-American siege of Yorktown began. By early October the town was completely invested by land and water, "caught," the Virginia General George Weedon exulted, "handsomely in a pudding bag."[138] Unable to conduct foraging expeditions, the beleagured garrison was quickly faced with critical shortages of forage and provisions. To prevent them from starving to death, Cornwallis ordered all of the artillery and baggage horses slaughtered and their remains thrown into the York River. Several days later the bloated bodies of the dead animals "came back in heaps with the tide" to foul the air with the stench of death. With the same unflinching determination Cornwallis ordered the expulsion of the black followers of the army to extend the dwindling supplies of food and thereby save his hungry and ailing troops to fight another day. As French and American forces battered at their crumbling works, the British "drove back to the enemy all of our black friends, whom we had taken along to despoil the countryside." Despite his admission that "I would just as soon forget to record [it]," a shamed Hessian officer, Johann Ewald, registered the sordid details of the army's final obscene betrayal of its black allies. "We had used them to good advantage," Ewald admitted, "and set them free, and now, with fear and trembling, they had to face the reward of their cruel masters." Later while on a sneak patrol, Ewald encountered "a great number of these unfortunates." Afraid that the half-starved outcasts "would have soon devoured what I had," Ewald drove them away by force. "This harsh act had to be carried out," he explained, "because of the scarcity of provisions; but we should have thought more about their deliverance at this time."[139]

In the end sacrificing the black auxiliaries proved futile. Hungry, exhausted, dispirited, devastated by smallpox, the worn and wasted fighters were forced to capitulate. On Friday, October 19, their regimental colors

[137] See Wickwire and Wickwire, *Cornwallis*, 1–3, 358–59, 366–68, 374–82 for details.

[138] General G. Weedon to Nathanael Greene, September 5, 1781, Commager and Morris, eds., *Spirit of 'Seventy-Six*, 1218.

[139] Ewald, *Diary*, 335–36.

furled and cased, their drums covered with black handkerchiefs, beating a slow march, Cornwallis's entire army filed out and grounded their arms, some of the soldiers throwing them violently onto the pile to protest their humiliation. Their commander, pleading illness, was not present at the surrender ceremonies. All about the town he yielded, sprawled the bodies of the black victims of disease. After viewing the scene, St. George Tucker, the great Virginia jurist, recorded in his journal a dismal epitaph for the slaves who searched for freedom with Cornwallis: "An immense number of Negroes have died in the most miserable manner in York."[140]

When news of the defeat reached London the following month, Lord North, whose ministry was forced to resign as a result of it, responded as though he had "taken a ball in his breast." Pacing up and down his apartment on Downing Street, North repeatedly exclaimed in anguish, "O God! it is all over!"[141] In fact, sporadic fighting continued for two more years before a peace treaty could be successfully negotiated.

[140] Edward M. Riley, ed., "St. George Tucker's Journal of the Siege of Yorktown, 1781," *William and Mary Quarterly*, 3d ser., 5 (1948): 392–93.

[141] Memoirs of Sir Nathaniel Wraxall, Commager and Morris, *Spirit of 'Seventy-Six*, 1243–44.

SIX

THE COMING OF PEACE: BRITISH

EVACUATION AND AFRICAN-AMERICAN

RELOCATION

THE REVOLUTIONARY WAR in the South produced a vast movement of people. Until 1782 the migratory movement had been almost wholly within the region and was precipitated by the profound disruptions of war. The emigration of loyalists at the end of the war was the largest net outward movement from the former British colonies in North America. Accurate statistics for this movement are difficult to obtain, but estimates suggest a global figure of one hundred thousand exiles.[1] In the British evacuation in 1782 from three American ports—Savannah, Charleston, and New York—and from the Spanish port of St. Augustine in 1783, black loyalists and blacks who were the property of white loyalists comprised the largest group in the emigrating population.[2] The majority of the black exiles were slaves who were forced to move with their migrating loyalist owners; some of the black émigrés held British certificates of freedom and were resettled in England and other parts of the British Empire; some were eventually repatriated to Africa. By their very numbers, the movement of the black loyalists facilitated the transmission of culture, experience, and revolutionary sentiment to other parts of the world and ultimately tied the history of black people of the United States, the Caribbean islands, and West Africa together.

The restoration of peace between Britain and America "diffused universal joy among all parties, except us, who had escaped from slavery, and taken refuge in the English army," wrote the young Boston King, formerly the property of Richard Waring of Charleston, South Carolina. Rumors that all slaves held by the British army were to be delivered over to their former masters "filled us with inexpressible anguish and terror, especially when we saw our old masters coming from Virginia, North-Carolina, and other parts, and seizing upon their slaves in the streets of New-York, or even dragging them out of their beds. . . . For some days," King remem-

---

[1] Wallace Brown, *The Good Americans. The Loyalists in the American Revolution* (New York: William Morrow, 1969), 227.

[2] Christopher Moore, *The Loyalists. Revolution, Exile, Settlement* (Toronto: Macmillan, 1984), 101.

bered, "we lost our appetite for food, and sleep departed from our eyes." But "the English had compassion upon us in the day of our distress, and issued out a Proclamation, importing, 'That all slaves should be free, who had taken refuge in the British lines, and claimed the sanction and privileges of the Proclamation respecting the security and protection of Negroes.' "[3]

The surrender of Cornwallis at Yorktown practically ended the revolutionary war and brought down the ministry of Lord North. On March 27, 1782, a new government led by the Marquis of Rockingham came to power in England. Cornwallis's capitulation and reports of badly deteriorating conditions in the South led the new government to abandon the war effort. The task of evacuating British-held posts fell to Sir Guy Carleton, former governor of Quebec and commander of forces in Canada, who had recently been named to replace Henry Clinton as commander in chief in America. Because of an acute shipping shortage and poor planning, the evacuation took three years. It began in July 1782 with the withdrawal from Savannah and ended in August 1785, when the evacuation of East Florida was finally completed.[4]

Rumors of the decision to evacuate the southern posts touched off a bitter contest for possession of the bondmen in British lines: between patriots and loyalists, loyalists and the military, the banditti and the privateers. Against them all the black bondmen struggled for their freedom. Carleton's orders to prepare the city of Savannah for evacuation reached Governor Wright in mid-June. Eager to secure the slave labor force, the Georgia Assembly spread the nets of the law over loyalist estates, confiscating and selling at public auction all property appropriated, including over £40,000 of goods belonging to Governor Wright.[5] But the much embattled loyalists had managed to conceal "a considerable number of Negroes" in Savannah. When a British fleet of transports appeared off the bar, the assembly reacted quickly. Noting that the removal by the British of slaves belonging to the good people of the United States, would be "a manifest injury to this country," the assembly unanimously approved a resolution to allow commissioners for the sales of forfeited estates to enter British lines for the purpose of recovering slaves and urged the governor to grant private citizens the same right.[6] While the British fleet lay at Tybee Island for several days after the evacuation was complete, flags passed back and forth but to no avail. The Georgia Assembly watched helplessly as

[3] Quoted in Phyllis R. Blakeley, "Boston King: A Negro Loyalist Who Sought Refuge in Nova Scotia," *Dalhousie Review* 48 (Autumn 1968): 351.

[4] Eldon Jones, "The British Withdrawal from the South, 1781–1785," in Higgins, ed., *Revolutionary War in the South*, 259–85.

[5] Wright to Carleton, May 30, 1782, Carleton Papers, PRO30/55/41.

[6] Candler, *RRG* 2:341, 3:119–20, 130.

Crown officials and loyalists "hurried away with our Negroes," as Governor Wright described the British withdrawal.[7]

How many slaves were removed from Georgia is not clear. Contemporary estimates range from four to six thousand.[8] British immigration records suggest a figure of about thirty-five hundred.[9] Unfortunately the reliability of these records is questionable; the records are fragmentary and confusing. Because the number of refugees and slaves was greater than anticipated, there were not enough military transports to complete the evacuation. To accommodate them, all of the empty shipping in the harbor, including private vessels, were freighted with blacks, whites, and movable property for transportation to East Florida. When even private shipping proved inadequate, "many Indians, refugees and Negroes" were embarked in canoes and other small craft and proceeded to St. Augustine by way of inland swamps, while still others travelled the difficult overland route.[10] Because the available statistical information pertains principally to blacks removed by white loyalists at the evacuation of Savannah, it is a distortion to generalize from it about Georgia's loss in slave population. The impression gained from qualitative and limited statistical information is that if wartime losses to belligerent armies, partisan bands, shipsmasters, and gangs of banditti as well as to disease were added to the official figures, the number of blacks who were relocated or lost was perhaps as much as two-thirds of Georgia's total prewar black population of approximately fifteen thousand.[11]

Although an actual count of slave losses during the evacuation of Charleston lies beyond historical recovery, the evidence permits a reasoned guess of about ten thousand, a figure that is substantially higher than General Nathanael Greene's estimate of five to six thousand.[12] Illicit traffic in slaves was a constant feature of the war in the South, but reports of British plans to evacuate Charleston that began circulating early in 1782 stimulated the traffic, particularly in sequestered slaves. Because blacks were dispersed through the various departments of the army or were leased to loyalists, it was difficult to maintain control over sequestered blacks, even within the limited confines of the city of Charleston. By all accounts British army and naval officers were directly involved in their removal. According

[7] Candler, *CRG* 39:404–12.

[8] See, for example, Moultrie, *Memoirs* 2:340; *Royal Gazette*, July 27, 1782; "Miscellaneous Papers of James Jackson, 1781–1798," Lilla M. Hawes, ed., *Georgia Historical Quarterly* 37 (1953):78.

[9] Coleman, *American Revolution in Georgia*, 145–46.

[10] Captain William Swiney to Carleton, June 12, 1783, Carleton Papers, PRO30/55, Carleton to Shelburne, August 15, 1782, CO5/106/329.

[11] Coleman, *American Revolution in Georgia*, 145–46.

[12] Nathanael Greene to R. R. Livingston, December 19, 1783, M247, reel 175, item 55, 2:599, Papers of the Continental Congress.

to the new state governor, John Mathews, "half of some, two thirds of others and the whole of a few [sequestered] estates have been deprived of the Negroes and stock that were on them when put under sequestration." Although sequestration generally meant only temporary deprivation of property, Mathews protested to Leslie, "most of your officers have construed this word into a very different meaning," and "every species of prop-·erty, Negroes, plate, household furniture, horses, carriages, cattle, etc. have been indiscriminately torn from their owners by persons now under your immediate command and have been either sent beyond seas for the benefit of those who have taken—I had almost said plundered—them, or now remain within your lines and in either case lost to their owners."[13]

There is little doubt that sequestered slaves were being removed on military vessels sailing from Charleston harbor. A "number of Negroes" who had served as servants to the officers of the Nineteenth and Thirtieth regiments were discovered on board a group of military transports as they prepared to sail from Charleston for Jamaica. In a sternly worded rebuke Leslie ordered the slaves released into the custody of the Board of Claims, authorized by him to register all blacks, slave and free, who still remained within British lines. Those certified as the property of loyalists were to be returned to their owners, the rest would continue to serve as military laborers.[14] In addition to those removed by the military, many sequestered slaves were deceived by private individuals who, under the "pretense of bringing Negroes from Carolina to prevent them from being punished by their owners," transported them to the Windward Islands for sale there.[15]

The documented charges of slave traffic exposes the impasse into which the Philipsburg proclamation had led. To satisfy military manpower needs and to demoralize the South by depriving it of its labor force and resources, the military command had fashioned a policy that promised freedom to slaves at the same time it condoned the practice of traffic in captured slaves as spoils of war. To some extent the exigencies of war had papered over the fundamental contradictions in the policy. But the competing claims of rival groups for the same spoils—to say nothing of the greater moral claim of the slaves themselves—laid bare their absolute incompatibility. Torn by the conflicting appeals of conscience and politics, Leslie turned to the commander in chief for guidance. What, he asked

[13] Mathews to Leslie, April 12, 1782, CO5/109/340–42.

[14] Leslie to O'Hara, May 3, 1782, Leslie Letter Book, Emmet Coll. 15539; *Royal South Carolina Gazette*, April 30, 1782.

[15] According to John Cruden, individuals named Gray and Gillespie carried on a lucrative trade in sequestered blacks in Jamaica and Tortola, the main island of the British Virgin Islands in the Lesser Antilles; see Cruden to George Nibbs, March 16, 1783, Extract of a Letter to Hon. J. Fahia, March 24, 1783, and Cruden to Major C. Nesbit, March 25, 1783, CO5/109/375, 377.

Carleton, should be done with sequestered slaves, many of whom had been useful in the siege of Savannah and elsewhere and were as a consequence of their service entitled to freedom.[16] Should rebel-owned slaves taken in action be regarded as the possession of officers who, Leslie explained, "look on the Negroes as their property"?[17] What should be done about loyalists whose property was confiscated by the South Carolina assembly and who "expect some compensation may be made for their losses" out of what remained of the sequestered property in slaves?[18]

Rather than choose between equally unsatisfying alternatives, Carleton instructed Leslie to free those slaves who held a British promise and to use his discretion with respect to the rest.[19] Leslie tried to compromise by issuing strict orders to officers against removing "any Negroes that does not belong to them."[20] But between August 7, when the evacuation announcement was made, and October 14, when the first contingent of refugees sailed from Charleston for East Florida, the military command was inundated by complaints from loyalists.[21] The full dimensions of the contest between military officers and loyalists over slaves and its tragic implications for the black bondmen who were at the center of it are best illustrated by a petition signed by 103 loyalists. The petitioners reproached the military command for its failure to halt the traffic in rebel-owned slaves, upon which loyalists' hopes for indemnification rested. Despite their transparent self-interest, however, the petitioners were also moved by sympathy for the plight of the slaves in question, "who although reduced to slavery in this country, are entitled to humanity, which forbids the separation of them from their kindred, and the dispersion of them in countries where their *Bondage would be more grievous*."[22]

What loyalists' petitions had failed to effect by persuasion, state authorities tried to achieve by coercion. To build up dwindling food supplies in Charleston and to stock adequate provisions for the evacuees, Leslie had requested permission of Governor Mathews and General Greene to purchase supplies from people in the countryside. Greene refused on the grounds that "the more scanty we can render their supplies of provisions, the sooner [evacuation] will happen and the fewer Negroes they will have in their power to take with them."[23] Mathews resisted by course of law.

[16] General Leslie's Queries, June 27, 1782, Carleton Papers, PRO30/55/43.

[17] Leslie to Carleton, October 18, 1782, Carleton Papers, PRO30/55/52.

[18] Leslie to Carleton, August 10, 1782, Leslie Letter Book, Emmet Coll. 15630.

[19] Answers to General Leslie's Queries, Carleton Papers, PRO30/55/44.

[20] Headquarters, August 13, 1787, Miscellaneous Manuscripts, SCHS.

[21] Rawlins Lowndes to Carleton, August 8, 1782, Mary Butler to Cornwallis, September 16, 1782, Carleton Papers, PRO30/55/49.

[22] The Memorial and Humble Representation of Divers Loyal Inhabitants of South Carolina, September 9, 1782, CO5/397/428–31.

[23] Greene to Marion, August 9, 1782, Horry Papers, Peter Force Transcripts.

Unless slave removals were halted, he warned Leslie, the state would seize on the debts due to British merchants, the confiscated estates and the claims on those estates by marriage settlements.[24] Anxious to guarantee the debts of British merchants and to forestall further confiscations of loyalist property, Leslie agreed to negotiate. On October 10 an accord was reached whereby Leslie agreed to restore all slaves belonging to citizens of South Carolina except those who held a British promise of freedom. Representatives of both sides would appraise the latter group and appropriate compensation would be made to their owners within six months. In exchange Mathews agreed that the state would cease sequestering loyalist property and would open its courts to suits by loyalists for estates already confiscated.[25]

However well-intentioned Leslie's efforts to reconcile the interests of the contesting parties, the October 10 agreement was a leap in the dark. At issue were several thousand slaves valued at tens of thousands of pounds. In June as he began developing plans for the evacuation of Charleston, Leslie had estimated that some ten thousand slaves were within British lines: six thousand belonging to loyalists; four thousand more the property of rebels.[26] When in August he ordered all persons who wished to leave the city to register with the army, 4,230 whites and 7,163 blacks were enrolled. According to the committee of loyalists named by Leslie to complete the departure list, it was "far from complete due to short notice allowed for people to give in their names." Missing from the list as well were the sequestered blacks and those attached to army departments, "of which there are several thousands." When stressing the need for additional ships, the committee of loyalists pointed out that "many Negroes [were] still expected from the country." Although the evidence is hardly precise, it does argue strongly that the British held no less than ten thousand blacks, perhaps as many as twelve thousand.[27]

As word of the pending evacuation circulated, slaves clamored at the gates of freedom, demanding to be counted among those described as "obnoxious" by reason of their service to Britain and, therefore, entitled to liberty. Recognizing the moral legitimacy of their claims, Leslie appointed a special committee of army officers and loyalists to examine "the numbers

[24] Mathews to Leslie, August 17, 1782, CO5/1093/44–45.

[25] Agreement Between A. Wright and James Johnson and Edward Rutledge and Benjamin Guerard, Carleton Papers, PRO30/55/51.

[26] General Leslie's Queries, June 27, 1782, Carleton Papers, PRO30/55/43.

[27] Return of the Number of Persons and Quantity of Effects to be Removed from Charleston . . . , August 29, 1782, Carleton Papers, PRO30/55/97; Ralph Izard to His Wife, October 7, 1782, Miscellaneous. Ralph Izard, Letters Concerning the British Evacuation of Charleston, 1782, New York Public Library.

and pretensions" of those claiming protection.[28] The response stunned the British general, who had by the terms of the October 10 accord, agreed to monetary compensation to American owners. In an urgent plea to Carleton for advice, Leslie warned that "from the Numbers that may expect to be brought off, including their wives and children, if to be paid for will amount to a monstrous expense." The potential cost of compensation was further inflated by the claims of loyalists, who dispatched representatives to New York in August to plead their case personally with Carleton, and by the demands of the army.[29]

Reluctant to commit the London government to such an expenditure, Carleton instructed Leslie to try to extend the compensation period from six months to a year to allow the home government time to decide the question. He did, however, reiterate the army's commitment to free those slaves entitled to British protection, and he ordered that none should be removed by the army departments.[30] The order came too late. On October 14 American searchers discovered 136 slaves concealed on the outbound St. Augustine fleet, and other searchers were the same day denied permission to board navy galleys. Frustrated by repeated delays and angered over reports that Haddrell's Point near Charleston was being used as an assembly point for the removal of contraband slaves, Mathews abrogated the short-lived agreement.[31]

Although the costly obligation of compensation was now eliminated, Leslie had still to contend with the thorny problem of how to deal with the conflicting claims of loyalists and military officers. The board of field officers and loyalists appointed by him to adjudicate the matter broke apart almost immediately, apparently as a result of a dispute over the military conduct of the quasi-judicial proceedings. After Major Moncrief "picked out about 260 able men" apparently for service as military slaves in St. Lucia, the loyalist members resigned.[32] Former state governor John Rutledge and other prominent Carolinians later maintained that the board of officers subsequently used its discretionary authority to report as obnoxious "almost every Negro, man, woman and child, that was worth the carrying away."[33] According to John Cruden "upward of 300 Negroes was passed by the Board."[34]

[28] Appointment of Robert Powell, Gideon Dupont et al., October, 1787, Leslie Letter Book, Emmet Coll. 15675.

[29] Leslie to Carleton, October 18, 1782, Secret, Carleton Papers, PRO30/55/52.

[30] Carleton to Leslie, November 12, 1782, Carleton Papers.

[31] Blake and Saunders to Mathews, October 14, 1782, CO5/109/354; Mathews to Leslie, October 19, 1782, CO5/397/442.

[32] 100 (a secret correspondent) to no direction, November 8, 1782, Horry Papers, Peter Force Transcripts.

[33] J. Rutledge, David Ramsay et al. to Carleton, March 27, 1783, CO5/109/304.

[34] Extract of a Letter to Hon. J. Fahia, March 24, 1783, CO5/109/377.

After the British fleet bearing the last troops and evacuees went to sea early in December, virtually no sequestered slaves remained of the original five thousand. As is the case with Georgia, British immigration records cannot be taken as precise indicators of the numbers of South Carolina blacks lost by desertion, death, or removal. Evacuation records compiled by John Winniett account for between five and six thousand.[35] This does not include those clandestinely removed by the army at the time of the evacuation or during the course of the war. Neither does it include those removed by gangs of banditti and slave traders, those who died of disease, or the more fortunate ones who escaped to freedom. If these were added to the official count, it is likely that the total wartime figure would approach the estimate of twenty-five thousand usually given by contemporaries.[36]

East Florida was the last British post in North America to be evacuated. Acquired by Britain from Spain by the Treaty of Paris of 1763, as late as 1782 it was still a sparsely settled colony of mostly large landholdings averaging 20,000 acres, many of which were uncultivated and owned by absentee landowners. The small population, which consisted of civil and military officials, two merchants, a few shopkeepers, and a number of artisans, clustered in the little town of St. Augustine.[37] Beginning in 1776 with the establishment of a revolutionary government in Georgia, East Florida began to receive the first white loyalist émigrés. Following Dunmore's defeat in Virginia, numbers of Virginia loyalists and "some Negroes," possibly brought there by Dunmore's fleet, began to arrive.[38] Historically a haven for black runaways, by 1779 East Florida's black population had quadrupled, principally as a result of a large influx of black fugitives and kidnapped slaves after the British invasion of the South in 1779. With a black-white ratio of three to one, the local assembly, many members of which were from among the original refugees from Georgia and South Carolina, authorized Governor Tonyn to seize all fugitive slaves and employ them under white overseers in building fortifications for the defense of the colony.[39]

In January 1782 East Florida was designated by the Crown as an asylum

[35] A Return of Refugees and Their Slaves Arriving in East Florida . . . to November 14, 1782, A Return of Refugees and Their Slaves Arriving in the Province of East Florida . . . December 23, 1782, and A Return of Refugees and Their Families and Negroes Who Came to the Province of East Florida . . . , CO5/560/477/507, 811–20.

[36] See, for example, *South Carolina Gazette and General Advertiser*, November 29–December 2, 1783; Moultrie, *Memoirs* 2:356.

[37] William Drayton, Force Papers, ser. 8D, entry 37.

[38] Tonyn to Germain, October 10, 1776, Tonyn to William Knox, November 1, 1776, CO5/557/3,193.

[39] An Act for Empowering . . . , June 30, 1781, CO5/624/77–79; Tonyn to Germain, July 30, 1781, CO5/560/124.

for loyalists. By May approximately three hundred destitute refugees from Georgia had arrived, although the official evacuation was not yet underway. From July through December a steady stream of emigrants poured into the colony, some of them substantial merchants, many of them impoverished farmers and backwoodsmen. The planters and farmers were given grants of land and tools and subsistence for their slaves; the merchants were provided with houses in town. The evacuation of Savannah and Charleston, together with Cornwallis's surrender at Yorktown, added some eleven thousand inhabitants to East Florida, of whom three out of five were black.[40] Because of the poor soil around St. Augustine, many of the new arrivals settled on the bluffs of the St. Johns River, forty miles from St. Augustine or on the fertile banks of the St. Marys River around Mosquito Inlet. Provided with hoes and axes, broadaxes and grindstones, they rapidly cleared the land and began to cultivate rice, Indian corn, and indigo. Because it was less labor intensive, and because of the possibility of higher profits, many of the new settlers turned to the production of tar and turpentine from the plentiful pine stands. In less than two years, lumber and naval stores ranked with indigo as the principal exports of the colony.[41]

Although East Florida had become "a commodious asylum" for refugees, the British government signed a preliminary peace treaty with Spain on January 20, 1783, which retroceded East Florida to Spain.[42] News of the impending evacuation sparked again a struggle over possession of the approximately nine thousand blacks in East Florida. The state of South Carolina immediately dispatched William Livingston as special commissioner under a flag of truce to try to prevent their removal by invoking article seven of the preliminary articles of peace between Britain and the United States.[43] Equally anxious to secure liberal treatment for South Carolina loyalists, John Cruden, the former commissioner of sequestered estates, appointed Dr. James Clitherall, one-time surgeon to the South Carolina Royalists, to assist in the recovery of slaves claimed by the citizens of South Carolina.[44] Governor Tonyn had other ideas, however. In an effort to hold on to as many slaves as possible until the southern state assemblies took action to repeal the confiscation acts, or in the event they refused to

[40] Speech of Tonyn to Both Houses, January 21, 1782, Tonyn to Germain, May 22, 1782, Tonyn to Earl of Shelburne, November 14, 1782, Memorial of Tonyn to the Lords Commissioners of the Treasury, CO5/560/177, 211, 235, 268; McArthur to Carleton, May 23, 1783, Carleton Papers, PRO30/55/70.

[41] Tonyn to Thomas Townshend, March 31, 1783, CO5/560/260; McArthur to Carleton, May 23, 1783, Carleton Papers, PRO30/55/70.

[42] The articles of peace are reprinted in Joseph B. Lockey, ed., *East Florida 1783–1785. A File of Documents Assembled and Many of Them Translated* (Berkeley and Los Angeles: University of California Press, 1949), 54–57.

[43] Guerard to Tonyn, April 19, 1783, May 6, 1783, CO5/560/331.

[44] Cruden to Clitherall, April 24, 1783, Carleton Papers, PRO30/55/68.

do so, to use the sequestered slaves to indemnify loyalists whose estates had been confiscated, Tonyn refused to cooperate. Instead he threatened to enforce an East Florida law making it a felony to remove any Negro or to assist in their escape on penalty of death without benefit of clergy and to require all ships masters to post bond of £200s. upon entering any East Florida port as surety against the illegal transportation of slaves.[45]

But the competition for slaves had still another dimension. As the revolutionary war wound down, the bands of banditti that had ravished the countryside for most of the war, shifted their activities to East Florida, the scene of fleeing loyalists with their slaves and countless runaways. Bands of "lawless banditti," among others the notorious Daniel McGirth, John Linder, Jr., formerly a tory militia officer, and his close friend Belay Cheney, William Cunningham, the Virginia marauder whose reprisal activities in South Carolina earned him the sobriquet "Bloody Bill," hovered along the frontiers of the province, plundering slaves and murdering and robbing their owners, until they were finally forced to retreat into the swamps by a posse of citizens organized by John Cruden. When in July 1784 the Spanish took possession of East Florida, five of the bandit leaders accepted the Spanish governor's offer of voluntary exile to one of the Spanish possessions. McGirth and Cunningham refused but were later exiled briefly to Havana.[46] Belay Cheney, John Linder, Jr., and his father John Linder, Sr. emigrated to the Mobile District, a political division of Spanish West Florida created in 1780 after the Spanish capture of Fort Charlotte from British forces. Both of the former bandits were given large land grants in the rich valleys of the Tensaw and Tombigbee rivers north of Mobile, which until the American Revolution was populated by a scattering of creole French families.

The Revolution spawned a significant influx of settlers, many with sizeable holdings of slaves and livestock, to the wilderness of southern Alabama. By 1788, census reports showed that the Mobile District had 556 whites and 836 blacks. The influx of immigrants, black and white, played an important role in the economic development of the new frontier, particularly in livestock grazing, which experienced remarkable growth during the early nineteenth century and remained an important occupation until the rich pasturelands of the public domain became sufficiently settled by farmers and planters to interfere with the grazing of the herds of cattle and swine.[47]

[45] Proclamation, *East Florida Gazette*, May 3, 1783, CO5/110/39; Clitherall to Cruden, May 25, 1783, Charles Johnston, James Clitherall, and Robert Willson to Cruden, May 30, 1783, Carleton Papers, PRO30/55/70.

[46] Tonyn to Evan Napean, October 1, 1783, Tonyn to Lord North, CO5/560/359–60, 741–46; Lockey, *East Florida*, 195–96, 215.

[47] Jack D. L. Holmes, "Alabama's Forgotten Settler: Notes on the Spanish Mobile District,

On August 29, 1785, the last group of evacuees departed East Florida on HMS Cyrus. According to British immigration records approximately ten thousand emigrants, 3,398 of them white, 6,540 of them black, left for different parts of the British Empire.[48] The great majority of the black émigrés were slaves forced by white planters to relocate with them. Almost half of them ended up in Jamaica and the Bahamas; the rest were scattered throughout the British West Indies, Europe, Nova Scotia, and Spanish West Florida. Altogether perhaps twenty thousand slaves were removed by white loyalists during the evacuation of Savannah, Charleston, and St. Augustine or were clandestinely carried off by officers of the British army and navy along the spreading lines of retreat, the ends of which reached into the brutal slave systems of the British West Indies. Their removal produced a marked effect on the social and economic conditions of the islands.

Only 714 slaves were removed from East Florida to Jamaica. For most of the war, however, Jamaica had been receiving loyalists from New England, the Chesapeake, the Carolinas, and Georgia, and they continued to drift in in smaller numbers for several years after the war was over. No accurate count exists of the total numbers of American slaves transported to Jamaica, however, because the Jamaica Assembly exempted loyalists from the payment of duties and imposts on the slaves they carried into the country for a period of seven years.[49] An official computation put the total number of loyalist-owned slaves at between forty-five hundred and five thousand,[50] but according to church registers 183 white families accompanied by approximately five thousand slaves emigrated from Georgia and settled in St. Elizabeth's parish alone.[51] Moreover, although a significant proportion of the booty seized by the army in America was consumed by the army, high quantities of staples and slaves were apparently disposed of in the West Indies. Circumstantial evidence suggests that many of the slaves ended up in Jamaica. During a twenty-year period beginning in 1768, the slave population of the island increased dramatically from 166,914 to 240,000.[52] Over sixty-five thousand of the seventy-three thou-

---

1780–1813," *Alabama Historical Quarterly* 33 (1971): 87–97; Jack D. L. Holmes, "The Role of Blacks in Spanish Alabama: The Mobile District, 1780–1813," ibid. 37 (1975): 5–18; Robert V. Haynes, *The Natchez District and the American Revolution* (Jackson: University Press of Mississippi, 1976), 30–33; Frank L. Owsley, *Plain Folk of the Old South* (Baton Rouge: Louisiana State University Press, 1982), 25–30.

[48] Tonyn to Sydney, August 29, 1785, Return of Persons Who Emigrated from East Florida to Different Parts of the British Dominions, May 2, 1786, CO5/561/709, 817.

[49] Archibald Campbell to Thomas Townshend, April 5, 1783, CO137/83.

[50] Account of Slaves in Jamaica Taken from the Poll-Tax Rolls, 1788, Add. MSS 12435, British Library, London.

[51] "Lists of Loyalists From Georgia Who Settled in Jamaica," *New England Historical and Genealogical Magazine* 62 (1908): 300–1.

[52] Estimates of Cattle and Negroes, 1768, Add. MSS 18273, British Library, London.

sand new slaves were apparently brought into the port of Kingston between 1775 and 1785.[53] Extant records reveal, however, that the principal
"African Factors" for Jamaica imported almost no African slaves during the
same period.[54] Because the records do not indicate the source of the increase, it is impossible to say with certainty that they were removed from
America, but many of them likely had been.

What became of them is unclear. Some of the loyalist émigrés settled in
Kingston and were sufficiently successful in business to arouse popular resentment over their temporary exemption from taxation. Others were so
impoverished that the island governor, Archibald Campbell, who probably
knew many of the Georgia émigrés, organized a "public subscription" for
their benefit. Although the London government had approved the granting of unpatented lands to the emigrants, much of it was rocky or mountainous and unsuitable for cultivation.[55] Some of the first Georgia emigrants resorted to the Jamaican system of jobbing, hiring out their slaves
to do the heavy work on local estates. Because work was plentiful, field
hands could earn up to three shillings plus provisions.[56] But the return of
peace, which permitted the reopening of the slave trade, greatly reduced
the demand for jobbing gangs and forced the planters to search for other
ways to employ their slaves. As a temporary expedient some planters sold
the provisions that had been provided by the government for the maintenance of their slaves. A series of hurricanes, which swept over the island
for seven successive seasons and destroyed the plantain walks, which were
the principal source of food for island slaves, exacerbated the problem of
food supplies for American slaves. To make matters worse, yellow fever,
brought to Jamaica by a ship from Philadelphia, flared in epidemic proportions. Prevalent among newcomers, it killed as many as seventeen persons a day. Overworked and undernourished, American slaves were among
the fifteen thousand island slaves who died as a result of that series of disasters.[57]

[53] Imports in British Bottoms into the Port of Kingston . . . Thomas Davison, Collector,
March 19, 1785, CO137/85/237.

[54] Account of Negroes Imported from Africa Sold by Hibberts and Jackson from 1764–
1774, Account of Negroes Imported from Africa Sold by Mssrs. Coppels, 1782, Account of
Negroes Imported from Africa Sold by Messrs. Rainfords, Account of Negroes Imported
and Sold by Messrs. Mures and Dunlop from Africa from 1781–1786, MS, West Indies S.10,
Rhodes House Library, Oxford, England.

[55] A. Campbell to Thomas Townshend, April 5, 1783, Earl of Shelburne to Campbell,
November 26, 1782, CO137/82/83; William James Gardner, *A History of Jamaica from Its
Discovery by Christopher Columbus to the Present Time* (London: E. Stock, 1873), 161.

[56] Campbell to the Earl of Shelburne, September 20, 1782, CO137/82; Leslie to Carleton,
November 18, 1782, Carleton Papers, PRO30/55/54.

[57] Report of the House of Assembly of Jamaica on the Slave Trade and the Treatment of
Negroes, 1788, MS West Indies S.10, Rhodes House Library; Clarke to Sydney, May 16,

Desperate for a way to recover their failing fortunes, a group of indigo planters from Georgia and South Carolina tried to revive the cultivation of indigo, which had flourished in Jamaica in the seventeenth century, by requesting that the bounty formerly granted to indigo planters in the mainland colonies be extended to Jamaica.[58] Their efforts apparently failed because as late as 1834 indigo remained a minor export, amounting in value to only £5,822.[59] With the encouragement of Governor Campbell a group of loyalists petitioned the home government to transport them and their slaves to the vast, thinly settled Mosquito Coast of Central America. A tropical, forested lowland, well watered and well suited to the cultivation of both indigo and sugar, they expected that the Mosquito Coast could be quickly changed from a coastal wilderness inhabited principally by the peaceful Mosquito Indians, into a British settlement "of consequence to the nation."[60] Provided with four months' provisions for themselves and their slaves, some thirty loyalist families with about one hundred slaves settled around Black River to the east of Cape Honduras, and at Cape Gracias a Dios, to the south of the cape,[61] and began establishing sugar plantations. In August fifty more families with nearly two hundred slaves arrived from East Florida.[62] Settlers continued to arrive and to establish small colonies along the coast. Within less than six months the principal settlement at Black River had 334 white families and 1,299 slaves, which when added to smaller settlements elsewhere, brought the total population to 448 white families and 1,891 slaves. In 1786, however, Spain claimed sovereignty over the Mosquito Coast under the terms of the Treaty of Paris. When Britain agreed to relinquish possession of the area, the settlers were forced to once again relocate, this time in Honduras.[63]

According to British immigration records, the Bahama Islands received one of the largest contingents of American evacuees.[64] Although title to the Bahamas had been granted by Charles II to the proprietors of Carolina

1785, CO137/85/153; Charles Ogilvie and Gideon Dupont, Agents for Loyalists in Jamaica, to Carleton, April 8, 1783, Carleton Papers, PRO30/55/66.

[58] Gardner, *History of Jamaica*, 83; Campbell to Lord North, August 1, 1783, CO137/83.

[59] Gardner, *History of Jamaica*, 323.

[60] Campbell to Lord North, July 14, 1783, Campbell to Sydney, July 3, 1784, CO137/83/84.

[61] Add. MSS 18270, 9.

[62] Campbell to Sydney, July 3, 1784, Alured Clarke to Sydney, August 15, 1784, CO137/84/137.

[63] Sydney to Clarke, November 18, 1784, A List of Settlers, Their Slaves, etc. on the Mosquito Shore, October 16, 1786, Sydney to Clarke, July 7, 1786, July 31, 1786, James Lurie to A. Clarke, June 19, 1787, CO137/84/86.

[64] For a general history of the Bahamas, with special emphasis on the loyalist period, see Sandra Riley, *Homeward Bound: A History of the Bahama Islands to 1850 with a Definitive Study of Abaco in the American Loyalist Plantation Period* (Miami, Fla.: Island Research, c. 1983).

in 1670 as part of an attempt at systematic colonization, until 1784 the population of the islands amounted to only 1,722 whites and 2,333 blacks, a sizeable number of whom were free. During the revolutionary war the islands were briefly held by Spain but were retaken by Britain, whose possession was confirmed by the Treaty of Paris of 1783. Upon the evacuation of East Florida approximately one thousand whites and nearly four thousand blacks emigrated to the islands, the majority of them settling on New Providence, Great Abaco, and Exuma.[65] Discouraged, perhaps, by reports that the thin, rocky soil and the lack of contiguous tracts of land made the islands unsuitable for large gangs of slaves, only a handful of large slave-owners were among the first arrivals.[66] In 1787, however, the Crown purchased the Bahamas from the proprietors, and, in an effort to attract settlers and provide new homes for American loyalists, offered forty acres of land to every male head of household who emigrated and twenty acres to every white or black man, woman, or child in a family plus exemption from quitrents for a period of ten years.[67]

Within two years the white population had doubled, increasing by l,600, and the black population had trebled, growing by 5,700.[68] The arrival of the newcomers had a significant demographic impact. Whereas most of the old population had been concentrated on New Providence, Eleuthera, and Harbour islands, several of the Out Islands, including Exuma, Long Island, Turks, Cat and Great Abaco islands, were settled for the first time. Although most of the land on Great Abaco was held by absentee owners, they agreed to relinquish title, and 658 refugees evacuated through New York established a settlement there, which they named Carleton in honor of the British commander in chief.[69] Within a few days of their arrival dissent broke out and two-thirds of the group left Carleton for Marsh's Harbour, where they laid out another town. Other small settlements were made on Cat Island and on Exuma.[70]

The early spirit of cooperation that existed between the loyalists and the old inhabitants quickly degenerated into a bitter, sometimes violent power struggle. Although there were several sources of friction, legal problems involving ownership of slaves were among the most important. Because of the proximity of the islands to the North American mainland, American

[65] McArthur to Carleton, July 5, 1783, Carleton Papers, PRO30/55/74; An Account of the Quantity of Land and the Number of Inhabitants, CO37/23/3.

[66] Return of Loyalists Who Arrived in the Bahama Islands from North America, June 4, 1784, CO23/23/131.

[67] Michael Craton, *A History of the Bahama Islands* (London: Collins, 1962), 163.

[68] Report Relating to the Bahamas, 1790, Liverpool Papers, Add. MSS 38350.

[69] Johann David Schoepf, *Travels in the Confederation 1783–1784*, 2 vols. (New York: Burt Franklin, 1968), 2:259, says Abaco was settled by North American refugees.

[70] Archibald McArthur to Lord Sydney, March 1, 1784, CO23/25/68–70.

slaveowners were, according to Governor John Maxwell, "daily pestering me with applications" for the restoration of slaves held by transplanted loyalists. Maxwell believed that the loyalists had acquired their slaves either by "Plunder or false promises," and that Americans had recovery rights to them under the terms of the Treaty of Paris of 1783, but he was also deeply troubled by the betrayal of British promises to black Americans. His anguish at their continuing exploitation is apparent in his plea to the assembly to provide legal protection to slaves against "the inhuman severities" of their masters: "the poor slave obtained his freedom by doing an act, which all nations protect: which is, most of these wretches deserted from their masters in the field: our Generals gave them protections: and in shifting for themselves, the masters deceive them and pretend a bill of sale for them on landing."[71]

Maxwell's departure for England in February 1785 and his replacement by acting Governor James Edward Powell led to the abatement, if not the disappearance, of mutual irritations. Powell's death and the subsequent appointment of John Murray, Earl of Dunmore, as governor in 1787, quickly revived the old conflicts. Still posing as the Great Liberator, Dunmore set up a Negro Court to decide all questions of property claims. The new court, which consisted of three persons appointed to serve at Dunmore's pleasure, had no jury. Dunmore then dispatched a boat to Great Abaco to "take away all the rebel property Negroes." Prevented from boarding the vessel by their new white owners, a number of slaves ran away, others armed themselves and went into open rebellion in the area around Spencer's Bight. Fearing "nothing less than an insurrection of their Slaves, and eventually to be obliged to relinquish their houses and plantations, destitute of every subsistence for themselves, their wives and children," the planters turned to Dunmore for help.[72] Anxious to lull the planters' fears and calm the growing racial tensions, Dunmore personally led the members of the Negro Court to Great Abaco and there extended a general invitation to all blacks to come in to claim their freedom before the court. Not surprisingly, only thirty blacks appeared, twenty-nine of whom were adjudged to be slaves, only one to be entitled to freedom. The grateful planters thanked Dunmore for the "fair, candid and impartial Trials which have been afforded our runaway Slaves, and the quiet and peaceful restoration of most of them to their lawful owners."[73]

[71] Observations on the Within Message and Extract, Message from Governor to General Assembly, September 29, 1784, CO23/25/196, 197.

[72] Memorial of the Planters and Other Inhabitants of the Island of Abaco, Residing at Spencer's Bight, in William Wylly, *A Short Account of the Bahama Islands, Their Climate, Productions, etc.* (London: n.p., 1789), 140 app. 9. Although Wylly, a loyalist who emigrated to the Bahamas in 1787 and became Solicitor General in 1787 and 1788, and Dunmore were bitter enemies, his account is generally corroborated by other sources.

[73] Ibid., 22–23, 41.

The coming of the loyalists, black and white, also had a decided effect on the social and economic life of the Bahama Islands. The addition of some five thousand slaves substantially increased the black ratio of the population and heightened racial consciousness. By contrast to other slave systems in the hemisphere where miscegenation was common, white loyalists and their descendants maintained rigid racial purity by intermarriage among white families. More importantly, the introduction of thousands of slaves reinforced the frail plantation system. Although slavery had been introduced into the Bahamas in 1671,[74] no single system of labor predominated nor did any single economic activity prevail. The four thousand inhabitants eked out a living by fishing, salt raking, wood cutting, and wrecking, the perennial Bahamian trade in plunder salvaged from vessels wrecked off the island's rocky coast. Agricultural production was limited, with only an estimated 500 acres of cultivated land on all of the islands,[75] most of it in small family plots of one to three acres, which was devoted to the production of fruit, yams, cassava, and sugar cane. The value of all Bahamian exports to Britain in 1773–1774 was a mere £5,216, most of which was in wrecked goods.[76]

The arrival of white loyalists and nearly five thousand slaves with diverse skills dramatically altered the Bahamian economy. By 1785 the number of acres under cultivation had increased to 2,470; five years later 18,000 acres were under cultivation, most of it in cotton, which was introduced into the Bahamas by American loyalists in 1785.[77] By 1788 the black loam soil was producing 250 tons of cotton annually, which was an important source for the British textile industry.[78] The introduction of a cotton gin in 1790 by Joseph Eve, a loyalist, revolutionized the industry and enabled it to withstand the attacks of the chenille bug, a disastrous hurricane that devastated the island in 1796, and overworking of the thin soils. The failure of the crop of 1800, however, precipitated an exodus of loyalists; an estimated three thousand returned to Georgia. The industry finally collapsed following the abolition of slavery in 1838.[79]

Other Bahamian products also benefited from the influx of black and white American loyalists. Until 1785 most of the Bahamian salt exported to provision ships, the New England fisheries, and the Newfoundland cod fisheries came from the Exuma salt ponds. Exuma, with a black population of 638 and only 66 whites,[80] continued to be a big supplier of salt for the

[74] Craton, *History of the Bahama Islands*, 189, 256.

[75] [William Wylly], A Short Account of the Bahama Islands by a Barrister at Law, Add. MSS, 6058, British Library, London.

[76] Trade Statistics, Bahamas, 1785, Liverpool Papers, Add. MSS 38346, 56.

[77] Report Relating to the Bahamas, 1790, Liverpool Papers, Add. MSS 38350, 217–26.

[78] Wylly, Short Account, Add. MSS 6058.

[79] Riley, *Homeward Bound*, 84, 190; Craton, *History of the Bahama Islands*, 170, 180, 181.

[80] Craton, *History of the Bahama Islands*, 166.

northern fisheries, producing in one year 50,000 bushels.[81] Only 75 whites and 41 blacks were raking salt on Turks Island at the southeast end of the island chain. By 1787 Turks Island had approximately 800 inhabitants, over half of them black, engaged in raking salt. So rapid was the growth of salt production on Turks Island that 600 blacks had to be brought in from Bermuda for the raking season.[82] This black Bermudian element led the inhabitants of Turks Island to repudiate their connection with the Bahamas, which in turn led Bermuda to make an unsuccessful claim to Turks Island in 1790.[83]

Although not strictly part of the West Indies, Bermuda was one of the "jewels" in the curving chain of British Caribbean islands. In 1767 the flat, rocky islands became a base for the British fleet. Until 1785 most of its inhabitants were engaged in fishing or in constructing sloops and schooners from the cedar trees that covered much of the islands. Comparatively few of the inhabitants were involved in agriculture; only about thirteen hundred of the cultivable acres on the islands were planted with sweet potatoes, barley, and a little wheat.[84] Unlike the West Indian sugar islands, most of which were disproportionately black, Bermuda's black-white ratio was nearly equal. In 1783 the islands had a white population of 5,462 and a black population of 4,919. By 1790 the total number of inhabitants had increased to fourteen thousand partly from the arrival of "many families" from North America.[85] The exodus of white and black Americans spawned by the revolutionary war modified the island's economy and led to important new adaptations in its slave labor system. Few of the island's slaves, all of whom were purchased from North America and the West Indies,[86] were engaged in the production of cash crops before 1785–1786, when loyalist-owned slaves planted the first 200 acres with cotton. Within three years one-eighth of all slaves were employed in the cultivation of cotton, and within five years Bermuda's "most fertile spots" were devoted to cotton culture.[87] Although sugar continued to be the most important crop in all of the British islands of the Caribbean, cotton rose to second place. Until

[81] Extract of a Letter from a Gentleman Settler in Exuma, n.d., CO37/23/19.

[82] An Account of the Quantity of Land and the Number of Inhabitants, CO37/23/3.

[83] Sir Alan Cuthbert Burns, *History of the British West Indies* (London: George Allen and Unwin, 1965), 560, 601.

[84] Additional Heads of Inquiry to Be Transmitted to the Agents for the Different Islands in the West Indies, CO37/38/1–2.

[85] Henry Hamilton to Lord Hawkesbury, June 15, 1790, An Account of the Number of Inhabitants in the Island of Bermuda, February 7, 1783, CO37/23/184–86, CO37/39.

[86] An Account of the Number of Negroes Imported into the Island of Bermuda, March 29, 1788, CO37/38/14.

[87] Additional Heads of Inquiry Transmitted to the Agents for the Different Islands in the West Indies, March 20, 1788, CO37/38/16–17; Henry Hamilton to Lord Hawkesbury, June 15, 1790, CO37/23/184–86.

United States grown cotton became a serious competitor, the British Caribbean colonies supplied over 70 percent of the cotton imported by Britain.[88]

Although most of the loyalists who emigrated to British islands settled in the Bahamas or Jamaica, a number also emigrated to Dominica and other West Indian islands. The long dispute between France and Britain over ownership of Dominica, St. Lucia, and St. Vincent, had been temporarily resolved in 1763, when Dominica was transferred by France to Britain, along with Tobago, St. Vincent, and Grenada. During the American Revolution the islands again fell to France, along with the adjacent islands of Guadeloupe, Martinique, and St. Lucia,[89] and even after the Treaty of Paris confirmed British possession France made several abortive attempts to recapture it. Despite a mountainous backbone, the rugged island had fertile soil, and coffee was quickly established as a staple by early French settlers. Between them, the 1,400 British and French subjects who shared the island of Dominica in 1780 owned 12,713 slaves, the majority of whom were employed on some 250 coffee plantations and 67 sugar plantations.[90]

In 1784 the assembly passed a law exempting loyalists and their slaves from all public taxes for a period of fifteen years and offered to furnish impoverished emigrants with tools and building materials. Despite the attractive offer, the first groups to arrive heard the discouraging news from Governor John Orde that most of the ungranted land was "in general tops of mountains," and, therefore, unsuitable for cultivation. Another contingent that arrived in the spring of 1785 at the beginning of the rainy season found "not a house or shed to be got here to cover them, every place is full." Only a few of the white émigrés were planters, most being skilled craftsmen, such as coopers, ships carpenters, shipwrights, and saddlers, or small shopkeepers and tavernkeepers who had to be subsidized by the government to survive in the island's planting society.[91] The reduction of the duties on coffee in 1783, however, made its cultivation in the West Indies far more profitable than formerly and in the seven years following tax reduction production trebled.[92] Several large planters, among them former Crown officials such as Governor Tonyn and Lord Hawke, and a number

[88] Burns, *History of the British West Indies*, 536.

[89] Ibid., 520.

[90] A Sketch of the State of This Island with Respect to Lands, Inhabitants, Slaves, April 10, 1784, CO71/8/190.

[91] Resolves of the Council and Assembly of Dominica, May 27, 1784, Orde to Lord Sydney, November 25, 1784, June 20, 1785, CO71/8/212–13, 40, 178; Meeting of His Majesty's Council, Minutes, August 23, 1785, CO71/9/258–59.

[92] Bryan Edwards, *The History, Civil and Commercial, of the British West Indies*, 4 vols. (Philadelphia: James Humphreys, 1806) 3:124.

of small planters, who were prevented from selling their slaves in East Florida by a Spanish policy forbidding Spanish colonials to emigrate to East Florida during the eighteen-month period British subjects were allowed to dispose of their property, transported their slaves to Dominica to take advantage of the active slave market there.[93] Although Dominica's black-white ratio had reached an incredible fourteen to one, slave mortality was exceptionally high, with a five-year average natural increase of only one hundred and forty-five.[94] It is not possible to trace them but most of the slaves transported and sold in Dominica likely wound up on a coffee walk. Disease, probably malaria or yellow fever, apparently killed many of them, because in February 1786 Governor Orde reported that sickness "has been so great" among the American slaves that he was obliged to order the garrison surgeon to supply them with medicine from the king's stores.[95]

Although the vast majority of slaves who were forced to migrate ended up as estate slaves in the Caribbean, hundreds, perhaps several thousand, became military slaves. Early in the eighteenth century European nations, including Britain, began to take advantage of the special demographic character of West Indian society by recruiting slaves to serve in the military and thereby conserve the strength of European troops, for whom service in the West Indies was a veritable death sentence. Generally, black recruits served on a temporary basis as military laborers. The British experience in the American Revolution, however, demonstrated the possibility of using slaves as a permanent military force. The prototype for the standing indigenous army in the West Indies was the Black Carolina Corps organized by General Leslie in South Carolina in 1779. After the war the unit was distributed among several British islands. By 1795 most members of the Black Carolina Corps were veterans with fifteen years' experience and had seen service in Grenada, Martinique, and other British islands.[96] Soon other British islands had similar corps, most of them organized by British army officers who were veterans of the American Revolution. At the behest of Archibald Campbell, a veteran of the Seven Years' War and of the American Revolution in the South and later military governor of Jamaica, a battalion of free blacks and "people of Color" was raised in America for the defense of Jamaica.[97] In response to a suggestion by General Edward Mathews, commander in chief in the Leeward Islands, Carleton ordered two hundred black recruits raised in South Carolina for service in St. Lucia,

[93] Orde to Sydney, August 24, 1785, CO71/8/193.
[94] Dominica, State of Negroes, of Free Persons of Color and of White Inhabitants in This Island, CO71/14, pt. 1.
[95] Orde to Sydney, February 6, 1786, CO71/10/4.
[96] Buckley, *Slaves in Red Coats*, 4, 6.
[97] A. Campbell to Carleton, December 6, 1782, December 21, 1782, Carleton Papers, PRO30/55/56, 57.

which had great strategic value because of its proximity to the French island of Martinique. The 241 blacks removed by Major Moncrief at the
evacuation of Charleston were apparently destined for that service.[98] Despite Britain's growing reliance on black auxiliary corps such as these, there
was as yet no standing black army.

The French Revolution and Napoleonic Wars, the first phase of which
opened in 1793, created an enormous demand for manpower among the
European belligerents. As a result both belligerents began groping toward
the creation of permanent black armies. France, which had proclaimed the
abolition of slavery in all French possessions in 1794, already enjoyed a
substantial military advantage from the militarization of large numbers of
blacks and coloreds. The first sustained British effort to create a standing
black army was by General Sir John Vaughan, a veteran of campaigns in
the West Indies during the American Revolution. Convinced that the only
way to offset the military advantage enjoyed by France was to resort to
permanent black regiments similar to the Black Carolina Corps, Vaughan
waged an unrelenting campaign over the vigorous opposition of West Indian merchants and planters. Faced with a rapidly deteriorating military
situation, the London government grudgingly agreed and in April 1795
authorized Vaughan to raise two black regiments. By the end of the century black soldiers were playing a major role in Britain's defense of her
mercantile empire in the Caribbean. The creation of the West Indian regiments and the subsequent "Africanization of the entire British colonial military structure," as one historian of the Caribbean has called it, had profound implications for British Caribbean society. In the short run, by
effectively defending the plantocracy the West India regiments helped to
preserve slavery; in the long run, however, the manumission of all black
soldiers by an act of Parliament in 1807 created a military caste of free and
fully enfranchised blacks whose very existence helped eventually to undermine the existence of slavery.[99]

The more immediate effects of revolutionary influence were felt in the
great revolt in Haiti, known in the eighteenth century as Saint Domingue.
Although the Haitian Revolution coincided with and is generally considered a by-product of the French Revolution, a number of prominent black
leaders of the revolution received their military education in the American
Revolution. In 1779 the Count D'Estaing was ordered to recruit men in
Saint Domingue, which for years had had a colored militia, for an auxiliary
army destined for service in the South. Between six hundred and eight
hundred black and mulatto freedmen volunteered. Known as Fontages Le-

[98] Edward Matthew to Henry White, July 2, 1782, Carleton to Leslie, September 2, 1782,
Carleton to General Matthew, n.d., Carleton Papers, PRO30/55/48; *Gazette of the State of
South Carolina*, November 22, December 6, 1784.
[99] Buckley, *Slaves in Red Coats*, 2, 9, 12–13, 18–19, 142.

gion after the Viscount de Fontages, its commander, the black men of the
Antilles fought with the French and American armies at the siege of Savannah. Whether or not they derived their revolutionary vitality directly from
that experience, on their return many members of the black Saint Domingue legion, including André Rigaud, Jean-Baptiste Villatte, Louis-
Jacques Beauvais, Christophe and Martial Besse, and Jean Savary, became
involved in the struggle for political liberty in Saint Domingue. Beauvais,
who served in Europe with the French army, returned to fight in the revolution and in 1791 became captain general. Rigaud and Villatte, who
became generals under the convention, and Henri Christophe, the future
king of Haiti, who was wounded during the siege of Savannah, were all
leaders of the revolution that culminated in the defeat of France and made
Haiti the second republic, after the United States, in the Americas.[100]

Although the majority of slaves removed from the southern states were
condemned to wretched slavery, several thousand were freed, either by
their own efforts or by the British army in keeping with the promises made
by successive military commanders. According to article seven of the preliminary articles of peace signed in Paris on November 30, 1782, the British pledged to withdraw from all occupied posts or garrisons without causing any destruction or "carrying away any negroes" or other property of
Americans. Although it had been common practice since ancient times for
the peace treaty to provide for the mutual restoration of fugitive slaves,[101]
slaves who remained within British lines refused "to be delivered in so un-
warrantable a manner," according to Hessian Adjutant General Major Carl
Leopold Baurmeister. Writing during the evacuation of New York, Baurmeister noted that although half of the slaves who had responded to Clinton's Philipsburg proclamation "are no longer alive, and the greater part
of the rest have gone on board the ships," those still with the British "insist
on their rights under the proclamation, and General Carleton protects
these slaves, although those who desire to return may do so."[102] Objections, of course, were immediately raised by the commander in chief of the
Continental armies, who as a slaveowner himself recognized that for many
white planters, if not for all white Americans of the revolutionary generation, preservation of the institution of slavery had the highest priority. According to General Washington's construction of the treaty, the provisional article prohibited the removal of all blacks. By contrast, Carleton,
with the full support of the London government, argued that such a pro-

[100] S. V. Jean-Baptiste, *Haiti: sa lutte? pour l'emancipation* (Paris, 1957), 84–85; Theophilus
G. Steward, "How the Black St. Domingo Legion Saved the Patriot Army in the Siege of
Savannah, 1779," American Negro Academy occasional papers, no. 5 (Washington, D.C.,
1899), 12–14.
[101] Finley, *Ancient Slavery*, 112.
[102] Baurmeister, *Revolution in America*, 569.

hibition was inconsistent with prior promises made to blacks by successive British army commanders.[103] Ironically, the British interpretation of article seven rested on the juristic conception of the rights of conquest, which gave the army title to slaves, fugitive or captured, "as to any other acquisition or article of prize." Because the preliminary articles contained no "explicitly unequivocal cession or act of restitution," British removal of slaves was not an infraction of the treaty; indeed by protecting those slaves who were manumitted before the treaty was signed, the army satisfied the terms of the agreement. To do otherwise, Carleton added in moving to the high ground, would be "a flagrant injustice to the slaves [Britain] has manumitted."[104] Suffering from a shortage of revenue and credit, Congress, over vigorous protests from the southern states, decided against making "an express declaration that the British had violated the [treaty]" for fear that "a renewal of hostilities might be a consequence of such declaration."[105] Filled "with joy and gratitude," as Boston King put it, approximately three thousand former slaves crowded aboard military transport ships in New York for resettlement elsewhere in the empire.[106]

The major migration of freed blacks settled in Nova Scotia. Before the American Revolution only a few slaves were in the Maritimes. During the war, however, the area became both a haven for runaways and a minor market for slaves sold by British officers, and Detroit Indians, among others. The evacuation of New York produced the largest influx of blacks, both slave and free, and at least temporarily strengthened slavery in Canada. No less than thirteen hundred slaves belonging to loyalists were brought into the maritime area in the postwar period and were taken to Quebec, the Bay of Quinte, Adolphustown, Johnstown, Delta in Leeds County, Camden, Edwardsburgh, the Eastern Townships east of Montreal, and various other white loyalist settlements. As a reward for their wartime services, 1,336 men, 914 women, and 740 children were given British certificates of manumission and were transported as free men and women to the cold, bleak land of Nova Scotia, where they were settled in segregated areas on substantially smaller land allotments than were granted to white settlers.[107]

The first contingent arrived in Nova Scotia in July 1783 and established themselves at Birchtown. Later arrivals settled at Digby, St. John N.B.,

[103] North to Carleton, August 8, 1783, CO5/110/62–72, 92, December 4, 1783, CO5/111/92.

[104] Negroes, PRO30/8/344/109–11.

[105] Ralph Izard to Arthur Middleton, May 30, 1783, 38–45–1, Middleton Papers.

[106] Inspection Roll of Negro Emigrants, April 17–23, 1783, M332, reel 7, p. 5, Miscellaneous Papers of the Continental Congess, 1774–1789, National Archives.

[107] Robin Winks, *The Blacks in Canada. A History* (New Haven, Conn.: Yale University Press, 1971), 29–30, 33.

Port Roseway, renamed Shelburne, Preston and other smaller communities. The majority of the Black Pioneers, an all black regiment commanded by Colonel Stephen Bluck, an educated mulatto, settled in Annapolis County and along the St. John River. Many of the black migrants were skilled workers who found employment in Halifax, Shelburne, and other larger centers, but the greater number were former field hands from the Chesapeake or the low country. The black loyalists had been given the poorest land on the barren Atlantic coast of Nova Scotia.[108] Unaccustomed to the thin soils or the severe winters, they fared poorly in the frontier communities, and within a few years most became tenant farmers or sharecroppers, working land owned by white men for half its produce.[109] By 1791 most of the black settlements were experiencing famine. To survive many of the poorest black settlers signed indenture contracts with local merchants whereas others were forced to sell their land, their clothing, even their bedding.[110]

In 1791–1792 there was a mass exodus of blacks from the maritime areas to West Africa. The movement back to Africa began simultaneously in England and in Nova Scotia. The first black refugees began arriving in London in 1772 following the Somerset decision. The evacuation of New York brought hundreds more to London's crowded streets. By 1786 there were more than twelve hundred free blacks in London, many of them destitute and reduced to begging in the streets. A group of city businessmen anxious to relieve the "calamitous situation" of black American refugees in London, organized a "Committee to Aid the Black Poor" to provide medical care and direct monetary assistance. When it became clear that private charity was only a temporary expedient for what many perceived was a growing social problem, the government reluctantly began paying modest subsistence allowances to the blacks. Anxious to be relieved of the burden of public support, the Lords of the Treasury and the Black Poor Committee quickly endorsed a proposal made by Henry Smeathman, an amateur botanist with experience on the African coast, to transport the indigent blacks to Sierra Leone on the West Coast of Africa. Smeathman died in 1786 before the project got under way, but the Black Poor Committee continued to try to persuade impoverished blacks to emigrate to Sierra Leone. When that plan was not immediately successful, the committee proposed to settle the blacks on the island of Great Inagua in the Bahamas, where it was hoped they would have a better chance of survival than in crowded London. Fifteen of the black leaders in question, however, de-

[108] Blakeley, "Boston King," 352.
[109] Winks, *Blacks in Canada*, 24–26; John N. Grant, "Black Immigrants into Nova Scotia, 1776–1815," *Journal of Negro History* 58 (1973): 253–61.
[110] Blakeley, "Boston King," 353. For a detailed treatment of the migration to Africa, see Ellen Gibson Wilson, *The Loyal Blacks* (New York: Capricorn Books, c. 1976), 135–256.

clared themselves to be "totally disinclined" to locate "in any situation where Traffick in slaves is carried on," and the Sierra Leone plan was revived.[111]

In April 1787 347 blacks, perhaps half of them former American slaves, and 104 white adults departed England for West Africa. After a difficult voyage 377 of the original passengers landed at a site purchased by the captain of the naval sloop from a local chief, a place of exceptional beauty situated on the left bank of the fast-flowing Sierra Leone River. There they founded the first settlement, Granville Town in what was called the Province of Freedom, at the beginning of the rainy season.[112] Plagued by "fevers, fluxes and bilious complaints," and by the raids of local slave traders and tribal chiefs, the settlers were driven away three years later by their Temne neighbors and Granville Town was destroyed. To save the foundering project, Granville Sharp, the antislavery leader responsible for bringing Somerset before Lord Mansfield, Thomas Clarkson and William Wilberforce, leaders of the abolitionist movement in Britain, organized the Sierra Leone Company to frame laws for the colony, promote its trade and provide new settlers.[113]

Coincidentally with the efforts of the white abolitionists, Thomas Peters, a former sergeant in the Black Pioneers regiment, arrived in England carrying a petition from 200 black Nova Scotian and New Brunswick families. Citing their disillusionment over their failure to receive the land promised them, or to be confirmed in it, they asked for "some establishment where [they] may attain a competent settlement for themselves and be enabled by their industrious exertions to become useful subjects to His Majesty."[114] Peters's memorial was submitted to the Sierra Leone Company through Sharp, and plans proceeded to relocate the unhappy black loyalists. In August Peters returned to Nova Scotia with Lieutenant John Clarkson, an agent of the Sierra Leone Company, to organize the mass migration of Maritime blacks. Within a few days of their arrival in Shelburne, Clarkson began to screen the applications of blacks who wished to settle in Sierra Leone. Although many were strongly suspicious that the whole project was part of a scheme to lure them back into the center of the slave trade, almost one-third of the Maritime black loyalist population agreed to undertake the great migration. In February 1792 a fleet of fifteen ships carrying 1,196 blacks from various parts of Nova Scotia and New Brunswick and an assortment of family pets sailed from Halifax for Sierra Leone. After a passage of forty days the fleet arrived in the estuary at the

[111] Mary Beth Norton, "The Fate of Some Black Loyalists of the American Revolution," *Journal of Negro History* 58 (1973): 411.

[112] For details see ibid., 402–26.

[113] Winks, *Blacks in Canada*, 61, 63.

[114] Quoted in ibid., 63.

site of the destroyed settlement of Granville Town. According to legend, as they were led ashore by Thomas Peters, the settlers sang "The day of jubilee is come, return ye ransomed sinners home."[115] In the beginning they lived in tents improvised from ship sails while they constructed circular huts of wattle plastered with clay after the native pattern. On the instructions of the board of directors of the Sierra Leone Company, Clarkson called the new settlement Freetown.[116]

The great migration to Africa stripped the Maritime area of its most stable and highly skilled black inhabitants. The group as finally assembled by Clarkson and local black religious leaders, Boston King, Moses Wilkinson, the blind Methodist preacher, and David George, the former Virginia slave and Baptist preacher, represented the "flower" of the black settlements, young and healthy men and women of varied skills, the majority of whom Clarkson decided "are better than any people in the labouring line of life in England: I would match them for strong sense, quick apprehension, clear reasoning, gratitude, affection for their wives and children, and friendship and good-will toward their neighbours." They were also, Clarkson discovered "rather enthusiasts in religion." Almost all of David George's Baptist congregation and most of Moses Wilkinson's Methodist church members elected to go, leaving behind, *The Weekly Chronicle* bitterly complained, "the maimed, the halt, the blind and the lazy," who were in accordance with Clarkson's instructions not permitted to emigrate. Some white merchants and farmers, who feared that the loss of cheap labor would be injurious to the growth and prosperity of the province, resorted to harsh countermeasures, including physical abuse, forged indenture contracts and false claims of unsatisfied debt, to detain them, but to no avail.[117]

The Nova Scotians, as the black loyalists called themselves, were apparently motivated by a strikingly common set of aspirations, which can be discerned in their conduct: in their insistence at the evacuation of American ports that the British command live up to the promises of freedom contained in the various slave proclamations; in the Peters memorial, which protested against the betrayal of those promises and the conditions under which as freed men and women they were required to live and work; in the uncommon resolution of four New Brunswick men, Richard Crankipine, William Taylor, Sampson Heywood, and Nathaniel Ladd, who

[115] Gary B. Nash, "The Forgotten Experience," in William M. Fowler, Jr. and Wallace Coyle, eds., *The American Revolution. Changing Perspectives* (Boston: Northeastern University Press, 1970), 34; Christopher Fyfe, *A Short History of Sierra Leone* (London: Longman, 1979), 36–37.

[116] Christopher Fyfe and Eldred Jones, eds., *Freetown. A Symposium* (Freetown: Sierra Leone University Press, 1968), 26, 118–19.

[117] Charles Bruce Fergusson, ed. *Clarkson's Mission to America, 1791–1792* (Halifax, Nova Scotia: Public Archives, 1971), 51, 81–82, 91, 92–93.

were prevented from embarking with Peters and so walked 340 miles from St. John, around the Bay of Fundy to Halifax, because they wanted to "quit a country . . . whose inhabitants treated them with so much barbarity"; in the fierce determination of the 104-year-old woman who begged Clarkson to take her to Sierra Leone so that she might "lay her bones in her native country." Beyond this and above all they were animated, as Clarkson discovered, not by "the idea of improving their own condition, but for the sake of their children whom they wished to see established (as they expressed it) upon a better foundation." Perhaps the most dramatic articulation of their familial ideals was provided by a slave, John Cottress, "who came to me," Clarkson remembered, "in order to resign his wife and family who were free." With tears streaming down his cheeks the slave told Clarkson "that though this separation would be as death to himself, yet he had come to a resolution of resigning them up forever, convinced as he was, that such a measure would ultimately tend to render their situation more comfortable and happy." Moved by "the noble and elevated sentiments of this poor *slave*," the deeply moved Clarkson tried unsuccessfully to buy Cottress.[118]

It is also clear from their conduct that the black émigrés of Sierra Leone felt the revolutionary impact of republicanism. Like their white owners they viewed themselves as heirs of the Revolution, entitled therefore to its promises of liberty, equality, and happiness, which for former slaves translated to mean freedom from slavery for themselves and their families; the right to security in the small farms promised them and escape from the racial intolerance they discovered in western Nova Scotia and New Brunswick, which constantly threatened their dignity and in many cases their freedom. In their struggle to make Sierra Leone the literal land of Freedom, the principles they advanced were the same ones upon which their former masters had based a successful revolution. They resisted with surprising boldness company efforts to raise revenue through taxes. Under the leadership of the colony's first governor, John Clarkson, the struggling settlement survived the hot sun and heavy rains caused by the southwest monsoons, attacks from the Temnes, and pillaging and destruction by a French ship in 1794 only to succumb to two rebellions, ironically inspired by a dispute over taxes, which the new governor, William Dawes, tried to impose contrary to a promise former Governor Clarkson had made.[119]

Mindful of the fact that their birthright also included the right of revolution and of self-government, in 1800 the Nova Scotians joined a rising aimed at limiting the authority of the governor and council to matters in-

[118] Ibid., 56–57, 91, 102.

[119] Fyfe and Jones, *Freetown*, 16; John Joseph Crooks, *A History of the Colony of Sierra Leone Western Africa* (reprint, Northbrook, Ill.: Metro Books, 1972), 46–47.

volving only the affairs of the Sierra Leone Company. Continued resistance to quitrents by the Nova Scotians had induced the company directors to petition the home government to increase the powers of the governor and council. The charter granted in July 1799 granted lawmaking powers to the governor and his council, subject to the revision of the court of directors of the company and placed criminal jurisdiction in their hands as well. Even before the charter arrived, an insurrection broke out. The insurgents were routed by a detachment of soldiers from the Twenty-fourth Regiment, three of the leaders were tried and executed, thirty-two more were expelled from the colony.[120] An apparent link between the rebellion against the Sierra Leone Company in 1800 and revolutionary America is seen in the involvement of Henry Washington, who once worked as a slave on the Mount Vernon estate of George Washington. The owner of a small farm on the slopes to the southeast of Freetown, Washington joined the revolt against the company led by a neighboring farmer, Nathaniel Wansey. For his part in the insurrection, Washington was banished to the Bulom Shore.

The effects of the vast uprooting on blacks, slave and freed, is not entirely clear. By and large, the response of the various groups of emigrants was determined by their status, whether slave or free, and upon their final destination. Freed blacks, about whom we know somewhat more, rapidly adjusted to their new surroundings and eventually evolved a distinctive culture in the environments in which they found themselves. The remarkable resilience and independence of the Nova Scotians is, for example, apparent in the speed with which they abandoned company plans for the development of an agricultural settlement in the poor soil along the coast, in favor of more lucrative occupations as craftsmen or in trade. As the population of Freetown grew as a result of the arrival of Jamaican maroons augmented by recaptives, mostly Yorubas rescued from slave ships, the inland trade in produce prospered. The growing demand in Europe for timber, groundnuts, and palm produce, and in Freetown for imported manufactures, gave rise in the nineteenth century to the import-export trade. The capital the successive settlers had accumulated, the specialized economic services and organizational skills they had developed, their mastery of specialized crafts, formed the foundations for the growth of overseas commerce, which by midnineteenth century was basic to Sierra Leone's economy.[121]

Black émigrés apparently eased the problems of resettlement by resorting to various forms of association, principally the family and the com-

[120] Crooks, *History of Sierra Leone*, 55–56. See also Wilson, *Loyal Blacks*, 383–401, which stresses the fact that the objective of the revolution was the overthrow of white rule.
[121] Fyfe, *Freetown*, 3, 15, 103–4.

munity. Although the majority of black loyalists were from disparate communities in North Carolina, South Carolina, and Virginia, they emigrated principally in family groups. Once in Nova Scotia they settled mainly in Shelburne, Annapolis, and Sydney counties, which enabled them to preserve the family structure and to recreate quickly new black communities. The geography of Freetown enabled them to maintain their social identity. Originally designed by company authorities as a planned city whose nine broad streets were laid out in geometrical form on a site only about eighty acres in area, the town grew up instead with unplanned clusters of houses crowded together on single lots in defiance of company regulations.[122] The existence of kindred and neighborhood groups, united by cultural and religious ties and living together in cohesive communities, ensured the survival of the Nova Scotians as a distinct group and provided the basis for their political and cultural hegemony in Sierra Leone until the modern period.[123]

By contrast to the Nova Scotians, colonies of freed blacks who emigrated to other slave systems had to resort to different strategies to survive. Among the new arrivals in the Bahamas were approximately five hundred blacks, "who by escapes and various other fortuitous circumstances were disentangled from the disgraceful shackles of slavery."[124] Although they had been promised freedom and land, no preparations had been made before their arrival in June 1784. Perhaps because as Bahamian Governor John Maxwell put it, the black refugees were "sitting themselves down where they can and without order,"[125] or perhaps because of the dramatic increase in the black population of the islands generally, the Bahamian Assembly passed a new Act for Governing Slaves, which contained stringent provisions punishing verbal abuse or assault of whites by blacks.[126] The chronic concern of the white planters over slave restiveness does not appear to have been misplaced. Extant evidence strongly suggests that a period of conspicuous unrest followed the importation of freed blacks into the Bahamas. Determined to protect their hard-won freedom, freed and runaway American blacks built a large village behind Government House in the town of Nassau on New Providence Island and another near Fort Charlotte. The villages served as asylums for runaways where "no white Person dares make his appearance within it, but at the risk of his life." Whether the villages survived or for how long is unknown. Several of the leaders were arrested and prosecuted for assault on whites, although Dunmore's

[122] Fyfe, *Freetown*, 4.
[123] Winks, *Blacks in Canada*, 76.
[124] Report Relating to the Bahamas, 1791, Liverpool Papers, Add. MSS 38350, 217–26.
[125] Maxwell to Sydney, June 19, 1784, CO23/25/132.
[126] Ibid., CO23/26.

critics charged that the governor intervened to protect them from punishment. The free black population of the islands did, however, continue to grow and to receive new infusions of former American slaves.[127]

Although patterns of life necessarily differed between the planting societies of the British West Indies and the west coast of Africa, everywhere religion was one of the central forces of cohesion in the transplanted black communities. The fact that Christianity took deep root among blacks was due almost entirely to the zeal of black preachers, many of them former American slaves who from the beginning played a crucial role in spreading the ideas they had accepted, absorbed, and in many cases shaped. David George, the former Virginia slave who was one of the early architects of black Christianity in the lower South, introduced the Baptist faith among black loyalists in Nova Scotia. Evacuated from Charleston, South Carolina, in the fall of 1782, George went to Nova Scotia and was given land and government provisions at Shelburne. Shortly after his arrival he began "to sing in the woods," drawing crowds of blacks from nearby settlements. Soon George began to hold nightly meetings for "these poor creatures who had never heard the gospel before." On one-quarter acre of land given to him by John Parr, governor of Nova Scotia from 1782 to 1791, George built a hut and a small meeting house and formed a Baptist church with six members, only the second Baptist church in Nova Scotia.[128]

By the summer of 1783 George's congregation had grown to fifty members. However, when he attempted to baptize two white persons, William and Deborah Holmes, forty to fifty disbanded soldiers came with ship's tackle and pulled over his house and the houses of other black families, beat George severely with sticks, and drove him into a swamp. Subsequently, George moved to Birchtown and began to preach to blacks from "house to house" until he ran afoul of Colonel Stephen Bluck, commandant of the Black Militia in the District of Shelburne and later schoolmaster at Birchtown. Fleeing from the persecution of black Anglicans, George returned to Shelburne and built a sizeable congregation there, while serving at the same time as an itinerant preacher at Ragged Island, Fredericton, and St. John, some two hundred miles from Shelburne. Altogether George established seven churches in Nova Scotia: at Shelburne, Birchtown, Jones Harbor, Ragged Island, St. John, Preston, and Halifax.[129] He trained other black preachers, including Peter Richards, who took over at St. John; Sampson Colbert, who replaced Richards on his death; and Hector Peters, who took over the Baptist church at Preston near Halifax. One of the principal organizers of the mass exodus of blacks from the Maritimes,

[127] Wylly, Short Account, 22, 41, 42.
[128] The first Baptist church was established at Horton in 1778; see Wilson, *Loyal Blacks*, 83. Wilson also gives a detailed history of black religion in Nova Scotia, 117–31.
[129] Ibid., 123.

George led almost all the black Nova Scotian Baptists to Sierra Leone. Upon their arrival in Freetown, they built "a hovel for a Meeting house." Made of poles and grass, it was the first Baptist church in the Moslem land of West Africa.[130]

Several hundred black Nova Scotians also embraced Methodism. In 1784 when William Black, the first Wesleyan missionary in the province, preached in Birchtown, two hundred black Methodists already had been organized into fourteen classes by the blind black preacher Moses Wilkinson. Among the sixty persons baptized by Black was Violet King, the wife of Boston King. Two years later when Freeborn Garrettson, the young American preacher, came to Shelburne to resolve some differences among members of the society and to organize classes, he was warmly received by the blacks, although a white mob pelted him with eggs. Among Garrettson's converts was Boston King, who began to preach in Birchtown and Shelburne. In 1791 King took over the black Methodist society of Preston, which comprised then about thirty-four members. Later that year both he and Wilkinson joined the exodus of blacks to Sierra Leone. At first King worked for the Sierra Leone Company and preached to the native inhabitants. With Governor Clarkson's encouragement, he opened a school and offered regular instruction to fifteen to twenty students. In 1794 the company sent King to study at the Kingswood School in Bristol, England. After two years, during which time he "found a more cordial love to the White People than I had ever experienced before," King returned to Freetown and resumed his work as schoolmaster and preacher.[131] From the small, autonomous Methodist and Baptist churches planted by the Nova Scotians, a flourishing Christian life developed in the land of Islam. Included in the new growth they sent out were the Protestant values of respect for hard work and individual achievement, which helped make the Nova Scotians the dominant group in the Freetown community.[132]

Whereas black preachers received support and encouragement from the Sierra Leone Company, the spread of Christianity among slaves in the planting societies of the British West Indies encountered significant opposition from slaveowners, who feared that for their slaves' minds to be "considerably enlightened by religion . . . would be attended with the most dangerous consequences." With a handful of white missionaries, black preachers, principally former American slaves, laid the foundations for the expansion of Christianity among slaves in the British West Indies. George Liele, the father of the black Baptist church in Georgia and South Carolina,

[130] "An Account of the Life of Mr. David George," in John Rippon, ed., *The Baptist Annual Register for 1790/1793*, 473–84.

[131] Blakeley, "Boston King," 353–56.

[132] For the subsequent history of Christianity in Sierra Leone, see Wilson, *Loyal Blacks*, 337–56.

established the first Baptist church in Kingston, Jamaica, in 1784. Evacuated from Savannah as an indentured servant of Colonel Kirkland, Liele worked out his contract in two years and then began to preach in a small private home in Kingston to "a good smart congregation." His first church there consisted of "four brethren from America besides myself."

Soon Liele's preaching began to attract slaves from nearby sugar estates and cattle pens, which led to a period of active persecution. As the cost of bringing the Christian message to slaves, Liele introduced a policy of close collaboration between church and state. He refused, for example, to baptize any slave without permission of the owner and he put up a steeple bell "to give notice to our people and more particularly to the owners of slaves that are in our society, that they may know the hour on which we meet, and be satisfied that their servants return in due time."[133] The black preacher's success in persuading "the gentlemen of the legislature, and the justices, and magistrates" that religious instruction "keeps [slaves] in mind of the commandments of God," led the Jamaican Assembly to approve Liele's petition for "freedom to worship Almighty God according to the tenents of the Bible." Official recognition of the slaves' right of religious worship dampened the fanaticism and prejudice of several white owners of large estates, who invited Liele to proclaim the gospel to their slaves.

From a sporadic and localized phenomenon the evangelizing of slaves was transformed into a dynamic process, which reached slaves on sugar estates and cattle pens, in dense forests and on mountaintops. Liele's method was to send out black converts to spread Christian teaching among slaves: John Gilbert, a free black, began preaching on the sugar estates and mountain plantations in St. George's parish on the north side of the island; George Gibbs, a free mulatto, received permission to preach to the slaves on the Dove Hall sugar estate in St. Thomas in the Vale parish, some sixteen miles from Spanish Town, the Jamaican capital. At the invitation of Isaac Lascelles Winn, the owner of Stretch and Sett sugar estate 140 miles west of Kingston, Moses Baker, an American and one of the most successful of the black Baptist preachers, began preaching to the slaves in St. James parish in northwestern Jamaica, an area of large sugar estates and high slave concentration. When slaves from other plantations began to "come of their own accord to Brother Baker," some owners objected, and Baker met with "a great deal of persecution and severe trials." Presumably because religion caused a reformation in slaves' morals, however, slaveowners actively began to seek Baker's services. Soon Baker was preaching on twenty different estates, whose slave populations frequently numbered three or four hundred, and had fourteen hundred "justified believers" and approximately three thousand adherents in St. James parish. When he was invited to

---

[133] Rippon, *Baptist Annual Register for 1790/1793*, 344.

preach by a planter from Westmoreland parish fifty miles away, Baker called for assistance and George Vineyard, another former American slave, was dispatched in his place.

By 1802 Thomas Nichols Swigle, a white Baptist missionary, was able to report that the Baptist church in Jamaica "abundantly thrives among the Negroes, more than any denomination."[134] In addition to the flourishing center of Baptist strength in St. James parish in the interior, black Baptists were well established in Kingstown. George Liele's congregation had outgrown the original meeting house and had built a new church, which boasted 8 deacons, 6 exhorters, and 610 members. In addition to the churches in St. Thomas and Westmoreland parishes, a church had also been established at Clifton Mount Coffee plantation in St. Andrews parish, which had 254 members. By the time the black Baptists called on the Baptist Missionary Society for support in 1813, a small but flourishing Baptist community had been established, largely by the efforts of George Liele and Moses Baker.[135]

Although Dr. Thomas Coke visited the island in 1789 and subsequently sent out a dozen missionaries, Methodism fared less well in Jamaica, perhaps because Methodist missionaries permitted slaves into their societies without first obtaining permission of their owners. Once Methodism began to lose some of its strong antislavery fervor, however, previously antagonistic white owners welcomed the missionaries, and by the turn of the century approximately 400 slaves were in society in Jamaica, compared to 216 in 1792.[136] Methodism was more successful on other Caribbean islands, where the Wesleyan movement among blacks began as early as 1758, when John Wesley baptized the first black in Antigua.[137] Whites on the islands, as elsewhere, had little use for Wesley's theological or political ideas or for the itinerants' "enthusiastic" style of preaching. As a consequence, Methodism in the West Indies was predominantly a black movement. In 1789 Thomas Coke reported only 70 whites and 2,740 blacks in society in Antigua; on St. Christopher, 50 whites and 650 blacks; on St. Eustatius, 8 whites and 250 blacks; on Dominica, 24 blacks; on Barbados, six whites; St. Vincent, 250 white and 139 blacks.[138]

[134] "Rise of the Early Negro Churches," 85.
[135] F. R. Augier et al. eds., *The Making of the West Indies* (London, 1961), 139. For details of the later history of the black church in Jamaica see Mary Turner, *Slaves and Missionaries: The Disintegration of Jamaican Slave Society, 1787–1834* (Urbana, Ill.: University of Illinois Press, c. 1982), especially 7–30.
[136] "Rise of the Early Negro Churches," 76, 85; Rippon, *Baptist Annual Register, 1801–1802*, 974.
[137] Joseph C. Hartzell, "Methodism and the Negro in the United States," *Journal of Negro History* 8 (1923): 301.
[138] Thomas Coke, *A Farther Account of the Late Missionaries to the West Indies in a Letter from the Reverend Dr. Coke to the Reverend John Wesley* (London, 1789), 12.

Black preachers, several of them former American slaves, also played a significant role in spreading the Methodist message. Joseph Paul, one of George Whitefield's black converts, purchased his freedom and evacuated from New York with the British. After stopping briefly in Abaco, Paul and his wife settled in Nassau in the Bahamas, where Paul reportedly preached to a congregation of about three hundred people, who gathered under a tamarind tree every Sunday. Between 1790 and 1793, Paul's congregation built a small church at the corner of Augusta and Heathfield streets, the first Methodist church in the Bahama Islands. Paul was also the first master of the Associates School, the earliest private school for blacks in Nassau.[139]

It seems likely that Methodism was also planted in St. Eustatius by a former American slave named Harry, who was brought to the Dutch island, which served as a supply base for the colonies, during the revolutionary war. When Coke arrived on St. Eustatius in 1787, Harry, a Methodist convert, had already converted twenty slaves. According to Coke's account "Harry did so grieve in spirit at the wickedness of the people around him, that at last the fire broke forth, and he bore a public testimony for Jesus." At first white authorities raised no objections, but after Harry's emotional style of preaching caused slaves to fall down "as if they were dead," the governor ordered Harry to stop preaching. The day after "Harry's mouth was stopped," Coke landed "to the joy of [Harry's] poor little flock." Before his departure Coke formed six regular classes, three of which "I gave to the care of Harry, which I expect will soon multiply." When Coke returned to St. Eustatius two years later, however, he found that Harry had been publicly whipped "in a most unmerciful manner" and banished for "praying with the people."[140]

By drawing upon the remarkable sources of spiritual energy that black preachers like Harry, George Liele, Moses Baker, George Vineyard, David George, Boston King, and countless others released into the world, blacks, both slave and free, found a way to deal with the vast confusion and anxiety that accompanied the dispersions spurred by the revolutionary war. Deprived of their social identity, they achieved an identity and power of their own in religion, which helped bind together the family group and sustain the black community above and beyond its ordeals in time and space. A movement generated by black people, most of whom had their first encounter with Christian teachings in forbidden meetings in isolated slave quarters in the plantation South, it emerged in the British West Indies as an intricate subculture that provided the psychological and moral resources

---

[139] Riley, *Homeward Bound*, 140.

[140] Thomas Coke, *A Continuation of Dr. Thomas Coke's Journal in Two Letters to the Reverend John Wesley* (London: J. Paramore, 1787), 10–11; idem, *A Farther Continuation of Dr. Thomas Coke's Journal in a Letter to the Reverend John Wesley* (London: J. Paramore, 1787), 3; idem, *Farther Account*, 5.

to deal with slavery. In Sierra Leone the absorbed values and skills generally comprehended by the phrase "Protestant ethic," fused with traditional West African qualities of spirituality and enthusiasm for trade, to evolve a distinctive Afro-European culture, which forms the basis for the cultural and economic patterns of life in westernized Africa today.[141]

The scattering of blacks, slave and free, to all parts of the world at the closing of the American Revolution thus had important cultural and economic implications, not the least significant of which was the transplantation of African-American religious culture to the British West Indies and West Africa; the Africanization of the British military structure in the West Indies; and the reinvigoration of the plantation systems in some of the British islands, most notably Bermuda and the Bahamas. The dislocations of war were also the generating force behind even more profound and enduring changes in the southern states of the new American republic.

[141] See, for example, John Peterson, "The Sierra Leone Creole: A Reappraisal" and Robert July, "The Sierra Leone Legacy in Nigeria: Herbert Macaulay and Henry Carr," in Fyfe and Jones, eds., *Freetown*, 100–117, 212–24.

SEVEN

THE AFTERMATH OF WAR:

DEMOGRAPHIC AND ECONOMIC

TRANSFORMATIONS

T HIS CURSED WAR has ruined us all," the Georgia planter Robert Baillie wrote in 1781 from East Florida, where he had gone to
try to recover his slaves before they could depart or be removed to
another location.[1] Years of occupation and bitter warfare and the savage
internecine struggle that characterized the war in the lower South had devastated vast areas of the country, left the southern plantation economies in
ruins, and the traditional structures and sources of authority in a state of
collapse. Crime was widespread in the backcountry areas of Georgia and
South Carolina, and riotous mobs of artisans, mechanics and sailors demonstrated in Charleston for "Democracy and the Revolution."[2] Major devastation of vast areas of South Carolina bore witness to the prolonged warfare. After he was exchanged as a prisoner of war, General William
Moultrie, commanding officer of the Second South Carolina Regiment,
left Philadelphia for his home in South Carolina. In late September he traveled south through Winyah to General Nathanael Greene's camp on the
Ashley River, a "dull, melancholy, dreary ride" of about one hundred
miles. Once teeming with animal life, the area was, Moultrie sadly observed, now destitute of livestock and wild game: "It had been so completely checquered by the different parties, that not one part of it had been
left unexplored; consequently, not the vestiges of horses, cattle, hogs, or
deer, etc. was to be found. The squirrels and birds of every kind were totally destroyed. The dragoons, told me," Moultrie continued, "that on
their scouts, no living creature was to be seen, except now and then a few
camp scavengers, picking the bones of some unfortunate fellows, who had
been shot or cut down, and left in the woods above ground."[3]

The ugly scars of war also greeted Captain Francis Richardson upon his
return to his plantation in the Sumter District of central South Carolina.
The "general doom and destruction which fell on every part of the State,"

---

[1] R. Baillie, July 17, 1791, "Papers of Lachlan McIntosh, 1774–1779," Lilla Mills Hawes,
ed., GHS, *Coll.* 12 (1957): 99.

[2] Nadelhaft, *Disorders of War*, 109.

[3] Moultrie, *Memoirs* 2:354–55.

Richardson noted, struck with the "most crushing force" in the High Hills of Santee region, where a disproportionate number of battles had been fought. As a result of the massive flight of slaves "the large cotton and rice plantations which had been cultivated by their labor had shrunk," Richardson wrote, "into small truck patches; stock of every description had been taken for the use of the British army; fences gone . . . , and rank thistle nodded in the wind."[4] Across the state a similar scene awaited Reverend Archibald Simpson, pastor of the Independent Presbyterian Church, whose plantation at Stoney Creek near the Georgia border had been alternately occupied by both armies and by several hundred refugees fleeing the war in Georgia: "All was desolation," he wrote plaintively, "and indeed all the way [home] there was a gloomy solitariness. Every field, every plantation showed marks of ruin and devastation. Not a person was to be met with in the roads. All was gloomy." Of the land surrounding his own parsonage he sighed : "It is impossible to describe in words how altered these once beautiful fields are; no garden, no enclosure, no mulberry, no fruit trees, nothing but wild fennel, bushes, underwood, briars, to be seen—and a very ruinous habitation."[5]

The scene was the same in Georgia. The disorganization caused by war, occupation, and the incessant partisan raids had left churches, public buildings, streets, bridges, and roads, which were vital to the recovery of trade and travel, in "a ruinous state."[6] Hundreds of planters and merchants who had fled the state during occupation were economically ruined or impoverished. The experience of Joseph Clay, a Savannah merchant, was typical of many. When he left the state at the time of the British invasion, Clay owned a plantation with a good dwelling house, a barn, slave quarters and the usual outbuildings, livestock, horses, and carriages. When he returned after the evacuation of the king's troops in July 1782, "not a vestige of any thing was left—every building was destroyed, not any fence or the least traces of any kind of Stock or property whatever—all was desolate."[7]

Prospects looked somewhat brighter once old inhabitants began slowly to drift back to the state and migrants from neighboring states began to arrive. Eager "to catch and nurse the present flame and thirst for imigrating [sic] to this Country," the state opened a land office in February 1783 to promote settlement of the backcountry.[8] But with much of the country's

[4] Francis Du Bose Richardson Memoirs, M3010, SHC.

[5] "Simpson's Journal," in Howe, *Presbyterian Church in South Carolina*, 2 vols. (Columbia, S.C.: Duffie and Chapman, 1870), 1:464–65.

[6] The Presentments of the Grand Jurors for the County of Chatham, October 3, 1782, File no. 71, item 70, Bevan Papers.

[7] To James Thompson Jun'r Sterling, June 7, April 24, 1790, "Letters of Joseph Clay," 226.

[8] Ibid., 167, 175.

prerevolutionary leadership still in exile and with the backcountry areas plagued by widespread crime, efforts at establishing even the most rudimentary government services that were essential to economic and social recovery were severely hampered. The "Lawless Savage and unprincipled Banditti," which Lachlan McIntosh complained "nearly depopulated and ruined this fine Country," continued to cover much of the countryside, and "no man is Safe one Night in his House in any part of this State or even in the Town Savannah, or traveling a Mile upon the Roads."[9] The road from Savannah to Augusta was so infested with robbers that when state officials tried to open a land court in Augusta, they had to be escorted from one county line to another by militia units.[10] As Clay surveyed "the ravaged situation we found our Country in the absence of many of our most valuable inhabitants and the slaves," and the "convulsed state" of government, he glumly concluded that planters and local merchants and factors would be obliged "to begin the World again."[11]

The repeated overrunning of the low country by the military forces of both belligerents depleted stock and seed, destroyed roads and ferries, fields and fences, and the irrigation works that were crucial to the rice economy. Two years before the British withdrawal Governor Wright reported that "there would not be above 2,000 barrels of Rice beat out for Market this season," compared to 35,000 barrels that were exported annually before the war.[12] Although the geographical shift of the rice industry from inland swamps to river tidal swamps and technical developments in the methods of cultivation reduced the labor required, normal production was not resumed until 1784, and that crop, according to Joseph Clay, "was very short of what it used formerly to be, and very inadequate to our wants and very disproportionate to the Amount of our Imports."[13]

The crippling effects of the war on South Carolina's economy are suggested by such statistics as survive. No data are available for 1780 and 1781, although it can be presumed that little was produced given the extensive wartime destruction, the massive desertion of slaves, and the necessity of redirecting the labor of many of them from agriculture to the production of "articles of primary necessity," such as cotton cloth, or to labor on public fortifications. Anything that was produced was probably consumed locally, "alternatively by friend and foe." Figures are available for South Carolina's exports beginning in 1783, however. Compiled for the

[9] "Papers of Lachlan McIntosh," 103.

[10] Candler, *RRG* 2:622.

[11] To Nathaniel Hall, April 16, 1783, "Letters of Joseph Clay," 185.

[12] "Proceedings and Minutes of the Governor and Council," January 10, 1780, GHS, *Coll.* 10:79; Lachlan McIntosh to General Washington, February 16, 1776, in George White, ed., *Historical Collections of Georgia* (New York: Pudney and Russell, 1854), 92.

[13] Joseph Clay to John Wilcock, April 22, 1784, "Letters of Joseph Clay," 211.

state assembly by George Abbott Hall, collector of the customs, they reveal a drastic decline in staple crops from prewar levels. Production of rice, South Carolina's most important staple, plunged dramatically. In the prewar years inland swamp plantations had produced up to 155,000 barrels of rice a year, most of which was exported to Britain and from there reshipped to Holland, Germany, France, or to British dependencies.[14] But the loss of slave labor, crucial to the labor-consuming ditching and canal work, and to the cutting, harvesting, threshing, and pounding operations, and the destruction of levees and irrigation canals, forced production down to little more than 23,000 barrels in 1782. Although 65,000 barrels were transported in 1783, that amount barely equalled what had been exported forty-seven years earlier in 1736.

In time the labor of enslaved workers reclaimed the rice fields, and the low-country industry recovered, with, however, an important difference: northern banking and credit facilities now provided the credit, and northern merchants and factors received and marketed the crops, three-fourths of which were destined for domestic ports in the north. The supply disruptions caused by the American Revolution contributed significantly to the erosion of South Carolina's foreign rice markets, which had dominated the western rice trade throughout the colonial period. Over the next decades, other regions would supplant the South Carolina trade, and the state slowly slipped into economic decline.[15]

Indigo, after rice the chief staple of South Carolina, suffered even more disastrous effects. First introduced into South Carolina in 1745, indigo production averaged 500,000 pounds a year, most of which was shipped to Britain. By 1782 production had dropped to only 827 casks. The industry enjoyed a brief resurgence, growing to 2,052 casks in 1783 before topping out in 1792, when 839,666 pounds were exported. As a result of the loss of the British bounty, however, the cultivation of indigo ceased to be profitable and land normally devoted to it was turned to cotton production.[16]

Five years after the revolutionary war had ended, Thomas Jefferson sadly reflected that "History will never relate the horrors committed by the Brit-

[14] Hall's report was sent to Jefferson as an enclosure in his letter of June 10, 1785; see Boyd, *Papers of Jefferson* 8:200.

[15] See Peter A. Coclanis, *The Shadow of a Dream. Economic Life and Death in the South Carolina Low Country, 1670–1920* (Chapel Hill: University of North Carolina Press, 1988). For the development of the factorage system see Smith, *Slavery and Rice Culture*, 76–89.

[16] John Drayton, *A View of South-Carolina as Respects Her Natural and Civil Concerns* (Charleston: W. P. Young, 1802), 127, 165, 167, 173. Drayton served in the South Carolina House of Representatives from 1792 to 1798. At age 32 he was elected lieutenant governor and became governor upon the death of Edward Rutledge in January 1800. He was perhaps the first governor to see most of the state firsthand and wrote a penetrating survey of it.

ish army in the Southern states of America."[17] The history of human misery and suffering caused by this or any war can never be fully recounted, it is true. Although little statistical evidence exists for the Chesapeake, it is clear that the region also suffered extensive material damage. Not a single battle was fought on Maryland's soil, but the shores of the Chesapeake around which most of Maryland's population clustered was the scene of almost constant naval warfare. One or other of the warring factions confiscated or destroyed hundreds of the boats that were the livelihood of rivermen. Continual interruptions of the tide of east coast traffic cut deeply into merchant profits. Damage to homes and personal property, the confiscation of crops and livestock, the destruction of fences and farm tools, and the desertion of slaves injured most of the great planters, whose spacious plantations rimmed the bay, and many of the small farmers and tenants farther inland. In one Maryland county, St. Marys on the Western Shore, forty-six claimants filed for losses in slaves, livestock, farm and household implements totaling £16,179.3.1.[18]

The heaviest damage occurred in areas of Virginia through which the British army passed. Throughout the James River valley horses and livestock were gone, farm buildings and bridges were destroyed, tobacco warehouses and wharves were wrecked, commerce was checked, developing industries were ruined, and the labor supply was severely depleted. Although no complete statistics exist, the extent of the damage is suggested by the lists of claimants compiled by county magistrates in 1782 at the behest of the state assembly. Although it is fragmented, this collection represents the only source that provides extensive statistical information of any kind. One of the most comprehensive sets of records was prepared by the magistrates of St. Bride's parish in Norfolk County near the mouth of the James River. According to their report, damages suffered by inhabitants added up to £39,543.5.3, most of it in buildings, livestock, household goods and plantation implements, and grain, forage, and tobacco. Inhabitants of neighboring Nansemond County presented claims for losses totaling over £37,000.[19] Estimated losses in St. David's parish in King Wil-

---

[17] To Dr. William Gordon, July 16, 1788, Boyd, *Papers of Jefferson* 13:364. See also Madison to Philip Mazzei, July 7, 1781, Hutchinson and Rachal, eds. *Madison Papers* 3:180: "No description can give you an adequate idea of the barbarity with which the enemy have conducted the war in the South."

[18] A List of Property Taken and Destroyed by the Enemy during the Late War, [1781?], Maryland State Papers, Rainbow Series, Blue Book 5:3.

[19] Losses in Virginia during the Revolution Occasioned by the Enemy, Legislative Department, House of Delegates. Speaker, Letters Received, November, 1783, Virginia State Library, Richmond, Va. The author is grateful to Brent Tarter and the staff of the Virginia State Library for locating this box of documents for me. The lists follow no regular pattern and the kind of information varies from county to county, with some counties reckoning losses in pounds sterling rather than by specific reference to property.

liam County on the York River were £13,280.5.11 and for the county as a whole £22,200.[20] Based on data gathered at the time, perhaps from sources such as these, Jefferson estimated that during the six-month period when British armies "raged in Virginia," economic losses to the state amounted to approximately three million pounds sterling.[21]

The extraordinary flight of slaves during the war years also contributed to the planters' crisis of confidence in the postwar era. It is difficult to say with precision how many slaves actually left their owners. Estimates range from eighty thousand to one hundred thousand.[22] The exact number is, at any rate, less important than the general changes their departures produced. The slave exodus engendered by the British invasion and occupation created a severe labor shortage that destroyed the basis of the South's productive economy and weakened the wealth and the power of its richest families. Feeling threatened by impending economic collapse and the breakdown of the traditional labor system upon which their hopes for economic recovery depended, the planter-merchant elite struggled to resurrect the weakened plantation system: by resorting to the massive importation of slaves to rebuild the collapsed economies; by enacting repressive slave codes, which testify to the tension and coercion in the relationship between masters and slaves in the postwar era; by formulating a patriarchal ideology, which drew upon scriptural sanctions and revolutionary ideology, and proclaimed for the first time that the characteristics of the social order were authorized, if not decreed, by God, nature, and reason. In the process, they created a racial community bound into a common religious and cultural framework.

Most, if not all white planters and merchants of the revolutionary generation were convinced that full economic recovery was inseparably linked to the restoration of slave labor. In the months immediately following the British evacuation of Savannah only between seventy and eighty slaves re-

---

[20] Elizabeth Cometti, "Depredations in Virginia During the Revolution," in Darret B. Rutman, ed., *The Old Dominion. Essays for Thomas Perkins Abernethy* (Charlottesville: University Press of Virginia, 1964), 145, 147.

[21] To Dr. William Gordon, July 16, 1788, Boyd, *Papers of Jefferson* 13:364.

[22] Wilson, *Loyal Blacks*, 2. Contemporary estimates are approximately the same. George Abbott Hall maintained that over twenty thousand slaves from South Carolina were carried off by the British, or died of smallpox or camp fevers in British military camps; see Enclosure 11 in From Ralph Izard, June 10, 1785, Boyd, *Papers of Jefferson* 8:199. Jefferson estimated that Virginia lost thirty thousand slaves in the single year 1781; see Boyd, *Papers of Jefferson* 13:364; James Jackson, revolutionary soldier, governor of Georgia, and United States Senator, maintained that between five and six thousand slaves left with the British at the evacuation of Savannah, "Miscellaneous Papers of James Jackson," *Georgia Historical Quarterly* 37:78. In all, Georgia lost approximately two-thirds of her prewar slave population, or about ten thousand slaves.

portedly were available for sale in the entire state.[23] The extreme scarcity drove prices up from an average of £40. for a "seasoned Negro" in 1776, to 200 guineas in 1782.[24] High prices did not, however, dull the planters' voracious appetite for slaves. The "Negro business," as Joseph Clay explained it to a business associate in London, "is a great object with us, both with a View to our Interest individually, and the general prosperity of this State and its commerce, it is to the Trade of this Country, as the Soul to the Body, and without it no House can gain a proper Stability, the Planter will as far in his power sacrifice every thing to attain Negroes."[25] The pent-up demand resulted in a massive influx of Africans from the Windward and Leeward coasts of Africa and from the West Indies, pushing Georgia's slave population up to 20,000 by 1787 and 29,264 by 1790, almost double the prewar figures.[26]

Although South Carolina's economy was on the upswing by 1784, George Abbott Hall frankly predicted that the enslaved population must be replaced "before the produce of this Country will be equal to what it was formerly."[27] Most rice planters and merchants agreed with Hall's grim equation of slave labor and agricultural prosperity. From the beginning slaves had played a large, even a determinative, role in the development of rice cultivation in South Carolina. By the time rice had emerged as South Carolina's premier crop, most planters were firmly convinced that their profits were inextricably tied to slavery. "Rice is raised so as to buy more negroes," the German traveler Johann David Schoepf observed after a visit to the state in 1794, "and negroes are bought so as to get more rice."[28] Although the geographical shift from inland swamp to river tidal swamp cultivation, which began in the late colonial period and was stimulated by the Revolution, significantly reduced the work regime, rice remained a labor-consuming industry.[29]

Low crop yields in 1783, 1784, and 1785 fed the slave hunger of rice planters and created an extreme postwar demand. Breaking temporarily with patterns of the prewar years, low-country slaveholders obtained some

[23] Georgia House of Representatives to President of Congress, January 12, 1782, folder 8, item 48, Bevan Papers.
[24] A List of the Landed and Personal Property in Georgia of Anthony Stokes, Candler, CRG 34:51–52; Colonel James Armstrong to Governor Thomas Burke, August 25, 1782, Clark, SRNC 16:646.
[25] Joseph Clay to James Jackson, February 16, 1784, "Letters of Joseph Clay," 194–95.
[26] Clay to Messers. Scott Dover Taylor and Bill, April 15, 1783, "Letters of Joseph Clay," 187; Evarts B. Greene and Virginia D. Harrington, American Population before the Federal Census of 1790 (New York: Columbia University Press, 1932), 8, 182.
[27] Boyd, Papers of Jefferson 8:199.
[28] Schoepf, Travels in the Confederation 2:182.
[29] Lewis Cecil Gray, History of Agriculture in the Southern United States to 1860, 2 vols. (New York: Peter Smith, 1941), 2:721; see also Morgan "Black Society," 98, 105.

of the slaves they needed from the Chesapeake, whose declining tobacco industry left planters with a surplus of slaves.[30] The majority of slave imports came, however, from Africa. Soon after the cessation of hostilities, a group in Charleston formed a company for the purpose of "carrying on the slave-trade to the coast of Africa."[31] According to the figures compiled for the state assembly by George Abbott Hall, 1,003 Negroes were imported from Africa and the West Indies in 1783, and 167 more were returned from St. Augustine for a total of 1,170. In 1784 , 4,020 were brought from Africa and the West Indies, and 1,372 were brought back from St. Augustine by loyalists who were permitted to return to the state. Within the space of two years, an estimated 6,562 slaves were imported into South Carolina.[32]

When the frenzied pace of slave imports threatened to produce economic havoc, the South Carolina General Assembly in 1787 temporarily suspended the slave trade. Between 1790 and 1800, in response to the heightened demand for slave labor generated by the expansion of the short-staple cotton industry after improvements increased efficiency of the cotton gin, an estimated fourteen thousand slaves were either imported into the state or were brought in by white migrants to the backcountry. From 1800, when South Carolina opened the trade, to 1807, when it was closed by federal law, a total of 39,075 slaves were imported into Charleston.[33] One of the effects of the massive influx of slaves in the postrevolutionary era was to entrench slavery in the low country and to extend it into the backcountry areas of Georgia and South Carolina.

Military operations during the war had provided "the means of spreading a very general knowledge" of the Georgia backcountry.[34] Bounties in land and slaves given by the state government to veterans formed the basis for a postwar rush to Georgia's backcountry. According to laws passed during the Revolution, all veterans, including those from other states as well as native Georgians, who had served in the state militia or with the Continental army in Georgia, were entitled to a land grant. In the postwar period the state granted over three million acres of land, including headrights and bounty grants, to approximately nine thousand veterans, of whom only about two thousand were native Georgians.[35] Within a six-

[30] Morgan, "Black Society," 84–85.

[31] Schoepf, *Travels in the Confederation* 2:221n.

[32] Drayton, *View of South-Carolina*, 167.

[33] Patrick S. Brady, "The Slave Trade and Sectionalism in South Carolina, 1787–1808," *Journal of Southern History* 38 (1972): 602 n. 2, 608, 612, 614–15; Virginia had prohibited the trade in 1778, Maryland in 1783, and Georgia in 1798, and North Carolina imposed a prohibitory tax on imported slaves.

[34] To Joachim Noel Fanning, April 23, 1783, "Letters of Joseph Clay," 191.

[35] James C. Bonner, *A History of Georgia Agriculture 1732–1860* (Athens: University of Georgia Press, 1964), 32.

month period in 1783, five hundred families settled in the backcountry.[36] The increase in the amount of land awarded under the old headright system to two hundred acres,[37] attracted hundreds of additional settlers, leading the state government to lay out several new counties. Franklin and Washington, where most of the bounty lands were located, were opened for settlement in 1784, Greene in 1786.[38] This area later became the first center for the production of green-seed upland cotton.[39]

The revolutionary war produced equally dramatic demographic consequences in South Carolina. Throughout most of the colonial period South Carolina's white population was clustered in the low country. After 1750, however, the backcountry received a heavy influx of white settlers from northern colonies.[40] By the 1760s the backcountry probably contained about 50 percent of South Carolina's white population. By contrast, the black population was heavily concentrated in the low country, which held an estimated 90 percent of all of the colony's slaves compared to only 10 percent for the backcountry.[41] The Revolution interrupted the flow of settlers to the backcountry, but upon the restoration of peace the great tide rolled once more as "multitudes from Europe and the middle and eastern states of America, poured into South Carolina."[42] By the end of the decade, the white population of the backcountry had grown to an astonishing 111,504, whereas the white population of the low country numbered a mere 28,645. In recognition of the growing political importance of the backcountry, the state government established a new town called Columbia about 140 miles from Charleston and designated it the new state capital.[43]

The distribution of the slave populations of Georgia and South Carolina followed a similar if less spectacular pattern. Whereas in 1775 two-thirds of Georgia's slaves lived within twenty miles of the coast, by 1790 over half of them lived in the backcountry.[44] In keeping with trends established in the prewar years, slaves continued to be heavily concentrated in the low country of South Carolina. Blacks constituted a clear majority of the population in all but two of the twelve parishes that made up the Georgetown

[36] Clay to Noel Fanning, April 23, 1783, "Letters of Joseph Clay," 191.

[37] Coleman, *American Revolution in Georgia*, 217.

[38] White, *Historical Collections*, 459, 477, 676.

[39] Bonner, *History of Georgia Agriculture*, 33. The statistics in figure 1 are derived from Sutherland, *Population Distribution*, 260.

[40] Drayton, *View of South-Carolina*, 102.

[41] Weir, *Colonial South Carolina*, 211; Morgan, "Black Society," 85, table 1.

[42] Drayton, *View of South-Carolina*, 103.

[43] Schoepf, *Travels in the Confederation* 1:222n; Drayton, *View of South-Carolina*, 184. The statistics used are derived from Greene and Harrington, *American Population*, 177–79.

[44] White, ed. *Historical Collections*, 92; Sutherland, *Population Distribution*, 259–60.

District. They outnumbered whites by almost four to one in Beaufort District. As a percentage of the total slave population, however, the low-country's share of slaves declined while that of the backcountry increased proportionately. Although no backcountry district had a black majority, every parish in every district contained slaves, a fact that was not, perhaps, without importance for the history of slavery in South Carolina, given the new political importance of the backcountry.[45]

Although it is not possible to establish an exact connection, it appears likely that bounties in slaves given by the state governments as part of pay and recruitment procedures led to a wider distribution of slaveholding in both South Carolina and Georgia. During the war hundreds of slaves were taken from private citizens by Sumter's Brigade and by other whig units and were given to state troops in lieu of payment.[46] The formalization of the procedure by the general assembly convened at Jacksonboro, attracted recruits from as far away as North Carolina and Virginia.[47] With the restoration of peace the assembly was deluged with claims for payment from private soldiers, like Richard Richardson, a former sergeant of the Second South Carolina Regiment, whose petition for the slave promised by the Jacksonboro assembly "to be given as a gratuity to such of the old Soldiers as were then in Service," was approved by the House, as was a similar petition by Derick Drigous, Continental soldier in the First Regiment of Foot. But the very limited supply of slaves available in the postwar period made it increasingly difficult for the state to meet its obligations. According to a report made by a joint committee of the state assembly in March 1784, 570¾ adult blacks and 44⅜ children were still owed to Sumter's troops and 101 adults and 9 children were still owed to Colonel Samuel Hammond's troops. Unable to meet the demand, the assembly resorted to the liquidation of its obligation with interest-bearing treasury certificates. Although some needy veterans sold their slave bounty rights to speculators for a fraction of their value, it is highly probable that the majority of veterans seized the opportunity to realize their social and economic ambitions with the aid of slave labor.[48]

The demographic consequences of the Revolution in the Chesapeake were also considerable. Repeated British invasions and continual naval assaults led to the movement farther inland of the population of once prosperous and populous tidewater towns. Williamsburg, the capital of Virginia until 1780, lost half of its prewar population of over one thousand.

---

[45] Greene and Harrington, *American Population*, 177–79. For the political effects of the population shift see Nadelhaft, *Disorders of War*, especially 12–13, 209–10.

[46] See for example, Thompson, *Journals*, 309, 458, 103, 482, 303, 389.

[47] Porter v. Dunn (1787) S.C. 1 Bay 53.

[48] Thompson, *Journals*, 303, 389, 545, 255, 256.

Among the migrants were professors from the College of William and Mary, lawyers, merchants, and "other considerable residents." Norfolk, burned early in the war, lost most of its six thousand inhabitants.[49] As late as 1790 the first federal census showed only 2,959 black and white residents.[50] Portsmouth, captured and burned during the war, and Yorktown, the scene of a prolonged siege, also lost population.[51] The short-range migrations of large numbers of people hastened the economic decline, under way since the 1750s, of formerly important tidewater towns. Suffolk, for example, before the war "drove a good trade in pitch, tar, timber and other products" with North Carolina. Captured and burned by the British in 1779, only three houses out of one hundred still stood at the end of the war.[52] In 1786 Suffolk appeared "very poor indeed" to a foreign traveler.[53] In Jamestown, the oldest settlement in Virginia and the first seat of government, only one or two out of nearly one hundred houses remained, leaving the little tobacco port "merely the rubbish of a town," with "no appearance of trade."[54] The trade of Norfolk, a thriving community before the war, and of Portsmouth was "diverted to other channels" during the war.[55]

The wartime movement of people and of trade, which hastened the decay of tidewater towns, contributed to the rise in economic and political prominence of several newer inland cities. Although an English traveler in 1785 described Richmond as "one of the dirtiest holes of a place I was ever in,"[56] the decision made during the war to move the capital there from Williamsburg because it was "more safe and central than any other town situated on navigable water," greatly advanced its economic and political importance. From a frontier trading village with muddy streets and a population in 1775 of roughly 600, almost half of whom were black, Rich-

[49] Schoepf, *Travels in the Confederation* 2:80–81, 99; Abbé Robin, *New Travels Through North America* (Philadelphia: Robert Bell, 1783), 52.

[50] United States Bureau of the Census. *Heads of Families at the First Census . . . , 1790: South Carolina* (Washington, D.C., 1908), 10.

[51] Schoepf, *Travels in the Confederation* 2:98, 99, 85.

[52] Mullin, *Flight and Rebellion*, 125; Schoepf, *Travels in the Confederation* 2:96.

[53] Louis B. Wright and Marion Tinling, eds., *Quebec to Carolina in 1785–1786. Being the Travel Diary and Observations of Robert Hunter, Jr., a Young Merchant of London* (San Marino, Calif.: Huntingdon Library, 1943), 263.

[54] Schoepf, *Travels in the Confederation* 2:87; Nicholas Cresswell, *Journal of Nicholas Cresswell 1774–1777* (Port Washington, N.Y.: Kennikat Press, 1968), 206–7.

[55] Schoepf, *Travels in the Confederation* 2:98–99; Peter C. Stewart, "Elizabeth River Commerce During the Revolutionary Era," in Richard A. Rutyna and Peter C. Stewart, eds., *Virginia in the American Revolution. A Collection of Essays*, 2 vols. (Norfolk: Old Dominion University, 1977, 1983), 1:55–72, shows that despite the rapid recovery of commercial activities in Norfolk in the postwar era, the level remained more or less the same as in the prewar period.

[56] Wright and Tinling, *Quebec to Carolina*, 236.

mond "prodigiously increased"[57] to become by 1790 the most populous city in the state, with 3,761 inhabitants, less than half of whom were black.[58] Next in importance to Richmond was Petersburg, already "a flourishing town" by 1782. Situated on the south side of the James River and at the falls of the Appamattox River, it was the entrepôt for all of the export commodities produced in southern Virginia and increasingly for North Carolina exports as well. "Tempted by the advantages of the trade and shipping there," new settlers continually moved in, and by 1790 Petersburg's population was 2,828, over half of whom were black.[59]

The economic prosperity of both towns was based in part on the tobacco trade. Carried downriver to Westham on canoes lashed together and from there transported by land carriage to Richmond or Petersburg, the tobacco was then sent by barge to Norfolk for transshipment to France and England. Although Petersburg was captured by the British in 1781, most of its tobacco warehouses were spared, perhaps out of friendship of the British generals Phillips and Arnold for Mrs. Robert Bolling, who owned most of the warehouses and in whose house Phillips died, perhaps because they meant to seize and market the tobacco themselves.[60] Because of its large and numerous warehouses, Petersburg quickly became known as the "first place in America in that line," its public inspectors inspecting approximately twenty-five thousand hogsheads of tobacco a year to Richmond's fifteen thousand.[61]

Merchants from the two towns also did a lively trade "in all manner of stores" with the planters who were rapidly filling up the back parts of Virginia. Beginning in the 1740s a steady stream of migrants moved into Virginia, spreading settlement well beyond the fall line by the 1750s.[62] The current gained force during the following decade as settlers from Pennsylvania and Maryland advanced down the Blue Ridge Mountains into Virginia's piedmont. The flow was temporarily interrupted during the revolutionary war, although the series of British invasions swelled it once again. When hostilities ended, the tide of settlement resumed and began to roll over the mountains into Kentucky and Tennessee. Driven by soil exhaustion, low crop yields and rising land prices, thousands of farmers and their families sold their land in Virginia and traveled over the mountains with

[57] Maurice Duke and Daniel P. Jordan, eds. *A Richmond Reader 1733–1983* (Chapel Hill: University of North Carolina Press, 1983), 6, 9, 24.

[58] U.S. Census, *Heads of Families*, 10.

[59] Chastellux, *Travels in North America* 2:426; Schoepf, *Travels in the Confederation* 2:72; U.S. Census, *Heads of Families*, 10.

[60] Chastellux, *Travels in North America* 2:420–21.

[61] Wright and Tinling, *Quebec to Carolina*, 237, 260.

[62] Thomas Anburey, *Travels Through the Interior Parts of America, by an Officer*, 2 vols, (reprint, New York: New York Times, c. 1969), 2:207. By the 1750s, Bedford, Dinwiddie, Fauquier, Halifax, Loudoun, Prince Edward, and Sussex counties had been formed.

their horses, oxen, sheep, and even poultry to Kentucky, where fertile land was plentiful and cheap enough to guarantee each child "a sufficient portion."[63]

The western migration of whites was accompanied by a massive movement of the black population. Although thousands of black Virginians had either escaped from slavery or died of disease during the war, Virginia's slave population continued to grow from 165,000 in 1776 to 270,762 in 1782. Growth was far less dramatic in Maryland, but the slave population there also gained slightly from 80,000 in 1776 to 83,362 in 1782. In both states the slave populations continued to increase through the end of the century. By 1790 Virginia's slave population was 292,627, Maryland's 103,036.[64] More significant than the growth in size, however, was the geographic expansion of slavery in Virginia. The inland migration of farmers and wartime dislocations caused by the movement of planters with their slaves during the various British invasions contributed to broad demographic shifts in the slave population of Virginia. Although the tidewater counties remained an area of high slave concentration, there was a conspicuous shift in the black population to developing areas, such as Northumberland, Richmond, and Westmoreland counties on the Northern Neck, and to counties abutting the tidewater, such as Isle of Wight, Sussex, Southampton, Brunswick, Dinwiddie, Amelia, Chesterfield, and Cumberland, and to piedmont couunties bounding the Blue Ridge Mountains, such as Culpeper, Orange, and Albemarle.[65] Maryland, by contrast, was "rapidly giving way to emancipation," as an English traveler put it in 1801. Unlike Virginia, which had extensive undeveloped western lands, Maryland had "no *backlands*, and no territory of any great value west of the mountains" into which to expand her agricultural economy and the slave labor system upon which it rested.[66] The result was a significantly greater increase in the size of the free black population from 4 percent in 1755 to over 20 percent by 1810.[67]

[63] Ibid. 2:235–36; Schoepf, *Travels in the Confederation* 2:36, 88n. In Frederick, Berkeley, Augusta, and Shenandoah counties, land was selling for from £6 to £10 an acre in 1783. For an important discussion of western migration, see Kulikoff, "Uprooted Peoples: Black Migrants in the Age of the American Revolution, 1790–1820," in Berlin and Hoffman, eds., *Slavery and Freedom*, 143–71.

[64] The figures used here are quoted in Gray, *History of Agriculture* 2:1025. Growth was apparently the result of natural increase; African imports showed a sharp drop after 1765, and in 1778 Virginia prohibited the slave trade. See James A. Rawley, *The Transatlantic Slave Trade. A History* (New York: Norton, 1981), 404.

[65] Dunn, "Black Society in the Chesapeake," 58–59, map 2.

[66] William Strickland, "Observations on the Agriculture of the United States of America," in William Strickland, *Journal of a Tour in the United States of America*, Reverend J. E. Strickland, ed. (New York: NYHS, 1971), 19.

[67] Dunn, "Black Society in the Chesapeake," 62. This trend was consistent with patterns

Black and white expansion westward, which coincided with disturbances in marketing conditions occasioned by the war, had important implications for economic life in the Chesapeake and ultimately for slavery as
well. Among the most significant effects were changes in the patterns of
agricultural production, most notably the spread of tobacco cultivation
southward and a gradual shift from tobacco to wheat production. Although the transition to grain cultivation began in the 1760s on Maryland's Eastern Shore, down to the Revolution tobacco remained Virginia's
principal export commodity.[68] The loss of thousands of field hands, the
destruction of warehouses and wharves, the shortage of draught horses
and water carriage, and the confiscation of thousands of pounds of tobacco
by British raiding parties severely damaged the industry, particularly in the
older producing areas along the Potomac and the lower James River. From
an annual average of 62,247 hogsheads from 1770 to 1773, tobacco exports from Virginia fell to only 49,497 hogsheads in the 1783–1784 season. Faced with high labor costs, low crop yields, and fluctuating prices
for tobacco, planters in Maryland and in northern Virginia in increasing
numbers gave up the culture of tobacco to sow grain instead, thus accel-
erating the prerevolutionary movement of the center of tobacco culture
inland to the south side of the James River and the Appomattox River
valley.

With the end of hostilities the tobacco industry began slowly to revive.
Aided by the expansion of cultivation in the piedmont, by 1787 production had returned to prewar levels in Virginia. By the end of the decade,
however, many planters in northern Virginia, including George Washington, had completely abandoned tobacco for wheat. The overall decline in
the commercial importance of tobacco and the expansion of the wheat
market are reflected in export figures: in the year ending in September
1792 Virginia exported 61,203 hogsheads of tobacco. Maryland's tobacco
exports dropped to only 28,292 hogsheads, down from a prewar average
of 30,000 hogsheads. During the same period Maryland exported 140,121
bushels of wheat and 191,799 bushels of flour while Virginia exported
393,376 bushels of wheat and 108,824 bushels of flour.[69] Wartime developments had, however, insured the collapse of tidewater cultivation.

---

apparent throughout the colonial period; see Wax, "Black Immigrants," 30–45, especially p.
35.

[68] Clemens, *Atlantic Economy*, 168, 174. The shift was most apparent in Maryland, where
some Eastern Shore planters had already abandoned tobacco. In Kent County, for example,
wheat was the principal crop.

[69] Jacob M. Price, *France and the Chesapeake. A History of the French Tobacco Monopoly, 1674–
1791, and of Its Relationship to the British and American Tobacco Trade*, 2 vols. (Ann Arbor,
Mich.: University of Michigan Press, 1973), 2:729, table 1A; Gray, *History of Agriculture*
2:605.

Competition from Georgia and South Carolina and from the developing industry along the Mississippi and Ohio rivers threatened the future prosperity of tobacco planters in the Chesapeake. Although the American tobacco export trade declined drastically between 1776 and 1782, the conditions of the war years generally favored the growth of the industry. Introduced into Georgia on the eve of the Revolution by planters from Virginia, tobacco grew well in the fertile soil around Augusta. A longer growing season allowed planters to produce two crops a year of a quality "rather superior" to that grown in Virginia.[70] First produced for export in 1770, tobacco shipments grew rapidly from 3,030 pounds the first year to 13,447 pounds in the period from January 1770 to January 1771, to 176,732 pounds in the year ending in January 1773.[71] The conclusion of a contract with the Farmers General of France and of an agreement with a Spanish mercantile firm increased the demand for tobacco at a time when naval and military activity in the Chesapeake had begun to depress production there. As a result of high prices, the tendency toward tobacco cultivation was distinct in Georgia before 1779. Had not the British invasion interrupted, "two-thirds of the planters, in the year 1779, would have turned their attention almost wholly upon tobacco, it being in more demand than rice or indigo."[72] British occupation and control of the ports of Charleston and Savannah after 1779 made it possible for Georgia and South Carolina tobacco planters to gain access to British markets. From 643 hogsheads in 1782 South Carolina's annual production grew rapidly to 5,019 hogsheads by 1787. By 1790 Georgia was exporting an average of 5,600 hogsheads a year.[73] The industry continued to grow until the beginning of the nineteenth century, when it was supplanted by sea-island cotton, experiments in which were being carried on at least as early as 1789.[74]

Introduced into South Carolina in 1754, cotton was grown as a supplement to rice in predominantly rice-growing districts and as the principal crop in estuarine tidewater regions and the sea islands, which were unsuitable for rice cultivation. Only small crops, never enough for export, were raised, however, and South Carolina remained heavily dependent upon textile goods imported from Britain. The closing of the British textile industry to American markets during the war accelerated the shift from indigo to cotton, as planters were forced "to originate articles of primary

[70] Gray, *History of Agriculture*, 591.

[71] Bernard Romans, *A Concise Natural History of East and West Florida* (reprint, New York: Pelican Publishing, 1961), 74–75.

[72] "Observations upon the Effects of Certain Late Political Suggestions, By the Delegates of Georgia," in White, ed., *Historical Collections*, 107.

[73] Price, *France and the Chesapeake* 2:730, table 1B.

[74] Plantation Journal, 1786–1801, no. 485, [Richard] Leake Papers, 1780–1801, GHS.

necessity," particularly "Negro cloth," woven from a mixture of cotton and wool. The impetus provided by the Revolution and improvements in the cotton gin, formed the basis for the cotton boom that occurred at the beginning of the nineteenth century.

After Eli Whitney refined the cotton gin while living at the Nathanael Greene plantation near Savannah, extraordinary profits led to the rapid development of cotton as an export commodity. In Georgia, cotton production was centered in a broad belt that began at the foothills of Wilkes County and continued south below Augusta and west to Columbus. By 1830 Middle Georgia, as this fertile region of red clay was known, was the leading cotton area of the South. As the population shifted to the upper reaches of the Savannah River, Augusta, a port town where tobacco roads converged and cotton buyers gathered to purchase seed cotton for ginning in their own mills, became a new focus of political and economic importance.[75] The success of the industry in Georgia led to its rapid spread into the rich, high swamplands of the middle and upper country of South Carolina and into reclaimed salt marshes in the lower country and on the sea islands. Production soared from 68,520 pounds in 1792 to 8,301,907 pounds exported in 1800 from the port of Charleston alone, which surpassed in value the greatest crops of rice or indigo ever harvested in South Carolina.[76]

Changes in patterns of agricultural production necessitated adjustments in the labor system. This was especially true of the Chesapeake. By contrast to tobacco, which required constant attention in transplanting, weeding, worming, picking, curing, rolling, and packing, wheat was less labor intensive. To maintain the profitability of slavery, therefore, many owners marketed their surplus slaves in newer regions or hired them to other planters outside the plantation. Between 1780 and 1810 an estimated seventy-five thousand slaves were moved across the Allegheny Mountains to frontier plantations in the new states of Kentucky and Tennessee, and another fifteen thousand were conveyed to the rapidly developing backcountry of Georgia and South Carolina and to the Mississippi and Louisiana frontiers. Following the closing of the external slave trade to the United States in 1808, the internal slave trade began to flourish, and between 1810 and 1820 an estimated 137,000 Chesapeake slaves were transported and sold by professional slave traders to planters in territories and states west of the Mississippi.[77]

[75] Bonner, *History of Georgia Agriculture*, 41, 48, 49, 50, 54, 56; Lee Soltow, "Socioeconomic Classes in South Carolina and Massachusetts in the 1790s and the Observations of John Drayton," *South Carolina Historical and Genealogical Magazine* 81 (1980): 297; Kulikoff, *Tobacco and Slaves*, 429.

[76] Drayton, *View of South-Carolina*, 128.

[77] Kulikoff, "Uprooted Peoples," 148, 149, 151.

Compelled by the changes in plantation agriculture, Chesapeake slave masters with a surplus of slave labor also increasingly resorted to the practice of renting slaves to work in local industries and urban occupations, as domestics in the homes of wealthy persons, or most commonly as workers on small farms and tenements.[78] Tenancy apparently first developed on the Northern Neck of Virginia before the war, when impoverished small planters began to lease their land. The practice gradually spread among larger planters in Frederick, Berkeley, Fauquier, and Loudoun counties. As a result of the demographic shifts in the white population that both preceded and accompanied the war, tenancy expanded into eastern Virginia as well.[79] Prevented by small profit margins from hiring free labor or purchasing slave labor, tenants and small farmers composed a thriving market for slaves who could not otherwise be profitably employed by their owners.

In the lower South, shifts in patterns of agricultural production also resulted in changes in labor arrangements. The severity of the work regimen was reduced somewhat as the tidewater rice culture developed, which eliminated the need for heavy hoeing, at least during the summer months. Although the task system remained the dominant method of labor arrangement in the low country, the spread of cotton, which was less demanding than either rice or indigo, contributed to the wider use of the gang system of labor than had previously been known in the lower South. Although most slaves continued to work as field hands, the growth in plantation unit size created new opportunities for skilled workers, and the number of slaves holding specialized positions increased significantly, at least temporarily.[80]

The revolutionary war did not launch any of these changes, but it did propel them. The wartime migration of whites with their slaves helped to sustain the westward movement of the tidewater and low-country populations and to nourish the fragile roots of slavery in the backcountry everywhere. Heavy wartime damage to the staple economies in the older producing areas accelerated shifts in patterns of agricultural production, which in turn necessitated the more rapid adaptation of the labor supply. By making it profitable to slaveowners, "hiring out" helped keep slavery viable in Virginia. By making slaves accessible to nonslaveowners, hiring out helped

[78] Sarah S. Hughes, "Slaves for Hire: The Allocation of Black Labor in Elizabeth City County, Virginia, 1782–1810," *William and Mary Quarterly*, 3d ser., 35 (1978): 268–69.
[79] Williard F. Bliss, "The Rise of Tenancy in Virginia," *Virginia Magazine of History and Biography* 58 (1950): 428–29. According to Hughes, approximately one-third of the free farm workers of Elizabeth City County were tenants by 1782; see Hughes, "Slaves for Hire," 274–75.
[80] Morgan, "Black Society," 97–107; Morgan, "Work and Culture," 577.

to disperse support for slavery through society. By the same token, the sale of surplus slaves stimulated the growth and development of slavery in the piedmont of Virginia and the backcountry of Georgia and South Carolina and in the new states of Kentucky and Tennessee. As ownership and sympathy for it became more widespread, as it grew more flexible and expanded spatially, slavery became more entrenched everywhere but in Maryland.

Paradoxically, the war and the social and economic changes engendered by it—all of which helped to implant slavery firmly in the South—also contributed to the vulnerability of the slave regime. Long years of war and occupation had led to the breakdown of the traditional agencies of social control that slaveholders relied upon to regulate community relations. The enslaved population was quick to take advantage of the new possibilities for greater freedom. African-Americans had emerged from the Revolution with a heightened self-awareness, which manifested itself in economic assertiveness and intensified rebelliousness. The wartime experience had also spawned a small nucleus of black leaders, "new men" who believed in violent rebellion for the sake of the abstract principle of freedom. In the postwar period, they undertook the organization of resistance.

The assertiveness of slaves is apparent in the dramatic rise in unsanctioned commercial activity, which seriously challenged the system of racial control. Provision plot agriculture, which grew out of the special labor arrangements of tasking, had traditionally allowed rural slaves the opportunity to produce agricultural commodities for their personal use. Over time the practice had become sufficiently institutionalized so that masters accepted the slaves' rights in their produce and in many cases in the marketing of surpluses. On some low-country plantations masters traded with their slaves on a cash basis, purchasing the fish, hogs, corn, or fowl they raised or foraged, or the baskets, chairs, brooms, horse or mule collars, wooden bowls and ladles, or other small items they produced during leisure hours. Most transactions were carried out at night in the small shops or stores usually situated at crossroads in the rural South.[81] Slaves often traded with one another, exchanging corn for the beans, potatoes, or melons that they grew in their small patches.

One of the most significant signs of growing autonomy was the extension to the cotton plantations of the practice of hiring-their-own-time, formerly an urban phenomenon.[82] At the height of the cotton season, slaves

[81] Schoepf, *Travels in the Confederation* 2:201, 221; William Grimes, *Life of William Grimes, the Runaway Slave. Written by Himself* (New York: n.p., 1825), 38–39; Charles Ball, *Slavery in the United States: A Narrative of the Life and Adventures of Charles Ball. A Black Man* (Lewistown, Pa.: John W. Shugert, 1836), 128, 144, 147, 149, 220, 261, 385, 391.

[82] According to Morgan, "Black Life in the Eighteenth-Century Chesapeake," 191, the practice of self-hire was almost exclusively urban in the eighteenth century.

on plantations around Augusta and on the Congaree River in South Carolina commonly hired themselves out to overseers or to planters on neighboring plantations to pick beyond the normal day's standard quantity, or to pick on Sunday, normally a day of rest. Some forty of the two hundred and sixty slaves from the Morgan County Court House plantation near Augusta, where Charles Ball was a slave, went out to work for other planters on neighboring plantations on Sundays. Others worked the overseer's twenty-acre cotton patch for twenty cents a day. Ball often hired himself out and claimed to have worked for over fifty people.[83]

Urban areas offered the greatest opportunities for economic advancement. The new movement toward urbanization generated by the war had allowed numbers of enterprising blacks to accumulate property, much of which went toward increasing the free black population through self-purchase, and to develop a relatively independent economic life. Although the practice was forbidden by law, many slaves as well as free blacks, "work and labour for themselves in several trades and occupations," for the privilege of which they paid their owners a portion of their earnings.[84] Low-country towns such as Charleston swarmed with slave butchers, cobblers, tailors, carpenters, masons, cartwrights, coopers, even goldsmiths, whose skills were hired out by their owners or who hired themselves out. Slave mechanics often found work in the countryside building houses, cotton gins, or horse mills. Slave tailors sought employment from house to house. Many Savannah slaves went out to work when and where they pleased, collected their own wages, provided their own subsistence, and at the end of the week, paid a percentage of their earnings to the owner. With their earnings, which ranged from ten shillings a year for a hatter or a ropemaker, to twenty shillings a year for a carpenter or mason, slaves were able to buy luxuries, such as Sunday clothing for the family, extra blankets, or food to supplement the regular slave diet, and in many cases, to purchase freedom, their own, or that of family members.[85]

During the war and in the depressed postwar years, skilled slaves enjoyed a temporary advantage over white artisans and mechanics. Their willingness to work for low wages brought them into economic competition with poor white workers and was a source of considerable hostility. In 1783, for example, the house carpenters and bricklayers of Charleston protested that "Jobbing Negro Tradesmen, who undertake work for little more than the Stuff would cost," deprived them of the means to earn a living and requested that the assembly pass a law prohibiting Negroes from

[83] Ball, *Slavery in the U.S.*, 144, 147, 150; Grimes, *Life of William Grimes*, 38–39.

[84] Chap. 6, sec. 8, Clark, *State Records* 24:15, 727.

[85] Morgan, "Black Life in Eighteenth-Century Charleston," 194, maintains that a "significant proportion" of eighteenth century manumissions involved slaves who purchased their own freedom or that of family members.

"undertaking work on their Own Account." A committee of the House of Representatives found the petitioners' grievances to be "well grounded" and, therefore, recommended legislation prohibiting "any Negro from working at any Mechanical operation" and prescribing penalties for persons who employed them.[86] The North Carolina Assembly enacted a similar measure in 1785 for the towns of Wilmington, Fayetteville, Washington, and Edenton, on the grounds that self-employed slaves occasioned "robberies and frauds" and deprived "poor white inhabitants" of "the means of earning their subsistence by labour."[87] The slave pilots' monopoly of the river traffic also provoked a series of protests from white pilots in the postwar years. For reasons of economy, however, the slave pilots were generally supported by Wilmington merchants, and the general assembly did not take action until 1800, and then only by requiring the owners of slaves to secure licenses and guarantee the conduct of their slaves.[88] Such actions by state assemblies and town authorities were an important source of white unity in the postwar period, particularly in towns such as Charleston, where serious internal divisions along class lines had begun to emerge during the conflict with England and threatened to create new political forces.[89]

Intensified slave rebelliousness in the postwar era was in many ways the climax of these developments. Although it is not possible to extrapolate a pattern of black behavior for the South as a whole, surviving court records from Virginia offer insights into the difficulty of maintaining racial discipline in the postwar era. Between 1785 and 1794 the number of deadly assaults by blacks on whites increased markedly. During that period over one hundred and forty-eight black persons were convicted of murdering whites; more than twenty-four were found guilty of attempted murder; ten were executed or transported for assault. Significantly, the rise in the incidence of racial violence generally coincided with a number of insurrection scares and actual episodes.[90]

More physical proximity promoted among urban-centered African-Americans a feeling of solidarity that was increasingly channeled into intricate forms of cooperative action. The egalitarian atmosphere created by the ideological and political developments of the period played an important role in the political awakening of urban blacks. The growth during the prewar years of urban-centered Afro-Christianity provided both an ideology and a structure for the first conscious attempts at organized resistance.

[86] Thompson, *Journals*, 237.

[87] Chap. 6, sec. 8, Clark, *State Records* 24:727.

[88] James Howard Brewer, "Legislation Designed to Control Slavery in Wilmington and Fayetteville," *North Carolina Historical Review*, 30 (1953): 163–64.

[89] Nadelhaft, *Disorders of War*, 8–12.

[90] Schwarz, *Twice Condemned*, 231, 247.

The revolt of African slaves in the French colony of Saint Domingue in the 1790s provided the inspiration. The progressive history of slave resistance shows that although slave rebellions retained vital links to the African past, insurrectionary activity was increasingly influenced by revolutionary ideology and evangelical religion.

The postwar period was marked by a rise in maroon activity, slave plots, and insurrections. Despite temporal variations, insurrectionary activities occurred over the entire slave region and shared some common elements. Most, if not all of the postwar outbreaks, had ideological overtones and were linked in one way or another to revolutionary experiences and to the changing social and political environment. The leaders and many of the participants had gained military experience, usually with the British army, during the war. Although the number of participants was quantitatively negligible and few of the outbreaks turned into genuine rebellions, they did represent a psychological threat that stirred slaveholders' worst fantasies.

Maroon activities increased in all of the southern states during the unsettled postwar years. During the revolutionary war a sizeable number of slaves ran away and set up camps in the swamps or in woods remote from the reaches of white power. A typical example was the case of runaways from Virginia and North Carolina, who organized themselves into bands and fled into the Dismal Swamp. Secure from the pursuit of patrols, they built cabins, planted corn, raised poultry and livestock and generally "lived in security and plenty" at least into the 1790s. Although they often waged defensive guerrilla warfare, their aims were limited, by and large, to personal escape from slavery.[91]

But black experience in the Revolution, particularly in the lower South where blacks had greater opportunities to gain military experience with occupying British forces, and the revolutionary ideas current in society at the time were powerful catalysts in moving slave resistance beyond these inchoate forms of violent resistance. In the immediate aftermath of the revolutionary war, something close to warfare developed in the coastal areas of Georgia and South Carolina. As soon as the fighting stopped, bands of armed blacks formed during the war years began to harrass coastal areas, causing general restiveness among the rural black population.[92] After the British evacuation substantial numbers of male and female runaways from Georgia and South Carolina fled to the swamps bordering the lower Savannah River and established a camp on a cleared site some 700 yards long and 120 yards wide. A breastwork of logs and cane standing 4 feet high

[91] Smyth, *Tour* 2:101–2; Schoepf, *Travels in the Confederation* 2:99–100.
[92] Governor Mathews to General Marion, October 6, 1782, Horry Papers; Wilkinson, *Letters of Eliza Wilkinson*, 25.

protected the land approach to the village, which consisted of twenty-one houses, surrounded by rice fields; large fallen logs defended the creek side of the camp from water attack. Although the legislatures of both states attempted to hunt the fugitives down and regularly offered bounties for their capture or death, they were generally regarded only as dangerous nuisances until 1787, when their numbers increased. Then authorities began to perceive a collective consciousness for large-scale revolt. Not content merely to remain at large, beginning in the spring of 1787 approximately one hundred armed men led by "Captain Cudjoe" and "Captain Lewis" and a group of armed runaways, who called themselves "the King of England's Soldiers," launched a series of guerrilla attacks on plantations on both sides of the Savannah River. In May they boldly attacked two detachments of Georgia state troops.

Such subversive actions threatened white plantation society. Aware of the "strong charms of allurement" marooning had for slaves, an alarmed Georgia legislature immediately dispatched state troops to rout the maroons from their village. A combined force of state troops and Indians succeeded in destroying the village and killing six of "their head men" and wounding a number of others. Most of the fugitives fled through the swamps into South Carolina, however, and persisted in harrassing whites and fomenting slave rebellion. Haunted by visions of racial anarchy, James Jackson, commanding officer of the Georgia militia, wrote an urgent warning to the governors of Georgia and South Carolina: "If something cannot be shortly done, I dread the consequences." Although there was no evidence of a plot, the fugitives, Jackson warned, "are as dangerous as any, and from thier [sic] independent state, from the ease they enjoy in South Carolina, forbode what I dread to express, a capital insurrection." Calling attention to the fact that "Their leaders are the very fellows that fought, and maintained their ground against the brave Lancers at the seige of Savannah," Jackson urged the two executives to launch a joint military expedition to hunt down and destroy the entire maroon force. The camp was routed by the militia and Lewis was taken prisoner. Tried and convicted of murder and robbery, he was sentenced to be hanged, his head severed and stuck on a pole on the island of Marsh in the Savannah River.[93]

Small armed bands, but with collective potential, continued to harrass coastal areas of both states. In August, the Berkeley County militia had to be called out to break up a band of armed blacks, "too numerous to be quelled by the usual parties of patrol," who were raiding plantations in the

[93] Trial of Negroe Man Slave named Lewis, the property of Oliver Bowen, Telamon Cuyler Collection. Box 71, file Georgia Slavery; folder, Georgia. Slavery, Trials, University of Georgia Library. I am grateful to Betty Wood for sharing this citation with me.

vicinity of Stono, near Charleston.[94] In neighboring North Carolina, the scene of several wartime plots and pervasive violence between master and slave,[95] a male slave belonging to William Bryan of troubled Craven County was killed "in suppressing of Rebel Slaves."[96] Slave-hunting militia units eventually destroyed or dispersed the large camps, although marooning itself survived throughout the history of slavery. Despite a number of insurrectionary scares, low-country slaveowners were able thereafter to maintain relatively tranquil control.

In the meantime, however, the momentum of rebellion was accelerated and intensified by the example of the successful slave revolt in the French colony of Saint Domingue in the 1790s. The Saint Domingue slave rebellion began August 22, 1791, on the northern plain encircling Cap Français. A number of the leaders of the rebellion had fought as volunteers in Fontages Legion with the French and American armies at the siege of Savannah. Their participation in the American Revolution forged the first vital link in a connected series of rebellions in new world slave societies. News of the Saint Domingue rebellion was transmitted to the North American slave population through an intricate interregional communication network operated by black seamen from American merchant ships trading in the West Indies.[97] As public interest in developments in Saint Domingue intensified, urban blacks gathered information from the proliferating political literature—pamphlets, handbills, and newspapers—developed by political factions to reach the grassroots of the white electorate. In Charleston, black workers at Peter Freneau's republican daily, the *City Gazette*, apparently appropriated over two hundred additional copies of the paper, which had been printed to meet the unusual public demand for information on events in Saint Domingue, presumably for distribution within the black community.[98]

The circulation of the politics of revolution from its generating source in North America through Europe and the French Caribbean and back to its starting point reinspired American slaves to mount their own rebellions. The first tremor of slave rebellion occurred in Northampton County, Virginia, in 1792. Rumors of an insurrection reached ever-vigilant white au-

[94] Adele Stanton Edwards, ed., State Records of South Carolina, *Journals of the Privy Council, 1783–1789* (Columbia: University of South Carolina Press, 1971), 203.

[95] Crow, "Slave Rebelliousness," 79–89.

[96] Senate Journal, Clark, *State Records* 19:258.

[97] See Julius S. Scott, "The Common Wind: Currents of Afro-American Communication in the Era of the Haitian Revolution," (Ph.D. diss., Duke University, 1986), 203, 204, 205, 288. See also Alfred N. Hunt, *Haiti's Influence on Antebellum America. Slumbering Volcano in the Caribbean* (Baton Rouge: Louisiana State University Press, 1988), 31.

[98] Ebenezer Smith Thomas, *Reminiscences of the Last Sixty-Five Years*, 2 vols. (Hartford, Conn.: Case, Tiffany and Burnham, 1840), 1:77–78. Peter Freneau, the brother of Philip Freneau, was editor of the *City Gazette*, which Thomas purchased January 1, 1810.

thorities before events had progressed very far. Although the leaders had apparently neither settled upon a date for the projected rising nor had they acquired arms or ammunition to carry it off, a dozen slaves suspected of leading the conspiracy were arrested, and the county militia was called out to prevent further meetings and to control slave movements. Restrictions on their right to meet and on their freedom to be at large were "extremely irksome" to the slaves because they "abridged them of those privileges which they had been taught by many white people of this County to believe they were entitled to," an apparent reference to the political ideas transmitted by whites themselves to their slaves through indiscreet conversations or filtered down to them through the instruments of partisan education. Instead of submitting quietly, six slaves organized a plan to "destroy those enemies of their liberty." Armed only with clubs, they attacked a militia patrol but were successful only in knocking off the hat of one of the patrollers. The following day five of the six were apprehended and summarily tried, and three of the five were executed.[99]

The next reported incident occurred in New Bern, North Carolina, in September 1792. A report that slaves had "in contemplation to rise against their masters and to procure themselves their liberty" produced spasms of fear in the white community. The rumored insurrection never materialized because of a general white alert. In July 1793 "a desperate Gang of Negroes" killed a Dr. St. John in Liberty County, Georgia.[100] The Garvin conspiracy of 1793 in Virginia and South Carolina suggests the first direct connection between insurrectionary activities in the South and the slave revolt in Saint Domingue. The conquest of the Plaine du Nord by the insurgents in June 1793 and the collapse of Cap Français, which took the lives of over ten thousand people, drove thousands of whites from the burning plains and the gruesome scenes of the harbor town to American ports.[101] The first contingent arrived in Norfolk in July, many of them sick or wounded and without clothing or resources of any kind. Appalled by the excesses of the slave revolt, sympathetic white Virginians offered the distressed refugees immediate assistance. As planters and slaves from Saint Domingue settled in the country, however, white Virginians saw the influence of Saint Domingue at work.

Early in August there were alarming reports from Point of Fork at the confluence of the Rivanna and Hardware rivers in Albemarle County that several slaves had armed themselves with spikes fixed on sticks and were robbing plantations. One runaway went to his master "with a sword made out of a Reap hook, and told him to his face that he would not serve him

---

[99] Palmer et al., eds., *Calendar of Virginia State Papers* 5:534–35, 555, 625.

[100] "Miscellaneous Papers of James Jackson, 1781–1798," GHS, *Coll.* 11 (1955): 81, 91.

[101] Thomas Ott, *The Haitian Revolution, 1789–1804*, 1st ed. (Knoxville: University of Tennessee Press, 1973), 65–72.

unless he was allowed certain privileges." Frightened planters believed that their slaves were encouraged by events in Saint Domingue: "The insolence of those people," Elias Langham wrote to the governor, "is almost a common talk on the Court Green, particularly since the arrival of the French from C. F." The first rumors of an actual conspiracy began to circulate in Richmond. Near the end of July, John Randolph of Richmond overheard a late-night conversation between several slaves concerning a plot to kill the white population of Richmond. When one of the slaves questioned whether the projected plot would ever be carried out, the apparent leader responded, "you see how the blacks has killed the whites in the French island and took it a little while ago."[102]

That the purported plot was not simply careless talk by angry slaves soon became clear. On August 8 William Nelson, Jr. wrote to Governor Henry Lee describing a letter found in the streets of Yorktown. Signed "Secret Keeper, Richmond," the letter was ostensibly written by Garvin, an itinerant preacher and black organizer of the revolt.[103] The letter detailed plans for a massive slave rebellion, which would include South Carolina as well as Virginia and would rely upon fire as the method of destruction because "the Negroes of Cape Francois [sic] have obtained their liberties by this method and they will proceed here in the same manner." Lieutenant Colonel Thomas Newton, commander of militia in the borough of Norfolk, warned that the slaves from Saint Domingue "would be ready to operate against us with the others."[104] Nelson expressed doubt that "no such plan as laid down in the letter [could] be completely executed," but he acknowledged the gravity of the situation and suggested that Lee consider arming the citizens of the state. Copies of Garvin's letter and of Randolph's deposition were sent to authorities in Petersburg, who also thought it "improbable that the negroes could ever make a stand," but, having ample reason to fear the revolutionary potential of their slaves, they requested that the state provide the Petersburg militia with arms.

Despite the frightened concern, Governor Lee took no action. Although surviving evidence suggests that no carefully considered plans for a massive revolution existed, the plot had some basis in fact. In September a number of slaves from different parts of the county were discovered in an old schoolhouse in Powhatan County. Some of the slaves taken confessed that "three hundred was to meet there" to launch a rebellion. Because they could not be tied to the Richmond plot, the slaves were whipped and released. When the citizens of Richmond learned of the slaves' covert meeting, they were horrified, and Mayor Robert Mitchell wrote to Governor

[102] Palmer et al., eds., *Calendar of Virginia State Papers* 6:436, 437, 438, 453, 470.
[103] Ibid., 475.
[104] Quoted in Ott, *Haitian Revolution*, 54.

Lee to express surprise that "the Governor had not advised their Lt.-Col. of the County of the suspicion of the negroes, that they be prepared against the worse."[105]

The decision of the leader of the Saint Domingue rebels, Toussaint Louverture, to join the French against the Spanish and the English, followed by news of the French emancipation decree in February 1794, copies of which were circulated in Charleston,[106] made Saint Domingue the symbol for black liberation struggles throughout the hemisphere and touched off a series of new insurrectionary attempts.[107] During the summer of 1795, Wilmington, North Carolina, was held in the grip of fear by the sporadic attacks of a band of runaways led by the "General of the Swamps." Posses eventually killed the rebels, including the general. In 1798 panic descended on coastal Bertie County when evidence of a conspiracy involving 150 slaves was discovered. The rebellion was never fully realized and the three leaders were convicted of a high misdemeanor instead of rebellion; they suffered thirty-nine lashes and cropped ears rather than death.[108] In the fall of 1795 "a Negro alarm" in Bryan County caused uneasy whites in Georgia to purchase "up most of the powder retailing to prevent the Negroes from purchasing [it]."[109] That same year a parish-wide conspiracy among the French-speaking slaves on the Julien Poydras plantation was discovered in Louisiana's Pointe Coupee parish. A Spanish court sent twenty-six black conspirators to the gallows, sentenced others to prison terms and hard labor, and transported two.[110]

Stunned by the military successes of the Saint Domingue insurgents and sensing the spread of revolutionary fervor, white southerners moved forcefully to break up the black communication networks and isolate their slaves from news from Saint Domingue. Governor Charles Pinckney of South Carolina wrote a tense message of sympathy to the Saint Domingue Colonial Assembly that summed up white fears that the rampaging army of

[105] Palmer et al., eds., *Calendar of Virginia State Papers* 6:475.

[106] Scott, "Common Wind," 8.

[107] France declared war on England February 1, on Spain March 7, 1793; Jacobin emissaries of the French government offered freedom to slaves in return for their support against England and Spain. On February 4, 1794, the convention abolished slavery.

[108] This paragraph relies heavily on Crow, "Slave Rebelliousness," 93–94.

[109] "Miscellaneous Papers of James Jackson," GHS, *Coll.* 11:91.

[110] Scott, "The Common Wind," 273. For details of the Pointe Coupee revolt, see Jack D. L. Holmes, "The Abortive Slave Revolt at Point Coupee, Louisiana, 1795," *Louisiana History* 11 (1970): 341–62. The ideals of the democratic revolutions of the eighteenth century persisted through the nineteenth century in the romantic literary movement among free black intellectuals in New Orleans; Caryn Cosse Bell and Joseph Logsdon, "The Impact of the Revolutionary Upheaval in France and the French Caribbean on Nineteenth Century Black Leadership" (Paper presented at the fifteenth annual conference of the French Colonial Historical Society, Guadeloupe, 1989).

slaves in Saint Domingue would touch off slave revolts at home: "When we recollect how nearly similar the situation of the Southern States and St. Domingo are in the profusion of slaves—that a day may arrive when they may be exposed to the same insurrections—we cannot but sensibly feel for your situation."[111] Convinced now of the error of admitting French slaves, the white authorities attempted to bar their entry. In Louisiana Spanish Governor Baron Hector de Carondelet closed the port of New Orleans to slave imports.[112] In 1795 North Carolina passed a law prohibiting the entry of all West Indian slaves over the age of fifteen. When French refugees accompanied by their slaves arrived in Wilmington later that year, local citizens refused to allow them to disembark. The effort to suppress the ideology of the Haitian Revolution received official sanction in 1798, when Governor Samuel Ashe issued a proclamation urging that the landing of all Negroes from the islands be blocked.[113] Alexander Garden of South Carolina advocated the more extreme measure that all slaves from Saint Domingue be expelled. Georgia and South Carolina responded by temporarily suspending the foreign slave trade itself.[114] But the fear that the upheaval in Saint Domingue might ignite a general slave rebellion gained potency and persisted for the remainder of the decade.[115] It provided the incentive and the opportunity for building a new social order in the South, the basis of which was the ideology of paternalism.

Christian slaveholders of the South had inherited a patriarchal ideology that had been handed down through the ages from the seigneurial world of medieval Europe and carried to the New World with the first English settlers.[116] The patriarchal ethic persisted through most of the colonial period until the development of a market economy began to dilute its influence. Slaveholders of the revolutionary generation rejected the fundamental elements of patriarchalism and embraced the conflicting values of revolutionary ideology without, however, acknowledging its implications for southern slaveholding society. During the tumultuous postwar years, the patriarchal ethic enjoyed a rapid resurgence. But the inability of slaveowners to maintain social and ideological control by coercion alone obliged them to reinterpret the ideology of patriarchy. The more benevo-

---

[111] Quoted in Ott, *Haitian Revolution*, 53.

[112] Scott, "Common Wind," 273.

[113] Crow, "Slave Rebelliousness," 94.

[114] Ott, *Haitian Revolution*, 54. In the wake of the Vesey Plot of 1822 the South Carolina legislature enacted the Free Colored Seamen's Act, requiring that all free blacks employed on incoming vessels be detained in jail while their ships were in port to prevent the contamination of the local black population by radical ideas; see Hunt, *Haiti's Influence on Antebellum America*, 120.

[115] See, for example, William H. Freehling, *Prelude to Civil War: The Nullification Controversy in South Carolina* (Chapel Hill: University of South Carolina Press, 1968), 384.

[116] Genovese, *Roll, Jordan, Roll*, 5.

lent ethos of paternalism elaborated by evangelical churchmen during the Second Great Awakening offered a more relevant alternative. Institutionalized in law, it functioned as the matrix of slaveholding society through which images and role definitions were disseminated, creating in the end a complex of institutionalized social and cultural values that gave to the region a distinctive character. When and by what process the paternalistic ideology became institutionalized and internalized and with what consequences for the slave community, continues to be a subject of ongoing debate among historians.[117]

The postwar reemergence and growth of the ideology of paternalism was a development of enormous complexity and evaluating its contributory elements is exceedingly difficult. In fact, the different elements of the ideology of paternalism appear to have developed separately and in response to different external and internal pressures.[118] The principle of divinely ordained inequality and its necessary corollary, the doctrine of dominance, was first given expression in racial legislation, which had its origins in the urgent need of white society in the postwar decade to contain and control the slave population. The historical prelude for the wave of racial antipathy that swept the South in the late eighteenth century began in the late seventeenth century, when black slavery was first institutionalized. Lo-

[117] Eugene D. Genovese's sweeping revision of previous interpretations has revived scholarly interest in the paternalistic aspects of plantation life. Genovese redefined the term paternalism to mean a social order at once benevolent and oppressive. Paternalism's emphasis on mutual obligations "brought whites and blacks together and welded them into one people with genuine elements of affection and intimacy." In its most destructive aspects, however, the recurring idea of mutual obligations had the potential to undermine slave solidarity by creating a tendency for slaves to identify with their masters—although Genovese himself maintained that slaves developed their own interpretation of paternalism and used it as a powerful defense against slavery. See Genovese, *Roll, Jordan, Roll*, 3–7, 74 and throughout. See also Eugene D. Genovese, "The Southern Slaveholders' View of the Middle Ages," in *Medievalism in American Culture*, Bernard Rosenthal and Paul E. Szarmach, eds. (Binghamton, N.Y.: Medieval and Renaissance Texts and Studies, 1984), 31–52, especially p. 44, in which Genovese argues that during the nineteenth century interest revived among southern intellectuals in medieval feudalism and the seigneurial manor. Despite considerable ambiguity toward the Middle Ages, their "commitment to plantation slavery compelled [southern intellectuals] to uphold medieval social relations" and to insist upon the "continuity of their class" and of southern civilization with medieval institutions and values.

[118] A recent essay by Philip D. Morgan, "Three Planters and Their Slaves: Perspectives on Slavery in Virginia, South Carolina, and Jamaica, 1750–1790," in Winthrop D. Jordan and Sheila L. Skemp, eds., *Race and Family in the Colonial South* (Jackson: University Press of Mississippi, 1987), 37–79, distinguishes between patriarchalism and paternalism, the former describing more severe, inflexible social relations, the latter more sentimental and generous treatment of dependents. According to Morgan, a shift from patriarchalism to paternalism is seen in embryo at the close of the eighteenth century. I essentially agree with Morgan's interpretation. I attribute the change to the influence of evangelical religion, which led to improved norms of slave treatment among Christian slaveowners; see chapter 10 this volume.

cal ordinances and provincial laws helped to shape customs and conventions and to define popular perceptions of the social roles of African-Americans. They provided a heritage of prejudice to which was added the racial hostility generated by the revolutionary war, the burgeoning size of the slave population and the growth of the free black population, the emergence of the antislavery movement, and the social turbulence in Saint Domingue. Feeling weak and threatened, southerners sought to gain a sense of security through the development of protracted and systematic repression, the psychological foundation for which they laid by repudiating all moral responsibility for slavery.

Beginning in the 1790s, state assemblies and the courts charged with enforcing the laws remorselessly translated popular prejudice into public policy. Differences in values between the mature plantation societies of the upper South and the more recent slave societies of the lower South and differences in the legal inheritance of each state combined with the more punishing wartime experience of the lower South produced differences in jurisprudence between the states. These differences notwithstanding, the postwar period witnessed the creation of a unified law of slavery, which for the first time incorporated a racist ideology. A broad range of measures designed to correct weaknesses in the existing slave system and to guarantee a permanent supply of docile laborers was adopted by all of the southern states. The first major slave code had been enacted in Virginia between 1680 and 1682. In acts passed during the next one hundred years minor revisions were made in the codes, but no substantial changes occurred until 1792, when the state assembly passed an omnibus slave act aimed at reinforcing the structure of slavery. Between 1777 and 1787 the North Carolina assembly enacted a series of laws to correct weaknesses in the system. In South Carolina, where comprehensive laws of slave police had existed since 1712, no laws respecting blacks were passed between 1776 and 1787. Thereafter, concern that the proportion of slaves in relation to white inhabitants was endangering the safety of the state led to the enactment of statutes limiting importations.[119]

Although the function of these codes was, in some respects, clearly admonitory, they are nonetheless important: first, because they illuminate problems of social relations and social control, and second, because they reflect and refract the preponderant values of white society. Among the most striking features of the codes is the image of the black as a social danger. Proscriptions against freedom of assembly and movement and against the bearing of arms or the handling of drugs had existed since 1680. The codes approved in the postwar era recapitulated the individual legislation of the previous period, developed more elaborate restrictions

---

[119] For a general history of the early slave codes, see Higginbotham, *In the Matter of Color*.

on slave meetings, and imposed absolute prohibitions on the right of slaves to carry weapons of any kind. White fears of a slave conspiracy also manifested themselves in the compulsory pass system; in the initiation of curfews; in the expansion of municipal police forces in a number of urban areas; in laws severely circumscribing the economic activities of slaves and free blacks in principal southern towns; in the operation of a complex surveillance system and the obligatory involvement of all white members of the community in the implementation of the laws.

The assumption of white southern society that color and physiognomy rendered blacks unalterably distinct was also given legal substance in the postrevolutionary codes. In its earliest formulation, physical difference, particularly color, had formed the basis for racial categorization. During the revolutionary era the propagation of the idea of racial distinctiveness was powerfully assisted by the adoption, first in Virginia in 1792, of regulations establishing a distinct legal category based on the percentage of "black blood."[120] Racial policies requiring total separation, adopted for the first time during the postrevolutionary period, divided the races socially and by implication declared persons of "Negro blood" to be inalterably inferior to whites. Proscriptions against teaching slaves to read or to write or to gather for the purpose of religious instruction or "mental improvement," which had existed since colonial times, were extended in 1805 to include black and mulatto children, the effect being to consign blacks to a morally and intellectually inferior status and to give credence to the theory that there was a hierarchy of capability and attainment among the races.[121]

The postwar codes also paid heightened attention to the formal rules regulating relationships between the races. Although southerners had not yet fully formulated the patriarchal ideology that planters later used to justify slavery, they laid the basis for it by writing into the laws of slavery the patriarchal traits of dominance and coercion on the one hand and subordination and dependence on the other. Laws in every state made the person (body) of the white inviolable by prescribing corporal punshment or, in Georgia, death for bodily assault or attempted assault on a white man, and castration or death for the rape or attempted rape of a white woman.[122] The same laws that institutionalized the notion of white supremacy stripped slaves not only of their right of personal liberty, but, in the words

[120] Samuel Shepherd, ed., *The Statutes at Large of Virginia, from the October Session 1792, to the December Session, 1806*, 3 vols. (Richmond: S. Shepard, 1835–36), 1:123, chap. 41, sec. 10.

[121] Chap. 11, sec. 5, ibid.; Laws of North Carolina, Clark, *State Records* 24:729, 921, chap. 6, sec. 15; chap. 28, sec. 25.

[122] Shepherd, ed., *Statutes at Large*, chap. 41, sec. 17, 18.; Thomas R. R. Cobb, *A Digest of the Statute Laws of the State of Georgia* (Athens, 1851), chap. 62, sec. 1.

of St. George Tucker, "either wholly annihilated or reduced to a shadow" their right of bodily security, generally regarded as inherent in all humans.

From the beginning of American slavery the master's right to punish his slaves had been unquestioned. Carolina's *Fundamental Constitution*, drawn up by John Locke in 1669, gave to the master "absolute power and authority over his negro slaves." A Virginia law of the same year not only acknowledged the owner's right to use coercive force but decreed that should such force result in the death of the slave, the law would not treat it as a felony because "it could not be presumed that prepensive malice, which alone makes murder felony, should induce any man to destroy his own estate." Operating under that premise, in North Carolina prior to 1774 no white person ever suffered capital punishment for murdering a black person. Although South Carolina had laws restraining whites in their treatment of blacks, few whites were ever tried, much less convicted, for cruelty or excessive punishments.[123]

The belief in the owners' right to use coercive force led in the eighteenth century to the development of a dual system of law: formal law, which struggled toward universal principles of justice, and an extralegal system of punishment known as plantation justice, which tolerated the most gross violations of those same basic values. In the upper South slave offenses were customarily punished on the spot, usually by an overseer equipped with a twisted cowhide whip or a hickory switch. In the lower South plantation justice frequently took the form of "settlements," according to which one evening a week was set aside for punishing all breaches of plantation discipline, such as the failure to pick the standard quantity of cotton fixed by the overseer, or theft, the most common slave "crime." Brutally ingenious variations, such as hanging a whipping victim by the thumbs, sometimes with a fence rail tied to the feet, or following the whipping by nailing the victim's ear to a post before severing it, or "cat-hauling," forcibly dragging a tomcat by the tail along the bare back and thighs of the victim, were considered exemplary forms of punishment that all slaves were required to witness "for their moral improvement."[124]

Plantation justice took the most brutal forms in areas of high slave concentration, where the prevailing philosophy was "a blow against one white man is a blow at all . . . the muttering and upheaving of volcanic fires,

[123] Michael Hindus, "Black Justice Under White Law: Criminal Prosecutions of Blacks in Antebellum South Carolina," *Journal of American History* 63(1976): 581; The Fundamental Constitution of Carolina, Drawn Up by John Locke, 1 March 1669, Clark, *State Records* 25:135.

[124] Josiah Henson, *Father Henson's Story of His Own Life* (Boston: John O. Jewett, 1858), 6; Ball, *Slavery in the United States*, 42, 149, 163, 286, 292–93; Charles William Janson, *The Stranger in America: Containing Observations Made during a Long Residence in That Country* (London: Albion Press, 1807), 376; Grimes, *Life of William Grimes*, 9, 11.

which underlie and threaten to burst forth and utterly consume the whole social fabric."[125] The ineradicable anxiety over slaves' alleged lust for white women, considered the most gross violation of the color line, provoked white communities to resort to the most naked forms of terror. When a slave in Chowan County, North Carolina boasted of his preference for white women, his owner summarily ordered him castrated. For actual rape, appeal to civil authority was considered an inadequate solution. Driven by the pathological fear of slaves' lust, a vigilante committee of Chowan County seized a slave suspected of raping a white woman and burned him alive without benefit of a trial.[126] In South Carolina, where criminal prosecution of whites for excessive punishment rarely resulted in conviction, whites performed the most grotesque ritual executions with impunity. Two slaves suspected of kidnapping and raping a planter's daughter were captured, stripped, and tied, their limbs extended by forked poles, their mouths tightly bound to prevent them from screaming, and in that defenseless position they were left to be eaten alive by the crows and buzzards that swarmed through the rural South.[127] Nor was this an exceptional case. As he wandered through "a pleasant wood" in South Carolina, the French traveler, J. Hector St. John Crevecoeur, happened upon "a dreadful scene of agonizing torture": a black man accused of killing a white overseer was suspended in a cage, where left for two days, he was being slowly devoured by birds and swarms of insects. Recoiling in horror, Crevecoeur gave "the wretched sufferer" a drink of water before fleeing the shocking scene. Later his hosts explained to their grossly offended guest that "the laws of self-preservation rendered such executions necessary."[128]

Such breathtaking savagery was deplored by thoughtful whites as a gross violation of democratic values, which pointed up the need for voluntary controls that would halt the bloodletting and resolve the profound conflict of values. Torn between a vision of their own benevolent humanity and a desire to guarantee the tractability and productivity of their slaves, the southern states adopted a number of marginal reforms which mitigated the most intolerable cruelties of the slave system, but at the same time entrenched slavery's fundamental values. Through the incorporation of certain protective features, the individual owner's full coercive power was to some degree disciplined. In 1788, for example, the Virginia legislature repealed an act defining the killing of a slave by excessive punishment as manslaughter only, although the law did not clearly declare the offense a fel-

[125] Henson, *Father Henson's Story*, 6.

[126] Janson, *Stranger in America*, 379–80.

[127] Ball, *Slavery in the United States*, 198.

[128] J. Hector St. John de Crevecoeur, *Letters from an American Farmer and Sketches of Eighteenth-Century America* (1782; reprint, Garden City, N.Y.: Dolphin Books, 1963), 171–72.

ony.[129] In statutes passed in 1774, 1791, and 1817, the North Carolina assembly gradually extended to slaves full protection against deliberate homicide. Although slave offenders of the law continued to be tried by special tribunals called "slave courts," between 1780 and 1820 several states extended to slaves procedural privileges, including the right of trial by jury, the right to counsel in felony cases, the right to challenge jurors, and the right of appeal. Owners were, moreover, obliged by the protective features of the law to exercise their authority responsibly. Designated as providers, they were expected to furnish sustenance and shelter.[130]

Ameliorative features should not, however, necessarily be construed as disinterested humanitarianism. Frequently it was a response to pressures exerted by the collective action of slaves. South Carolina's omnibus slave code of 1740 was passed in the wake of the Stono Rebellion. Its protective features, including requirements that owners provide food and clothing and refrain from excessive punishment of their slaves, were predicated on the notion that excessive cruelty might precipitate other slave rebellions. Although Virginia's law of slavery was modified numerous times between 1705 and 1792, no significant improvement in the legal condition of slaves occurred until the revision of 1792, which coincided with the first serious attempted slave insurrection in Northampton County in the postwar period.

The protective features of the codes were, moreover, as often as not nullified by state courts, so that, in practice, the sovereign will of the master remained unlimited. It is in court decisions, where law and practice are reconciled, that the public conscience is most visible. Unrestrained by the civil guarantees of the constitution, except where procedural rights were concerned, the courts as often violated as obeyed the legal prescriptions respecting the slave's right to personal security, or as the great Baptist preacher John Leland, put it, they "protect their lives and limbs, but do not protect their skin and flesh."[131] Because special courts dealt with most cases involving slaves, state courts ordinarily handled questions arising out of the slave's legal status as property. Presided over by men obsessed with the idea that the rights of property must inexorably prevail lest society come apart, the courts created a body of precedent that offered the broadest possible affirmation of the notion that the property right is basic.

Using their broad discretionary power to decide how much physical force was necessary to establish labor discipline, state courts violated or

[129] Chap. 23. Hening, ed., *Statutes of Virginia* 12:681.

[130] Chap. 58 (1811), chap. 60 (1815), Cobb, *Digest of Statute Laws*, 986, 987; Ernest James Clark, Jr., "Aspects of the North Carolina Slave Code, 1715–1860," *North Carolina Historical Review* 39 (1962): 148–64.

[131] John Leland, *The Virginia Chronicle: With Judicious and Critical Remarks, Under XXIV Heads* (Fredericksburg, Va.: T. Green, 1790), 9.

significantly qualified the statutory protections of the life of the slave. In the *Thomas Sorells Case*, a defendant accused of the murder of a slave was acquitted by the Virginia General Court "directly contrary to the evidence," according to the eminent jurist St. George Tucker.[132] Although a 1791 act had declared that the willful and malicious killing of a slave should be adjudged as murder and punishment be the same as for killing a white man, the Supreme Court of North Carolina consistently found extenuating circumstances. In *State v. Weaver* the Court declared that if a slave offered resistance to a master "endeavor[ing] to exact obedience by force," and was as a result killed by his master, his death was "not murder, not even manslaughter, but justifiable."[133] In *State v. Boon* the court expressed its abhorrence at the act of murder, but decided in favor of the defendant on the grounds that the 1791 act did not clearly differentiate the various degrees of homicide.[134] By an act of 1817 the legislature finally clearly designated the killing of a slave a felony, but in *State v. Tackett* the court ruled that the intent of the law "was to make the homicide of a slave, extenuated by legal provocation, *manslaughter*, and to punish it as such." Resting it's decision on the proprietary relationship between slave and master, the court explained "that the relationship between a white man and a slave is different from that between free persons, and, therefore, many acts will extenuate the homocide of a slave, which would not constitute a legal provocation if done by a white person." The court-created nostrum that "it is competent for one charged with murder of a slave to give evidence that the deceased was turbulent; that he was insolent and impudent to white persons," left owners arguably immune from all constitutional restraints in the exercise of their coercive powers.[135]

Fearful of the violent or retaliatory potential of slaves, the courts by their interpretations of the laws rendered slaves powerless to defend themselves, even against violent assault by a white person. In *State v. Pivar*, which came before a North Carolina court in 1799, the issue was raised whether a slave could resist a white man. The case involved a thirteen- or fourteen-year-old white boy, who blocked the path of a passing slave and made a "jocular" threat to shoot him. The slave shoved the boy aside and continued on his way, whereupon the youth shot and killed him. In acquitting the boy, the court ruled the slave's act of shoving a white person justified the taking of his life.[136]

[132] Sorrell, In re (1786) 1 Va. Cas. 3 Va. 253.

[133] State v. Weaver (1798) 3 N.C. (2 Hayw.) 54.

[134] State v. Boon (1801) 1 N.C. Tayl. 246.

[135] State v. Tackett (1820) 8 N.C. (1 Hawks) 210. See also Betty Wood," 'Untill He Shall Be Dead,' " 377–98, which finds no evidence that the American Revolution caused Georgians "to seriously reappraise or fundamentally alter the judicial procedures they applied to slaves," 397.

[136] State v. Pivar (1799) 3 N.C. (2 Hayw.) 79.

The degree to which racist ideology pervaded southern society is strikingly apparent in the treatment of free blacks. Because free blacks were viewed as a peculiar problem, most states imposed limitations on manumissions. Although some ten thousand slaves were manumitted in Virginia as a result of the state's 1782 revision of the code, the wave abruptly ended around 1790, and in 1806 the legislature passed a law requiring free blacks to leave the state within one year after manumission. In 1777 North Carolina proscribed "the evil and pernicious practice of freeing slaves," except by judicial action and in 1801 Georgia forbade emancipation except by act of the legislature, thereby preventing owners themselves from taking any action that directly interfered with the institution of slavery or fortified the insidious presence of freedmen.[137]

The idea that blackness was itself prima facie evidence of inferiority, if not of slave status, reached its apotheosis in the quarter century after the Revolution in a cluster of court cases involving legislative formulations of the natural rights philosophy. During debates over the adoption of the Virginia Declaration of Rights, a "certain set of aristocrats" led by Robert Carter Nicholas had tried to expurgate the declaration's ringing assertion that "all men are by nature equally free," on the grounds that it would lead to "civil convulsions." Supporters of the first article, with as Edmund Randolph put it, "too great indifference to futurity," insisted that "slaves not being constituent members of our society could never pretend to any benefit from such a maxim," and the clause was incorporated.[138] Such an argument represented standard whig assumptions about the qualifications for citizenship, among them being the conviction that only freemen possessed of a clear and conscious attachment to republican principles should be eligible to partake of the rights and privileges of the political community. Although constitutional classifications based on race had existed since the seventeenth century, until the Revolution there had been little need to constitutionally deny rights of citizenship to blacks. By and large, the most explicit legal proscription related to militia service.[139]

But the adoption of state bills of rights modeled after Virginia's Declaration of Rights inevitably raised questions about slaves and particularly about the implications of the natural rights philosophy for free blacks. Accordingly, most of the original southern state constitutions expressly excluded blacks from voting and from the exercise of certain civic duties, such

[137] Chap. 6 (1777), Clark, *State Records* 24:14–15; Act Prescribing the Mode of Manumitting Slaves in this State (1801), Oliver H. Prince, comp., *A Digest of the Laws of the State of Georgia* (Athens, 1837), 787.

[138] Randolph, *History of Virginia*, 252. See also Kate Mason Rowland, *The Life of George Mason*, 2 vols. (New York: Russell and Russell, 1964), 1:240.

[139] Jordan, *White Over Black*, 410–14.

as serving on juries.[140] Only in North Carolina, whose constitution extended the franchise to every taxpaying freeman of the age of twenty-one, and Maryland, which granted suffrage to "every man having property in a common interest with, and attachment to the community," were free blacks not debarred. In North Carolina free blacks apparently vigorously exercised their citizenship rights until 1835, in Maryland until 1810, when they were shorn of the right by constitutional amendment.[141]

There were, moreover, other rights which could be inferred from the rights specified in the several bills of rights, and in the United States Constitution, the implications of which free blacks were quick to grasp. In 1791 three free black men of Charleston—Thomas Cole, a bricklayer, and two butchers, P. B. Mathews and Mathew Webb, submitted a petition in behalf of the free black community. In it, they made a sweeping claim to citizenship under the Three-Fifths Compromise of the United States Constitution: "That in the Enumeration of Free Citizens by the Constitution of the United States for the Purpose of Representation of the Southern States in Congress Your Memorialists have been considered under that description as part of the Citizens of this State." Their status as citizens, they further maintained, secured for free blacks the fundamental legal and judicial rights that attach to citizenship in a "Free Independent State."[142]

The petition was rejected by the legislature, perhaps because civil rights for free blacks implied a humanity that white society was unwilling to concede as a right. In 1806 the Georgia Superior Court decided that the legal rights of free blacks were the same as those of slaves, including rules of evidence and the form of a trial. "The constitution of this state," the court explained, "was not made to establish the rights and liberties of slaves or free negroes; . . . as free negroes, persons of colour, and slaves, can derive no benefit from the constitution, so neither can they be included by any general principles within the pale of its provisions."[143] Although the Virginia Supreme Court acknowledged that the "leading and most prominent feature" of the Declaration of Rights was "the equality of civil rights and liberty," yet the court maintained it "never was contemplated . . . to extend to the whole population of the State."[144] These reverses notwithstanding, the bold attempt of the free blacks of Charleston to turn the Constitution

[140] Francis Newton Thorpe, ed. and comp., *The Federal and State Constitutions, Colonial Charters, and Other Organic Laws of the States, Territories, and Colonies Now or Heretofore Forming the United States of America*, 7 vols. (Washington, D.C.: USGPO, 1909), 2:779, 6:3251.

[141] Ibid. 3:1687, 1705; 5:2796.

[142] "Eighteenth Century Petition of South Carolina Negroes," *Journal of Negro History* 31 (1946): 98–99.

[143] Ex parte George (1806), Thomas U. P. Charlton, *Reports of Cases Argued and Determined in the Superior Courts of the Eastern District of the State of Georgia, 1805–1811* (New York: Stephen Gould and Son, 1824), 90–91.

[144] John Aldridge v. The Commonwealth (1824) 2 Va. Cas. 447.

into a significant instrument for the protection of individual rights against infringement by the state constituted a powerful historical antecedent, which eventually found its way through the channels of the due process and equal protection clauses of the fourteenth amendment.

In the self-describing language of privilege, hierarchy, and dominance that they wrote into the laws and court decisions, the slaveholding class derived and confirmed its own identity. Through the discourse of dominance, whites sought to inhibit or negate even negative capacities such as hate or revenge that blacks shared with whites, and thereby to define black people as quintessentially different and, therefore, proper subjects of domination, a stereotype that was quickly given literary and historical expression.[145] Complemented by threats, harassment, and personal violence, the repressive laws and the courts' elaboration of them effectively translated the images of white superiority and black inferiority into everyday reality. Thus they contributed significantly to the formulation of the doctrine of dominance, which condoned and advanced the worst tendencies of the patriarchal ethos. The communal fear of an alien and menacing population and the legislation of white superiority it engendered gave to all white southerners an intimate sense of cultural, spiritual, and racial identity that became in time the centerpiece of white southern historical consciousness and of southern unity.

[145] See, for example, Captain Hugh McCall, *History of Georgia* (Atlanta, Ga.: B. Caldwell, 1784; reprint, Atlanta, Ga.: A. B. Caldwell, 1909), 3–4; Randolph, *History of Virginia*, 96; St. George Tucker, *The Valley of Shenandoah. Or Memoirs of the Graysons* (Chapel Hill: University of North Carolina Press, 1970), chap. 4, especially pp. 59–71, in which Tucker concedes the immorality of slavery, but emphasizes its benevolent aspects.

EIGHT

THE CHRISTIAN SOCIAL ORDER:

REFORMULATING THE MASTER'S

IDEOLOGY

THROUGH THE USE of the repressive apparatus of the state, southern slaveowners had created a hegemonic ideology to maintain economic power.[1] Slaveholders were not, however, entirely comfortable with their monstrous creation. Their internal conflict stemmed in part from the disjunction between the view they chose to have of blacks and the reality of their shared humanity, in part from a self-conscious sense of the vulnerability of their crudely rationalized violence. Driven by guilt, anxiety, and fear, they sought an escape from the moral implications of their actions. In the religiously inspired doctrine of mutual obligations, they found a shield to protect themselves from the disturbing realities of slavery and to render tolerable their own participation in it. The restraining force of the principle of mutual obligations arose almost simultaneously with the doctrine of dominance, but on foundations laid by evangelical religion.

Beginning in 1785 and extending to 1829, slaveholders' attitudes towards the humanization of slavery and the Christianization of slaves evolved from open hostility to a gradual recognition of the advantages that religious conversion of slaves could offer in resolving the masters' internal conflict and in stabilizing the slave system. One prominent scholar has suggested that, as evangelical Protestantism became the dominant religion of slaveholders, the churches "felt strong pressure to back down from their overt opposition to bondage."[2] In fact, evangelical Protestantism did not become the dominant religion until after the churches abandoned their support for antislavery. Although small slaveholders joined Baptist and Methodist churches in substantial numbers, the slaveholding aristocracy did not embrace evangelical religion until southern evangelical churchmen succeeded in dispelling some of the phobias that had for over a century encumbered white attitudes toward the proselytization of slaves. Unable

---

[1] Genovese, *Roll, Jordan, Roll*, 24–49, emphasizes the hegemonic function of the law.

[2] James Oakes, *The Ruling Race: A History of the American Slaveholders* (New York: Alfred A. Knopf, 1982), 108.

to mold the culture on the question of slavery, the evangelical churches were increasingly influential in shaping the paternalistic ethos that was to become the distinguishing mark of antebellum society.

Like the metaphorical brushfire that evangelicals frequently used to describe the Second Great Awakening, revivals burst into existence on the banks of the James River in 1785. Launched by roving Methodist preachers, the movement spread rapidly through the upper South until 1791–1792, and then quickly subsided into what one itinerant called "dull times." Despite the independence of the Virginia Anglican church, because of its ties to England and the suspect allegiance of many of its clergymen, the established church had suffered irreversible damage during the revolutionary war. Although the weak and struggling Methodist movement had experienced a period of active persecution, the flight of Anglican clergy and a shortage of ordained priests to administer the sacraments allowed Methodism to make inroads in the Chesapeake after 1778.[3] The support of Baptists for the patriot cause, which contributed significantly to the success of the Revolution, had also improved the fluctuating fortunes of the Baptists in Virginia.[4] Both groups thus emerged from the war in strengthened positions.

Their positions were, however, quickly jeopardized by the association of evangelical religion with the budding antislavery movement in the North. Building upon a religious tradition persistently hostile to slavery, antislavery forces, most of them in the North, accepted the insights of revolutionary ideology and brought it into the service of the incipient abolitionist movement.[5] Their success in the North led to the creation there of a strange new cosmos based on a revolutionary alteration in the accepted concept of man. With the restoration of peace the evangelicals' exalted vision of a brotherhood of man was carried into the Chesapeake by English churchmen and northern missionaries bent on transforming southern society. The evangelicals' separate rendition of transcendent truth was fundamentally alien to the value system of the South, however, and led in the 1780s to open and bitter conflict.

The Methodists were the first publicly to denounce slavery. Although the Methodist Conference of 1780 had agreed that slavery was morally wrong and contrary to religious principles, Methodism was then still a weak movement struggling to establish itself in the South, and no action

[3] William Henry Williams, *The Garden of American Methodism: The Delmarva Peninsula 1769–1820* (Wilmington, Del.: Scholarly Resources, 1984), 41, 50, 53.

[4] Bonomi, *Under the Cope of Heaven*, 185–86; William Parks, "Religion and the Revolution in Virginia," in Rutyna and Stewart, eds., *Virginia in the American Revolution* 1:50–51; Beeman, *Evolution of the Southern Backcountry*, 140–46.

[5] For a detailed discussion of the relationship between republicanism and evangelicalism, see James D. Essig, *The Bonds of Wickedness: American Evangelicals Against Slavery, 1770–1808* (Philadelphia: Temple University Press, 1982), especially pp. 73–96.

was taken other than to admonish members of the society to free their slaves. The conferences of 1783 and 1784 debated whether to suspend local preachers who held slaves, but decided only to suspend those in states where slavery was illegal and to postpone action in Virginia for another year.[6] Beginning with the arrival in 1784 of Thomas Coke, the English cleric authorized by Wesley to organize the Methodists into a distinct church, Methodist spokesmen began to attack slavery.

On his first tour of Virginia, Coke decided to "exhort our Societies to emancipate their Slaves" and to "bear a public testimony against slavery." Far from converting slaveholders to repentant emancipation, however, Coke's sermon created outrage. The next time he tried to preach, an armed mob appeared, intent, the somewhat daunted Coke concluded, "to fall upon me as soon as I touched on the subject of slavery." On one occasion a prominent Virginia woman offered a reward of fifty pounds to anyone who would whip the English preacher, and an armed man bent on silencing him by assassination pursued Coke relentlessly. Alarmed for his own safety, Coke adopted a more pragmatic approach, usually opening his sermons by admonishing his black listeners "in a very pathetic manner on the Duty of Servants to Masters." Coke's breach of public dogma was not so easily forgiven, however, and shortly after he completed his first tour of Virginia a bill against him "as a Seditious Person" was presented before the grand jury of Halifax County and was found by the jury. As he prepared to leave for England, a posse of almost one hundred men was formed to follow Coke and bring him back to face charges, "but their hearts failed them."[7]

Although Coke had diluted his own moral principles to avoid personal injury, the Methodist Conference that he led in 1784 formulated a policy on slavery that reflects the conjunction of religious antislavery and republican ideology. Dominated by European churchmen and northern preachers, the Baltimore conference pushed through a set of rules that badly divided the Virginia church. Declaring that slavery was "contrary to the laws of God, of men, and of nature, and that it was hurtful to society and contrary to the dictates of conscience and pure religion," the so-called "slave rules" called upon all members of the society to free their slaves within twelve months, except in Virginia and there within two years, under pain of expulsion.[8] Having made an explosive social issue fundamental to their cause, Methodist churchmen then briefly attempted to use the state as a

[6] *Minutes of the Methodist Conferences, Annually Held in America, From 1773 to 1794, Inclusive* (Philadelphia: Henry Tuckness, 1795), 1783, 1784, 39, 62, 71, 73.

[7] Thomas Coke, *Extracts of the Journals of the Reverend Dr. Thomas Coke's Five Visits to America* (London: G. Paramore, 1793), 33, 36–37; idem, *A Farther Continuation of Dr. Thomas Coke's Journal in a Letter to the Reverend John Wesley* (London, 1787), 6–7.

[8] Virginia churchmen were attending a state meeting at the time, see Lee, *Short History*, 70, 72, 101.

moral instrument of religious policy. During the summer and fall of 1785, churchmen led by Coke began circulating emancipation petitions aimed at the legal abolition of slavery. A delegation headed by Coke visited Mount Vernon in an effort to persuade Washington to join the crusade. Although Washington privately confessed that he favored the formation of an anti-slavery society in Virginia, he refused to sign the petition, or even publicly to support Methodist efforts, on the grounds that "it would be dangerous to make a frontal attack on a prejudice which is beginning to decrease."[9]

The antislavery policy adopted by the Baltimore conference was an ideological leap ahead of what most white Virginians, including the rank-and-file evangelical church members, apparently believed. The controversial slave rules produced defiant rebuttals by subordinate churches and in some cases threatened to divide clergymen against their congregations and congregations against the church. In Brunswick County, a stronghold of Methodism, "a great many principal friends" met with Coke and other church leaders to insist upon repeal of the slave rules.[10] Some congregations refused to tolerate sermons on the subject. When John Lee, brother of the prominent preacher Jesse Lee, was reproached by another Methodist preacher for failing to speak out against slavery, Lee explained that he "did not find freedom to say anything about that delicate subject in public, as in his judgment it would neither profit the master or the slave."[11] When he later published his journal in England, Coke himself confessed "that however just my sentiments may be concerning Slavery, it was ill judged of me to deliver them from the pulpit."[12] In his *Short History of the Methodists*, Jesse Lee, the first historian of Methodism, also conceded that "however good the intention of the preachers might be in framing [the slave rules], we are well assured that they never were of any particular service to our societies."[13]

Eventually persuaded that the slave rules "were offensive to most of our southern friends," and "were so much opposed by many of our private members, local preachers and some of the travelling preachers," the Methodists suspended the emancipation rule in 1785, barely six months after it was adopted. For the next twenty-four years individual ministers continued to offer sporadic, if ineffectual, opposition and general conventions of the Methodist church adopted rules about slavery, but they were never

[9] Thomas Coke, *A Farther Continuation of Dr. Thomas Coke's Journal*, 8; Coke, *Extracts of the Journals*, 39, 45.

[10] Coke, *Extracts of the Journals*, 39.

[11] Jesse Lee, *A Short Account of the Life and Death of the Reverend John Lee, A Methodist Minister in the United States of America* (Baltimore, Md.: John West Butler, 1805), 126.

[12] Coke, *Farther Continuation*, 7.

[13] Lee, *Short History*, 88.

"attended with that success which was expected."[14] In a reflective mood, Methodist Bishop Francis Asbury wrote in his journal in 1798 "that slavery will exist in Virginia, perhaps for ages," because even "Methodists, Baptists, Presbyterians, in the highest flights of rapturous piety, still maintain and defend it."[15] By contrast, the Philadelphia annual conference continued to maintain an unequivocal opposition to slavery, and thousands of slaves from the Delmarva Peninsula, which includes all of Delaware and the Eastern Shore of Maryland and Virginia, were manumitted, most of them by Methodists.[16] The failure of the slave rules of 1784 left the Methodist church in the anomalous position of condemning slavery in one portion of its geographical territory and permitting the same institution to exist, under the full sanction both of disciplinary statute and public opinion, in another.[17]

The story was the same among the Baptists. The congregationally organized Baptist church could offer no general pronouncement on slavery; however, representatives from the different churches and associations of Virginia approved a resolution at the Virginia Baptist General Committee Meeting in 1785, which declared "heredit[ar]y slavery to be contrary to the word of God."[18] In 1787 the Ketocton Association, which included parts of Loudoun, Fairfax, Prince William, Stafford, Fauquier, Culpeper, and Frederick counties, debated the question and agreed that slavery was a breach of divine law. Accordingly, a committee was appointed to develop a plan for general emancipation. When the plan was circulated, however, member churches of the association "remonstrated so decidedly, that the association resolved to take no further steps in the business."[19] Nevertheless, in 1790 the Baptist General Committee approved a resolution presented by John Leland, itinerant preacher from Massachusetts, whose circuit included parts of Orange, Culpeper, Spotsylvania, and Louisa counties. The resolution declared "that slavery is a violent deprivation of the rights of nature, and inconsistent with a representative government; and therefore recommends it to our Brethren to make use of every legal measure to extirpate the horrid evil from the land and pray Almighty God, that our Honourable Legislature may have it in their power, to proclaim the general jubilee, consistent with the principles of good policy."[20]

[14] Ibid., 102; Albert M. Shipp, *The History of Methodism in South Carolina* (Nashville, Tenn.: Southern Methodist Publishing, 1884), 468.

[15] Asbury, *Journal and Letters* 2:151.

[16] Williams, *Garden of American Methodism*, 161–63.

[17] Shipp, *History of Methodism in South Carolina*, 468.

[18] W. Harrison Daniel, "Virginia Baptists and the Negro in the Early Republic," *Virginia Magazine of History and Biography* 80 (1972): 64.

[19] Semple, *History*, 392.

[20] Quoted in Daniel, "Virginia Baptists and the Negro," 66.

Only two associations responded to the resolution, neither favorably. The Roanoke Association confessed that "we are not unanimously clear in our minds whether the God of nature ever intended that one part of the human species should be held in an abject state of slavery to another part of the same species"; yet, the association continued, "the subject with us is so very abstruse and such a set of complex circumstances attending the same, that we suppose neither the general committee nor any other Religious Society whatever has the least right to [unclear] as a society, but leave every individual to act at discretion."[21] In the spring of 1792 the Strawberry District Association took up the question, "(which is answered thus), we advise them not to interfere with it."[22] When the Baptist General Committee again debated the issue in 1793, it decided in favor of noninterference on the grounds that slavery was a matter that "belongs to the legislative body."[23] Widespread negative reaction and the commitment of Baptists generally to the separation of church and state probably accounts for the decision to leave the issue to civil authorities.[24]

For the next quarter-century the evangelical movement sporadically debated the propriety of slavery. The Methodist Discipline continued to oppose the slave trade and the General Conference to offer sporadic resistance, but the rules were inconsistently enforced and the opposition was generally ineffectual. Nevertheless, individual Methodist preachers achieved a small measure of success, particularly among Delmarva Methodists, who manumitted thousands of slaves between 1787 and 1833.[25]

Several Baptist associations also continued to debate the question of slavery but none was able to reach a consensus. At its 1796 meeting the Portsmouth Association agreed that the leading cause of the "present wretched and distressing times" was the fact that leading Christians "hold and retain in *abject slavery*, a set of poor fellow creatures, *contrary to the laws of God and nature*," but could not settle upon a course of action.[26] A year later the Ketocton Association agreed that slavery was a transgression of divine law but decided that in view of "the variety of circumstances attend-

[21] June, 1790, Roanoke Baptist Association Minutes, 1789–1831, Virginia Baptist Historical Society, University of Richmond, Richmond, Va. (hereafter cited as VBHS).

[22] May, 1792, Strawberry Association Minutes, 1787–1822, VBHS.

[23] Rippon, *Baptist Annual Register*, 66.

[24] Essig, *Bonds of Wickedness*, 68–69, maintains that the Baptist response to Leland's resolution was also due in part to resistance to ecclesiasticism.

[25] Williams, *Garden of American Methodism*, 162–64; Shipp, *History of Methodism in South Carolina*, 468; William Glendinning, *The Life of William Glendinning, Preacher of the Gospel. Written by Himself* (Philadelphia: W. W. Woodward, 1795), 101–2; Joseph Travis, *Autobiography of the Reverend Joseph Travis*, Thomas Osmond Summers, ed. (Nashville, Tenn.: E. Stevenson and J. E. Evans, 1856), 46–47.

[26] May, 1796, Portsmouth (Virginia) Association Minutes, 1791–1800, 1801–1840, VBHS.

ing the situation of those distressed people, and the perplexing circumstances of many of their holders, respecting themselves, their connexions, and in many instances, their just creditors," gradual emancipation was the best, perhaps the only approach.[27] In 1823 the Goshen Association emphatically denounced the slave trade "as an unfeeling and unchristian practice, by no means to be tolerated in the Church of Christ," but the association did not translate its hatred of slavery into disciplinary action.[28] Some local preachers and church members deplored the abomination of slavery as a violation of religious teachings and republican principles and several native preachers, including David Barrow, freed their slaves, as did numerous individuals.[29] Slavery was accepted by the majority of white Baptists, however, and except in Maryland, most church members were apparently slaveholders themselves and, therefore, shared the racial prejudices of the majority.[30]

Smothered by the deadening pall of racial prejudice, the small antislavery movement died a quick death. The antislavery policies adopted by the Methodist Conference in 1784 and the Baptist General Committee in 1785 and 1790 had led the struggling evangelical movement into a tense and disruptive relationship with the larger society at precisely the moment when it was most actively engaged in an effort to achieve disestablishment and religious freedom. Fearful of losing the political leverage they had gained from their support of the Revolution, the evangelicals drew back from the political precipice created by the antislavery movement. With the support of prominent Republican leaders such as Jefferson and Madison, who believed that religious freedom was a prerequisite for civil liberty, they won the fight for disestablishment. The enactment of the Virginia Statute for Religious Freedom in December 1786, which signified official recognition of their accommodation to political realities, gave the evangelicals legal status and helped transform a small embattled movement into formidable, respectable denominations.

The religious issue continued to be important in Virginia politics during the 1790s. Eager to advance the principle of separation of church and state, dissenting sects, especially the Baptists, continued to petition the assembly to institute a statewide sale of the glebe lands belonging to the Episcopal parishes and to use the proceeds for state-administered educational and

[27] Primitive Baptists, *Virginia Ketocton Association*, Minutes of the Ketocton Baptist Association, Held at Frying-Pan, Loudoun County (American Imprint, 1797).

[28] October, 1823, Goshen Baptist Association Minutes, VBHS.

[29] Luther Jackson estimates that between 1783 and 1810 the number of free Negroes in Virginia increased from three to thirty thousand; see Jackson, *A Short History of the Gillfield Baptist Church of Petersburg, Virginia* (Petersburg, Va.: n.p., 1937), 5.

[30] See, for example, Robert W. Gardner, "Virginia Baptists and Slavery, 1759–1790," *The Virginia Baptist Register* 24 (1985): 1218–19.

poor relief programs. Republican leaders like Madison, who recognized in the growing Baptist movement a potential Republican constituency, supported the Baptists on the question of glebe lands, and in 1799 divestiture was finally accomplished. Despite repeated Federalist warnings that the Republicans were the enemies of Christianity, the Baptist Association of Virginia, which had once challenged gentry rule, tended thereafter to align with Republicans and to support Republican policies, in part because of their suspicion of all government, particularly centralized government, in part because of their anxiety to protect and advance religious freedom.[31]

The settlement of the glebe lands issue was an important step in the cultural accommodation between evangelical religion and civil government. Republican leaders had offered a political compromise that the evangelical churches implicitly accepted. Their acceptance into the establishment was of tremendous significance in transforming the cultural history of the South. Beginning around 1800, revivalism in the upper South experienced phenomenal growth. Several factors contributed to the success of the Second Great Awakening in the South. First, the situation in the postrevolutionary South created a psychic need for religion. The general social strain caused by changing economies and innovations in politics and shifting social norms and moral dislocations attendant on the economic transformation of southern society created a sense of disconnection with the past and a profound feeling of helplessness. The evangelical movement, with its conception of the church as a society of people capable of changing their own lives, provided a means to regain some sense of direction and purpose and to reassert control over events. Second, the decline of the antislavery movement nationally helped to allay popular fears that the spread of evangelicalism would disrupt the slave system. Except for the abolition of the slave trade, which many expected Congress to prohibit after 1808, most of the major goals of antislavery evangelicals had been realized in the North, thus draining the movement of its vitality. The withdrawal of evangelicals from organized antislavery activity after 1785 and the decision of ecclesiastical bodies to relegate responsibility for slavery to the political sphere were crucial to the progress of revivalism. Without religious accommodation on the issue of slavery there probably would have been no religious revival in the upper South. Accommodation made it possible and made it possible too for slaveholders, including the privileged classes of society, to embrace at last the evangelical churches.[32]

Methodists had always enjoyed the support of the lower economic and social orders, and in the area south and west of Maryland two of every five

[31] Richard R. Beeman, *The Old Dominion and the New Nation, 1788–1801* (Lexington: University Press of Kentucky, 1972), 93–95, 115–16, 198.
[32] Essig, *Bonds of Wickedness*, 113–14; Beeman, *Evolution of the Southern Backcountry*, 191.

Baptists were black.[33] A significant number of all new converts after 1785 were, however, from the ranks of the upper social and economic classes. The conversion of Robert "Councillor" Carter in 1778, when Baptists were still a persecuted and despised sect, was extremely important to the establishment of the Baptist church in Virginia. Perhaps the wealthiest man of Virginia, Carter was in a unique position to influence public policy. He was a leading force in the opposition to the general assessment bill in 1784 and participated in the struggle against inequitable marriage and vestry laws. A faithful church member of the Morattico Baptist Church, he led in organizing the Nomini Baptist church in Westmoreland and the Yeocomico Church on one of his own plantations. As a member of the Virginia Baptist General Committee and as a lay leader, he brought public recognition and newfound respectability for Baptists among the planter class on the Northern Neck. His home, Nomini Hall, in Westmoreland County was the major center for evangelism in the area.[34]

Although many still disdained the "grimaces, howlings, and contortions" of the Methodists, Methodism was also gaining acceptance among the wealthy and powerful.[35] In describing the great revivals that exploded across the Chesapeake after 1785, Jesse Lee observed that "Many of the wealthy people, both men and women, were seen lying in the dust, sweating and rolling on the ground, in their fine broad cloths or silks, crying for mercy."[36] On his third tour in 1788, Dr. Coke returned to Halifax County, where he had "met with much persecution" four years earlier. Now almost all of the "great people of the county," including at least five colonels, came to hear him preach. Among the recent converts was Coke's would-be assassin. On his sixth tour in 1796 Coke was invited to preach in the North Carolina House of Commons to an audience of senators and representatives.[37] When Asbury was invited to preach in Abingdon, in 1796, "by the will of the judges" the county court adjourned. The afternoon service conducted by Asbury was attended by "the judges, some of the lawyers, and very few of the citizens."[38]

The access of evangelical leaders to the court, the center of political life in the county, and to the assembly room, the locus of the larger society around it, emphasizes the dynamic of change in the relationship between

[33] John Asplund, ed., *The Universal Annual Register of the Baptist Denomination in North-America. For the Years 1794 and 1795* (Hanover, N.H.: Dunham and True, 1796), 68.

[34] William L. Lumpkin, "Colonel Robert Carter, A Baptist," *Virginia Baptist Register* 8 (1969): 339–55.

[35] Beeman, *Evolution of the Southern Backcountry*, 187–88.

[36] Lee, *Short History*, 131.

[37] Coke, *Extracts of the Journals*, 108; idem, *Farther Continuation*, 7; idem, *Extracts of the Journals of the Late Reverend Thomas Coke, LL.D.* (Dublin: R. Napper, 1816), 238.

[38] Asbury, *Journal and Letters* 2:84.

the evangelical churches and the political arena. Through the kinds of communication that were developing between the plain-dressed itinerants and the bewigged gentlemen justices and assemblymen, law and religion were slowly beginning to penetrate each other's domains. Through doctrinal borrowings from one another, they were becoming mutually influential. The rising level of acceptance by white society lessened somewhat the evangelicals' emotional identification with the lowly and oppressed. Their declining interest in converting slaves and the growing popularity of Methodism in the larger towns of Virginia led to a decrease in the number of black church members until the camp meeting was introduced into Virginia between 1803 and 1810.[39]

The camp meeting, which originated in Tennessee in 1799, was introduced into Virginia by Jesse Lee.[40] The first meeting was held in a grove of trees some three miles south of Duck Creek Cross Roads on what is now the Delmarva Peninsula. The prototype for all camp meetings, it began on July 25 and was attended by thousands of people who came by wagon and cart to hear Lee deliver the opening sermon on a text from Isa. 33:12: "And the people shall be as the burnings of lime, as thorns shall they be burned in the fire." For days and nights without interruption preacher followed preacher, praising, exhorting, condemning, whipping the crowds into such emotional frenzy that their shouts and cries of ecstasy could be heard three miles away. According to Lee's estimate, two hundred whites and "many among the blacks" were converted. From that meeting revivalism spread like an unchecked fire across the Eastern Shore of Maryland and through the lower counties of Delaware, almost revolutionizing the peninsula in the process.[41]

After a long period of decline following the revolutionary war, the backcountry areas of the lower South also experienced localized and sporadic revivalism. In South Carolina, ten years after the Revolution the remains of churches burned by the British still dotted the countryside, and, a foreign traveler wryly noted, "they are in this country not very anxious to build them up again."[42] Many of the parish churches remained closed and only here and there throughout the state was there a Baptist or a Presby-

---

[39] Semple, *History*, 307; Jackson, "Religious Development of the Negro," 182.

[40] Williams, *Garden of American Methodism*, says the camp meeting originated in Logan County, Kentucky, in 1800; Reverend Henry Boehm, *Reminiscences, Historical and Biographical, of Sixty-Four Years in the Ministry* (New York: Carlton and Porter, 1865), gives the origin as Tennessee.

[41] Lee, *Short History*, 31, 272–73; Boehm, *Reminiscences*, 128–29, 133, 147. For details of the progress of revivalism on the Delmarva Peninsula, see Williams, *Garden of American Methodism*, 78–87.

[42] François Alexandre Frederic, duc de La Rouchefoucauld-Liancourt, *Travels Through the United States of North America in the Years 1795, 1796, and 1797*, 2 vols. (London: T. Davison, 1799), 1:599.

terian congregation. Although Baptists made gains following disestablishment in 1778, in 1793 the Charleston Association, the second Baptist association in America, had twenty-four churches but only 1,987 communicants. The largest church in the association, the Charleston Church, had only 265 members, whereas Welsh Neck, Edisto, Euhaw, Upper Fork of Lynches Creek and Rocky River all had fewer than one hundred and fifty members each. The remaining churches had under one hundred members. The backcountry's Bethel Association, constituted in 1789, had twenty-eight churches and 1,360 communicants. Only one church, Jamey's Creek, had over one hundred members.[43] Except for Baptist and Quaker meetings, organized Christian religion was almost nonexistent in Georgia after the war. Baptists, who were nearly unanimous in their support of the revolution, actually gained adherents during the war, often at the expense of the Presbyterians and Lutherans.[44] By 1790 there were forty-two Baptist churches with 3,211 members in the state.[45]

Outside North Carolina, where Methodism enjoyed its greatest success outside the Chesapeake, Methodism still engendered suspicion and distrust. With only twenty-eight members, the denomination had made almost no progress in Georgia. In 1786 the Virginia Conference decided to send preachers into Georgia and in 1788 Asbury visited the state, but no permanent Methodist society was established there until 1790, when Hope Hull, a pioneer in Georgia, was sent to Savannah to preach in a chair-makers shop. Hull, driven out by mob violence, was followed by a series of Methodist itinerants, whose spiritual labors seemed "only to increase the existing prejudices of the people against the Methodists."[46] Methodism also had to struggle to gain acceptance by whites in South Carolina. In 1785 the newly ordained superintendent, Francis Asbury, accompanied by Woolman Hickson, Jesse Lee, and Henry Willis traveled by horseback to organize the Methodist Church in South Carolina. In Georgetown they converted William Wayne, the first recorded Methodist in the state. Four days later, Lee preached the first Methodist sermon in Charleston and made the first Charleston convert, Edgar Wells, a wealthy merchant. Although the mission was not conspicuously successful, it did

[43] Baptists, South Carolina Charleston Association, *Minutes of the Charleston Association, held at the High Hills of Santee, the 2d of November 1793* (Charleston, 1793), 4; Baptists, Bethel Association, *Minutes of the Bethel Association, held at the Baptist Church on Jamey's Creek, Spartanburg County, South Carolina. Begun on Saturday, August 13, 1791* (n.p., 1791[?]), 4–5.

[44] Reba C. Strickland, *Religion and the State in Georgia in the Eighteenth Century* (New York: Columbia University Press, 1939), 152, 160, 162–63.

[45] John Asplund, ed., *The Annual Register of the Baptist Denomination, in North-America: To the First of November, 1790. Containing An Account of the Churches and their Constitutions, Ministers, Members, Associations* (Richmond Va.: n.p., 1791), 44–46.

[46] Nathan Bangs, D.D., *A History of the Methodist Episcopal Church*, 2 vols. (New York: T. Mason and G. Lane, 1839), 2:192–93.

result in the establishment of the Cumberland Street Church, the first Methodist meetinghouse. Known as the "blue meeting house" to distinguish it from the "white meeting house," or the Circular Congregational Church, it was completed in 1787 and had a mixed congregation of forty white members and fifty-three blacks.[47] At the same time, Methodist preachers ranged through the countryside, laying out circuits named for the broad streams that coursed the length of the state.

Charleston was, however, the *point d' appui* . To Asbury, pleasure-loving Charleston with its fashionable racetrack and theaters was "the seat of Satan, dissipation, and folly." The "white and worldly people," he complained, "are intolerably ignorant of God; playing, dancing, swearing, racing."[48] Even more humble folk in rural communities, who lacked the worldly pleasures available in sophisticated Charleston, preferred to pass the Sabbath in fishing, hunting, drinking, or fighting. Slaves, too, spent their free hours "in tumultous sports and licentiousness," such as dancing, singing, and playing the banjo for their own entertainment, or racing, wrestling, and fighting one another without weapons for the amusement of their owners, who laid wagers on favorites.[49]

Many of the itinerants were, like Asbury, "deeply dejected" by their reception. Still they persevered, wandering through sand hills and grass-covered forests where cattle and hogs ranged; seeking out settlements along the creeks and rivers; visiting from house to house, reproving and rebuking; stopping to preach in groves of oak and hickory, in pole-cabins in the country, and in plantation kitchens and courthouses. The very peculiarity of the circuit preachers, with their straight-breasted coats and broad-brimmed hats pulled down over closely cropped hair neatly brushed down over their foreheads, brought out congregations, mostly, Asbury sadly reflected, "women and Africans."[50] Attachment to the religious formalism of the Protestant Episcopal church still influenced many low-country whites, who scorned and ridiculed the emotional preaching of the Methodists, which they thought suitable to the lower classes and blacks, "whose passions were the strongest and their understandings weakest."[51] Enlivened

[47] Asbury, *Journal and Letters* 1:535 n. 17, 2:691, 716; Shipp, *History of Methodism in South Carolina*, 164. See also, Richard N. Cote, "South Carolina Methodist Records," *South Carolina Historical Magazine* 85 (1984): 51–57; Durwood T. Stoke, "The Baptist and Methodist Clergy in South Carolina and the American Revolution," *South Carolina Historical Magazine* 73 (1972): 87–96.

[48] Asbury, *Journal and Letters* 2:7, 41.

[49] Janson, *Stranger in America*, 101; Henry Bibb, *Narrative of the Life and Adventures of Henry Bibb, An American Slave, Written By Himself* (reprint, New York: Negro Universities Press, 1969), 23.

[50] Asbury, *Journal and Letters* 2:41.

[51] Rochefoucauld, *Travels* 2:17; William Capers, "Autobiography," in William May Wightman, ed., *Life of William Capers, D.D.* (Nashville Tenn.: Southern Methodist Publishing, 1859), 164.

by emotive preaching and stirring hymns, evangelical services often produced "strange and unaccountable bodily exercises" commonly called the jerks, or the jumping or dancing exercise, and culminated at times in spiritual ecstasy. Physical manifestations of spirit, they frightened many people, who believed that there was something magical or wizardly about evangelical preaching.[52] Thus Asbury complained, the Baptists, who had modified their peculiarities somewhat, "take the rich; and the commonalty and the slaves fall to us."[53] In fact, because of planter resistance to the proselytism of slaves, little effective mission work was done for slaves. The minutes of the General Conference of 1787 list only 121 black members of the society in South Carolina compared to 1,645 white members.[54] At the conference, however, the first official step toward the evangelization of slaves was taken.

Never quite ready to identify wholly with slaveholding society, the participants of the General Conference of 1787, adopted a rule directing all Methodist ministers and preachers to "leave nothing undone for the spiritual benefit and salvation of the negroes." Three years later the General Conference approved the establishment of Sunday schools where black and white children could be taught to read.[55] To slaveholders, Methodist intermeddling with slavery lay wholly beyond the range of ecclesiastical jurisdiction. Memories of the abortive slave rules persisted among planters in the low country from Cape Fear to the Savannah River. There Methodist preachers still "lay under the ban of suspicion as disorganizers who could not be trusted among the negroes without danger to the public peace."[56] In 1795 at the height of the panic created by the heavy influx of refugees from Saint Domingue with their chilling stories of black revolutionary fervor, a group of twenty-three Methodist itinerants met in Charleston and adopted a strong statement condemning ministers who held slaves "to the Scandal of the Ministry, and the strengthening of the hands of Oppression." Alone among religious groups in the city to speak out in favor of emancipation, they insisted that all ministers of the Charleston Association who held slaves "Ought immediately to Emancipate them where the Laws will permit it: And where they will Not, that they Ought to make them compensation for their Labour; And *will* them free." Whoever refused "Shall forfeit both his seat in conference, and Letters of Ordination."[57]

Although the General Rules maintained a discreet silence on the subject

[52] Shipp, *History of Methodism in South Carolina*, 585.

[53] Asbury, *Journal and Letters* 2:424.

[54] *Minutes of the Methodist Conferences*, 1787, 102.

[55] *Minutes Taken at the Several Annual Conferences of the Methodist Episcopal Church for the Year 1824* (New York, 1824), 104, 640–41.

[56] Capers, "Autobiography," 136–37.

[57] Quoted in George C. Rogers, Jr., *Charleston in the Age of the Pinckneys* (Columbia, S.C.: University of South Carolina Press, 1980), 143.

of slavery, in 1800 the Articles of Agreement among the Preachers were adopted at the General Conference in May. Drawn up by a committee composed of Ezekial Cooper, William M'Kendree, and Jesse Lee, and signed by Bishops Thomas Coke, Francis Asbury, and Richard Whatcoat, the address briefly recalled the long history of Methodist opposition to slavery "as repugnant to the unalienable rights of mankind, and to the very essence of civil liberty, but more especially to the spirit of the Christian religion." It then introduced two new paragraphs: the first calling on all circuit preachers to emancipate their slaves under pain of expulsion, the second directing the annual conferences, the main business meetings for the state conferences, to draw up petitions urging states that had not already done so, to enact laws providing for the gradual emancipation of slaves.[58]

Although the original version was not circulated in the South, a copy of the address was discovered in a box of books by a Methodist minister in Charleston named John Harper. Harper, an Englishman, indiscreetly showed the broadside to a few persons and the contents became publicly known. Harper burned the offensive documents in the presence of the mayor, but it was not enough to satisfy public outrage and a mob of two hundred people descended on the home of the benighted preacher. Harper escaped, but the infuriated crowd seized one of his clerical associates, George Dougherty, dragged him through the street to a water pump, held his head under the spout and pumped water down his throat. Dougherty, in feeble health, was rescued from drowning by a Mrs. Kingsley, who stuffed her shawl into the mouth of the spout. Dougherty was then led to safety by a gentleman armed with a drawn sword.[59]

The Methodist antislavery address alone posed a significant danger to slave society and heightened perceptions of the threat of evangelical religion. The fact that it coincided with the first large-scale, organized, broadly motivated slave revolt produced a wave of insurrectionary hysteria that rolled over the entire South beginning in 1800. By contrast to the spontaneous and localized insurrectionary scares that had proceeded it, Gabriel's Revolt in Virginia in 1800 represented an elaborate attempt to wage war to the death against the slavocracy. Conceived of by two slave blacksmiths, Jack Bowler or Ditcher, the property of William Bowler of Caroline County, Virginia, and Gabriel Prosser, the property of Thomas Prosser, the carefully drawn plans called for an army of slaves raised in Henrico and the surrounding counties of Hanover, Louisa, Goochland, and Caroline to assemble at Prosser's blacksmith shop in the woods. Equipped with

[58] The Address of the General Conference of the Methodist Episcopal Church, to all their Brethren and Friends in the United States, Broadside Collection 29, no. 1, Library of Congress.

[59] Bangs, *History of the Methodist Episcopal Church* 2:125.

swords made by slave blacksmiths and formed in ranks behind a silk flag emblazoned with the words "Death or Liberty," the slave army was then to march in three columns on Richmond, there to seize the arsenal, mills, and treasury; to fire the warehouse district and the bridges leading across the James River into the city; and to take as hostage Governor James Monroe. If the assault succeeded, the leaders planned then to call by proclamation on poor whites and Indians and all "friends of humanity" to join in a war "to subdue the whole of the country where slavery was permitted but no further."[60]

On August 30 at 2:00 P.M. of the day the march was to take place, "whispers of an intended insurrection among the negroes at Petersburg," were reported to Governor Monroe.[61] The discovery of an elaborate scheme involving hundreds of armed slaves shook the white community: "It is unquestionably the most serious and formidable conspiracy we have ever known of this kind," a distraught Monroe confided to fellow Virginian Thomas Jefferson.[62] The mobilization of the militia and a torrential rain, which fell about the time appointed for the slaves' rendezvous, quashed the great slave plot for the destruction of slavery. Authorities moved quickly to identify and try suspected slaves and to execute the leaders. Confident that the failure of Gabriel's plot had broken the spirit of resistance, Virginia authorities gradually relaxed military measures.[63] But the fever was not over. In December rumors began to circulate that slaves from the coal pits outside Richmond were plotting an insurrection. They were followed in January by reports of a plot among Southampton County slaves. Over the next year a wave of insurrectionary hysteria rolled through southeast and central Virginia, breaking finally in the Albemarle area of North Carolina in the spring of 1802. At least six Virginia counties and seven North Carolina counties conducted conspiracy trials, prosecuted hundreds of slaves, executed dozens, whipped, mutilated, and deported scores more.[64]

[60] Palmer et al., eds., *Calendar of Virginia State Papers* 9:141–47, 151, 152, 153, 159, 165. Douglas R. Egerton, "Gabriel's Conspiracy: Unsuccessful Coda to the American Revolution" (Paper presented at the annual meeting of the Organization of American Historians, March 1988) describes Gabriel's conspiracy as built upon politics and class as well as racial lines. It depicts Gabriel as not just "a black republican," but also as "a black Republican."

[61] Palmer et al., eds., *Calendar of Virginia State Papers* 9:128.

[62] Stanislaus Murray Hamilton, ed., *The Writings of James Monroe*, 7 vols. (New York: AMS Press, 1898–1903), 3:201–5, 208.

[63] Joshua Coffin, *An Account of Some of the Principal Slave Insurrections, and Others, which Have Occurred, or Been Attempted, in the United States and Elsewhere, during the Last Two Centuries* (New York: American Antiquarian Society, 1860), 212.

[64] John Scott Strickland, "The Great Revival and Insurrectionary Fears in North Carolina: An Examination of Antebellum Southern Society and Slave Revolt Panics," in Orville Vernon Burton and Robert C. McMath, Jr., eds., *Class, Conflict, and Consensus. Antebellum Southern*

The news of Gabriel's Revolt, coming hard on the heels of the *Address of the General Conference,* aroused dark suspicions in South Carolina about the activities of Methodist preachers, who in their zeal for souls had begun to teach slaves during the evening hours because their masters would not excuse them from work during the day, and precipitated a period of active persecution of Methodists in Charleston.[65] Although there were fewer than one thousand black communicants in South Carolina,[66] several of the early Methodist churches in the state were predominantly black. In 1795 the Methodist meeting house in Georgetown, South Carolina, had "a number of very modest, attentive hearers, and a good work among the blacks." Ten years later, the church had only twenty white members and nearly 400 blacks.[67] In 1793 Bethel, the "New Church," in Charleston, reported 500 members, over 300 of whom were black. Sensing that the mood of the black community was changing under the compelling influence of religion, the South Carolina assembly hastily approved a law prohibiting slaves from meeting, even in the presence of whites, for religious instruction or worship before sunrise or after sunset. Civil and military officers and the patrol were authorized to "do whatever may be necessary to disperse them, and inflict on them such reasonable corporeal [sic] punishment as they may think proper, not exceeding twenty lashes."[68] When James Jenkins, presiding elder of the Camden district, visited the city three years later, he found the galleries erected for black members of the Methodist churches bare.[69]

Significantly, southern evangelical leaders played a critical intermediary role. The Baptists, who had already dissociated slavery from the legitimate concerns of the church, adapted more readily to the prevailing mood. Dr. Richard Furman, pastor of the First Baptist Church of Charleston and later

---

Community Studies, Contributions in American History, no. 96 (Westport, Conn.: Greenwood Press, 1982), 57–95, treats the insurrectionary scares as white hysteria, a response to social strains that "threatened consensual unity." Crow, "Slave Rebelliousness," 95–101, finds evidence of actual plots. Both attribute the insurrectionary fever to social strains of the time, and both emphasize the role of religion. In a more recent work, "Equal Justice: Afro-American Perceptions of the Revolution in North Carolina, 1775–1800" (Paper presented at the annual meeting of the Organization of American Historians, March 1988) Crow argues that blacks were keenly aware of revolutionary ideology and believed that it applied to all people and were inspired by it to engage in collective resistance.

[65] Bangs, *History of the Methodist Episcopal Church* 2:65. Lieutenant Governor John Drayton wrote to Governor Monroe for details about the plot, see Hamilton, *Writings of James Monroe* 3:216–18.

[66] Bangs, *History of the Methodist Episcopal Church* 2:63.

[67] Asbury, *Journal and Letters* 1:747, 2:70, 424.

[68] Joseph Brevard, *An Alphabetical Digest of the Public Statute Law of South Carolina,* 3 vols. (Charleston: John Hoff, 1814), 2:254.

[69] Reverend Abel McKee Chreitzberg, *Early Methodism in the Carolinas* (Nashville, Tenn.: Methodist Episcopal Church, South, 1897), 82.

one of the most prominent Baptist leaders of the South, gave dynamic and systematic statement to the ideas of southern Baptists. It was customary at each yearly Baptist association meeting to appoint a minister to write on a particular subject for the next year; these pastoral letters were then circulated through the member churches of the association. Dr. Furman's "Of Religious and Civil Duties," written in 1800, was a deliberate effort to allay white fears and suspicions and to unchain the Baptist church in the South from the antislavery theology associated with it in the North and with Methodism in the South.[70]

Like a fugue, Furman's letter played out the familiar themes introduced earlier in the century by the conventional churches and repeated with variations thereafter. Displaying a readiness to defend slavery that soon came to characterize the Charleston Association of South Carolina, Furman justified the institution on familiar biblical grounds. He then repeated the promise, implicit in the annual sermons of the Anglican bishops over the century, that the disciplinary power of Christianity would be used to cultivate virtues appropriate to slaves: "The scriptural doctrine on the station and duties of servants is clear and decided. It requires of them faithfulness, submission, quietude and obedience, in respect of the wise and sovereign order of God's providence, which has placed them in that situation; and it directs them to perform their duty on conscientious principles, 'As to the Lord and not to men.' The scriptures also give assurances, that this faithfulness will meet with peculiar approbation and gracious reward of Heaven; but that a contrary conduct will provoke the Divine displeasure."

If slaves must live according to the dictates of Scripture so must masters, Furman continued. Just as God had ordained that some humans should rule over others, so had He willed that they should rule "with justice and moderation; to afford [slaves] a reasonable portion of the comforts, as well as necessaries of life; and to regard with seriousness their religious interests, as of persons who are placed by the Divine government under their care and direction." Furman concluded by enjoining all Christians to act in strict accordance with the divine mandate: "Let us adhere to these scriptural principles, and perform these duties, so clearly laid down in the volume of inspiration. On these we may and ought to insist."[71] In the theo-

[70] Essig, *Bonds of Wickedness*, 120, attributes the letter to Wood Furman. That is doubtful inasmuch as Wood, the father of Richard, was a schoolteacher and justice of the peace, who was, however, an early historian of Methodism. Richard, a convert to Baptist principles, was licensed to preach in 1773 and served as pastor of High Hills Church until 1787, when he accepted a call to the Charleston church, where he remained until his death. He was very active in the Charleston Association; see Townsend, *South Carolina Baptists*, 32 n. 113.

[71] Wood Furman, comp. , *A History of the Charleston Association of Baptist Churches* (Charleston, S.C., 1811), 149.

logical ground taken by Furman lay the roots of southern paternalistic benevolence.

Furman's pastoral letter made it clear that evangelical religion could be counted upon to exhort and encourage all members of society, black and white, to make their thoughts and behavior conform to the basic ethical code of society as it was incorporated into law. It fit the political realities of slaveholding society and made it possible for white southerners to embrace evangelical religion. With the support of prominent state leaders, including Charles Cotesworth Pinckney, Thomas Pinckney, and William Henry Desaussure, a Baptist petition to the South Carolina legislature for an amendment to the law of 1800, which imposed restrictions on religious meetings for blacks, was renewed successfully in 1802, although all religious meetings were required to have a majority of whites present.[72]

At the next meeting of the General Conference, the Methodists abjured the controversial paragraphs in the Articles of Agreement among the Preachers and substituted a new recommendation calling on preachers to "admonish and exhort all slaves to render due respect and obedience to the commands and interests of their respective masters."[73] Even Asbury, who had signed the address, now regretted it: "Sure nothing could so effectually alarm and arm the citizens of South Carolina against the Methodists as the *Address of the General Conference*," he conceded. "The rich among the people never thought us worthy to preach to them: they did indeed give their slaves liberty to hear and join our church: but now it appears the poor Africans will no longer have this indulgence."[74] Bowing to political expediency, in 1804 the Methodists finally agreed to accept two disciplines, one for the northern churches and another for the southern.[75] In 1812 the General Conference agreed to give to each Annual Conference the right to form its own regulations respecting slavery.[76]

Although many individuals and an occasional group continued to resist the weighty pressure to conform to the majority socioreligious point of view, even the intrepid Dougherty, who later returned to Charleston and established a Negro school, confided to his bishop, "I humbly hope the storms in Charleston have taught me some useful lessons."[77] By 1809 Asbury himself had decided to resign the issue of slavery to the moral control of southern society: "Would not an *amelioration* in the condition and treat-

[72] Benedict, *General History*, 709. See also Cooper and McCord, *Statutes of South Carolina* 2:69, 8:343, 364, 385, 393, 410, 413, 440, 448.

[73] Quoted in Shipp, *History of Methodism in South Carolina*, 473–74.

[74] Asbury, *Journal and Letters* 2:281.

[75] Rogers, *Charleston in the Age of the Pinckneys*, 143–44.

[76] William W. Bennett, *Memorials of Methodism in Virginia, From Its Introduction into the State in the Year 1772, to the Year 1829* (Richmond, Va.: Author, 1871), 640.

[77] Chreitzberg, *Early Methodism*, 82.

ment of slaves have produced more practical good to the poor Africans, than any attempt at their emancipation," he asked himself. Grudgingly he answered his own question: "The state of society unhappily, does not admit of this: besides, the blacks are deprived of the means of instruction; who will take the pains to lead them into the way of salvation, and watch over them that they may not stray, but the Methodists? . . . What is the personal liberty of the African which he may abuse, to the salvation of his soul; how may it be compared?"[78]

Southern Methodist itinerants like Reuben Ellis of Virginia, one of the earliest circuit preachers in South Carolina, tied the knot between theological and sociopolitical attitudes even more securely. Eager to convince wary planters that Methodism posed no threat to slavery, Ellis visited plantations like that of Elias Ball, among the wealthiest and most influential planters on the Cooper River, and proposed "to make an experiment" by collecting Ball's slaves on the broad piazza attached to the mansion for Ellis to preach to them. Ball consented and was so pleased by what he heard that he invited Ellis back and later offered him board and a salary of $600.00 to serve as a permanent plantation chaplain.[79] Although evangelizing activities among slaves proceeded unevenly, a few itinerants were eventually able to schedule Sabbath appointments to preach to plantation slaves and occasionally to preach regularly on a particular plantation.

Private negotiations like those between Ellis and Ball and the more circumspect behavior of evangelical preachers in general gradually succeeded in gaining the support of the ruling aristocracy, if not of the general populace. The shift in official attitudes is apparent in the trend late in the century toward positive promotion of prominent evangelists in the political arena. Although the rural courthouse in South Carolina did not attain the politicolegal or social importance it represented in the Chesapeake and in the tidewater of North Carolina, as counties continued to be created in the postwar period, a number of new courthouses and other public buildings were constructed, especially in capital towns. Sturdy structures, usually situated at a major crossroads, they dwarfed the rough frame or log meetinghouses that survived the war and thus symbolized the preeminence of the secular over the sacred in postrevolutionary American society.

Convinced of evangelical sincerity on the issue of slavery, justices and lawyers entrusted with responsibility for maintenance of the public morality, openly and deliberately embraced the evangelicals. When Coke visited Edenton, North Carolina, he was invited to preach in the courthouse, one of the most imposing buildings in the state. Shortly afterward, Edenton

[78] Asbury, *Journal and Letters* 2:591.
[79] Capers, "Autobiography," 137–38.

was admitted to the Camden circuit.[80] As a young circuit preacher William Capers was invited by a prominent lawyer to preach at the Lancaster Courthouse. When Capers arrived, he found it was "sale-day," and the courthouse yard was filled with carts retailing cakes and cider, and probably peach brandy and whiskey because the preaching had to be postponed until evening so that the customers would be sufficiently sober to attend.[81] Many county seats such as Marion Courthouse in the Great Pee Dee Valley and Salisbury, North Carolina, had no churches, and itinerants, like the lame Joseph Travis, regularly used the courthouses for religious services. At the invitation of the chaplain, in 1812 Asbury preached in the South Carolina state assembly hall in Columbia "and had the members for a part of my congregation." Gradually the converts made by the evangelists filled the courthouses and legislative halls.[82] One of the most telling signs of the emerging relationship between the civil and ecclesiastical was that of Claiborn Clifton, a wealthy veteran of the revolutionary war, an influential lawyer and Methodist preacher from Columbia, who when at the bar, at times forgot and addressed the jury as "dear brethren."[83] The convergence of the lines of religion and law was pivotal in the cultural history of the South.

Having surrendered their efforts to emancipate bondmen from the chains of slavery, the evangelicals were increasingly free to work for their deliverance from the shackles of sin. At Asbury's insistence, the Methodists renewed their efforts in the lower South beginning late in1803 at a meeting house called Rehoboth in Warren County, Georgia.[84] In 1806 Samuel Dunwody was dispatched to Savannah, where he set up a school in a small room. At the end of a year his ministerial labors had produced only five white and seven black converts.[85] Beginning in 1808, however, the "sacred flame" began to spread across Georgia and South Carolina and up the Yadkin River in North Carolina. As in the upper South, the medium of revivalism was the camp meeting.

From the cities and villages, the small farms and great plantations, hundreds and sometimes thousands of people, traveling down the roads in carriages and carts, or along the water courses in sloops or steamboats, with their bedding, cooking utensils, and provisions for four or five days, came to attend the "general meetings," which were in the beginning often jointly conducted by Methodist, Presbyterian, and Baptist preachers. The greatest impact was felt in Georgia and North Carolina. Although enthu-

---

[80] William L. Grissom, *History of Methodism in North Carolina from 1772 to the Present Time*, (Nashville, Tenn.: Methodist Episcopal Church, South, 1905), 163–64.

[81] Capers, "Autobiography," 109.

[82] Asbury, *Journal and Letters* 2:715.

[83] Travis, *Autobiography*, 61, 91.

[84] Lee, *Short History*, 290.

[85] Bangs, *History of the Methodist Episcopal Church* 2:93.

siasm for revivalism was less in South Carolina, tours by Bishops Asbury and William M'Kendree and the itinerants Henry Boehm and James Gwin in 1808, 1809, and 1818 eventually bore fruit. By the time the initial thrust of the movement had spent itself, the Baptist and Methodist communions had been transformed from despised religious sects to the two most important evangelical bodies in the region.

As a natural consequence of their growth in the South, Baptists and Methodists had reached large numbers of slaves. Even so the black constituency of the churches remained comparatively small and many planters on the great rice and cotton plantations still viewed the evangelicals as apostles of violence and social revolution. The association of slave rebellion and slave religion crystallized in the Vesey Conspiracy of 1822. The themes and proposed methods of the rebellion planned by Denmark Vesey, a free black and master carpenter, and fellow slave conspirators Ned and Rolla Bennet, Monday Gill, Peter Poyas, and a physician and conjurer named Jack Pritchard, or Gullah Jack, bore a striking resemblance to the Prosser conspiracy. A war of liberation, the details of which were worked out at evening prayer meetings over a four-year period, the rebellion involved by some accounts as many as nine thousand slaves who had been recruited from plantations as far north as South Santee and south as far as the Euhaws, James, and Johns islands. Like Prosser's plot the Vesey conspiracy called for black troops, armed with weapons made by slave armorers, to be divided into three forces; one to cross from James Island, land on South Bay and march into Charleston to seize the arsenal and guardhouse; a second to advance simultaneously up the neck; while a third prepared to rendezvous in the vicinity of the mills. The army would then sweep the town with fire and sword, killing all whites.[86]

Although the black revolutionaries failed to achieve their broader purpose, they seemed to open up prospects for future risings. Trial testimony, which suggested that some of the Vesey plotting was done in class meetings, convinced local authorities that "religious fanaticism" and the African schism had "formed a hot bed" for revolt.[87] The retaliation taken against

[86] For the trial records, see James Hamilton, Jr., *Negro Plot. An Account of the Late Intended Insurrection among a Portion of the Blacks of the City of Charleston, South Carolina* (Boston: Joseph W. Ingraham, 1822), 25–26, 35–38, 40; Lionel H. Kennedy and Thomas Parker, *An Official Report of the Trial of Sundry Negroes, Charged With an Attempt to Raise an Insurrection in the State of South Carolina* (Charleston, 1822). Kennedy and Parker were presiding magistrates of the court. For secondary accounts, see John Lofton, *Denmark Vesey's Revolt: The Slave Plot That Lit a Fuse to Fort Sumter* (Kent, Ohio: Kent State University Press, 1983); Eric Foner, "Black Conspiracies," *New York Review of Books* 17 (1971): 39; Richard C. Wade, "The Vesey Plot: A Reconsideration," *Journal of Southern History* 30 (1964): 143–61; Robert S. Starobin, ed. *Denmark Vesey: The Slave Conspiracy of 1822* (Englewood Cliffs, N.J.: Prentice-Hall, 1970).

[87] Hamilton, *Negro Plot*, 31; see also C. C. Pinckney's comment quoted in William Pope

black Methodists in the wake of the abortive insurrection, put an end to the separate existence of the African Methodist Episcopal church in Charleston and effectively ended the city's independent black church movement until after the Civil War. Although some of the seceders returned to the Methodist Episcopal church, black church membership did not recover for another fifteen years. The Vesey plot also produced charges that religious teachings had made slaves "insubordinate to proper authority." Anxious to shore up the gains evangelical religion had struggled for almost a century to achieve, the southern clergy abandoned the antislavery posture taken by early churchmen, and, in their anxiety to mute white fears concerning the radicalizing effects of Christianity, they led in the formulation of the scriptural proslavery defense and thus did their ironic part to strengthen the institution of slavery.

By 1815 the pioneering first generation of evangelicals, whose rejection of slavery had branded them as antisocial revolutionaries, was passing from the scene, to be replaced by local preachers like William Capers and Richard Furman. Typical of the second generation of evangelical leadership, Capers and Furman, like many southern churchmen, were slaveholders who, however, coveted their faith for everyone, including slaves. Born in St. Thomas parish, South Carolina, in 1790, Capers was converted to Methodism and in 1808 became an itinerant minister. For the next forty-six years Capers served the church in the Carolinas and Georgia. The most powerful orator in the Conference, he exercised more influence among the wealthy of the state than any other Methodist. Forced by northern opposition to decline the office of bishop in 1832, when the Methodists split in 1845 Capers became bishop of the Methodist Episcopal Church, South.[88] Although Furman was born in New York, he was brought by his parents to South Carolina at ten months of age and spent most of his youth in High Hills of Santee. At age sixteen he was converted to Baptist principles and was ordained to the ministry in 1774. Exceedingly active in church work, Furman was the creator and president of the South Carolina Baptist Convention and a leading influence in the shaping of the Southern Baptist Convention, also organized in 1845.[89]

Under the leadership of Furman and Capers, the evangelical movement in the lower South passed from a small but aggressive antislavery movement committed to the notion that the whole tenor of the New Testament was hostile to slavery, to a proslavery auxiliary dedicated to the conviction that the conservative writings of St. Paul reflected both the spirit and the

Harrison, comp. and ed., *The Gospel among the Slaves. A Short Account of Missionary Operations among the African Slaves of the Southern States* (Nashville, Tenn.: Methodist Episcopal Church, South, 1893), 114.

[88] Wightman, *Life of William Capers*, 413.
[89] Townsend, *South Carolina Baptists*, 32 n. 113.

letter of the New Testament. At the height of the Vesey crisis, the South Carolina Baptist Convention, speaking through its president, Richard Furman, issued a statement titled "Exposition of the Views of the Baptists to the Coloured Population of the United States," which disclaimed any interference with slavery. To prove that Christianity was no enemy to slavery, Furman reiterated the scriptural defenses that had been elaborated over the years and put the Convention on record as opposed to emancipation. In doing so Furman contributed significantly to the ideological foundation of paternalism by accepting its major propositions that blacks were different, that slavery was an inherent part of God's design, and that emancipation would not only produce no benefit to slaves, but would be "extremely injurious to the community at large." He defended the Christianization of slaves as a stabilizing force, noting that although "a considerable number of those who were found guilty [of insurrectionary activity] and executed, laid claim to a religious character," there were "multitudes of the best informed and truly religious among them, who, from principle, as well as from prudence, would not unite with them, nor fail to disclose their machinations, when it would be in their power to do it."[90] In his defense of slavery as a humane institution, Furman went well beyond the limited claims of his predecessors. His sweeping generalization that slavery created a family, over which the master presides as "guardian and even father of his slaves," molded the scaffolding to support the paternalistic ideology. His insistence that by caring for children, the aged, the sick, and disabled, slavery accomplished "what is effected, and often at a great public expense, in a free community, by taxes, benevolent institutions, bettering houses, and penitentiaries"[91] laid the ground for the extreme defense of slavery as a superior form of social organization.[92]

Despite his outspoken defense of slavery as a moral foundation of an orderly, righteous society, Furman also felt compelled to push the battle to the gates on the question of religious instruction for slaves. "Though they are slaves," he insisted, "they are also men; and are with ourselves accountable creatures; having immortal souls, and being destined to future eternal reward." The divinely sanctioned power of the master over the body of his slaves, Furman maintained, was attended by a God-given responsibility for

[90] Vesey, a free black, and thirty-six slaves were executed.

[91] Richard Furman, *Reverend Dr. Richard Furman's Exposition of the Views of the Baptists, Relative to the Coloured Population of the United States* (Charleston, S.C.: A. E. Miller, 1823), 4, 6, 7–8, 10, 14.

[92] Eugene D. Genovese, "Slavery Ordained of God" (Gettysburg, 1985), 17. Hilrie Shelton Smith, *In His Image, But . . . Racism in Southern Religion, 1780–1910*, (Durham, S.C.: Duke University Press, 1972), 53–54, acknowledges that Furman "submitted an important paper to Governor John L. Wilson, in which he set forth the convention's attitudes toward Negro Slavery." He does not, however, see it as a pivotal point in the history of evangelical religion in the South and in the development of the paternalistic ideology.

the welfare of their souls. Speaking for the convention, Furman, one of the principal religious architects of the developing paternalistic ideology, positively asserted that the slaves' religious interests "claim a regard from their masters of the most serious nature."[93]

The gradual internalization of the paternalistic ideology articulated by churchmen like Furman and Capers, took place in the hundreds of small biracial churches that sprang up in the South between 1785 and 1829. Although the great majority of urban African-Americans became members of separate black churches whose relative independence invited the participation of their creative energies, beginning with Gabriel's Revolt, growing numbers of farm and plantation slaves worshipped in biracial churches under the close supervision of white members. The meeting places of black and white cultures, the biracial churches were the filters through which the paternalistic ethos radiated in all directions through southern society.

Historians agree that evangelical religion was a dominant shaping force in southern culture but they disagree about its meaning for slaves. Some stress the biracial aspects of evangelical religion: the fact that black and white southerners worshipped together; that black deacons and elders served alongside their white counterparts; that black preachers were admitted to the clergy; that blacks were subject to the same moral standards as whites and enjoyed the same procedural rights in disciplinary matters.[94] Other historians maintain that the origins of segregation are to be found in the systematic separation of the races in early evangelical churches, which, however, afforded black Christians the opportunity to "escape from paternalism."[95] As these studies suggest, the story is paradoxical and cannot be easily comprehended because so much is contradictory. Certainly slaveholders sought in Christianity a framework for a hegemonic ideology, but, as Eugene Genovese has observed, "The strategy of using religion as a method of social control could never have served its purpose had it been only that." The success of the strategy was due to the fact that it "combined

[93] Furman, *Exposition of the Views of the Baptists*, 16. Gallay, "Origins of Slaveholders' Paternalism," 369–94, also maintains that one of the principal sources of paternalism was the evangelicals' attempt to reform slavery during the First Great Awakening. The aim of Whitefield and the network of Christians he established was the evangelicalism of slaves and the amelioration of the conditions of slavery. Never, Gallay insists, did they seek radical change in the institution itself.

[94] See, for example, Kenneth K. Bailey, "Protestantism and Afro-Americans in the Old South: Another Look," *Journal of Southern History* 41 (1975): 451–72; John B. Boles, *Black Southerners 1619–1869* (Lexington: University Press of Kentucky, 1983), 158–62.

[95] See, for example, John Lee Eighmy, "The Baptists and Slavery. An Examination of the Origins and Benefits of Segregation," *Social Science Quarterly* 49 (1968): 666–73. See also Robert L. Hall, "Black and White Christians in Florida, 1822–1861," in John B. Boles, ed., *Masters and Slaves in the House of the Lord. Race and Religion in the American South, 1740–1870* (Lexington: University Press of Kentucky, 1988), 81–98.

self-interest with a genuine concern for the spiritual welfare of their slaves and indeed themselves."[96]

To a society based on the ownership of slaves, the idea of spiritual brotherhood posed a troublesome question of morality that was not merely rhetorical, but was a matter affecting the entire character of southern society.[97] Many masters and ministers were devout Christians who were genuinely convinced of the moral responsibility they bore for the salvation of their slaves' immortal souls. Their concern is apparent in church covenants. Written by outstanding members of the church or by committees, the covenants were statements of principles, which represented what Baptists believed and tried to practice. On a day set aside specifically for that purpose, the covenant was read and signed by members of the congregation. Thereafter it was read regularly at monthly meetings. The typical covenant called on the signers to love one another, to observe and support the articles of faith, to abstain from wicked company and vain pleasures, such as cards, dice, dancing, and horse racing, to discharge civil and religious duties conscientiously, and to instruct children in the principles of religion.

Some church covenants also contained statements respecting the master-slave relationship. The covenant adopted by the biracial Welsh Neck Church in 1785 and the amended version of 1814 are typical examples of Baptist beliefs on the subject: "We promise that if we should be possessed of Negroes or other slaves, that we will act a truly Christian part by them; by giving them good advice, laying our commands on them to attend the worship offered in public on Lords days and in private in our families when convenient, and we also promise that we will not treat them with cruelty, nor prevent their obtaining a religious knowledge and will endeavour to prevent their rambling and will encourage those who can read, at proper times to instruct others, and in all things endeavour to act in our families as to obtain the blessings of God."[98] Article 11 of the covenant of the Cashaway Baptist Church on the Pee Dee River traced the origins of mutual obligations to the biblical injunction, "Masters give unto your servants that which is just and equal; knowing that ye also have a master in heaven" (Col. 4; Eph. 6.9) and reminded members that by it corresponding privi-

[96] Genovese, Roll, Jordan, Roll, 186, 189, 190. See also Creel, A Peculiar People, 176–77, which notes the significance of the fact that the Christian conversion movement "originated with an appeal from planters." Creel questions how long the issue of slave conversion in South Carolina might have "lain dormant except for the efforts intended to stabilize the plantation system."

[97] For a discussion of the psychological conflict experienced by Christian slaveholders, see Oakes, Ruling Race, 96–122, especially p. 105. Oakes argues that "the important place of religion in the proslavery defense is an indication of how deeply slaveholders felt the need to bring their ethical convictions into line with their daily practices."

[98] Church Covenant, June 18, 1785, April 2, 1814, Minutes Welsh Neck Baptist Church, South Carolina Baptist Historical Society (hereafter cited as SCBHS).

leges were granted to owner and slave: just as "obedience is due from them to us, we feel bound to avoid acts of cruelty toward them" and to "support them with food and raiment becoming their station and worthy of the Christian character which we sustain."[99]

How well white southerners kept the covenant is suggested by surviving church records. In keeping with religious egalitarianism, slaves were accepted for church membership by both Methodist and Baptist congregations. Among Baptists the prerequisites for admission into the fellowship consisted of evidence of personal salvation, competent understanding of the Scriptures, and proof of an upright life followed by baptism according to Scriptual prescription, that is, by immersion.[100] Church records reveal that the principal criterion for the admission of slaves was to be able to "relate an experience of grace."[101] Baptized slaves were entitled to participate fully in church services, although throughout the South racial bias manifested itself in spatial arrangements. Seating in all of the biracial churches was allocated according to a hierarchy that corresponded to social divisions, and slaves generally occupied the aisles or galleries.[102] It is significant that the founding of the separate black churches was, for the most part, a protest against just such segregation and discrimination.

According to church rules, black Baptists were eligible to participate as ordained preachers and deacons and on occasion even to conduct ordination rites. In the spring of 1802, for example, Henry Francis, a former slave "of handsome ministerial abilities,"[103] was ordained at the Savannah African Baptist Church. The ordination sermon was delivered by one of Georgia's pioneer black preachers, Jesse Peter or Galphin. After Francis was publicly examined on matters of doctrine, his call to the ministry, and his ideas of church government, he knelt down before Andrew Bryan, pastor of the first all-black Baptist church in Savannah, for the ordination prayer and the imposition of hands. The ordained white ministers present then "gave the right hand of fellowship to Mr. Francis."[104]

On occasion, white churches actively recruited black preachers. In 1792, for example, the Roanoke Association unanimously agreed to do every-

[99] Covenant of the Mechanicsville Baptist Church, n.d., Cashaway (Mount Pleasant) Baptist Church Book, 1765–1805, SCBHS.

[100] Baptists. South Carolina, *A Summary of Church Discipline . . . by the Baptist Association, in Charleston, South Carolina* (Wilmington, S.C.: James Adams, 1783), 15–18.

[101] November, 1811, June 6, 1812, September 5, 1812, April 3, 1813, May 1, 1813, South Quay Baptist Church Minutes, 1775–1827; September 7, 1800, Wallers (Goshen) Baptist Church Minutes, 1799–1818, Virginia Baptist Historical Society (hereafter cited as VBHS).

[102] Alfred J. Morrison, ed., *Travels in Virginia in Revolutionary Times* (Lynchburg, Va., 1922), 88; Rouchefoucauld, *Travels* 1:588.

[103] Rippon, *Baptist Annual Register*, (1798–1801), 263.

[104] See *Georgia Analytical Repository*, Reverend Henry Holcombe, ed., 6 vols., 2d ed. (Savannah, 1802–03), 1:20–22 for details of the ordination of Henry Francis.

thing possible to purchase Simon, the property of John Davis of Mecklen-burg County, and set him free "as we think him ordained of God to preach the Gospel."[105] A few white churches chose black ministers, although these were the exceptions rather than the rule. After the Baptist church at Gloucester, Virginia, was left without a minister, the congregation "at length did, what it would hardly have been supposed, would have been done by Virginians," and chose William Lemon, a black man, as pastor. When Thomas Armistead resigned, the Portsmouth church employed the black Jacob Bishop, as pastor, but Bishop was eventually forced to leave.[106] In 1821 Big Creek Baptist Church in the South Carolina backcountry gave the slave Ceasor permission to preach "whare he is called or as far as his master will allow him to go for one year provid [sic] he preaches sound Doctrin." Three years later at Ceasor's request the church issued him a permit to "exercise his gift" in Georgia. Sometimes the gifted black preacher led the Big Creek congregation in prayers and singing and even conducted services.[107]

The Methodist General Conference also adopted a rule approving the ordination of "our African brethren." Because of the strong opposition of preachers from the southern states, the rule was never printed in the Form of Discipline and as a consequence it was little known, even among Meth-odist preachers themselves.[108] The first black to receive ordination from the Methodist Episcopal church was Richard Allen of Philadelphia, and in 1824 David Payne, a "man of color," was ordained deacon by the Virginia Conference.[109] Many black preachers were, however, licensed to preach without receiving ordination. The famous "Black Harry," or Harry Hosier, considered by Coke to be one of the best preachers in the world, traveled with Coke and frequently preached to black and white congregations. In Wilmington, North Carolina, Asbury was assisted by a black preacher named John Charles, and black preachers were often used in missionary service, particularly in South Carolina.[110]

Most black members of biracial churches probably served as lay exhort-ers rather than preachers, however. An emotional form of preaching that followed the sermon, but was ordinarily devoid of scriptural references, the

[105] October 16, 1792, Roanoke Baptist Association Minutes.

[106] Semple, *History*, 355; Lemuel Burkitt and Jesse Read, *A Concise History of the Kehukee Baptist Association from Its Original Rise to the Present Time* (Halifax, N.C., 1803), 253.

[107] October 4, 1823, June 5, 1825, May 6, 1826, December 31, 1831, Big Creek Baptist Church, Williamston, Minutes, 1801–1936, SCBHS.

[108] Lee, *Short History*, 270–71.

[109] In 1794 Allen founded the Bethel African Methodist Episcopal Church (MEC) in Phil-adelphia, "Mother Bethel" as it came to be called. In 1799 Asbury ordained Allen, and in 1816 the African Methodist Episcopal Church was established with Allen as bishop; Asbury, *Journal and Letters* 3:366, ed. note.

[110] Ibid. 1:298, 403, 2:530; Coke, *Extracts of the Journals*, 18.

exhortation was generally designed to encourage sinners to repent or to persuade the unsaved to accept salvation. Methodist exhorters were usually licensed, and, although exhortation was not treated as a church office among Baptists, Baptist congregations generally required candidates to obtain permission to exhort from a church committee.[111] Numerous black members of biracial Baptist churches, particularly in the upper South, applied for and were granted permission to "exercise their gift within the bounds of the church," although some candidates were denied permission on the grounds that their preaching was "not thought profitable."[112] Many black exhorters apparently tried to use exhortation as a stepping stone to the ministry by, for example, administering the rites of the church, or by using a Bible passage as a text, functions normally performed only by ordained ministers.[113]

The complexity of the interaction of the races and the limits of racial egalitarianism are most apparent in the administration of church discipline. Theoretically at least, both black and white church members were subject to the same church discipline, administered at the local level by Methodist congregations, class meetings, or ad hoc committees, among Baptists by the local congregation at monthly or quarterly meetings. In actual practice, black Christians were denied access to substantive power, as the records of Virginia Baptist churches reveal. In the early years, some Virginia Baptist churches allowed all members, male and female, bond or free, to participate in church discipline and government; others admitted all male members, whether slave or free. Dissatisfaction with the practice was apparently widespread and an effort was made to introduce uniformity and white control over disciplinary matters. In 1797 the Roanoke Association declared that it was the duty of every church to "rule her members." Because blacks were unable to attend church meetings, the association recommended that member churches set aside one Sunday of each month "to settle and Reg-

[111] For a discussion of the differences between exhortation and preaching, see Jerry L. Tarver, "Exhortation among Early Virginia Baptists," *Virginia Baptist Register* 5 (1966): 228–36.

[112] March 31, 1792, May 1799, Berryville (Buck Marsh) Baptist Church Minutes, 1785–1803; September 3, 1809, February 4, 1809, Berryville Baptist Church Minutes, 1803–1841; March 4, 1814, South Quay Baptist Church Minutes, VBHS. The practice was less common in South Carolina, perhaps because of the demographic characteristics of the black population. For similar examples, however, see June 27, 1827, and February 1827, Lower Fork of Lynches Creek Baptist Church (Gum Branch) Minutes, 1796–1887, SCBHS.

[113] See, for example, June 19, 1790, Upper King and Queen Baptist Church Minute Book, 1774–1816; August, 1791, Berryville (Buck Marsh) Baptist Church Minutes; March 4, 1814, South Quay Baptist Church Minutes, VBHS; Baptists, Virginia, *Minutes of the Baptist Dover Association, 1798–1832* (Richmond, Va.: Samuel Pleasants 1798–1832), 1816, 9, 10. For South Carolina, see August 1, 1809, Big Creek Baptist Church Minutes; September 6, 1829, Black Creek Baptist Church, Dovesville, Records, 1798–1896, SCBHS.

ulate all disorders that may be among the black Members."[114] In 1802 the
Dover Association decided that "The degraded state of the minds of slaves,
rendered them totally incompetent to the task of judging correctly respecting the business of the church, and in many churches there was a majority
of slaves: and in consequence of which, great confusion often arose." The
association, therefore, directed that the subject be treated in a circular letter, which argued that although all members were entitled to church privileges, "none but free male members, should exercise any authority in the
church."[115]

In casting about for a way to reconcile the cherished religious principle
of egalitarianism with the practice of hierarchy in church government, the
association hit upon a theory that had already recommended itself to civil
authorities faced with explaining away constitutional qualifications based
upon race and sex: the secular theory of natural rights. Church officers, the
association maintained, were endowed by God with special authority; no
one could exercise that authority "whose situation in social life renders it
his duty to be under obedience to the authority of another, such as minor
sons, and servants," whose minds were not "sufficiently independent to
give an impartial decision." Because women, minors, and servants had
been conspicuously "useful in certain stages of discipline," the association
conceded to them certain limited benefits: to "admonish, reprove, or rebuke, either singly or united to others," to "cite refractory members to
appear before the church," and to act as witnesses for or against those so
accused. The association concluded with a recommendation that in disciplinary matters, churches should appoint persons whose situation was similar to that of the offender, that is, females if the case involved a woman,
"the most considerable and experienced servant members" if a slave.[116] A
number of Virginia Baptist churches did appoint black deacons to "see [the
black brethren], hold prayer with and amongst them, admonish and stir
them to holy duties."[117] Although the practice was less common, Baptist
churches in the lower South also appointed black deacons "as a guard for
the black members."[118]

The actual adminstration of discipline was in the hands of white male
members. Perhaps because "the state of the slaves," as the Dover Association of Virginia put it, was "of so singular and delicate a nature, that no
general rule could apply," individual churches adapted their proceedings

[114] October 7, 8, 9, 1797, Roanoke Baptist Association Minutes.

[115] Semple, *History*, 101.

[116] *Minutes of the Baptist Dover Association*, 1802, 10–11.

[117] October 4, 1788, June 4, 1813, South Quay Baptist Church Minutes, August, 1808,
August 3, 1811, Wallers (Goshen) Baptist Church Minutes, VBHS,

[118] September 6, 1829, Black Creek Baptist Church Records, SCHS.

according "to the nature of each case, in the most prudent way."[119] Regardless of the procedure, it is in the administration of discipline that the severe limits of biracialism are most apparent. Extant church records suggest that church discipline was used to establish the standards of conduct and morality and the values and social mores that came to characterize white southern society. Above all, disciplinary records indicate the great importance of the family and the emphasis upon legitimacy in a Christian society. An examination of the various sexual relationships that males and females, black and white, might enter suggests which relationships were deemed acceptable and which were not. By and large, acceptable behavior varied according to race and gender. White males, for example, were allowed greater sexual freedom than white females. The reasons for preoccupation with female sexual morals were attributable to two concerns: the perpetuation of the family and the preservation of family estates, and the maintenance of racial purity, upon either of which the infidelity of the woman could cast doubts. The idea of the family-centered patriarchy was later elaborated into a general social philosophy.[120]

Christian churches also tried to inculcate in slaves moral values appropriate to their race and status in society. Although they cast the role of the black family differently, they tried in the interest of social stability to implant in their slaves the familial values of evangelical religion, which dictated monogamous fidelity. Although slave marriages were not recognized at law, church policy considered them valid before God. Caught on the horns of this dilemma, individual congregations like Virginia's South Quay Baptist Church seriously debated whether slave marriages should be made obligatory; no decision was reached and the question was referred to the association. The problem was complicated further by the slave practice of "double marriage," and by the forcible separation of slave families by sale and inheritance practices. The Buck Marsh church discussed the problem of slaves "parting with former wives and Taking of [sic] with others" and decided that "Such Members Shall be Call'd to account for such conduct and also all such as shall (and has been encouragers of such a conduct) shall be equally chargeable for so doing." When a black woman asked permission of the Buck Marsh church to marry a man who had previously been married, the church replied that it "countenances no such Proceeding."[121] When Giles complained to the Berryville Baptist Church that his

[119] Semple, *History*, 93–94.

[120] For a discussion of the evolution of the domestic patriarchy see Kulikoff, *Tobacco and Slaves*, 165–204, and Michael Johnson, "Planters and Patriarchy: Charleston, 1800–1860," *Journal of Southern History*, 46 (1980). For a discussion of the use of church discipline in shaping gender roles, see Jean E. Friedman, *The Enclosed Garden. Women and Community in the Evangelical South, 1830–1900* (Chapel Hill: University of North Carolina Press, 1985).

[121] August, 1791, April 5, 1794, Berryville (Buck Marsh) Baptist Church Minutes.

wife had voluntarily left him and requested church approval for remarriage, the church refused.[122] Churches in the lower South also struggled with the same problem. When Sam requested permission of the Lynches Creek Baptist Church to take another wife, the five-man disciplinary committee ruled that "he should Cleave to the Wife he has last taken."[123] Big Creek Baptist Church expelled Anne "for the sin of Adultery for marering and having a former [husband] yet living" and refused Black Will's request to be "received into our church having two wifes living."[124]

Church discipline was also used as an instrument to support and encourage marital integrity and the stability of the black family unit. Adultery was considered equally sinful among blacks as among whites and, if proven, was usually punished by excommunication. The fact that almost twice as many female as male slaves were excommunicated for adultery suggests the operation of a double sexual standard for black as well as white couples.[125] The most conspicuous contradiction in the churches' efforts to accord the same sacred status to slave marriages as to white marriages, involved the owner's right to separate married couples. John Leland complained that "What promises soever they make, their masters may and do part them at pleasure" and he chastised both church and state for the obvious hypocrisy: "If their marriages are as sacred as the marriage of freemen, the slaves are guilty of adultery when they part voluntarily, and the masters are guilty of a sin as great, when they part them voluntarily."[126]

Leland's ethical point troubled conscientious Christian slaveowners and led eventually to efforts to obtain legal sanction for slave marriages. In the meantime, churches put up only feeble resistance to the owners' disruption of the marriage bond between slaves. Although the Kehukee Association determined that a member church was not duty bound "to hold a member in fellowship who breaks the marriage of servants" by forcibly separating husband and wife,[127] individual churches rarely excommunicated Christian masters for disrupting slave marriages. In 1816 the Dover Association urged member churches to adopt some policy that would stabilize slave

[122] December 1, 1804, ibid.
[123] October 17, 1828, Lynches Creek Baptist Church Minutes.
[124] June 4, 1803, January 2, 1812, Big Creek Baptist Church Minutes.
[125] October 5, 1782, April 5, 1794, March 3, 1810, August 31, 1811, June 4, 1813, July 30, 1814, South Quay Baptist Church Minutes; June 6, 1795, March 31, 1792, June 5, 1802, Berryville (Buck Marsh) Baptist Church Minutes; April 2, 1808, October 11, 1817, Berryville Baptist Church Minutes; July 26, 1822, Tussekiah Baptist Church Minutes, 1784–1826; VBHS. For the lower South see February, 1825, Big Stephens Creek Baptist Church, Edgefield District, Records, 1803–1901, January 19, 1822, September 5, 1822, September 3, 1823, Welsh Neck Baptist Church, SCBHS.
[126] John Leland, *The Virginia Chronicle: With Judicious and Critical Remarks, under XXIV Heads* (Fredericksburg, Va.: T. Green, 1790), 9.
[127] Burkitt and Read, *Concise History*, 54.

marriages, but three years later the association decided that "fornication clearly proven" was adequate grounds for a church to dissolve a slave marriage, thus freeing the slave couple to remarry. But "as it concerns those who are in a state of freedom, we are of opinion that those only sanctioned by law, as being legally divorced, will justify a man in marrying again."[128] For all their deliberations, the practical consequence of the churches' inability to formulate a coherent policy on the subject was that the sale or separation of a slave was tantamount to a virtual decree of divorce, recognized by usage and by virtual decree of the evangelical churches.[129]

The practical utility of religion as an effective social control clearly commanded the support of planters who were neither pious nor orthodox but simply recognized that religion could be used to foster paternalistic ideals. Both Baptist and Methodist church leaders consistently maintained that slaveholders had a religious obligation to treat their slaves in a humane and Christian manner. Yet no association ever formulated a policy concerning slave abuse by masters. When the issue was put before the Dover Association in 1813, the association was unable to reach accord. To the question "Is there no restriction on believing masters in the chastisement of their servants?" the association replied that it was impossible "to fix a certain rule in these cases," but recommended instead that member churches "take notice" of excessive or improper punishment and "deal with the transgressor as they would with offenders in other crimes."[130] Individual churches did occasionally discipline Christian masters, however. In 1792, for example, the Black Creek Baptist Church excommunicated James Johnson for beating a black man. The Mountain Creek Baptist Church excluded a Brother Howard for the same offense.[131] White members of South Carolina's Big Creek Baptist Church encouraged and supported Judy when she was brought before the church's disciplinary committee for using "ill language" against her master and mistress. Judy rested her defense on the fact that "she had not enough to Eat given her from them." Anxious to evade church censure, Judy's contrite owners publicly repented, he saying "if he has hurt aney of his Bretherns feelings by whipping his servant, or saying aney thing or doing aneything Els, he is sorey for it, Sister Johnson [the slave mistress] says that she is sorry for saying that they would sell Judy, and that it should not be to her satisfaction." Despite the sympathy of the congregation for her plight, because Judy refused "to confess her faultes," she was expelled from fellowship. The Mill Swamp Baptist Church of South Carolina considered charges brought against William Boyce for

---

[128] *Minutes of the Baptist Dover Association*, 1819, 5.

[129] W.E.B. DuBois, ed., *The Negro Church* (Atlanta, Ga.: n.p., 1903), 56.

[130] *Minutes of the Baptist Dover Association*, 1813, 11.

[131] Daniel, "Virginia Baptists and the Negro," 64; June, 1815, Mountain Creek Baptist Church, Anderson, Minutes and Historical Sketch, 1798–1956, SCBHS.

"uncommon cruelties to his slaves," but found insufficient evidence to warrant discipline. In a similar case, Morgan's Baptist Church appointed a committee to visit Sister Sally Egnew to "make inquiry into her alleged conduct toward a negro woman," but apparently took no action.[132]

On the other hand, the disciplinary power of the church was routinely used to reinforce plantation discipline. Although slaves rarely accused their masters of transgressions, owners routinely brought charges against their slaves. The white male-dominated disciplinary conferences routinely punished running away and disobedience to masters by excommunication.[133] Moral offenses such as drinking, theft, and disorderly conduct were also punished by excommunication, although white offenders were generally accorded the same treatment.[134] The intervention of evangelical preachers into the relationship between master and slave, long viewed as an alarming intrusion into the affairs of the plantation with potential for producing disorder and instability, gradually came to be accepted as an important, perhaps the most important, means of promoting social stability.

The paternalistic ethos forged in the anxious discussions of hundreds of small evangelical churches satisfied the social, religious, philosophical, and moral needs of the Christian slaveholding community. Its concepts were not only intellectually persuasive to the slaveholding elite, but extraordinarily useful as ideological supports for the slave society they had helped to create. Embraced by lawyers and jurists, the paternalistic ideology found expression in the growing tendency after 1823 for state courts to protect the slave from the absolute control of the master by fixing legal limits to the master's coercive power at punishment short of death. In *Commonwealth v. Booth*, the Virginia General Court scrupulously upheld the master's right to punish his slaves, which the court maintained "is justified by the relation of master and slave," but it established the rule that assault "becomes unlawful by subsequent excess and inhumanity."[135] Although it proceeded somewhat cautiously, the North Carolina Supreme Court moved even more dramatically to seriously modify the legal rule that the power of the master was absolute. In 1823 in the case of *State v. Reed*, the court gave a new interpretation "founded upon the laws of nature and con-

[132] September 10, 1823, Big Creek Baptist Church Minutes, March 27, 1802; Mill Swamp Baptist Church Minutes, 1774–1790, January 14, 1819, Morgan's (Goose Creek) Baptist Church Minutes, 1787–1821, VBHS.

[133] January 4, 1782, October 4, 1782, July 1, 1785, April 2, 1791, December 3, 1813, South Quay Baptist Church Minutes; March 6, 1805, Berryville Baptist Church Minutes. For the lower South, see February 1809, January 1812, June 1812, October, July 1815, Big Stephens Creek Baptist Church Records, June 8, 1794, Little River Baptist Church, Fairfield County, Minutes, Rolls, 1794–1820, SCBHS.

[134] January 2, 1790, February 6, 1790, February 2, 1796, March 3, 1810, May 30, 1810, South Quay Baptist Church Minutes.

[135] Commonwealth v. Booth (1824) 2 Va. Cas., 4 Va. 394.

firmed by revelation." Writing for the majority, Justice Henderson reasoned that "the *life* of a slave being in no way necessary to be placed in the powers of the owner for the full enjoyment of his services the law takes care of that; and with me it has no weight to show that by the laws of ancient Rome or modern Turkey, an absolute power is given to the master over the *life* of his slave. I answer, these are not the laws of our country, nor the code from which they were taken." Concluding that it was "abhorrent to the hearts of all those who have felt the influence of the mild precepts of Christianity," Henderson held that "absolute control" meant that the masters' powers extended only over the services of slaves, not over their lives, an interpretation that became the prevailing rule of the Court.[136]

Ten years later in the landmark *State v. Negro Will* case, the North Carolina Supreme Court established the slave's right to life. For the first time in the history of slavery, the court recognized the right of a slave to defend himself against his master in protection of his own life. Rather than argue from the point of law, Will's counsel, B. F. Moore, who later became one of the most famous pleaders of the state bar, made his plea on moral grounds: if the condition of slavery required "that the slave be disrobed of the essential features that distinguish him from a brute, the relation must adapt itself to the consequences and leave its subjects the instinctive privileges of a brute," the young lawyer began. "I am arguing no question of abstract right," he continued, "but I am endeavoring to prove that the natural incidents of slavery must be borne with because they are inherent to the condition itself; and that any attempt to restrain or punish the slave for the exercise of a right, which even absolute power cannot destroy, is inhuman and without the slightest benefit to the security of the master or to that of society at large." In deciding to free Will, the court went to considerable lengths to protect the owner's right to punish his slaves: "Unconditional submission is the general duty of the slave; unlimited power, is in general, the legal right of the master." But, the court admitted, there is an exception to the rule: punishment "shall not reach the life of the offending slave." Just as "It is certain that the master has not the right to slay his slave," the majority opinion maintained, it is "equally certain that the slave has the right to defend himself against the unlawful attempt of his master to deprive him of life." Thus did the court draw a careful line between the lawful and unlawful exercise of the formerly absolute power of the master and establish in law the right of slaves to resist wanton or cruel attempts to destroy their lives.[137]

The religiously inspired theory of reciprocal obligations had even more

[136] State v. Reed (1823) 9 N.C. (2 Hawks) 454.

[137] State v. Negro Will (1834) 18 N.C. (1 Dev. and B.) 121. Compare to State v. Pivar, 397.

far-reaching social and political consequences. To the extent that it devised an apparently practical moral system that all Christians could embrace, it became a beneficial instrument for humanizing slavery. Subsequently, perhaps even simultaneously, the doctrine of mutual obligations, whose broad outlines were already incorporated in law, was restated and amplified by the courts. The earliest judicial exposition of the doctrine is found in *Fairchild v. Bell*. The defendant in this 1807 South Carolina case had severely beaten one of his female slaves and had then driven her away from home. The plaintiff, a physician, found the woman "in a miserable condition, almost naked, shockingly beaten, and having an iron on her leg of fifteen pounds weight." Contrary to the owner's orders, the physician treated the injured woman and then sued to recover costs. Although the jury found for the defendant, the court, through the judge's charge, laid the ground for the doctrinal development of mutual obligation. Giving at least implicit recognition to the slave's humanity, the court asserted the duty of the master to provide for and protect his slaves: "For as the master is bound by the most solemn obligation to protect his slave from suffering, he is bound by the same obligation to defray expenses or services of another, to preserve the life of his slave, or preserve the slave from pain and danger." At the same time, however, the court emphatically affirmed the reciprocal obligation of the slave to labor for his master: "The slave lives for his master's service. His time, his labor, his comforts, are all at his master's disposal."[138]

Despite its appearance as a reasoned, humane judgment, the judicially arranged marriage between oppressor and oppressed had significant implications for the perpetuation of slavery. As Eugene Genovese has argued, by satisfying the most basic material needs of slaves, the system of mutual obligations minimized the danger of protest and, at least ideally, fostered the slaves' internalization of the authority of the paternal figure. Thus the system and the duality which gave it rise was designed to operate as an instrument of domination by which slaves were effectively controlled, if not rendered passive. That it functioned as a conscious instrument of social control is made clear by *Gayle v. Cunningham*. Called upon to decide whether the child of a female slave, born after the execution of the will but before the death of the testator, should go with the mother to the person to whom she was bequeathed, the court ruled on two grounds that the child should follow the mother. Speaking for himself and two others, Justice William Henry Desaussure maintained that "The original foundation of property was derived from labor bestowed upon it, whereby its value was created or augmented." With doubtful reasoning the court, through Desaussure, continued: "The issue of a female slave would often be valueless but for her exertions and suffering, all of which are at the risk

---

[138] Fairchild v. Bell (1807) S.C. 2 Brevard 129.

of her master or owner. Equality is equity. Those who incur the risk are reasonably entitled to the gain."

Having reduced slaves to chattel, the court then admitted their humanity: "If then this case were more doubtful than it is, humanity obviously dictates that the children should follow their mothers; a contrary decision would separate even sucking infants. . . . Such a separation would be revolting; we cannot therefore be called upon in a doubtful case, to decide in such a way." Although humane motives were probably present, the court's concluding argument shows how the duality was exercised to turn unwilling blacks into compliant, dependent slaves: "Sound policy, as well as humanity, requires that every thing should be done to reconcile these unhappy beings to their lot, by keeping mothers and children together. By cherishing their domestic ties, you have an additional and powerful hold on their feelings and security for their good conduct."[139]

Eighteen years later a Virginia court added a new dimension to the theory of reciprocal obligations, one which reflects the familial values of evangelical religion as well as the preoccupation of republican ideology with human happiness. In *Allen v. Freeland* (1825) the court affirmed for the first time that "Slaves are not only property, but they are rational beings, and entitled to the humanity of the Court when it can be exercised without invading the right of property."[140] Three years later in *Randolph v. Randolph* the court, using *Allen v. Freeland* as a precedent, held that "The master has not only his own pecuniary interest to consult, and his own affections and predilections to gratify, in all of which he will be aided by the Courts; but, he owes a duty to the slave, as well as the slave does to the master, and which he ought to perform; the duty of protection from a violent seizure and sale, which may terminate in the destruction of his happiness, and in breaking asunder all his family ties and connections."[141]

It was in claiming religious rights for slaves that evangelical religion exerted its most considerable influence in coordinating Christian ethics and law. Intent on survival, evangelical preachers had concluded that slavery was divinely sanctioned, but they had at the same time tirelessly and uncompromisingly insisted upon the fundamental Christian position that "though they are slaves, they are also men; and are with ourselves accountable creatures; having immortal souls, and being destined to future eternal reward."[142] A few church leaders like John Leland had gone so far as to insist that liberty of conscience "is the right of slaves beyond contradiction."[143] In its reply to the question "What shall the master of a family do

139 Gayle v. Cunningham (1819) S.C. Harp. Eq. 124.
140 Allen v. Freeland (1825) 3 Rand. 24 Va. 170.
141 Randolph v. Randolph (1828) 6 Rand. 27 Va. 194.
142 Furman, *Exposition of the Views*, 16.
143 Leland, *Virginia Chronicle*, 9.

with slaves who refuse to attend public prayers in the family?" the Kehukee Association came close to endorsing Leland's position: it "is the duty of every master of a family to give his slave liberty to attend the worship of God in his family; and likewise it is his duty to exhort them to it, and endeavour to convince them of their duty; and then leave them to their own choice."[144]

Gradually that belief penetrated deeper into society and made its mark on the system when in 1818 a South Carolina court recognized freedom of conscience as a formal right of slaves. *John Bell, ads. Dempsey Graham* involved charges that the slave patrol, or persons assuming that identity, had repeatedly interrupted Methodist church services at Shady Grove, South Carolina. Under pretense of enforcing the act of 1803, which required that a majority of the participants be white and that slaves in attendance must carry written permisson from their owners, the patrol had apprehended black congregants and whipped them with hickory switches, "the usual instruments with which they executed their commission." In deciding the case the court ruled that the religious service was, in fact, amenable to the law. Reflecting the theories of the day, the court then, for the first time, accepted as an historic truth the religious argument of the slave's right of conscience: "To worship God, after the dictates of our consciences, is a privilege that all men claim as a birth right from heaven. Millions have shed their blood in defence of it; and a conviction of its justness has sustained the martyr at the stake. But feeble indeed, would be the protection of our inestimable constitution, which professes to secure to us this privilege, if a petty patrol officer was permitted to mar and disturb our devotions at his pleasure, and with impunity. The English Common Law held this privilege so sacred, that it would not justify one in striking, even in his own defense, during worship; and it is a principle so clear that those who unlawfully disturb the devotion of a religious assembly, by any indecency or violence, may be punished by indictment, that authorities are unnecessary to support it."[145]

Although the court had, in this instance, chiseled out a basic principle, popular suspicion of the radicalizing effects of religion did not disappear completely. Five years after *John Bell, ads. Dempsey Graham* the aborted slave revolt led by Denmark Vesey produced charges that religious teachings had made slaves "insubordinate to proper authority." These were, however, only temporary obstacles, and by and large southern courts generally encouraged the extension of religion to slaves and enforced with increasing vigor owners' obligations to provide food, housing, and medical care for slaves.

[144] Burkitt and Reed, *Concise History*, 70.
[145] Bell v. Graham (1818) S.C. 1 Nott and McC. 278.

The dual transformations in law and religion ultimately led to a gradual amelioration of some aspects of slavery. Although variation existed in slave life generally at any given time, the growing acceptance of norms of slave treatment among Christian slaveowners led to progressively better treatment of slaves. Beginning around 1790, attempts at "improved housing" were marked by the gradual replacement of the mud-wall African-styled slave houses with European-style frame houses constructed of more permanent materials and presumed, therefore, to be superior. On some plantations raised wooden flooring replaced the old earth-floored cabins and provided a more sanitary environment. In time, some planters did away with the old communal style "barracks" in favor of single-family slave dwellings, although these may have been reserved for privileged house servants and slave artisans.[146] The standardization of slave housing, which was well under way by the 1830s, was accompanied by a shift away from the use of locally produced African-style colonoware pottery to imported, mass-produced European housewares.[147]

Statistical comparisons of mortality and health reveal that relatively better nutrition, diet, housing, and working conditions, and retention of the family unit produced at least minimal improvements in longevity and childbirth. Although regional and gender variations in mortality were significant, general mortality rates of farm and plantation slaves shifted from thirty-six years for females and thirty years for males in the eighteenth century to almost thirty-five for females and better than thirty-six for males in the nineteenth century. Birthrates, estimated at two per slave mother in the eighteenth century, increased to an estimated three and a half per mother in the nineteenth century, the result perhaps of better maternal health.[148]

[146] See Genovese, *Roll, Jordan, Roll*, 524, and William M. Kelso, "Mulberry Row Slave Life at Thomas Jefferson's Monticello," *Archaeology* 39 (1968): 29, 34.

[147] Theresa A. Singleton, "An Archaeological Framework for Slavery and Emancipation, 1740–1880," in Mark Leone and Parker B. Potter, Jr., eds., *The Recovery of Meaning: Historical Archaeology in the Eastern United States* (Washington, D.C.: Smithsonian Institution Press, 1988), 354–88.

[148] Jennifer O. Kelley and J. Lawrence Angel, "Life Stresses of Slavery," *American Journal of Physical Anthropology* 74 (1987): 199, 200, 202–3; Kelley and Angel's findings are based on an analysis of skeletal evidence of 120 black individuals from twenty-five sites in Maryland, Virginia, and the Carolinas, over a period between 1690 and c. 1860. See also Ted A. Rathbun, "Health and Disease at a South Carolina Plantation: 1840–1870," ibid. 74(1987): 239–53. Rathbun's analysis of thirty-six human skeletons discovered during a cemetery relocation near Charleston also reveal gender differentiations in mortality, with average age at death for males of thirty-five, for females forty. Compare to the mortality rates of free blacks of Philadelphia, whose adult life expectancy was 38.9 for females, and 44.8 for males; see J. Lawrence Angel, Jennifer Olsen Kelley, Michael Parrington, and Stephanie Pinter, "Life Stresses of the Free Black Community as Represented by the First African Baptist Church, Philadelphia, 1823–1841," ibid. 74(1987): 213–29. Peter Kolchin, *Unfree Labor. American Slavery and Russian Serfdom* (Cambridge, Mass.: Harvard University Press, 1987), 134, 137, 162, main-

The alliance between religion and law was also the catalyst for the launching of the church mission movement, which greatly accelerated the Christianization of slaves. Mission work among slaves had always enjoyed a high priority among Methodists. Until the creation of a special ministry for slaves, however, it had to be carried out by individual southern clerics, often under the pressure of persecution. The South Carolina Conference was the first to carry on organized mission work among slaves. Beginning as early as 1809, the Conference appointed James H. Mellard as missionary to the slaves in the area from the Ashley to the Savannah River and James E. Glenn missionary from the Santee to the Cooper. Both Glenn and Mellard, who had earlier been driven away from Georgetown by the local patrol, resigned their commissions, apparently because of strong white opposition.[149]

In 1829, however, the first Methodist plantation missions were launched in the South Carolina Conference by William Capers at the behest of Charles Cotesworth Pinckney. Impressed by the results achieved by a Methodist overseer among the slaves of a fellow planter in Georgia, Pinckney invoked the aid of William Capers, then Superintendent of Missions, in procuring the services of a Methodist exhorter for his Santee River plantation. Shortly afterwards two Pon Pon planters, Charles Baring and Colonel Lewis Morris, asked that missionaries be regularly sent to their plantations to preach to their slaves. With the approval of the bishop and Missionary Board, two missions were established, one to the south of Ashley River, the other south of the Santee and Pee Dee rivers. Assured by Capers that only ministers "deemed competent and safe" would be sent as missionaries,[150] Pinckney threw his considerable influence behind the plantation mission movement. In an address to the South Carolina Agricultural Society, Pinckney reasoned that "Nothing is better calculated to render man satisfied with his destiny in the world than a conviction that its hardships and trials are as transitory as its honors and achievements." With his own ancestral lands as an example, he announced that white southern missionaries would be available for the oral instruction of plantation slaves on the river deltas of the low country.[151]

The movement grew rapidly, spreading first among planter friends of the Pinckneys in Beaufort District. In nearby St. Luke's parish, "a large and respectable meeting of gentlemen" agreed to adopt the missionary sys-

---

tains that the "relative material comfort" of slaves in the United States was higher than that of slaves in other countries and "also in comparison with most of the world's population."

[149] Travis, *Autobiography*, 52, 53, 55; Chreitzberg, *Early Methodism*, 309–10.

[150] Wightman, *Life of William Capers*, 292.

[151] Charles Cotesworth Pinckney, *An Address Delivered in Charleston before the Agricultural Society of South Carolina at Its Anniversary Meeting, on Tuesday, the 18th of August, 1829* (Charleston, S.C. 1829).

tem, as did a number of planters on the Pee Dee and Black rivers. By 1831 there were four separate missions to slaves: three in South Carolina, one in Georgia. In the tenth year of operation, the mission movement extended from Waccamaw Neck and Pee Dee River on the east to the Savannah River on the west and embraced 234 plantations served by 17 missionaries, who had under their pastoral charge 5,556 adults and 2,525 children under regular catechetical instruction. Within a single generation, the number of white Methodists increased over 100 percent; black Methodists increased over 170 percent.[152] Although the plantation mission movement centered in the South Carolina Conference, mission work gradually spread to other southern states. In the process, the religious configuration of the southern states was transformed as the evangelical churches, particularly the Baptists and Methodists, rapidly supplanted the Anglican church, which since colonial times had enjoyed a privileged position in the South.

To a large extent the spread of the mission movement was due to the fact that southern Methodist leadership had rejected not only the antislavery vision of society that had been a central part of Methodist church policy from 1785 to roughly 1815 but equally their method of achieving it. In his Report of the South Carolina Conference Missionary Society in 1836, Capers denounced the burgeoning abolitionist movement in the North as "utterly erroneous and altogether hurtful." In a radical departure from the tradition of Coke and Asbury, Capers embraced the negative theory of government subscribed to by Baptists. The question of abolition was, he insisted, "a civil one, belonging to the State, and not at all a religious one, or appropriate to the Church." Far from giving any countenance to the "delusion" of abolitionism, Holy Scriptures "unequivocally authorize the relation of master and slave." With the Bible as their sheet anchor, "Our missionaries inculcate the duties of servants to their masters . . . as indispensably important. We hold that a Christian slave must be submissive, faithful and obedient, for reasons of the same authority with those which oblige husbands, wives, fathers, mothers, brothers, sisters, to fulfill the duties of these relations. We would employ no one in the work who might hesitate to preach thus; nor can such a one be found in the whole number of the preachers of this Conference."[153]

The impact of evangelical Christianity upon master-slave relations and upon the institution of slavery itself was as ambivalent as the religious teachings to which formal religion bore witness. On the one hand, church leaders not only abandoned antislavery but, in their anxiety to mute white fears concerning the radicalizing effects of Christianity, they led in the for-

[152] Shipp, *History of Methodism in South Carolina*, 450, 552–53; Wightman, *Life of William Capers*, 294–95; Chreitzberg, *Early Methodism*, 309–10, 311.
[153] Quoted in Wightman, *Life of William Capers*, 295–96.

mulation of the scriptural proslavery defense and thus did their part to strengthen the institution of slavery. On the other hand, by insisting that slaves were not mere chattel but human beings, they led public opinion and the courts to recognize certain human rights for slaves. Their success in identifying moral goals that could be shared by the white majority made it possible for evangelical religion to have a decisive effect in humanizing slavery by mitigating some of the hardships attending the conditions of slavery. In the new social order, slaves were forced to develop new defenses against the dehumanizing effects of slavery and to create new forms of cultural autonomy. Their efforts to respond with integrity within the narrowly delimited options open to them led to the creation of Afro-Christianity, a black rendition of Christian theology and morality that was not identical with the Christian goals of planters and not anticipated by the white missionaries' vision of Christianity.

NINE

THE AFRICAN-AMERICAN RESPONSE:
BLACK CULTURE WITHIN A
WHITE CONTEXT

FOR SLAVEHOLDERS, the idea of the egalitarian fellowship of all humans in Christ was a way to resolve both the problem of social control and their own psychic need to escape responsibility for the brute system that continually disturbed and wrenched their consciences. For the slaves who embraced the faith of their masters, evangelical religion was something very different. For the individual, acceptance of Christianity was a symbolic assertion of self, the chief means by which chattel property again became human. For the group, the small, well-defined community of believers became the spiritual, social, material, and, above all, symbolic center of the slave community, the fountainhead of their unity and survival, of their cultural and ultimately ethnic identity, in a very real sense, of their freedom. Unlike Anglo-Americans, for whom the concept of freedom implied autonomy, for African-Americans, as for their African forebears, freedom meant social bonds, attachment to a group. Wrenched from home and family, stripped of social personality and identity, robbed of customs and family, African-Americans ultimately found their need for incorporation into a collectivity satisfied through membership in the transcendent human family. Through it and in it they found spiritual freedom, although freedom from chattel slavery still eluded them.[1]

African-American Christianity was a product of white Protestantism. Within the white evangelical structure, however, blacks created their own institutions and fashioned an intricate subculture capable of providing them with the psychological and moral resources necessary to withstand slavery. Their struggle was, as Charles H. Long has suggested, both adap-

---

[1] Kopytoff and Miers, "African 'Slavery,' " in Miers and Kopytoff, eds., *Slavery in Africa*, 17, maintain that the Euro-American concept of freedom, which implies the autonomous individual, does not apply to traditional African society, wherein freedom is defined as membership in a group. John Mbiti, the African theologian puts it this way: in Africa "a person cannot be individualistic, but only corporate." The Yoruba expression quoted in Mbiti, "I am because we are, and since we are therefore I am," aptly summarizes it; see, Mbiti, *African Religions and Philosophy*, 209, 214.

tive and creative.[2] The period beginning with the Second Great Awakening in 1785 and ending with the launching of the plantation mission movement in 1829 forms a critical phase in the long struggle of African-Americans to sustain their religious and cultural identity against the massive program of cultural genocide developed and efficiently managed by slaveowners. The creation of separate black churches led by charismatic black preachers provided at last a formal institutional basis for the development of culture and community.

The idea that Christianity could serve as an instrument of social control and stability enjoyed the support of a number of powerful planters. It remained a minority opinion, however, and missionary activity among slaves was not extensive prior to 1829.[3] Until then, religious conversion of slaves was primarily a black enterprise, conducted by an urbanizing black elite. Throughout the South, black preachers succeeded in organizing separate black churches with relatively distinctive attributes given the social context in which they operated. Their existence made it possible for African-Americans to affirm their African heritage rather than identify with the dominant white culture by joining white churches. The pattern of racial separation continued until Gabriel's Revolt and the Vesey Plot led an alarmed white society to press for the incorporation of blacks into biracial churches. By the time the new racial pattern was inaugurated, the tradition of separate churches was well established and was to persist and reemerge during Reconstruction.

The earliest growth points of the Afro-Baptist church were in urban areas of high black concentration: the eastern corner of Virginia, from Portsmouth and Norfolk to Petersburg and Richmond along both banks of the James River; Savannah and the surrounding area extending up the Savannah River to Augusta in Georgia; the area around Welsh Neck on the Pee Dee River and the Beaufort church in the Sea Island region of South Carolina. The denominational origin of the Afro-Baptist church in the South was Virginia. It was in Virginia that the earliest black churches were established, and it was from the Virginia church that many of the early black leaders emerged and, in their movements throughout the country, started new congregations in towns and villages throughout the South and the developing southwest.

Despite the wartime exodus of the black and white populations from older tidewater communities, the black Baptist church established on the eve of the Revolution continued to expand, even through the 1790 decade of general religious decline. Between 1785 and 1810, a number of new

[2] Charles H. Long, "Perspectives for a Study of Afro-American Religion in the United States, *History of Religion* 11 (1971): 57.

[3] Creel, *A Peculiar People*, 217, says that it did not become dominant in South Carolina until after 1845.

separate black Baptist churches sprang up in the developing urban centers along the James River leading to Richmond. The leadership of the separate church movement was made up almost entirely of members of Virginia's large free black population. The majority of these first black churches were formed by a coalescence of black congregations that had broken away from white congregations. The first instance of blacks separating themselves from a white congregation was apparently the Williamsburg African Church, the early forerunner of the Afro-Baptist church in Virginia. Expelled from the biracial church for defying a rule of the Dover Association prohibiting blacks from preaching on pain of excommunication, Gowan Pamphlet not only continued to preach but also formed his own church, which grew to approximately five hundred members and was admitted to the association in 1791.

After the white minister, John Williams, left the Allen's Creek Baptist Church in Mecklenburg County, Virginia, some black "preachers of talent . . . commenced the administration of ordinances, without ordination." Although they were persecuted, they baptized over a hundred new black members, who then "branched out" and formed new churches. When Reverend Williams returned and attempted to "settle them into order," the "most orderly" agreed to rebaptism, but "Many refused to give up their independent state."[4] Gillfield Church, a biracial church when constituted in 1788, was organized in 1797 under similar circumstances as the Second African Church of Petersburg, as was the Harrison Street Baptist Church of Petersburg, established about the same time under the leadership of a free black named John Benn. The First Baptist Church of Norfolk formed in 1800 was expanded in 1805 to include most of the separating black members of the previously biracial Portsmouth Baptist Church, established in 1789. In 1817 the 25 white members of the 252 black member Norfolk Church withdrew to form the all-white Cumberland Street Baptist Church of Norfolk.[5]

One of the largest and most active centers of black Baptist activity was in the Richmond area. Predominantly a black movement whose rise was intimately linked with the prewar activities of black preachers and exhorters enlisted by white Baptists, the development of the early church took place within the biracial First Baptist Church of Richmond. Although growth stalled during the 1790s, a large following developed from among Richmond's burgeoning industrial slave population, many of whom were employed in the city's tobacco factories. In 1823, ninety-one free black Baptists petitioned the state legislature for permission to establish an African church but were denied. By 1828 black membership in the First

[4] Semple, *History*, 115, 222.
[5] Jackson, "Religious Development of the Negro," 191.

Church had expanded to one thousand, compared to a white membership of only three hundred. Embarrassed by membership in an overwhelmingly black church, the First Church of Richmond finally agreed to separate, and, in 1841, the First African Baptist Church of Richmond opened its doors with 940 members. Its phenomenal growth led to the creation in 1845 of the Second African Baptist Church, and of the Ebenezer or Third African Baptist Church in 1858.[6]

In the meantime, the Afro-Baptist church had also reached neighboring Charles City County, where preaching and prayer meetings were being held as early as 1775 in a meetinghouse known as the "old log church." There was no organized church, however, and black Baptists had to make the long and difficult trip by dugout canoe up the James River to Petersburg on the Appomattox River to worship in the Gillfield Baptist Church. In an 1809 revival, a free black farmer named Abram Brown was converted and subsequently led the movement to form a separate black church. In 1810, it was constituted as the Elam Baptist Church, and, in 1813, it was admitted to the Dover Association.[7]

Virginia's urban-born black churches remained the dynamic centers of growth and expansion of the Afro-Baptist church in the decades before the plantation mission movement was inaugurated. Although Virginia did not have a single slave mission until 1841, in 1845 blacks constituted two-thirds of the Rappahannock Association, the area extending roughly from the mouth of the York River to the Mattaponi, north in a line from Caroline County to King George County, to the Potomac River and south to Chesapeake Bay. The Portsmouth Association, which extended from Portsmouth and Norfolk to Petersburg, contained some of the largest and most active black churches in Virginia, including the Portsmouth and Norfolk churches, Davenport's, southeast of Petersburg in Prince George County, and the First African of Petersburg.[8] Zealous Virginia blacks were among the chief instruments for the expansion of the Afro-Baptist Church north into Maryland. The Maryland Afro-Baptist church dates from 1835, when a former Virginia slave named Moses Clayton organized the First Colored Baptist church in Baltimore. In 1847 another Virginia black, Noah Davis, organized the Second Colored Baptist Church in Baltimore.[9]

The same ingredients of African-American initiative and indigenous leadership were present in the development of the Afro-Baptist church in

---

[6] John T. O'Brien, "Factory, Church and Community: Blacks in Antebellum Richmond," *Journal of Southern History* 44 (1978): 522–23, 526, 527.

[7] *Organization and Development of the Elam Baptist Church, 1810–1910* (Ruthville, Va., 1976), 10–13; See also *Minutes of the Baptist Dover Association*, 1813, 5.

[8] Benedict, *General History*, 663.

[9] Edward D. Smith, *Climbing Jacob's Ladder* (Washington, D.C.: Smithsonian Institution Press, c. 1988), 79, 80.

Georgia, the second vital center of Afro-Baptist growth. The success of Andrew Bryan's African Baptist Church in Savannah eased the process of slave conversion in Georgia. By 1788, Bryan's congregation had grown to 225 members in full communion with approximately 350 adherents. Under the patronage of some prominent white men of Savannah, Bryan began a campaign to obtain permission to establish an autonomous black church. A petition drawn up by Lachlan McIntosh was circulated among the leading men of the city and county. It emphasized that the black Baptist society had a standing rule to admit no slave without the permission of his or her owner. It stressed the Christianizing effects on slave discipline, pointing, for example, to black Christians "meek and obedient behaviour to their Masters and Mistresses." It argued for the usefulness of religion as an instrument of social control, noting that as a result of hearing Andrew Byran preach, a number of "bad and evil disposed Negroes and Slaves" had been "entirely reclaimed." Citing the "irreproachable character" of Pastor Bryan, the petition brushed aside white fears that religious worship might be used for "base ends," and insisted instead that should there be "any disorder brooding" among the black congregants, "their Pastors, Deacons, and leading members would be the first to recommend and the best to depend upon for every information." Finally, the petition dismissed the idea that blacks should be admitted to white churches on the grounds "that when they are assembled in large numbers, from constitutional peculiarities, they are extreamly [sic] disagreeable to every audience." Concluding that there were no other alternatives but "to permit them to assemble at thier [sic] own house, and in thier [sic] own way, or entirely deprive them [of] the privilege of attending public worship," the petition recommended that they be allowed to worship "according to the dictates of their consciences and in thier [sic] own way." Although the petition was denied by the mayor and aldermen of the corporation, an appeal was made to the commander of the county militia, and with the support of white sympathizers permission was granted for Bryan and his followers to conduct religious services during daylight hours in a barn provided by Bryan's owner, on condition that all in attendance carry written passes from their owners and that they "conduct themselves with due decency and order."[10] Shortly afterwards Bryan, who had purchased his freedom from the Bryan family heirs for £50, bought a lot in Savannah and built upon it a frame structure called the Bryan Street African Baptist Church, the first black Baptist church in Georgia, and the first Baptist church, black or white, in Savannah.

[10] The petition is quoted in full in Joseph M. Simms, *The First Colored Baptist Church in America Constituted at Savannah January 20, 1788* (Philadelphia: J. B. Lippincott, 1888), 26–29, 46–47.

Bryan's African church was in fact well established before Newington, the oldest white Baptist church in Savannah, was organized. Indeed, it might be argued that the Newington church owed its origin to emerging black talent. In 1789 a black preacher "preached in the neighbourhood in a negro yard under some peach trees." Among the curious whites who came to hear the unnamed preacher was a prominent revolutionary war veteran, Major Thomas Polhill. Both Polhill and his wife were converted by "this poor sable creature." After his conversion Polhill became the patron of the Baptist cause and a leading promoter and organizer of meetings, which ultimately led to the establishment of the Newington church in 1793. A year after it was constituted, the white Newington church still had only eight or ten members, whereas the African church, "through the instrumentality of their own men," increased rapidly both in the city of Savannah and in the outlying areas.[11] By 1800, Bryan's church had 700 members. To accommodate the numbers, members of Bryan's congregation formed the First African Baptist Church of Savannah and elected as pastor Henry Cunningham, a slave. The following day 250 members were dismissed from the First African to form the Ogeechee Colored Baptist Church fourteen miles south of Savannah, and Henry Francis assumed its pastorate.[12]

Up the Savannah River in Augusta, Jesse Peter Galphin had organized another thriving center of Afro-Baptist strength. With the nucleus of his old Silver Bluff Church, Galphin formed the Springfield Baptist Church, apparently in 1793, in the upper end of the city. At its peak ,the Springfield church had five hundred members and was one of the largest churches in the Georgia Association.[13] The mother Baptist church in Augusta, the Springfield African Church predated the white First Baptist Church, which was not organized until 1818, and it was the parent body of Augusta's second black Baptist church. Organized in 1840 as the Independent Baptist Church and renamed Thankful in 1844, the second church was formed by members and deacons of the Springfield church in an effort to accommodate the large numbers of slaves who worked on plantations and in brickyards in the extreme southeastern part of the city, and who had to travel across town to worship at Springfield.[14]

From these urban centers black preachers fanned out into outlying areas, generating an unprecedented religious awakening among slaves and drawing thousands of them into African-American church communities and bi-

[11] Benedict, *General History* 2:185; Henry Holcombe, D.D., *The First Fruits, In a Series of Letters* (Philadelphia: Author, 1812), 115.

[12] Rippon, *Baptist Annual Register*, (1798–1801), 366–67.

[13] Benedict, *General History* 2:194.

[14] Clarence M. Wagner, *Profiles of Black Georgia Baptists* (Atlanta: Bennett Brothers Printing, 1980), 26, 35.

racial churches. Of the twelve churches that formed the Savannah River Association in 1803, three black churches—the First and Second African of Savannah, and the Ogeechee—represented over 65 percent of the total membership. In 1813 the Savannah River Association divided the body into two associations, those churches on the Georgia side of the river forming the new Sunbury Association. Probably no association in the state contained as large a proportion of black members as Sunbury. In 1846 the association reported 4,300 members, less than 500 of whom were white. Approximately one-half of the association's twenty churches were entirely black, and, with few exceptions, blacks constituted a majority of the memberships of the remaining churches. The First African of Savannah was the largest church in the association.[15]

South Carolina slaves from the neighboring sea islands sometimes joined or attended the black Baptist churches of Savannah.[16] Only two autonomous black churches were formed in South Carolina, both of them short-lived. The Silver Bluff Church, formed by Jesse Peter Galphin in 1781, had 210 members in 1792. But the church either disappeared or was amalgamated with the African church of Augusta after Galphin moved to Georgia.[17] Welsh Neck Baptist Church, the mother church of all Baptist churches in the Pee Dee River area, was all white when formed, but black membership quickly outgrew white. Eighty-seven blacks were baptized during the summer of 1779 following a long period of general decline in white church membership. On August 24 they were constituted into a separate church. Their autonomy was short lived, however. In September a substantial number of the new converts were excommunicated on the grounds that they were "very ignorant of the nature of true religion." Unable to find their own pastor, in 1782 forty-six black members accepted the invitation of Reverend Edmund Botsford to rejoin the white church.[18]

The biracial Welsh Neck Baptist Church regularly sent out black members to the various plantations in the Pee Dee valley, a major center of Baptist influence in the state, to "preach to their own colour on Lords-day evenings, and at other times" when no services were scheduled in the meetinghouse. According to Reverend Botsford, pastor of the Welsh Neck church, the conversion of "a great number of rich planters," and the discovery by a number of them "that their slaves are of increasing value to them when they become religious," led to intense evangelizing activities among native-born and African imports in the backcountry areas of South

[15] Benedict, *General History* 2:742 n. 7.

[16] Creel, *A Peculiar People*, 216.

[17] Townsend, *South Carolina Baptists*, 259.

[18] Minutes of the Welsh Neck Baptist Church, Historical Sketch, June 27, July 21, August 1, August 7, August 24, September 5, 1779, April 1782.

Carolina and in upper Georgia and contributed to a dramatic expansion of black membership in evangelical churches in the Pee Dee valley.[19]

The majority of black Baptists in South Carolina were, however, members of biracial congregations, several of which had comparatively large black memberships. Blacks constituted roughly half of the membership of the Welsh Neck church for some years. There were a number of biracial churches in the backcountry, including Tyger River, Little River, Buffalo Creek, and Cashaway. In the low country the Charleston Baptist Church had about sixty-three black members.[20] The Sea Island region was among the last to receive white missionaries, although preaching to blacks did occur in isolated pockets. Jacob H. Dunham, the first white person baptized in Liberty County, Georgia, preached among the settlements of poor people along the Altamaha River and among the Gullahs around Darien and the islands of St. Catherines and Sapelo, and Baptist missionaries set up a number of preaching places in the Beaufort District. Joseph B. Cook preached to blacks in the little town of Beaufort and at Euhaws. In 1802 he baptized thirty-two, "all poor unlettered negroes excepting one." The majority of Cook's congregation at Beaufort was black.[21] Henry Holcombe, born in Virginia but reared on the Little River of Saluda, preached at different places in Euhaws and baptized a number of blacks in local rivers. Blacks constituted a majority of the Black Swamp Baptist Church[22] and they apparently formed the nucleus of the first Baptist church in Beaufort in 1794.[23] In 1804 about one hundred black persons living on the islands around Sandy Creek were dismissed to join the Beaufort church.[24] The number of black Baptists in the South Carolina low country remained negligible, however. Of the 10,560 communicants in South Carolina's 130 Baptist churches in 1806, most of them in the up-country, only 3,500 were reportedly black, and the number did not increase substantially until the 1840s, when Baptist missionaries invaded the Sea Island region.[25]

Like the Afro-Baptist church, the denominational origins of the Afro-Methodist church are found in the Chesapeake. The Methodist movement was introduced into western Maryland in 1764 under the bold leadership of Robert Strawbridge. Through the work of a number of gifted native American preachers "raised up" by Strawbridge, it spread south into Brunswick County in southeastern Virginia and into Bute and Halifax

[19] Botsford to the editor, April 25–August 1790, Rippon, *Baptist Annual Register* (1790–1793), 105, 107.

[20] Ibid., 256, 257.

[21] Ibid. (1801–1802), 935.

[22] Creel, *A Peculiar People*, 132, 133, 138, 218.

[23] Holcombe, *First Fruits*, 49, 50–52.

[24] Townsend, *South Carolina Baptists*, 257.

[25] Creel, *A Peculiar People*, 210.

counties in the area of Albemarle Sound in northeastern North Carolina. In 1786 preachers were dispatched to new circuits in South Carolina and Georgia. Until 1825, however, Maryland comprised the heartland of Methodism. Although Francis Asbury, Thomas Coke, Henry Boehm, Richard Whatcoat, to say nothing of native preachers like Freeborn Garrettson and William Watters, preached to slaves during their tours, Afro-Methodism developed as an indigenous movement under the leadership of black preachers. Like midwives, Wesley's itinerating missionaries brought black people into Christ, and then left them. Through their work they had, by 1784, formed a sort of spiritual communion among Maryland blacks. But native black leadership formed the church.

Afro-Methodism in Maryland began in two racially integrated societies "settled" by Asbury in Maryland: Lovely Lane, the oldest meetinghouse in America, and Strawberry Alley, the first of the two houses to begin construction in 1773 but the last to be finished. As in other urban areas of the South, black Methodists of their own accord sought separation and a distinct organization. Several factors prompted their withdrawal, the most immediate being a reaction to increased discrimination. The conscious identification of Methodism with antislavery meant, among other things, that belonging to a Methodist society constituted, at least for blacks, a protest against slavery or against discrimination. When the white membership of Lovely Lane and Strawberry Alley meetinghouses forbade black church members to take communion with whites, black members, led by Jacob Fortie, withdrew from the white society and began meeting separately.[26] That they preferred to establish and maintain their own churches was clear from their importuning of Asbury to allow them to form a distinctly "African yet Methodist church," which "in temporals, shall be altogether under their own direction." Annoyed at their insistence upon "greater privileges than the white stewards and trustees ever had a right to claim," Asbury refused his permission. Eventually, however, the secessionists were able to establish two black Methodist churches in Baltimore, Sharp Street and Bethel.[27]

The pattern of racial separation clearly preferred by black Christians spread more slowly elsewhere in the South. In North Carolina two all-

[26] See Bettye C. Thomas, *History of the Sharp Street Memorial Methodist Episcopal Church, 1787–1920* (Baltimore, Md., 1977), for a detailed history of these developments. See also Julie Winch, *Philadelphia's Black Elite: Activism, Accommodation, and the Struggle for Autonomy, 1787–1848* (Philadelphia: Temple University Press, 1988), 4–5, 10, which suggests that the establishment of the separate church was more than a reaction to prejudice. According to Winch the Free African Society (FAS), a social and benevolent organization established by Richard Allen and Absalom Jones, was already moving in that direction as early as September 1790.

[27] Asbury, *Journal and Letters* 2:65.

black churches were formed: one by William Meredith, a follower of William Hammet, the controversial founder of the Primitive Methodist movement, the other by Henry Evans, a black preacher from Virginia. In both Wilmington and Fayetteville, Methodism was first implanted among the slave population. In 1784 William Meredith began to preach in Wilmington. His first congregation of Primitive Methodists was composed entirely of blacks. Public hostility to the Slave Rules led to active persecution. Although he was harrassed by the white community and thrown into jail, Meredith continued to preach through the grates of his window and eventually succeeded in building a small meetinghouse, which was subsequently burned to the ground. With the "penny collections" of slaves, Meredith built a second church on the site of the first, which at his death he willed to the Methodist church. In 1797 the first class of whites formed in Wilmington was joined to the black church, but when William Capers, then an itinerating preacher, was appointed to the Wilmington station in 1813, the majority of the communicants were still black.[28]

Methodism was introduced into Fayetteville, North Carolina, by a black preacher named Henry Evans. A free black from Virginia and a shoemaker by trade, Evans converted to Methodism while still a young man. Although he was licensed to preach in Virginia, Evans decided to move to Charleston, South Carolina. En route he stopped in Fayetteville on the Cape Fear River in North Carolina, which had a small Presbyterian congregation but not a single church building. Appalled at the "profanity and lewdness" of the slave community, Evans decided to remain in Fayetteville and began preaching to the blacks. Although his preaching violated no law, the town council ordered him to stop. Evans withdrew to the sandhills outside of town and conducted nightly meetings in the the woods. A mob quickly formed to break up the services, and Evans was forced to relocate his meetings nightly. But his charismatic preaching soon produced a noticeable decline in drunkenness and a general improvement in the public morals of slaves, "particularly as regarded their habits on Sunday," the young preacher William Capers remembered. The mob was called off, and Evans was allowed to preach in town and to build "a tolerably good-looking Methodist meeting house" some 50 feet long and 30 feet wide.

According to Capers' memoirs, a highly respected white woman, the former preceptress of the local female academy, who was impressed by the personal piety and powerful preaching of the black man, joined Evans' church, and prejudice against the preacher began to "melt like wax before

---

[28] Capers, *Autobiography*, 162–63; Lee, *A Short History*, 207–9. Hammit, a missionary brought from the West Indies to Charleston, pronounced Coke and Asbury tyrants and the AMC in schism because preachers did not wear robes or show sufficient respect for Wesley. He then formed the Primitive Methodist Church and established several churches in Charleston, Georgetown, Savannah, and Wilmington; see Asbury, *Journal and Letters* 1:706 n. 11.

the flame." As Evans' fame spread through the white community, blacks were crowded out of the church and "seemed likely to lose their preacher." Sheds were, therefore, added to each side of the original building to accommodate black members, while whites occupied the center. When Evans died in 1810, the entire community turned out to mourn the brilliant yet self-effacing man Bishop Capers called "the father of the Methodist Church in Fayetteville."[29]

Despite deep and lingering, and sometimes rabid, opposition to Methodism, urban blacks also succeeded in establishing a separate church in South Carolina. In keeping with the common pattern, South Carolina's separate black Methodist church was formed when blacks withdrew from biracial churches in which they constituted a majority but were denied equal rights and privileges. To protest their demeaned position in the house of God, they abandoned the white-dominated churches and established their own. From the beginning, blacks represented a substantial majority of the urban churches of South Carolina and played a prominent role in the expansion of the church into rural areas before 1829. The first Methodist society was formed in Charleston in 1785 by Henry Willis and John Tunnell. At the end of its first year, the struggling little society reported only thirty-five white and twenty-three black members, who worshipped together in an abandoned Baptist meetinghouse on Church Street. Evicted from the meetinghouse, they met for a year in private homes until they were able to build a church on Cumberland Street, known originally as the "Blue Meeting House." Although they were relegated to the galleries, black people were attracted to Methodism, and by 1789 they were in a majority by 119 to 66 in the Cumberland church.[30]

Methodism had driven down a stake in Charleston, but long years of struggle to keep it implanted followed the establishment of the Cumberland Street Church. Between 1789 and 1791 two events shook the church to its center and nearly destroyed the weak Methodist movement in South Carolina. The first was a schism led by William Hammet, who accused Asbury of being unfaithful to Wesleyan Methodism, and led a secessionist movement to which he gave the name Primitive Methodists.[31] The second was the adoption by the General Conference of 1787 of a rule exorting Methodist ministers and preachers to "leave nothing undone" in the spiritual instruction of slaves.

[29] Capers, "Autobiography," 124–29; Travis, *Autobiography*, 101–2. Both Capers and Travis were stationed in Fayetteville, Capers at the time of Evans's death.

[30] Reverend Charles F. Deems, ed., *Annals of Southern Methodism for 1855* (New York: J. A. Gray's Fire-Proof Printing Office, 1856), 239, 240, 242.

[31] Hammet built two Primitive churches in Charleston, Trinity and St. James Chapel, one in Georgetown, one in Savannah, and one in Wilmington; Albert Deems Betts, *History of South Carolina Methodism* (Columbia, S.C.: Advocate Press, 1952), 66.

At the 1788 meeting of the South Carolina Conference in Charleston, whites resentful of the "obnoxious" slave regulations rioted during the opening sermon of the conference. During the evening session, while Bishop Asbury was preaching to a crowded audience, the meetinghouse was pelted with rocks and brickbats, one narrowly missing the bishop, who, however, completed his sermon. The Charleston newspapers poured bitter invective and fiercely denounced the Methodist clergy and all things Methodist. Methodist societies, almost two-to-one black in Charleston, were watched, ridiculed, and openly assailed. Methodist churches were denounced as "negro churches," their preachers, "negro preachers." Within two years, the number of white Methodists in South Carolina declined by over one thousand. Some Methodist societies, such as the flourishing band on Edisto, disbanded and never reformed.[32]

For the next ten years, the predominantly black Cumberland congregation withstood regular and frequent attacks from mobs. Bishop Asbury, who presided over the sessions of the South Carolina Conference held in Charleston every year from 1794 through 1800, was greeted with "sneers, hurrahs, and shouts" by the crowds who awaited his every appearance. Despite active persecution, perhaps because of it, the determined little society decided to build a new church on a lot on Pitt Street. Dedicated in 1797, Bethel became the center of the black Methodist movement in Charleston. Harrassed and persecuted by white mobs, blacks steadily withdrew from the more accessible Cumberland church to Bethel, located in a more remote part of the city.[33] Growing racial friction caused by the news of Gabriel's revolt led to renewed harrassment of black Methodists. In 1807 a large body of the city guard, dressed in full uniform and armed with muskets, surrounded Bethel. The surprised congregation was rounded up and deposited *en masse* in the Sugar House, the local jail for slaves.[34]

Continuous harrassment led to a declining membership of both black and white Methodists in Charleston. In 1811, however, the Charleston societies reported an increase of 81 white and 415 black members. In the same year the South Carolina Conference reported 22,383 white and 16,789 black Methodists.[35] The upsurge in the number of black Methodists was due essentially to two related developments: the appointments to Charleston of Bennet Kendrick and his successor, William Capers, both of whom encouraged the Christianization of slaves, and the launching of a dynamic black-led mission movement to plantations in outlying parishes. According to Capers, the future Methodist bishop of the Southern divi-

---

[32] Deems, *Annals of Southern Methodism*, 241, 242, 243, 245.
[33] Ibid., 248, 253; Chreitzberg, *Early Methodism*, 73.
[34] Deems, *Annals of Southern Methodism*, 253.
[35] Chreitzberg, *Early Methodism*, 351.

sion, the only persons who were zealous enough and trusted enough to win access to low-country slaves were a group of "extraordinary colored men" from the Charleston churches. Skilled town slaves, and in some cases freed blacks, they were known and respected by the planters for whom they often worked. Designated as "agents," they were sent out as missionaries to various plantations on Goose Creek and on the Cooper, the Wando, and Pon Pon rivers; to St. Paul's parish, and to James, Johns and Wadmalaw islands. Welcomed and given board by some owners, their meetings "only winked at" by others, they preached and conducted classes, admitted and excluded members, all the while reporting regularly to their church in Charleston.[36] Discouraged about the prospects of Methodism among whites in the low-country, Asbury doubted whether "we have joined more than one hundred and seventy-eight members of the fair skin in twenty years," but he gratefully observed that "by our coloured missionaries the Lord is doing wonders among the Africans."[37]

In the meantime, under the leadership of a remarkable group of black men and women, Bethel gained a surprising degree of autonomy, generating and disbursing enough income to finance its own expansion and maintain its own separate conferences. When in 1815 white church leaders attempted to limit the church leaders financial control, "offense was taken" and black church people developed a secret plan to "Secure Bethel church for themselves, on the grounds that the church had been built largely through contributions of black members." The failure of that effort, followed by a dispute over the building of a hearse house on the black burial ground adjoining Bethel, led to a massive and dramatic demonstration of the rapidly developing unity of the black Christian community: the walkout of over four thousand black Methodists and the creation of a separate church, the African Methodist Episcopal Church, which was admitted in full connection with Bishop Richard Allen's African Methodist Episcopal Society in Philadelphia.[38] In 1818, the Charleston AME reported a membership of 1,848, making it the seond largest AME church in the United States after Philadelphia with 3,311 members.[39]

Just as the pattern of separate black churches was getting established in South Carolina and elsewhere in the South, the great Vesey Plot of 1822 dealt it a deadly blow. Since Vesey and several of his conspirators were members of Bethel, the city government leveled a series of harsh reprisals against the congregation and demolished its church. Morris Brown, the minister in charge, fled Charleston for Pennsylvania, where he later became

---

[36] Capers, "Autobiography," 138–39.

[37] Asbury, *Journal and Letters* 2:584.

[38] Chreitzberg, *Early Methodism*, 156–57.

[39] Daniel A. Payne, *History of the African Methodist Episcopal Church*, C. S. Smith, ed. (reprint, New York: Arno Press and the New York Times, 1969), 27.

a bishop of the African Methodist Episcopal Church. Thereafter in South Carolina, and indeed throughout the South, the growth of black religion took place within biracial churches, a pattern that prevailed until Reconstruction. That the Baptist and Methodist denominations progressed most rapidly where separate churches existed is compelling proof that indigenous black leadership was indispensable to the development of Afro-Christianity.

No docile sheep led by white shepherds, early black Christians often embraced the faith before their masters, and not infrequently were the instruments of their owners' conversions. The churches they established were in several significant instances the parent bodies of white churches. In parts of the South, evangelical Christianity was first implanted by African-Americans or by white churchmen among the African-American population. Although the proportion of black Christians within the black community still remained small, by 1829 Afro-Christianity had been planted in most of the counties of Maryland's Eastern and Western Shores. In Virginia, Afro-Baptist and Afro-Methodist churches flourished in Alexandria, Richmond, Petersburg, Williamsburg, Portsmouth, Norfolk, Charles City, Goochland, Lynchburg, and Pocorone, and blacks constituted a sizeable percentage of most of the state's biracial chuches. Georgia, dominated religiously by Baptists, had several large and independent black congregations in Savannah and Augusta, and these were pushing out in all directions. In North Carolina, blacks made up a substantial percentage of all Methodists in the Neuse and Roanoke districts in the Albemarle Sound region, and they constituted a majority in the Cape Fear area. Despite strenuous opposition, urban blacks had built large Methodist societies in Charleston, Georgetown, Beaufort, Euhaws, and Black Swamp and sent black preachers among the Gullahs in the Sea Island region.

Afro-Christianity had also made its way into the great region between the Alleghenies and the Mississippi River, carried there by the populations pushing westward from Virginia and North Carolina to Kentucky, and southwest to Alabama. Although most of the black migrants were forcibly removed, some were free blacks in search of a better life, a few were slaves who had been able to purchase their freedom. The black Christians among them laid the foundations for the spread of Afro-Christianity. As early as 1801, several black preachers were reported preaching to all-black crowds in Lexington.[40] In 1822 a former Virginia slave, who had obtained his freedom and moved to Lexington, organized the first black church in the state of Kentucky. Completely autonomous, the church had a membership of some five hundred, mostly free blacks, and a school with thirty-two chil-

[40] Rippon, *Baptist Annual Register* (1801–02), 807.

dren enrolled.[41] In 1832 a family of free blacks who had migrated into Indiana from North Hampton County in North Carolina decided to build a Methodist meetinghouse on land belonging to James Roberts, a member of the founding family of Roberts Settlement, one of the oldest black communities in Indiana. The local black community raised funds and built the first African Methodist Episcopal meetinghouse in the state in Hamilton County near Westfield.[42]

The first Baptists in the present state of Alabama were reported in 1808, near the Tombigbee River in Clarke and Washington counties. By 1821 there were seventy churches in the state, including the African Huntsville Baptist Church, which joined the Flint River Association in 1821. In his history of the Baptists in Alabama, published in 1840, Reverend Hosea Holcombe reported that "a great number" of the state's Baptists were black, that there were three or four all-black churches, including the African Huntsville and African Cottonfort in Lancaster, and that the membership of many other churches were from one-half to two-thirds black.[43]

In short, African-Americans themselves provided the opening wedge for the operation of the religious missions. Although the Christianization of slaves after 1829 was a white-directed movement, Afro-Christianity had acquired certain definite characteristics in its formative period that were to survive all subsequent modifications and set it apart from the white Protestant denominations from which it sprang. Given the social context in which it operated, Afro-Christianity was obliged to follow established patterns of church organization. Pastors, church leaders, class leaders, and elders performed most of the same functions as their white counterparts. Closely supervised by white organizations, they publicly adhered to orthodox doctrine and regulations. Within the African-American spiritual community, however, they began to forge a unique spiritual and cultural identity based upon a complex interweaving of traditional, namely African, cultural elements with Christianity. The expedient harmony of traditional beliefs and adaptive norms and practices that distinguished African-American Christianity helped shape the collective mentality of the emerging church community.[44]

[41] Edward Strutt Abdy, *Journal of a Residence and Tour in the United States of North America. From April, 1833 to October, 1834*, 3 vols. (London: John Murray, 1835), 2:346–47.

[42] Contract, 1832, Roberts Family Papers, 1734–1944, Library of Congress.

[43] Holcombe, *First Fruits*, 45, 61,110,111.

[44] Historians do not agree about the extent of African survivals in the worship of black churches. Melville Herskovits maintained that specific African survivals could be found in certain types of black churches—in African "motor behavior" and spirit possession and in the practice of baptism by immersion, which he links to Nigerian and Dahomean water cults. In a chapter whose title, "Death of the Gods," richly suggests the author's thesis, Albert J. Raboteau, the pioneer historian of African-American Protestantism, challenges much of Herskovits' argument, although Raboteau does concede that there were probably two areas of com-

The performance of religious ritual was the chief means by which African-Americans expressed their communal feelings. Little is known about the actual practice of religion in the first black churches, but evidence, much of it provided by white observers, suggests that, by and large, African-Americans, particularly those who were members of independent black churches, decided for themselves which aspects of religious ritual were more significant. According to John Leland, black Baptists preferred "to sing, pray and exhort, and sometimes preach, and seem to be unwearied in the procession." Their exhortations and their music tended to be noisy and emotional and, according to most white observers, "more subject to bodily exercise."[45] The description of all-night prayer meetings held in humble slave cabins written by James L. Smith, the slave of Thomas Langsdon of Northumberland County on Virginia's Northern Neck, provides the most detailed account of black worship: "The way we worshipped is almost indescribable," the black exhorter recalled. "The singing was accompanied by a certain ecstasy of motion, clapping of hands, tossing of heads, which would continue without cessation about half an hour; one would lead off in a kind of recitative style, others joining in the chorus. The old house partook of the ecstasy; it rang with their jubilant shouts, and shook in all its joints."[46]

Although early black Christians learned to sing from white hymnals, particularly Isaac Watts' hymn books, they clearly built upon African forms. Africans had a distinct musical system, characterized by idiosyncratic use of pitch, of chords, counterpoint, harmony, tempo, and rhythm and incremental leading lines with choral repetitions. Smith's description of the call and response points to the strong influence of these African elements. Lacking instruments, slaves replicated the syncopated rhythms by clapping their hands and patting their feet, or by swaying their heads and bodies, which substantially modified the increasingly austere musical

monality between African and European religion "where mutual reinterpretation and syncretism possibly occurred: ecstatic behavior and magical folk-belief"; see Raboteau, *Slave Religion*, 55–92, especially p. 59. Sterling Stuckey's more recent work, which makes the ring shout the focus of black culture, has renewed the debate over African religious retentions. Although Stuckey suggests that there was "a greater consciousness" of African values among low-country slaves than anywhere else, which he attributes to the concentration of BaKonga peoples in the low country, there is no compelling evidence that the theology of any one group predominated elsewhere. See Stuckey, *Slave Culture*, 43. Rather, the religious concepts that survived were those that most African groups held in common or which had the most functional value under slavery.

[45] Leland, *Virginia Chronicle*, 13; Mederic Louis Elie Moreau de Saint-Mery, *Moreau de Saint-Mery's American Journal (1793–1798)*, Kenneth Roberts and Anna M. Roberts, trans. and eds. (Garden City, N.Y.: Doubleday, 1947), 48; Asbury, *Journal and Letters* 1:89, 222.

[46] James L. Smith, *Autobiography of James L. Smith* (Norwich: Press of the Bulletin Company, 1881), 27.

traditions of white Christians. The simple, powerful camp hymns that swept the South during the Second Great Awakening, represented a new type of song whose message of Christian liberty was a powerful and compelling catalyst of black spiritual expression.[47]

The performance of religious rituals to commemorate momentous events formed the basic locus for the creation of cultural unity and communal solidarity. Christianity introduced a new set of beliefs and practices. Fundamental traditional values were not, however, entirely supplanted, nor for that matter did Christian religious ritual completely take the place of traditional ritual. Instead an adaptation of both Christian and traditional forms produced distinctive ritual patterns through which African-Americans were able to affirm their own separate cultural identity within the continuing process of assimilation. Burial rituals, the principal repositories of slave values, were the most dramatic representation of the new spiritual traditions around which the church community formed.[48]

Because the conditions of burial were often determined by the slave-owner, not all slaves were buried in formal ceremonies. James W. C. Pennington, a Maryland slave who escaped from bondage to become the first African-American to graduate from a European university, remembered that when slaves died, their remains were often consigned to the grave without ceremony.[49] Such documentary sources as exist, however, indicate that traditional burial practices continued in the functioning of the Afro-Christian church. The African custom of mourning and wake-keeping, for example, apparently was incorporated into Christian funerary rites, as the rituals conducted for Aunt Fanny, a Christian slave woman in antebellum Virginia, suggest. As her horrified owners looked on, Aunt Fanny's fellow slaves crowded around the deathbed: "Joining hands they performed a savage dance, shouting wildly around her bed. This was horrible to hear and

[47] Two general histories of African-American music are Eileen Southern, *The Music of Black Americans* (New York: W. W. Norton, 1971), and Dena J. Epstein, *Sinful Tunes and Spirituals: Black Folk Music to the Civil War* (Urbana: University of Illinois Press, 1977); see also Lazarus Ekwueme, "African-Music Retention in the New World," *Black Perspective in Music* 2 (1974): 128–43, and Olly Wilson, "The Significance of the Relationship between Afro-American Music and West African Music," ibid. 2 (1974): 3–22.

[48] The earliest efforts to demonstrate the possible extent of African retentions are John M. Vlach, "Graveyards and Afro-American Art," *Southern Exposure* 5 (1977): 61–65; idem, *The Afro-American Tradition in Decorative Arts* (Cleveland, Ohio: Cleveland Museum of Art, 1978); and Robert Farris Thompson, *Flash of the Spirit* (New York: Vintage Books, 1984), a broader work that shows the influence of five African Civilizations—Yoruba, Kongo, Ejaghan, Mende, and Cross River, on New World cultures; for Kongo-Angolo influences on burial practices, see 132–42. See also Robert Farris Thompson, and Joseph Cornet, *The Four Moments of the Sun: Kongo Art in Two Worlds* (Washington, D.C.: National Gallery of Art, 1981).

[49] *Five Slave Narratives. A Compendium* (New York: Arno Press and the New York Times, 1968), xx, 67.

see," one white witness recalled, "especially as in this family every effort had been made to instruct their negro dependents in the truth of religion."[50] The former slave, Peter Randolph, recalled that slaves in Prince George County kept all-night vigils at which they sang and prayed continuously until the body was interred.[51] The Rhode Island journalist, Hezekiah Butterworth, described similar deathbed rituals in slave cabins in Florida. Called "consolation meetings," they were held when a fellow slave was very ill or near death and consisted of prayers and "wild hymns" sung in the "sweet, weird, haunting cadences" carried from Africa.[52]

The historical relationship between African-American wakes and the all-night vigils in African villages, which sometimes lasted for days or even weeks, is indirect but apparent. In the context of the West African funeral, the aesthetic content is closely connected to the imperatives of ancestor worship. Although ancestors are normally benign or function as guardians of the family, the "wandering dead," who have not yet received a proper funeral, represent a danger to the welfare of the community and even to succeeding generations. Although funeral rituals serve different functions, the first and central purpose of the music and dance is to appease the spirit of the departed ancestor and thereby ward off potential danger.

The ideology of the ancestors is an underlying tenet of African-American death rites as well. The plaintive and poignant songs described by white southerners were almost certainly derived from the musical eulogies sung during West African rites by friends and relatives of the deceased. The "savage dance" performed by African-American slaves was also clearly derived from the ritual dances performed by groups of dancers at West African wakes and funerals. For African-Americans, as for their African forebears, the long period of mourning and the ritualized activities associated with it, served not only to propitiate the dead but to recall the life of the deceased, to provide sustaining support for family and friends, to celebrate, at least symbolically, the human conquest over death, and ultimately, to strengthen social bonds.[53]

The communal mentality is also evident in the insistence of African-American Christians that their own communal leaders conduct burial ser-

[50] Letitia M. Burwell, *Plantation Reminiscences* (n.p.: Page Thacker of Kentucky, 1878), 57.

[51] Peter Randolph, *Sketches of Slave Life* (Boston: Author, 1855), 13.

[52] Hezekiah Butterworth, *A Zigzag Journey in the Sunny South: Or Wonder Tales of Early American History* (Boston: Estes and Lauriat, 1887), 225–31. For a general discussion of mortuary rites, including preparation of the body, the funeral procession, burial sermons, and postburial practices, see David R. Roediger, "And Die in Dixie: Funerals, Death and Heaven in the Slave Community, 1700–1865," *Massachusetts Review* 22 (1981): 163–83.

[53] Lynne F. Emery, *Black Dance in the United States. From 1619 to 1970* (Palo Alto, Calif.: National Press Books, 1972), 40–45, 117–19, discusses funeral dances in the New World. See also Ekwueme, "African-Music Retentions," 131–32.

vices. When white preachers attempted to take over funeral rituals, black Christians resisted. Recognized as the trusted representatives of the slave community by slaves and their owners alike, Virginia's numerous black preachers enjoyed a near monopoly over black funeral preaching. As a missionary to the blacks in Charlotte County, Virginia, John H. Rice observed that when "they are unrestrained by the presence of the whites," black Christians reverted to the "savage customs of Africa." The mourners, Rice disdainfully reported, "cry and bawl, and howl around the grave, and roll in the dirt, and make many expressions of the most frantic grief." Anxious to "put a stop to these things," and to "have it in my power more frequently to preach to the black people," Rice proposed that he preside over all funeral services for black members of his Cub Creek congregation. But, Rice ruefully admitted "this proposal was for some time neglected."[54]

The archaeological record of black church cemeteries and plantation slave cemeteries in the antebellum South confirms a dynamic process of adaptation of both Christian and traditional forms in interment practices. A geographical and chronological comparison of historic and contemporary black burials in coastal and interior parts of South Carolina and in Hanover County, Virginia, reveals a fundamental shift in the culture and ideology of the African-American graveyard.[55] All of the sites show the intrusion of Christian customs: the hexagonal coffin shape, the presence of nails and coffin hardware, and the use of burial shrouds. Beginning in the nineteenth century, the symbolism of the Second Great Awakening began to appear in the form of Bibles, doves, and, on contemporary graves, styrofoam head and foot markers shaped as crosses, lambs, or Bibles.

All sites, however, reveal various expressions of African heritage. Predictably the most abiding evidence of African influence is found in planta-

[54] Report of the Reverend John H. Rice, a Missionary to the Blacks in Charlotte County, Virginia, to the Committee of Missions, in *The Evangelical Intelligencer*, n.s., 3 (1809): 391–92.

[55] The following discussion is based on these sources: for coastal South Carolina see John D. Combes, "Ethnography, Archaeology and Burial Practices among Coastal South Carolina Blacks," *Conference for Historic Site Archaeology Papers* 7 (1974): 52–61; Cynthia Connor, "Sleep on and Take Your Rest": Black Mortuary Behavior on the East Branch on the Cooper River (Master's thesis, University of South Carolina, 1989), an analysis of over eight hundred black and white historic and contemporary burials in an area of the coastal plain of South Carolina some twenty miles north of Charleston. For late nineteenth-century eyewitness accounts, see H. Carrington Bolton, "Decorations of Graves of Negroes in South Carolina," *Journal of American Folk-Lore* 4 (1891): 214, and Ernest Ingersoll, "Decoration of Negro Graves," *Journal of American Folk-Lore* 5 (1892): 68–69. For a general discussion of the subject, see Elizabeth A. Fenn, "Honoring the Ancestors. Kongo-American Graves in the American South," *Southern Exposure* 13 (1984): 42–47. The Virginia burials were analyzed by the author. I am grateful to Reber Dunkel for calling the sites to my attention and to George Winston, deacon of the Providence Baptist Church near Ashland, for taking me to the Hickory Hill Plantation site.

tion slave cemeteries, most of which were located in groves or densely wooded areas, traditionally considered to be sacred abodes of spirits. Graves, most of them visible only as depressions in the ground, are randomly arranged and are invariably dug east and west, with many of the graves intruding through previous burials. At the Charles Towne Landing low-country site, several burials, especially of children, are facedown, a technique to trick malevolent spirits. In South Carolina the African aesthetic perspective is apparent in the presence of grave goods. The practice of marking graves with a wide assortment of material possessions—common among the BaKongo peoples of central Africa, and the roughly equivalent practice of honoring the dead with ceramic ornaments among the Akan people of Ghana and the Ivory Coast—was widespread at coastal and interior burial sites in South Carolina, although it was not apparent in Virginia. The interaction of various African cultures is, however, visible in the common practice of marking graves with living plants and, in a significant number of cases, with cedar trees, which in traditional religion often function as a symbolic representation of the immortal spirit of the deceased.[56] Wooden markers, possibly representing the rudimentary human form, appear on graves in Middleburg and Charles Towne Landing in South Carolina and at the Hickory Hill plantation cemetery near Ashland in Hanover County, Virginia. Similar in design to the wooden headmarkers described by John Vlach, they are perhaps related to the West African woodworking tradition, which commonly utilizes the human form, or to the wooden grave sculptures found in the BaKongo region of Africa.[57]

The perpetuation of traditional belief elements is also apparent in the continuance of the second funeral, which was by the nineteenth century an established custom in Virginia.[58] According to William E. Hatcher, the white pastor of the Grace Street Baptist Church of Richmond, "There was one thing which the negor greatly insisted upon . . . that their dead [not] be put away without a funeral." Masters often gave slaves a day "of their own choosing" to celebrate the funeral because a service at the time of burial "was never according to their notions." Consequently the all-day service usually took place several weeks after the burial. Conducted by funeral preachers like the celebrated John Jasper of Fluvanna County, the service was ordinarily held in the woods and was attended by hundreds of slaves from the surrounding area, who came to "sing and dance and drink

[56] Thompson, *Four Moments of the Sun*, 190.

[57] Vlach, "Graveyards and Afro-American Art," 164; Vlach, *Afro-American Tradition in Decorative Arts*, 145–47, 117–19.

[58] Raboteau, *Slave Religion*, 231, briefly discusses the funeral sermon, or second funeral, but he concludes only that it is "difficult to say whether the practice reflected an African system of multiple funerals or was simply a necessity dictated by the uncertainty of permission and the lack of time available to slaves to attend such services."

the dead to his new home, which some believe to be in old Guinea."[59] Even as members of biracial churches, African-Americans showed remarkable resistance to changes in ancestor-related funeral practices. Church minutes frequently complain of the "disorder" at black funerals, of competition among black preachers "as to whose privilege it is to preach," and of the libation and dancing, which in traditional African practice dramatized the belief in the return of the deceased to the land of the ancestors, the continuity and culmination of the life cycle, which all members of the community were expected to celebrate.[60]

As graveyard ideology suggests, many African-Americans continued to hold to the standard African concept of death as a transition to a hereafter, which they viewed as a continuation of sorts, of life in its human form.[61] Growing numbers of African-American Christians had, however, come to accept the orthodox Christian position on the hereafter, the final judgment, resurrection, heaven and hell. By contrast to the Christian view of death as a punishment for the fall of man, traditional African religion held that God's punishment is imposed in this life, usually in the form of personal misfortunes or family or community catastrophes. Except for the Yorubas, who believed in a future righteous judgment,[62] most Africans expected neither judgment nor reward in the hereafter.[63]

The orthodox Christian position that faithful service and meek resigna-

[59] For nineteenth century descriptions of slave funerals see Hatcher, *John Jasper*, 37–38; Adam Hodgson, Esq., *Remarks During a Journey through North America in the Years 1819, 1820, and 1821. In A Series of Letters* (Westport, Conn.: Negro Universities Press, 1970), 14; Henry Cogswell Knight, *Letters from the South and West; By Arthur Singleton, Esq.* [pseud.] (Boston: Richardson and Lord, JHA Frost, 1827), 77; Robert Sears, ed., *A New and Popular Pictorial Description of the United States* (New York: Author, 1848), 348. Randolph, *Sketches of Slave Life*, 14, is a slave account.

[60] *Minutes of the Baptist Dover Association*, 1821; April, 1791, Berryville (Buck Marsh) Baptist Church Minutes; May 6, 1827, Welsh Neck Baptist Church Minutes. For African traditional practices, see Parrinder, *West African Religion*, 106–7; Zahan, *Religion, Spirituality and Thought*, 44. It is possible, as Mechal Sobel has observed, that the second funeral of blacks influenced white burial pratices. By the late eighteenth century visitors to Virginia had begun to remark on the delayed funeral services among whites. At a loss to explain the unusual custom, nineteenth-century travelers attributed it to an earlier period when clergy were scarce and burials had to await their arrival. Inasmuch as whites adopted other African-American practices at their graveyards and burials, it is entirely conceivable that the delayed funeral was of Afro-American origin.

[61] Robert C. Mclean, ed., "A Yankee Tutor in the Old South," *North Carolina Historical Review* 47 (1970): 64; Henry Benjamin Whipple, *Bishop Whipple's Southern Diary, 1843–1844*, Lester B. Shippen, ed. (New York: Da Capo Press, 1968), 21.

[62] Jonathan Olumide Lucas, *The Religion of the Yorubas* (Lagos, Nigeria: CMS Bookshops, 1948), 256.

[63] Mbiti, *African Religions and Philosophy*, 161, 210; idem, *Death and the Hereafter in the Light of Christianity and African Religion* (Kampala: Department of Religious Studies and Philosophy, Makerere University, 1974), 11–12.

tion to the sorrows of this world would lead to bliss in the next was clearly consolatory to many slaves. But while African-American Christians accepted the notion that goodness was to be compensated, they also believed that evil was to be punished. What issued from this was a distinctive vision of heaven formulated to suit the slaves' special psychic needs. Encouraged by white Christian preachers to look forward to the day when all distinctions of color and condition would be abolished and they would find equality in the sight of God and peace in the company of their masters, mistresses, and even overseers, slaves eagerly embraced the idea of eternal rest from earthly sufferings, but, as the slave Charles Ball writes, "they by no means so willingly admit the master and mistress to an equal participation in their enjoyments." Instead of perfect equality slaves expected a revolution in the conditions of master and slave; instead of reconciliation they expected revenge, for did not the Bible everywhere lay down "that those who have possessed the good things of this world, and have lived in ease and luxury, at the expense of their fellow men, will surely have to render an account of their stewardship, and be punished, for having withheld from others the participation of those blessings, which they themselves enjoyed."[64]

African-American Christians' moral preference for justice over equality, which is embodied in the idea of a social revolution in paradise, was according to Ball "the cornerstone" of the slaves' religious creed. Disseminated in "the religious meetings of the slaves themselves," it bears witness to the fact that the white Christian argument that one race could legitimately enslave another race was considered by African-American Christians to be both morally repugnant and sinful. This represents a divergence not only from the traditional Christian view but also from the traditional African view in favor of the radical biblical interpretation offered by religious antislavery forces. According to the slave Lunsford Lane, a Baptist convert, one "very kind hearted Episcopal minister," was extremely popular with slaves. But "after he had preached a sermon to us in which he argued from the Bible that it was the will of heaven for all eternity we should be slaves, and our masters be our owners, most of us left him; for like some of the faith hearted disciples in early times we said,—'This is a hard saying, who can bear it.' "[65]

In the logic of the fundamental proposition that justice enjoyed a biblically preferred position, slaves found justification for their own distinctive concepts of social morality. In some instances they redefined Christian notions of morality in their own terms. Running away is a case in point. In their search for a way to harmonize the historic Christian faith of the Bible

[64] Ball, *Slavery in the United States*, 169–71.
[65] *Five Slave Narratives*, 21.

with the needs of plantation society, white evangelicals fell upon Paul's Epistle to Philemon, in which Paul sent Onesimus, a runaway slave, back to Philemon, his owner. They found moral justification for the more sweeping claim to slave loyalty, even to a vicious and inhumane master, in the biblical story of the bondwoman Hagar, who fled from an abusive owner only to be commanded by an angel of the Lord to return and become submissive. The influence of Christian instruction did persuade some slaves to acquiesce in their bondage and to look upon loyalty as a religious commitment. Josiah Henson, a slave who lived on a farm near Port Tobacco, Maryland, wrote that despite a passion for freedom, "I had never dreamed of running away," which Henson ascribed to his long tutelage by "ministers and religious men," on "the duties of the slave to his master as appointed over him in the Lord. . . ." Henson's acceptance of the white Christian doctrine of endurance and submission had tragic consequences for his fellow slaves.

In 1825 Henson's financially strapped owner instructed his faithful slave to lead all of his other slaves to his brother's farm in Kentucky, where they would be free from the claims of creditors. Traveling with a pass from his owner, Henson led nearly two hundred slaves, including his own wife and two children, through Virginia to Harper's Ferry and over the mountains via the National Turnpike to Wheeling. At Cincinnati, "crowds" of free blacks tried to dissuade them from surrendering themselves to a new owner and to claim freedom instead. Blind to the ironies and hypocrisies of the situation, Henson delivered himself, his family and his fellow slaves back into bondage. Only after it was too late, did Henson appreciate the cost of his loyalty: "my soul has been pierced with bitter anguish at the thought of having been thus instrumental in consigning to the infernal bondage of slavery so many of my fellow-beings."[66]

From all indications, however, the assimilation of the white Christian doctrine of the duty of servants to their masters did not proceed very far. Thousands of slaves, like the half-white Henry Bibb, "learned the art of running away to perfection . . . made a regular business of it, and never gave it up," until they achieved freedom or died trying. Bibb's owner "tried to speculate on my Christian character" to prospective buyers "to make it appear that I was so pious and honest that I would not runaway for ill treatment, which was," Bibb defiantly declared, "a gross mistake, for I never had religion enough to keep me from running away from slavery in my life."[67] Others, like the Virginia-born slave William Grimes, turned to Scripture to refute white Christian arguments for religious acquiescence in slavery. After he was severely abused by a series of masters, Grimes fled

[66] Henson, *Father Henson's Story*, 53.
[67] Bibb, *Narrative*, 102.

from his Savannah owner by hiding out on the Boston brig *Casket*. Befriended by Yankee sailors, he escaped to freedom in Connecticut. But Grimes' conscience troubled him and so he "went up on a high mountain, and prayed to the Lord, to teach me my duty, that I might know whether or not I ought to go back to my master." Picking his way through the maze of contradictions between the teaching and the practice of Christian slaveowners, Grimes came down from the mountain satisfied "that the Lord heard my prayers, when I was a poor wretched slave, and delivered me out of the land of Egypt, and out of the house of bondage, and that it was his hand, and not my own artfulness and cunning, which had enabled me to escape."[68]

Anthony Burns, who later became a symbol in the struggle between North and South over the issue of fugitive slaves, not only ran away but discovered in the religion of his oppressors justification for doing so. Impelled to action by his own expulsion from a white Virginia Baptist church for the sin of running away, Burns began by challenging the usual references to St. Paul's letter to Philemon. St. Paul had sent Onesimus back to Philemon not as a slave, Burns insisted, but rather "that he should be no longer a slave, but a brother beloved unto his former master." Burns's efforts to resolve the apparent contradiction between the principle inculcated by St. Paul and the story of Hagar led him to undertake an exegesis of Scripture. The same ambiguities in Christianity that nurtured proslavery defenses served as the theological groundwork for Burns' antislavery attack. The Bible, Burns concluded, " set forth only one God for the black and the white races, that He had made of one blood all the nations of the earth, that there was no divine ordinance requiring one part of the human family to be in bondage to another." Further Burns insisted "that there was no passage of Holy Writ by virtue of which Col. Suttle [Burns' owner] could claim a right of property in him, any more than he could in Col. Suttle." His biblical arguments reverberating with the secular rhythms of natural rights, Burns rejoiced that "Paul was on his side, [and] the whole spirit of the Gospel sanctioned his desires. . . . From that moment, with a clear conscience and full integrity of Christian character, he applied himself to the recovery of his inalienable right to liberty and the pursuit of happiness." To the Virginia congregation that had expelled him Burns defiantly wrote, "God made me a man, not a slave, and gave me the same right to myself that he gave the man who stole me to himself."[69]

In their attitudes toward property, African-American Christians drew a fine ideological distinction between stealing and taking.[70] "I never was ac-

---

[68] Grimes, *Life of William Grimes*, 28–29.

[69] Charles Emery Stevens, *Anthony Burns. A History* (New York: Arno Press and the New York Times, 1969), 174–75.

[70] See Schwarz, *Twice Condemned*, 214.

quainted with a slave who believed that he violated any rule of morality, by appropriating to himself any thing that belonged to his master if it was necessary to his comfort," the slave Charles Ball avowed.[71] What to their owners was a deliberate act of sinfulness was to slaves part of a moral struggle to win support for themselves and those they cared for. "No white knight, rescuing fair white ones from cruel oppression, ever felt the throbbing of a chivalrous heart more intensely than I, a *black* knight, did, in running down a chicken in an out-of-the-way place to hide till dark and then carry to some poor overworked black fair one, to whom it was at once food, luxury, and medicine," the Maryland slave Josiah Henson proudly pronounced. "No Scotch borderer, levying black mail or sweeping off a drove of cattle, ever felt more assured of the justice of his act than I of mine, in driving a mile or two into the woods a pig or a sheep, and slaughtering it for the good of those Riley [the slaveowner] was starving. I felt good, moral, heroic."[72]

Like thousands of other slaves, Henson was a man of deep religious convictions. The fact that he recognized no moral guilt for robbing his master was due not to the absence of ethical convictions but rather to the fact that they were at variance with the white religious perspective. "The slave sees his master residing in a spacious mansion, riding in a fine carriage, and dressed in costly clothes, and attributes the possession of all these enjoyments to his own labor; while he who is the cause of so much gratification and pleasure to another, is himself deprived of even the necessary accommodations of human life," Charles Ball explained.[73] The accuracy of Ball's testimony is confirmed by white church records.

Although Baptist congregations generally punished slave thievery by excommunication, black church members openly repudiated white morality and with equal moral earnestness defended slave "thievery" as compatible with God's law and with natural law. The records of the Goshen Association of Virginia are full and explicit on this point. In October 1816 the minutes declared "that many Coloured persons, who are Members of our Church, hold the abominable opinion that it is no crime, in the sight of God, to steal their master's property, arguing that it is taking their own labour; . . . many of them, acting upon this principle, have thereby brought great reproach upon the cause of Religion." The association therefore recommended to member churches that each "call upon their Coloured Members one by one, to avow their opinions upon this point, and where this opinion is avowed and the party cannot be convinced of his or

---

71 Ball, *Slavery in the United States*, 231.
72 Henson, *Father Henson's Story*, 21–22.
73 Ball, *Slavery in the United States*, 231.

her error, after full and fair investigation, that they exclude them from their fellowship."[74]

Although African-American Christians believed that they were entitled to the product of their own labor, they condemned theft from a member of the slave community as an offense against the community. Each slave community probably had its own form of punishment for various offenses. According to Jacob Stroyer, born of African slave parents on a South Carolina plantation near Columbia, slaves on the Singleton plantation had different ways of detecting thieves. One method involved a Bible suspended from a string, which was attached to a stick held by one member of a four-man examining committee. During the formal testing process, one member of the committee informed the suspect of the charges, a second pronounced his guilt, a third his innocence. The fourth held the suspended Bible while reciting three times the incantation: "Bible, in the name of the Father and of the Son and of the Holy Ghost, if [John] stole that chicken, turn." A turning Bible was taken as proof of guilt.[75] A variation of the same practice, known as the "sifter ordeal," was still being performed near the turn of the century. Significantly, the sifter turner was usually a prominent member of the church and the incantation invoked the saints: "By St. Peter, by St. Paul, by the Lord who made us all, if John Doe did thus and so, Turn, sifter, turn and fall."[76] Another method of detection involved a concoction of dust from a recent grave, mixed with water. The same testing process was used with a similar incantation: "In the name of the Father, and the Son and the Holy Ghost, if you have taken Sam's

---

[74] October, 1816, Goshen Baptist Association Minutes. Historians have recognized the disjunction between the moral precepts held by Christian slaveowners and those held by Christian slaves, particularly where theft was concerned. Raboteau, *Slave Religion*, 295–96, attributes slave attitudes to practical concerns and to a disdain for white hypocrisy; Creel, *A Peculiar People*, 238–39, notes that Gullahs viewed theft as a violation of the "collective interests and values." In fact, the African-American concept of property might have had African ethical antecedents. Among most West African peoples, title to all land was theoretically vested in the king or chief. In actual practice, the land belonged to the community collectively. The concept of private property was recognized to the extent that individual households were entitled to use land as required for agricultural purposes, and to ownership of the house built, the trees planted, the produce grown, and the utensils made or used. Unused land was open to anyone in the chiefdom for hunting or fishing, and uncultivated or overgrown land usually reverted to the community. See Melville J. Herskovits, *Dahomey. An Ancient West African Kingdom*, 2 vols. (New York: J. J. Augustin, 1938), 1:51–63, 78–98; Alfred B. Ellis, *The Yoruba-Speaking Peoples of the Slave Coast of West Africa* (Oosterhout (N.B.), Netherlands Anthropological Publications, 1966), 188–89; Samuel Johnson, *The History of the Yorubas*, 5th ed. (Lagos, Nigeria: CMS Bookshops, 1950). A similar concept of property also persisted in the French West Indian islands, where Dahomean influence preponderated; see Gwendolyn Midlo Hall, *Social Control in Slave Plantation Societies. A Comparison of St. Domingue and Cuba* (Baltimore, Md.: Johns Hopkins University Press, 1971), 66–67.

[75] *Five Slave Narratives*, 57–59.

[76] "Folk-Lore Scrap-Book," *Journal of American Folk-Lore* 5 (1892): 63.

chicken don't drink this water, for if you do you will die and go to hell and be burned in fire and brimstone, but if you have not you may take it and it will not hurt you."[77]

All three rituals are clearly divinatory techniques, analogous if not identical to divination methods found among all West African peoples. A religious activity, divination was used to comfort, advise, council, warn, and judge people, as well as to reveal secrets, including theft. Methods and paraphernalia varied widely and some systems, such as the highly developed Yoruba *Ifa*, used symbols, verses and couplets, the mastery of which required years of training. The conditions of slavery required slaves to find substitutes for the elaborate paraphernalia and to forego the prolonged formal training. But belief in the art of divination as a psychological process and as a religious activity clearly survived both the destructive effects of slavery and the transforming power of Christianity.[78] The rituals present a compelling study of beliefs and practices of a religious culture in transition.

In the Bible ritual it is difficult to tell where traditional religion ends and Christian belief begins. The incorporation of the Bible as a symbolic representation of the Christian deity implies acceptance of the potency and efficacy of the Christian God. The ritual form is, however, unmistakably West African. Although Christianized paraphernalia and incantations were used, both were ultimately derived from West African prototypes. The African belief that offenses against the community must be punished by the corporate community of the living and the dead is strikingly present in the use of graveyard dust to identify a thief. Among many West African societies ancestral spirits were regarded as guardians of moral values and tribal ethics, their graves functioning, in the words of Robert F. Thompson, "as an unseen court of last appeal," to which the aggrieved might repair to seek vengeance.[79] Fear of the moral vengeance of the dead was a powerful force for moral order in the slave community as it was in the ancestral African village.

At the same time that Afro-Christianity provided the context for the continuation of relevant traditional norms, it also helped to promote an alternative set of values. This was accomplished through the introduction of different values, first to individual converts, then to the larger population by the converts themselves. The cumulative modification of existing

[77] *Five Slave Narratives*, 57–59.

[78] Mbiti, *African Religions and Philosophy*, 177; J. Omosade Awolalu, *West African Traditional Relgion* (Ibadan, Nigeria: Onibonoje, 1979), 146–49; Philip M. Peek, "The Divining Chain in Southern Nigeria," in Simon Ottenberg, ed., *African Religious Groups and Beliefs: Papers in Honor of William R. Bascom* (Meerut, India: Archana Publications, c. 1982), 187–209.

[79] Mbiti, *African Religions and Philosophy*, 207, 213; Thompson, *Four Moments of the Sun*, 186.

indigenous values that resulted is apparent in changing marital values. Although it is risky to extrapolate from white records a pattern of black behavior, disciplinary records from biracial churches offer compelling evidence that although in general slave converts received evangelical beliefs, many continued to reject the Christian ideal of monogamous fidelity. Fidelity assumed a more or less equal sex ratio or the alternatives of celibacy or infidelity; many opted instead in favor of African marriage forms, which were uniquely appropriate to the conditions of slavery. Approximately one-third of all the offenses involving black members of seventeen Virginia Baptist churches concerned some aspect of plantation discipline. Offenses involving sexual behavior account for nearly two-thirds of the rest. The most common transgressions among black Baptists in South Carolina's biracial churches were adultery and "double marriage."[80]

The persistence of African prototypes was largely the result of a conscious selection of cultural behavior that had positive value for survival. By 1800 the sex ratio was equal in the tidewater of Virginia but there were roughly 120 men per 100 women in the piedmont.[81] Although the postwar trend was toward larger plantation units, many Chesapeake slaves still lived on small or middling units[82] and nearly half of South Carolina's slave population lived on plantations of fewer than fifty slaves.[83] Slaves often had to find partners on neighboring plantations. In states such as Georgia, where the the numbers of men and women were equal on only about 17 percent of estates, roughly half of the slave mothers listed in colonial inventories analyzed by Betty Wood were living apart from their husbands.[84] Moreover, during the postwar period the slave population was in a constant state of flux due to the growing practice of hiring slaves out. The forced migration of tidewater slaves to the new Southwest in the postrevolutionary era permanently disrupted the lives of thousands of black fami-

---

[80] June 4, 1803, January 2, 1812, Big Creek Baptist Church Minutes; June 1810, August 1815, February 1825, Big Stephens Creek Baptist Church Minutes; January 19, 1822, October 20, 1822, September 3, 1823, Society Hill (formerly Welsh Neck) Baptist Church Minutes; October, 1819, October 17, 1828, Lower Fork Lynches Creek Baptist Church Minutes; January 9, 1808, Turkey Creek Baptist Church, Abbeville County, South Carolina, 1785–1869, SCBHS; November, 1808, Albemarle Association Minutes, 1815–1840; May 18, 1774, August 24, 1782, March 22, 1783, July 7, 1805, Broad Run Baptist Church Minutes, 1762–1872, October 2, 1811, Carmel Baptist Church Minutes, 1799–1819; December 1811, August 1812, Lyles (Albemarle) Baptist Church Minutes, 1800–1835; April 19, 1794, April 20, 1799, Mill Swamp Baptist Church Minutes, VBHS; July 1829, Records of the Little Ogeechee Baptist Church, Stetson Memorial Library. For Gullah attitudes toward sex and marriage, see Creel, *A Peculiar People*, 245–47.

[81] Morgan, "Slave Life in the Virginia Piedmont," figure 1. For the size of plantation units, see Kulikoff, *Tobacco and Slaves*, 337–38.

[82] Dunn, "Black Society in the Chesapeake," 69–70.

[83] Morgan, "Black Society," 93.

[84] Wood, "Some Aspects of Female Resistance," 606–7, 609.

lies.[85] Gifts of slaves to married sons and particularly to daughters to provide a measure of economic security frequently splintered slave families.[86]

Under these conditions, African family types were more functional than the European-based conjugal type. Summoned by their churches to answer charges of adultery or polygamy, Christian slaves defended their distinctive life-styles with a brand of morality derived from African culture and reinforced by the social environment of slavery. The case of Bob is representative. Bob, the Christian slave of a Christian master, Jerome Millar, lived in Lane Creek, South Carolina, where he married a slave woman "according to costom of slaves." Subsequently Millar moved to Skull Shoals and took Bob with him, leaving behind Bob's wife and child, who apparently lived on another plantation. After settling in Skull Shoals both Bob and his master were baptized into the Baptist fellowship at Skull Shoals (Pacolet). Shortly thereafter Bob remarried without seeking permission of the church.

In keeping with typical Baptist practice of watching over one another's morals, a church conference summoned Bob to answer charges of violating church discipline. Bob frankly admitted having taken a second wife because he "had it not in his power to stay with or near his [first] wife," and he did not think that the church would "exclude him from marriage when he served his master in faithfulness, and leaving his former wife and child on the account of the love he had for his master." Perceiving their obligation to promote stable slave marriages as morally requisite, the church conference persuaded Millar to sell Bob so that he could live with, or at least near, his first wife. Bob, motivated perhaps by a calculated awareness that his situation might deteriorate under a new owner, refused, explaining that he "thought it most advisable as a Slave to serve a Christian master, and one he was acquainted with and loved," rather than risk the uncertainty of life with a new owner. The conference then asked if Bob would put away his second wife and return to the first provided that he could be sold to a Christian master. Bob's response indicates that although his theological learning was not profound, he clearly believed that the social structure of slavery validated his morals: "He answered he was not willing to change his master for any Christian master as he thought there was not that happiness enjoyed between the Christian slave and his wife as there was between the Christian freeman and his wife and believed he did not sin against the Lord in taking a wife when his master moved him from his former wife." For his refusal to acknowledge his sin as well as for his "self-sufficiency" and lack of a "humble spirit," Bob was excommunicated. Twenty years later Bob, "professing to be restored from his backsliding,"

[85] Kulikoff, "Uprooted Peoples," 359.
[86] See Lee, "Problem of Slave Community," 333–61.

asked for reinstatement, but the church "agreed that their non-fellowship is yet with Bob until satisfaction can be obtained."[87] As Bob's defense of double marriages suggests, it was not weakness in the slave family that afflicted slave society. The problem of double marriage was one of the crippling consequences of slavery.

The logic implicit in Bob's argument, that norms and customs from traditional society were appropriate because alternative norms were unavailable or unacceptable, was ultimately accepted by the evangelical churches, which grappled unsuccessfully with the problem before reluctantly accommodating to the social realities of slavery. Unable to agree, the association in 1794 ordered the query expunged from the record.[88] In 1792 the Strawberry Association discussed the feasibility of allowing slaves to remarry following involuntary separation. Although it disapproved the practice, the association declined either to recommend separation of the offending couple or to expel them from the church.[89] In 1817 the Shiloh Association also took up the question, but, unable to agree on a recommendation, passed responsibility on to the individual churches.[90] Two years later the Accomac Association adopted a forthright policy that declared that in the event that involuntary separation precluded the possibility of ever being united, "under such a peculiar situation, the wife may be considered as dead to her husband, and that he can marry again without committing adultery."[91] The Goshen Association considered whether separation for a period of seven or eight years effectively dissolved the marriage of a slave couple, but decided to leave the matter to the discretion of the individual churches.[92]

During the 1820s the Welsh Neck Baptist Church of South Carolina also engaged in prolonged soul searching over the pervasive problem of "double marriages" by black members. In meeting after meeting the small planters prayed and deliberated over how to integrate black members into the community of shared norms. Finally they settled upon a basically pragmatic solution. In deference to the "memory of the Fathers of the Church" in South Carolina, who had sanctioned plural marriages, they decided to retain in fellowship black members who were received into the church in that condition. Setting aside their moral concerns, they also agreed to al-

[87] May 19, 1798, April 20, 1799, July 18, 1819, Skull Shoals (Pacolet) Baptist Church, Cherokee County, Minutes, 1785–1805, SCBHS. See also Janet Cornelius, "Slave Marriages in a Georgia Congregation," in Burton and McMath, eds., *Class, Conflict and Consensus*, 128–45. Cornelius's study of Midway Congregational Church records in the antebellum period reveals the persistence of these marital patterns.

[88] May 26, 1792, May, 1794, Portsmouth (Virginia) Association Minutes, VBHS.

[89] 1792, Strawberry Association Minutes, VBHS.

[90] 1817, Shiloh Baptist Association Minutes, 1804–1839, VBHS.

[91] 1819, Accomac Association Minutes, 1815–1824, VBHS.

[92] October, 1819, Goshen Baptist Association Minutes.

low slave couples who were involuntarily separated by their owners and lived at such a distance from one another as to "be considered as virtually dead to one another," to take a second spouse while the first still lived.[93]

The progressive integration of slaves into the community of shared marital norms was, to a large extent, the achievement of black churches. The principal social authority in the slave community, the black church functioned as an adaptive institution. Such church records as survive suggest that black churches enjoyed increasing success in their efforts to inculcate Christian marital ideals. Although the state did not recognize legal marriages, black Baptist churches published bans and encouraged a Christian ceremony. Anthony Burns regularly performed the marriage rite for slaves.[94] Andrew Bryan required candidates for baptism to furnish proof of marriage or to be married in the church.[95] After joining George Liele's black Baptist congregation, many Jamaican slaves, who had once "lived in the sinful state of fornication," married and "put away that deadly sin."[96] Religious ceremonies clearly comforted and sustained black families and in some cases, perhaps, acted as a constraint upon masters. The former Maryland slave, James W. C. Pennington, observed that after obtaining permission to marry according to slave custom, some slaves on his master's plantation "would ask further leave to go to a minister and be married."[97] Pennington himself performed the marriage ceremony that united Anna Murray, a free black woman, and Frederick Douglass, the ex-slave abolitionist.[98]

Church deacons exercised primary responsibility for preserving stable marital relationships. Although black preachers and deacons performed many of the same functions as their white counterparts, in matters of church discipline their powers were more extensive. In some black churches, deacons had exclusive control over disciplinary matters. Reports of misconduct were investigated by the deacons, who also conducted the trials and determined penalties for those found guilty of infractions. Deacons worked hard to reconcile differences between married couples and to reform sinners, but church members who violated the norms of marital fidelity were punished by immediate expulsion from the church. In recognition of the realities of slavery and in keeping with traditional custom,

[93] December 2, [1828], January 2, 18, 31, [1829], Welsh Neck Baptist Church Minutes. See also April, 1832, Records of the Little Ogeechee Baptist Church, and October, 1809, 1825, 1833, Minutes of the Georgia Baptist Association, Georgia, 1803–1905, Stetson Memorial Library, Macon, Ga.

[94] Stevens, *Anthony Burns*, 167.

[95] Simms, *First Colored Baptist Church*, 44.

[96] "Rise of the Early Negro Churches," 88.

[97] *Five Slave Narratives*, 68.

[98] Frederick Douglass, *Narrative of the Life of Frederick Douglass, An American Slave. Written By Himself* (New York: New American Library, 1968), 113.

black churches, like their white counterparts, granted divorces to slaves whose marriages were broken by forced separation.[99] By thus promoting stable marital relationships, black churches contributed significantly to the preservation of the ideal of family life, the bedrock of social stability in the quarters.

The concept of the family, which survived the massive disruptions of separation and forced migration, found reinforcement within the evangelical structure, wherein individuals viewed one another as brothers and sisters. Fictive kinship ties, consonant with the African belief that the individual exists only as a member of a large and intrinsically interrelated social group, such as the clan, bound the family into the community and extended it beyond the bounds of affinal and consanguinal kinship. Family ties thus became a crucial link in the chain of the developing black community. Through the church communion, socioreligious networks were developed, linking disparate individuals and groups into new and different sets of social relationships, which in certain respects replicated or replaced tribal organization.

Care for members of the community, central to the internal values of African society, functioned as the core of developing African-American community life. Associations for mutual self-help characterized all phases of life among West African peoples. Diverse types of societies, ranging from weavers' cooperatives to communal burial societies, were traditionally composed of persons who belonged to the same sib or extended family.[100] There are no known instances of exact replication of the large corporate kin groups and structured associations among African-Americans. African-Americans did, however, adapt this social organization to the black community in an innovative manner to reassert some of the social solidarity that had operated in Africa and to carry out similar social and economic functions.

In both the North and the South, this inherited cooperative spirit provided the cultural motivation for the development of organized social life among African-Americans.[101] The urban African-American churches and free urban blacks, who usually had strong links with the church, provided the leadership for the establishment of schools, beneficial societies, and burial societies. The tradition of education for blacks arose under the spon-

[99] O'Brien, "Factory, Church and Community," 528–30; June 2, June 24, June 30, July 15, August 3, October 13, 1827, Gillfield Baptist Church Records, 1817–1939, Alderman Library, University of Virginia, Charlottesville, Microfilm.

[100] Herskovits, *Dahomey* 1:75–77; Lucas, *Religion of the Yorubas*, 198–99, 228.

[101] For the development of northern black communities, see Gary B. Nash, *Forging Freedom: The Formation of Philadelphia's Black Community, 1720–1840* (Cambridge, Mass.: Harvard University Press, 1988); and William Dillon Piersen, *Black Yankees* (Amherst: University of Massachusetts Press, 1988).

sorship of a variety of institutions and agencies. The groundwork was laid by the Society for the Propagation of the Gospel as part of the efforts of the Church of England to encourage the conversion of Negroes and Indians. The school established in Charleston by the Reverend Alexander Garden in 1743 provided a rudimentary education for the children of free blacks until it closed its doors in 1764.[102] During the 1790s, Methodist Sunday schools were established in a number of places. Usually located near the church, they offered instruction to black "scholars" from books compiled by the church council.[103]

Although the early white schools were not particularly successful, education quickly developed as part of the function of the black churches. In Kingston, Jamaica, George Liele organized a free school for children, both slave and free, which had a black deacon as a schoolmaster. A number of adults in Liele's congregation were also taught to read and "all are desirous to learn."[104] Members of Gowan Pamphlet's African church in Williamsburg also learned how to write and kept their own church records.[105] Approximately fifty members of Bryan's African Baptist church in Savannah were taught to read the Bible, the Baptist Confession of Faith, and some of Bunyan's works, among other things. In cooperation with the white Independent Presbyterian church of Savannah, the First African Baptist Church established the first sabbath school in the city and taught an average of two hundred students.[106] Three were able to write. Henry Francis also conducted a school for black children in Georgia.[107] Almost all Virginia cities with large black populations, among them Alexandria, Petersburg, Fredericksburg, and Richmond, operated sabbath schools. By 1821 there were approximately six hundred children enrolled in Sunday schools in Baltimore.[108]

In addition to the church-operated sabbath schools, which served both the slave and free populations, a number of schools were established under the auspices of denominational societies and beneficial organizations, the members of which were frequently connected with one of the African churches but whose activities were confined to relieving poverty and operating schools to serve the free black community. The first mutual self-

[102] C. W. Birnie, "Education of the Negro in Charleston, South Carolina Prior to the Civil War," *Journal of Negro History* 12 (1927): 13–14.

[103] Lee, *Short History*, 162–63.

[104] "Rise of the Early Negro Churches," 72, 73.

[105] Semple, *History*, 115.

[106] Edgar Garfield Thomas, *The First African Church of North America* (Savannah, Ga.: n.p., 1925), 48. See also Rippon, *Baptist Annual Register* (1790), 342, 541.

[107] Rippon, *Baptist Annual Register* (1790–93), 342; "Rise of the Early Negro Churches," 83, 87.

[108] Luther Jackson, "Early Strivings of the Negro in Virginia," *Journal of Negro History* 25 (1940): 32–33; Hodgson, *Remarks*, 55.

help association was the Free African Society of Philadelphia, organized in 1787 by Absalom Jones, an Episcopal preacher, and Richard Allen, founder of the African Methodist Episcopal church. A benevolent organization whose members made monthly contributions for the support of the needy, the Free African Society was the model for similar societies in other northern cities.[109] The first step in the development of an organized social life among African-Americans in the South was made by members of the economically independent free black community, who with the black churches laid concurrently the basis for benevolent associations, schools, and burial societies.

The pioneer benefit society in the South was formed in Charleston in 1790. Composed exclusively of free brown men, the society maintained a continuous existence for over a hundred years, after which time it became known as the Century Fellowship Society.[110] Within a year after the Brown Society was established, a group of free blacks responded to the exclusionist organization by forming the Free Dark Men of Color, or Humane Brotherhood. In 1803 the Minors' Moralist Society was established by James Mitchell, Joseph Humphries, William Cooper, Carlos Huger, Thomas S. Bonneau, William Clark, and Richard Holloway, all free black men associated with the Charleston Methodist society.[111] Among the largest and best-known schools in Charleston was that operated by Bonneau until his death in 1828 or 1829. The school was later operated by Daniel Payne, who subsequently became a bishop of the African Methodist Episcopal church. Before 1833 a number of other benevolent associations were established in Charleston, some as auxiliaries to the church. Among them were the Friendly Union, the Brotherly, the Unity and Friendship, the Cumberland Society, the Asbury Association, and the Capers Missionary Society.[112]

In Virginia benefit societies generally functioned as auxiliaries to the African church. The earliest society was formed in Richmond in 1815 as the Burying Ground Society of the Free People of Color of the City of Richmond. The Beneficial Society of Free Men of Color of the City of Petersburg was established about the same time and enjoyed continuous growth up to the Civil War.[113] In Richmond the First African church established

[109] Leo McGee, "Early Efforts Toward Educating the Black Adult," *Negro History Bulletin* 34 (1971): 88–89.
[110] E. Horace Fitchett, "The Traditions of the Free Negro in Charleston, South Carolina," *Journal of Negro History* 25 (1940): 144.
[111] Daniel A. Payne, *Recollections of Seventy Years* (reprint, New York: Arno Press and the New York Times, 1968), 14.
[112] Birnie, "Education of the Negro," 15–16.
[113] Jackson, "Early Strivings of the Negro," 33; Browning, "Beginnings of Insurance Enterprise," 429–30.

the poor Saints Fund to provide aid for indigent members of the community.[114] The Gillfield Baptist church also provided a range of services, including funds to purchase freedom for individual members of slave families.[115] Beneficial societies were functioning in Baltimore as early as 1820 and by 1835 there were an estimated thirty-five to forty societies, each with a membership of thirty to one hundred and fifty persons.[116]

Some of these benefit societies, like the Burying Ground Society of Richmond, were established to perform funeral ceremonies. One of their principal functions was to turn out en masse for the funeral of a deceased member. Charles Colcock Jones, one of Georgia's large slaveholders and the founder of one of the Presbyterian churche's most successful missions to slaves, attributed the "weird" funeral processions to some "unknown antiquity."[117] Although such organizations had been significantly modified, conceptually and functionally they bore marked similarity to West African funeral guilds, such as the Ogboni, the Egungun or the women's Orisa Oko among the Yoruba, and the Mo of the Ibos. Partly religious and partly social, West African secret societies were responsible for funeral obsequies.[118] In recreating these social organizations, African-Americans maintained their functional, if not ritualistic, features. They provide another example of the persistence of traditional spiritual concepts and values, particularly in the concern with the proper performance of funeral ceremonies as a necessary condition for the return of the soul to the world of spirits. They express as well the deeply rooted African concept of the relationship of the family to the ancestors.

The social composition of some of these early associations suggests that clear distinctions existed within the black community of Charleston: between slave and free, between brown and black, between those who enjoyed better socioeconomic conditions and those who did not.[119] Cutting across the local cultural stratification, however, were bonds of common

[114] O'Brien, "Factory, Church and Community," 530.

[115] Jackson, "Religious Development of the Negro," 232.

[116] James B. Browning, "Beginnings of Insurance Enterprise among Negroes," *Journal of Negro History* 22 (1937): 432.

[117] Charleson Colcock Jones, Jr., *Memorial History of Augusta, Georgia, from Its Settlement in 1735 to the Close of the Eighteenth Century* (Syracuse, N.Y.: D. Mason, 1890), 386. Benefit societies in Augusta wore distinctive uniforms: a black cape with a purple band for female members of some societies, a white cape with a black band in others.

[118] Lucas, *Religion of the Yorubas*, 197–98, 227–35.

[119] Some historians cite the Brown Fellowship Society and the Humane Brotherhood as evidence of color consciousness and caste distinctions within the urban black community. A recent analysis of the two voluntary associations casts doubt on whether color consciousness was a primary factor in the social relations among Charleston's free black community and emphasizes instead differences in wealth, age, and occupation. See Robert L. Harris, Jr., "Charleston's Free Afro-American Elite: The Brown Fellowship Society and the Humane Brotherhood," *South Carolina Historical Magazine* 82(1981): 289–310, especially p. 310.

history and cultural motivation, which expressed themselves in the stated purposes of the various organizations: to provide for the education of orphans and to relieve the poverty of widows and indigents; to protect members of the group against sickness, accident, or personal misfortune; to provide burial grounds for deceased persons. Several of the organizations allowed members to borrow from the treasury to make business or home improvements or to carry them through hard times.[120]

It would be a mistake to exaggerate the achievements of the early black churches and their auxiliary organizations. Few black children received more than a rudimentary education, and most slave children received none at all. The economic and social services offered by the beneficial societies were limited to a select portion of the free urban black population and were not available to the vast majority of plantation slaves. Nevertheless, the schools did foster the development in urban areas of a literate cadre of churchmen, who eventually formed the basis of the modern black church. By providing opportunities for the acquisition and development of administrative skills and to learn principles of organization and management of church property, the churches and their ancillary operations contributed to the emergence of powerful black leaders. A number of extraordinary black church leaders, among them Andrew Bryan, Andrew Marshall, Henry Hosier, Henry Evans, Morris Brown, and Daniel Payne, became well-known public figures throughout the country and abroad. Countless lesser known figures emerged as community leaders for their own people. Revered by their congregations, respected by whites, they assumed broad powers within their own churches and, as a concomitant, enjoyed status and prestige within the black community. The tradition of religious leadership established in the early churches provided the basis for the articulate and effective political leadership roles played by black churchmen after emancipation. Even in modern times, the black community's most outstanding political leaders have been churchmen.[121] The educational, social, and economic structures created by the church-related beneficial societies appear to have also contributed significantly to the development of local black leadership and to the growth of the black urban community. The formation of organizations such as the local burial societies, which reflect the religious beliefs that shaped African and African-American attitudes towards death, dramatized and strengthened the new sense of social identity, for which the self-designation "African" became increasingly common.

The existence of various forms of collective action based on a common sense of identity provided a potential basis for the mobilization of the black

[120] Browning, "Beginnings of Insurance Enterprise," 426.
[121] Bailey, "Protestantism and Afro-Americans," 471.

community. Black churches were sometimes used for political and social purposes. Under powerful black leaders such as Gabriel Prosser, Denmark Vesey, and Nat Turner, some churches were used to launch rebellions.[122] The details of the separate schemes unfolded during Gabriel's Revolt and the various plots and conspiracies that swept Virginia and North Carolina in 1802 suggest that, perhaps for the first time in the history of slavery, African-Americans had acquired a sufficient consciousness of shared identity and common interests to enable them to organize effectively to challenge the system. Their growing sense of identification sprang from several sources. First was the experience of slavery itself. As a result of the increasingly homogeneous character of the slave population of the upper South and their concentration on larger units and in towns, slaves were gradually developing an awareness of a common heritage of suffering and humiliation, which in the early history of slavery had been hampered by cultural diversity and wide dispersal.

The emergence of an egalitarian creed with its emphasis on the values of liberty, equality, and brotherhood, lexiconized by white revolutionaries during the struggle with Britain, constituted a powerful impetus to unified, violent efforts to escape lifetime servitude. The brooding spirit of the Declaration of Independence infuses the claim made by Jack Bowler that "we have as much right to fight for our liberty as any men."[123] The black conspirators apparently also appropriated one of the Revolution's most compelling symbols for their own widely divergent purposes. According to a lawyer present at the trial, one of the accused men reportedly responded to the court's invitation to speak in his own defense by declaring, "I have nothing more to offer than what General Washington would have had to offer, had he been taken by the British and put to trial by them. I have adventured my life in endeavouring to obtain the liberty of my countrymen, and am a willing sacrifice in their cause."[124] The accused man's representation of himself as the black counterpart of George Washington reveals the difficulty white Southerners had in controlling the starting premises they had helped create.

What is most distinctive about Gabriel's Revolt and the series of plots and conspiracies that followed in 1802 is the religious impulse. The evi-

[122] The issue of whether Christianity made slaves passive, and thus defused the potential for rebellion, has been debated by historians. Raboteau, *Slave Religion*, 290–318, especially 291, maintains that Christianity supported both accommodation and rebelliousness. Although he concedes that "such slaves as Vesey and Turner were proof to American slaveholders that slave Christianity could become a double-edged sword," his emphasis is on nonviolent forms of resistance and self-assertion. In Vincent Harding's, *There Is a River*, religion plays a far more prominent role in the history of black rebellion.

[123] Palmer et al., eds., *Calendar of Virginia State Papers* 9:149, 160.

[124] Robert Sutcliff, *Travels in Some Parts of North America, In the Years 1804, 1805, and 1806*, 2d ed. (York and London, 1815), 68. The author thanks Betty Wood for this citation.

dence presented at the trials of all of the conspirators suggests a combination of both evangelical and traditional religious elements in the inspiration and coordination of conspiratorial activity. Gabriel's Revolt and the various insurrection plots were precipitated by an emerging group of African-American Christians, of whom Gabriel was the most outstanding example. They all occurred in areas that had been exposed to evangelical preaching and where churches and religious meetings proliferated. The established network of meetings provided the Christian revolutionaries with new levels of organization. Gabriel's recruiters enlisted dozens of slaves at the Hungry Meeting House and at the "preachings" at Littlepage's Bridge in Caroline County. Organizational meetings for the revolt were frequently held at William Young's "under pretext of attending preachment." Gabriel's decision to exempt Quakers and Methodists from the intended mass slaughter of whites suggests that the identification of Methodism with antislavery had been made by slaves as well as by their owners.[125]

The insurrectionary scares of 1802 broke out at the height of a season of intense religious revivalism. Trial testimony revealed that the conspiratorial headquarters were Halifax County, Virginia, and Bertie County, North Carolina. The Catawba Meetinghouse was reportedly the center for planning and recruiting for the rising, which was scheduled to begin on April 16, Good Friday. The Bertie conspiracy was promulgated at night preachings, and recruiting was carried out at the Wiccacon Meetinghouse. The march was to be launched from a black religious meeting at Outlaws Old Field and was to culminate in a surprise attack on the quarterly union meeting of the five Baptist churches in Bertie County, which often drew as many as three to four thousand white persons.[126] Although Gabriel himself apparently disdained the use of traditional cultic practices, George, one of his recruiters, proposed that he "travel down country to what he called the 'pipeing tree,' and enlist the Outlandish people, 'for they were suposed [sic] to deal with Witches and Wizards and this would be useful to armies to tell when any calamity was about to befall them.' "[127]

As details of the Vesey Plot in South Carolina unfolded at the trials, an apparent connection between Methodism and slave revolt was uncovered. Despite a spate of books and articles on the Vesey Plot, the close connection that existed between slave revolts and independent African churches has not been fully explored, although Vincent Harding has suggested that organized rebellion had "already been built deeply into the structure of black church life in Charleston" by the resignation in 1817 of 4,376 black

[125] Ibid., 150, 151, 152, 153, 158, 165, 167.
[126] T. C. Parramore, "Conspiracy and Revivalism in 1802: A Direful Symbiosis," *Negro History Bulletin* 43 (1980): 28–31. For details of the revival, see Burkitt and Read, *Concise History*, 141–60. The estimate of attendance at union meetings is on 147.
[127] Quoted in Mullin, *Flight and Rebellion*, 159.

Methodists from the regular Methodist church.[128] The unprecedented withdrawal of blacks was the result of an attempt by a white minister, Anthony Senter, to reassert control over the largely autonomous black Methodists, who hitherto had held their Quarterly Conferences separately and had collected and disbursed their own revenues. The failure of an attempt to take over the predominantly black Bethel Church followed by a decision by the white trustees to construct a hearse house on the black burial lot adjoining Bethel Church precipitated the resignation of almost every black class leader and the massive walkout of over four thousand members. The seceders successfully built a separate church on the corner of Hudson and Calhoun streets and were admitted into full connection with Bishop Richard Allen's African Methodist Society in Philadelphia, which suggests that slaves in urban areas were aware of the activities of free blacks in the North despite white efforts to suppress such information.[129]

The argument that stirrings of independence in the religious sphere are likely to be carried over into the political sphere finds corroboration in the trial records, which suggest that Vesey's ideas sprang up in the soil of the African independent church movement. According to Benjamin Ford, a young white witness, Vesey's general conversation was "about religion which he would apply to slavery, as for instance, he would speak of the creation of the world, in which he would say all men had equal rights, blacks as well as whites."[130] Various witnesses testified that Vesey prepared his followers by preaching liberation from the Bible. Among his favorite texts was Zechariah 14:1–3: "Behold the day of the Lord cometh, and thy spoil shall be divided in the midst of thee. For I will gather all nations against Jerusalem to battle; and the city shall be taken, and the houses rifled, and women ravished, and half of the city shall go forth into captivity; and the residue of the people shall not be cut off from the city. Then shall the Lord go forth, and fight against those nations, as when he fought in the day of battle."[131]

Vesey's frequent use of the salvation history theme to galvanize his followers is significant. The message that the salvation of the Jews was about to be reenacted among African-Americans was relevant to the religious and social needs of slaves. It invested rebellion with divine sanction and gave redemptive meaning to it. Vesey claimed the highest moral and religious sanction for his command to kill all whites: "and they utterly destroyed all

[128] Vincent Harding, "Religion and Resistance among Antebellum Negroes, 1800–1860," in August Meier and Elliott Rudwick, eds., *The Making of Black America. Essays in Negro Life and History* (New York: Atheneum, 1969), 184–85.

[129] Chreitzberg, *Early Methodism*, 156–57.

[130] Denmark Vesey, *The Trial Record of Denmark Vesey*, introduction by John Oliver Killens (Boston: Beacon Press, 1970), 64.

[131] Ibid., xv, 159.

that was in the city, both men and women, young and old, and ox, and sheep, and ass, with the edge of the sword" (Joshua 6:21). He also used biblical texts to create and sustain social and moral solidarity among his followers: "He that is not with me is against me" (Luke 11:23).

Following the example of the great leader of the Haitian Revolution, Toussaint L'Ouverture, who was both a Christian and an astute political leader, Vesey also utilized elements of traditional religion as a device for uniting his followers. His link to non-Christian slaves was Gullah Jack, a native of Angola. A physician and conjurer, Jack was considered invulnerable, a belief confirmed and perpetuated by Vesey, who told potential recruits that Jack "could not be killed."[132] In imitation perhaps of the black hougan, or priest of vodun, named Boukman, who conducted the ritual ceremony that launched the Haitian Revolution,[133] at the planning meetings Gullah Jack and other military leaders "roasted a fowl, and ate it half raw, as an evidence of union."[134] Reminiscent of traditional oathing rites used to enforce loyalty to the group, the ceremony appealed to tribal heritage and thus served as a symbolic instrument of unity. Jack also drew upon traditional warfare magic to provide his troops with moral and even physical courage. As an immunity from danger during the impending revolt, he ordered his troops to eat only parched corn and ground nuts, and, as a guarantee of protection and invulnerability to the white man's bullets, he instructed them to keep a crab claw in their mouths.[135]

The symbolic fusing of Christian theology and traditional rituals enabled Vesey to forge a militant revolutionary force and to direct its smoldering rage against the institution of slavery into political action. Although Gabriel's Revolt and the Vesey Plot were modest in comparison with armed outbreaks in the British Spanish Caribbean, Saint Domingue, and elsewhere, it would be a mistake to underestimate their importance. Although they had neither the strength nor the measure of force necessary to challenge white power successfully, the ability of charismatic leaders like Prosser, Vesey, and Gullah Jack to inspire unity among different groups demonstrated anew that African-Americans had revolutionary potential in their own right. The challenge they raised to the fundamental theoretical formulations concerning the concept of equality marks a new stage in ac-

[132] Ibid., 63.

[133] George Eaton Simpson, "The Belief System of Haitian Vodun," *American Anthropologist* 47 (1945): 35–59, especially 36–37, 57. As C.L.R. James has written, "Voodoo was the medium of the [Haitian Revolution]"; see C.L.R. James, *The Black Jacobins. Toussaint L'Ouverture and the San Domingo Revolution*, 2d ed., rev. (New York: Vintage Books, 1963), 86.

[134] Vesey, *Trial Record*, 63.

[135] Vesey, *Trial Record*, 76; Lofton, *Denmark Vesey's Revolt*, 142, mentions Gullah Jack's "own peculiar methods for boosting morale," but fails to recognize the African antecedents. For a discussion of West African belief in amulets see Winterbottom, *Account of the Native Africans* 1:251–62.

tion and provides the basis for, and tradition of, emancipatory movements in the black world. The tradition is repeated in a variety of settings: in the independent church movement started by the former Virginia slave George Liele in Jamaica from which the "Baptist War" of 1831–1832 was launched;[136] in the Southampton County, Virginia, revolt of 1831 led by the religious charismatic, "Prophet Nat" Turner; in the church-connected mass resistance movements waged against colonial rule in twentieth century Africa, the most notable example of which is the Nyasaland Rising of 1915 led by the Virginia-educated John Chilembwe.[137]

Although the idea of militant mobilization failed, with the growth and expansion of black Christianity the churches became the principal organizations for the solving of certain social and political problems. In Sierra Leone, Cato Perkins of the Countess of Huntingdon's Connection, a splinter group of the Anglican church, and the Baptist leader David George, mobilized their congregations to oppose government policies of taxes and rent increases and to elect representatives from their own church communities. Early in the century black American evangelists launched a missionary movement to West Africa. In 1815 Lott Carey, a Charles City County slave, and Colin Teague with Carey, pastor of the First Church in Richmond organized the African Missionary Society, the first in the country. With $700.00 raised for African missions, Carey and Teague led a handful of members of their Richmond congregation to Monrovia, where in 1821 they founded the Protestant Baptist church, the first church in Liberia. In 1820 Daniel Coker of Baltimore, a founder member of the African Methodist Episcopal church, and a small group travelled to Sierra Leone and for several years carried out missionary work among the Africans. Carey, Teague, and Coke were the forerunners of the black-led effort to Christianize West Africa that flourished from the 1870s to 1900.[138] The contacts and exchanges between African-American and African civilizations made it possible during the ensuing century to formulate the concept of a black world community.

The organizing efforts of the black community, combined with the appearance of William Lloyd Garrison's *Liberator* and the insurrection led by Nat Turner in Southampton County, Virginia, in 1831, produced a strong reaction from the slaveholding community. Convinced of a connection between the activities of the black churches and black militancy, the General

---

[136] Mary Turner, *Slaves and Missionaries. The Disintegration of Jamaican Slave Society* (Urbana, Ill.: University of Illinois Press, 1982), 148–78.

[137] George Shepperson and Thomas Price, *Independent African. John Chilembwe and the Origins, Setting and Significance of the Nyasaland Rising of 1915* (Edinburgh: University Press, 1987), 422–25.

[138] Peter B. Clarke, *West Africa and Christianity* (London: E. Arnold, 1986), 35, 53–54, 160, 198.

Assembly of Virginia passed a law prohibiting slaves and free blacks from assembling for the purpose of learning to read or write, regardless of whether the instructor was white or black. The following year the assembly decreed that "no Negro ordained, licensed or otherwise" could hold assemblies or meetings of any type, day or night. Various Baptist associations in the state also took steps to establish white control over the independent black churches. The Portsmouth Association, for example, ordered the Gillfield Baptist and the First African, or Harrison Street, churches of Petersburg to represent themselves at association meetings through white delegates from white churches. The African Baptist church of Williamsburg was closed by the Dover Association.[139] In 1834 the General Assembly of South Carolina also enacted legislation aimed at preventing the teaching of slave and free children and at abolishing black schools.[140] As a result of this act, Daniel Payne was forced to close his private school.[141] Schools conducted by white schoolmasters did continue to operate in Charleston and a number of "secret schools" were organized and continued to function through the antebellum period.[142]

The overall effect of such repressive legislation, however, was virtually to destroy the young schools and to cripple the independent church movement. The launching of the plantation mission movement by the South Carolina Methodist Conference in 1829 marked the beginning of the white-directed evangelical movement and a concerted effort to extinguish all vestiges of traditional African religion. By the time that happened, African-Americans had created a new historical community, its strong community spirit rooted in an encompassing kinship system, which affirmed various aspects of their African identity and culture. During the historical process of interaction between traditional and Christian cultures, African-Americans had been Christianized, but they had also "traditionalized" Christianity itself.

[139] Jackson, "Religious Development of the Negro," 204–10.
[140] Birnie, "Education of the Negro," 17–18.
[141] Payne, *Recollections*, 27–28, 35–36.
[142] Fredrika Bremer, *The Homes of the New World. Impressions of America*, Mary Houitt, trans., 2 vols. (New York: Negro Universities Press, 1968), 2:499.

CONCLUSION

THE AMERICAN REVOLUTION marked a major turning point in the history of slavery and of the South. The outbreak of revolutionary conflict in the 1760s signaled thousands of slaves to declare and claim their freedom. Although most slaves were probably aware of Britain's role as the world's leading slave-trading nation, they quite correctly perceived that their best chances for freedom lay with a British victory, or at least with the disruption of the existing social order. Resorting to patterns of resistance inherited from their African past, some slaves deserted to form maroon communities; some attempted to forge large-scale rebellion; most fled to British forces in the South. As much as any other single factor, their readiness to enter into open rebellion created the dynamic for revolution in the South.

Although the British army did not create slave resistance, it lost no time in trying to exploit it. The seductive idea of employing slave labor to satisfy manpower needs and to intimidate independence-minded white southerners was broached early in the conflict by Crown officials, but rejected by Parliament as too dangerous. Although Britain's stated policy was tolerant of slavery, the pressure exerted by thousands of black fugitives and the salutary effect of black desertions on white owners drew the army irresistibly into a position it had tried to avoid but ultimately could not—the appearance, but not the reality, of intervention in domestic slavery. Neither British policy nor practice involved actual emancipation, but it raised the specter of emancipation and, in so doing, became a critical variable in propelling white southerners toward independence. Seeing in British actions the potential for violent and disastrous insurrection, the southern gentry responded by joining battle with the forces of revolution. To a large extent their support for independence and for the war effort generally was part of a desperate effort to reassert their hegemony over their slaves and thereby preserve their fragmenting world. The turbulence of the war and the racial anarchy it spawned rocked the slave system to its foundations and substantially heightened racial tensions. The revolutionary war in the South thus became a war about slavery, if not a war over slavery.

In the North, the social ferment of the war years helped to forge an inextricable link between evangelical Christianity and republican ideology, which gave rise to an organized antislavery movement and led ultimately to the gradual extinction of slavery there. In the South, military occupation, continuous naval assaults, and bitter internecine warfare led to total socioeconomic dislocation, precipitated in part by British efforts to use slavery as a matter of tactics, in part by the massive desertion of slaves and the breakdown of the rural agricultural order it engendered. The damage to production facilities during the war, the dramatic breakdown in labor discipline, and the extreme shortage of labor and capital in the immediate postwar period, in the long run contributed to the transformation of agricultural patterns. In the upper South, the shift from the production of tobacco to wheat, already underway since the 1760s, was accelerated by the disruptions of war. Through diversification, Virginia and Maryland eventually were able to overcome the serious economic setbacks brought on by the war. In the lower South, supply disruptions in the rice industry led European markets to turn to new sources of supply and ultimately contributed to the geographical shift of the domestic rice industry to Louisiana, Arkansas, and Texas. In the short run, efforts to rebuild the old agricultural order produced an economic resurrection of sorts. Over the long run, the revolutionary war really marked the beginning of the end of the rice industry in the low country.

In their desperate efforts to save their economy, low-country planters imported thousands of Africans. To some extent, dominating economic problems in the immediate postwar era had overshadowed the more specific problem of a fragmenting social order. Nevertheless, the burgeoning black population, the emergence of a short-lived religious antislavery movement in the South, and an extended period of revival disorder (which encouraged various forms of iconoclastic behavior), conjoined with the racial anarchism spawned by the war, exposed the extreme vulnerabilty of the social order. Galvanized by the obsessive fear that white society was about to be engulfed by a mounting black population, or destroyed by a black rising, or swallowed up by miscegenation, the slaveholding elite developed a new set of sanctions coercive enough to guarantee efficient and full use of slave labor power and created a culture tied directly to color and blood, redefining in the process the social rules and expectations of both races.

Convinced that religious antislavery had placed the future of evangelical religion in jeopardy in the South, a new generation of southern-born evangelical leaders began consciously to separate the southern evangelical movement from the national struggle to eradicate slavery, thus prefiguring the divisions on the question of secession in the antebellum South. They abandoned, too, the emphasis on political action, the hallmark of the early Methodist movement, in favor of hortatory moralism, whose aim was not to abolish slavery but to operate it in a moral manner. The paternalistic ethos southern evangelical leaders helped to formulate was eagerly embraced by slaveholding society. Disseminated by the courts and such institutions of cultural formation as churches and schools, it became a principal instrument for the reassertion of slaveholders' hegemony over their slaves.

The effect was to rivet the chains of slavery more tightly than ever before and thereby to consolidate the political power of the slaveholding class.

Black hopes for freedom from the bonds of slavery were thus thwarted and deflected, but they were not destroyed. Black southerners emerged from the Revolution with a deeper sense of strength and of kind, with a greater awareness of the universality of the black struggle, and a more viable political consciousness. In the postwar period, this changing political consciousness manifested itself in several ways. The liberation rhetoric of the Revolution and the renewed emphasis on the equality of persons before Christ in the Second Great Awakening that swept the South after 1785 inspired a certain portion of the black population to resort to massive, organized resistance. A more effective, militant leadership, whose tactics, strategy, and organizational concepts were patterned after Euro-American models, but whose immediate inspiration was the black revolution in Saint Domingue, planned several large-scale rebellions, the most serious of which were Gabriel's Revolt of 1800 in Virginia and the great Vesey Plot of 1822 in South Carolina.

The majority of African-Americans, whose spirit was no less revolutionary, resorted to cultural assertiveness. Many assumed innovative and largely autonomous economic roles, displacing in some cases free white labor. During the various phases of the Second Great Awakening, thousands turned to religion, arguably the most important counterbalancing force to the disintegrating forces operating within plantation society. Although the phenomenal growth of Afro-Christianity after 1800 necessarily took shape within the perimeters of white religion, African-Americans were able to develop their own institutions and parallel structures. The establishment of separate black churches throughout the South was a radical departure from anything that had gone before. By refusing to accept discrimination in the biracial churches, African-American Christians implicitly rejected the hierarchical structure of white Protestantism and, by implication, the notion of white supremacy upon which it rested. By insisting upon their own ritual patterns and by asserting certain specifically African aspects of moral values separate from the values of the dominant white culture, they established a claim to cultural power. Ultimately, of course, white southerners realized that such subversive behavior raised a direct challenge to white cultural hegemony and posed a threat to the structure of white southern society and so they acted to quash it. By then Afro-Christianity had a distinct and rooted life.

Although Afro-Christian churches faced many difficulties in unifying the black community and giving it direction, the churches quickly became the primary vehicles of unity and community among otherwise isolated black communities. Through this medium, ethnic differences were submerged into a common spiritual solidarity. As the organizing symbol for African-

Americans, the black churches were the source for the creation of new forms of social organization, of black cemeteries and burial societies, of fraternal and charitable associations, and of Bible societies and schools. The success of African-American Christians in resisting total incorporation into the white Christian structure contributed significantly to the creation of the two racially distinct value systems and cultural communities that came to characterize southern society. In the end, by insisting upon blacks' common humanity and their equal endowment with moral if not political power, southern blacks, slave and free, raised the most effective challenge to the ideological structures that sustained the slave system.

BIBLIOGRAPHY

CONTENTS

SELECTED BIBLIOGRAPHY

PRIMARY SOURCES: UNPUBLISHED

British Library: London

Liverpool Papers, Add. MSS 38190–38489.
Miscellaneous Documents, 1660–1799, Add. MSS 12435.
Order Book of the 43d Regiment at Yorktown, 1781, Add. MSS 42449–42450.
Papers, Tracts, and Histories Relating to Jamaica Collected by Charles Edward Long, Add. MSS 18270, 18273.
[Wylly, William], "A Short Account of the Bahama Islands by a Barrister at Law," Add. MSS 6058.

National Army Museum: London

Order Books, Letter Books, Journals, Letters, and Other Documents of Lt. General Sir Eyre Coote Relating to the American War of Independence, 1776–1782, 6912/14, nos. 31–50.

Public Record Office: London

OFFICIAL RECORDS

Colonial Office Papers (Class 5): America and the West Indies, 1607–1807

Correspondence, Original, Secretary of State: East Florida, 1777–1786, CO5/557–59, 560–61.
Correspondence, Original, Secretary of State: South Carolina, 1780–1784, CO5/397.
Letters from Governor Wright, 1761–1780, CO5/658–65.
Letters to the Secretary of State, 1772–1780, CO5/679–80.
Military Dispatches, 1779–1783, CO5/106, 109, 110, 111.
Plantations General, 1780–1783, CO5/8.
Proceedings of the Board of Police, 1780–1782, CO5/519–24.
Correspondence, Original, CO5/1353, 1373.

Colonial Office Papers (Class 23): Bahamas. Original Correspondence, 1767–1786

Correspondence, Original, Secretary of State, 1780–1786, CO23/25/26.
Letters from the Secretary of State, 1784–1788, CO23/24.

Colonial Office Papers (Class 37): Bermuda. Original Correspondence, Secretaries of State

Bermuda and Turks Island, 1779–1790, CO37/23.
Dispatches, 1778–1784, CO37/38.
Miscellaneous, 1778–1784, CO37/39.

Colonial Office Papers (Class 71): Dominica. Original Correspondence, Board of Trade

Dispatches, 1783–1786, CO71/8–14.

Colonial Office Papers (Class 137): Jamaica. Original Correspondence.

Correspondence, Original, Secretaries of State, 1781–1787, CO137/82–87.

Treasury Papers (Class 1): In-Letters

Letters from Governor Wright of Georgia, T1/560.
Papers from Clinton to Gage, 1781–1782, T1/571.
Treasury. Miscellaneous Papers, 1774–1783, T1/580.

OTHER COLLECTIONS

Carleton Papers, Records of British Army Headquarters (BHP) in America, 1775–83, PRO30/55.
Chatham Papers, PRO30/8.
Cornwallis, Charles (1738–1805), second earl of Cornwallis and first marquis of Cornwallis, Papers, 1614–1854, PRO30/11.

Rhodes House Library: Oxford

MS West Indies S.10.

Scottish Record Office: Edinburgh

Cunningham of Thorntoun Muniments, 1746–1782, 1876–1883. Notebooks Containing the Journal of Lt. John Peebles of the 42d or Royal Highland Regiment during the War of Independence, GD 21.

Libraries and Archives

ALDERMAN LIBRARY, UNIVERSITY OF VIRGINIA, CHARLOTTESVILLE.
Gillfield Baptist Church Records, 1817–1939, Microfilm.
Goose Creek Baptist Church Records. Fauquier County, 1775–1853. Photostat no. 4496.

CAROLINIANA LIBRARY, UNIVERSITY OF SOUTH CAROLINA, COLUMBIA.
Bee, Thomas (1725–1812).
Porcher, Philip E., Papers (1730–1800).

GEORGIA HISTORICAL SOCIETY, SAVANNAH.
Bevan [Joseph Vallence] Papers, 1733–1812.
Buffington, [Moses], Papers, 1779.
Habersham, Joseph, Papers, 1769–1802.
King, [Mark], Papers, 1782.
Leake, [Richard], Papers, 1780–1801.
Zubly, [John Joachim], Papers, 1770–1781.

HOWARD-TILTON MEMORIAL LIBRARY, TULANE UNIVERSITY, NEW ORLEANS, LOUISIANA.
British Headquarters [Sir Guy Carleton] Papers, PRO 30/55. Microfilm.
Candler, Allen D., comp. The Colonial Records of the State of Georgia. Copies made from original records in England. Microfilm.

LIBRARY OF CONGRESS, WASHINGTON, D.C.
American Revolution MSS, 1777–1779. Transcripts.
Bounetheau, Peter, Papers, 1685–1877. Account Books, Business and Personal.
Force, Peter, Collection, 1762–1814. Force Transcripts.
Force, Peter, Historical Manuscripts, 1501–1866. Force Papers.
Honyman, Robert, 1747–1824. Diary 1776–1782.
Lincoln, Benjamin, Papers, October–December 1778, September–October 1779. Microfilm.
Maryland State Papers, Rainbow Series. Red Books, vols. 1–33; Brown Books, vols. 1–9; Black Books, vols. 6–10; Blue Books, vols. 1–5. Microfilm.
Minor, Garrett, Plantation and Family Records and Accounts, 1774, 1780–81, 1784–85, 1788–89.
Orderly Books. Regimental Order Book, British Army, Siege of Savannah, 2 July– 2 October 1779.
Sumter, Thomas, Papers, 1780–1832. Draper mss., ser. VV, Whi.

MARYLAND HALL OF RECORDS, ANNAPOLIS.

Maryland State Papers

Rainbow Series. Red Books 4557–4606; Brown Books 4608–17; Black Books 4629–36; Blue Books 4639–44.
Executive Papers. A-6636.

MARYLAND HISTORICAL SOCIETY, BALTIMORE, MARYLAND.
Davis, John. Account Book, 1751–1782, MS 1475.
Revolutionary War Collection, MS 1814.

NATIONAL ARCHIVES, WASHINGTON, D.C.
Papers of the Continental Congress, 1774–1789 (M247). Records of the Continental and Confederation Congresses and the Constitutional Convention, Record Group 360. Microfilm.
Miscellaneous Papers of the Continental Congress, 1774–1789 (M332).

NEW YORK PUBLIC LIBRARY, NEW YORK CITY.
Leslie, General Alexander. Letter Book. Letters from and to Nesbit Balfour, Emmet Collection.
Miscellaneous. Ralph Izard. Letters Concerning the British Evacuation of Charleston, 1782.
Papers Relating to South Carolina in the Revolution, Chalmers Collection.

NORTH CAROLINA HISTORICAL COMMISSION, RALEIGH.
Caswell, Richard, Papers, 1774–1789.
Cogdell, Richard, Papers, 1761–1784.
Davie, William Richardson, Papers, 1778–1817.
Dickson Manuscripts, 1784–1790.

SOUTH CAROLINA BAPTIST HISTORICAL SOCIETY, FURMAN UNIVERSITY LIBRARY,
GREENVILLE. MICROFILM.
Big Creek Baptist Church, Williamston, Minutes, 1801–1936.
Big Stephens Creek Baptist Church, Edgefield District, Records, 1803–1901.
Black Creek Baptist Church, Dovesville, Records, 1798–1896.
Brushy Creek Baptist Church, Greenville County and Association, Records, 1795–
    1927
Buffalo Baptist Church, Cherokee County, Minutes, 1805–1810.
Cashaway (Mount Pleasant) Baptist Church Book, 1765–1805.
First Baptist Church, Georgetown, Minutes, 1805–1821.
Little River Baptist Church, Fairfield County, Minutes, Rolls, 1794–1820.
Lower Fork of Lynches Creek Baptist Church (Gum Branch), Minutes, 1796–
    1887.
Mountain Creek Baptist Church, Anderson, Minutes and Historical Sketch, 1798–
    1956.
Skull Shoals (Pacolet) Baptist Church, Cherokee County, Minutes, 1787–1805.
Turkey Creek Baptist Church, Abbeville County, South Carolina, 1785–1869.
Tyger Baptist Church, Greenville County Minutes, 1801–1833.
Welsh Neck Baptist Church, Society Hill Minutes, 1737–1841.

SOUTH CAROLINA HISTORICAL SOCIETY, CHARLESTON.
Grimké, John Faucheraud, Military Records.
Grimké, John Faucheraud, Papers, 1761–1866.
Jenkins Reverend Mr., Papers, Memorandum Book, 1773–1782.
Middleton, Arthur, Papers, 1767–1783.
Miscellaneous Manuscripts.
Pinckney Family Papers, 1703–1847.
Prioleau Papers.
Smith, Josiah, Jr., Diary, 1780–1782.

SOUTH CAROLINA STATE ARCHIVES, COLUMBIA.
General Assembly Papers, 1776 (1782)–1830. Record Group 0010, ser. 003.
Comptroller General, Accounts Audited of Claims Growing Out of the Revolu-
    tion, 1778–1804. Record Group 0015, ser. 003.

SOUTHERN HISTORICAL COLLECTION, UNIVERSITY OF NORTH CAROLINA LIBRARY,
CHAPEL HILL.
Brevard and McDowell Family Papers, 1754–1903.
Burke, Thomas (c. 1747–1783), Papers, 1763–1852.
Davie, William Richardson (1756–1820), Papers, no. 1 (Addition).
Pendleton, Edmund (1721–1803), Letters, 1776–1779.

Richardson, Francis Du Bose, Memoirs.
Smith, Josiah, Jr. (1730–1826), Lettercopy Book, 1771–1784.

STETSON MEMORIAL LIBRARY, MACON, GEORGIA. MICROFILM
Minutes of the Georgia Association, Georgia, 1803–1905.
Records of the Little Ogeechee Baptist Church, Screven County, Georgia, 1797–
     1905.
Savannah River Baptist Association, South Carolina, 1803–1829.

VIRGINIA BAPTIST HISTORICAL SOCIETY, UNIVERSITY OF RICHMOND, RICHMOND.
Accomac Association Minutes,1815–1824.
Albemarle Association Minutes,1815–1840.
Antioch Baptist Church (Boar Swamp) Minutes, 1787–1827.
Antioch Baptist Church (Racoon Swamp) Minutes, 1772–1837.
Appomattox Association Minutes, 1805–1860.
Berryville Baptist Church Minutes, 1803–1841.
Berryville (Buck Marsh) Baptist Church Minutes, 1785–1803.
Broad Run Baptist Church Minutes, 1762–1872.
Carmel Baptist Church Minutes, 1799–1819.
Chestnut Grove (Albemarle) Baptist Church Minutes, 1773–1811.
Emmaus Baptist Church Minutes, 1792–1841.
Goshen Baptist Association Minutes, 1795.
Lyles (Albemarle) Baptist Church Minutes, 1800–1835.
Middle District Baptist Association Minutes, 1791–1852.
Mill Swamp Baptist Church Minutes, 1774–1790.
Morgan's (Goose Creek) Baptist Church Minutes, 1787–1821.
Portsmouth (Virginia) Association Minutes, 1791–1800, 1801–1840.
Roanoke Baptist Association Minutes, 1789–1831.
Shiloh Baptist Association Minutes, 1804–1839.
South Quay Baptist Church Minutes, 1775–1827.
Strawberry Association Minutes, 1787–1822.
Tussekiah Baptist Church Minutes, 1784–1826.
Upper King and Queen Baptist Church Minutes Book, 1774–1816.
Wallers (Goshen) Baptist Church Minutes, 1799–1818.

VIRGINIA STATE LIBRARY, RICHMOND.
Legislative Department. House of Delegates, Speaker. Letters Received, November 1783.
Legislative Petitions.

WILLIAM L. CLEMENTS LIBRARY, ANN ARBOR, MICHIGAN.
Clinton, Sir Henry, 1731[?]–1795, Papers, 1750–1812.
Germain, George Sackville, first viscount of Sackville, 1776–1785, Papers, 1683–
     1785.
Howe, General Sir William, Orderly Books.
Moncrief, James, Letter Book, 1780–1782.
Wray, George, Papers, 1770–1793.

WILLIAM R. PERKINS LIBRARY, DUKE UNIVERSITY, DURHAM, NORTH CAROLINA.
Jones, Seaborn, Jr., Papers, 1781–1847.

PUBLIC DOCUMENTS

Records of the Federal and State Governments

Clark, William Bell, ed. *Naval Documents of the American Revolution*. 5 vols. Washington, D.C.: USGPO, 1968.

Ford, Worthington C., ed. *Journals of the Continental Congress, 1774–1789*. 34 vols. Washington, D.C.: USGPO, 1904–37.

Smith, Paul H., Gerard W. Gawalt, and Ronald M. Gephart, eds., *Letters of Delegates to Congress, 1774–1789*. 15 vols. to date. Washington, D.C.: Library of Congress, 1985–.

Thorpe, Francis Newton, ed., and comp. *The Federal and State Constitutions, Colonial Charters, and Other Organic Laws of the States, Territories, and Colonies Now or Heretofore Forming the United States of America*. 7 vols. Washington, D.C.: USGPO, 1909.

United States Bureau of the Census. *Heads of Families at the First Census . . . 1790: South Carolina*. Washington, D.C. 1908.

State Documents

Adams, Lark Emerson, ed. State Records of South Carolina. *The Journals of the House of Representatives, 1775–1785*. Columbia: University of South Carolina Press, 1979.

Brevard, Joseph. *An Alphabetical Digest of the Public Statute Law of South Carolina*. 3 vols. Charleston: John Hoff, 1814.

Browne, William Hand, Clayton C. Coleman, and Bernard C. Steiner, eds. *Archives of Maryland*. 71 vols. to date. Baltimore: Maryland Historical Society, 1883–.

Candler, Allen D., comp. *The Colonial Records of the State of Georgia. (1732–1782)*. 27 vols. Atlanta: C. P. Byrd, 1904.

————, comp. *The Revolutionary Records of the State of Georgia*. 3 vols. Atlanta: Franklin-Turner, 1908.

Clark, Walter, ed. *The State Records of North Carolina*. 26 vols. Raleigh: P. M. Hale, 1886–1907.

Cobb, Thomas R. R. *A Digest of the Statute Laws of the State of Georgia*. Athens: Christy, Kelsea and Burke, 1851.

Cooper, Thomas, and David J. McCord, eds. *The Statutes at large of South Carolina*. 10 vols. Columbia, S.C.: A. S. Johnston, 1836–41.

Edwards, Adele Stanton, ed. State Records of South Carolina. *Journals of the Privy Council, 1783–1789*. Columbia: University of South Carolina Press, 1971.

Hemphill, William Edwin, ed. *Extracts from the Journal of the Provincial Congress of South Carolina, 1775–1776*. Columbia: South Carolina Archives Department, 1960.

Hening, William W., ed. *The Statutes at Large: Being a Collection of All the Laws of Virginia from the First Session of the Legislature in the Year 1619*. 13 vols. Richmond: Samuel Pleasants, Jr., 1809–1823.

Palmer, William P., Sherwin McRae, Raleigh E. Colsten, and Henry W. Flournoy, eds. *Calendar of Virginia State Papers and Other Manuscripts, 1652–1869, Preserved at the Capitol in Richmond*. 11 vols. Richmond: Samuel Pleasants, Jr., 1875–93.

Prince, Oliver H., comp. *A Digest of the Laws of the State of Georgia*. 2d ed. Athens: Author, 1837.

Saunders, William L., ed. *The Colonial Records of North Carolina*. 10 vols. Raleigh: Printers to the State, 1886–90.

Shepherd, Samuel, ed. *The Statutes at Large of Virginia, from the October Session 1792, to December Session 1806*. 3 vols. Richmond: S. Shepherd, 1835–36.

Thompson, Theodora J., ed. The State Records of South Carolina. *Journals of the House of Representatives of South Carolina, 1783–1784*. Columbia: University of South Carolina Press, 1977.

Reports of Judicial Decisions

Catterall, Helen T., ed. *Judicial Cases Concerning Slavery and the Negro*. 4 vols. Washington, D.C., 1926.

Charlton, Thomas U. P. *Reports of Cases Argued and Determined in the Superior Courts of the Eastern District of the State of Georgia, 1805–1811, by Thomas U. P. Charlton*. New York: Stephen Gould and Son, 1824.

NORTH CAROLINA LAW REPORTS
Taylor (4) 1798–1802
Haywood (2–3) 1797–1806
Hawks (8–11) 1820–1826
Devereaux and Battle (18–22) 1834–1839

SOUTH CAROLINA LAW REPORTS
Bay (1–2) 1783–1804
Brevard (3–5) 1793–1816
Harper's Equity–1824
Nott and McCord (10–11) 1817–1820

VIRGINIA LAW REPORTS
Virginia Cases, Criminal 1789–1826
Randolph 1821–1828

PRINTED PRIMARY SOURCES

Newspapers

Gazette of the State of South Carolina, 1777–1780, 1783–1785.
Georgia Gazette, 1763–1775, 1788–1790.
Royal Gazette, 1781–1782.
Royal Georgia Gazette, 1779–1782.
Royal South-Carolina Gazette, 1781–1782.
South Carolina and American General Gazette, 1764–1781.

Virginia Gazette Dixon and Hunter 1751–1778
Pinkney 1766–1776
Dixon and Holt 1783–1789
Nicolson and Prentis 1781–1790

Books and Articles

Adair, William. "The Revolutionary War Diary of William Adair." Harold B. Hancock, ed. *Delaware History* 13 (October 1968): 154–65.

Abdy, Edward Strutt. *Journal of a Residence and Tour in the United States of North America. from April, 1833, to October, 1834.* 3 vols. London: John Murray, 1835.

Allaire, Anthony. *Diary of Lieutenant Anthony Allaire.* Reprint. New York: New York Times, 1968.

Alzelius, Adam. *Sierra Leone Journal, 1795–1796.* Alexander Peter Kup, ed. Uppsala, Sweden: Almqvist and Wiksells, 1967.

Anburey, Thomas. *Travels through the Interior Parts of America.* 2 vols. New York: New York Times, c. 1969.

Asbury, Francis. *An Extract from the Journal of Francis Asbury, Bishop of the Methodist Episcopal Church from August 7, 1770, to December 29, 1778.* Philadelphia: Joseph Crukshank, 1792.

Asbury, Francis. *The Journal and Letters of Francis Asbury.* Elmer T. Clark, J. Manning Potts, and Jacob S. Payton, eds. 3 vols. London: Epworth Press; Nashville, Tenn.: Abingdon Press, 1958.

Asplund, John. *The Annual Register of the Baptist Denomination, in North-America: To the First of November, 1790. Containing an Account of the Churches and Their Constitutions, Ministers, Members, Associations.* Richmond, Va: n.p., 1792.

————, ed. *The Universal Annual Register of the Baptist Denomination, in North America, For the Years 1794 and 1795.* Hanover, N.H.: Dunham and True, 1796.

Ball, Charles. *Slavery in the United States: A Narrative of the Life and Adventures of Charles Ball: A Black Man.* Lewistown, Pa.: John W. Shugert, 1836.

Ballagh, James Curtis, ed. *The Letters of Richard Henry Lee.* 2 vols. New York: Macmillan, 1914.

Bangs, Nathan. *A History of the Methodist Episcopal Church.* 2 vols. New York: T. Mason and G. Lane, 1839.

BAPTISTS

South Carolina

A Summary of Church Discipline . . . by the Baptist Association, in Charleston, South Carolina. Wilmington: James Adams, 1783.

Bethel Association. *Minutes of the Bethel Association, Held at the Baptist Church on Jamey's Creek, Spartanburg County, South Carolina, Begun on Saturday, August 13, 1791.* N.p., c. 1791.

Charleston Association. *Minutes of the Charleston Association, Held at the High Hills of Santee, October 30, 1790–3, November 1790.* N.p., 1790.

Minutes of the Charleston Association, held at Welch Neck, Pee Dee, November 5, 1791. Charleston, 1791.

Minutes of the Charleston Association, Held at Coosawhatchie, the 3d of November, 1792. Charleston, 1792.

Minutes of the Charleston Association, Held at the High Hills of Santee, the 2d of November, 1793. Charleston, 1793.

Minutes of the Charleston Association, Held at the Upper Fork of Lynches Creek, 1 November, 1794. Charleston, 1794.

Virginia

Minutes of the Baptist Dover Association, 1798–1832. Richmond: Samuel Pleasants, 1798–1832.

Baurmeister, Carl Leopold. *The Revolution in America. Confidential Letters and Journals, 1776–1784, of Adjutant General Baurmeister of the Hessian Forces*. Bernhard A. Uhlendorf, trans. New Brunswick, N.J.: Rutgers University Papers, 1957.

Benedict, David. *A General History of the Baptist Denomination in America*. New York: Lewis Colby, 1848.

Bennett, William W. *Memorials of Methodism in Virginia, From Its Introduction into the State in the Year 1772, to the Year 1829*. Richmond: Author, 1871.

Bibb, Henry. *Narrative of the Life and Adventures of Henry Bibb, An American Slave, Written by Himself*. Reprint. New York: Negro Universities Press, 1969.

Boehm, Reverend Henry. *Reminiscences, Historical and Biographical, of Sixty-Four Years in the Ministry*. New York: Carlton and Porter, 1865.

Bogin, Ruth. " 'Liberty Further Extended': A 1776 Antislavery Manuscript by Lemuel Hayes." *William and Mary Quarterly*, 3d ser., 40, no. 1 (1983): 85–105.

Boyd, Julian P., and Lyman H. Butterfield, eds. *The Papers of Thomas Jefferson*. 24 vols. to date. Princeton, N.J.: Princeton University Press, 1950–.

Bremer, Fredrika. *The Homes of the New World. Impressions of America*. Mary Houitt, trans. 2 vols. New York: Negro Universities Press, 1968.

Brewster, Jarvis. *An Exposition on the Treatment of Slaves in the Southern States, Particularly in the States of Maryland, Virginia, North Carolina, South Carolina and Georgia*. New Brunswick, N.J.: D. and J. FitzRandolph, 1815.

Brickell, John. *The Natural History of North-Carolina*. New York: Johnson Reprint, 1969.

Brissot de Warville, Jacques Pierre. *New Travels in the United States of America, 1788*. Durand Echeverria, ed. Cambridge, Mass.: Harvard University Press, Belknap Press, 1964.

Burke, Edmund. *The Speeches of the Right Honourable Edmund Burke, in the House of Commons, and in Westminister-Hall*. 4 vols. London: Longman, Hurst, Rees, Orme and Brown, 1816.

Burkitt, Lemuel, and Jesse Read. *A Concise History of the Kehukee Baptist Association from Its Original Rise to the Present Time*. Halifax, N.C.: A. Hodge, 1803.

Burwell, Letitia M. *Plantation Reminiscences*. N.p.: Page Thacker of Kentucky, 1878.

Butterfield, L. H., ed. *Diary and Autobiography of John Adams*. 4 vols. Cambridge, Mass.: Harvard University Press, Belknap Press, 1962.

Butterworth, Hezekiah. *A Zigzag Journey in the Sunny South: Or Wonder Tales of Early American History*. Boston: Estes and Lauriat, 1887.

Campbell, Colin, ed. *Journal of an Expedition against the Rebels of Georgia in North America. Under the Orders of Archibald Campbell, Esquire*. Printed for the Richmond County Historical Society. Darien, Georgia: Ashantilly Press, 1981.

Capers, William. "Autobiography." In William May Wightman, ed., *Life of William Capers, D. D.* Nashville, Tenn.: Southern Methodist Publishing, 1859.

Cappon, Lester J., ed. *The Adams-Jefferson Letters*. For the Institute of Early American History and Culture. Chapel Hill: University of North Carolina Press, 1959.

Carman, Harry J., ed. *American Husbandry*. Port Washington, N.Y.: Kennikat Press, 1964.

Carter, Clarence E., ed. *The Correspondence of General Thomas Gage with the Secretaries of State, and with the War Office and the Treasury*. 2 vols. Hamden, Conn.: Archon Books, 1969.

Chastellux, François Jean, Marquis de. *Travels in North America in the Years 1780, 1781, and 1782*. Howard C. Rice, Jr., ed. For the Institute of Early American History and Culture. Chapel Hill: University of North Carolina Press, 1963.

Clinton, Sir Henry. *Memorandums etc. Respecting the Unprecedented Treatment which the Army Have Met with Respecting Plunder Taken after a Seige, and of Which Plunder the Navy Serving with the Army Divided Their More Than Ample Share, Now Fourteen Years Since*. Memo. London, 1794.

Cobbett, William, and T. C. Hansard, eds. *The Parliamentary History of England from the Earliest Period to the Year 1803*. 36 vols. London: T. C. Hansard, 1806–20.

Coffin, Joshua. *An Account of Some of the Principal Slave Insurrections, and Others, which Have Occurred, or Been Attempted, in the United States and Elsewhere, during the Last Two Centuries*. New York: American Antiquarian Society, 1860.

Coffin, Levi. *Reminiscences of Levi Coffin*. New York: Augustus M. Kelley, 1968.

Coke, Thomas. *A Continuation of Dr. Thomas Coke's Journal in Two Letters to the Reverend John Wesley*. London: J. Paramore, 1787.

———. *Extracts of the Journals of the Late Reverend Thomas Coke, LL.D.* Dublin: R. Napper, 1816.

———. *Extracts of the Journals of the Reverend Dr. Coke's Five Visits to America*. London: G. Paramore, 1793.

———. *A Farther Account of the Late Missionaries to the West Indies in a Letter from the Reverend Dr. Coke to the Reverend John Wesley*. London: n.p., 1789.

———. *A Farther Continuation of Dr. Thomas Coke's Journal in a Letter to the Reverend John Wesley*. London: J. Paramore, 1787.

Coke, Thomas, and Henry Moore. *The Life of the Reverend John Wesley, A.M. Including An Account of the Great Revival of Religion in Europe and America*. Philadelphia: Larry Hall, 1793.

Commager, Henry Steele, and Richard B. Morris, eds. *The Spirit of 'Seventy-Six. The Story of the American Revolution. As Told by Participants*. New York: Harper and Row, 1967.

Crary, Catherine S., ed. *The Price of Loyalty. Tory Writings from the Revolutionary Era*. New York: McGraw-Hill, 1973.

Cresswell, Nicholas. *Journal of Nicholas Cresswell, 1774–1777*. Port Washington, N.Y.: Kennikat Press, 1968.

Cruden, John. *Report on the Management of the Estates Sequestered in South Carolina*. In *Winnowings in American History. Revolutionary Narratives*, Paul Leicester Ford, ed. Brooklyn, N.Y.: Historical Printing Club, 1890.

Dalcho, Frederick. *An Historical Account of the Protestant Episcopal Church in South Carolina. From the First Settlement of the Province, to the War of the Revolution*. Charleston, S.C.: E. Thayer, 1820.

Dann, John C., ed. *The Revolution Remembered. Eyewitness Accounts of the War for Independence*. Chicago: University of Chicago Press, 1977.

Davies, Samuel. *The Duty of Christians to Propagate Their Religion Among Heathens, Earnestly Recommended to the Masters of Negro Slaves in Virginia. A Sermon Preached in Hanover, January 8, 1757*. London: J. Oliver, 1758.

De Braham, John Gerard William. *Report of the General Survey in the Southern District of North America*. Louis De Vorsey, Jr., ed. Columbia: University of South Carolina Press, 1971.

Deems, Charles F. *Annals of Southern Methodism for 1855*. New York: J. A. Gray's Fire-Proof Printing Office,1856.

De Saussure, Wilmot Gibbes. *An Account of the Seige of Charleston, South Carolina in 1780*. Charleston: News and Courier Book Presses, 1885.

Donnan, Elizabeth, ed. *Documents Illustrative of the History of the Slave Trade to America*. 4 vols. Washington: Carnegie Institution of Washington, 1930–35.

Drayton, John. *A View of South-Carolina, as Respects Her Natural and Civil Concerns*. Charleston: W. P. Young, 1802. .

———. *Memoirs of the American Revolution, From Its Commencement to the Year 1776, Inclusive; As Relating to the State of South-Carolina*. 2 vols. Charleston: A. E. Miller, 1821.

Duke, Maurice, and Daniel P. Jordan, eds. *A Richmond Reader 1733–1983*. Chapel Hill: University of North Carolina Press, 1983.

Easterby, James Harold, ed. *Wadboo Barony. Its Fate As Told in Colleton Family Papers, 1773–1793*. Columbia: University of South Carolina Press, 1952.

Eddis, William. *Letters from America*. Aubrey C. Land, ed. Cambridge, Mass.: Harvard University Press, Belknap Press, 1969.

Edwards, Bryan. *The History, Civil and Commercial, of the British West Indies*. 4 vols. Philadelphia: James Humphreys, 1806.

Ewald, Captain Johann. *Diary of the American War. A Hessian Journal*. Joseph P. Tustin, trans. and ed. New Haven, Conn.: Yale University Press, 1979.

Fawcett, Benjamin. *A Compassionate Address to the Christian Negroes in Virginia, and Other British Colonies in North-America*. 2d ed. London: J. Eddowes and J. Colton, 1756.

Fergusson, Charles Bruce, ed. *Clarkson's Mission to America, 1791–1792*. Halifax, Nova Scotia: Public Archives of Nova Scotia, 1971.

Fitzpatrick, John C., ed. *The Writings of George Washington from the Original Manuscript Sources, 1745–1799*. 39 vols. Washington, D.C.: USGPO, 1931–40.

Five Slave Narratives. A Compendium. New York: Arno Press, 1968.

"Folk-Lore Scrap-Book." *Journal of American Folk-Lore* 5 (1892): 63.

Force, Peter, ed. *American Archives . . . A Documentary History of . . . the North American Colonies.* 4th ser., 6 vols. (March 7, 1774–August 21, 1776); 5th ser., 3 vols. (May 3, 1776–December 31, 1776), 1837–53.

————, comp. *Tracts and Other Papers Relating Principally to the Origin, Settlement and Progress of the Colonies in North America, from the Discovery of the Country to the Year 1776.* 4 vols. Washington, D.C.: Peter Force, 1836–46.

Ford, Paul Leicester, ed. *The Writings of Thomas Jefferson.* 10 vols. New York: Putnam's, 1892–99.

Fortescue, Sir John, ed. *The Correspondence of King George the Third from 1760 to December 1783.* 6 vols. London: Macmillan, 1927–28.

Franklin, Benjamin. "Observations Concerning the Increase of Mankind, Peopling of Countries, etc." *Magazine of History* 16 (1918): 217–24.

Fries, Adelaide, ed. *The Records of the Moravians in North Carolina.* 11 vols. Raleigh: Edwards and Broughton, 1922–69.

Furman, Richard. *Reverend Dr. Richard Furman's Exposition of the Views of the Baptists, Relative to the Coloured Population of the United States.* Charleston, S.C.: A. E. Miller, 1823.

Furman, Wood, comp. *A History of the Charleston Association of Baptist Churches.* Charleston, S.C.: J. Hoff, 1811.

Garrettson, Freeborn. *The Life of the Reverend Freeborn Garrettson.* Nathan Bangs, comp. 4th ed. For the Methodist Episcopal Church. New York: G. Lane and C. B. Tippett, 1845.

Georgia Analytical Repository. Reverend Henry Holcombe, ed. 6 vols. 2d ed. Savannah: Seymour, Woolhopter, and Stebbins, 1802–3.

Georgia Historical Society, *Collections.* Savannah, Ga.: Georgia Historical Society, 1840–19–.

"Account of the Siege of Savannah, 1779, from a British Source" 5:129–39.

"Letters from Governor Sir James Wright to the Earl of Dartmouth and Lord George Germain, Secretaries of State for America, from August 24, 1774, to February 16, 1782" 3:180–375.

"Letters of Joseph Clay Merchant of Savannah, 1776–1793" 8:12–259.

"Letters of the Honorable James Habersham, 1756–1775" 6 (1904): 9–245.

"Miscellaneous Papers of James Jackson, 1781–1798." Lilla Mills Hawes, ed. 11:1–101.

"Papers of Lachlan McIntosh, 1779–1779." Lilla Mills Hawes, ed. 12:1–162.

"Proceedings of Minutes of the Governor and Council of Georgia, October 4, 1774–November 7, 1775, and September 6, 1779–September 20, 1780." Lilla Mills Hawes, ed. 10:1–129.

"Selected Eighteenth Century Manuscripts" 20:4–174.

Georgia Writers Project. *Drums and Shadows. Survival Studies Among the Coastal Negroes.* Athens: University of Georgia Press, c. 1986.

Gibbs, Robert W., ed. *Documentary History of the American Revolution.* 3 vols. New York: D. Appleton, 1855.

Glendinning, William. *The Life of William Glendinning, Preacher of the Gospel. Written by Himself.* Philadelphia: W. W. Woodward, 1795.

Graham, Samuel. "An English Officer's Account of His Services in America, 1779–1781: Memoirs of Lt. General Samuel Graham." *Historical Magazine* 9 (1865): 241–49, 267–74, 301–8, 329–35.

Gray, Robert. "Colonel Robert Gray's Observations on the War in Carolina." *South Carolina Historical and Genealogical Magazine* 11 (1910): 139–59.

Greene, Evarts B., and Virginia D. Harrington. *American Population Before the Federal Census of 1790*. New York: Columbia University Press, 1932.

Grimes, William. *Life of William Grimes, the Runaway Slave. Written by Himself*. New York: n.p., 1825.

Gummere, Amelia Mott, ed. *The Journal and Essays of John Woolman*. New York: Macmillan, 1922.

Hales, Stephen. *A Sermon Preached Before the Trustees for Establishing the Colony of Georgia in America*. London: T. Woodward, 1734.

Hamilton, James, Jr. *Negro Plot. An Account of the Late Intended Insurrection among a Portion of the Blacks of the City of Charleston, South Carolina*. Boston: Joseph W. Ingraham, 1822.

Hamilton, Stanislaus Murray, ed. *The Writings of James Monroe*. 7 vols. New York: AMS Press, 1898–1903.

Harrison, William Pope, comp. and ed. *The Gospel among the Slaves. A Short Account of Missionary Operations among the African Slaves of the Southern States*. Nashville, Tenn.: Methodist Episcopal Church, South, 1893.

Hatcher, William E. *John Jasper. The Unmatched Negro Philosopher and Preacher*. Reprint. New York: Negro Universities Press,1969.

Hawes, Lilla Mills, ed. "Minute Book, Savannah Board of Police, 1779." *Georgia Historical Quarterly* 45(1961): 245–57.

Hawes, Lilla Mills, ed. "Miscellaneous Papers of James Jackson, 1781–1798." *Georgia Historical Quarterly* 37(1953): 54–81.

Henson, Josiah. *Father Henson's Story of His Own Life*. Boston: John P. Jewett, 1858.

Hewatt, Alexander. *An Historical Account of the Rise and Progress of the Colonies of South Carolina and Georgia*. 2 vols. London: Alexander Donaldson, 1779.

Higginbotham, Don, ed. *The Papers of James Iredell*. 2 vols. Raleigh, N.C.: Division of Archives and History, 1976.

Hodgson, Adam, Esq. *Remarks During a Journey through North America in the Years 1819, 1820, and 1821. In A Series of Letters*. Westport, Conn.: Negro Universities Press, 1970.

Holcombe, Henry, D. D. *The First Fruits, In a Series of Letters*. Philadelphia: Author, 1812.

Holcombe, Rev. Hosea. *A History of the Rise and Progress of the Baptists in Alabama*. Philadelphia: King and Baird, 1840.

Hutchinson, William T., and William M. E. Rachal, eds. *The Papers of James Madison*. 16 vols. to date. Chicago: University of Chicago Press, 1962–.

Janson, Charles William. *The Stranger in America: Containing Observations Made during a Long Residence in That Country*. London: Albion Press, 1807.

Jones, Charles Colcock, Jr. *Memorial History of Augusta, Georgia, from Its Settlement in 1735 to the Close of the Eighteenth Century*. Syracuse, N.Y.: D. Mason, 1890.

Jones, E. Alfred, ed. *The Journal of Alexander Chesney, A South Carolina Loyalist in the Revolution and After.* Columbus: Ohio State University Press, 1920.

Kemble, Francis Anne. *Journal of a Residence on a Georgian Plantation in 1838–39.* New York: Harper and Bros., 1863.

Kennedy, Lionel H., and Thomas Parker. *An Official Report of the Trials of Sundry Negroes, Charged with an Attempt to Raise an Insurrection in the State of South Carolina.* Charleston, 1822.

Knight, Henry Cogswell. *Letters from the South and West: By Arthur Singleton, Esq.* [pseud.] Boston: Richardson and Lord, 1824.

Knox, William. *Three Tracts Respecting the Conversion and Instruction of Free Indians and Negro Slaves in the Colonies. Addressed to the Venerable Society for the Propagation of the Gospel.* London: J. Debrett, 1789.

Laing, Alexander Gordon. *Travels in the Timannee, Kooranko, and Soolima Countries.* London: J. Murray, 1825.

Lambert, John. *Travels through Canada and the United States of North America, in the Years 1806, 1807, and 1808.* 2d ed. 2 vols. London: C. Craddock and W. Joy, 1814.

Laurens, Henry. *The Papers of Henry Laurens.* Philip H. Hamer and George C. Rogers, eds. 10 vols to date. For the South Carolina Historical Society. Columbia: University of South Carolina Press, 1968–.

Lee, Jesse. *A Short Account of the Life and Death of the Reverend John Lee, A Methodist Minister in the United States of America.* Baltimore, Md.: John West Bulter, 1805.

———. *A Short History of the Methodists in the United States of America; Beginning in 1766, and Continued till 1809.* Baltimore, Md.: Magill and Clime, 1810.

Leland, John. *The Virginia Chronicle: With Judicious and Critical Remarks, under XXIV Heads.* Fredericksburg, Va.: T. Green, 1790.

Lennon, Donald R., and Ida Brooks Kellamals, eds. *The Wilmington Town Book. 1743–1778.* Raleigh, N.C.: North Carolina Department of Cultural Resources, 1973.

Letter to a Member of the General Assembly of Virginia, on the Subject of the Late Conspiracy of the Slaves. Baltimore, Md.: Bonsal and Niles, 1801.

"Letters of Patrick Carr, Terror to British Loyalists, to Governors John Martin and Lyman Hall, 1782–1783." *Georgia Historical Quarterly* 1(1917): 337–43.

"Letters Showing the Rise and Progress of the Early Negro Churches of Georgia and the West Indies." *Journal of Negro History* 1, no. 1 (1916): 69–92.

Lockey, Joseph B., ed. *East Florida 1783–1785. A File of Documents Assembled and Many of them Translated.* Berkeley and Los Angeles: University of California Press, 1949.

Loewald, Klaus G., Beverly Starika, and Paul S. Taylor, eds. "Johann Martin Bolzius Answers a Questionnaire on Carolina and Georgia." *William and Mary Quarterly,* 3d ser., 14, no. 2 (1957): 218–61.

McLean, Robert C., ed. "A Yankee Tutor in the Old South." *North Carolina Historical Review* 47 (1970): 51–85.

McLoughlin, William G., ed. *The Diary of Isaac Backus.* 3 vols. Providence, R.I.: Brown University Press, 1980.

Mays, David John, ed. *Letters and Papers of Edmund Pendleton, 1734–1803*. 2 vols. Charlottesville: University Press of Virginia, 1967.

Mereness, N. D. *Travels in the American Colonies*. New York: Macmillan, 1916.

Minutes of the Methodist Conferences, Annually Held in America, From 1773 to 1794, Inclusive. Philadelphia: Henry Tuckness, 1795.

Minutes Taken at the Several Annual Conferences of the Methodist Episcopal Church for the Year 1824. New York: Bangs and Emory, 1824.

Mitchell, Robert Gray, ed. "Sir James Wright Looks at the American Revolution." *Georgia Historical Quarterly* 53, no. 4 (1969): 509–18.

Moreau de Saint-Mery, Mederic Louis Elie. *Moreau de St. Mery's American Journal [1793–1798]*. Kenneth Roberts and Anna M. Roberts, trans. and eds. Garden City, N.Y.: Doubleday, 1947.

Morrison, Alfred J., ed. *Travels in Virginia in Revolutionary Times*. Lynchburg, Va.: J. P. Bell, 1922.

Morse, Jedidiah. *The American Geography*. 3d ed. Dublin: John Jones, 1792.

Moultrie, William. *Memoirs of the American Revolution*. 2 vols. New York: David Longworth, 1802.

Muhlenberg, Henry Melchior. *The Journals of Henry Melchior Muhlenberg*. Theodore G. Tappert and John W. Doberstein, eds. 3 vols. Philadelphia: Philadelphia Evangelical Lutheran Ministerium of Pennsylvania and Adjacent States, 1942–58.

Mullin, Michael, ed. *American Negro Slavery. A Documentary History*. Columbia: University of South Carolina Press, 1976.

Murdoch, David H., ed. *Rebellion in America. A Contemporary British Viewpoint. 1765–1783*. Santa Barbara, Calif.: Clio Books, 1979.

Newsome, A. R., ed. "A British Orderly Book, 1780–1781." *North Carolina Historical Review* 9 (1932): 57–58, 163–86, 273–98, 366–92.

New York Historical Society, *Collections*. New York: The New-York Historical Society, 1868–19–.

Bunbury, Henry E., ed. Lee Papers 4:1–480; 7:1–427.

"Letters to General Lewis Morris" 8: 433–512.

"Official Letters of Major-General James Pattison" 8:1–430.

Nunis, Doyce B., Jr., ed. "Colonel Archibald Campbell's March from Savannah to Augusta, 1779." *Georgia Historical Quarterly* 45, no. 3 (1961): 275–86.

"Official Correspondence Between Brigadier-General Thomas Sumter and Major-General Nathanael Greene from A.D. 1780 to 1783." *Year-Book City of Charleston, South Carolina, 1899*. Charleston, 1899: 4–135.

"Official Letters of Governor John Martin, 1782–1783." *Georgia Historical Quarterly* 1 (1917): 281–335.

Pace, Antonio, ed. and trans. *Luigi Castiglioni's Viaggio. Travels in the United States of North America 1785–1787*. Syracuse, N.Y.: Syracuse University Press, 1983.

"Papers of the Second Council of Safety of the Revolutionary Party in South Carolina, November, 1775–March, 1776." *South Carolina Historical and Genealogical Magazine* 4 (1903): 195–214.

Payne, Daniel A. *History of the African Methodist Episcopal Church*, C. S. Smith, ed. Reprint. New York: Arno Press; New York Times, 1969.

Payne, Daniel A. *Recollections of Seventy Years*. Reprint. New York: Arno Press; New York Times, 1868.

Perry, William Stevens, ed. *Historical Collections Relating to the American Colonial Church*. Reprint, 5 vols. in 4. New York: AMS Press, 1969 [1870–78].

Pierce, Major William. "Letters of Major William Pierce to St. George Tucker." *Magazine of American History* 7 (1881): 431–45.

Pilmore, Joseph. *The Journal of Joseph Pilmore, Methodist Itinerant, for the Years August 1, 1769 to January 2, 1774*. Frederick E. Mason and Howard T. Maag, eds. For the Historical Society of the Philadelphia Annual Conference of the United Methodist Church. Philadelphia: Message Publishing, 1969.

Pinckney, Charles Cotesworth. *An Address Delivered in Charleston before the Agricultural Society of South Carolina at Its Anniversary Meeting, on Tuesday the 18th of August, 1829*. Charleston, S.C.: n.p., 1829.

Porter, Dorothy, ed. *Negro Protest Pamphlets*. New York: Arno Press; New York Times, 1969.

Primitive Baptists. *Virginia Ketocton Association*. Minutes of the Ketocton Baptist Association, Held at Frying-Pan, Loudoun County, August 1797. N.p., 1797.

Proceedings of the Convention of Delegates for the Counties and Corporations in the Colony of Virginia, Held at Richmond Town, in the County of Henrico, March 20, 1775. Richmond, Va.: Ritchie, Truehart, and DuVal, 1816.

Ramsay, David. *History of the Revolution of South Carolina*. 2 vols. Newberry, S.C.: W. J. Duffie, 1858.

Randolph, Edmund. *History of Virginia*. Arthur H. Shaffer, ed. Charlottesville: University Press of Virginia, 1970.

Randolph, Peter. *Sketches of Slave Life*. Boston: Author, 1855.

Reed, William Bradford, ed. *Life and Correspondence of Joseph Reed, Military Secretary of Washington, at Cambridge*. . . . 2 vols. Philadelphia: Lindsay and Blakiston, 1847.

Richmond College Historical Papers. 2 vols. Richmond, Va., 1915.

Riley, Edward M., ed. "St. George Tucker's Journal of the Siege of Yorktown, 1781." *William and Mary Quarterly*, 3d ser., 5 (1948): 375–95.

Rippon, John. *The Baptist Annual Register. (1790/93–1801/02)*. 4 vols. London: n.p., 1793–1802.

Robin, Abbé. *New Travels Through North America*. Philadelphia: Robert Bell, 1783.

Rochefoucauld-Liancourt et D'Estissac, François-Alexandre-Frédéric, duc de la. *Travels Through the United States of North America in the Years 1795, 1796, and 1797*. 2 vols. London: T. Davison, 1799.

Rogers, George C., Jr., ed. "Letters of Charles O'Hara to the Duke of Grafton." *South Carolina Historical and Genealogical Magazine* 65, no. 3 (1964): 158–80.

Romans, Bernard. *A Concise Natural History of East and West Florida. 1775*. Reprint. New York: Pelican Publishing, 1961.

Rutland, Robert A., ed. *The Papers of George Mason, 1725–1792*. 3 vols. Chapel Hill: University of North Carolina Press, 1970.

Schaw, Janet. *Journal of a Lady of Quality. Being the Narrative of a Journey from*

Scotland to the West Indies, North Carolina, in the Years 1774 to 1776. Evangeline Walker Andrews, ed. New Haven: Yale University Press, 1939.

Schoepf, Johann David. *Travels in the Confederation 1783–1784*. 2 vols. Research and Source Works Series, no. 206. New York: Burt Franklin, 1968.

Sears, Robert, ed. *A New and Popular Pictorial Description of the United States*. New York: Robert Sears, 1848.

Semple, Robert A. *A History of the Rise and Progress of the Baptists in Virginia*. Richmond, Va.: John O'Lynch, 1810.

Serle, Ambrose. *The American Journal of Ambrose Serle, Secretary to Lord Howe, 1776–1778*. Edward H. Tatum, ed. San Marino, Calif.: Huntington Library, 1940.

Shipp, Albert M. *The History of Methodism in South Carolina*. Nashville: Southern Methodist Publishing, 1884.

Siebert, Wilbur Henry, ed. *Loyalists in East Florida 1774–1785. The Most Important Documents Pertaining Thereto*. 2 vols. Deland, Fl.: Florida State Historical Society, 1929.

Simcoe, John Graves. *Simcoe's Military Journal: A History of the Operations of a Partisan Corps Called the Queen's Rangers . . . during the War of the American Revolution*. 1844. Reprint. New York: New York Times and Arno Press, 1968.

Simms, Joseph M. *The First Colored Baptist Church in America Constituted at Savannah January 20, 1788*. Philadelphia: J. B. Lippincott, 1888.

Simms, William G. *The History of South Carolina from Its First European Discovery*. Charleston: S. Babcock, 1840.

"Sir James Wright Looks at the American Revolution." Contributed by Robert G. Mitchell. *Georgia Historical Quarterly* 53 (1969): 509–18.

Smith, James L. *Autobiography of James L. Smith*. Norwich: Press of the Bulletin Company, 1881.

Smith, Richard. "Diary of Richard Smith." *American Historical Review* 1, no. 3 (1896): 288–310.

Smyth, J.F.D. *A Tour of the United States of America*. 2 vols. Dublin: G. Perrin, 1784.

South Carolina Historical Society, *Collections*. Charleston, The South-Carolina Historical Society, 1875–1897.

    "Journal of the 2d Council of Safety, Appointed by the Provisional Congress, November 1775" 3:35–271.

"State of the Virginia Baptists in 1797: Excerpts from the Letters of Isaac Backus." *Virginia Baptist Historical Register* 8 (1969): 381–94.

Stedman, Charles. *The History of the Origin, Progress and Termination of the American War*. 2 vols. Dublin: P. Wogan, P. Byrne, 1794.

Strickland, William. "Observations on the Agriculture of the United States of America." In William Strickland, *Journal of a Tour in the United States of America*. Reverend J. E. Strickland, ed. New York: New-York Historical Society, 1971.

Stuart-Wortley, Hon. Mrs. E., ed. *A Prime Minister and His Son. From the Correspondence of the 3d Earl of Bute and of Lieutenant-General the Hon. Sir Charles Stuart, K.B.* London: John Murray, 1925.

Sutcliff, Robert. *Travels in Some Parts of North America, In the Years 1804, 1805, and 1806.* 2d ed. York and London: W. Alexander, 1815.

Sutherland, Stella H. *Population Distribution in Colonial America.* New York: AMS Press, 1966.

Syrett, Harold C., and Jacob E. Cooke, eds. *The Papers of Alexander Hamilton.* 7 vols. New York: Columbia University Press, 1961–87.

Tarleton, Banastre. *A History of the Campaigns of 1780 and 1781, in the Southern Provinces of North America.* London: T. Cadell, 1787.

Thomas, Ebenezer Smith. *Reminiscences of the Last Sixty-five Years.* 2 vols. Hartford: Case, Tiffany and Burnham, 1840.

Tilden, John Bell. "Extracts from the Journal of Lt. John Bell Tilden, 2d Pennsylvania Line, 1781–1782." *Pennsylvania Magazine of History and Biography* 19 (1895): 51–63, 208–33.

Travis, Joseph. *Autobiography of the Reverend Joseph Travis.* Thomas Osmond Summers, ed. Nashville, Tenn.: E. Stevenson and J. E. Evans, 1856.

Tucker, St. George. *A Dissertation on Slavery: With a Proposal for the Gradual Abolition of It, in the State of Virginia.* Westport, Conn.: Negro Universities Press, 1970.

[———]. *To a Member of the General Assembly of Virginia, on the Subject of the Late Conspiracy of the Slaves.* Baltimore, Md., 1801. Virginia State Library. Microfilm.

Uhlendorf, Bernard A., ed. and trans. *The Siege of Charleston. With an Account of the Province of South Carolina: Diaries and Letters of Hessian Officers from the von Jungkenn Papers in the William L. Clements Library.* Ann Arbor, Mich.: University of Michigan Press, 1938. Reprint. New York: New York Times and Arno Press, 1968.

Uhlendorf Bernhard A., and Edna Vosper, eds. "Letters of Major Baurmeister during the Philadelphia Campaign, 1777–1778." *Pennsylvania Magazine of History and Biography* 59 (1935): 392–419.

Van Schreeven, William J., Robert L. Scribner, and Brent Tarter, eds. *Revolutionary Virginia: The Road to Independence. A Documentary Record.* 6 vols. to date. For the Virginia Independence Bicentennial Commission. Charlottesville: University Press of Virginia, 1973–.

Vesey, Denmark. *The Trial Record of Denmark Vesey.* Introduction by John Oliver Killens. Boston: Beacon Press, 1970.

Watters, William. *A Short Account of the Christian Experience, and Ministerial Labours, of William Watters. Drawn Up by Himself.* Alexandria, Va.: S. Snowden, 1806.

Weld, Isaac, Jr. *Travels Through the States of North America, and the Provinces of Upper and Lower Canada, during the Years 1795, 1796, and 1797.* London: John Stockdale, 1799.

Whipple, Henry Benjamin. *Bishop Whipple's Southern Diary, 1843–1844.* Lester B. Shippen, ed. New York: Da Capo Press, 1968.

White, George, ed. *Historical Collections of Georgia.* New York: Pudney and Russell, 1854.

Wilkinson, Eliza [Yonge]. *Letters of Eliza Wilkinson.* Caroline Gilman, ed. New York: New York Times, 1969.

Winterbottom, Thomas Masterman. *An Account of the Native Africans in the Neigh-bourhood of Sierra Leone*. 2d ed., 2 vols. London: Frank Cass, 1969.

Wright, Louis B., and Marion Tinling, eds. *Quebec to Carolina in 1785–1786. Being the Travel Diary and Observations of Robert Hunter, Jr., a Young Merchant of London*. San Marino, Calif.: Huntington Library, 1943.

Wylly, William. *A Short Account of the Bahama Islands, Their Climate, Productions, etc. to which Are Added, Some Strictures upon Their Relative and Political Situation, the Defects of Their Present Government etc. by a Barrister at Law, Late His Majesty's Solicitor General of Those Islands, and King's Counsel for the Provinces of Nova Scotia and New Brunswick*. London: n.p., 1789.

SELECTED SECONDARY SOURCES

Ajayi, J. F. Ade. *Yoruba Warfare in the Nineteenth Century*. Cambridge, England: Cambridge University Press, 1964.

Akers, Charles W. " 'Our Modern Egyptians': Phillis Wheatley and the Whig Campaign against Slavery in Revolutionary Boston." *Journal of Negro History* 60 (1975): 397–410.

Alden, John Richard. "John Stuart Accuses William Bull." *William and Mary Quarterly*, 3d ser., 2 (1945): 313–20.

———. *The South in the Revolution. 1763–1789*. Vol. 3 of *A History of the South*. Wendell Holmes Stephenson and E. Merton Coulter, eds. Baton Rouge: Louisiana State University Press, 1957.

Allen, Gardner W. *A Naval History of the American Revolution*. 2 vols. Williamstown, Mass.: Houghton, 1913.

Angel, J. Lawrence, Jennifer O. Kelley, Michael Parrington, and Stephanie Pinter. "Life Stresses of the Free Black Community as Represented by the First African Baptist Church, Philadelphia, 1823–1841." *American Journal of Physical Anthropology* 74 (1987): 213–29.

Aptheker, Herbert. *American Negro Slave Revolts*. London: P. S. King and Staples, 1943. New York: Columbia University Press, 1977.

———. *Negro Slave Revolts in the United States, 1526–1860*. New York: International Publishers, 1945.

———. *To Be Free. Studies in American Negro History*. New York: International Publishers, 1948.

Asante, Molefi, and Kariamu Welsh Asante, eds. *African Culture. The Rhythms of Unity*. Westport, Conn.: Greenwood Press, 1985.

Aufderheide, Arthur C., Fraser D. Neiman, Lorentz E. Wittmers, Jr., and George Rapp. "Lead in Bones II: Skeletal-Lead Content as an Indicator of Lifetime Lead Ingestion and the Social Correlates in an Archaeological Population." *American Journal of Physical Anthropology* 55 (1981): 285–93.

Awolalu, J. Omosade. *West African Traditional Religion*. Ibadan, Nigeria: Onibonoje, 1979.

Bailey, Kenneth K. "Protestantism and Afro-Americans in the Old South: Another Look." *Journal of Southern History* 41 (1975): 451–72.

Basden, George Thomas. *Among the Ibos of Nigeria*. London: Seeley, Service and Co., 1921.

Basden, George Thomas. *Niger Ibos*. London: Frank Cass and Co. 1966.

Bastide, Roger. *African Civilizations in the New World*. London: C. Hurst, 1971.

Beeman, Richard R. *The Evolution of the Southern Backcountry. A Case Study of Lunenburg County, Virginia, 1746–1832*. Philadelphia: University of Pennsylvania Press, 1984.

———. *The Old Dominion in the New Nation, 1788–1801*. Lexington: University Press of Kentucky, 1972.

Berlin, Ira. "The Slave Trade and the Development of Afro-American Society in English Mainland North America, 1619–1775." *Southern Studies* 20 (1981): 122–36.

———. "Time, Space, and the Evolution of Afro-American Society in British Mainland North America." *American Historical Review* 85 (1980): 44–78.

Berlin, Ira, and Ronald Hoffman, eds. *Slavery and Freedom in the Age of the American Revolution*. For the United States Capitol Historical Society. Charlottesville: University Press of Virginia, 1983.

Betts, Albert Deems. *History of South Carolina Methodism*. Columbia: Advocate Press, 1952.

Birnie, C. W. "Education of the Negro in Charleston, South Carolina, Prior to the Civil War." *Journal of Negro History* 12 (1927): 13–21.

Blackburn, George, and Sherman L. Ricards. "The Mother-Headed Family Among Free Negroes in Charleston, South Carolina, 1850–1860." *Phylon* 42 (1981): 11–25.

Blakeley, Phyllis R. "Boston King: A Negro Loyalist Who Sought Refuge in Nova Scotia." *Dalhousie Review* 48 (Autumn 1968): 347–56.

Blassingame, John. *The Slave Community. Plantation Life in the Antebellum South*. Rev. and enl. ed. New York: Oxford University Press, 1979.

Bliss, Willard F. "The Rise of Tenancy in Virginia." *Virginia Magazine of History and Biography* 58 (1950): 427–41.

Boles, John B. *Black Southerners 1619–1869*. Lexington: University Press of Kentucky, 1983.

———, ed. *Masters and Slaves in the House of the Lord. Race and Religion in the American South, 1740–1870*. Lexington: University Press of Kentucky, 1988.

Bolton, H. Carrington. "Decoration of Graves of Negroes in South Carolina." *Journal of American Folk-Lore* 4 (1891): 214.

Bonner, James C. *A History of Georgia Agriculture 1732–1860*. Athens: University of Georgia Press, 1964.

Bonomi, Patricia U. *Under the Cope of Heaven: Religion, Society and Politics in Colonial America*. New York: Oxford University Press, 1986.

Bonomi, Patricia U., and Peter R. Eisenstadt. "Church Adherence in the Eighteenth-Century British American Colonies." *William and Mary Quarterly*, 3d ser., 39 (1982): 245–86.

Bowler, Arthur R. *Logistics and the Failure of the British Army in America, 1775–1783*. Princeton, N.J.: Princeton University Press, 1975.

Boyd, William K. "Methodist Expansion in North Carolina after the Revolution," *Historical Papers*. Trinity College Historical Society, Series no. 12 (1916): 37–55.

Brady, Patrick S. "The Slave Trade and Sectionalism in South Carolina, 1787–1808." *Journal of Southern History* 38 (1972): 601–20.

Brewer, James H. "Legislation Designed to Control Slavery in Wilmington and Fayetteville." *North Carolina Historical Review* 30 (1953): 155–66.

Brooks, Walter H. "The Evolution of the Negro Baptist Church." *Journal of Negro History* 7 (1922): 11–22.

———. "Priority of the Silver Bluff Church and Its Promoters." *Journal of Negro History* 7 (1922): 172–96.

Broussard, James H. *The Southern Federalists 1800–1816*. Baton Rouge: Louisiana State University Press, 1978.

Brown, Paula. "The Igbira." In *Peoples of the Niger-Benue Confluence*. 1955. Reprint. London: International African Institute, 1970.

Brown, Richard Maxwell. *Strain of Violence: Historical Studies of American Violence and Vigilantism*. New York: Oxford University Press, 1975.

Brown, Wallace. *The Good Americans. The Loyalists in the American Revolution*. New York: William Morrow, 1969.

———. *The King's Friends; The Composition and Motives of the American Loyalist Claimants*. Providence, R.I.: Brown University Press, 1965.

Browning, James B. "The Beginnings of Insurance Enterprise among Negroes." *Journal of Negro History* 22 (1937): 417–32.

Buckley, Roger Norman. *Slaves in Red Coats. The British West India Regiments, 1795–1815*. New Haven, Conn.: Yale University Press, 1979.

Burns, Sir Alan Cuthbert. *History of the British West Indies*. 2d ed., rev. London: George Allen and Unwin, 1965.

Burnston, Sharon Ann. "The Cemetery at Catoctin Furnace, Maryland: The Invisible People." *Maryland Archaeology* 17 (1981): 19–31.

Burton, Orville Vernon, and Robert C. McMath, Jr., eds. *Class, Conflict, and Consensus. Antebellum Southern Community Studies*. Contributions in American History, no. 96. Westport, Conn.: Greenwood Press, 1982.

Calhoon, Robert M. *Evangelicals and Conservatives in the Early South, 1740–1861*. Columbia: University of South Carolina, 1988.

Chreitzberg, Reverend Abel McKee. *Early Methodism in the Carolinas*. Nashville, Tenn.: Methodist Episcopal Church, South, 1897.

Clark, Ernest James, Jr. "Aspects of the North Carolina Slave Code, 1715–1860." *North Carolina Historical Review* 39 (1962): 148–64.

Clarke, Peter B. *West Africa and Christianity*. London: E. Arnold, 1986.

Clemens, Paul G. E. *The Atlantic Economy and Colonial Maryland's Eastern Shore. From Tobacco to Grain*. Ithaca, N.Y.: Cornell University Press, 1980.

———. "The Operation of an Eighteenth-Century Chesapeake Tobacco Plantation." *Agricultural History* 49 (1975): 517–31.

Clowse, Converse D. *Economic Beginnings in Colonial South Carolina, 1670–1730*. 1st ed. For the South Carolina Tricentennial Commission. Columbia: University of South Carolina Press, 1971.

Cody, Cheryll Ann. "Naming, Kinship and Estate Dispersal. Notes on Slave Family Life on a South Carolina Plantation, 1786 to 1833." *William and Mary Quarterly*, 3d ser., 39 (1982): 192–211.

Coleman, Kenneth. *The American Revolution in Georgia. 1763–1789*. Athens: University of Georgia Press, 1958.

Combes, John D. "Ethnography, Archaeology and Burial Practices Among Coastal South Carolina Blacks." *Conference for Historic Site Archaeology Papers* 7 (1974): 52–61.

Connor, Cynthia. "Sleep On and Take Your Rest": Black Mortuary Behavior on the East Branch of the Cooper River, South Carolina. Master's thesis, University of South Carolina, 1989.

Cooper, Frederick. *Plantation Slavery on the East Coast of Africa*. New Haven, Conn.: Yale University Press, 1977.

Cote, Richard N. "South Carolina Methodist Records." *South Carolina Historical Magazine* 85 (1984):51–57.

Curtin, Philip D. *The Atlantic Slave Trade. A Census*. Madison: University of Wisconsin Press, 1969.

Craton, Michael. *A History of the Bahama Islands*. London: Collins, 1962.

———. *Searching for the Invisible Man. Slaves and Plantation Life in Jamaica*. Cambridge, Mass.: Harvard University Press, 1978.

———. *Testing the Chains: Resistance to Slavery in the British West Indies*. Ithaca, N.Y.: Cornell University Press, 1982.

Creel, Margaret Washington. *"A Peculiar People": Slave Religion and Community-Culture Among the Gullahs*. New York: New York University Press, 1988.

Crooks, John Joseph. *A History of the Colony of Sierra Leone Western Africa*. Reprint. Northbrook, Ill.: MetroBooks, 1972.

Crow, Jeffrey J. "Slave Rebelliousness and Social Conflict in North Carolina, 1775–1802." *William and Mary Quarterly*, 3d ser., 37 (1980): 79–102.

Crow, Jeffrey J., and Larry E. Tise, eds. *The Southern Experience in the American Revolution*. Chapel Hill, N.C.: University of North Carolina Press, 1978.

Crum, Mason. *Gullah. Negro Life in the Carolina Sea Islands*. Durham, N.C.: Duke University Press, 1940.

Curtin, Philip D. *The Atlantic Slave Trade. A Census*. Madison: The University of Wisconsin Press, 1969.

Daniel, W. Harrison. "Virginia Baptists and the Negro in the Early Republic." *Virginia Magazine of History and Biography* 80 (1972): 60–69.

Davis, David Brion. *The Problem of Slavery in the Age of Revolution. 1770–1823*. Ithaca, N.Y.: Cornell University Press, 1975.

Davis, Harold E. *The Fledgling Province. Social and Cultural Life in Colonial Georgia. 1733–1766*. For the Institute of Early American History and Culture. Chapel Hill: University of North Carolina Press, 1976.

Davis, Richard Beale. *Intellectual Life in the Colonial South. 1758–1763*. 3 vols. Knoxville: University of Tennessee Press, 1978.

"Divination and the Sifter." *Journal of American Folk-Lore* 5 (1892): 63.

Douglass, John E. "Judiciary Without Jurisdiction: South Carolina's Experiment with a County and Precinct Court System, 1720–1730." *South Carolina Magazine* 90 (1989): 237–56.

Dunn, Richard S. "A Tale of Two Plantations: Slave Life at Mesopotamia in Jamaica and Mount Airy in Virginia, 1799 to 1828." *William and Mary Quarterly,* 3d ser., 34 (1977): 32–65.

Earle, Carville V. *The Evolution of a Tidewater Settlement System: All Hallow's Parish, Maryland, 1650–1783.* University of Chicago: Department of Geography Research Paper no. 170, 1975.

Earle, Carville V., and Ronald Hoffman. "Urban Development in the Eighteenth-Century South." *Perspectives in American History* 10 (1976): 7–78.

Edwards, Paul, and James Walvin. *Black Personalities in the Era of the Slave Trade.* Baton Rouge: Louisiana State University Press, 1983.

Egnal, Marc. "The Origins of the Revolution in Virginia: A Reinterpretation." *William and Mary Quarterly,* 3d ser., 37 (1980): 401–28.

Eighmy, John Lee. "The Baptists and Slavery: An Examination of the Origins and Benefits of Segregation." *Social Science Quarterly* 49 (1968): 666–73.

Ekirch, A. Roger. *"Poor Carolina." Politics and Society in Colonial North Carolina, 1729–1776.* Chapel Hill: University of North Carolina Press, c. 1981.

Ekwueme, Lazarus. "African-Music Retentions in the New World." *The Black Perspective in Music* 2 (1974): 128–43.

Elkins, Stanley M. *Slavery. A Problem in American Institutional and Intellectual Life.* Chicago: University of Chicago Press, 1959.

Eller, Ernest McNeill, ed. *Chesapeake Bay in the American Revolution.* Centreville, Md.: Tidewater Publishers, 1981.

Ellis, Alfred B. *The Yoruba-Speaking Peoples of the Slave Coast of West Africa.* Oosterhout. Netherlands: Anthropological Publications, 1966.

Emery, Lynne F. *Black Dance in the United States From 1619 to 1970.* Palo Alto, Calif.: National Press Books, 1972.

Epstein, Dena J. *Sinful Tunes and Spirituals: Black Folk Music to the Civil War.* Urbana: University of Illinois Press, 1977.

Essig, James D. *The Bonds of Wickedness: American Evangelicals Against Slavery, 1770–1808.* Philadelphia: Temple University Press, 1982.

Fairbanks, Charles H. "The Plantation Archaeology of the Southeastern Coast." *Historical Archaeology* 18 (1984): 1–14.

Fenn, Elizabeth A. "Honoring the Ancestors. Kongo-American Graves in the American South," *Southern Exposure* 13 (1984): 42–47.

Finley, Moses L. *Ancient Slavery and Modern Ideology.* New York: Viking Press, 1980.

Fisher, Allan G. B., and Humphrey J. Fisher. *Slavery and Muslim Society in Africa.* 1st U.S.A. ed. Garden City, N.Y.: Doubleday, 1971 [1970].

Fitchett, E. Horace. "The Traditions of the Free Negro in Charleston, South Carolina." *Journal of Negro History* 25 (1940): 139–52.

Foner, Philip. *Blacks in the American Revolution.* Westport, Conn.: Greenwood Press, 1976.

Forde, Cyril Daryll. *The Yoruba-Speaking Peoples of South-Western Nigeria.* London: International African Institute, 1969.

Frazier, E. Franklin. *The Negro Family in the United States.* Chicago, 1939.

———. *The Negro in the United States.* Rev. New York: Macmillan, 1957.

Frey, Sylvia R. "Between Slavery and Freedom: Virginia Blacks in the American Revolution." *Journal of Southern History* 49 (1983): 375–98.

———. "The British and the Black: A New Perspective." *Historian* 38 (1976): 225–38.

———. "British Armed Forces and the American Victory." In John Ferling, ed., 165–83. *The World Turned Upside Down*. Westport, Conn.: Greenwood Press, 1988.

———. *The British Soldier in America. A Social History of Military Life in the Revolutionary Period*. Austin: University of Texas Press, 1981.

Fyfe, Christopher. *A Short History of Sierra Leone*. London: Longman, 1979.

Fyfe, Christopher, and Eldred Jones, eds. *Freetown. A Symposium*. Freetown: Sierra Leone University Press, 1968.

Galenson, David. *White Servitude in Colonial America*. Cambridge, England: Cambridge University Press, 1981.

Gallay, Allan. *The Formation of a Planter Elite. Jonathan Bryan and the Southern Colonial Frontier*. Athens: University of Georgia Press, 1989.

———. "The Origins of Slaveholders' Paternalism: George Whitefield, the Bryan Family, and the Great Awakening in the South." *Journal of Southern History* 53 (1987): 369–94.

Gamble, David P. *The Wolof of Senegambia*. London: International African Institute, 1957.

Gardner, Robert W. "Virginia Baptists and Slavery, 1759–1790." *Virginia Baptist Register* 24 (1985): 1212–20.

Gardner, William James. *A History of Jamaica from Its Discovery by Christopher Columbus to the Present Time*. London: E. Stock, 1873.

Garlan, Yvon. *War in the Ancient World. A Social History*. London: Chatto and Windus, 1975.

Gaspar, Barry David. *Bondsmen and Rebels*. Baltimore: Johns Hopkins University Press, c. 1985.

Genovese, Eugene D. *From Rebellion to Revolution. Afro-American Slave Revolts in the Making of the Modern World*. Baton Rouge: Louisiana State University Press, 1979.

———. *Roll, Jordan, Roll. The World the Slaves Made*. New York: Vintage Books, 1976.

———. *The World the Slaveholders Made. Two Essays in Interpretation*. New York: Vintage Books, 1971.

Gibson, James R., ed. *European Settlement and Development in North America: Essays on Geographical Change in Honour and Memory of Andrew Hill Clark*. Toronto: University of Toronto Press, 1978.

Grant, John N. "Black Immigrants into Nova Scotia, 1776–1815." *Journal of Negro History* 58 (1973): 253–70.

Gray, Lewis Cecil. *History of Agriculture in the Southern United States to 1860*. 2 vols. New York: Peter Smith, 1941.

Greene, Jack P., ed. *The American Revolution. Its Character and Limits*. New York: New York University Press, 1987.

Grissom, William L. *History of Methodism in North Carolina from 1772 to the Present Time*. Nashville: Methodist Episcopal Church, 1905.

Gutman, Herbert G. *The Black Family in Slavery and Freedom, 1750–1925*. New York: Pantheon Books, 1976.

Hall, Gwendolyn Midlo. *Social Control in Slave Plantation Societies. A Comparison of St. Domingue and Cuba*. Baltimore, Md.: Johns Hopkins University Press, 1971.

Handler, Jerome S. *The Unappropriated People: Freedmen in the Slave Society of Barbados*. Baltimore: Johns Hopkins University Press, 1974.

Harding, Vincent. *There Is a River. The Black Struggle for Freedom in America*. 1st ed. New York: Harcourt Brace Jovanovich, c. 1981.

Harris, Robert L., Jr. "Charleston's Free Afro-American Elite: The Brown Fellowship Society and the Humane Brotherhood." *South Carolina Historical Magazine* 82 (1981): 289–310.

Hartzell, Joseph C. "Methodism and the Negro in the United States." *Journal of Negro History* 8 (1923): 301–15.

Herskovits, Melville J. *Dahomey. An Ancient West African Kingdom*. 2 vols. New York: J. J. Augustin, 1938.

———. *The Myth of the Negro Past*. Boston: Beacon Press, 1958.

Higginbotham, A. Leon, Jr. *In the Matter of Color. Race and the American Legal Process. The Colonial Period*. New York: Oxford University Press, 1978.

Higgins, W. Robert, ed. *The Revolutionary War in the South: Power, Conflict and Leadership*. Durham, N.C.: Duke University Press, 1979.

Hill, Samuel S., ed. *Varieties of Southern Religious Experience*. Baton Rouge: Louisiana State University Press, 1988.

Hindus, Michael. "Black Justice Under White Law: Criminal Prosecutions of Blacks in Antebellum South Carolina." *Journal of American History* 63(1976): 575–99.

Hoffman, Ronald. *A Spirit of Dissension. Economics, Politics, and the Revolution in Maryland*. Baltimore, Md.: Johns Hopkins University Press, 1973.

Holmes, Jack D. L. "Alabama's Forgotten Settler: Notes on the Spanish Mobile District, 1780–1813." *Alabama Historical Quarterly* 33 (1971): 87–97.

———. "The Role of Blacks in Spanish Alabama: The Mobile District, 1780–1813." *Alabama Historical Quarterly* 37 (1975): 5–18.

Holt, Bryce R. "The Supreme Court of North Carolina and Slavery." *Historical Papers*. Trinity College Historical Society, ser. 17 (1927): 7–73.

Howe, George. *History of the Presbyterian Church in South Carolina*. 2 vols. Columbia, S.C.: Duffie and Chapman, 1870.

Hudgins, Carter L. "Historical Archaeology and Salvage Archaeological Excavations at College Landing. An Interim Report." Virginia Research Center for Archaeology, 1977.

Hughes, Sarah S. "Slaves for Hire: The Allocation of Black Labor in Elizabeth City County, Virginia, 1782–1810." *William and Mary Quarterly*, 3d ser., 35 (1978): 260–86.

Hume, Ivor Noel. *1775. Another Part of the Field*. New York: Alfred A. Knopf, 1966.

Hunt, Alfred N. *Haiti's Influence on Antebellum America. Slumbering Volcano in the Caribbean*. Baton Rouge: Louisiana State University Press, 1988.

Idowu, E. Bolaji. *African Traditional Religion*. Maryknoll, N.Y.: Orbis Books, 1973.

Imasogie, Osadolor. *African Traditional Religion*. Ibadan, Nigeria: University Press, 1985.

Ingersoll, Ernest, ed. "Decoration of Negro Graves." *Journal of American Folk-Lore* 5 (1892): 68–69.

Isaac, Rhys. *The Transformation of Virginia, 1740–1790*. For the Institute of Early American History and Culture. Chapel Hill: University of North Carolina Press, 1982.

Jackson, Harvey H. "Hugh Bryan and the Evangelical Movement in Colonial South Carolina." *William and Mary Quarterly*, 3d ser., 43 (1968): 594–614.

Jackson, Luther P. "Early Strivings of the Negro in Virginia." *Journal of Negro History* 25 (1940): 25–33.

———. "Religious Development of the Negro in Virgina from 1760 to 1860." *Journal of Negro History* 16 (1931): 168–239.

James, C.L.R. *The Black Jacobins. Toussaint L'Ouverture and the San Domingo Revolution*. 2d ed., rev. New York: Vintage Books, 1963.

Jernegan, Marcus W. "Slaves and Conversion in the American Colonies." *American Historical Review* 21 (1916): 504–27.

Johnson, Michael P. "Planters and Patriarchy: Charleston, 1800–1860." *Journal of Southern History* 46 (1980): 45–72.

———. "Runaway Slaves and the Slave Communities in South Carolina, 1799 to 1830." *William and Mary Quarterly*, 3d ser., 38 (1981): 418–41.

Johnson, Samuel. *The History of the Yorubas*. 5th ed. Lagos, Nigeria: C.M.S. Bookshops, 1950.

Jones-Jackson, Patricia. *When Roots Die. Endangered Traditions on the Sea Islands*. Athens: University of Georgia Press, 1987.

Jordan, Winthrop D. *White Over Black. American Attitudes Toward the Negro, 1550–1812*. Chapel Hill: University of North Carolina Press, 1968.

Jordan, Winthrop D., and Sheila L. Skemp, eds. *Race and family in the Colonial South*. Jackson, Miss.: University Press of Mississippi, 1987.

Joyner, Charles W. *Down by the Riverside*. Urbana: University of Illinois Press, 1984.

Kaplan, Sidney. *The Black Presence in the Era of the American Revolution, 1770–1800*. Washington, D.C.: New York Graphic Society and Smithsonian Institution Press, 1973.

———. "The 'Domestic Insurrections' of the Declaration of Independence." *Journal of Negro History* 61 (1976): 243–55.

Kelley, Jennifer O. "The Workers of Catoctin Furnace." *Maryland Archaeology* 19 (1983): 2–17.

Kelley, Jennifer O., and J. Lawrence Angel. "Life Stresses of Slavery." *American Journal of Physical Anthropology* 74 (1987): 199–211.

Kelso, William M. *Kingsmill Plantations 1619–1800. Archaeology of Country Life in Colonial Virginia*. Orlando, Fla.: Academic Press, 1984.

Kilson, Martin L., and Robert I. Rotberg, eds. *The African Diaspora. Interpretative Essays*. Cambridge, Mass.: Harvard University Press, 1976.

Klein, Rachel. "The Rise of the Planters in the South Carolina Backcountry, 1767–1808." Ph.D. diss., Yale University, 1979.

Klingberg, Joseph. *The Anti-slavery Movement in England*. New Haven: Yale University Press; London: Humphrey Milford; London: Oxford University Press, 1926.

Klingelhofer, Eric. "Aspects of Early Afro-American Material Culture: Artifacts from the Slave Quarters at Garrison Plantation, Maryland." *Historical Archaeology* 21 (1987): 112–19.

Kolchin, Peter. *Unfree Labor. American Slavery and Russian Serfdom*. Cambridge, Mass.: Harvard University Press, Belknap Press, 1987.

Kulikoff, Allan. "The Origins of Afro-American Society in Tidewater Maryland and Virginia, 1700–1790." *William and Mary Quarterly*, 3d ser., 35 (1978): 226–59.

———. "A 'Prolifick' People: Black Population Growth in the Chesapeake Colonies, 1700–1790." *Southern Studies* 16 (Winter 1977): 391–414.

———. *Tobacco and Slaves. The Development of Southern Culture in the Chesapeake, 1680–1800*. For the Institute of Early American History and Culture. Chapel Hill: University of North Carolina Press, 1986.

Lambert, Robert Stansbury. *South Carolina Loyalists in the American Revolution*. Columbia: University of South Carolina Press, 1987.

Lawrence, James B. "Religious Education of the Negro in the Colony of Georgia." *Georgia Historical Quarterly* 14 (1930): 41–57.

Lee, Jean Butenhoff. "The Problem of Slave Community in the Eighteenth-Century Chesapeake. *William and Mary Quarterly*, 3d ser., 43 (1986): 333–61.

Leone, Mark P., and Parker B. Potter, eds. *The Recovery of Meaning: Historical Archaeology in the Eastern United States*. Washington, D.C.: Smithsonian Institution Press, 1988.

Levine, Lawrence W. *Black Culture and Black Consciousness. Afro-American Folk Thought from Slavery to Freedom*. Oxford: Oxford University Press, 1977.

Levtzion, Nehemia. *Ancient Ghana and Mali*. New York: Africana Publishing, 1980.

Lewis, Ronald L. *Coal, Iron and Slaves. Industrial Slavery in Maryland and Virginia, 1715–1865*. Westport, Conn.: Greenwood Press, 1979.

Libourel, Jan M. "Galley Slaves in the Second Punic War." *Classical Philology* 68 (1973): 116–19.

Little, Kenneth L. *The Mende of Sierra Leone. A West African People in Transition*. Rev. London: Routledge and Kegan Paul; New York: Humanities Press, 1969.

Littlefield, Daniel C. *Rice and Slaves. Ethnicity and the Slave trade in Colonial South Carolina*. Baton Rouge: Louisiana State University Press, 1981.

Livermore, George. *An Historical Research Respecting the Opinions of the Founders of the Republic on Negroes as Slaves, as Citizens, and as Soldiers*. 4th ed. Boston: A. Williams, 1863.

Lofton, John. *Denmark Vesey's Revolt. The Slave Plot That Lit a Fuse to Fort Sumter*. Kent, Ohio: Kent State University Press, 1983.

Long, Charles H. "Perspectives for a Study of Afro-American Religion in the United States." *History of Religion* 11 (1971): 54–66.

Long, Richard A. *Africa and America: Essays in Afro-American Culture*. Atlanta, Ga.: Atlanta University, 1981.

Lovejoy, Paul E., ed. *The Ideology of Slavery in Africa*. Beverly Hills, Calif.: Sage Publications, 1981.

Lucas, Jonathan Olumide. *The Religion of the Yorubas*. Lagos, Nigeria: C.M.S. Bookshops, 1948.

Lumpkin, William L. "Colonel Robert Carter, A Baptist." *Virginia Baptist Register* 8 (1969): 339–55.

McColley, Robert. *Slavery and Jeffersonian Virginia*. 2d ed. Urbana: University of Illinois Press, 1973.

McCowen, George Smith. *The British Occupation of Charleston, 1780–1782*. For the South Carolina Tricentennial Commission. Columbia, S.C.: University of South Carolina Press, 1972.

McCrady, Edward. *The History of South Carolina in the Revolution 1780–1783*. 3 vols. New York: Russell and Russell, 1969.

McGee, Leo. "Early Efforts Toward Educating the Black Adult." *Negro History Bulletin* 34 (1971): 88–89.

MacLeod, Duncan J. *Slavery, Race and the American Revolution*. Cambridge, England: Cambridge University Press, 1974.

Mair, Lucy P. *African Marriage and Social Change*. London: Frank Cass and Co., 1969.

Manoukian, Madeline. *Akan and Ga-Adangme Peoples of the Gold Coast*. For the International African Institute. London: Oxford University Press, 1950.

Mathews, Donald G. *Religion in the Old South*. Chicago: University of Chicago Press, 1977.

Mbiti, John S. *African Religions and Philosophy*. New York: Frederick A. Praeger, 1969.

———. *Death and the Hereafter in the Light of Christianity and African Religion*. Kampala: Department of Religious Studies and Philosophy, Makerere University, 1974.

———. *Love and Marriage in Africa*. London: Longman, 1973.

Meier, August, and Elliott Rudwick, eds. *The Making of Black America. Essays in Negro Life and History*. New York: Atheneum, 1969.

Menard, Russell R. "From Servants to Slaves: The Transformation of the Chesapeake Labor System." *Southern Studies* 16 (Winter 1977): 355–90.

———. "The Maryland Slave Population, 1658–1730: A Demographic Profile of Blacks in Four Counties." *William and Mary Quarterly*, 3d ser., 32 (1975): 29–54.

Merrens, Harry Roy. *Colonial North Carolina in the Eighteenth Century. A Study in Historical Geography*. Chapel Hill: University of North Carolina Press, 1964.

Middleton, Arthur Pierce. *Tobacco Coast. A Maritime History of Chesapeake Bay in the Colonial Era*. Newport News, Va.: Mariner's Museum, 1953.

Miers, Suzanne, and Igor Kopytoff, eds. *Slavery in Africa. Historical and Anthropological Perspectives*. Madison: University of Wisconsin Press, 1977.

Miller, John C. *The Wolf by the Ears: Thomas Jefferson and Slavery*. New York: Free Press, 1977.

Miller, Randall M. "A Backcountry Loyalist Plan to Retake Georgia and the Carolinas, 1778." *South Carolina Historical Magazine* 75 (1974): 207–14.

Moore, Christopher. *The Loyalists. Revolution, Exile, Settlement*. Toronto: Macmillan, 1984.

Morgan, Edmund S. *American Slavery, American Freedom*. New York: Norton, 1975.

Morgan, Philip D. "Black Life in the Eighteenth-Century," In *Perspectives in American History*, n.s., 1 (1984): 187–232.

———. "The Development of Slave Culture in Eighteenth Century Plantation America." Ph.D. diss., University College, London, 1977.

———. "Slave Life in Piedmont Virginia." In *Colonial Chesapeake Society*, Lois Green Carr, Philip D. Morgan, and Jean B. Russo, eds., 433–84. For the Institute of Early American History and Culture. Chapel Hill: University of North Carolina Press, 1988.

———. "Slave Life in the Virginia Piedmont, 1720–1780: A Demographic Report." Conference on "The Colonial Experience: The Eighteenth Century Chesapeake," Baltimore, Md., 1984. Mimeograph.

———. "Three Planters and Their Slaves: Perspectives on Slavery in Virginia, South Carolina, and Jamaica, 1750–1790." In *Race and Family in the Colonial South*, Winthrop D. Jordan and Sheila L. Skemp, eds., 37–79. Jackson, Miss.: University Press of Mississippi, 1987.

———. "Work and Culture: The Task System and the World of Lowcountry Blacks, 1700 to 1880." *William and Mary Quarterly*, 3d ser., 39 (1982): 563–99.

Mullin, Gerald W. *Flight and Rebellion. Slave Resistance in Eighteenth-Century Virginia*. New York: Oxford University Press, 1972.

Nadelhaft, Jerome J. *The Disorders of War. The Revolution in South Carolina*. Orono, Maine: University of Maine at Orono Press, 1981.

———. "The Somerset Case of Slavery: Myth, Reality, and Repercussions," *Journal of Negro History* 51 (1966): 193–208.

Nash, Gary B. *Forging Freedom: The Formation of Philadelphia's Black Community, 1720–1840*. Cambridge, Mass.: Harvard University Press, 1988.

Neiman, Fraser D. "Domestic Architecture at the Clifts Plantation: The Social Context of Early Virginia Building." *Northern Neck Historical Magazine* 28 (1978): 3096–128.

Noel, Donald L., ed. *The Origins of American Slavery and Racism*. Columbus, Ohio: Charles E. Merrill, 1972.

Norton, Mary Beth. "The Fate of Some Black Loyalists of the American Revolution." *Journal of Negro History* 58 (1973): 402–26.

Oakes, James. *The Ruling Race: A History of American Slaveholders*. New York: Alfred A. Knopf, 1982.

Obichere, Boniface I. "The Social Character of Slavery in Ashanti and Dahomey." *Ufahama* 12 (1983): 191–205.

O'Brien, John T. "Factory, Church and Community: Blacks in Antebellum Richmond." *Journal of Southern History* 44 (1978): 509–36.

Okihiro, Gary, ed. *In Resistance. Studies in African, Caribbean, and Afro-American History.* Amherst: University of Massachusetts Press, 1981.

Olson, Gary D. "Thomas Brown, Loyalist Partisan, and the Revolutionary War in Georgia, 1777–1782." *Georgia Historical Quarterly* 54 (1970): 1–19.

Olwell, Robert A. " 'Domestick Enemies': Slavery and Political Independence in South Carolina, May 1775–March 1776." *Journal of Southern History* 55 (1989): 21–48.

Organization and Development of the Elam Baptist Church, 1810–1910. Ruthville, Va.: n.p., 1976.

Ott, Thomas. *The Haitian Revolution, 1789–1804.* 1st ed. Knoxville: University of Tennessee Press, 1973.

Ottenberg, Simon, ed. *African Religious Groups and Beliefs: Papers in Honor of William R. Bascom.* For the Folklore Institute. Meerut, India: Archana Publications, c. 1982.

Ottenberg, Simon, and Phoebe Ottenberg, eds. *Cultures and Societies of Africa.* New York: Random House, 1960.

Owens, Loulie. *Saints of Clay: The Shaping of South Carolina Baptists.* Columbia, S.C.: R. L. Bryan, 1971.

Owsley, Frank L. *Plain Folk of the Old South.* Baton Rouge: Louisiana State University Press, 1982.

Pancake, John S. *This Destructive War: The British Campaign in the Carolinas, 1780–1782.* University: University of Alabama Press, 1985.

Parramore, T. C., "Conspiracy and Revivalism in 1802: A Direful Symbiosis." *Negro History Bulletin* 43 (1980): 28–31.

Parrinder, Edward Geoffrey. *Sex in the World's Religions.* New York: Oxford University Press, 1980.

———. *West African Religion. A Study of the Beliefs and Practices of Akan, Ewe, Yoruba, Ibo and Kindred Peoples.* New York: Barnes and Noble, 1970.

Phillips, Ulrich B. *American Negro Slavery. A Survey of the Supply, Employment and Control of Negro Labor.* Baton Rouge: Louisiana State University Press, 1966.

Pierre, C. E. "The Work of the Society for the Propagation of the Gospel in Foreign Parts among the Negroes in the Colonies." *Journal of Negro History* I (1916): 349–60.

Piersen, William D. *Black Yankees.* Amherst: University of Massachusetts Press, 1988.

———. "White Cannibals, Black Martyrs: Fear, Depression, and Religious Faith as Causes of Suicide Among New Slaves." *Journal of Negro History* 2 (1977): 147–59.

Porter, Dale H. *The Abolition of the Slave Trade in England, 1784–1807.* Hamden, Conn.: Archon Books, 1970.

Price, Jacob M. "The Economic Growth of the Chesapeake and the European Market, 1697–1775." *Journal of Economic History* 24 (1964): 496–511.

———. *France and the Chesapeake. A History of the French Tobacco Monopoly, 1674–*

1791, and of Its Relationship to the British and American Tobacco Trades. 2 vols. Ann Arbor, Mich.: University of Michigan Press, 1973.

Price, Richard, ed. *Maroon Societies: Rebel Slave Communities in the Americas.* 2d ed. Baltimore: The Johns Hopkins University Press, 1979.

Proctor, Samuel, ed. *Eighteenth-Century Florida and the Revolutionary South.* Gainesville, Fla.: University of Florida Press, 1978.

———, ed. *Eighteenth-Century Florida. Life on the Frontier.* Gainesville, Fla.: University of Florida Press, 1976.

Quarles, Benjamin. *The Negro in the American Revolution.* Chapel Hill: University of North Carolina Press, 1961.

Raboteau, Albert J. *Slave Religion. The "Invisible Institution" in the Antebellum South.* New York: Oxford University Press, 1978.

Radcliffe-Brown, A. R., and Cyril Daryll Ford. *African Systems of Kinship and Marriage.* For the International African Institute. London: Oxford University Press, 1950.

Ragatz, Lowell Joseph. *The Fall of the Planter Class in the British Caribbean, 1763–1833.* New York: Century, 1928.

Rankin, Hugh F. "The Moore's Creek Bridge Campaign, 1776." *North Carolina Historical Review* 30 (1953): 23–60.

———. *The North Carolina Continentals.* Chapel Hill: University of North Carolina Press, 1971.

Rathbun, Ted A. "Health and Disease at a South Carolina Plantation: 1840–1870." *American Journal of Physical Anthropology* 74 (1987): 239–53.

Rattray, Robert S. *Ashanti Law and Constitution.* New York: Negro Universities Press, 1969.

Rawick, George P. *From Sundown to Sunup: The Making of a Black Community.* Vol. 1, ser. 1 of *The American Slave: A Composite Autobiography,* Contributions in Afro-American and African Studies. Westport, Conn.: Greenwood Publishing, 1972.

Rawley, James A. *The Transatlantic Slave Trade. A History.* New York: Norton, 1981.

Rice, Charles Duncan. *The Rise and Fall of Black Slavery.* London: Macmillan, 1975.

Riley, Sandra. *Homeward Bound: A History of the Bahama Islands to 1850 with a Definitive Study of Abaco in the American Loyalist Plantation Period.* Miami, Fla.: Island Research, c. 1983.

Robinson, Donald L. *Slavery in the Structure of American Politics, 1765–1820.* New York: Harcourt Brace Jovanovich, 1971.

Roediger, David. "And Die in Dixie. Funerals, Death and Heaven in the Slave Community, 1700–1865." *Massachusetts Review* 22 (1981): 163–83.

———. "The Meaning of Africa for the American Slave." *Journal of Ethnic Studies* 4 (1977): 1–15.

Rosenthal, Bernard, and Paul E. Szarmach, eds. *Medievalism in American Culture.* Binghamton, N.Y.: Medieval and Renaissance Texts and Studies, 1984.

Rutman, Darret B., ed. *The Old Dominion. Essays for Thomas Perkins Abernethy.* Charlottesville: University Press of Virginia, 1964.

Rutyna, Richard A. and Peter C. Stewart. *Virginia in the American Revolution. A Collection of Essays.* 2 vols. Norfolk, Va.: Old Dominion University, 1977, c. 1983.

Schmidt, Leigh Eric. " 'The Grand Prophet,' Hugh Bryan: Early Evangelicalism's Challenge to the Establishment and Slavery in the Colonial South." *South Carolina Historical Magazine* 87 (1986): 238–30.

Schwarz, Philip J. *Twice Condemned. Slaves and the Criminal Laws of Virginia, 1705–1865.* Baton Rouge: Louisiana State University Press, 1988.

Scott, Julius S. "The Common Wind: Currents of Afro-American Communication in the Era of the Haitian Revolution." Ph.D. diss., Duke University, 1986.

Sheldon, Marianne Burnoff. "Black-White Relations in Richmond, Virginia, 1782–1820." *Journal of Southern History* 45 (1979): 27–44.

Shepperson, George, and Thomas Price. *Independent African. John Chilembwe and the Origins, Setting and Significance of the Nyasaland Rising of 1915.* Edinburgh: University Press, 1958.

Sheridan, Richard B. "The Jamaican Slave Insurrection Scare of 1776 and the American Revolution." *Journal of Negro History* 61 (1976): 290–309.

Shyllon, Folarin. *Black People in Britain, 1555–1833.* For the Institute of Race Relations. London: Oxford University Press, 1977.

————. *Black Slaves in Britain.* For the Institute of Race Relations. London: Oxford University Press, 1974.

Sieber, Roy, and Roslyn A. Walker. *African Art in the Cycle of Life.* For the National Museum of African Art. Washington, D.C.: Smithsonian Institution Press, c. 1987.

Siebert, William Henry. *Loyalists in East Forida. 1774–1785.* 2 vols. Deland, Fla.: Florida State Historical Society, 1929.

Simpson, George Eaton. "The Belief System of Haitian Vodun." *American Anthropologist* 47 (1945): 35–59.

Singleton, Theresa A., ed. *The Archaeology of Slavery and Plantation Life.* Orlando, Fla.: Academic Press, 1985.

Sirmans, M. Eugene. *Colonial South Carolina: A Political History, 1663–1763.* Chapel Hill: University of North Carolina Press, 1966.

————. "The Legal Status of the Slave in South Carolina, 1670–1740." *Journal of Southern History* 28 (1962): 462–73.

Smith, Edward D. *Climbing Jacob's Ladder.* For the Anacostia Museum of the Smithsonian Institution. Washington, D. C.: Smithsonian Institution Press, c. 1988.

Smith, Hilrie Shelton. *In His Image, But . . . Racism in Southern Religion 1780–1910.* Durham, N.C.: Duke University Press, 1972.

Smith, Julia Floyd. *Slavery and Rice Culture in Low Country Georgia, 1750–1860.* Knoxville: University of Tennessee Press, 1985.

Sobel, Mechal. *Trabelin' On: The Slave Journey to an Afro-Baptist Faith.* Westport, Conn.: Greenwood Press, c. 1979.

————. *The World They Made Together. Black and White Values in Eighteenth-Century Virginia.* Princeton, N.J.: Princeton University Press, c. 1987.

Southern, Eileen. *The Music of Black Americans.* New York: W. W. Norton, 1971.

Stampp, Kenneth M. *The Peculiar Institution*. New York: Vintage Books, 1956.

Starobin, Robert S. *Denmark Vesey: The Slave Conspiracy of 1822*. Englewood Cliffs, N.J.: Prentice-Hall, 1970.

Starr, J. Barton. *Tories, Dons and Rebels. The American Revolution in West Florida*. Gainesville, Fla.: University Presses of Florida, 1976.

Stegmaier, Mark J. "Maryland's Fear of Insurrection at the Time of Braddock's Defeat." *Maryland Historical Magazine* 71 (1976): 467–83.

Stevens, Charles Emery. *Anthony Burns. A History*. New York: Arno Press; New York Times, 1969.

Steward, Theophilus G. "How the Black St. Domingo Legion Saved the Patriot Army in the Seige of Savannah, 1779." American Negro Academy occasional papers, no. 5. Washington, D.C.: Academy, 1899.

Stoke, Durwood T. "The Baptist and Methodist Clergy in South Carolina and the American Revolution." *South Carolina Historical Magazine* 85 (1984): 87–96.

Strickland, Reba C. *Religion and the State in Georgia in the Eighteenth Century*. New York: Columbia University Press; London: P. S. King and Son, 1939.

Stuckey, Sterling. "Remembering Denmark Vesey—Agitator or Insurrectionist?" *Negro Digest* 15 (1966): 29–41.

———. *Slave Culture. Nationalist Theory and the Foundations of Black America*. New York: Oxford University Press, 1987.

Suttles, William C., Jr. "African Religious Survivals as Factors in American Slave Revolts." *Journal of Negro History* 6 (1971): 97–104.

Tarver, Jerry L. "Exhortation among Early Virginia Baptists." *Virginia Baptist Register* 5 (1966): 228–36.

Thomas, Bettye C. *History of the Sharp Street Memorial Methodist Episcopal Church, 1787–1920*. Baltimore, 1977.

Thomas, David Hurst, Stanley South, and Clark Spencer Larsen. *Rich Man, Poor Men: Observations on Three Antebellum Burials from the Georgia Coast*. Vol. 54, pt. 3, Anthropological papers of the American Museum of Natural History, New York, 1977.

Thomas, Edgar Garfield. *The First African Church of North America*. Savannah, Ga.: n.p., 1925.

Thompson, Robert Farris. *Flash of the Spirit*. New York: Vintage Books, 1984.

Thompson, Robert Farris, and Joseph Cornet. *The Four Moments of the Sun: Kongo Art in Two Worlds*. Washington, D.C.: National Gallery of Art, 1981.

Tise, Larry. "Proslavery Ideology: A Social and Intellectual History of the Defense of Slavery in America, 1790–1840." Ph.D. diss., University of North Carolina, 1975.

Toth, Charles W., ed. *The American Revolution and the West Indies*. Port Washington, N.Y.: Kennikat Press, 1975.

Townsend, Leah. *South Carolina Baptists 1670–1805*. Florence, S.C.: Florence Printing, 1935.

Turner, Lorenzo Dow. *Africanisms in the Gullah Dialect*. Chicago: University of Chicago Press, 1949.

Turner, Mary. *Slaves and Missionaries. The Disintegration of Jamaican Slave Society*. Urbana: University of Illinois Press, c. 1982.

Van Deburg, William L. *Slavery and Race in American Popular Culture*. Madison, Wis.: University of Wisconsin Press, 1984.

Vlach, John M. *The Afro-American Tradition in Decorative Arts*. Cleveland, Ohio: Cleveland Museum of Art, c. 1978.

———. "Graveyards and Afro-American Art." *Southern Exposure* 5 (1977): 61–65.

Wade, Richard C. "The Vesey Plot: A Reconsideration." *Journal of Southern History* 30 (1964): 143–61.

Wagner, Clarence. *Profiles of Black Georgia Baptists*. Gainesville, Ga.: Author, 1980.

Walker, James W. St. George. *The Black Loyalists: The Search for a Promised Land in Sierra Leone and Nova Scotia, 1783–1870*. New York: Africana Publishing, 1976.

———. "Blacks as American Loyalists: The Slaves' War for Independence." *Historical Reflections* 2 (1975): 51–67.

Wallace, Willard M. *Traitorous Hero. The Life and Fortunes of Benedict Arnold*. New York: Harper and Brothers, 1954.

Walvin, James, ed. *Slavery and British Society 1776–1846*. Baton Rouge: Louisiana State University Press, 1982.

Washington, James Melvin. *Frustrated Fellowship. The Black Baptist Quest for Social Power*. Macon, Ga.: Macon University Press, 1986.

Wax, Darold D. "Black Immigrants: The Slave Trade in Colonial Maryland." *Maryland Historical Magazine* 73 (1978): 30–45.

———. " 'New Negroes Are Always in Demand': The Slave Trade in Eighteenth-Century Georgia." *Georgia Historical Quarterly* 68 (1984): 193–220.

———. "Preferences for Slaves in Colonial America." *Journal of Negro History* 58 (1973): 371–401.

Weir, Robert M. *Colonial South Carolina. A History*. Millwood, N.Y.: KTO Press, 1983.

White, David O. *Connecticut's Black Soldiers, 1775–1783*. Chester, Conn.: Pequot Press, 1973.

Wickwire, Franklin, and Wickwire, Mary. *Cornwallis. The American Adventure*. Boston: Houghton Mifflin, 1970.

Wiecek, William M. "The Statutory Law of Slavery and Race in the Thirteen Mainland Colonies of British America." *William and Mary Quarterly*, 3d ser., 34 (1977): 258–80.

Williams, William Henry. *The Garden of American Methodism: The Delmarva Peninsula, 1769–1820*. For the Peninsula Conference of the United Methodist Church. Wilmington, Del.: Scholarly Resources, 1984.

Willis, William S. "Divide and Rule: Red, White, and Black in the Southeast." *Journal of Negro History* 48 (1963): 157–76.

Wilson, Ellen Gibson. *The Loyal Blacks*. New York: Capricorn Books, c. 1976.

Wilson, Olly. "The Significance of the Relationship between Afro-American Music and West African Music." *Black Perspective in Music* 2 (1974): 3–22.

Winch, Julie. *Philadelphia's Black Elite: Activism, Accommodation, and the Struggle for Autonomy, 1787–1848*. Philadelphia: Temple University Press, 1988.

Winks, Robin. *The Blacks in Canada. A History*. New Haven, Conn.: Yale University Press; Montreal: McGill-Queen's University Press, 1971.

Wood, Betty. *Slavery in Colonial Georgia, 1730–1775.* Athens: University of Georgia Press, 1984.

———. "Some Aspects of Female Resistance to Chattel Slavery in Low Country Georgia, 1763–1815." *Historical Journal* 30 (1987): 603–22.

———. " 'Untill He Shall Be Dead, Dead, Dead': The Judicial Treatment of Slaves in Eighteenth-Century Georgia." *Georgia Historical Quarterly* 71 (1987): 377–98.

Wood, Peter H. *Black Majority. Negroes in Colonial South Carolina. From 1670 through the Stono Rebellion.* New York: Alfred A. Knopf, 1974.

Wright, J. Leitch, Jr., "Blacks in British East Florida." *Florida Historical Quarterly* 54 (1976): 425–42.

Zahan, Dominique. *Religion, Spirituality and Thought of Traditional Africa.* Chicago: University of Chicago Press, 1979.

Zilversmit, Arthur. *The First Emancipation: The Abolition of Slavery in the North.* Chicago: University of Chicago Press, 1967.

INDEX

Act for the speedy prosecution of slaves committing Capital crimes, 17

African. *See* West African

African retentions: communal values, 315; dance, 42, 300–301; funeral practices, 42, 300–304; housing patterns, 30; linguistic derivations, 29, 48; marriage forms, 311–12; music, 299–301; patterns of slave resistance, 45–48

African-American Christianity: and resistance, 225, 230, 320–24; beliefs and morality, 305–15; expansion of, 297–98; millennialism in, 24, 62. See also *Individual Christian denominations*

African-Americans: and community formation, 37, 299, 315–19; and creation of institutional life, 315–19; and creation of religious culture, 27, 37

African Methodist Episcopal Church, 317, 322, 324

Afro-Baptist church: in Georgia, 288–90; in South Carolina, 290–91; in Virginia, 285–87

Afro-Methodist church: in Maryland, 292–93; in North Carolina, 293–94; in South Carolina, 294–97

Allaire, Anthony, 116

Allen, Richard, 269, 317, 322

American Revolutionary War: and black liberation movement, 4, 57, 59, 61, 62, 66, 80, 118–19, 142, 167, 169; demographic consequences of, 166, 211, 212n, 214–15, 216–18; and entrenchment of slavery, 218–19, 222–23; and patterns of agricultural production, 219–21; and patterns of labor use, 221–22; and patterns of slave resistance, 225–32; as a triangular war, 45

Anglican church, 18, 19

antislavery movements, 44, 75, 250, 326

Aptheker, Herbert, 2

Arbuthnot, Admiral Marriot, 158

arming of slaves: American plans to, 77, 79, 86; British national debate over, 67, 70–76, 79–80; by northern states, 77, 79; in West Indies (*see* slaves, European militarization of); royal officials proposals to, 68–69, 100, 136, 139–40; southern proposals to, 78, 86, 136

Arnold, Benedict, 153, 165

Asbury, Bishop Francis, 23, 43, 247, 251, 253, 254, 255, 256, 260, 263, 269, 292, 295, 296

Augusta (Ga.), 38, 101, 103, 111, 220, 221, 224

Balfour, Lieutenant Colonel Nisbet, 120, 129, 130, 135

Ball, Charles, 224, 305, 308

Ball, Elias, 261

Baltimore (Md.), 36, 161

Baltimore Conference of 1784, 245, 246

Baker, Moses, 202

Baptist: antislavery, 247, 248; church discipline, 270, 271, 272–75; churches, 25, 38, 39, 200, 203; missionaries to slaves, 23; revivals of, 23

Barnes, Colonel Richard, 161

Barrow, David, 249

Bastide, Roger, 29

Baurmeister, Adjutant General Major Carl Leopold, 192

Beauvais, Louis-Jacques, 192

Bennet, Ned and Rolla, 263

Bermuda, 188

Besse, Martial, 192

Bethel (Baptist) Association, 253

Bibb, Henry, 306

Bishop, Jacob, 269

Black Carolina Corps, 190, 191. *See also* slaves, as soldiers; slaves, European militarization of

Black preachers: and funerals, 302, 303–304; and spread of Christianity, 37–39, 200–204, 285, 292, 295, 296–98, 324; licensing of, 268–70; reputation of, 314–15, 319

Black religious societies. *See* religious and beneficial societies, African-American

Black, William, 19, 201

Blacks. *See* African-Americans; black preachers; Free Blacks